Puerto Rico

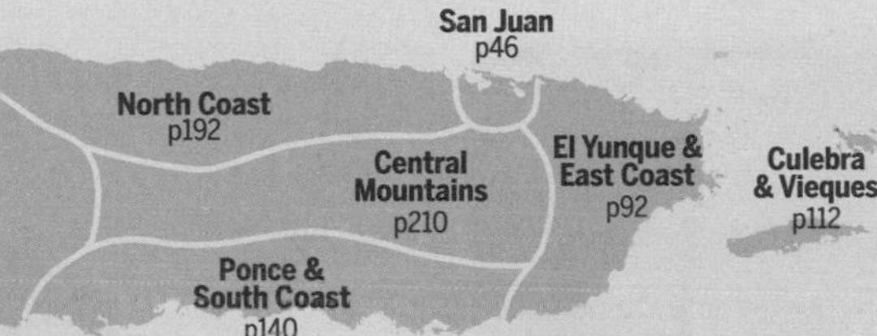

THIS EDITION WRITTEN AND RESEARCHED BY

Ryan Ver Berkmoes, Luke Waterson

PLAN YOUR TRIP

ON THE ROAD

DANITA DELIMONT/GETTY IMAGES ©

HACIENDA BUENA VISTA P153

BRYAN MULLENNIX/GETTY IMAGES ©

EL MORRO P47

ERIC PURCELL/GETTY IMAGES ©

Contents

UNDERSTAND

SURVIVAL GUIDE

MACAW

SPECIAL FEATURES

Welcome to Puerto Rico

With endless sand, swashbuckling history and wildly diverse tropical terrain, locals fittingly call this sun-washed medley of Spanish and American influences the 'Island of Enchantment.'

Tropical Beaches

Puerto Rico is the fodder of many a Caribbean daydream for good reason: it can satisfy both the lethargic beach bum or the budding big-wave surfer – all in a long weekend. Its coral reefs host a riot of tropical fish and the sands shimmer like crushed pearls. On some beaches you'll have plenty of company, but in other places like Vieques you might have some of the best stretches of sand in the world all to yourself.

Cultural Vibrancy

Those curious enough to look beyond San Juan's condo towers and congested roads reap big rewards from the vibrant culture of this island. You'll get a whiff of it in the tempting smoke that rises from roadside *lechoneras* (eateries specializing in suckling pig). You'll hear it in the distorted thump of a rowdy, beer-soaked weekend in Boquerón or the intoxicating patter of a salsa beat. You'll see it down the quiet hallways of museums celebrating everything from failed revolution to classical European painting. Puerto Rican traditions have been shaped by generations of cultural synthesis, celebration and setback, and it emerges today as distinct, spirited and indomitable.

History

Puerto Rico's history lessons – told through cannon fire and colonization, repression and revolt – offer a palpable sense of the island's dynamic past. There's a bit of legend in every direction: from the fortress walls pocked by cannon fire to the crumbling towers of the sugar refineries that once fired the island's economy. Free-trading colonialists built sparkling European plazas in the harbor cities, while political revolutionaries plotted revolt in tiny villages in the central mountains. Those with a passion for history can wander precolonial Taíno ball courts or steamy coffee plantations, and even if your interest is scant, it's hard not to get caught up in Puerto Rico's fascinating story in the stunning confines of Old San Juan. The most amazing thing about this island's past is the beguiling weave it creates with the present.

Rainforest Playground

The limestone caves in the misty central mountains resound with the chirp of coquí frogs hidden among giant tree ferns. Hiking Puerto Rico's unique collection of forests – some of the wettest in the Caribbean – is an explorers dream, and few ever forget time spent on the dripping trails of El Yunque.

Why I Love Puerto Rico

By Ryan Ver Berkmoes, Author

It was a balmy January evening on a back street of Old San Juan and I noticed a tiny corner bar where a TV was showing a football game being played in a blizzard. How could I not walk right in, order a cold beer, and enjoy the incongruity? Later, as the night progressed, I was struck by the local families out strolling, giving authenticity to a place that could easily be just a tourist cliché. The next day it was luscious *lechonera* in Guavate, and then it was losing count of all the perfect untrod beaches in Vieques.

For more about our authors, see page 288

Above: El Yunque National Forest (p93)

Puerto Rico

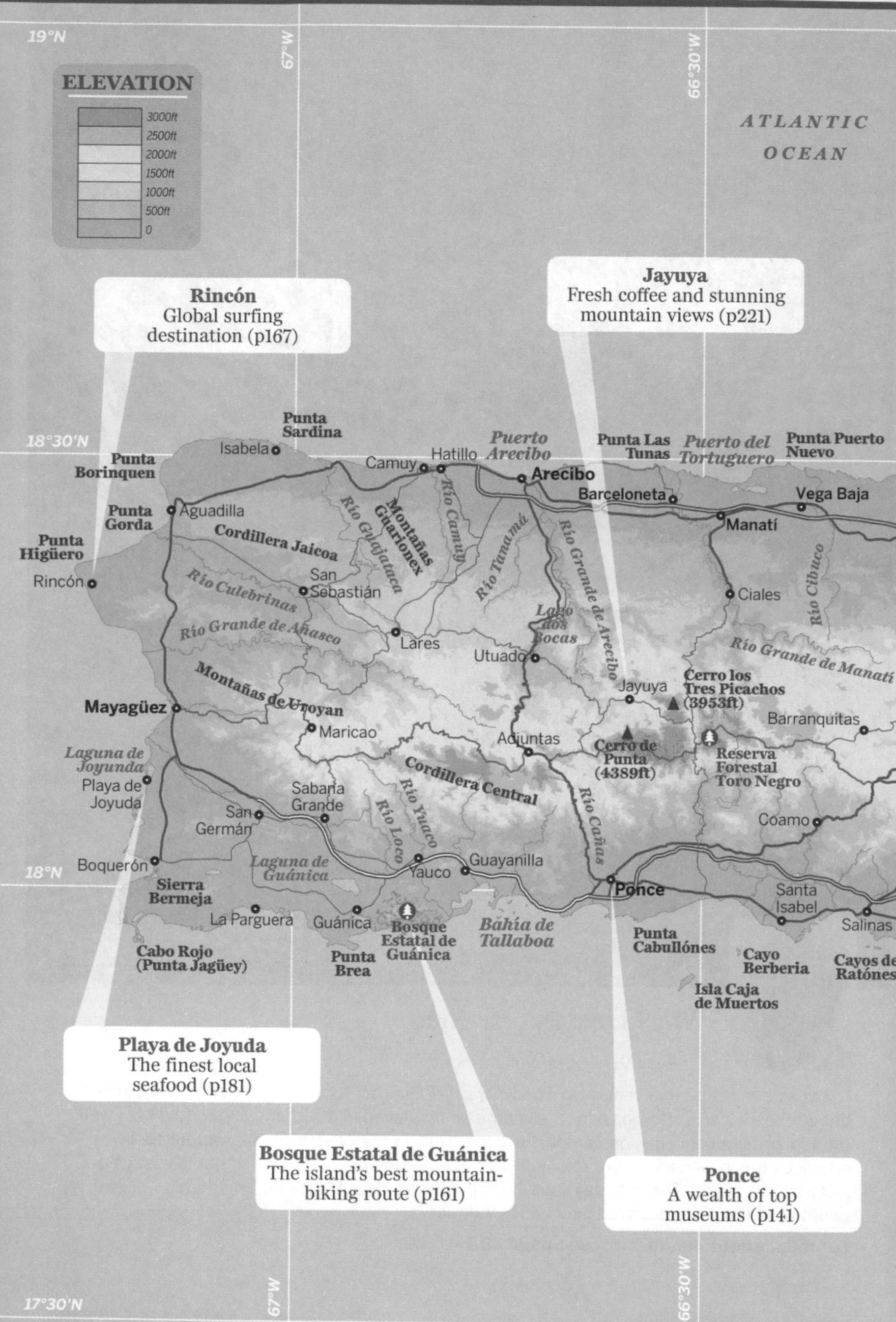

19°N
67°W
66°30'W
ELEVATION
3000ft
2500ft
2000ft
1500ft
1000ft
500ft
0
ATLANTIC OCEAN
Rincón
Global surfing destination (p167)
Jayuya
Fresh coffee and stunning mountain views (p221)
18°30'N
Punta Sardina
Punta Borinquen
Isabela
Camuy
Hatillo
Puerto Arecibo
Arecibo
Punta Las Tunas
Puerto del Tortuguero
Punta Puerto Nuevo
Barceloneta
Vega Baja
Manatí
Punta Gorda
Aguadilla
Punta Higüero
Rincón
Cordillera Jaicoa
Montañas Guarionex
Río Camuy
Río Guajataca
Río Tanamá
Río Grande de Arecibo
Río Cibuco
Río Culebrinas
San Sebastián
Ciales
Río Grande de Añasco
Lares
Lago dos Bocas
Utuado
Río Grande de Manatí
Montañas de Uroyan
Jayuya
Cerro los Tres Picachos (3953ft)
Mayagüez
Maricao
Adjuntas
Cerro de Punta (4389ft)
Barranquitas
Reserva Forestal Toro Negro
Laguna de Joyunda
Playa de Joyuda
Cordillera Central
Río Yauco
Río Loco
Río Cañas
Sabana Grande
San Germán
Coamo
18°N
Boquerón
Laguna de Guánica
Yauco
Guayanilla
Sierra Bermeja
Ponce
Santa Isabel
La Parguera
Guánica
Bosque Estatal de Guánica
Bahía de Tallaboa
Salinas
Punta Cabullónes
Cabo Rojo (Punta Jagüey)
Punta Brea
Cayo Berberia
Cayos de Ratónes
Isla Caja de Muertos
Playa de Joyuda
The finest local seafood (p181)
Bosque Estatal de Guánica
The island's best mountain-biking route (p161)
Ponce
A wealth of top museums (p141)
17°30'N

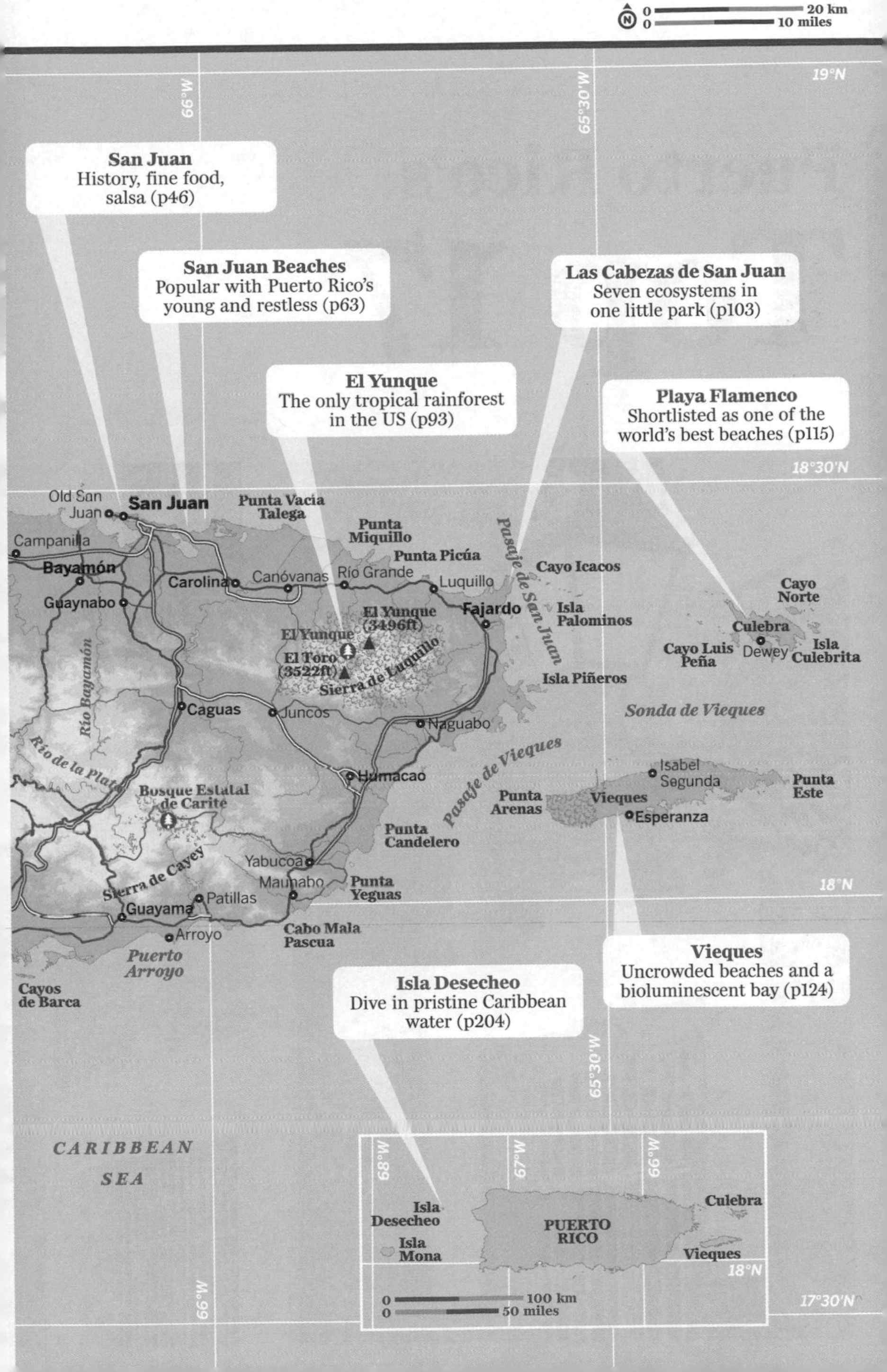

0 — 20 km
0 — 10 miles

San Juan
History, fine food, salsa (p46)

San Juan Beaches
Popular with Puerto Rico's young and restless (p63)

Las Cabezas de San Juan
Seven ecosystems in one little park (p103)

El Yunque
The only tropical rainforest in the US (p93)

Playa Flamenco
Shortlisted as one of the world's best beaches (p115)

Vieques
Uncrowded beaches and a bioluminescent bay (p124)

Isla Desecheo
Dive in pristine Caribbean water (p204)

66°W
65°30'W
19°N
18°30'N
18°N
17°30'N
Old San Juan
San Juan
Punta Vacía Talega
Punta Miquillo
Punta Picúa
Campanilla
Bayamón
Carolina
Canóvanas
Río Grande
Luquillo
Guaynabo
Pasaje de San Juan
Cayo Icacos
Fajardo
Isla Palominos
Cayo Norte
Culebra
Cayo Luis Peña
Dewey
Isla Culebrita
El Yunque (3496ft)
El Yunque
El Toro (3522ft)
Sierra de Luquillo
Isla Piñeros
Río Bayamón
Caguas
Juncos
Naguabo
Sonda de Vieques
Río de la Plata
Pasaje de Vieques
Isabel Segunda
Punta Este
Humacao
Bosque Estatal de Carite
Punta Arenas
Vieques
Esperanza
Punta Candelero
Yabucoa
Sierra de Cayey
Maunabo
Punta Yeguas
Patillas
Guayama
Arroyo
Cabo Mala Pascua
Puerto Arroyo
Cayos de Barca
CARIBBEAN SEA

68°W
67°W
66°W
Isla Desecheo
Isla Mona
PUERTO RICO
Culebra
Vieques
18°N
0 — 100 km
0 — 50 miles

Puerto Rico's Top 17

1

Evocative Old San Juan

1 Even those limited to a quick visit find it easy to fall under the beguiling spell of the cobblestone streets, pastel-painted colonial buildings and grand fortresses of Old San Juan (p47). From the ramparts of El Morro, the allure of this place is evident in every direction – from the labyrinth of crooked lanes to the endless sparkle of the Atlantic. By day, lose yourself in historical stories of blood and drama; by night, float along in crowds of giggling tourists and rowdy locals.

Glorious Beaches

2 The rub of sand between your toes, the brilliant sparkle of turquoise water and the rhythmic shush of cresting waves – Puerto Rico's beaches have the qualities of a daydream. Take your pick from the golden, crescent-shaped heaven of Playa Flamenco (p115; considered among the world's best beaches); the embarrassment of riches on Vieques; the coconut-oil-scented crowds of Playa Isla Verde (p63), San Juan's little slice of Brazil; the secluded, mangrove-shaded hideaways in the south; or the roaring surf of the west. Below right: Playa Isla Verde

DANITA DELIMONT / GETTY IMAGES ©

2

GREG JOHNSTON / GETTY IMAGES ©

Ponce

3 Ponce (p141), the so-called 'Pearl of the South,' boasts a wealth of museums with enough diversity to satisfy the most intellectually rapacious museum hunter. Those interested in the island's music should start with the Museo de la Música Puertorriqueña, before touring the lovingly restored plantation at Hacienda Buena Vista or the Caribbean's best art museum, the Museo de Arte de Ponce. Add in the town's beautiful Plaza Las Delicias (p142), home to the eclectic Parque de Bombas, to round out your visit. Below: Parque de Bombas (p145)

Bioluminescent Bays

4 Few experiences can inspire the awe of floating on inky waves under a canopy of stars and witnessing one of nature's most tactile magic tricks: the otherworldly sparkle of bioluminescent waters. Kayaking into Puerto Rico's bioluminescent bays and seeing the jeweled flicker of water drip from your hands or illuminate a paddle stroke promises an experience of profound wonder. Or you can just glide along on an electric boat. Best bets: the bioluminescent bay at Vieques (p128) or at Laguna Grande (p106) near Fajardo.

BRYAN MULLENNIX / GETTY IMAGES ©

TRAVELART / ALAMY ©

INGE SCHEPERS SPORTS AND EVENTS PHOTOGRAPHY / ALAMY ©

JHEINIMANN / ALAMY ©

ANTON GORBOV / ALAMY ©

Catch Some Baseball

5 The bleachers at island *béisbol* (baseball) stadiums reveal a lot more than nine innings of play – they offer a glimpse at the Caribbean love affair with this sport. Even if their numbers are sometimes small, Puerto Ricans love the low-key games and dirt-cheap tickets that get fans right up to the Winter League Baseball action. Witness upstart farm leaguers looking for their big shot facing off against fading stars of the Major League looking to go out in a blaze of glory in San Juan's Hiram Bithorn Stadium (p85).

Las Cabezas de San Juan

6 The diverse ecosystem of the Las Cabezas de San Juan nature reserve (p103) is only a quick day trip from the high-rises of San Juan's urban core and highlights the island's ecological assortment at every turn. After a quick trip through the visitor center, travelers begin the compact tour of the flora and fauna. The sea grass waves along mangrove forest and coral-protected lagoons, while giant iguanas scuttle from underfoot and crabs scurry along the rocky shores. At night, there's bioluminescent action. Top right: Iguana at Las Cabezas de San Juan

San Juan's Great Food

7 San Juan's restaurants impress their international audiences with the most inventive fine dining in the Caribbean. Recent years have seen a revolving door of hot restaurants in Old San Juan – only the most innovative survive – while in the edgy Santurce district (p78) you'll find ever-creative, high-profile eateries by name-brand chefs. Expect the traditional, elemental essence of Puerto Rican flavors fused with preparations from across the globe. And don't miss the casual pleasures of dining at the many fine cafes across the capital. Above: Shrimp *mofongo*

BRYAN MULLENNIX / GETTY IMAGES ©

TIM DRAPER / GETTY IMAGES ©

GEORGE OZE / ALAMY ©

Architectural Gems

8 If you tried to savor every single example of colonial grandeur – all the fountains and historic squares, every dignified plantation house and buttressed 19th-century town hall – Puerto Rico's architectural gems would demand a month-long stay. But if just one location outside of Old San Juan earns time on your agenda, take a stroll around Ponce and its historic main square (p142). In the west, Puerto Rico's second-oldest city, San Germán (p187), dates to 1511, an age that blows away anything in the continental US. Top left: Fuente de los Leones (p142), Ponce

Mountain Biking

9 Spend half a day rumbling down the rocky, cactus-lined paths of Bosque Estatal de Guánica (p161) and you will traverse some of the most interesting mountain-biking terrain in the Caribbean. They're not well groomed or technical, but trails in this Unesco-protected site, or those in less-traveled karst country forests like Bosque Estatal de Susúa (p159), bring the DIY thrills of the sport to Puerto Rico's unique subtropical wilds. For calmer rides, consider the rough yet quiet nature reserve roads on Vieques or the pleasant paths along San Juan's beaches. Top right: Cacti in Bosque Estatal de Guánica

Seafood at Playa de Joyuda

10 Pork takes a backseat to seafood at the string of restaurants known island-wide as the Milla de Oro del Buen Comer (Gourmet Golden Mile) at Playa de Joyuda (p181). Here the oysters, crab, shrimp and much more are ultrafresh and served up in a dozen family-owned joints along a 3-mile oceanfront stretch of highway. And if your visit doesn't bring you to the west coast, you'll also find seafood stands and restaurants at Playa Luquillo and Playa Húcares in the east. All draw mobs of fans on weekends. Above right: Blue crabs for sale

Island Wildlife

11 Maybe the syncopated polyrhythmic grooves of salsa rule the island's nightlife, but the chirp of the coquí frogs – whose sound is just like their name – rules the night. These little creatures are the unofficial mascot of the island. Puerto Rico's wild population also includes rare birds in the Bosque Estatal de Guánica and lazy reptiles on the remote Isla Mona (p190), often called the Galápagos of the Caribbean. In the waters offshore, the sea life adds to a naturalist's agenda, with tropical fish, coral, turtles and even manatee. Below: Coquí frog

El Yunque National Forest

12 Lush forests, verdant hills and crashing waterfalls attract visitors to El Yunque (p93), the only true rainforest in the US. It's a place to embark on a short hike through the oxygen-rich mist and gawk at Jurassic-sized ferns. You will get wet, so take a raincoat, but bring binoculars, too; of the 26 species found here and nowhere else in the world, you'll want to keep a sharp eye out for the Puerto Rican parrot, one of the 10 most endangered birds on earth.

11

12

Salsa

13 Let the scholars debate over whether the origins of salsa are rooted in the clubs of New York or the islands of the Caribbean and just feel it. There's no doubt that it lives on as the essential heartbeat of Puerto Rico (especially at venues in San Juan, p83). You'll hear the basic rhythm of the *clavé* (percussion instrument; literally 'keystone') driving Puerto Rican pop music and traditional songs. The secret to grooving to its rhythms on the dancefloor is handed down from one generation to the next.

Swimming & Snorkeling

14 Many of the island's snorkeling and swimming lies out of the heavily traveled tourist corridors, on satellite islands off the main island's east or south coast, and at coral reefs in the southwest. In the morning, waters in these areas are crystal clear and usually calm enough to enjoy visibility up to 75ft. And what a view – expect brightly colored fish, coral formations and, if you're lucky, a lazy ray or two. The consistently clear waters of Isla Desecheo (p204), off the island's west coast, also top any diver's wish list. Bottom: Diving at Isla Desecheo

13

LAWRENCE MANNING / CORBIS ©

14

STEVE SIMONSEN / GETTY IMAGES ©

15
STEVE SIMONSEN / GETTY IMAGES ©

16
TONY ARRUZA / GETTY IMAGES ©

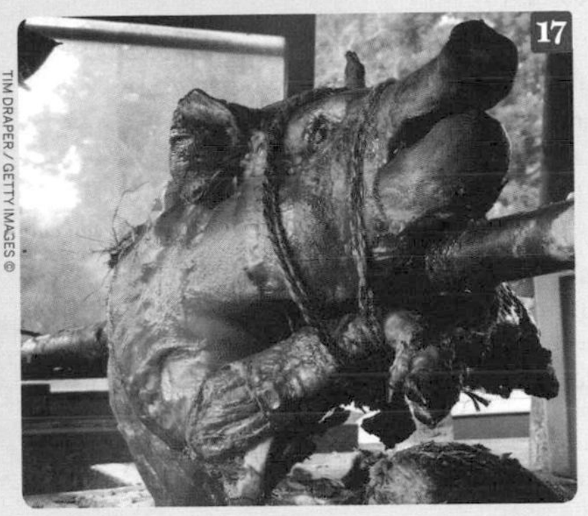
17
TIM DRAPER / GETTY IMAGES ©

Coffee in the Central Mountains

15 Puerto Rico's legendary coffee plantations offer caffeine junkies a rare opportunity. Here in the remote central mountains, you can sip a steaming cup of rich, fresh coffee while looking over the rolling hills and quiet valleys where the beans are grown, roasted and brewed. The winding Ruta Panorámica, a white-knuckled scenic route through the peaks, takes travelers past one picturesque plantation after the next and through the village of Jayuya (p221), in the heart of coffee country.

Big-Wave Surfing at Rincón

16 In winter, the cold weather brings righteous swells to the island's west-coast surfing capital of Rincón (p167), where some of the most consistent, varied and exciting surf locations in the Caribbean can be found. And while the double overheads and excellent tubes attract an international set of would-be pros, beginners can paddle out to tamer breaks nearby. At sunset, crowds of locals and visitors replenish themselves with inexpensive eats and ice-cold beer while they mingle in laid-back beach bars and around bonfires on the sand.

Feast on Roast Pork

17 If you were to draw the Puerto Rican food pyramid, it might only have four elements: rice, beans, plantains and pork. Of these, pork rules the roost; you'll find it fried, grilled, stewed and skewered. But it's the mighty *lechón* (savory, smoky, suckling pig, spit-roasted for up to eight hours) that remains the island's favorite lunch. On the weekends, the roadsides near Guavate (p218) are a virtual parking lot for *lechoneras* (eateries specializing in suckling pig), with locals and visitors feasting alike. Above: *Lechón*

Need to Know

For more information, see Survival Guide (p259)

Currency
US dollars ($)

Language
Spanish, some English (for more on language, see p271)

Visas
For US visitors it's the same as visiting another state; visitors from other countries must have a valid passport. Some nationalities will need a visa.

Money
ATMs common; credit and debit cards widely accepted.

Cell Phones
Most US cell phone plans include coverage in Puerto Rico. Travelers from other countries can easily buy a local SIM card.

Time
Atlantic Standard/Daylight Time (GMT/UTC minus four hours)

When to Go

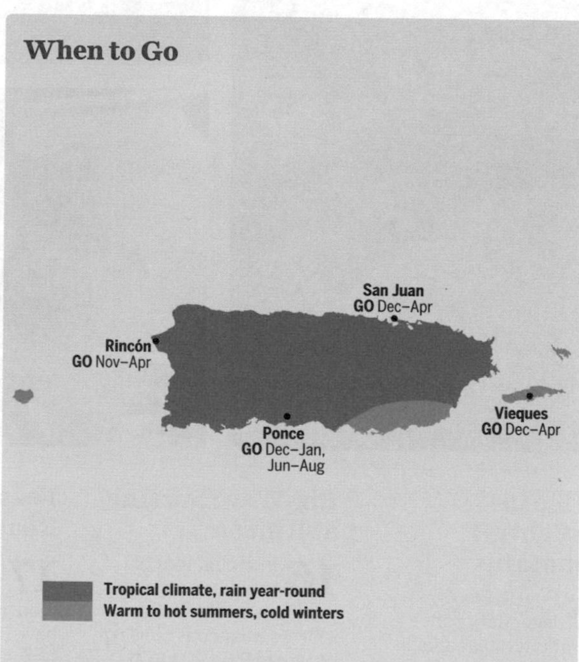

High Season
(mid-Dec–mid-Feb & Jul)

➡ Crowds escaping the frosty US mainland in winter see hotels rates go up and seasonal attractions come to life.

➡ In July, local families create a second high season, filling beach towns.

Shoulder
(Sep–Nov & mid-Mar–Jun)

➡ Puerto Rico's tourist infrastructure takes a breather to regroup during shoulder season, though there isn't a significant fluctuation in prices or services.

Low Season
(Aug–early Dec)

➡ Things get pretty lethargic during hurricane season; some resorts offer discounted packages, but prices at small hotels don't drop precipitously.

Useful Websites

See Puerto Rico (www.seepuertorico.com) Official tourist site.

Eye Tour Puerto Rico (www.eyetour.com) Excellent short videos.

Welcome to Puerto Rico (welcome.topuertorico.org) Part encyclopedia, part travel guide.

Puerto Rico Day Trips (www.puertoricodaytrips.com) Fun days out from cities across the Commonwealth.

Scurvy Dog's Puerto Rican Blog (www.robertospuertorico.com) Off-beat and less-touristy places to see.

Lonely Planet (www.lonelyplanet.com/puerto-rico) Destination information, hotel bookings, traveler forum and more.

Important Numbers

Puerto Rico's country code	☎1
International access code	☎011
Directory assistance	☎411
Emergency	☎911

Exchange Rates

Australia	A$1	$1.09
Canada	C$1	$1.05
Europe	€1	$1.48
Japan	¥100	$1.23
New Zealand	NZ$1	$0.80
UK	UK£1	$1.66

For current exchange rates see www.xe.com.

Daily Costs

Budget: Less than $120

- Public transportation: $10
- Double room in a budget guesthouse: $60–80
- Museum entry: free–$8

Midrange: $120–250

- Rental car: $25–45
- Double room in a midrange hotel: $80–200
- *Lechonera* meal and drinks: $15

Top End: More than $200

- Double room in a boutique hotel or resort: from $200
- Dinner and drinks for two at a top restaurant: from $80
- Guided tours of bioluminescent bays or snorkeling excursions: from $45

Opening Hours

Hours can vary from those posted, so check before setting off.

Banks 8am-4pm Mon-Fri, 9:30am-noon Sat

Bars 2pm–2am, often later in San Juan

Government offices 8:30am–4:30pm Monday to Friday

Museums 9:30am–5pm, often closed Monday and Tuesday

Restaurants 9am–9pm, later in San Juan

Shops 9am–6pm Monday to Saturday, 11am–5pm Sunday, later in malls

Arriving in Puerto Rico

Luis Muñoz Marín International Airport San Juan's LMM airport (SJU; p267) receives the vast majority of flights to Puerto Rico. It has all services, including major rental-car companies and fairly cheap, flat-rate taxis to the nearby tourist centers.

Old San Juan Piers Cruise ships dock at the busy port (p267) at the base of Old San Juan. Fabulous sites, food and drink are all nearby.

Getting Around

Most visitors drive themselves around Puerto Rico when they travel the island.

Bus Regular large urban buses run on routes convenient for visitors in San Juan.

Car Exploring Puerto Rico will be more rewarding with your own vehicle, although chaotic local driving habits and poor road conditions mean you won't want to plan any extended road trips. Note that a car is unnecessary while staying in San Juan: parking is scarce, traffic terrible.

Ferries & Planes Only used for trips to the major islands of Culebra and Vieques.

Públicos Minibuses (called *públicos*) serve most corners of the island. They're cheap and an adventure in themselves, but they're not quick, and what on a map looks like a short journey between popular sights can require time-consuming changes.

Taxi Within San Juan, taxis are reasonable.

For much more on **getting around**, see p267

First Time Puerto Rico

For more information, see Survival Guide (p259)

Checklist

➡ Reserve as far in advance as possible for flights and hotels in high season.

➡ Don't worry about a passport if you're a US citizen, a valid state ID or driver's license will do.

➡ Brush up on your high-school Spanish, a few simple phrases will be greatly appreciated.

➡ Stream some salsa to get a sense of the local beat (p244).

➡ Arrange for appropriate travel insurance (p264).

What to Pack

➡ Bathing suit

➡ Shorts

➡ Sandals

➡ Flash duds for salsa dancing

➡ Your US-cell phone – almost all plans include Puerto Rico

➡ Refillable water bottle – tap water is safe to drink

➡ Books, if you prefer printed versions

Top Tips for Your Trip

➡ Relax, Puerto Rico is easy. US citizens don't need passports and the currency is the US dollar. If you forget something you can easily buy it at familiar stores like Walgreens.

➡ Save time to just chill and save plenty of time for the beaches. While there are countless reasons to go exploring, you'll find that road conditions can make endless days in a car stressful. Also, as you do move around, hit the pause button in places like Vieques, which are much more rewarding over several days as opposed to a super-quick day trip from San Juan.

➡ Eat like a local. You can get great international fare or even slum it in familiar fast food outlets, but why bother? Stands, food trucks and humble open-air cafes dish up the Commonwealth's delicious cuisine, which boasts an enticing medley of Caribbean and Spanish flavors.

What to Wear

Puerto Rico is mostly quite casual. Shorts and a T-shirt will suffice anytime you're near a beach, whether it's for a daytime frolic or a sunset cocktail at an open-air bar. Long pants, shirts that tuck in and skirts will suffice for nicer restaurants in San Juan, although there's no limit to how snazzy you can be if you're hitting the cutting-edge clubs.

Sleeping

Puerto Rico has a wide range of accommodations; be sure to book ahead in high season. See p260 for more information.

➡ **Hotels** Available in all price ranges from $60 a night to $400 or more, with a good selection under $200. Locations range from Old San Juan to the myriad beaches to remote mountain hideaways.

➡ **Guesthouses** These range from places with one or two rooms to larger motel-like stays; many are family-run and/or have an eco bent.

➡ **Resorts** World-class properties line San Juan's beachfront and other coastal areas. There are, however, few all-inclusive resorts.

➡ **Camping** Possible on Culebra and in a handful of nature parks.

Money

ATMs dispensing US currency are easily found in all but the smallest of places. Credit and debit cards are widely accepted and you can use them in all but the most casual of food trucks and stalls. Watch for mandatory fees at upscale hotels and resorts.

Bargaining

Except for larger items like paintings in souvenir stalls, you'll find few places where it's appropriate to bargain. Prices in stores and most markets are firm and attempts at negotiation will not be welcome.

Tipping

Generally, you tip in Puerto Rico as you would on the US mainland.

- **Bars** $1 per drink.
- **Buffets** Tip staff 10% to 20% if they are serving you your drinks.
- **Luggage attendants** $1 to $2 per bag for anyone who helps with your luggage, whether it's a skycap, shuttle driver, bellhop etc.
- **Pool/beach attendants** $1 to $2 for each service rendered.
- **Restaurants** 15% to 20% of the bill.
- **Taxis** 15% of the fare.
- Check for service charges included in your bill at touristy restaurants, even for groups smaller than six.
- If possible, tip servers with cash even when paying by credit card; this precludes management taking a cut.

ENDELL METZEN / GETTY IMAGES ©

Woman looking at a quilt, San Juan (p46)

Etiquette

Puerto Rico is pretty laid back, but your welcome will be even warmer if you grasp a few principles of local etiquette.

- Meals, even a pause for a coffee, are meant to be unhurried affairs.
- When entering a restaurant or cafe, offer a general greeting to those around you: *'Buen provecho'* (enjoy your meal), coupled with a salutation appropriate to the time of day.
- Understand that Puerto Rico is part of the United States (residents pay taxes and serve in the military), but that it is not a state with voting rights in Congress, and know that questions about the Commonwealth's future political status are cause for intense local debate.

Language

Spanish is the main language spoken, although most people speak at least some English and many are fluent. Travelers with no Spanish-language skills will still have no problems as even locals who don't speak English are used to visitors who don't speak Spanish and know how to get by.

If You Like...

Perfect Beaches

If you've come to laze on the beach and do a whole lot of nothing, there's only one decision to make: where to spread your towel. Generally, the beaches of the north and east are best for swimming.

Balneario Escambrón Nice sand, good snorkeling and a nearby fort make this San Juan's most evocative beach. (p63)

Playa Flamenco Often short-listed among the world's best beaches, this pristine strip on Culebra is largely undeveloped. (p115)

Playa Santa This south-coast cove stands in the shadow of a majestic 19th-century lighthouse and is perfect for swimming with manatees. (p187)

Balneario Boquerón This Blue Flag–certified beach is excellent for strolling and soaking up the palm-lined Caribbean scenery. (p183)

Playa Caracas Just one of the amazing buffet of beaches on the south coast of Vieques. (p129)

Live Music

Building an itinerary around live music is a surprisingly difficult task in Puerto Rico, where many of the clubs prefer raging reggaetón to live salsa. Here are some of the best bets.

Nuyorican Café This is, bar none, the best place for live music; the musicians carry the torch of Puerto Rican's musical legacy, while the dance floor steams. (p84)

Nuestro Son On a moody Old San Juan back street, you'll hear the latest sounds of the island. (p84)

Museo de la Música Puertorriqueña With hands-on displays of instruments and occasional live performances, this museum in Ponce looks into Puerto Rico's groove history. (p145)

Romantic Escapes

With swaying palms and brilliant red sunsets, Puerto Rico suffers no lack of romance. Besides plush resorts, you'll also find fabulous hideaways around the island.

Condado Vanderbilt Hotel Recently restored in a lavish manner, this vast beachside palace is San Juan's hottest resort. (p73)

Horned Dorset Primavera For very special occasions, this secluded west-coast boutique resort is as romantic as they get. (p174)

Mary Lee's by the Sea These exceedingly fashionable, independently owned cliff-side apartments are made for couples who want no interruptions. (p160)

Blue Horizon Boutique Resort On a quiet beach in Vieques, the bungalows here make for a delightful escape. (p135)

Casa Grande Mountain Retreat Swing in a hammock on your porch whilst overlooking a gorgeous isolated valley. (p201)

Colonial Architecture

The grand edifices of Puerto Rico's past still sing the hymns of bygone colonial dignity. They're littered around the island, but shouldn't be missed.

Old San Juan There's a picture to be taken down every narrow alley of this historic port town, which has a wealth of lovingly restored buildings. (p47)

Plaza Las Delicias Ponce's historical core surrounds this, the grandest public plaza on the island, which boasts the magnificent Fuente de los Leones. (p142)

San Germán Tucked into the island's southwestern hills lies one of the oldest established cities, where beautifully restored historic homes stand beside

(Top) San Blás Catholic Church (p157), Coamo
(Bottom) Puerto Rican tody, El Yunque National Forest (p93)

the crumbling remains of the neglected ones. (p187)

Coamo Before soaking in the thermal baths, visit the city's remarkable San Blás Catholic Church at the edge of the historic central square. (p157)

Wildlife-Watching

Under sea and overhead, Puerto Rico's colorful wildlife is ever present.

El Yunque The only rainforest in the US's forest system is crawling with lizards and exotic birds; look for the exceptionally rare Puerto Rican parrot. (p93)

Bosque Estatal de Guánica This amazingly arid patch of dry forest is teeming with birds that nest in the cacti and scrub-covered hills. (p38)

Isla Mona The so-called Galápagos of the Caribbean is a scarcely traveled nature preserve where visitors can snorkel clear waters with octopus, colorful fish, eels and sharks, and hike past giant iguanas. (p190)

Bahía de Jobos Kayakers and hikers navigate the elaborate mangrove channels and coves to spot pelicans, herons and manatee. (p155)

Bosque Estatal de Guajataca Keep your eyes in the canopy of this karst-country forest and you might spot the rare Puerto Rican boa. (p201)

Diving & Snorkeling

Due to big swells on the north coast, most of the best diving and snorkeling lies away from San Juan.

La Parguera Just offshore from this southwestern town is 'The Wall,' which drops to over 1500ft and offers the chance to see rare black coral. (p164)

Fajardo Enormous coral heads and a great assortment of reef fish – including band-tailed puffers and parrot fish – make this a great destination in the east. (p103)

Humacao Excellent for advanced divers, this region has caves and jagged walls, and a mile-long reef frequented by dolphins. (p108)

Culebra & Vieques These two islands have charter trips to tiny, off-lying cays and snorkeling beaches within walking distance of each other. (p112)

Isla Desecheo Off Rincón, this island hosts great dives when the sea is calm, with reliable visibility over 100ft. (p204)

Pirates & History

Puerto Rico's strategic importance in the Atlantic channel made it a strong destination for the peg-leg and plundering set.

Faro y Parque Histórico de Arecibo Kids go crazy for the pirate-themed rides at Arecibo's family-oriented amusement park. (p199)

El Morro This fortress defended the gold of the Spanish crown from one group of pirates after the next; scanning the horizon for ships from its ramparts still captures the imagination. (p47)

Cabo Rojo Birthplace of Puerto Rico's most famous pirate, this remote corner of the island has diverse terrain for hiking and hunting for treasure. (p180)

Unique Shopping

From colorful *vejigantes* (Puerto Rican masks) to hand-carved saints, Puerto Rico's artisans make one-of-a-kind souvenirs.

Old San Juan Amid way too much tourist tat, you'll discover real treasure, especially at little shops like Olé and galleries along Calle del Christo and Calle Fortaleza. (p85)

Roadside fruit stands When driving through karst country, keep a keen eye out for local farmers hocking locally grown fruits, home-brewed spicy sauces and regionally harvested honey.

Uncharted Studio Every bit as funky as Rincón itself, this local art gallery is filled with affordable one-of-a-kind pieces. (p176)

Hiking

Don't expect much by way of well-marked trails, but Puerto Rico's hikes offer excellent DIY adventures.

El Yunque Short, easy hikes through this soaking rainforest should top every outdoors agenda. (p93)

Bosque Estatal de Guánica With amazing views and a bizarre landscape of cacti and scrub, this blazing hot hike is the weirdest on Puerto Rico. (p38)

Corozo Salt Flats, Punta Jagüey & Playa Santa Hike out to rugged cliffs, serene beaches or brackish salt flats in Puerto Rico's untamed southwest. (p186)

Bosque Estatal de Guajataca Navigate deep limestone sink-holes, karst-country terrain and sudden cliffs in this untouched state forest. (p201)

Cerro de Punta You could get here by car, but what fun would that be? Take a rugged DIY hike through the Reserva Forestal Toro Negro to reach the island's highest point. (p219)

Month by Month

TOP EVENTS

Día de los Reyes, January

Carnaval, February

Feria Dulce Sueño, March

Fiesta de San Juan Bautista, June

Festival Nacional Indígena, November

January

Travelers looking to escape the cold find balmy solace in Puerto Rico, where temperatures hover between the high 70s and 80s and there's little rainfall.

Día de los Reyes

The islandwide Día de los Reyes celebration on 6 January toasts the three kings (the Magi) and rivals the popularity of Christmas. Many small towns have festivals in their plazas, with food vendors and live music, and families exchange gifts to celebrate Epiphany.

Fiesta de la Calle San Sebastián

The Fiesta de la Calle San Sebastián is a week-long shindig of parades, food, dancing and music in Old San Juan. One of the island's hippest street carnivals, it's usually held over January's third weekend.

Whale-Watching

From late January to late March, migrating humpback whales can be seen off west-coast shores. Snorkeling and dive boats double as whale-watching operators, but you may also be able to spot the mammals from the lighthouses at Cabo Rojo and Rincón.

February

Though the mountains are coolest during this time of year, temperatures stay fairly consistent along the coast. It is also one of the driest times of year, with only rare, brief, afternoon showers.

Maricao Coffee Festival

Held mid month, the annual Maricao Coffee Festival has demonstrations of traditional coffee-making and local crafting. The rugged mountain setting is sublime, and the fresh air fills with the scent of roasting beans.

Carnaval

During the days preceding Lent, Ponce parties *hard* before giving up vices. While this event is not as wild as Rio de Janeiro's Carnival or New Orleans' Mardi Gras, it's a riot to see parading *vejigantes* (traditional horned masks) and beauty pageants.

Festival Casals de Puerto Rico

World-class instrumentalists play at San Juan's Festival Casals de Puerto Rico, honoring native cellist and composer Pablo Casals. For over 50 years, this month-long event from mid-February has offered top orchestral and chamber music events.

March

Snowbird tourists return north, but Puerto Rico's weather remains remarkably beautiful, with warm temperatures and little rain. This might be the slowest month of tourism all year, leaving parks virtually empty.

Feria Dulce Sueño

The streets of Guayama fill with the elegant gait of Paso Fino horses during the two-day Feria Dulce Sueño (Fair of Sweet Dreams). Competitions take place in a dignified rodeo atmosphere and the city goes horse crazy. It's held in early March.

Puerto Rico JazzFest

Hosted at the Tito Puente Amphitheater in San Juan, the Puerto Rico JazzFest (www.prheinekenjazz.com) draws international artists and jazz fans. It's usually held over the third weekend in March.

April

Trade winds bring a bit more precipitation to the north coast, though rainfall is mostly in the afternoon. As temperatures continue to increase, small festivals enliven mountain towns.

Saint's Day

Cities across Puerto Rico celebrate the birthday of patriot and revolutionary independence icon José de Diego (b April 16, 1867). It's a national holiday, celebrated with particular enthusiasm in Aguadilla, where he was born.

Ironwood Wine

Near Ponce, people in little Juana Díaz get tipsy with their Taíno heritage, celebrating Mavi Carnival and toasting a fermented drink made from the bark of an ironwood tree. Festivities include lots of costumes, food and fairly intense hangovers.

Semana Santa

The Catholic holiday of Easter gets celebrated for an entire week at Semana Santa festivals across the island. The most vivid festivals will have a procession through the streets to reenact the crucifixion – using a real person tied to a cross.

May

Many of the little agricultural towns of the south celebrate the arrival of spring with the fruit of their harvests – including a delicious assortment of coconut, mango, shrimp and oysters.

Semana de la Danza

Ponce's Semana de la Danza, held in mid-May, features a week of music and dance concerts that celebrate the stately music of string quartets and 19th-century ballroom dance. Many of the events are free.

June

Puerto Ricans switch to summer mode, with shorter work days and time off from school. The summer tourist season – when road-tripping locals join foreigners – swings into high gear.

Fiesta de San Juan Bautista

During the week preceding June 24, Old San Juan explodes with the island capital's *fiesta patronal* (patron saint's festival). Party animals eventually walk backwards into the sea (or sometimes fountains) to demonstrate their loyalty to the saint of Christian baptism.

Festival del Juey

Guánica's mid-June Festival del Juey delights crab eaters and brings an open-air fair to the town's seaside boardwalk. The crustaceans are consumed in every preparation imaginable and washed back with a whole lot of cold beer.

July

Blazing-hot temperatures drive Puerto Rican families to the beaches in droves. This is high season for sun-seeking locals, so expect plenty of company at the beach.

Puerto Rico Salsa Congress

The competition among professional dancers is intense during the Puerto Rico Salsa Congress (www.prsalsa.com), usually held in late July in San Juan. Spectators have the chance to see the dance at its highest form.

Fiesta de Santiago

Loíza Aldea's Fiesta de Santiago, held at the end of the month, brings Puerto Ricans of African descent to a festival worthy of Bahía in Brazil: parades, fabulous drum ensembles, masks and costumes revive saints and incarnations of West African gods.

August

Every weekend hosts parties for Puerto Rico's patron saints even as the tropical rains start to fall during the start of the hurricane season's peak.

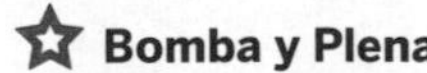

Bomba y Plena

The music of plantation workers fills the air at Bomba y Plena festivals during late summer. Explosive drumbeats and folk songs are the custom; reliably rowdy ones happen in Ponce, and in the nearby mountain villages of Juana Díaz and Aguas Buenas.

> **HURRICANE SEASON**
>
> Officially hurricane season on Puerto Rico runs from June through November. However, there have been tropical storms right into December and beyond. Realistically, however, the odds of a major storm affecting your visit are quite small. The last major hurricane swept through in 1998, some 60 years after the previous huge storm to hit the island. You may get more rain during hurricane season due to tropical fronts, but with modern forecasts the chances of you being caught out by a huge storm are slim.

October

Though this is the slow tourist season, the island's typical assortment of parties for patron saints are scattered throughout the month. A lack of crowds anywhere make this a great month for a visit.

Día del Descubrimiento de América

Though Christopher Columbus is loathed throughout most of Latin America, Puerto Rico celebrates his arrival – the so-called Día del Descubrimiento de América (Discovery of America Day) – with a smattering of parades and street festivals on October 12.

November

American tourists begin descending on the island as the weather turns cold in the north. Puerto Rico also sees many native sons and daughters return to the island for the holidays.

Festival Nacional Indígena

Although all pure-blooded Taíno have been gone for about 400 years, this Jayuya festival, held mid-month, revives the games, costumes, food and music of the original islanders. As with almost all Puerto Rican fiestas, there is a beauty pageant, this time with women in Native American dress.

Play Ball!

Winter League Baseball in Puerto Rico is in full swing and stadiums throughout the island host teams of aspiring major leaguers, young players hoping to get a bit more experience over the winter, and former Major League Baseball players in the twilight of their careers.

December

Twinkling lights make central plazas sparkle as Puerto Rico gets geared up for Christmas. Near the end of the month, every town celebrates the nativity.

Waves in the West

Cold fronts push huge waves to the island's west coast, making it the high season for surfing Rincón and beaches near Isabela and Aguadilla. With perfect tubes and tons of tourists, you'll need to reserve a board and lessons early.

Las Mañanitas

Mexican mariachis parade around the square in Ponce during Las Mañanitas, an annual celebration of the Virgin of Guadalupe, patron saint of Mexico. It's a brassy event, with lots of trumpets and drinking.

Hatillo Mask Festival

Held on December 28, the Hatillo Mask Festival features masked devils prowling the streets as incarnations of the agents of King Herod, who sent soldiers to find and kill the Christ child. Kids run and hide from the maskers.

Itineraries

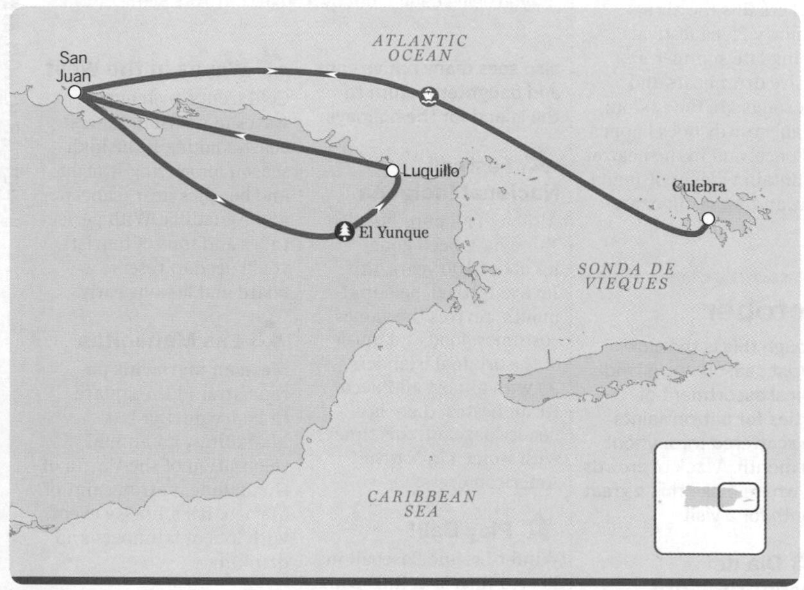

3 DAYS San Juan & Around

It's easy to get caught up in **San Juan**, from lazy days spent exploring the wonders of Old San Juan, to the urban beaches that include Isla Grande, and the edgy – and tasty – wonders of Santurce. But there is plenty to see and do just outside the capital that will give you a much broader picture of Puerto Rico's diverse pleasures.

At the very least, join one of the sailing day trips out to **Culebra**, where you'll get a taste of funky island life and enjoy some sensational snorkeling.

Although you can take more day-time tours, rent a car and do a little freelance exploring instead. Head up to the lush rainforest wonders of **El Yunque**. Driving Hwy 191, you'll climb ever higher into the misty peaks and you can pick your breaks for waterfalls and nature hikes. Consider also stopping off at one of the adventure parks where you can zip-line through the trees.

Spend the night at a mountain retreat before returning to San Juan via **Luquillo**, with its natural wonders, beaches and great food stands.

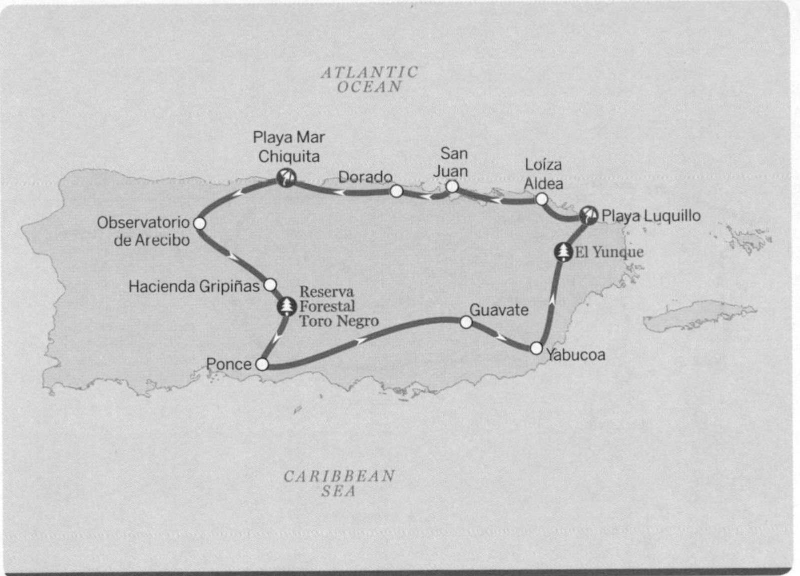

Essential Puerto Rico

Touch down in **San Juan** and get to the beaches, exploring Isla Verde, Condado and Ocean Park. Spend the next day weaving through the Unesco treasures of Old San Juan and posing by the ramparts of El Morro. Finish up with an evening among the rollicking scene of Santurce's bars and restaurants.

Start early on day three and go west, stopping first at **Dorado**, where you can take in some world-class golf or hide out at the beach at Punta Salinas.

Continue west and stop to watch the waves explode over the reefs at **Playa Mar Chiquita**, where you can picnic while enjoying the aquatic drama. Turn southwest, winding up the mountain road to the **Observatorio de Arecibo**. If you're extraordinarily lucky, this might be the day this mountain-sized icon detects life on another planet. Bunk nearby at the restored plantation of **Hacienda Gripiñas**.

Next morning, take full advantage of being in coffee country before finding your way along the Ruta Panorámica, heading up toward Puerto Rico's tallest peak in the **Reserva Forestal Toro Negro**. Come off your high and make your way to historic **Ponce** to dine and sleep. The next day start slow and enjoy the city's excellent museums, then head east to sample smoky pork at one of the famed roadside *lechoneras* (eateries specializing in suckling pig) in **Guavate**. Continue east to sleep at a beach house in **Yabucoa**. The cool, green interior of **El Yunque** and its magical rainforest starts day six, which finishes on the white sands of **Playa Luquillo**. At night, glide across the glowing waters of the bioluminescent bay at Laguna Grande.

Before returning to San Juan, have a meal from one of the famous *friquitines* (beach kiosks) at Playa Luquillo. Drive back via **Loíza Aldea**, where you can buy a *vejigante* (traditional horned mask), before passing the evening wandering the back streets of Old San Juan and stopping for a drink where you can watch locals and other visitors doing just the same.

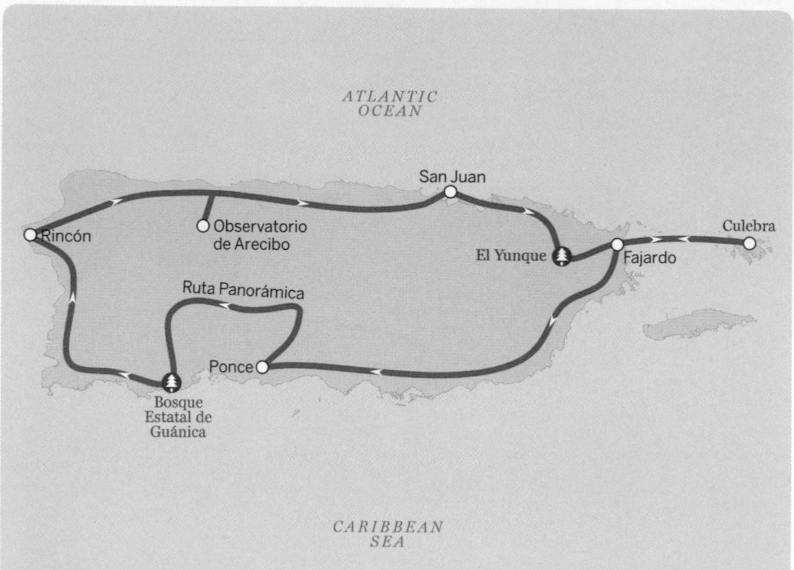

The Grand Tour

Spend four days in **San Juan** and the surrounding areas, getting plenty of beach time and making sure to see Old San Juan. Spend at least one night listening to live salsa and taking in the dance-floor action at Nuyorican Café, the best live music club on the island. Head to **El Yunque** for a day of hiking, then spend the night in **Fajardo** and experience the wonder of the bioluminescent bay at Laguna Grande.

The next morning head east aboard the ferry for **Culebra** – the more intimate cousin to Vieques. The next few days will go by too quickly, snorkeling and swimming at some of the best beaches in the world, and taking a charter trip off to the abandoned white-sand paradise of Isla Culebrita.

Now that your batteries are fully recharged, it's time to do some exploring. Make for the mainland and follow the quiet road past the sleepy sugar towns of the south coast toward **Ponce**. Spend a couple of days exploring the colonial buildings and excellent food in the so-called 'Pearl of the South.' You can visit La Guancha Paseo Tablado, Centro Ceremonial Indígena de Tibes or make a short detour up the mountain on the **Ruta Panorámica** to do some hiking and sip the island's famous coffee.

Definitely allow one day (preferably with an early morning start so you can be done by mid-afternoon when the sun is at its hottest) for the rugged, bone-dry forest of **Bosque Estatal de Guánica**. After hiking, drive scenic Rte 333 along the south coast and stop to swim at tiny mangrove-enclosed beaches and spend the night in an isolated resort.

You can either spend the day swimming the turquoise water of Playa Santa or head straight to the final destination, **Rincón**. The last few days of the trip will be spent surfing (or taking lessons) on perfect waves and soaking up the island's best sunsets with an icy rum drink in hand. Complete the circuit, breaking up the drive with a stop at the **Observatorio de Arecibo**, before arriving back in San Juan for your final evening, dining in style in Old San Juan or Santurce.

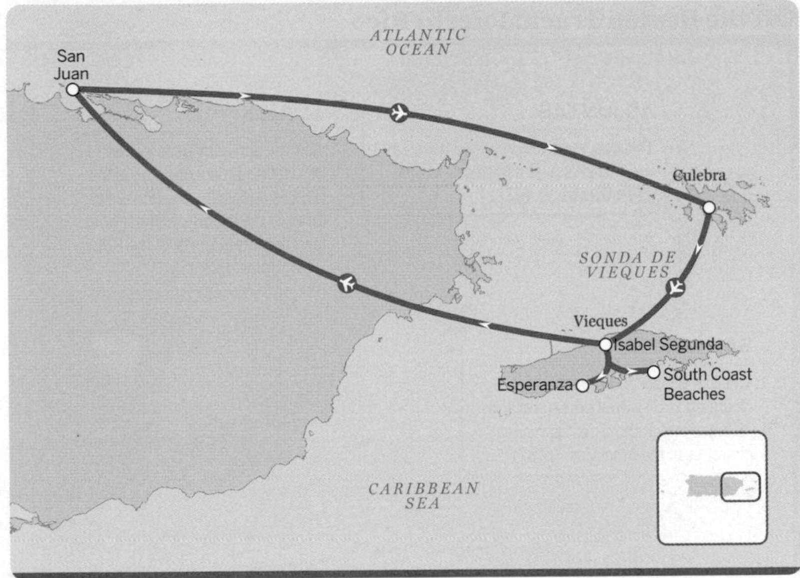

Escape to Culebra & Vieques

After time in the capital of **San Juan**, hightail it out of town for your island break. A trip to the islands of Culebra and Vieques displays Puerto Rico in its best light: perfect sand, laid-back atmosphere and ramshackle nightlife. Take a scenic flight to leave the capital: it's affordable and saves you the hassle and expense of getting to the ferries at Fajardo, plus the daredevil approach to Culebra rivals the best thrill ride.

Start in **Culebra**, which doesn't have much in the way of fancy resorts and clubs; the focus here is on the world-class beaches, reef snorkeling and wildlife refuges. With few cars on the island and long, deserted stretches of sand, Culebra offers the serenity that can be all too rare on the crowded Puerto Rican mainland. Visitors can soak in the expansive views of the ocean, breathe the fresh island air and explore beaches, from the renowned Playa Flamenco to the remote and enticing Playa Zoni. Save time for the beautiful snorkeling at Luis Peña Marine Preserve.

After dark, the little harbor at Dewey comes alive with affable expats whose love of karaoke crooning is only rivaled by their thirst for cold cans of Medalla.

Next up is surprising Vieques, the larger island just southwest of Culebra. You can take a ferry back to the mainland and another out to Vieques, but flying is vastly quicker and much more fun. Once you touch down in **Isabel Segunda**, hang around this atmospheric town for a bit before heading south to **Esperanza**, the perfect place to savor the slow pace of the tropics while enjoying some fine places to stay, eat and drink. You may not want to leave. Spend the next few days exploring the wealth of **south coast beaches** in the Vieques National Wildlife Refuge. You will be hard-pressed to choose your favorite as you marvel at small coves and deep bays and try in vain to find a crowd.

Save one night for the magically glowing waters of the Bioluminescent Bay, where you can paddle out in a quiet kayak or glide silently in an electric boat, before flying back to San Juan.

Off the Beaten Track: Puerto Rico

ADJUNTAS

This cool subtropical jungle haven in the hills is rich with bananas, coffee and citrus fruits. (p222)

JAYUYA

Visit the surreal Museo del Cemí in this isolated town, located in a steep-sided valley overlooked by three of the island's highest peaks, a few kilometers north of the Ruta Panorámica. (p221)

SAN GERMÁN

The island's second-oldest city (founded 1511) is well preserved and includes one of the oldest surviving churches in the Americas. (p187)

REFUGIO NACIONAL CABO ROJO

The southernmost extent of Puerto Rico is crowned by its iconic Los Morrillos Lighthouse; nearby is the beautiful beach of Playa Santa. (p186)

LA PARGUERA

Discover this low-key and funky seaside town, with its maze of mangrove canals running to the open ocean, which has a 40ft diving wall. (p162)

COAMO

The namesake thermal baths here are linked to Ponce de León's quest for the fountain of youth. (p157)

0 20 km
0 10 miles

BOSQUE ESTATAL DE CARITE

Enjoy beautiful hiking and swim in icy pools that are almost empty for much of the year. On your way, grab lunch from one of the *lechoneras* along the highway near Guavate. (p213)

HWY 3 SOUTH OF PLAYA HÚCARES

Enjoy low-key beaches, small villages and great eats on this drive that's well off the main road. (p108)

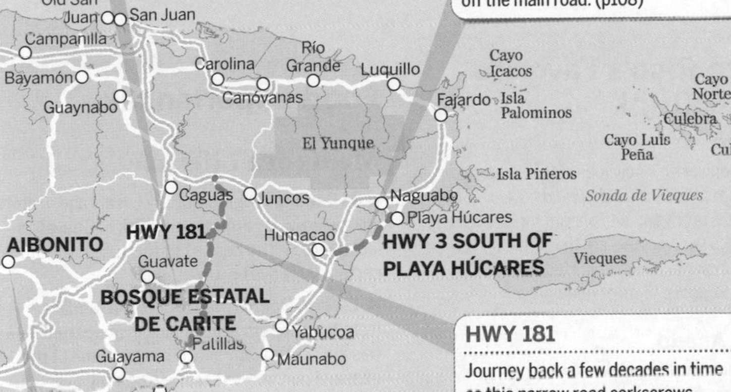

HWY 181

Journey back a few decades in time as this narrow road corkscrews through the lush mountains on the south side of El Yunque to the coast. (p111)

AIBONITO

Try to see both coasts of the island from the Mirador La Piedra Degetau before taking in the extraordinary spectacle of Puerto Rico's deepest canyon, the Cañón de San Cristóbal. (p214)

Plan Your Trip
Eat & Drink Like a Local

From trendy dining in San Juan to the roadside stalls of Guavate, Puerto Rico's food is the best and most varied in the Caribbean. *Comida criolla* (traditional Puerto Rican cuisine) is a blend of influences as wide-ranging as the Caribbean, African, Spanish and American forces that shape the culture itself.

Puerto Rico's Favorite Food & Drink

Mofongo

The Commonwealth's delicious staple, *mofongo* is made from plantains mashed and cooked with garlic, spices, broth and bits of pork for richness and flavor. No two versions are the same; it's so popular that plantains are imported from the Dominican Republic to meet demand.

Lechón Asado

The heavenly smell of *lechón asado* (roast suckling pig) wafts from countless stalls and simple open-air restaurants. Succulent, juicy and lavishly seasoned, it's always popular. In fact, many make the pilgrimage to Guavate, where scores of outlets compete for business, just for a plate or two.

Rum

As the home of Bacardí, the world's largest producer of rum, it's no surprise that Puerto Rico loves the spirit in its many forms, from crystal clear to amber, mild to complex. Look for sipping varieties in bars or just enjoy that perennial crowd pleaser, a fruity rum punch.

Food Experiences

Meals of a Lifetime

➡ **El Rancho Original** (p218) Locals and visitors alike will always argue over which of Guavate's *lechoneras* is the best – but this place will almost certainly always be a contender.

➡ **El Gato Negro** (p182) Join local families – from tiny nippers to gossiping grandparents – at this authentic waterside diner for some of the freshest and tastiest seafood you will ever eat.

➡ **José Enrique** (p78) For San Juan's best cuisine, head to Santurce, and for Santurce's best cuisine, head to José Enrique's eponymous restaurant to discover some of the best food Puerto Rico, and indeed, the Americas, has to offer.

➡ **Kasalta's** (p79) A classic San Juan cafe and restaurant with every local specialty you can imagine, from the soups to the superb desserts.

➡ **Manolín** (p75) An un-fancy gem in Old San Juan where staples like *mofongo* and *churrasco a la parrilla* (skirt steak) are given full honors – and at bargain prices.

Culinary Festivals

Festivals celebrating regional specialties take place year-round. Some favorites:

➡ **Maricao Coffee Festival** Held in mid-February, this celebration has demonstrations of traditional coffee-making and plenty of info on local brews. The rugged mountain setting is sublime, and the fresh air fills with the scent of roasting beans.

➡ **Carnaval de Salinas** Held in Salinas in April, this festival showcases the many varieties of local seafood.

➡ **Festival del Apio** In mid-April the small farming town of Barranquitas honors an unlikely culinary hero, the *apio*, a relative of celery. It's a tasty addition to *mofongo* and many other staples.

➡ **Festival del Guineo** Who knew there were so many types of banana? Try more than a dozen varieties at this festival (which also honors the hard-working local farmers) in Lares in mid-July. Marvel at the spectacle of the banana-eating contests.

➡ **Festival del Plátano** October in Corozal is all about plantains – mashed, fried and all ways in between. And, yes, they serve many variations on *mofongo*!

➡ **Festival de los Platos Típicos** Luquillo, home to the famous group of food stalls, is the perfect home for this mid-November celebration of popular local foods.

What to Eat & Drink

Pork & More

First things first: Puerto Ricans adore meat. They smoke it, stew it, fry it and fillet it. They make bold claims about it (apparently modern barbecue descends from the roast pork that the Taíno called *barbicoa*), they mash it up with all kinds of starches (*mofongo,* anyone?) and they form it into outlandish designs (such as *chuletas can-can*, fringed like a showgirl's skirt).

But fancy or no-frills, the top of the Puerto Rican food chain is a smoky, savory *lechón asado*, which is cooked on a spit over a charcoal fire. When it's done right, the pig is liberally seasoned with a distinctive seasoning called *adobo* (garlic, oregano, paprika, peppercorns, salt, olive, lime juice and vinegar worked into a paste). *Adobo* comes from Spain and is often associated with Filipino food. The meat is then basted with *achiote* (annato seeds) and juice from *naranjas* (the island's sour oranges). Finally, after it's cooked to crispness, the meat is served with *ajili-mójili* (tangy garlic sauce).

For less festive occasions, Puerto Rican dinners include roast *cabro* (kid goat), *ternera* (veal), *pollo* (chicken) or *carne mechada* (roast beef).

Seafood

Despite all that ocean, seafood takes a second place to pork on Puerto Rican menus. But that doesn't mean that it's not popular. A favored way to prepare seafood – from *pulpo* (octopus) to *mero* (sea bass) – is *en escabeche*. This technique yields a fried then chilled seafood, pickled in vinegar, oil, peppercorns, salt, onions, bay leaves and lime juice.

Fried fish is popular at beachside stalls and cafes. It's often topped with *mojo isleño* (a piquant sauce of vinegar, tomato sauce, capers and spices). Cheap and tasty, *bacalaitos* (fried codfish fritters) are ubiquitous.

Jueyes (land crabs) have long been a staple of islanders who can simply gather them from the beaches. An easy way to enjoy the taste is to eat *empanadillas de jueyes (*crab meat is picked from the shells, seasoned and baked in a wrap with *casabe* paste, which is made from yucca). Fish lovers should also try a bowl of *sopón de pescado* (fish soup), with its scent of onions, garlic and a subtle taste of sherry.

Shrimp and prawns are often marinated in garlic, grilled and served with *mofongo*, a heavenly pairing.

Soups & Stews

Soups and stews fill the humble cafeterias serving *comida criolla* and offer a genuine fusion of Taíno, European and African flavors. Many include island vegetables for texture: *yautia* (tanier; a starchy tuber that is very similar to taro), *batata* (sweet potato), yucca, chayote squash and *grelos* (turnip greens). *Sancocho* (Caribbean soup) blends these vegetables with plantains – peeled and diced – and coarsely chopped tomatoes, green pepper, chilis, cilantro, onion and corn. Cooks then add water, tomato sauce, chopped beef and pork ribs for flavoring.

Another delicious, common dish is *asopao de pollo,* a rich and spicy chicken stew soaked in *adobo*.

Fruits

Puerto Rico grows and exports bananas, papayas, fresh and processed pineapples, as well as a bewildering variety of exotic tropical fruits. It's also the third-largest producer of citron – behind Italy and Greece – and you'll see a long swath of fields around Adjuntas dedicated to this fruit. Markets and stalls selling fruits (and fresh vegetables like perfect ripe tomatoes) are common.

Desserts

Puerto Ricans love their sweets and even the smallest town will usually have a bakery where you can get fresh cakes and other treats. In larger cities, stylish cafes will have their own bakery section where you can choose from an array of temptations.

Look for the flavors of passion fruit and other tropical treats in desserts like flan. In fact this version of custard is customized in myriad ways; versions with chocolate are highly prized. *Arroz con Dulce* (rice pudding) is best when topped with a dusting of freshly ground cinnamon.

Coffee & Fruit Juices

Coffee, grown in Adjuntas and many of the mountain regions, is a staple at all hours. In fact Puerto Rico is fast gaining a reputation for some of the best coffee in the hemisphere. Locally owned coffee houses are springing up, with an especially impressive collection in Old San Juan.

COFFEE PLANTATIONS

Somewhat off the beaten path, Puerto Rico's historic coffee plantations let you enjoy a fresh brew amid trees laden with beans and with stunning scenery. The tortuous Ruta Panorámica takes travelers past one mountainside plantation after another. Among our favorites there and elsewhere:

- Hacienda San Pedro (p221), Jayuya
- Hacienda Gripiñas (p222), Jayuya
- Hacienda Buena Vista (p153), Ponce

Cafe con leche (coffee with milk) is a Puerto Rican version of a cafe latte and is a staple at breakfast. Easily tossed back, it's the perfect start to a day.

Fruit juices, such as *guanábana* juice, are locally made in both carbonated and noncarbonated varieties. *Mavi* is something like root beer, made from the bark of the ironwood tree. As in much of the tropics, beach and street vendors sell *cocos fríos* (chilled green coconuts) with tops lopped off on the spot and straws inserted to reach the uber-refreshing juice inside.

Rum & Beer

Simply put, *ron* (rum) is the national drink. Puerto Rico is the largest producer of rum in the world, and distilleries prop up the island's economy. The headquarters of the Bacardí Rum Factory is in Cataño, but most Puerto Ricans drink locally made Don Q or Castillo. Sipping a fine rum (flavors can include a rich medley of caramel and molasses) is a treat in many bars; Barrilito Three Star is aged in old sherry barrels for up to 10 years and is much lauded. Of course, many prefer their rum in one of the island's ubiquitous cocktails: piña colda and rum punch.

Medalla Light is a popular *very* light pilsner that many islanders drink like water; it usually costs no more than $2 in bars and cafes.

How to Eat & Drink

Dining out in Puerto Rico is easy and fun. Among areas notable for food, Old San Juan has a great range of places to eat, as do other areas of the capital such as Santurce, where food writers rave about the trendy restaurants. Cities such as Ponce and Rincón have many interesting options, as do the islands of Culebra and Vieques.

When to Eat

- **Breakfast** Typical Puerto Rican breakfasts are light and simple, except on weekends and holidays, when people have more time to cook fancy dishes or go out. Many just grab a coffee and a roll or a *la mallorca* (a sweet snack made of pastry covered with powdered sugar).

CHEAP TREATS

Cheap, cheerful and indisputably Puerto Rican, *friquitines*, also known as *quioscos*, *kioskos* or just plain food stalls, offer some of the island's best cheap snacks. Running the gamut from smoky holes-in-the-wall to mobile trucks that park on the roadside, these kiosks offer fast food that is invariably homemade, locally sourced and tasty.

The island's most famous cluster of permanent *friquitines* (more than 60 in all) lines the beachfront at Luquillo (p102). Other more movable feasts operate at weekends in places such as Piñones near San Juan and Boquerón on the west coast, although you can come across them almost anywhere. Even Vieques has a couple of superb food trucks.

Among the favorites on offer:

- *Surullitos* (fried cornmeal and cheese sticks)
- *Empanadillas* (meat or fish turnovers)
- *Alcapurrias* (fritters made with mashed plantains and ground meat)
- *Bacalaítos* (salt-cod fritters seasoned with oregano, garlic and sweet chili peppers)

But don't think your choices are limited: everything from fabulous Mexican to smokey barbecue and much more is on offer.

When it's hot, keep an eye out for *piragúeros*, vendors who sell syrupy *piraguas* (cones of shaved ice covered in sweet fruity sauces such as raspberry, guava, tamarind or coconut). Another treat are fresh smoothies made from your choice of an abundance of fruit.

- **Lunch** Puerto Ricans usually go cheap for lunch on weekdays, flocking to fast-food outlets for burgers and the like, or gathering around *friquitines* (street vendors) that sell a variety of fried finger foods. On weekends, longer lunchtime meals with groups of friends and families are favored, and roadside stands near local beaches are crowded. On Sunday afternoons, a big *cena* (lunch; 1pm to 4pm) in scenic spots is especially popular.
- **Dinner** This is the one meal of the day that busy Puerto Ricans are likely to enjoy in a restaurant. Especially on Thursday, Friday and Saturday nights, try to book a table at popular places, although you will likely just wait your turn with the jovial masses.

Where to Eat

- **Friquitines** These street vendors are found anywhere there are groups of people.
- **Repostelrías** In all but the tiniest of villages, the place for a morning *café con leche* and a couple of slices of *pan criollo* (a bit like French bread) is the local bakery.
- **Cafes** Come in many forms, from corner joints that serve all manner of drinks and simple foods, to ornate eateries where Puerto Rico's excellent local coffees are served with style.
- **Restaurants** Found in all shapes and sizes, from simple cafeterias where you can get cheap plates of local staples, to grand seaside venues noted for their fresh seafood.

Plan Your Trip

Puerto Rico Outdoors

Puerto Rico has it all: vistas of turquoise water, bushwhacking through dense jungle, kayaking over warm waves and heavenly surf breaks. The range of outdoor adventures in Puerto Rico is limited only by your ambition, and the island's diverse forests, balmy beaches and crinkled karst formations are calling.

Puerto Rico's Most Memorable Trails

La Mina Trail (p95)

Navigate through an old mine tunnel in the rainforest, ending at a lovely waterfall.

El Yunque Trail (p97)

This moderately challenging hike summits the highest point in Puerto Rico's rainforest.

Cueva del Viento (p202)

Test your navigation skills on the poorly marked trails of the Guajataca forest, and find this spooky cave.

Camino Ballena (p161)

Hike down a big hill in dry forest and, just when you're getting parched, take a dip in the Caribbean.

Los Morrillos Lighthouse (p186)

Scramble up to the windswept headlands and old lighthouse overlooking Puerto Rico's remote southwest corner.

Surfing

Lapped on four sides by warm ocean, Puerto Rico has earned the right to consider itself the 'Hawaii of the Atlantic,' with the most consistent surf breaks in the world. Thanks to legendary waves at beaches such as Tres Palmas, Crash Boat and Jobos, Puerto Rico has a deeply ingrained surfing culture based around some of the best breaks in the Americas.

When to Go

➡ **October–April** Winter is the time when cold fronts and low pressure systems from the north bring the biggest waves to Rincón and other surfing destinations on the west and north shores.

When Not to Go

➡ **December, June & July** Even though you can surf in the west year-round, rates spike in December, when hordes of Americans on Christmas vacation invade, making for crowded waters and competitive accommodations. In June and July there are smaller, if surfable swells, but vacationing Puerto Ricans arrive in droves and many accommodations enforce a three-night minimum stay.

SURF ESCAPES FROM SAN JUAN

If the west coast's waves are too big, or if its dudes are too cool or the drive is too far, there are a number of lesser-known options for surfers who want to make a quick day trip from San Juan. Along the north coast there are a few decent breaks for expert surfers around Manatí, and those with less experience can enjoy the shallow-water thrills of boogie boarding. There are even reasonable surfing lessons (p67) to be had in the capital, San Juan.

Die-hards will take what they can get at Balneario Escambrón in Puerta de Tierra, while the best stuff can be found over in Piñones at Los Aviónes. East of San Juan, the best place to surf barrels is at La Pared in Luquillo or the wildlife reserve at La Selva.

Where to Surf

Although there are opportunities to surf the north and east coasts (Luquillo has a popular break), the best of Puerto Rico's surfing is off the famous west coast.

➡ **Rincón** In 1968 the World Surfing Championships were held at Rincón (p167), and the island hasn't looked back since. Surfers from around the world come here for a long annual season. The huge variety of breaks include plenty of stuff for beginners and experts. This is Puerto Rico's surfing capital.

➡ **Aguadilla** Some locals actually favor the breaks near here (p203), which are generally a bit more challenging than those at Rincón.

➡ **Isabela** (p205) To avoid the crowds, rent an apartment on the cliff-edge out-of-the-way beach towns near Isabela. Playa Jobos, a long beach good for all levels, is here. Gas Chambers is a right-hand break for experienced surfers, while Surfer's Beach is kind to beginners.

Renting Boards & Taking Lessons

Anywhere there is surfing on Puerto Rico you can expect to find board rentals, surf shops and usually places for lessons. The local scene is popular enough that there is demand for good gear. In San Juan, especially, you'll find many highly promoted daytime surf camps for people of all ages.

Underwater Adventure

Most Caribbean islands boast a formidable diving scene and Puerto Rico is no exception, with an exciting selection of walls, drop-offs, reefs and underwater caves.

Where to Dive

➡ **Parguera Wall** The first of Puerto Rico's truly world-class dive areas is near La Parguera in the south. The underwater wall (p164) falls from 60ft to over 1500ft due to a huge drop in the continental shelf below the sea bed. With more than 25 named dive sites, the area is awash with trenches, valleys, coral gardens and colorful fish.

➡ **Isla Desecheo** Thirteen miles northwest of Aguadilla, Desecheo (p204) has a number of spectacular dive sites and visibility that is often at least 100ft.

➡ **Isla Mona** This is where real adventurers head for diving. It's expensive to charter a trip, but the unblemished waters (p190) are frequented by turtles and seals.

➡ **Culebra** The protected waters of the Luis Peña Marine Preserve (p118) gain more followers every year.

➡ **San Juan** If you can't stray far from the capital, there is good diving right off shore at Balneario Escambrón (p63).

Where to Snorkel

➡ **Culebra & Vieques** The best snorkeling in Puerto Rico can be found off the sheltered islands Culebra (p118) and Vieques (p131), where you can snorkel directly from the beach. The former offers Punta Melones, the Luis Peña Marine Preserve and the wonderfully isolated Playa Carlos Rosario; the latter boasts an array of options on the west and south coasts.

➡ **Isla Caja de Muertos** The south coast faces clear Caribbean waters that suffer low river runoff. Taking the day trip out to this island (p148) near Ponce can satisfy hikers as well.

➡ **La Parguera** These warm waters (p163) have some decent snorkeling, and DIY adventurers can access hidden mangrove beaches via kayak.

Dive Planning Basics

Generally speaking, the waters off the north and west coasts of Puerto Rico are rough and better suited to surfing. You may, however, get some luck on calm days snorkeling the fringe reefs off Condado and Playa Isla Verde in San Juan or at either Playa Shacks or Playa Steps in Rincón. Even though west-coast waters are calmer in summer, snorkeling still isn't great there.

Top Dive Operators

Dive operators run day trips out of the major ports and resort hotels around the island. If you are in the San Juan area, consider a dive trip to the caves and overhangs at Horseshoe Reef, Figure Eight or the Molar. There's decent diving along the chain of islands called 'La Cordillera,' east of Las Cabezas de San Juan (in the Fajardo area), with about 60ft to 70ft visibility. Catch the Drift or the Canyon off Humacao.

Many operators run highly promoted day trips on catamarans to Culebra and Vieques. These are fun outings and include beach visits along with time underwater.

Across Puerto Rico, you'll find good operators on the islands, and at Rincón, La Parguera and Fajardo among others.

Hiking

Hiking in Puerto Rico has plenty of potential. But what you actually get out of it depends largely on your individual expectations and how willing you are to strike out on your own (often without a decent map). It would be wrong to paint a picture of the island as some kind of hiker's nirvana. Although the scenery is invariably lush and the coastline wonderfully idyllic, a lack of well-kept paths and a dearth of accurate information are challenges.

Where to Hike

➡ **El Yunque National Forest** (p93) The most popular hikes by far are in the emblematic El Yunque rainforest, where a 23-mile network of largely paved trails has opened up the area to mass tourism. Hikes here are usually short and easily accessible, and there are plenty of ecominded tour operators happy to guide you through the main sights. The forest also contains Puerto Rico's only true backcountry adventure: the seven-hour trek to the top of El Toro (3522ft) and back.

➡ **Bosque Estatal de Guánica** The foil for El Yunque in every way, this forest (p161) is on the opposite corner of the island, the climate

SAFETY GUIDELINES FOR DIVING & SNORKELING

Before embarking on a scuba-diving, skin-diving or snorkeling trip, carefully consider the following points to ensure a safe and enjoyable experience:

➡ Possess a current diving certification card from a recognized scuba-diving instructional agency (if scuba diving).

➡ Be sure you are healthy and feel comfortable diving.

➡ Obtain reliable information about physical and environmental conditions at the dive site from a reputable local dive operation.

➡ Be aware of local laws, regulations and etiquette about marine life and the environment.

➡ Dive only at sites within your realm of experience; if available, engage the services of a competent, professionally trained dive instructor or dive master.

➡ Be aware that underwater conditions vary significantly from one region, or even one site, to another. Seasonal changes can significantly alter any site and dive conditions. These differences influence the way divers dress for a dive and what diving techniques they use.

➡ Ask about the environmental characteristics that can affect your diving and how trained local divers deal with these considerations.

HIKING ACROSS THE ISLAND

Fondo de Mejoramiento (www.fondodemejoramiento.org) runs day hikes covering the entire length of the island from east to west along the Cordillera Central (Central Mountains). The idea is to cover the whole Ruta Panorámica in different weekend segments over a period of three months (February to April). The 'Ruta' was actually designed by Luis Muñoz Marín in the 1950s primarily as a hiking route.

is bone-dry and instead of palms the trails are lined with cacti. This remote place doesn't have fantastic trails, but it's good for birdwatching and gorgeous views of the Caribbean.

➡ **Reserva Forestal Toro Negro** For more dramatic and isolated hikes, head toward the center of the island, on Puerto Rico's misty rooftop. Be prepared to get your shoes dirty here as clouds often shroud the peaks and the trails are invariably damp and muddy. Typical of the numerous forest reserves scattered along the Ruta Panorámica – others include Maricao, Carite and Guilarte – Toro Negro (p219) is rarely staffed in low season and you'll be lucky to spot more than a handful of fellow hikers enjoying the views.

➡ **Bosque Estatal de Guajataca** The 27-mile network of rough trails (p201) is good for a DIY hiker who doesn't mind a bit of bushwhacking, including a side trip to the spooky Cueva del Viento.

What to Expect

With its lush mountains, numerous protected parks and highly developed infrastructure, Puerto Rico ought to be a country perfectly suited to hiking. Yet in reality, decent well-signposted trails are few and far between, and many of the Commonwealth's carefully protected forest reserves are rarely utilized.

This paucity of backcountry information can be something of a shock to aspiring wilderness hikers fresh from bushwhacking their way through the Sierra Nevada or dragging their crampons across the European Alps. But, contrary to what the gushing tourist brochures would have you believe, Puerto Rico is no Yosemite. Nor are the Puerto Ricans – with some obvious exceptions – a nation of hikers.

Outside El Yunque National Forest, the island's two dozen or so forest reserves are invariably poorly staffed and lacking in any accurate trail maps. But plan ahead and a little-used Eden is yours for the exploring. Persistence is important. Try the Departamento de Recursos Naturales y Ambientales (p253) in San Juan, ask around at the various adventure tour agencies and – best of all – question the more outdoor-minded locals. You'll be surprised by what you can find.

Tour Companies & Guides

Numerous companies in San Juan can organize group trips to Toro Negro and El Yunque that incorporate hiking with various other activities such as zip-lining and climbing with a harness up a waterfall.

To make an organized trek in the company of serious Puerto Rican hikers, take a weekend hike through the Cañón de San Cristóbal near Barranquitas, where steep cliffs and spectacular waterfalls contribute to some of the island's most serendipitous scenery.

Private guide Robin Phillips (p99) leads all kinds of custom tours of El Yunque's less-traveled south side, including trips to petroglyphs.

Cycling

On an island often clogged with cars, cycling is not a contender. Still, you'll find that places to pedal and bicycle rentals – or leads to same – are becoming more common at guesthouses and hotels. San Juan has some good bike tours and rides along the beaches suitable for even the most casual cyclist.

Where to Cycle

➡ **Vieques** The protected wildlife refuges on this beautiful island (p131) are great places to cycle with minimal auto intrusion – although be prepared for road conditions that favor the sturdiest of mountain bikes.

➡ **Cabo Rojo** The secondary roads on the southwest coast of the island (p180) pass gently rolling hills around Guánica, Cabo Rojo and Sabana Grande. There are enough roads here for a two- or three-day trip, including rough trails around the Cabo Rojo lighthouse.

ALTERNATIVE OUTDOOR ADVENTURES

- There's a lot of rewarding **kayaking** through the bays, mangroves and nature preserves of San Juan and the east. There are many tours to choose from, the most popular and memorable being the nighttime journeys over the glowing waters of the bioluminescent bays near Fajardo (p106) and Vieques (p128).
- Hit the Reserva Forestal Toro Negro with San Juan–based adventure company, Acampa Nature Adventure Tours (p220), and you could find yourself **rappelling** off 60ft cliffs and **zip-lining** above the tree line.
- **Kitesurfing** has taken off on Playa Isla Verde (p63) in San Juan. Get kited out at the locally based 15 Knots (p67).
- Rincón (p172) is the best place to go for **whale-watching**; humpbacks appear in the Pasaje de la Mona around December. You can organize a boat trip or sometimes catch a glimpse from outside the Punta Higüero lighthouse.
- Of the various **yoga** retreats on the island, the most transcendental in both mood and setting has to be the early-morning classes at the Casa Grande Mountain Retreat (p201).

- **Isabela Coast** The coastal bike path (p204) is great for a casual afternoon ride. You'll pass the crashing surf and plenty of coastal beaches to take a dip. You can rent bikes right along the roadside.
- **Piñones** The specially designed bike trails in Piñones (p89) make for an easy, enjoyable ride on this small island.
- **Central Mountains** (p217) The Toro Verde Nature Adventure Park has a professionally groomed single-track trail that offers the island's best mountain biking.

Before You Go

If you want to do serious cycling in Puerto Rico, you'll find that it's more cost-effective to fly with your bike. The options for long-term rentals on the island are scarce and expensive. Also, remember to bring plenty of extra tubes, a spare tire, basic tools and a couple of replacement spokes so the island's combination of rough roads and scarce bike shops doesn't leave you out of commission.

Plan Your Trip

Travel with Children

Combining comforts of home and lots of all-ages outdoor adventures, Puerto Rico is an excellent destination for travelers with children. The options for family activities on the island are extensive and happen mostly outdoors. Snorkeling, cave exploring, rainforest adventures and just plain beach fun are some of the highlights.

Puerto Rico for Kids

Puerto Rico is a safe and fun destination for kids, with perhaps the best services for families in the Caribbean. Facilities are comfortable, and you'll receive fewer icy stares from curmudgeonly yachters than you might do elsewhere. Families will find it easy to fill their agendas.

Children's Highlights

Families will have the most fun on Puerto Rico if they plunge into its beloved outdoor charms: playing on sandy beaches, swimming in warm water and exploring the island's wildlife. However if it rains, many of the island's museums have programs for kids and there's a small kids' museum in San Juan.

Beaches

- **Condado** (p63) San Juan's most famous beach is also a family winner. Beautiful sand, gentle surf and lots of nearby places for treats.
- **Isla Verde** (p63) San Juan's other main beach can be a little quieter than Condado, which makes for more sand-castle-building solitude.
- **Sun Bay** (p130) The original public beach on Vieques has the facilities some of the wilder beaches around the island lack: changing rooms, bathrooms and picnic benches.

Best Regions for Kids

San Juan

Young travelers will be thrilled by San Juan's vibrant culture, wide beaches and kid-friendly museums. San Juan's historic sights have a lot of diversions for kids, and the tunnels and turrets of El Morro and Fuerte San Cristóbal capture young imaginations with stories of pirates and seafaring adventure.

Culebra & Vieques

Snorkeling and swimming in the clear, calm waters is excellent for kids, and the islands boast holiday home and apartment rentals, which can be an affordable option for families.

El Yunque & East Coast

Rainforests and frogs, drippy palms and mountain lookouts – the easy hikes of the El Yunque rainforest are thrilling. The bioluminescent waters of Fajardo are also magical.

West Coast

The west coast has excellent surfing and boogie boarding, with waves big enough or small enough to match all abilities. And it's fun to get off the beaten path.

➡ **Playa Flamenco** (p115) Culebra's famous beach is also famously fun for families. The gentle surf offers a relaxing frolic, while there are many vendors selling beach toys, snacks and other treats.

➡ **Playa Luquillo** (p100) Visiting families can join scores of local families at this beach popular with young and old. There's plenty of shade and the famous stalls sell every treat imaginable.

➡ **Playa Jobos** (p205) Watch surfers offshore beyond the reef, while enjoying protected waters close to shore. There are some good cafes for lunch.

➡ **Playa Shacks** (p205) Older kids will enjoy the underwater caves here for snorkeling at this somewhat secluded beach.

Hikes

The best hikes for the whole family are in the rainforest of El Yunque (p93). Unlike virtually every other forest on the island, these trails are well marked, easy to follow and easy enough for shorter legs. A favorite is the popular Big Tree Trail, which ends at a waterfall where kids who are brave enough can take an icy dip. The rainforest also has informative ranger-led walks.

Remember that the trails in El Yunque can get pretty crowded after 11am, so it's good to start early. Also, it's essential to bring water on your hike, as there are no facilities on the trails.

The Las Cabezas de San Juan (p103) nature reserve is another great natural area for families, with mini tours through a diverse coastal environment, a tram and lots of skeletons of marine animals.

Adventures

Families will also find a number of more adventurous activities in parts of the island further afield, though the winding hairpin turns of the central mountains are not recommended. Following the coast, there's lots to keep a family busy: you can ride a horse along the beach in Isabela (p204), explore the mysterious subterranean caves at the Río Camuy (p198) or hit the pirate-themed historical amusement park in Faro y Parque Histórico de Arecibo (p199).

MIND-BLOWING SIGHTS FOR CHILDREN

Bioluminescent bays Near Fajardo (p106) in the east and on Vieques (p128), the waters glow on dark nights, which produces many a delighted shriek as you float along by kayak or small electric boat.

Observatorio de Arecibo (p198) This mountain-top radio telescope is like a giant ear listening to the heavens.

Marine life in Culebra Coral, tropical fish and clear waters make for excellent snorkeling (p118).

Rainforest flora of El Yunque The soggy trails of the US forest system's only rainforest (p93) lead past fascinating flora and fauna.

Watching whales and surfers at Rincón Gaze out to migrating whales and surfers from the cliffs above the waters (p167).

Planning

Although fast-food chains and strip malls can be a bit off-putting for more adventuresome adults, the familiar sights make Puerto Rico more comfortable for kids. That said, there are several things parents can do to ensure a delightful visit.

➡ **Call ahead** Puerto Rican attractions can be notoriously unpredictable with their hours of operation – particularly in state-operated parks – so confirm opening hours before you go.

➡ **Know your accommodations** Look carefully at your hotel options to see what offerings they have for kids. Even though many of the hotels have swimming pools, some are tiny and not kid-friendly; others splash out with mini water parks. Check if resorts have evening programs designed to occupy younger travelers, which can give parents time for a moonlit stroll down the beach. Many major resorts offer 'kids clubs' during the day with myriad activities.

➡ **Consider an apartment** Holiday rental apartments are common and often quite affordable. Besides a lot more space than a hotel room, they offer cooking facilities for the vagaries of young appetites. Many have pools and are close to a beach.

➡ **Find a sitter** Getting someone to mind the kids is not always easy. Resorts and large hotels usually have agencies they recommend, but elsewhere finding a sitter you trust can be haphazard.

Regions at a Glance

San Juan

Nightlife
History
Beaches

Dine, Drink & Dance

The rollicking drinking and sensational eating of the Santurce district is reason enough to head out for the night in San Juan. Old San Juan is another great option; join locals and tourists dancing to the libidinous late-night rhythms of a salsa band. Still not done? The casinos are open all night.

Old San Juan

In Old San Juan history of the Americas comes alive in full color. From the ramparts of grand forts, visitors take in pastel-painted facades and tight cobblestone streets in one direction and the endless sparkle of the Atlantic in the other.

Beaches

This is the little Rio of the Caribbean, where the young, the old and the oily arrive to play under ever-present sunshine on beaches from Condado to Isla Verde.

p46

El Yunque & East Coast

Rainforest
Bio Bays
Beaches

El Yunque

The trails leading into El Yunque's humid hills are loaded with surprises: misty waterfalls, the colorful shock of a tropical bird or flower and unexpected views of the canopy-covered hills. And El Yunque is only the beginning of the fabulous natural attractions here.

Laguna Grande

Though Puerto Rico is blessed with several bodies of glowing bioluminescent waters, the one at Laguna Grande near Fajardo is fab. Those who haven't experienced the phenomenon will float along in awe.

Playa Luquillo

If you don't leave the main island for Culebra or Vieques, Playa Luquillo is Puerto Rico's best beach, perfect for swimming, snorkeling and surfing.

p92

Culebra & Vieques

Beaches
Snorkeling
Relaxation

Beaches

Bar none, these are Puerto Rico's loveliest and most diverse beaches – some of which are commonly listed among the best in the world. Visitors splash around and soak up the essence of the Caribbean daydream.

Snorkeling

The clear water, variety of fish and coral structures are mesmerizing. Unlike snorkel destinations that require a boat, these are within a short swim of the sandy beach.

Chillin'

Both islands have a funky, laid-back charm that is irresistible. A mix of characterful locals and long-term idiosyncratic expats combine to create an utterly mellow lifestyle.

p112

Ponce & South Coast

Architecture
Museums
Archaeology

Colonial Ponce

A mix of elegantly restored colonial mansions and tattered historic structures on the verge of collapse, Ponce has some of the most interesting architecture on the island.

Museums

Ponce hosts museums on political revolution, musical heritage and history, but the one that might be worth the trip from San Juan in its own right is the recently renovated Museo de Arte de Ponce.

Taíno Heritage

Just outside the southern capital is the largest Taíno site in the Caribbean, where quiet ceremonial ball courts pay homage to the island's distant past.

p140

West Coast

Surfing
Diving
Adventure

Rincón Breaks

The Beach Boys didn't sing about Rincón for nothing. The immaculate breaks near the point make for some of the best surfing on the planet. It's a great place to learn, too.

Diving

You can leave any number of west coast towns for excellent deep-water expeditions, including a trip to the pristine waters near Isla Desecheo and the illusive Isla Mona.

Cabo Rojo

The lonely Cabo Rojo point is a great place for a short cycling tour, but even if you arrive by car, a scramble up the lighthouse-crowned point overlooking the Caribbean is heart-racing.

p166

North Coast

Golf
Surfing
Caving

Dorado's Links

Dorado's long fairways, challenging courses and jaw-dropping views attract golfers from around the globe. You'll find some of the best courses in the Caribbean within chipping distance of one another.

Lesser-Known Breaks

Some claim that while Rincón gets all the glory, the serious surfing happens just to the north, near ramshackle seaside towns like Aguadilla and Isabela.

Vast Cave Systems

The karst country's limestone soft hills have made a kind of geological Swiss cheese. This part of the island has enormous networks of caves that are perfect for exploring alone or on underground tours.

p192

Central Mountains

Remote Roads
Hiking
Rural Culture

Ruta Panorámica

Travel along the Ruta Panorámica and you'll discover a part of Puerto Rico that few tourists see. The jagged spine of the central mountains includes coffee plantations, hidden villages and forgotten jungle.

Backcountry Walks

Wild scenery and isolation make the untrammeled forests here appealing to gutsy outdoor adventurers. Sure, none of the trails are marked or maintained, but that's part of the fun, right?

Tiny Villages

The little towns seem lonely until you stumble on the right *lechonera,* where a plate of smoky pork and a spontaneous dance party appear out of nowhere.

p210

On the Road

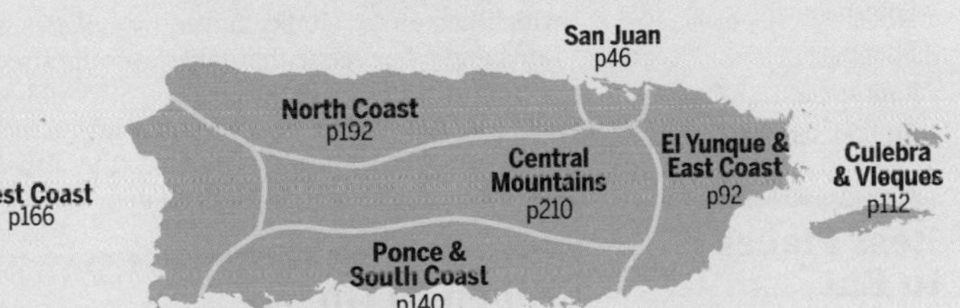
San Juan
p46
North Coast
p192
El Yunque &
East Coast
p92
Central
Mountains
p210
Culebra
& Vieques
p112
West Coast
p166
Ponce &
South Coast
p140

San Juan

POP 389,000

Includes ➡

Best Places to Eat

- José Enrique (p78)
- Santaella (p79)
- Kasalta's (p79)
- Carli's Café Fine Bistro & Piano (p75)
- Marmalade (p77)

Best Places to Stay

- Hotel El Convento (p71)
- La Concha (p72)
- Casablanca Hotel (p70)
- Andalucía Guest House (p73)

Why Go?

Established in 1521, San Juan is the second-oldest European-founded settlement in the Americas and the oldest under US jurisdiction. Shoehorned onto a tiny islet that guards the entrance to San Juan harbor, the old town was inaugurated almost a century before the Mayflower laid anchor in present-day Massachusetts, and is now a historic wonderland that juxtaposes historical authenticity with pulsating modern energy.

Beyond its timeworn 15ft-thick walls, San Juan is far more than a collection of well-polished colonial artifacts – it's also a mosaic of ever-evolving neighborhoods such as Santurce, which has a raw vitality fueled by galleries, superb restaurants and a bar scene that takes over the streets at night.

And then there are the beaches. Silky ribbons of sand line San Juan's northern edge from swanky Condado to resort-filled Isla Verde. You can land at the airport and be out splashing in the azure waters an hour later.

When to Go

Winter is the most popular time to visit San Juan as the frozen masses from colder climes come to thaw out. Old San Juan's streets fill with cruise-ship passengers, and bookings are essential at the hottest hotels and restaurants. The boisterous street party of Fiesta de la Calle San Sebastián in mid-January is a high point, especially for locals.

At other times of the year, San Juan is much quieter, even though the beaches remain alluring year-round. From April to October you'll find plenty of deals and diminished crowds.

From December through to May, the weather is at its best – highs in the mid-80s, lows in the high 70s and little humidity.

History

When the Spaniards arrived with their colonization plans in the early 1500s, San Juan was merely a deserted spit of land dominated by dramatic headlands and strong trade winds.

However, their low-land outposts encountered constant Indian attacks and mosquito-borne malaria, so in 1521 the colonists retreated to the rocky outcrop and christened it Puerto Rico (Rich Port). A few years later a Spanish cartographer accidentally transposed Puerto Rico with San Juan Bautista – the name the Spaniards had given to the whole island – and the name change stuck.

The gigantic fortress, El Morro, with its 140ft ramparts, soon rose above the ocean cliffs, and the Catholic Church built a church, a convent and a cathedral.

For the next three centuries, San Juan was the primary military and legislative outpost of the Spanish empire in the Caribbean and Central America. But economically it stagnated.

That all changed after the Spanish-American War of 1898. The US annexed the island as a territory and designated San Juan the primary port. Agricultural goods such as sugar, tobacco and coffee flowed into the city. *Jíbaros* (country people) flocked into the port for work, and old villages such as Río Piedras were swallowed up.

WWII brought capital and development as the US beefed up its military defense of the island and the Caribbean. After the war, the monumental economic initiative called Operation Bootstrap began changing Puerto Rico from an agricultural to a manufacturing-based economy, and hundreds of US factories relocated to San Juan after the island gained commonwealth status in 1951, to take advantage of tax breaks. Foreign and US banks arrived en masse, the first high-rise buildings went up, and tourist zones took shape along the beachfront of the burgeoning city.

The unchecked growth was a nightmare for city planners, who struggled to provide services, roads and housing. By the 1980s, unemployment was rampant and crime high. Ironically, Old San Juan was considered the epicenter of all that was wrong with the city. Tourists kept to the overdeveloped beaches of Condado, Isla Verde and Miramar.

In 1992, the 500-year anniversary of Columbus' 'discovery' of the Americas gave city leaders the impetus to restore Old San Juan.

The new millennium has brought several successful projects such as the super-efficient Tren Urbano (metro) that opened in 2005, a convention center in Miramar, and a series of redeveloped hotels in Condado.

Of late, San Juan has been hit hard by Puerto Rico's economic upheaval. Tourism is now more important than ever to the local economy.

Sights

Most of San Juan's major attractions, including museums and art galleries, are in Old San Juan. Beaches dominate the appeal of Condado, Ocean Park and Isla Verde (as they should), while Santurce offers buzzy, gritty delights. Be aware that most museums are closed on Mondays.

Old San Juan

Old San Juan is a colorful kaleidoscope of life, music, legend and history and would stand out as an unmissable sight anywhere, let alone on an island as small as Puerto Rico.

Somnolent secrets and beautiful surprises await everywhere. From the blue-toned, cobblestoned streets to the spectacle of over 400 historically listed buildings to the stunning views from old walls, there is a plethora of visual treats great and small.

Add to this the quarter's sensuous yet subtle mood swings: tranquil at dawn, languid during the midday heat, romantic at dusk and positively ebullient after dark.

Mixing ancient with modern, San Juan has embraced the present in the same way it has embraced every era that has gone before – with confidence, innovation and a palpable joie de vivre.

Far from being just another drop-off point on a busy cruise-ship itinerary, this is a city that lives for itself, never selling itself out to tourism: listen to the creaking rocking chairs on Calle de Sol, the clatter of dominoes in a local cafe or spontaneous African drumming echoing around Plaza de Armas. Prepare to be surprised, entranced and delighted – use our walking tour on p64 to help you explore.

★El Morro FORT

(Fuerte San Felipe del Morro; Map p52; ☎787-729-7423; www.nps.gov/saju; Calle del Morro; adult/child $3/free; ⏲9am-6pm) The star of Old San Juan, El Morro juts aggressively over bold headlands, glowering across the Atlantic at would-be conquerors. The 140ft walls (some

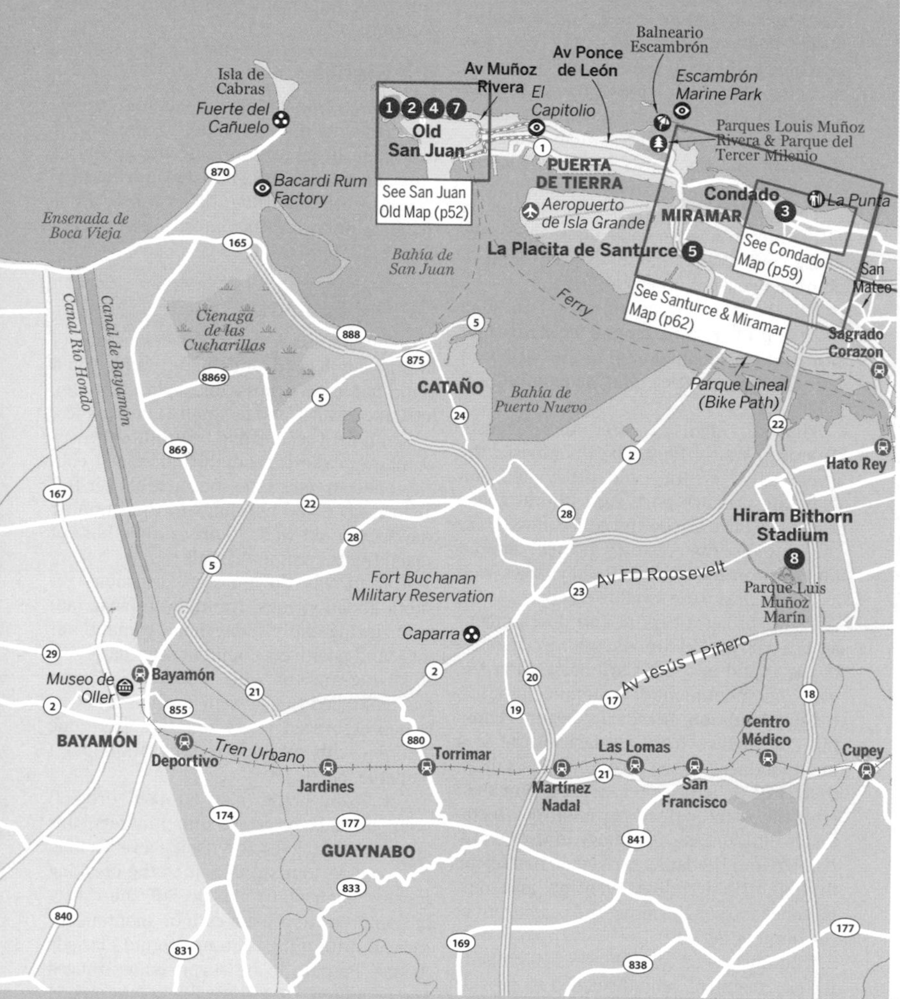

San Juan Highlights

❶ Journey back to the 16th century at **El Morro** (p47) and **Fuerte San Cristóbal** (p50).

❷ Feel the rhythm of Puerto Rico at a late-night salsa session at **Nuyorican Café** (p84).

❸ Hit some of the best urban beaches anywhere at **Condado**, **Isla Verde** (p63) and more.

❹ Be seduced by charm and beauty while wandering the characterful streets of **Old San Juan** (p47).

❺ Lose yourself in the narrow streets around Santurce's

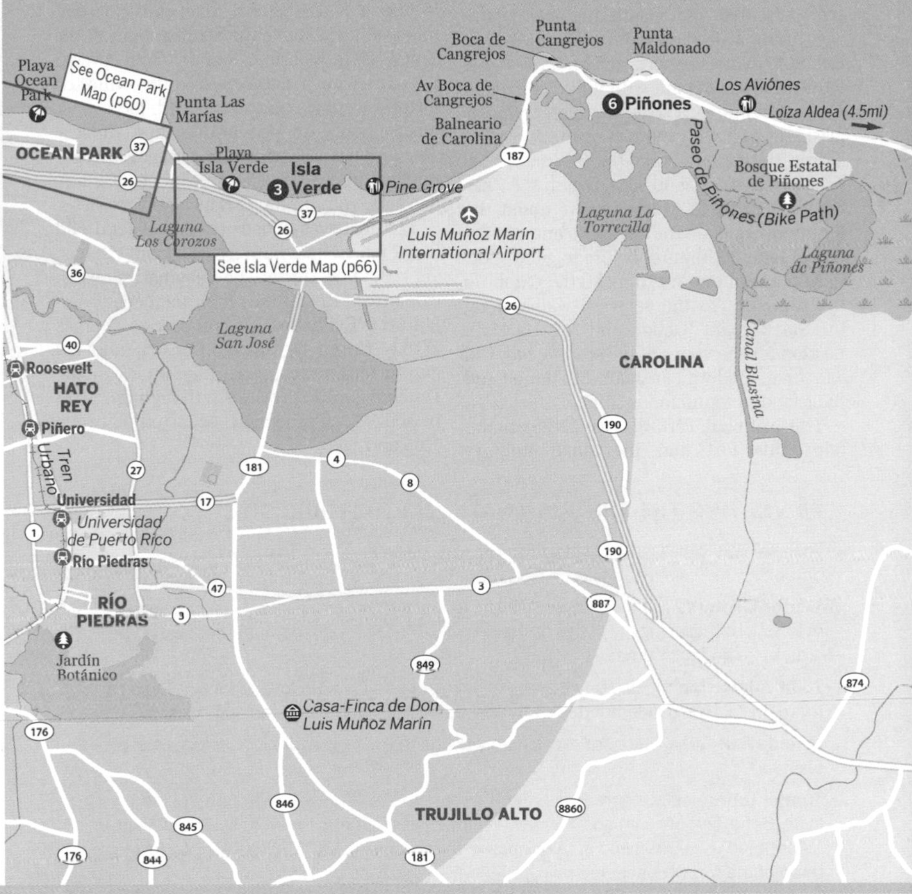

La Placita de Santurce (p83), where you'll find great restaurants, cafes and a fun bar scene.

❻ Explore bike paths, beaches and ramshackle restaurants in down-to-earth **Piñones** (p89).

❼ Savor locally grown coffee at one of the many exquisite **Old San Juan cafes** (p74).

❽ Cheer on the home baseball team as the Cangrejeros de Santurce knock it out of the park at **Hiram Bithorn Stadium** (p85).

up to 15ft thick) date back to 1539, and El Morro is said to be the oldest Spanish fort in the New World.

Displays document the construction of the fort, which took almost 200 years, as well as El Morro's role in rebuffing attacks on the island by the British, the Dutch and, later, the US military.

The gray, castellated **lighthouse** on the 6th floor has been in operation since 1846 (although the tower itself dates from 1906), making it the island's oldest light station still in use today. After suffering severe damage during a US navy bombardment during the 1898 Spanish-American War, the original lighthouse was rebuilt with unique Spanish-Moorish features, a style that blends in surprisingly well with the rest of the fort. Join a free **lighthouse talk** (10:30am Spanish & 2:30pm English Sat, 10:30am English & 2:30pm Spanish Sun) FREE to learn more about the lighthouse and get the chance to enter it. Arrive at least 30 minutes before to get a spot.

At a minimum, try to make the climb up the ramparts to the sentries' walks along the Sta Barbara Bastion and Austria Half-Bastion for the **views** of the sea, the bay, Old San Juan, modern San Juan, El Yunque and the island's mountainous spine.

The National Park Service (NPS) maintains this fort and the small military museum on the premises. It was declared a Unesco World Heritage site in 1983.

On weekends, the fields leading up to the fort are alive with picnickers, lovers and kite flyers. The scene becomes a kind of impromptu festival with food vendors' carts on the perimeter.

★Fuerte San Cristóbal — FORT

(San Cristóbal Fort; Map p52; 787-729-6777; www.nps.gov/saju; Av Muñoz Rivera; adult/child $3/free; 9am-6pm) San Juan's second major fort is Fuerte San Cristóbal, one of the largest military installations the Spanish built in the Americas. In its prime, San Cristóbal covered 27 acres with a maze of six interconnected forts protecting a central core with 150ft walls, moats, booby-trapped bridges and tunnels. The fort has a fascinating museum, a store, military archives, a reproduction of a soldier's barracks, and stunning Atlantic and city views.

The fort was constructed to defend Old San Juan against land attacks from the east via Puerta de Tierra. The imaginative design came from the famous Irish mercenary Alejandro O'Reilly and his compatriot Thomas O'Daly (hired by Spain). Construction began in 1634 in response to an attack by the Dutch a decade previously, though the main period of enlargement occurred between 1765 and 1783.

VISITING THE SAN JUAN NATIONAL HISTORIC SITE

To make your time visiting El Morro (p47) and Fuerte San Cristóbal, the two megastars of the San Juan National Historic Site, more rewarding, take note of the following:

Visitor Centers Each fort has a small and useful visitor center where you can learn more about these huge facilities and buy books that delve deeper into these amazing structures and their times.

Joint Admission You can buy a 24-hour ticket – good for both forts – for $5. If you can, try to do each on a different day so that all those walls don't start looking the same.

Orientation Talks There are short, highly useful free introductory talks every hour at each fort.

Tunnel Tours Hour-long free guided tours roam the tunnels at Fuerte San Cristóbal every Saturday (English) and Sunday (Spanish) at 10:30am. Come at least half an hour beforehand (or earlier) and put your name on the sign-up list. Guides walk you through three of the fort's tunnels, including one that's otherwise closed to the public.

Outworks Walk Hour-long free guided tours of the fortifications show how Fuerte San Cristóbal remained impregnable. The walks are held every Saturday (Spanish) and Sunday (English) at 2:30pm. Sign up at least half an hour beforehand (or earlier).

Life Inside the Fortification On the third Sunday each month, guides and re-creators give an idea of what life was like for a soldier in El Morro during the 18th century. Drills and duty dominated, and while the re-creations don't capture the smells of a time when bathing was rare, they do show what happens when you explode the black powder used in cannons.

Seven acres were lopped off the fort in 1897 to ease congestion in the old town, and the following year the Spanish marked Puerto Rico's entry into the Spanish-American War by firing at the battleship USS *Yale* from its cannon battery. The fort became a National Historic site in 1949 and part of the Unesco World Heritage site in 1983.

★La Fortaleza HISTORIC SITE

(Map p52; ☎787-721-7000; www.fortaleza.gobierno.pr; Recinto; suggested donation $3; ⊙tours 9am-3:30pm Mon-Fri) Guarded iron gates mark La Fortaleza, also known as El Palacio de Santa Catalina. This imposing building, dating from 1533, is the oldest executive mansion in continuous use in the western hemisphere. You can take a short guided tour that includes the mansion's Moorish gardens, the dungeon and the chapel.

Tour schedules change daily; call on the day you wish to visit to reserve a place, or stop by the gatehouse at the west end of Calle Fortaleza. Be prepared for a security gauntlet.

The original fortress for the young colony, La Fortaleza eventually yielded its military preeminence to the city's newer and larger forts, and was remodeled and expanded to domicile island governors for more than three centuries.

★Casa Blanca HISTORIC BUILDING

(White House; Map p52; ☎787-725-1454; San Sebastián; adult/child $2/1; ⊙8:30am-4:20pm Tue-Sat) First constructed in 1524 as a residence for Puerto Rico's pioneering governor, Juan Ponce de León (who died before he could move in), the Casa Blanca is the oldest continuously occupied house in the western hemisphere.

For the first 250 years after its construction it served as the ancestral home for the de León family. In 1783 it was taken over by the Spanish military, then with the change of Puerto Rico's political status in 1898, it provided a base for US military commanders until 1966. Today it is a historic monument containing a museum, a chain of fountains and an Alhambra-style courtyard. The interior rooms are decked out with artifacts from the 16th to the 20th centuries. Parts of the secluded grounds look like a fragment of tropical rainforest.

★Cuartel de Ballajá & Museo de las Américas MUSEUM

(Map p52; off Norzagaray; ⊙9am-noon & 1-4pm Tue-Sat, noon-5pm Sun) FREE Built in 1854 as a military barracks, the *cuartel* is a three-story edifice with large gates on two ends, ample balconies, a series of arches and a protected central courtyard that served as a plaza and covers a reservoir. It was the last and largest building constructed by the Spaniards in the New World. Facilities included officers' quarters, warehouses, kitchens, dining rooms, prison cells and stables. The small ground-floor cafe is a good place to pause and soak up the monumental courtyard's atmosphere.

The 2nd floor features the **Museo de las Américas** (Museum of the Americas; Map p52; ☎787-724-5052; www.museolasamericas.org; Cuartel de Ballajá, off Calle Norzagaray; adult/child $3/2; ⊙9am-noon & 1-4pm Tue-Sat, noon-5pm Sun), which gives an overview of cultural development in the New World. It features changing exhibitions, and Caribbean and European American art, most notably an impressive *santos* (small carved figurines representing saints) collection. The excellent shop is a good place to buy cultural books.

★Galería Nacional MUSEUM

(Map p52; ☎787-725-2670; 98 Norzagaray; adult/child $3/2; ⊙9:30am-noon & 1-5pm Tue-Sat) Next to the Iglesia de San José is the former Convento de los Dominicos, a Dominican convent that dates from the 16th century. The museum has been restored to its colonial grandeur and, with the adjoining Iglesia de San José, forms one of the oldest structures in the hemisphere. It houses galleries of Puerto Rican paintings from the 18th century to the present, including work by José Campeche and Francisco Oller. There are good special exhibitions.

Following centuries of use as a convent, the building became a barracks for Spanish troops and was later used as a headquarters for US occupational forces after the Spanish-American War of 1898.

Catedral de San Juan CHURCH

(Map p52; ☎787-722-0861; www.catedralsanjuan.com; 153 Calle del Cristo; ⊙8am-5pm) FREE Although noticeably smaller and more austere than other Spanish churches, the Catedral de San Juan nonetheless retains a simple earthy elegance. Founded originally in the 1520s, the first church on this site was destroyed in a hurricane in 1529. A replacement was constructed in 1540 and, over a period of centuries, it slowly evolved into the Gothic/neoclassical-inspired monument seen today.

Old San Juan

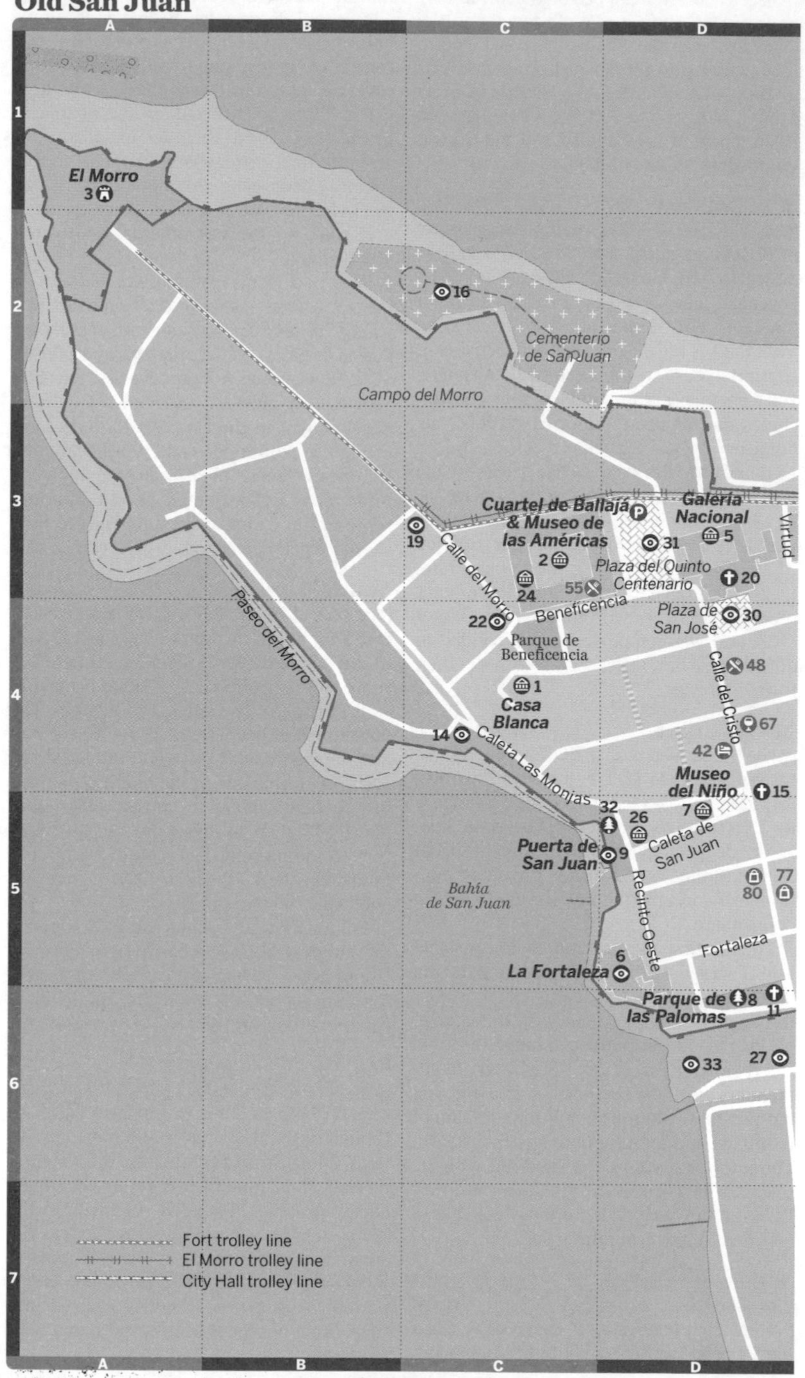
A
B
C
D
1
2
3
4
5
6
7
El Morro
3
16
Cementerio de San Juan
Campo del Morro
Cuartel de Ballajá & Museo de las Américas
Galería Nacional
Virtud
19
2
31
5
Plaza del Quinto Centenario
20
24
55
Calle del Morro
Beneficencia
Plaza de San José
30
22
Parque de Beneficencia
Calle del Cristo
48
1
Casa Blanca
Paseo del Morro
67
14
Caleta Las Monjas
42
Museo del Niño
15
7
32
26
Caleta de San Juan
Puerta de San Juan
9
Recinto Oeste
77
80
Bahía de San Juan
Fortaleza
6
La Fortaleza
Parque de las Palomas
8
11
33
27
Fort trolley line
El Morro trolley line
City Hall trolley line

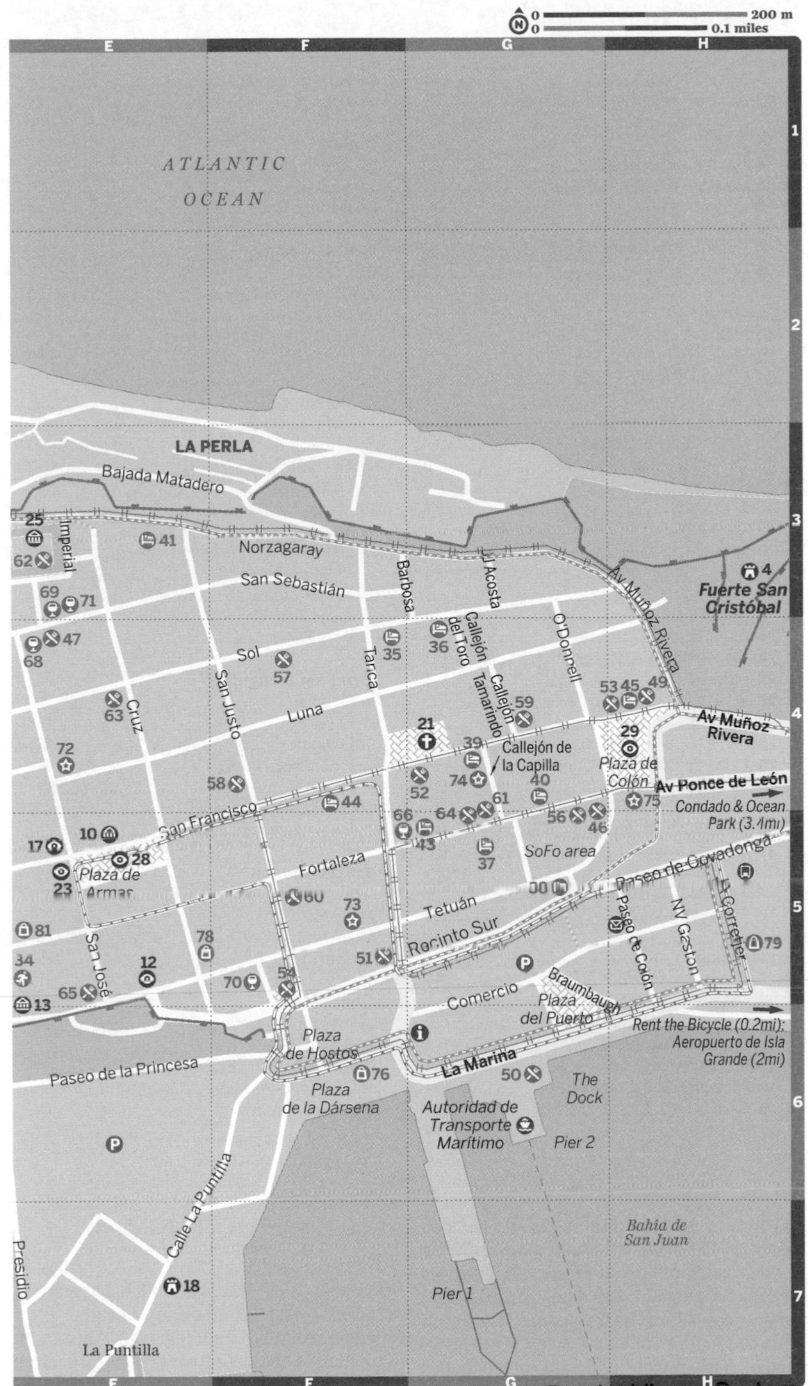
0 200 m
0 0.1 miles
ATLANTIC OCEAN
LA PERLA
Bajada Matadero
Norzagaray
Imperial
San Sebastián
Barbosa
Acosta
Av Muñoz Rivera
Fuerte San Cristóbal
Callejón del Toro
O'Donnell
Sol
Tanca
Callejón Tamarindo
San Justo
Cruz
Luna
Callejón de la Capilla
Plaza de Colón
Av Ponce de León
Condado & Ocean Park (3.4mi)
San Francisco
Fortaleza
SoFo area
Plaza de Armas
Paseo de Covadonga
Tetuán
Recinto Sur
San José
Paseo de Colón
NV Gastón
Corretjer
Comercio
Braumbaugh
Plaza del Puerto
Rent the Bicycle (0.2mi); Aeropuerto de Isla Grande (2mi)
Plaza de Hostos
La Marina
Paseo de la Princesa
Plaza de la Dársena
Autoridad de Transporte Marítimo
The Dock
Pier 2
Calle La Puntilla
Bahía de San Juan
Presidio
Pier 1
La Puntilla

Old San Juan

Top Sights

1 Casa Blanca ... C4
2 Cuartel de Ballajá & Museo de las Américas ... C3
3 El Morro ... A1
4 Fuerte San Cristóbal ... H3
5 Galería Nacional ... D3
6 La Fortaleza ... D5
7 Museo del Niño ... D5
8 Parque de las Palomas ... D6
9 Puerta de San Juan ... D5

Sights

10 Alcaldía ... E5
11 Capilla del Cristo ... D6
12 Casa de Ramón Power y Giralt ... E5
13 Casa del Libro ... E5
14 Casa Rosa ... C4
15 Catedral de San Juan ... D4
16 Cementerio de San Juan ... C2
17 Diputación ... E5
18 El Arsenal ... E7
19 Escuela de Artes Plásticas ... C3
20 Iglesia de San José ... D3
21 Iglesia San Francisco de Asís ... G4
22 Instituto de Cultura Puertorriqueña ... C4
23 Intendencia ... E5
24 Museo de las Américas ... C3
25 Museo de San Juan ... E3
26 Museo Felisa Rincón de Gautier ... D5
27 Paseo de la Princesa ... D6
28 Plaza de Armas ... E5
29 Plaza de Colón ... H4
30 Plaza de San José ... D4
31 Plaza del Quinto Centenario ... D3
32 Plazuela de la Rogativa ... D5
33 Raíces Fountain ... D6

Activities, Courses & Tours

34 Anam Spa & Cocktail Lounge ... E5

Sleeping

35 AlaSol Apartments ... F4
36 Casa Sol ... G4
37 Casablanca Hotel ... G5
38 Chateau Cervantes ... G5
39 Da House ... G4
40 Fortaleza Guest House ... G4
41 Gallery Inn ... E3
42 Hotel El Convento ... D4
43 Hotel Milano ... G5
44 Navona Studios ... F4
45 Posada San Francisco ... H4

Eating

46 Aguaviva ... G5
47 Anamu ... E4
48 Bodega Chic ... D4
49 Café Berlin ... H4
50 Café Cola'o ... G6
51 Café Cuatro Sombras ... F5
52 Cafeteria Mallorca ... G4
53 Caficultura ... H4
54 Carli's Café Fine Bistro & Piano ... F5
55 Don Ruiz ... C3
56 Dragonfly ... G5
57 El Jibarito ... F4
El Picoteo ... (see 42)
58 Finca Cialitos ... F4
59 La Madre ... G4
60 Manolín ... F5
61 Marmalade ... G4
62 Old San Juan Farmers Market ... E3
Patio del Nispero ... (see 42)
63 St Germain Bistro & Café ... E4
64 Trois Cent Onze ... G5
65 Verde Mesa ... E5

Drinking & Nightlife

66 Douglas' Bar ... F5
67 El Batey ... D4
68 La Factoria ... E4
69 La Taberna Lúpulo ... E3
Mezzanine ... (see 63)
70 Old Harbor Brewery ... F5
71 Rivera Hermanos Cash & Carry ... E3

Entertainment

72 Amigos del Corralón ... E4
73 Nuestro Son ... F5
74 Nuyorican Café ... G4
75 Teatro Tapia ... H4

Shopping

76 Artisans Fair ... F6
77 Bóveda ... D5
78 Butterfly People ... E5
79 Cigarros Antillas ... H5
80 Galeria Exodo ... D5
81 Olé ... E5

Most people come to see the marble tomb of Ponce de León and the body of religious martyr St Pio displayed under glass. However, you can get quite a show here on Saturday afternoons when the limos roll up and bridal parties requisition the front steps. The main entrance to the cathedral faces a beautiful shaded park replete with antique benches and gnarly trees. On Sundays and holy days, you'll see worshippers in their finery.

Museo de San Juan MUSEUM

(Map p52; ☎787-480-3530; 150 Norzagaray; by donation; ⏱9am-4pm Tue-Sun) Located in a Spanish colonial building, the Museo de San Juan is the definitive take on the city's 500-year history. The well-laid-out exhibition showcases pictorial and photographic testimonies from the Caparra ruins to the modern-day shopping malls. There's also a half-hour video about the history of San Juan and a small Saturday morning market in the pretty inner courtyard.

Iglesia de San José — CHURCH

(Map p52; ☎787-725-7501; Calle del Cristo; adult/child $1/free; ⏲noon-6pm 2nd & 4th Sat of month, mass 12:30pm 4th Sat) What it lacks in grandiosity it makes up for in age: the Iglesia de San José in the Plaza de San José is the second-oldest church in the Americas, after the cathedral in Santo Domingo in the Dominican Republic. Established in 1532 by Dominicans, this church, with its vaulted Gothic ceilings, still bears the coat of arms of Juan Ponce de León (whose family worshipped here), a striking carving of the Crucifixion and ornate processional floats.

For 350 years, the remains of Ponce de León rested in a crypt here before being moved to the city's cathedral, down the hill. It remains the final resting place of José Campeche, one of Puerto Rico's most revered artists, and the site of Puerto Rico's oldest fresco painting.

Long-term renovation has transformed the church into a construction site; it's a race against time as the National Trust for Historic Preservation has named the church one of America's most endangered old buildings due to deterioration. It's worth visiting during the church's limited public hours. The exposed structural details are fascinating, and an extensive bilingual exhibit highlights some of the archaeological discoveries made during the restoration process. Ask about a visit to the crypt below and always stop by when nearby as you might find the door open.

★Puerta de San Juan — GATE

(San Juan Gate; Map p52) Spanish ships once anchored in the cove just off these ramparts to unload colonists and supplies, all of which entered the city through a tall red portal known as Puerta de San Juan. This tunnel through the wall dates from the 1630s.

It marks the end of the Paseo de la Princesa, and stands as one of three remaining gates into the old city (the others lead into the cemetery and the enclave of La Perla). Once there were a total of five gates, and the massive wooden doors were closed each night to thwart intruders. Turn right after passing through the gate and you can follow the **Paseo del Morro** northwest, paralleling the old city walls for approximately three-quarters of a mile. Pause on one of the benches along the west side that have fine harbor and sunset views.

Plaza de Armas — PLAZA

(Army Plaza; Map p52) Follow San Francisco into the heart of the old city and it opens on to the Plaza de Armas. This is the city's nominal 'central' square, laid out in the 16th century with the classic look of plazas from Madrid and Mexico.

One of the highlights of the plaza is the **Alcaldía** (City Hall; Map p52; ⏲9am-4pm Mon-Fri), which dates from 1789 and has twin turrets resembling those of its counterpart in Madrid. This building houses the office of the mayor of San Juan and is also the site of periodic exhibitions.

At the western end of the plaza, the **Intendencia** (Administration Building; Map p52) and the **Diputación** (Provincial Delegation Building; Map p52) are two other functioning government buildings adding to the charms of the plaza. Both represent 19th-century neoclassical architecture, and come complete with cloisters.

In its time, the plaza has served as a military parade ground (hence its name), a vegetable market and a social center. Shade trees, banks of seats, and a couple of old-fashioned coffee booths still make the plaza the destination of choice for couples taking their evening stroll. The beat of a bomba drum has also been known to light up an otherwise humdrum evening.

Iglesia San Francisco de Asís — CHURCH

(Map p52; cnr Tanca & San Francisco; ⏲9am-6pm) Dating to 1756, this atmospheric old church is the perfect place to pause, even if you're not ready to get down on your knees and pray. Note the thickness of the original walls as well as the restored murals throughout. There are many ornately carved details. The tree-lined plaza out front is also good for a break.

★Parque de las Palomas — PARK

(Pigeon Park; Map p52) On the southern end of Calle del Cristo, Parque de las Palomas is in a tree-shaded cobblestone courtyard on the top of the city wall, with excellent views of Bahía de San Juan and the crisscrossing water traffic that includes Brobdingnagian cruise ships.

Paloma means 'dove' or 'pigeon' and it's the latter you'll encounter in the hundreds. With a lot more class than their often-scrabbling-about urban bretheren, these pigeons fly in and out of dovecote-like holes in the wall and offer up a chorus of coos when at rest. Some folks come to the park just to feed them; buy birdseed from a vendor by the gate.

Capilla del Cristo — CHURCH

(Christ's Chapel; Map p52; ⏲Tue afternoon & religious holidays) Over the centuries, tens of thousands of penitents have come to pray for miracles at the Capilla del Cristo, the tiny outdoor sanctuary at the end of a pedestrian street and adjacent to Parque de las Palomas.

You can see the chapel any time, but the iron fence across the front is only open on Tuesday afternoons and on religious holidays.

One story claims the church commemorates a miracle: during the city's San Juan Bautista festivities, a rider in a race was carried by his galloping horse down Calle del Cristo, off the top of the wall and into the sea, and miraculously survived. Over the years, believers of the fable have left hundreds of little silver ornaments representing parts of the body – called *milagros* (miracles) – on the altar as thanks for being cured of an infirmity.

★Museo del Niño — MUSEUM

(Children's Museum; Map p52; ☎787-722-3791; www.museodelninopr.org; 150 Calle del Cristo; adult/child $5/7; ⏲10am-4pm Tue-Thu, 10am-5pm Fri, noon-5:30pm Sat & Sun; 👪) Kids love the three floors of hands-on exhibits stuffed into this orange-and-green building that sits on the edge of a small shady park. Fun and interactive displays candy coat all sorts of serious and interesting topics. Favorites include a walk-through cave explaining bats and their sounds, a space exploration center, a climbing wall, a TV studio where you can make your own shows and a lot more. Even toddlers can get in on the fun in a special area just for them.

Casa del Libro — MUSEUM

(House of Books; Map p52; ☎787-723-0354; www.lacasadellibro.org; 199 Callejón de la Capilla; ⏲11am-4:30pm Tue-Sat or by appointment) FREE Bibliophiles will be in awe of this tiny but worthwhile collection of more than 5000 manuscripts and texts that date back 2000 years. The collection includes one of the most respected assemblages of incunabula (texts produced prior to 1501) in the Americas, including documents signed by King Ferdinand II and his wife Isabela. In 2014, the collection was temporarily relocated during construction work to Callejón de la Capilla (Chapel Alley) off 319 Fortaleza.

Plazuela de la Rogativa — PARK

(Map p52) This tiny gem of a plaza with lovely views of the bay is home to an interesting, stylized bronze sculpture of the bishop of San Juan and three women bearing torches.

According to legend, the women walked through this plaza one night in 1797 holding candles, which tricked British Lieutenant Abercromby (who was preparing to lay siege to San Juan with 8000 troops and a flotilla of over 50 vessels) into believing that reinforcements were flooding the city. Fearful of being outnumbered, Abercromby and his fleet withdrew.

SAN JUAN IN...

Two Days

Stay in Old San Juan (p47). Explore the historical sights of the **colonial quarter** and catch the sunset from an old wall. Wander till you find the perfect eatery before heading to Nuyorican Café (p84) for salsa music. Hit **Condado** (p59) on day two for some beach time and consider **Santurce** (p78) for dinner.

Four Days

Go on a museum crawl around Old San Juan and throw in a visit by ferry to the Bayamón Bacardí Rum Factory (p88). Join an ecotour company for a daytime tour of El Yunque (p64). Prowl the nightclubs of the big hotels in **Condado** and **Isla Verde** (p82), and try not to lose your wad in a glitzy resort casino.

One Week

Explore **Santurce's museums, galleries and market** (p60) by day. Hit classic local joints like Manolín (p75) and debate who makes the best *mofongo* (mashed plantains). Rent a bike and cycle to **Piñones** (p89). Round it up by hiring some beach toys at Balneario Escambrón (p63) and frolicking in the surf or snorkeling out to the coral.

SAN JUAN'S NEIGHBORHOODS

Metro San Juan, in common with many great cities, is an amalgamation of its neighborhoods, with each area exhibiting its own vicissitudes, atmosphere and charms. Here's a quick rundown of what to expect.

Old San Juan The soul of the city, Old San Juan's compact Unesco World Heritage site is packed with historical relics and endless opportunities for strolling, plus eclectic and alluring nightlife.

Puerta de Tierra This thin slither of land that links Old San Juan with the rest of the city is a strange amalgam of tatty housing projects, salubrious parks and one of the best municipal beaches on the island.

Miramar A leafy residential quarter of eclectic middle-class houses and plush lakeside condos.

Condado San Juan's original resort strip is a revitalized urban neighborhood replete with designer shops, pretty parks and massive beachside resorts.

Ocean Park Attractive beachside community with genteel guesthouses, high-rise condos and a quiet swath of beach.

Isla Verde The city's premier hotel strip mixes condo towers and swanky resorts in an architectural mishmash. The beach is sublime.

Santurce The city's hottest neighborhood has bounced back from decay with galleries, museums, offbeat cafes and a revitalized market quarter with great bars and restaurants.

Hato Rey San Juan's financial hub is a dense cluster of glass tower blocks.

Río Piedras The low-rise academic quarter boasts cheap shops, a thriving market and a lovely botanical garden.

Paseo de la Princesa PROMENADE

(Walkway of the Princess; Map p52) Evoking a distinctly European feeling, the Paseo de la Princesa is a 19th-century esplanade just outside the city walls. Lined with antique streetlamps, trees, statues, benches, fruit vendors' carts and street entertainers, this romantic walkway ends at the magnificent **Raíces Fountain** (Map p52), a stunning sculpture and water feature that depicts the island's eclectic Taíno, African and Spanish heritage.

Escuela de Artes Plásticas LANDMARK

(Academy of Fine Arts; Map p52; www.eap.edu; Norzagaray) The monumental columned building with a red-roofed dome across from El Morro is the Escuela de Artes Plásticas. Originally an insane asylum during the 19th century, this grand school with its arches, porticos and courtyards displays students' work at the end of each academic term. In the sculpture court on the right-hand side of the building, students can sometimes be seen sculpting granite.

Plaza de San José PLAZA

(Map p52) This small cobblestone plaza is dominated by a statue of Juan Ponce de León, cast from an English cannon captured in the raid of 1797.

El Arsenal FORT, ART GALLERY

(Map p52; ☎787-724-1877, 787-724-5949; ⏰hours vary) On the point called La Puntilla, this low fortress is a former Spanish naval station, and the last place to house Spanish forces after the US victory in the Spanish–American War. Today it is home to the fine- and decorative-arts divisions of the **Instituto de Cultura Puertorriqueña** (Institute of Puerto Rican Culture; Map p52; ☎787-724-0700; www.icp.gobierno.pr; Calle del Morro; ⏰8:30am-4:30pm Mon-Fri) FREE, and hosts periodic exhibitions in three galleries.

Plaza de Colón PLAZA

(Columbus Plaza; Map p52) Tracing its roots back more than a century to the 400-year anniversary of Columbus' first expedition, the Plaza de Colón is dominated by its towering statue of Columbus atop a pillar. Ringed with tall trees, the plaza sees a lot of action. At this end of Old San Juan the city wall was torn down in 1897, and the plaza stands on the site of one of the city's original gated entries, Puerta Santiago.

Museo Felisa Rincón de Gautier MUSEUM

(Map p52; ☎787-723-1897; www.museofelisarincon.com; 51 Caleta de San Juan; ⏰9am-4pm Mon-Fri)

FREE This museum, an attractive neoclassical townhouse, was the longtime home of San Juan's beloved mayor, Doña Felisa. She presided over the growth of the city with personal style and political acumen for more than 20 years during the Operation Bootstrap days of the 1940s, '50s and '60s.

Casa de Ramón Power y Giralt NOTABLE BUILDING
(Map p52; ☎787-722-5834; www.fideicomiso.org; 155 Tetuán; ⊙9am-5pm Tue-Sat) FREE Once the residence of a political reformer and Puerto Rico's first representative to the Spanish court, this 18th-century house is now the headquarters of the Conservation Trust of Puerto Rico. It contains small exhibits of Taíno artifacts and a gift shop. The trust provides information on the precariousness of the island's ecology, as well as information about tours in San Juan and at the trust's properties. Three environmental films can be shown upon request, in English or Spanish; one is an animated short for children.

Plaza del Quinto Centenario PLAZA
(Map p52) This modern square is shoehorned in among all the architectural landmarks and offers great views over El Morro and the ocean. Built in 1992 for a rumored $10 million to honor the 500-year anniversary of Columbus' first voyage to the Americas, it is dominated by a stylized granite and clay totem pole – **El Tótem Telúrico** – by Puerto Rican artist Jaime Suarez. Using clay from across the Americas, it is meant to signify the origins of the people of the Americas.

Cementerio de San Juan CEMETERY
(Map p52) Sitting just outside the northern fortifications of the old city, the neoclassical chapel in the cemetery provides a focal point among the graves. The colony's earliest citizens are buried here, as well as the famous Puerto Rican freedom fighter Pedro Albizu-Campos. This Harvard-educated chemical engineer, lawyer and politician led the agricultural workers' strikes in 1934 and was at the forefront of the movement for Puerto Rican independence until his arrest and imprisonment in 1936. A number of muggings have occurred here, so be careful.

Casa Rosa NOTABLE BUILDING
(Map p52) This tropical pink villa built in the 19th century served as the Spanish officers' quarters. The building has since been restored and is used for government work.

La Perla

Wedged tightly between the roaring Atlantic surf and San Juan's thick perimeter walls, the compact neighborhood of La Perla is a ramshackle hodgepodge of eye-catching pastel houses. A steep, narrow access road leads down from Norzagaray to one of San Juan's roughest neighborhoods.

Though it's picturesque from a distance, tourists should steer clear of La Perla, and enjoy its creative graffiti from the promenade above.

The neighborhood was the subject of a controversial 1966 nonfiction book called *La Vida* by American anthropologist Oscar Lewis. Lewis won a National Book Award for detailing what he described as a tragic cycle of poverty and prostitution, but many Puerto Ricans decried it as stereotypical.

During the mid-2000s, the Puerto Rican government made regular (unsuccessful) bids to buy out La Perla's residents and redevelop the area.

Puerta de Tierra

The area along the peninsula east of Old San Juan is less than 2 miles long and only a quarter of a mile wide. This district, Puerta de Tierra, takes its name from its position as the 'gateway of land' leading up to the walls of Old San Juan. When attacking by land, the waves of English and Dutch invaders had to come through here. Centuries ago, it was the neighborhood where free black and multiracial people lived, outside of the protection of the city walls, which harbored the Spaniards and *criollos* (islanders of European descent).

Today the district is the conduit for cars entering Old San Juan, though its north coast is an awe-inspiring sight: a dramatic wave-pummeled shore with the windswept Balneario Escambrón (p63), a public beach. Just offshore is Escambrón Marine Park, a preserve featuring an array of corals and underwater life popular with divers and snorkelers. Inland lies the sun-dappled Parque Muñoz Rivera, the grand Capitolio and, further east, the Fuerte San Gerónimo.

Fuerte San Gerónimo FORT
(Map p62) This fort at the east end of Puerta de Tierra was completed in 1788 to guard the entrance to Laguna del Condado. It was barely up and running in 1797 when the British came marching through to San Juan and a short-lived occupation. Restored in 1983, today San Gerónimo is hemmed in by tall ho-

Condado

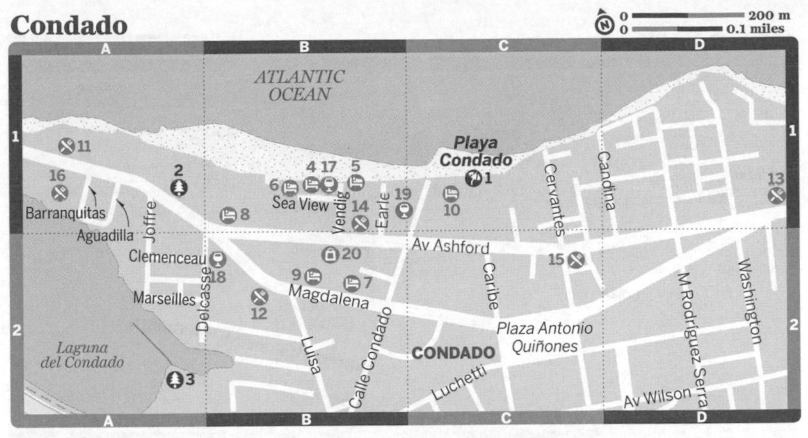

tels. The interior of the fort, entered via the walkway behind the Caribe Hilton, is rarely open, but the exterior walls are accessible and offer views of Condado across the inlet.

El Capitolio NOTABLE BUILDING
(Capitol; 787-724-2030, ext 4616; www.senadopr.us; off Ave Ponce de León; 9am-5pm) FREE The capital of the commonwealth is in an impressive columned and domed building in a commanding location overlooking Puerta de Tierra's wave-lashed coast. The much-revered constitution of the commonwealth, which moved the island further away from colonialism in 1951, is on display inside the 80ft rotunda. Regular sessions of the legislature meet inside, while rallies for and against statehood occur outside every time the government debates the issue.

Parques Louis Muñoz Rivera & Parque del Tercer Milenio PARK
Spanning the broad swath between the Atlantic and Av Ponce de León, Parque Louis Muñoz Rivera dates back over 50 years and injects much-needed breathing space into the surrounding urban landscape. Trails wind under shade trees to a kids' playground and a pavilion for community events.

Parque del Tercer Milenio was the site of the eighth Pan American Games, held in 1979, and is now home to an array of activities, a good playground, the popular Balneario Escambrón (p63) beach, and offshore diving at **Escambrón Marine Park**.

Condado

Top Sights
1 Playa Condado C1

Sights
2 Parque de la Ventana al Mar A1
3 Parque Laguna del Condado Jaime Benítez A2

Sleeping
4 Alelí by the Sea B1
5 Atlantic Beach Hotel B1
6 Condado Vanderbilt Hotel B1
7 Coral Princess Hotel B2
8 La Concha B1
9 Le Consulat Hotel B2
10 San Juan Marriott Resort & Stellaris Casino C1

Eating
11 Hacienda Don José A1
12 José José B2
Perla .... (see 8)
13 Pinky's D1
14 Pure And Natural B1
15 Via Appia C2
16 Yantar A1

Drinking & Nightlife
La Concha Lobby Bar .... (see 8)
17 Oceano B1
18 Small Bar B2
19 Splash Lounge B1

Shopping
20 Abitto B2

Condado

In the 1960s, Condado is where Puerto Rico's tourist boom was first ignited, spearheaded by exiled Cuban businessmen and rum-drunk Americans. But, as fashions ebbed and flowed, Condado went the way of Miami

Ocean Park

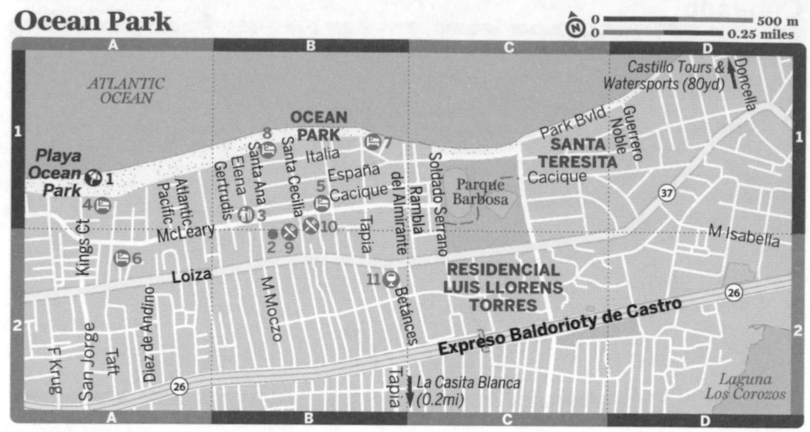

Ocean Park

Top Sights

1 Playa Ocean Park A1

Activities, Courses & Tours

2 Ashtanga Yoga Puerto Rico B2
3 Tres Palmas B1

Sleeping

4 Acacia Boutique Hotel A1
5 Andalucía Guest House B1
6 At Wind Chimes Inn A2
7 Hostería del Mar B1
8 Numero Uno B1

Eating

9 Kasalta's B2
10 La B de Burro B1
Niche .... (see 4)
Pamela's .... (see 8)

Drinking & Nightlife

11 Pa'l Cielo B2

Beach: a tawdry time in the 1970s and 1980s was followed by a rebirth.

Although no South Beach today, Condado buzzes with top-end resorts (including the newly revived grand Condado Vanderbilt Hotel), the odd celebrity and legions of beachgoers fleeing cold weather up north. In fact 2014's *22 Jump Street* filmed its spring break scenes with Jonah Hill and Channing Tatum on Condado's beaches.

Today, dotted in among the high-rises, you'll still find a few old eclectic 1920s villas, along with a handful of pretty parks that serve as spacious windows to the sea.

Besides having a wonderful water view, the **Parque Laguna del Condado Jaime Benítez** (Map p59; www.estuario.org), a park on the southeastern shore of the lagoon, has displays about ongoing mangrove habitat restoration.

Ocean Park

At the eastern end of Condado lies Ocean Park, with its associated neighborhood of Punta Las Marías, a largely residential collection of private homes and beach retreats that includes a handful of plush seaside guesthouses.

Santurce

Santurce is one of San Juan's most important – and most interesting – barrios, actually incorporating Condado and **Miramar**, but usually used to describe the area south of Expressway 26 and north of Hato Rey.

The '40s and '50s were a boom time here, when color and life seeped from Santurce's energetic streets, spurred on by the buoyancy of Operation Bootstrap. Back then, Santurce was a financial center and a residential quarter of some repute. The nosedive began in the 1970s when the business district headed south to Hato Rey and Santurce was left to fester.

Now, some 40 years later, Santurce has worked hard to turn the corner. Its renaissance has been spearheaded by art galleries, a performing arts center, trendy clubs, and some of the city's best and most popular restaurants, cafes and bars. Much of Santurce's current vibrancy can be found in and around **La Placita de Santurce** (Map p62), the small square that's home to the Santurce Mercado and many cafes, as well as along Avenida Ponce de León.

As you can see from the stunning street art, the local art scene is hot, with small galleries and cultural spaces organizing all manner of shows and events.

★ Santurce Mercado — MARKET

(Market; Map p62; La Placita de Santurce; ⏲ 6am-late) Santurce's revitalized *mercado* rocks just like old times. The show starts not long after dawn when bleary-eyed market traders stock up their permanent stalls with home-grown treats from around the island.

There's *chayote* from Barranquitas, pumpkin from Coamo, pineapple from Lajas and mango from Mayagüez – all glowing colorful, tasty and fresh in the morning sun.

Materializing mid-morning, inquisitive shoppers arrive en masse to finger and bag the best produce, before sitting down for a hearty lunch in one of the square's family-run cafes. Throughout the day, people pause at the little bar stalls for a drink or a snack. Many relax at the outdoor tables or ponder the huge bronze sculptures of avocados.

At 5pm, with the market winding down for the evening, the square undergoes a heady transformation, particularly late in the week. Still dressed in their smart work attire, office workers roll in to drink, chat, de-stress and unwind. The party can last for hours.

On any night, locals and visitors prowl the surrounding streets for some of San Juan's best eats. Come 6am and there's little left, save for a handful of all-night revelers nursing nascent hangovers and the familiar clatter of early-morning traders setting out their wares for another day of business.

★ Museo de Arte de Puerto Rico — MUSEUM

(MAPR; Map p62; ☎ 787-977-6277; www.mapr.org; 299 Av José de Diego; adult/student & senior $6/3; ⏲ 10am-5pm Tue-Sat, to 8pm Wed, 11am-6pm Sun) San Juan boasts one of the largest and most celebrated art museums in the Caribbean. Housed in a splendid neoclassical building that was once the city's Municipal Hospital, MAPR boasts 18 exhibition halls spread over an area of 130,000 sq ft.

The artistic collection includes paintings, sculptures, posters and carvings from the 17th to the 21st century, chronicling such renowned Puerto Rican artists as José Campeche, Francisco Oller, Nick Quijano and Rafael Ferrer.

But there's far more to this cultural tour de force than just a collection of paintings. Adding distinction to diversity, the facility also boasts a 2.5-acre sculpture garden, a conservation laboratory, a theater and a good shop.

Don't miss the gardens, where winding paths invite visitors to stroll past 16 sculptures and more than 100,000 plants in a scene reminiscent of Monet's water lilies.

Museo de Arte Contemporáneo de Puerto Rico — MUSEUM

(MAC; Map p62; ☎ 787-977-4030; cnr Av Ponce de León & Roberto H Todd; admission by donation; ⏲ 10am-4pm Tue-Sat, noon-4pm Sun) The Museo de Arte Contemporáneo de Puerto Rico sits just down the road from the Museo de Arte de Puerto Rico in an eye-catching classical Georgian building – the former Rafael M Labra school – dating from 1918. The museum displays art from the mid-20th century onwards and showcases artists from Puerto Rico, the Caribbean and Latin America. If you're lucky, you'll hear classical music being rehearsed in the atrium.

C787 Studios — ART GALLERY

(Map p62; www.c787studios.com; 734 Cerra; ⏲ hours vary) There are wide-ranging exhibitions in this gallery, as well as experimental music and performance art.

Espacio 1414 — ART GALLERY

(Map p62; ☎ 787-725-3899; www.espacio1414.org; 1414 Av Fernández Juncos; ⏲ hours vary, call for an appointment) Housed in an austere yet modern building, this gallery celebrates contemporary Latin American art. There are regular special shows in addition to the permanent displays of the Berezdivin Collection, which has works from across the region.

3X Man — ART GALLERY

(Map p62; 1416 Av Ponce de León; ⏲ hours vary) A quirky shop for clothing and paintings, 3X Man has art and music shows too. It's in the

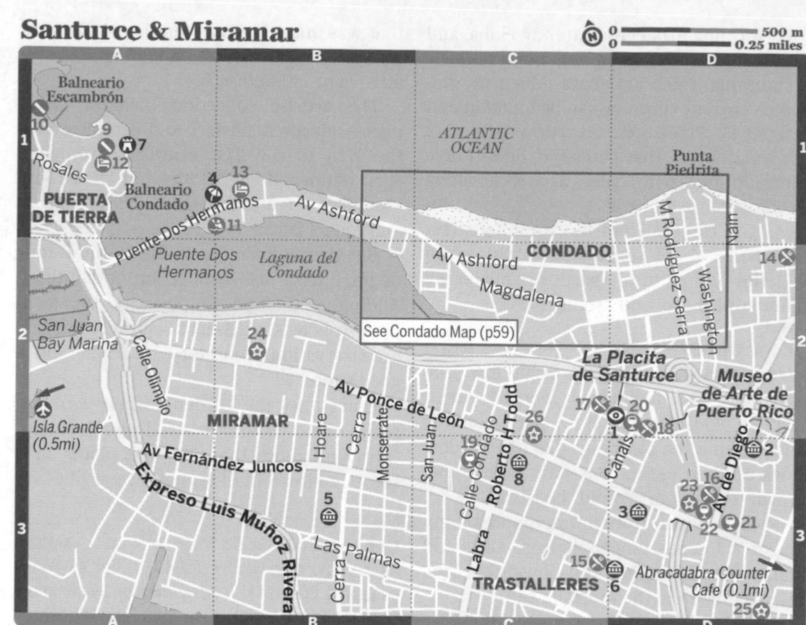

space of the signed, ground-breaking gallery Executive Manolo.

Hato Rey

South of Santurce, the urban grit of the former business district is replaced by the sleekness of its successor. Sagrado Corazón station is the gleeming first stop on San Juan's Tren Urbano. The mighty glass towers all around are the Caribbean's wannabe Wall St. That moaning you hear might be the bankers contemplating the island's perilous financial state.

Río Piedras

The flatness of Hato Rey soon gives way to the leafy uplands of Río Piedras. Founded in 1714 and existing as a separate town until 1951, Río Piedras is the home of the University of Puerto Rico and harbors a thriving academic community. You'll find cheap cafes, a cut-price shopping street (José de Diego), and the island's largest farmers market. The university is set in lush, palm-filled grounds and is distinguished by its signature minaret-like clock tower.

The Río Piedras stop of the Tren Urbano is right in the center.

Mercado de Río Piedras MARKET

(Paseo de Diego; ⏲9am-6pm Mon-Sat) If you like the smell of fish and oranges, the bustle of people, and trading jests in Spanish as you bargain for a bunch of bananas, this market is for you. As much a scene as a place to shop, the market continues the colonial tradition of an indoor market that spills into the streets.

Four long blocks of shops and inexpensive restaurants lining Paseo de Diego and facing the market have been closed to auto traffic, turning the whole area into an outdoor mall. You can shop or just watch as the local citizens negotiate for everything from *chuletas* (pork chops) to *camisas* (shirts). The market and stores along Paseo de Diego open from early morning to late evening, Monday to Saturday.

Jardín Botánico GARDEN

(Botanical Garden; ☎787-403-1789; off Hwy 1 at Hwy 847; ⏲6am-6pm) FREE This 75-acre tract of greenery is a good urban respite. Hiking trails through cathedrals of bamboo lead to a lotus lagoon, an orchid garden with more than 30,000 flowers, and a plantation of more than 120 species of palm. The air smells of heliconia blossoms, as well as of nutmeg and cinnamon trees.

Santurce & Miramar

Top Sights
1 La Placita de Santurce D2
2 Museo de Arte de Puerto Rico D3

Sights
3 3X Man D3
4 Balneario Condado A1
5 C787 Studios B3
6 Espacio 1414 .... D3
7 Fuerte San Gerónimo A1
8 Museo de Arte Contemporáneo de Puerto Rico C3
Santurce Mercado .... (see 1)

Activities, Courses & Tours
9 Caribe Aquatic Adventures A1
10 Scuba Dogs A1
11 Velauno B1

Sleeping
12 Caribe Hilton A1
13 Condado Plaza B1

Eating
14 Blonda Condado D2
15 Cafe Culturas C3
16 Hacienda San Pedro Coffee Shop D3
17 José Enrique C2
Pikayo .... (see 13)
18 Santaella D2

Drinking & Nightlife
19 Circo Bar C3
20 El Patio De LiLa D2
La Placita de Santurce .... (see 1)
21 Starz D3
22 Tia Maria's D3

Entertainment
23 El Centro de Bellas Artes Luis A Ferré D3
24 Fine Arts Miramar B2
25 La Respuesta D3
26 Metro Cinema C2

Pick up a free map at the small cafe and gift shop near the entrance. The garden is a 1.5km walk north from the Tren Urbano Río Piedras stop.

Beaches

San Juan has some of the best municipal beaches this side of Rio de Janeiro. Starting half a mile or so east of the old town, you can go from rustic to swanky and back to rustic all in the space of 7.5 miles.

★Balneario Escambrón BEACH

A sheltered arc of raked sand, decent surf breaks, plenty of local action and a 17th-century Spanish fort shimmering in the distance are the hallmarks of this fine beach only a stone's throw from Old San Juan and the busy tourist strip of Condado. Best of all, it's often uncrowded.

Perched on the north end of the slither of land that *is* Puerta de Tierra, it abuts majestic Parque del Tercer Milenio. This palm-fringed, yet rugged beach just might be one of the best municipal options offered anywhere. There are lifeguards, restrooms, gear rental stands and snack bars, along with a large parking lot.

★Playa Condado RESORT BEACH

(Map p59) Hemmed in by hotel towers and punctuated by rocky outcrops, Condado's narrow beaches are busier than Ocean Park's, but less exclusive than Isla Verde's. Expect splashes of graffiti, boisterous games of volleyball and plenty of crashing Atlantic surf.

The area's official public beach is **Balneario Condado** (Map p62), a small arc of sand, adjacent to the Dos Hermanos bridge, that faces west toward Fuerte San Gerónimo across the inlet. A line of rocks breaks the water here, making the sea calm and bathing relatively safe. Lifeguards police the area on weekdays, and snack bars are open daily, but bathrooms are few and far between. You can rent beach chairs.

Condado's Atlantic-facing beaches are very popular. Families congregate around the big hotels, while gay men like the beach at the end of Calle Vendig. **Parque de la Ventana al Mar** (Window to the Sea Park; Map p59; Ashford) has lovely waterfront views.

★Playa Ocean Park BEACH

(Map p60) Ocean Park's lesser fame is its hidden blessing. Fronted by leafy residential streets and embellished by the odd luxury B&B, its wide sweep of fine, diamond-dust sand is protected by offshore reefs and caressed by cooling seasonal trade winds. The neighborhood's namesake beach is perfectly tranquil, yet open to all: just pick a road through the low-rise gated community and follow it toward the water.

★Playa Isla Verde BEACH

(Map p66) With its legions of tanned bodies and dexterous beach bums flexing their triceps around the volleyball net, Playa Isla Verde basks in its reputation as the Copacabana of Puerto Rico. Serenity seekers may prefer to dodge the extended families and colonizing spring-break hedonists that stake space here and head west to Ocean Park. Whatever your view, this broad, mile-long wedge of sand that lies between Punta Las Marías and Piñones is an undeniable beauty.

Balneario de Carolina BEACH
(Rte 187; parking $3; 8am-5pm Tue-Sun) Wedged in between the high-rise-hotel strip of Isla Verde and rustic delights of Piñones, Balneario de Carolina is a fine, clean beach that lacks natural shelter and is positioned right in front of Luis Muñoz Marín International Airport. Equipped with plenty of lifeguards, bathrooms, showers and barbecue pits, the beach is usually uncrowded during the week.

Activities

All those glittering azure waters are an obvious draw for outdoor fun in San Juan. Beaches that open to the Atlantic are great for surfing, while the many reefs draw snorkelers and divers. On land you can get out and about in the nearby green hills.

★ **Acampa** OUTDOOR GEAR, TOURS
(787-706-0695; www.acampapr.com; 1221 Av Jesús T Piñero, Caparra; tours $80-160; 10am-6pm Mon-Fri, 10:30am-5:30pm Sat) One of the best places in town to buy or rent outdoor gear – including camping equipment – is Acampa. It also runs a number of excellent tours all over the island, including hiking, mountaineering, kayaking and paddleboarding.

Caving & Canyoning

Aventuras Tierra Adentro ADVENTURE TOUR
(787-766-0470; www.aventuraspr.com; 268a Av Jesús T Piñero, Río Piedras; day trip $150-175; store 10am-6pm Tue-Fri, 10am-4pm Sat, tour schedule varies) Aventuras Tierra Adentro is a favorite store for climbers and hikers in Puerto Rico. It's also a tour operator specializing in rock climbing and rappelling trips to the Río Camuy caves, and canyoning trips in El Yunque. Guides also lead zip-lining over the mouth of Camuy's Angeles sinkhole. It's one mile west of the university.

Cycling

Stick to the shore and cycling in San Juan can actually be good fun, as long as you know where to go. In fact, it is perfectly

City Walk
Old San Juan

START CAFÉ COLA'O
END LA TABERNA LÚPULO
LENGTH 2.75 MILES; THREE TO FOUR HOURS

Start with an early-morning pick-me-up at 1 **Café Cola'o** (p75) next to the cruise ships parked by Pier 2. Now stroll west and observe the soaring 12-story elegance of the 1937 2 **Banco Populare building** (cnr San Justo & Tetuán), an art-deco gem. Continue along 3 **Paseo de la Princesa** (p57), a shaded 19th-century esplanade that tracks alongside the formidable old city walls to the brink of the Bahía de San Juan.

Turn north briefly on Calle del Christo, then turn west on Fortaleza. Here you'll find buildings such as the 4 **Palacio Rojo**, that date back to the height of the colonial era. It's easy to see why this 1792 building is called the Red Palace. Its rouge walls once housed the Spanish commanding officers. Now, retrace your steps to the Paseo de la Princesa, to the pigeons of 5 **Parque de las Palomas** (p55).

As you feel the refreshing Atlantic breeze hit you face-on, you'll spy the city's legendary perimeter wall as well as the imposing bronze 6 **Raíces Fountain** (p57), which depicts Taíno, European and African figurines rising amid a shower of cascading water.

Behind the fountain, follow the Paseo de la Princesa as it cuts northwest along the waterfront. In the 17th and 18th centuries, Spanish ships once anchored in the cove just off these ramparts to unload colonists and supplies, all of which entered the city through a tall red portal known as 7 **Puerta de San Juan** (p55).

Pass through the gate and turn right onto Recinto Oeste. This short cobblestoned street leads to the guarded iron gates of 8 **La Fortaleza** (p51), which today is a classical palace. Head back northwest, taking a moment to gaze out over the water from the diminutive 9 **Plazuela de la Rogativa** (p56) and admire its bronze sculpture of a religious procession.

Follow the leafy Caleta de San Juan up the slope to the beautiful 10 **Plazuela Las**

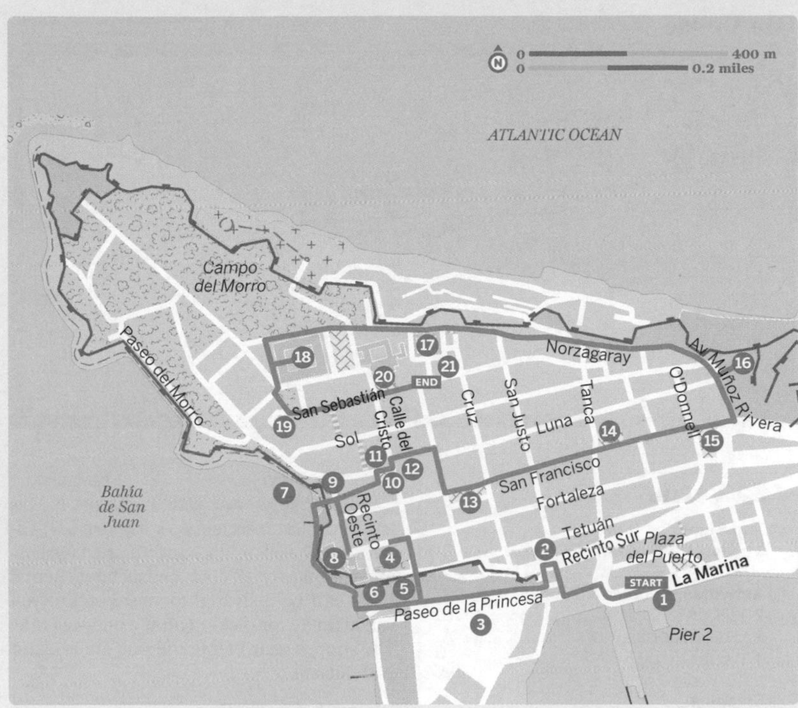

Monjas, where stray cats stretch and romantic couples linger. On the north side of the plaza is ⑪ **Hotel El Convento** (p71), Puerto Rico's grandest hotel, well worth a casual inspection. To the east lies the ⑫ **Catedral de San Juan** (p51), a relatively austere religious building whose importance is enhanced by its age (dating from 1540) and the fact that the remains of Juan Ponce de León rest inside.

Cut along Luna for a block before heading right down San José. Take a left onto San Francisco, which will bring you to the ⑬ **Plaza de Armas** (p55), a small but important square with government buildings that is the hub of the old city. Continue east on San Francisco, pausing at quirky shops and the ⑭ **Iglesia San Francisco de Asís** (p55), ending in the ⑮ **Plaza de Colón** (p57), named for the great Genoese explorer. Cut north up Av Muñoz Rivera and you'll come to ⑯ **Fuerte San Cristóbal** (p50), the old city's other major fortification.

Walking west along Norzagaray, you can look down at the faded pastel houses of La Perla, an impoverished neighborhood sprayed by the tempestuous Atlantic. Hidden in a former market building to your left is the ⑰ **Museo de San Juan** (p54). Just west, the intriguing ⑱ **Cuartel de Ballajá** (p51) houses the Museo de las Américas, a museum of changing exhibits on Caribbean and European art. Across the grassy expanses of Campo del Morro, picnickers fly kites and the stately fort of El Morro beckons. Stroll the former sentries' walks for iconic panoramic views of San Juan and the sea.

Head down Calle del Morro to the ⑲ **Casa Blanca** (p51), the ancestral home for 250 years of the descendants of Juan Ponce de León, and the oldest permanent residence in the Americas.

A stone's throw to the east lies the ⑳ **Plaza de San José** (p57), with its statue of Juan Ponce de León, cast from an English cannon captured in the raid of 1797. More antiquity overlooks the plaza from the north in the shape of the Iglesia de San José, the second oldest church in the Americas. From here, you'll probably be ready for a cold beer at ㉑ **La Taberna Lúpulo** (p81).

Isla Verde

Isla Verde

Top Sights

1 Playa Isla Verde....C1

Activities, Courses & Tours

2 15 Knots....B1
3 Ocean Sports....A1
4 WOW Surfing School....D1

Sleeping

5 Coqui Inn....B1
6 El Patio Guesthouse....A2
7 El San Juan Resort & Casino....D1
8 Hotel La Playa....D1
9 InterContinental San Juan Resort & Casino....C2
10 Ritz-Carlton....D1
11 Water & Beach Club....C1

Eating

12 Bajuice....C2
13 Casa Dante....A1
14 Ceviche House....A1
15 Don José Café....D2
16 El Estribo....A1
17 Las Canarias....D2
18 Metropol....D2
19 Yamiko....C2

Drinking & Nightlife

Club Brava....(see 7)
El San Juan Hotel Lobby....(see 7)
Mist....(see 11)

feasible to work your way safely along the coastline from Old San Juan out as far as Carolina and the bike paths of Piñones.

Rent the Bicycle BICYCLE RENTAL
(787-602-9696; www.rentthebicycle.net; 100 Del Muelle, Old San Juan; rental per day from $27) Offers tours and rents sturdy banana-yellow cruiser bikes with lock and helmet. Rental bikes can be delivered to your hotel or you can arrange for pick-up after a one-way ride. The shop is near Pier 6; the staff are brilliant with advice.

Diving & Snorkeling

While Puerto Rico is well known for its first-class diving, San Juan is not the best place for it: strong winds often churn up the water. Condado has an easy dive that takes you through a pass between the inner and outer reefs into coral caverns, overhangs, grottoes and tunnels.

★**Caribe Aquatic Adventures** DIVING, SNORKELING
(Map p62; 787-281-8858; www.caribe-aquatic-adventures.com; snorkel/1-tank dive incl equipment from $50/90) This outfit does dives near San Juan, but also further afield around the islands off the coast of Fajardo (Icacos for snorkeling, and Palominos and Palominitos for diving). The dives from the shore at Balneario Escambrón are highly recommended. Divemaster Karen Vega has decades of local experience and is excellent with children.

Scuba Dogs DIVING, SNORKELING
(Map p62; 787-783-6377; www.scubadogs.net; Parque del Tercer Milenio, Puerta de Tierra; dives from $70; hours vary) This large and long-running outfit has a shop in Parque del Tercer Milenio. It has been a tireless supporter

of the offshore coral wonderland that is Escambrón Marine Park. The Dogs offer gear rental, an array of shore and boat dive trips, plus training.

Eco Action Tours DIVING
(☎787-791-7509; www.ecoactiontours.com; two-tank dives from $70) In addition to diving, Eco Action Tours can do just about any tour imaginable, from rappelling to nature walks. It operates out of a van and comes to you. It offers San Juan area shore dives and dives on the east coast.

Ocean Sports DIVING
(Map p66; ☎787-268-2329; www.osdivers.com; 77 Av Isla Verde) Has a dive store in Isla Verde and organizes a wide range of dives and instruction. It has a full service facility that provides Nitrox, Trimix and rebreathers.

Fishing

San Juan is an excellent base for serious deep sea fishing for prized fish that include dolphin fish, tuna, wahoo, and white and blue marlin.

Castillo Tours & Watersports FISHING
(☎787-791-6195; www.castillotours.com; 101 Doncella, Punta Las Marías; boat charters from $700) The Castillo family offers deep-sea fishing for blue marlin, wahoo, tuna and mahimahi, as well as snorkeling and sailing excursions.

Magic Tarpon FISHING
(☎787-644-1444; www.magictarpon.com; Cangrejos Yacht Club; 4hr charters from $330) Huge tarpon up to 8ft long and weighing well over 200lbs lurk in the mangroves of San Juan's lagoons. This outfit uses small boats and light tackle; it offers special instruction to kids, who may be dwarfed by the fish they catch.

Spas

Most of the major resorts have in-house spas, which are also open to nonguests. Many are affiliated with international spa chains.

Anam Spa & Cocktail Lounge SPA
(Map p52; ☎787-962-6479; www.anamspacocktaillounge.com; 259 Calle del Christo; manicure from $15, massage from $40; ⏲11am-7pm) This friendly spa with fine views of the water and far-off mountains has hit upon a genius gimmick: offer free drinks to customers. Most treatments and sessions include at least one free cocktail and the expert bartenders will sell you more. While you tipple, your aches and pains can be rubbed away and your nails buffed.

Water Sports

San Juan doesn't match Rincón in the surfing stakes, but no matter. You'll find the best waves and biggest *surferos* scene east of Isla Verde out toward Piñones and beyond, when the morning and evening breezes glass off a 4ft swell. Popular breaks include Pine Grove and Los Aviónes along Hwy 187.

At most of the city's beaches, you'll find vendors that will rent you pretty much anything that floats, or simply take you for a ride: banana boats, wave runners, kayaks ($20 to $30 per hour), small catamarans (with captain; $60 to $70 per hour), jet skis, water skis and kneeboards. Or get airborne with some parasailing (from $60 per person).

★15 Knots KITESURFING
(Map p66; ☎787-215-5667; www.15knots.com; 4851 Av Isla Verde, Isla Verde; rental per hour from $50, lessons from $275) The often gusty conditions off San Juan's beaches make the waters prime kitesurfing territory. This good outfit offers rentals and lessons.

WOW Surfing School SURFING
(Map p66; ☎787-955-6059; www.gosurfpr.com; Playa Isla Verde; lessons from $50, rentals per day from $25) This outfit runs full surfing lessons from the Ritz-Carlton on Playa Isla Verde. Lessons for all ages include boards, stretching, safety drills, dry-land practice and the real thing. You can rent boards and jet skis.

Tres Palmas SURFING
(Map p60; ☎787-728-3377; www.trespalmaspr.com; 1911 McLeary, Ocean Park; rental per day from $40) Tres Palmas offers surfboard and boogieboard rentals and lessons, including ones geared towards children.

Velauno PADDLEBOARDING
(Map p62; ☎787-982-0543; www.velauno.com; 860 Av Ashford, Condado; 1hr paddleboard & kayak rental from $20, tours from $55; ⏲hours vary) Velauno offers stand-up paddleboarding classes and rentals. It also has kayak rentals and tours.

Courses

If you're feeling limber and loose – or would like to be – there are a number of venues offering dance instruction, and yoga classes aren't difficult to find.

SAN JUAN FOR CHILDREN

Puerto Rico is a family-friendly destination and children are quite a part of daily life across San Juan. Most resorts have children's clubs or programs; only a few boutique properties have age restrictions. Large swaths of the beaches are reef-protected so waves are gentle. Playa Ocean Park (p63) and Playa Isla Verde (p63) are not only very family friendly, they are also often uncrowded.

In and around San Juan there are several attractions that children really enjoy. The Museo del Niño (p56) is always a big hit – as are the many stray cats who nap outside it. In season, a winter-league baseball game (p85) is classic family fun.

Two very obvious sights to visit are El Morro (p47) and San Cristóbal (p50) in Old San Juan. What could be better than huge fortresses complete with tales of gold, plunder and pirates? Kids can explore the walls and tunnels for hours.

Dance

To learn a basic break step or show off your oh-so-effortless moves, the best venue in town is Nuyorican Café (p84) in Old San Juan, where free lessons are offered Wednesdays from 9pm to 11pm. Learn a few basic moves and you can join the masses who take to the floor after school's over.

Yoga

Many hotels and resorts these days offer yoga classes to guests.

Ashtanga Yoga Puerto Rico YOGA
(Map p60; ☎787-677-7585; www.itsyogapuertorico.com; 1950 McLeary, Ocean Park; classes from $17) Pilates and modified Ashtanga classes are offered at this long-running school. Discounts for multiple visits.

Tours

Many popular tours travel to the east end of the island (p92) for the amazing bioluminescent waters at Laguna Grande. Noted outdoor gear vendor Acampa (p64) also runs recommended adventure tours on land and water. Many of the other activities outfits can lead you on tours over land and water.

★ **Rent the Bicycle** BIKE TOUR
(☎787-602-9696; www.rentthebicycle.net; 100 Del Muelle, Old San Juan; tours from $40) San Juan's best bike outfit offers excellent tours of Old San Juan, the Condado beaches and Piñones.

★ **Legends of Puerto Rico** CULTURAL TOUR
(☎787-605-9060; www.legendsofpr.com; tours from $35; ⏲daily, schedule varies) Debbie Molina-Ramos is a well-respected guide for Legends of Puerto Rico, whose popular 'Night Tales in Old San Juan' books up early. She offers engaging discussions of history at places like old jails not usually seen by tourists, as well as movie locations. Other walking tours cover Old San Juan by day, food and cultural themes, and much more. Tours meet and depart from various locations.

Para la Naturaleza ECOTOUR
(Para la Naturaleza; www.paralanaturaleza.org) Operates a number of private nature reserves, including the very popular Cabezas de San Juan in the east near Fajardo. Part of the Conservation Trust of Puerto Rico, it hopes to protect fully one-third of the island in the coming decades. Check for its many excellent tours.

Flavors of San Juan FOOD TOUR
(☎787-964-2447; www.flavorsofsanjuan.com; tours from $70) If eating your way around the old town is your style, Flavors of San Juan conducts three-hour walking tours that give you a tasty dose of the local cuisine. You can also see the town on a rum tour or learn to cook *mofongo* at a cooking class.

Festivals & Events

Aside from Festival San Sebastián, which becomes more adult-oriented during the evening, festivals in San Juan retain a congenial atmosphere that is favorable to families.

Fiesta de la Calle San Sebastián CULTURAL
(⏲mid-Jan) For a full week around the third weekend in January, Old San Juan's Calle San Sebastián hums with semireligious processions, music, food stalls and larger-than-ever crowds. During the day, it's folk art and crafts; at night, it's raucous revelry.

Festival Casals CLASSICAL MUSIC

(www.festcasalspr.gobierno.pr; tickets $10-85; ⌚early Mar) Since 1956 renowned soloists and orchestras have come from all over the world to join the Puerto Rico Symphony Orchestra in performing virtuoso concerts night after night, primarily at El Centro de Bellas Artes Luis A Ferré. The performances usually stretch over about three weeks from late February into March.

Puerto Rico JazzFest JAZZ

(www.prheinekenjazz.com; ⌚mid-Mar) Puerto Rico's largest jazz fest is held for four days around the third weekend in March. It attracts the best Latin jazz artists from all over the Caribbean. The late, great Tito Puente sometimes played here, and Eddie Palmieri often still does.

Fiesta de San Juan Bautista CULTURAL

(⌚late Jun) Celebration of the patron saint of San Juan and a summer solstice party, Latin style. Staged during the week preceding June 24, the heart of the action is in Old San Juan.

But you can catch the action – including religious processions, wandering minstrels, fireworks, food stalls, drunken sailors and beauty queens (straight and otherwise) – in the rest of the city (and country). Playa Isla Verde is a major focus on the last day of the festival, when thousands of people march into the water backwards three times at midnight in order to cleanse themselves of evil spirits.

Festival de Cine Internacional de San Juan FILM

(San Juan International Film Festival; www.festivalcinesanjuan.com; ⌚Oct) Screens new films over one week in October, with an emphasis on Caribbean cinema. Given the number of Puerto Ricans/Nuyoricans making good on the big screen – J Lo, Benicio del Toro, Jimmy Smits (and Raul Julia, who was given a state funeral when he died of cancer in 1994) – this event has been pulling in bigger luminaries each year.

Sleeping

You'll find ample accommodations in San Juan, many situated right on its stunning beaches.

Choices are many. Upscale, midscale, boutique or B&B: take your pick. Old San Juan offers historical havens, including

SEVEN ESSENTIAL OLD SAN JUAN DETAILS

Don't miss these seven Old San Juan features that are the fabric of its appeal.

Garitas The iconic turreted guard towers carved into the thick city walls are distinctive conical structures that have become symbolic of Puerto Rico and its rich colonial history.

Streets Look down and you'll see beautiful paving bricks with a blue glaze on many streets. In the right light, the subtle variations in color change with every step you take. Also note the pink granite used for many of the curbs, and the sidewalks made from slate.

Cats Best seen on the Caleta de San Juan, the narrow street running west from the Catedral de San Juan, the city's cats lounge about here shaded by tropical trees arching overhead.

Windows Don't stare but at night you'll catch glimpses of family life behind lace curtains as you stroll past 200-year-old buildings that are still home to hundreds. It's a reminder that Old San Juan remains a vibrant neighborhood, despite the crush of visitors.

Iron Next to the gorgeous ironwork in the French Quarter of New Orleans, Old San Juan has the second most elaborate displays of New World metalwork. Spanish colonial styles favored wrought-iron creations that spoke of importance, strength and beauty.

Doors Made of stout wood, the doors on old buildings are often 16 or more feet in height. This matched the high ceilings inside that allowed heat to rise up and out of living spaces.

Sunset It shows off the many hues of the buildings to beautiful effect. Stroll the Paseo del Morro along the walls to the far tip of El Morro fort to see the golden light play off the old town and the restless Atlantic. Magic.

the exquisite El Convento. Condado and Ocean Park have the highest concentration of guesthouses and big resorts. Isla Verde has a few boutique options flanked by mega resorts.

There is no shortage of chain hotels, however there are quite a few interesting and at times quirky indie options, although few are in the budget category. Rates vary significantly from season to season. Note that the large hotels tack on substantial resort, service and parking fees.

You can also find a huge range of rental condos in the high-rises along the beaches listed on www.airbnb.com and www.vrbo.com. Some are excellent value.

Old San Juan

Fortaleza Guest House GUESTHOUSE $

(Map p52; ☎787-721-7112; www.fortalezaguesthouse.com; 303 Fortaleza; r with shared bathroom and fan/air-con $40/50;) Well located in Old San Juan – though not for the fussy – these basic budget rooms are a good place to meet other travelers. Tiny rooms have either air-con and no natural light or a fan with a somewhat loud streetside balcony. Perks include a small guest kitchen, and excellent Indian and natural food stores across the street. Bookable on www.hostelworld.com.

Posada San Francisco HOSTEL, GUESTHOUSE $

(Map p52; www.posada-colonial-puertorico.com; 405 San Francisco; dm $26, d with shared bathroom $72;) This family-run budget option makes up for lapses in service by being spacious and clean (one-use shower mats in the six shared bathrooms). Full- and twin-bedded rooms have high ceilings, fridges and classic tile floors. Exquisite 5th-floor-patio views and a guest kitchen top it off. The hostel can be difficult to contact; book on its website.

★**Casa Sol** B&B $$

(Map p52; ☎787-399-0105, 787-980-9700; www.casasolbnb.com; Sol 316; r $140-210;) A great new addition in the heart of the old town, this charming B&B has five very nicely decorated rooms. The restored 19th-century building has a bright central courtyard with a skylight. Fittingly for its name and address, it is done up in a radiant yellow. The owners are generous with their local knowledge and often lead tours.

★**Casablanca Hotel** HOTEL $$

(Map p52; ☎787-725-3436; www.hotelcasablancapr.com; 316 Fortaleza; r $180-200;) This stylish SoFo hotel blends a luxurious mix of colonial and contemporary styles. Five floors of rooms (but no elevator) are swathed in vibrant fabrics, and some of the bathrooms sparkle with gorgeous mother-of-pearl sinks. Greet the morning on the roof deck with inspirational views of El Morro and El Yunque, or swan around in one of the shaded soaking tubs.

Its restaurant fills out a Moorish-style lobby of eye-candy lounges and bold tile work, presided over by a sunburst chandelier.

Gallery Inn INN $$

(Map p52; ☎787-722-1808; www.thegalleryinn.com; 204-206 Norzagaray; r incl breakfast $178-200;) Get ready to do a double-take. This quirky artist-owned hotel will make you feel as if you've wandered inadvertently onto the set of a Harry Potter movie. Showcasing masks, caged birds, trickling water, antiques, paintings and well-thumbed books, this cavernous 18th-century compound perches romantically above the Atlantic waves with ocean breezes, 25 eclectic rooms and a stunning plunge pool.

Da House HOTEL $$

(Map p52; ☎787-977-1180; www.dahousehotelpr.com; 312 San Francisco; r $100-120;) One of Old San Juan's funkier hotels is also one of its best bargains, with boutique-style rooms kitted out with chic furnishings and eye-catching contemporary art. Each room in the creamy peach building is dedicated to a different local artist. For the musically inclined, one of San Juan's best salsa bars, the Nuyorican (p84), is downstairs; for the less enamored (or sleep-deprived), staff will ruefully give out ear plugs.

Hotel Milano HOTEL $$

(Map p52; ☎787-729-9050; www.hotelmilanopr.com; 307 Fortaleza; r incl breakfast $125-200;) Sandwiched into Calle Fortaleza, the Milano is a reliable, if slightly austere option. Rooms are straightforward, while up on the roof there's an open-air restaurant with glimpses of the harbor. You can't beat the central location and there is an elevator to hoist you and your gear up to higher floors. Note that the cheapest rooms have no windows.

DON'T MISS

SAN JUAN'S URBAN LAGOONS

While it's easy to focus on the beautiful waters off San Juan's beaches, the city also has some remarkable waters just inland. Estuaries back up most of the coastal lands and surround the airport. Here in the mangroves can be found over 100 species of birds, 300 types of plants, dozens of kinds of fish and even the odd manatee. Unfortunately you can also find a lot of the nastiness you expect in urban waterways. Recently, groups have begun cleaning up these sprawling lagoons and waterways, and while it is thought that a real clean-up would cost an unaffordable $600 million, locals realize that you have to start somewhere.

Three community groups offer ways to get out on these waters, which are truly the heart of the city. Away from the constant crash of traffic, you discover a serene side to San Juan.

Excursiones Eco (787-565-0089; www.excursioneseco.com; walking tours from $12, boat tours $40-55) offers guided trips through the Caño de Martín Peña, a 3.5-mile tidal channel that connects the Bahía de San Juan with the Laguna San José. Passengers explore its mangrove forest and bird habitat while learning about its history and the current struggles of the low-income neighborhoods surrounding it. Walking tours that visit these under-served former squatter communities, which now house some 27,000 people, are also on offer.

Expediciones Península (787-644-9769; www.expedicionespeninsula.com; tours Sat & Sun) has well-organized weekend tours of the main lagoons that focus on wildlife and the culture of the people living around the waters. Tours last up to three hours and combine a boat ride with walking. Call to reserve, as well as confirm times and meeting point. You can rent binoculars to spot the fauna for only $5.

Corporación Piñones Se Integra (COPI; 787-253-9707; www.copipr.com; per 90min $15; 9am-5pm), a community-based nonprofit working to improve life in Puerto Rico's poorer barrios, also works to protect the urban waterways. Headquartered in the **Centro Cultural Ecoturístico de Piñones** (Rte 187, Boca de Cangrejos, Loíza) situated to the right of Rte 187 immediately after you cross the bridge at Boca de Cangrejos, the group rents out kayaks for self-guided explorations of the adjacent Laguna Torrecilla, a beautiful mangrove-ringed body of water just east of the airport.

Navona Studios GUESTHOUSE $$
(Map p52; 787-721-7573; 258 San Francisco; r from $100;) A good low-key option in the heart of the Old Town, these small units have small fridges, smartly checked tile floors and unfussy decor. Many have large windows that open onto tiny balconies. The owners operate the jewelry store of the same name on the ground floor. There's a two-night minimum; weekly and monthly rates are available.

AlaSol Apartments APARTMENTS $$
(Map p52; 787-724-4456; sol.viejosanjuan@gmail.com; 318 Sol; apt per night/week $100/585;) These handy one-bedroom apartments (four-night minimum stay) have to be one of the best bargains in Old San Juan. Located on neighborly Sol with all of the restaurant and museum action just a hop away, the traditional but comfortable apartments have a double bed, futon, kitchenette, bathroom, living room, TV and – almost unheard of in Old San Juan – a parking space out front. Priceless!

★ **Hotel El Convento** PARADOR $$$
(Map p52; 787-723-9020; www.elconvento.com; 100 Calle del Cristo; r $265-385, ste $650-1460;) Historic monument, tapas restaurant, meeting place, coffee bar and evocative colonial building… El Convento is Puerto Rico's most complete atmospheric and multifaceted hotel. Built in 1651 as the New World's first Carmelite convent, the 67 rooms and five suites (2nd-floor rooms have the highest ceilings) are gorgeously decorated with Andalusian tiles, mahogany and thick rugs. Service is impeccable from reception to bar.

This sturdy baroque beacon is packed with priceless old-world relics and oozes subtle 'Siglo de Oro' (Golden Age) charm. Check out the Goya-esque tapestries in the hallway or the late-afternoon tranquillity of the enclosed inner courtyard. Plunge into the tiny rooftop pool and Jacuzzi with sweeping views over the cathedral and Old San Juan. The nightly wine and food reception may preclude outside dinner plans.

Chateau Cervantes HOTEL **$$$**
(Map p52; ☎787-724-7722; www.cervantespr.com; 329 Recinto Sur; r/ste from $220/265; ❄️📶) Twelve rooms on six floors, intimate decor and a stunning level of all-round opulence, the Cervantes is about as luxurious as Puerto Rico gets. Once inside, 'chateau' is definitely the right word to use in this Parisian-influenced city beauty with its eye-catching art (original, of course) and electronic gadgets deftly splashed around angular rooms that retain a tangible old-town feel.

Designed as a boutique hotel of the highest class by local guru Nono Maldonado, the hotel barely advertises itself from the street – probably because it doesn't need to.

Condado, Santurce & Miramar

Coral Princess Hotel HOTEL **$$**
(Map p59; ☎787-977-7700; www.coralpr.com; 1159 Magdalena; r incl breakfast $152-189; ❄️📶🏊) The Coral Princess is a small, 25-room boutique hotel that punches way above its weight. Sitting in Condado's midrange bracket, it offers all the luxuries of the fancy resorts – flat-screen TVs, marble floors and original art – but with enough intimacy and Latin flavor to remind you that you're still in Puerto Rico.

Alelí by the Sea GUESTHOUSE **$$**
(Map p59; ☎787-725-5313; alelibythesea@hotmail.com; 1125 Sea View; r $85-110; P❄️📶) A gift to budget-conscious travelers, this modest nine-room guesthouse is the final bastion of inexpensive seaside accommodations in Condado. Try for a room with an ocean view. There's a handy kitchen, and a spacious deck fronts the beach.

Le Consulat Hotel HOTEL **$$**
(Map p59; ☎787-289-9191; www.leconsulathotel.com; 1149 Magdelena; r $140-145; P❄️📶🏊) A mere two blocks from the beach, these comfortable smallish rooms are in a dynamite location within walking distance of Condado's restaurants and nightlife.

Atlantic Beach Hotel HOTEL **$$**
(Map p59; ☎787-721-6900; www.atlanticbeachhotel.net; 1 Vendig; r $96-138; P❄️📶) This oceanside spot has rooms that exude a black-and-white minimalism. Its great waterfront location trumps tired common areas and slapdash staff enthusiasm. It's close to a popular gay beach.

★**La Concha** RESORT **$$$**
(Map p59; ☎787-721-7500; www.laconcharesort.com; 1077 Av Ashford; r $340-380; P❄️@📶🏊) Popular La Concha will wow you. Spacious and serene white rooms pop with flashes of color, and blue-lit showers exude an otherworldly underwater glow. Add in its three pools (one adults-only), gorgeous indoor and

SANTURCE'S STREET ART

Colonial art might be more the thing in Old San Juan, but out in the neighborhood of Santurce the focus is decidedly more modern. Here, vibrant street art, in works as much as 50ft high, has helped transform a previously no-go area into one of the city's most dynamic districts.

Importantly, these artworks also offer a more colorful and in-depth answer to the question 'What is Puerto Rican culture?' than any colonial building can. Courtesy of a new international urban art festival, Los Muros Hablan ('the walls speak'), Santurce is an edgy new powerhouse of San Juan culture. Fanning out from the Placita Santurce, the street art here is not just eye candy but offers a stunning insight into Puerto Rico.

Look out for the not-so-idyllic farming scene of a bison hauling off a cart piled high with fast-food junk, a recumbent Taíno Indian with a cloth draped over his head being reclaimed by nature, a fat iguana (iguanas are big pests on the island) squatting down the length of one building, and a group of crabs (Santurce is reclaimed swampland and was once infested with crabs) clustering around a computer screen. To make sense of these murals and to see many of the others, Casa Sol B&B (p70), based in old San Juan, offers explanatory tours of the street art. To find out about alternative arts events hereabouts, head to the cool neighborhood hangout Abracadabra Counter Cafe (p78).

outdoor seating areas, hallways in crayon colors, a 24-hour casino, a sushi bar and the drop-dead gorgeous Perla restaurant (p77), and you won't feel the need to venture far.

In addition, the hotel lobby is a hip place to see and be seen in San Juan, with a sophisticated party scene on weekends. So bring a dazzling outfit or request a room tucked away from the action.

Condado Vanderbilt Hotel HOTEL **$$$**
(Map p59; ☎787-721-5500; www.condadovanderbilt.com; 1055 Av Ashford; r from $350; P ❄ @ 🛜 🏊) One of the most opulent hotels when it opened in 1919, the Condado Vanderbilt Hotel was set to reopen in 2014 after a lavish restoration and expansion. Its 323 rooms, including 90 rooms in the original building, are large, and a high percentage of them are suites. Service is tops, with concierges stationed on every floor. Public spaces are opulent.

A landmark on one of the choicest parts of Condado Beach, the Vanderbilt is sure to get a lot of attention in the coming years, especially as it had lain dormant since the 1990s and was even threatened with demolition.

Condado Plaza RESORT **$$$**
(Map p62; ☎787-721-1000; www.condadoplaza.com; 999 Av Ashford; r from $360; P ❄ @ 🛜 🏊) The Condado Plaza straddles the thin wedge of land that separates Condado's lagoon from the Atlantic Ocean, offering stunning views in both directions. Highlights include a swanky lobby reminiscent of a designer movie set, a 24-hour casino with live entertainment, a celebrated gourmet restaurant (Piyako), and a lovely arc of sand facing the formidable walls of Fuerte San Gerónimo across the inlet.

It's a Hilton property and has close to 600 brightly decorated rooms (most with balconies) in a complex straddling Avenida Ashford.

Caribe Hilton RESORT **$$$**
(Map p62; ☎787-721-0303; www.hiltoncaribbean.com/sanjuan; Rosales; r $279-479; P ❄ @ 🛜 🏊) The Caribe was constructed in 1949 and played host to numerous celebrities throughout the 1950s and '60s. Its recently renovated rooms are loaded with amenities, and the sprawling pool and beach area includes a lawn chessboard, scores of hammocks and an interesting mini-peninsula with lounge beds. Though it's a bit of an island unto itself, there's good beach access and Old San Juan is a not unpleasant 30-minute walk away.

Ocean Park

★ Andalucía Guest House GUESTHOUSE **$$**
(Map p60; ☎787-309-3373; www.andaluciapr.com; 2011 McLeary; d from $100; P ❄ @ 🛜) Within striking distance of Ocean Park's excellent restaurants and beaches, this comfortable guesthouse makes you feel like you're part of the neighborhood. Its 11 rooms sport pretty tiling and striking color schemes, and some have a kitchen or kitchenette. The super-helpful owners lend out boogie boards and beach chairs, and there's a cozy terrace deck and courtyard Jacuzzi.

Hostería del Mar GUESTHOUSE **$$**
(Map p60; ☎787-727-3302; www.hosteriadelmarpr.com; 1 Tapia; r $154-275; ❄ 🛜) With a desirable beachside location, and greeting guests with an artsy water feature and eye-catching antiques, this whitewashed Ocean Park guesthouse is quiet, intimate and definitively Caribbean. There's no pool, but there is an excellent restaurant in an enclosed gazebo overlooking the beach. Rooms are furnished with simple rattan comfort.

Acacia Boutique Hotel HOTEL **$$**
(Map p60; ☎787-727-0668; www.acaciaboutiquehotel.com; 8 Taft; r $165-260; ❄ 🛜) This mini-hotel with a profusion of elaborate staircases offers a smorgasbord: funky wall art, simple rooms (some with ocean views), an award-winning restaurant, and a pool-sized Jacuzzi.

At Wind Chimes Inn INN **$$**
(Map p60; ☎787-727-4153; www.atwindchimesinn.com; 1750 McLeary, cnr Taft; r from $150; ❄ 🛜 🏊) This remodeled two-story Spanish-style villa mixes intimacy with low-key luxuries in its 22 bright rooms. It's a pleasant antidote to the soulless feel of Condado's mega-resorts.

Numero Uno GUESTHOUSE **$$$**
(Map p60; ☎787-726-5010; www.numero1guesthouse.com; 1 Santa Ana; r $234-346; ❄ 🛜 🏊) Hidden behind the walls of a whitewashed 1940s beachfront house, surrounded by palms and topped by a luminous kidney-shaped swimming pool, the 12 rooms and four apartments here are run by a former New Yorker whose soaring vision has inspired an inn of spiffy rooms, intimate service and an exquisite on-site seafood restaurant.

Isla Verde

El Patio Guesthouse GUESTHOUSE $
(Map p66; 787-726-6298; 23 Mar de Bering; s/d/tr $60/70/75;) In the cheaper price bracket, this is a good Isla Verde bet. This little villa is walking distance to the beach and other attractions, and is run by a kind woman who bends over backwards to make sure that rooms are spick-and-span. There's a guest kitchen and laundry, and rooms have TVs and fridges.

Coqui Inn MOTEL $
(Map p66; 787-726-4330; www.coqui-inn.net; 36 Mar Mediterráneo; r $76-95; P) Bisected by a major expressway, Isla Verde has its ugly side and you'll get a face full of it here. Expect serviceable but bare-bones rooms with cable TV, free morning coffee and parking. Visitors with ear plugs can take comfort in the price and the proximity to the beach – a short walk across a concrete bridge. Housekeeping can be lax.

Hotel La Playa GUESTHOUSE $$
(Map p66; 787-791-1115; www.hotellaplaya.com; 6 Amapola; r $109-120;) Yes, you can stay oceanfront in Isla Verde without breaking the bank. And, be green about it – Hotel La Playa has solar hot-water heaters, low-power air-con units, a 2000-gallon water catchment system, and a sustainably sourced restaurant that recycles its cooking oil for biodiesel. Pretty rooms have tasteful Caribbean decor.

★**El San Juan Resort & Casino** RESORT $$$
(Map p66; 787-791-1000; www.elsanjuanhotel.com; 6063 Av Isla Verde; r from $335; P) Bedazzled by starburst chandeliers and animal-print sofas, the lobby of El San Juan is a theatrical backdrop for the fashion parade prancing in for the legendary nightly entertainment. It's renowned for its flashy casino and rollicking nightlife. If you want that plus ocean-view rooms, unlimited water features and snazzy restaurants, this is the place for you.

Water & Beach Club HOTEL $$$
(Map p66; 787-728-3666; www.waterbeachhotel.com; 2 Tartak; r from $288; P) One of Puerto Rico's most celebrated 'boutique' hotels, the Water & Beach Club has a reception area straight out of *Architectural Digest* and elevators that sport glassed-in waterfalls. The minimalist rooms are artfully designed and benefit from spectacular beach views, and you are in close proximity to its two trendy nightspots.

Ritz-Carlton RESORT $$$
(Map p66; 787-253-1700; www.ritzcarlton.com; 6961 Av Los Gobernadores; r from $720; P) Decked out in expensive marble and embellished with Alhambra-esque lions that line the path to the swimming pool, this is San Juan at its swankiest and is a favorite hangout of visiting celebrities. Rooms are plush, service heavy on the 'yes sirs and madams' and the communal areas shimmer like winning entries in an international design competition.

Parceled inside this carefully manicured tropical 'paradise' are a spa, tennis courts, numerous eating facilities and yes, that obligatory casino.

InterContinental San Juan Resort & Casino RESORT $$$
(Map p66; 787-791-6100; www.icsanjuanresort.com; 5961 Av Isla Verde; r $238-850; P) The InterContinental offers a full-on luxury beachside resort experience with all of the usual extras you'd expect. Though the nearly 400 rooms and facilities are spiffy enough, the El San Juan next door still wins first prize for character and panache. Some rooms have views of the airport, a highly efficient 10-minute ride by taxi.

Eating

Few would dispute the fact that San Juan offers the best eating in the Caribbean. From contemporary takes on traditional fare to cafes serving exquisite locally grown coffee to restaurants run by renowned chefs, you'll be spoiled for choice.

Old San Juan

Just wandering the streets of Old San Juan, you're likely to stumble onto great places for a meal, often no bigger than an especially generous hole in the wall. Years ago the SoFo area (for 'south of Fortaleza') had a rep for cutting-edge cuisine, but times have changed. Although this area still has some good choices, some of the most interesting newer places can be found in what might be called 'NoLu', the quieter streets north of Luna.

★**Finca Cialitos** CAFE $
(Map p52; 939-207-9998; www.fincacialitos.com; 150 San Justo; snacks from $3; 9am-5pm

Tue-Sun) Your best cup of San Juan coffee is at this funky find that calls itself the 'Cafe Espresso Art'. Beans for the brews here come from the family's coffee estate in the nearby lush hills and are roasted on site. Baked goods, comfy chairs for lounging, cool mags and more will convince you to hang.

Don Ruiz CAFE **$**

(Map p52; ☎787-410-9444; Cuartel de Ballajá, off Norzagaray; mains from $5; ⊙8:30am-4:30pm Tue-Thu, 8:30am-7:30pm Fri & Sat, 11am-5:30pm Sun) Among the many treasures inside the Cuartel de Ballajá is this fine little cafe that roasts its own coffee beans. Sit outside overlooking the historic courtyard or inside amongst the rich smells. Food includes fine baked goods and sandwiches. Settle everything down with a shot of fine rum.

Manolín PUERTO RICAN **$**

(Map p52; ☎787-723-9743; 251 San Justo; mains $5-12; ⊙6am-4:30pm Mon-Sat) Elbow in with the local office workers at this snaking grill, and fill up on excellent *mofongo* (mashed plantains) and *churrasco a la parrilla* (skirt steak). Other all-star local fare includes garlic shrimp, pork chops and the delectable pistachio pudding. Breakfasts, especially the fluffy omelettes, are worth crawling out of bed for – just get there by 10:30am.

Caficultura CAFE **$**

(Map p52; ☎787-723-7731; 401 San Francisco; mains from $7; ⊙8am-5pm) Once you drink your *café con leche*, you'll want another! Just assume you'll want to settle in at this atmospheric cafe that evokes the gaslight era with its high ceilings and marble-topped tables. Watch the masses from sidewalk tables.

Café Cuatro Sombras CAFE **$**

(Map p52; ☎787-724-9955; www.cuatrosombras.com; 259 Recinto Sur; snacks from $3; ⊙8am-5pm;) Those desperate for caffeine served exquisitely can tiptoe here from the cruise-ship port; others will be drawn in by the gleaming interior that looks more like a duty-free jewelry shop than a coffee emporium. The beans are locally grown and roasted. In the morning enjoy the iconic toast with guava butter.

Café Cola'o CAFE **$**

(Map p52; ☎787-724-4607; www.prcafecolao.com; Pier 2; snacks from $3; ⊙6:30am-6pm) Café Cola'o is very different from the coffee bar you might patronize at home. For one, it lacks a word that rhymes with 'ucks' in the name; for another, it serves coffee that is handpicked from various small farms in Puerto Rico's central mountains. Staff here have an encyclopedic knowledge of all things java.

St Germain Bistro & Café FRENCH **$**

(Map p52; ☎787-725-5830; 156 Sol; dishes $8-15; ⊙11:30am-3:30pm & 6-10pm;) Main-course salads are the stars at this casual, idiosyncratic and ultimately tasty French cafe. Light fare such as creative sandwiches and crepes are among the staples. The soup choice changes daily, while the homemade cakes are melt-in-your-mouth heavenly. The upstairs sibling bar Mezzanine is splendid for a drink.

Old San Juan Farmers Market MARKET **$**

(Map p52; www.mercadoagricolanatural.com; Museo de San Juan, 150 Norzagaray; snacks from $2; ⊙8am-1pm Sat) Stop by the courtyard of the Museo de San Juan to pick up some organic local produce or coffee, nibble on homemade chocolate, bread or cheese, peruse the handcrafted gifts or tuck into an inexpensive brunch.

★Carli's Café, Fine Bistro & Piano FUSION **$$**

(Map p52; ☎787-725-4927; www.carlisworld.com; 500 San Justo; mains $12-34; ⊙3:30-11pm Mon-Thu, to 1am Fri & Sat) As much a place for a quiet cocktail or a night of excellent jazz, Carli's has a wide menu of tapas, and mains bring a Puerto Rican flair to continental classics. Tables out front on the small plaza are prized. In the evening, Carli Munoz, the owner and noted jazz musician, often works the piano.

The venue is housed in the equally appealing old Banco Popular building, an art-deco classic from 1937.

Trois Cent Onze FRENCH **$$**

(Map p52; ☎787-725-7959; www.311restaurantpr.com; 311 Fortaleza; mains $24-36; ⊙6-10pm Tue-Sun) With its well-established French bistro, 311 evokes 'elegant,' 'refined' and 'sophisticated', without too many Latino-fusion makeovers (although the Caribbean lobster is always a treat). Glide into one of the island's most romantic interiors, awash with billowing white curtains, slowly rotating fans, flickering candles and delightful Moorish-Andalusian tiles.

Order from a menu replete with scallops, duck and foie gras. There's a wine list to rival anything in France.

DON'T MISS

CAFETERIA MALLORCA

If all the tourist glitz makes you wonder where to find the 'old' in Old San Juan, head right to timeless **Cafeteria Mallorca** (Map p52; ☎787-724-4607; 300 Calle San Francisco; mains $5-15; ⏰7am-6:30pm) near the Iglesia San Francisco de Asís. In fact you wouldn't be surprised to find an aged Sally Field still in her 1960s *Flying Nun* habit tucked into one of the tightly packed tables.

The namesake specialty is the sweet and soft Mallorca, a traditional round bun served with sugar on top. You can have yours sweet – with jam – or savory with a choice of meats and cheeses. The classic features ham and cheap Swiss cheese. It's placed in a sandwich press and lightly toasted. The result is a hot treat that's thin, slightly crispy and oozing with salty, cheesy goodness. Oh, and you get a dash of powedered sugar on top.

For the most fun, sit at the bustling counter where the veteran waitstaff will keep you plied with *café con leche* and where you can watch the Mallorcas prepared by the dozen. The rest of the menu features classic Puerto Rican fare as well as simple sandwiches you might have once enjoyed at drugstore counters, not unlike this one. Service is speedy and you'll be back out enjoying the glories of the old town in no time at all.

Bodega Chic FRENCH **$$**
(Map p52; ☎787-722-0124; 51 Calle del Cristo; mains $15-25; ⏰6-10pm Tue-Sun) Although this restaurant is bifurcated by the entrance to its vintage building, you won't be divided in your praise for its excellent French fare with a strong country accent. The food is hearty and has Algerian touches (think grains and bold flavors) thanks to chef Christophe Gourdain. Top dishes include mussels and frites (with aioli) plus hanger steak.

El Jibarito PUERTO RICAN **$$**
(Map p52; ☎787-725-8375; 280 Sol; mains $10-25; ⏰10am-9pm) Welcome to the neighborhood, *hermano* (brother). El Jibarito is the kind of unpretentious place that you just know will serve a good and garlicky *mofongo* (mashed plantains) or *arroz con habichuelas* (rice and beans). It does. A favorite of local families and visitors, the meals are simple but hearty, with good pork and prawns.

Anamu PUERTO RICAN **$$**
(Map p52; ☎787-977-7107; www.anamupr.com; 150 San Sebastián; mains $15-25; ⏰5:30pm-midnight Tue-Sat) Upscale local fare with international accents are the hallmarks of this tidy restaurant that resides in a prim and perfectly restored vintage house. Yes there's a fine *mofongo*, but there are also excellent seafood dishes and mains from further afield, such as the creamy risotto. Cocktails are a specialty.

El Picoteo SPANISH **$$**
(Map p52; ☎787-723-9020; Hotel El Convento, 100 Calle del Cristo; dishes $10-20; ⏰noon-2pm & 5-10pm Tue-Sun) One of El Convento's (p71) culinary highlights is this terrace tapas bar – perched above the hotel's central courtyard. Perennial favorites include tortilla, meatballs, garlic prawns, seviche and various cheeses. More substantial offerings include paella. Get a table at sunset and watch the rosy hues play off the shadows of the lovely courtyard.

La Madre MEXICAN **$$**
(Map p52; ☎787-647-5392; 351 San Francisco; mains $15-25; ⏰5-11pm Mon-Fri, from noon Sat & Sun) A sophisticated take on Mexican is the theme at this hip and lively restaurant-lounge. Start with delectable tamarind margaritas or opt for fruity alternatives like *parcha* (passion fruit) or *acerola* (cherry). The food boasts creative twists while the entertainment changes nightly – everything from oldies to salsa. Videos such as old cartoons may make boomers maudlin after their third mojito.

Patio del Nispero CARIBBEAN **$$**
(Map p52; ☎787-723-9020; Hotel El Convento, 100 Calle del Cristo; mains $12-30; ⏰6:30am-10pm) The shady courtyard at the El Convento (p71) is home to the hotel's all-day restaurant, so-named for the resident 350-year-old Nispero tree. Lunch and dinner feature dishes with local and regional flavors, however the best meal of the day is the breakfast, both for the setting and the excellent dishes such as the eggs Benedict.

Café Berlin INTERNATIONAL **$$**
(Map p52; ☎787-722-5205; 407 San Francisco; dishes $13-22; ⏰9am-10pm; 📶🅥) The view of the Plaza de Colon from the terrace here is

reason enough to stop. In a setting that's more Viennese than Caribbean, Café Berlin serves fresh food with a strong vegetarian (and vegan) bias. There are meaty mains but also tofu done any which way you want. Desserts are scrumptious. The breakfast menu is long.

★Marmalade FUSION $$$
(Map p52; ☎787-724-3969; www.marmaladepr.com; 317 Fortaleza; mains $20-35; ⏲6-10pm; 🍷) The personal vision of noted chef Peter Schintler, Marmalade was one of the first restaurants to bring real foodie recognition to Old San Juan more than a decade ago. This starkly minimalist eating establishment is decked out like the Korova Milk Bar in Stanley Kubrick's *A Clockwork Orange*.

The food takes full advantage of local sourcing and dishes are prepared with an intense passion for detail. The wine list is extensive, although the drink many will remember (or try to) is called 'global warming' and is an experience in changing tastes as spice-laden ice cubes melt.

Verde Mesa CARIBBEAN $$$
(Map p52; ☎787-390-4662; www.verdemesa.com; 107 Tetuán; mains $15-25; ⏲6-10pm Tue-Sat; 🍷) Hidden in plain sight amidst the tourist masses, this little gem of a restaurant is lauded for its vegetarian and seafood fare. Take a break from *mofongo* and enjoy fresh and flavorful food. Many of the ingredients are sourced from local organic farms. Pressed tin ceilings, antiques and moody lighting give meals a romantic patina. Don't miss the crème brûlée.

Dragonfly FUSION $$$
(Map p52; ☎787-977-3886; www.oofrestaurants.com; 364 Fortaleza; mains $18-28; ⏲6-11pm) One of SoFo's most stylish culinary innovators when it opened in 2000, this moody restaurant (think dark, red bordello – all dim lampshades and decorative mirrors) stays fresh with a changing menu of Pan-Asian fare with Latin accents. Sushi and sashimi are joined by more unusual fare such as the signature Peking duck nachos and brightly seasoned seafood.

Aguaviva SEAFOOD $$$
(Map p52; ☎787-722-0665; 364 Fortaleza; mains $28-45; ⏲6-10pm) This high-profile SoFo restaurant is owned by the same company as Dragonfly and Parrot Club – in fact there are drink specials designed to get you to try all three. There's an arty water/sea-life theme – all turquoise blues and brilliant whites. The house specialty is seafood; many come for the souvenir cocktail cups.

Condado

Pure and Natural CAFE $
(Map p59; ☎787-725-6104; 1125 Av Ashford; mains $6-12; ⏲11am-8pm; 🍷) A healthy haven amidst the temptations of resort fare, this storefront cafe isn't vegetarian but it does have a lot of veggie options. Choose from an array of fresh juices and then dig into a salad, sandwich or other casual meal. Service is far from rushed; bring something to read.

Pinky's CAFE $
(Map p59; ☎787-222-5222; 1451 Av Ashford; dishes $8-15; ⏲7am-10pm) Break free of hotel restaurants and come to Condado's popular delicafe for breakfasts, smoothies, sandwiches and wraps. A chance to make up for all that delicious, rich Puerto Rican food you've been eating, it's also an opportunity to hit a laid-back local hang.

Via Appia ITALIAN $
(Map p59; ☎787-725-8711; 1350 Av Ashford; pizzas $10-20; ⏲11am-11pm) The good thing about Condado is that it still retains a smattering of family-run jewels among all the Starbucks and 7-Elevens. Via Appia is one such gem, a no-nonsense Italian eatery where the pizza is the main event and the gentlemanly waiters could quite conceivably have walked off the set of *The Godfather*. Dine alfresco, as the multilingual mélange of Avenida Ashford goes strolling by.

And don't miss the delicious sangria.

Hacienda Don José MEXICAN, PUERTO RICAN $
(Map p59; ☎787-722-5880; 1025 Av Ashford; dishes $10-22; ⏲8am-11pm) Condado on the cheap – it can still be done. Indeed, the Don José is more reminiscent of a Mexican beach bar than a plush tourist trap. Waves lash the rocks within spitting distance of your *huevos rancheros* or tender fajitas, and busy staff shimmy around the tiled tables beneath colorful murals.

If your swanky hotel's all-you-can-eat buffet has worn you out, drop by here for a little bit of local hospitality.

Perla STEAKHOUSE, SEAFOOD $$$
(Map p59; ☎787-977-3285; La Concha, 1077 Av Ashford; mains $25-45; ⏲6-10pm) Dine inside an architectural oyster at romantic Perla, where hand-blown glass lamps cast a

flattering glow and pearlescent walls undulate and echo into the nighttime sea. Aquatic options feature on the menu along with steaks. A voluminous wine list (many by the glass) highlights French and Californian selections. Book ahead for the coveted window seats.

Yantar FUSION **$$$**

(Map p59; ☎787-724-3636; 1018 Av Ashford; mains $20-50; ⏲5.30pm-2am) Think mod mood lighting and fresh, creative Spanish fusion cuisine arranged just so. The warm, attentive staff will walk you through the menu, and they make a mean cocktail. Starters are tapas-inspired and mains are just plain delicious, prepared with impeccable attention to detail. Plan to take your time, and ask for a table overlooking the Condado Lagoon.

José José SPANISH **$$$**

(Map p59; ☎787-725-8496; 1110 Magdalena; dishes $25-40; ⏲noon-3pm Tue-Sun, 6-10pm Tue-Fri & Sun) From the Basque Country's San Sebastián, chef José Abreu crafts complex Spanish-influenced dishes, from lobster risotto to lamb. Or tell the kitchen what ingredients you crave and the chef will improvise a creative custom-made tasting menu. The wine selection and service may not always be up to par with the food.

Santurce & Miramar

Numerous small and atmospheric cafes are found in and around the La Placita de Santurce. This area is also ground zero for some of San Juan's best restaurants. By day or night, wander a little and see what grabs you.

★**Abracadabra Counter Cafe** CAFE **$**

(☎787-200-0447; 1661 Av Ponce de Leon; meals $6-10; ⏲8:30am-7pm Mon-Thu, 8:30am-11pm Fri, 10am-3pm Sat & Sun) As colorful as the neighboring street murals, this vibrant cafe draws in an eclectic crowd through the day and into the night. Fresh juices, fine coffees (with beans from Hacienda San Pedro up the street), sublime breakfasts, and a variety of casual fare and snacks are reasons to drop by.

Cafe Culturas CAFE **$**

(Map p62; ☎939-275-1595; www.neograff.wix.com/cafeculturas; Av Fernández Juncos, near Calle Hipódromo; mains $4-8; ⏲7am-8pm Tue-Thu, to 10pm Fri, noon-10pm Sat & Sun) One of San Juan's new cutting-edge cafes with prices aimed at the economically challenged masses, this upstairs retreat features farm-to-table fare and locally sourced coffee. Omelettes, wraps, sandwiches and more are infused with zesty local flavors and made with artisanal flair. On some nights there's live jazz, arty flicks and performance art. A traditional cafe is on the ground floor.

Hacienda San Pedro Coffee Shop CAFE **$**

(Map p62; ☎787-993-1871; 318 Av de Diego; snacks from $2; ⏲6:30am-6pm Mon-Fri, 9:30am-3pm Sat) An example of why San Juan has become a coffee mecca: beans grown and roasted locally are used in a fab range of coffee drinks, most at prices you won't find in touristy areas. Pastries are excellent and it's easy to let the hours slip by in the sleek surrounds or outside at a sidewalk table.

Blonda Condado CAFE **$$**

(Map p62; ☎787-993-5710; 1504 Av Ashford; mains $18-30; ⏲11:30am-10pm Mon-Fri, 9am-11pm Sat & Sun) Blonda is all about the weekend brunch. Linger over steak and eggs, or excellent eggs Benedict with crab, in an airy cafe with sleek wood tables and a boisterous crowd. The rest of the time, fresh well-prepared dishes range from pizza and pasta to tender salmon with asparagus.

★**José Enrique** FUSION **$$$**

(Map p62; ☎787-725-3518; www.joseenriquepr.com; 176 Duffaut; meals from $35; ⏲11:30am-10pm Tue-Fri, 6:30-10pm Sat) Discreetly hidden in a yellow house lacking a sign, you'll have no problems finding one of the hemisphere's best restaurants – just follow the excited hordes in the know. There are no reservations, so be prepared to wait; your meal is definitely worth the minor chaos. The namesake chef is a multiple-award winner and he combines local ingredients brilliantly.

Look for fresh fish with sides such as malanga (a taro-root mash), and local cheeses served with an amazing guava and papaya salsa. Novel details include providing chocolate sticks in place of spoons for eating the sublime chocolate mousse.

★**Santaella** PUERTO RICAN, FUSION **$$$**

(Map p62; ☎787-725-1611; www.santaellapr.com; 219 Canals; meals from $35; ⏲11:30am-11pm Tue-Fri, 6:30-11pm Sat) One of San Juan's best restaurants, Santaella buzzes with excitement, inspired by the superb drinks at the bar and the sensational fare. Dishes range from tapas-small to full-size and include a varying line-up of simple creations that are a

WORTH A TRIP

BEBO'S BBQ

Absolutely as unadorned as the bones left after you've scarfed down a plate of its ribs, **Bebo's BBQ** (☎787-791-7115; Marginal Los Angeles I-20, Carolina; meals $5-10; ⏰11am-11pm) is a frills-free local barbecue joint that pays homage to all things pork. Pick whichever of two lines is shorter and ask the no-nonsense order takers for a plate of ribs and roasted pork. Make certain you get a side of yucca and onions (trust us, it's as addictive as starch can be) and then find a spot at one of the picnic tables in the open-air eating area. Borrow some hot sauce from one of your greasy-fingered neighbors and dig in.

For ambience there's noisy Hwy 26 alongside Bebo's road frontage position, and just beyond is a busy runway at LMM airport. Try to decide if that roar you hear is a jet taking off or the sounds of your approval for a great – and cheap – meal. It's next to a McDonald's.

triumph of flavor. Although many are happy to wait in the alluring bar, those in the know book in advance.

Pikayo FUSION **$$$**
(Map p62; ☎787-721-6194; www.pikayo.com; Condado Plaza, 999 Av Ashford; mains $37-50; ⏰6.30-10pm) Wilo Benet is one of the island's platoon of celebrity chefs. He's uncovered the soul of Caribbean cooking by infusing colonial-era Puerto Rican cuisine with various African and Indian elements. This showcase restaurant is renowned not just for its menu of steaks and seafood but also its polished service.

Ocean Park

La Casita Blanca PUERTO RICAN **$**
(☎787 726 5501; 351 Tapia; mains $7-15; ⏰11:30am-4pm Mon-Wed & Sun, to 6pm Thu, to 9pm Fri & Sat) Down-home neighborhood cooking has been the order of the day at this low-key eatery for decades. Locals, including other chefs, come from far and wide to kick back at simple tables and feast on food their grandmother used to make. Expect true Puerto Rican street food and traditional dishes, and zero attitude.

Servers may not always speak English, but they'll help you sort it all out.

★**Kasalta's** CAFE **$$**
(Map p60; ☎787-727-7340; 1966 McLeary; mains $5-24; ⏰6am-10pm) Oh the garbanzo bean soup! Tucked into Ocean Park's residential enclave, Kasalta's is the sort of authentic Puerto Rican bakery and diner that you'll find yourself crossing town to visit daily. The coffee here is as legendary as the sweets that fill a long glass display case and include everything from Danish pastries to iced buns.

Plentiful seating, myriad newspapers and a buzzing local ambience add even more icing to the cake. Breakfasts are divine, while the lunchtime specials are scrumptious. The melted manchego cheese sandwich is extraordinary.

La B de Burro MEXICAN **$$**
(Map p60; ☎787-242-0295; 2000 McLeary; meals $10-30; ⏰11am-10pm Mon-Sat, to 9pm Sun) You don't need to wear a mask, tights and cape to sample the best burritos in the Caribbean, but you'd fit right in if you did. A popular hangout pumping out hearty chimichangas, a cool soundtrack and Old Harbor brew on tap, this funky *lucha libre* (free wrestling)–themed *taqueria* (taco shop) sports a purple wrestling-ring patio, Mexican altars and a ceiling full of *papel picado* (perforated paper) streamers.

Local kids plant and tend seedlings outside.

Pamela's SEAFOOD **$$$**
(Map p60; ☎787-726-5010; Numero Uno Guesthouse, 1 Santa Ana; mains $20-45; ⏰11am-10pm) Right on the beach, come to Pamela's for the waterfront setting and a leisurely drink or tapas-style small plate. Service can be slow so a full dinner is more of a commitment. The menu focuses on fresh seafood – think jalapeño-ginger shrimp and seafood chowder – though there are surprise twists with flavors from Puerto Rico to Asia.

The restaurant is part of the trendy Numero Uno guesthouse (p73), and diners sip wine and munch on scallops beside a teardrop-shaped swimming pool while the ocean crashes just feet away. Reserve ahead.

Niche INTERNATIONAL **$$$**
(Map p60; ☎787-268-2803; www.acaciaboutique-hotel.com; Acacia Boutique Hotel, 8 Taft; mains $25-40; ⏰7:30-11am & 6-10:30pm Mon-Sat, 11am-3pm

Sun) A neighborhood favorite, this super-intimate space inside the oceanfront Acacia Boutique Hotel (p73) oozes romantic atmosphere. Little windows in the floor peek down at water in the cistern, and the wave-shaped banquette seating makes it feel like you're in a seaside speakeasy. The emphasis is on fresh local seafood, with dishes such as mahimahi seviche and an award-winning lobster risotto.

The Sunday brunch gets rave reviews too. Only downside is that service can be hit or miss.

Isla Verde

Don José Café PUERTO RICAN $

(Map p66; ☎787-253-1281; www.restaurantedonjose.com; 6475 Av Isla Verde, Km 6.3; mains $4-18; ⊙24hr) No frills, no formalities, but good diner food – and it's open 24 hours, though you'd think it wasn't operating at all judging by the heavily tinted windows. Come here for breakfast after an exuberant all-night party and nip your hangover in the bud with eggs, bacon and ham washed down with strong coffee.

El Estribo PUERTO RICAN $

(Map p66; ☎787-463-0446; 35 Av Isla Verde; mains $10-25; ⊙11:30am-11pm Sun-Thu, to 1am Fri & Sat) Country cooking comes to town at this unassuming eatery. One favorite dish is the chicken stuffed with plantains, wrapped in bacon, and then drizzled with guava sauce, but all of the mains are sumptuous and the portions large. The owner often picks up his guitar and sings a few ditties, making the little place feel welcoming and lively every night of the week.

Bajuice CAFE $

(Map p66; ☎787-444-4779; Av Isla Verde, 5555 Cond Los Corales; smoothies $4.25-5.25, dishes $4-8; ⊙8am-8pm; 📶) Detoxify, baby! This casual juice bar makes a range of smoothies and fresh fruit blends, all posted on its chalkboard. Ingredients include açai, hemp, bee pollen and the like. The avocolada is a big hit, blending avocado, lemonade, pineapple, grapes, sea salt, vanilla, coconut water and agave. But it's got more tame offerings as well, and also serve healthy wraps, sandwiches, salads and breakfasts.

Las Canarias BAKERY, DELI $

(Map p66; ☎787-294-5441; Av Isla Verde, Marginal Biascoechea; dishes $7-10; ⊙6am-10pm) Start your day with fresh-baked pastries and *café con leche*. Later in the day choose between beef empanadas or fresh-made sandwiches, or put together a plate of the daily specials, arrayed in trays behind the counter. All of it is cheap, filling and fun. Locals and tourists alike come to this simple bakery and eat their fill.

Ceviche House PERUVIAN $$

(Map p66; ☎787-726-0919; 79 Av Isla Verde; mains $18-30; ⊙11:30am-10pm Mon-Thu & Sun, to 11pm Fri & Sat) Though the seviche here is grand, as one might expect, this casual Peruvian restaurant also cooks up delicious, juicy steaks and a full range of fresh seafood, like whole red snapper or mussels with salsa. The friendly staff are attentive without being overbearing.

Metropol PUERTO RICAN $$

(Map p66; ☎787-791-4046; http://metropolrestaurant.com; Av Isla Verde, Annexo Club Gallistico; dishes $11-22; ⊙11:30am-10pm) Find this neighborhood favorite right next to the cockfighting arena. It's well known for the plentiful portions and simple (but not plain) local and Cuban fare. The stuffed Cornish hen is popular – perhaps a casualty of the arena next door? There are several other locations around the island, though it's a family-run endeavor.

GAY & LESBIAN SAN JUAN

Considered to be the most gay-friendly destination in the Caribbean, San Juan has long buried its stereotypical macho image and replaced it with a culture known for its tolerance and openness.

Condado is an especially gay-friendly neighborhood. The beach at the end of Calle Vendig is a gay hangout and there are several popular cafes and restaurants nearby.

Santurce is the nexus of the club and cruising scene, with new places opening all the time.

The annual **Puerto Rico Queer Filmfest** (www.puertoricoqueerfilmfest.com) began in 2009, and takes place in mid-November; Pride events are held in early June.

Casa Dante PUERTO RICAN $$

(Map p66; ☎787-726-7310; 39 Av Isla Verde; dishes $10-26; ⏰11am-11pm) Casa Dante is a family-run restaurant that serves more variations of *mofongo* than one would think humanly feasible. All are delicious, and its steak and creole chicken get rave reviews as well.

Yamiko JAPANESE $$

(Map p66; ☎787-982-3322; 5960 Av Isla Verde; sushi $5-12, mains $11-20; ⏰3pm-1am Mon-Thu, to 4am Fri & Sat, to 3am Sun) What a genius move – late-night sushi! The decor is simple, but people come not for fancy wall hangings but for the warm hospitality and top-notch sushi with super-fresh ingredients. Yamiko also offers a full range of Japanese and Chinese mains.

Drinking & Nightlife

San Juan is a late-night town; you'll find places to party the night away right across the city. Old San Juan is good for strolling from venue to venue, while the beachfront neighborhoods like Condado are known for their glitzy resort venues. Meanwhile, you can go totally hip in Santurce, where cutting-edge places open (and close) regularly.

Old San Juan

Part of the fun of Old San Juan is simply exploring the streets and finding the little characterful bars and cafes that survive amidst the tourist throngs.

Besides being an unbeatable place for dinner, Carli's Café (p75) is a splendid spot for a civilized drink or a night of superb jazz.

★La Taberna Lúpulo BAR

(Map p52; ☎787-721-3772; 150 San Sebastián; ⏰6pm-2am Mon-Fri, from 3pm Sat & Sun) This beautiful old corner bar has been updated with Puerto Rico's best selection of microbrews. The line-up on the 30 taps is ever-changing and includes some of America's best and most unusual brews. Windows are open to the street on both sides and the neighborhood has a relaxed, leafy charm.

★El Batey BAR

(Map p52; 101 Calle del Cristo; ⏰11am-7am) If Hunter S Thompson's ghost wanted to relive his *Rum Diary* days, this is where you'd find him. Cool, crusty and unashamedly divey, the walls of this cavernous drinking joint are covered in graffiti, while the low-key lighting will have you groping in your pockets for spare change to light up the suitably retro jukebox.

El Batey is a place to down shots, shoot pool and ramble soulfully about when Elvis was king and the Bacardí bottles still came from Cuba.

Mezzanine COCKTAIL BAR

(Map p52; ☎787-724-4657; www.themezzaninepr.com; 156 Sol; ⏰noon-midnight Tue & Wed, noon-2am Thu & Fri, 10am-2am Sat, 10am-midnight Sun; 📶) A perfectly raffish 2nd-floor bar, Mezzanine has a raggedly refined atmosphere that seems timeless. The cocktails are inventive, the wine list good and it's on the floor above the very popular St Germain Bistro (p75). There's live jazz some nights, and the tapas dishes go down smoothly.

La Factoria BAR

(Map p52; cnr San Jose & San Sebastián; ⏰8pm-4am Tue-Sun) Gotta wedge your way in on weekend nights; DJs, acoustic guitars, sing-along sets and even a bit of patriotic fervor as the clock approaches midnight. And that's just the start. The so-named Hijos de Borinquen (or 'Sons of Borinquen') has been known to keep going until 6am. Great cocktails plus tapas for filler.

Rivera Hermanos Cash & Carry BAR

(Map p52; 157 San Sebastián; ⏰11am-midnight Mon-Sat) A nearly 40-year-old institution run by two Rivera sisters (who didn't bother to change the sign), this old liquor warehouse is a vibrant community hangout for local artists, hipsters and students, where live salsa and *boleros* (ballads) fill the evenings, and local poets recite to longtime patrons perched on the old wooden chairs sipping cheapo Medallas. You can even borrow an instrument for one of the frequent pick-up jam sessions.

Douglas' Bar BAR

(Map p52; cnr Fortaleza & Tanca; ⏰5pm-late) Open to the streets this tiny spot is almost as small as the corner pocket in the upstairs pool table. Stop in for a cold beer or a cocktail and join the genial vibe. Northerners will be forgiven for feeling smug if the lone TV is showing a frostbitten American football game.

Old Harbor Brewery BREWERY

(Map p52; ☎787-721-2100; 202 Tizol; ⏰11:30am-1am) Old Harbor concocts a handful of excellent varieties, including a crisp Coquí lager, a hearty Kofresí stout and various rotating seasonal choices. The gleaming copper kettles add plenty of atmosphere. However, most agree that you come for the beer, not the food.

Condado, Ocean Park & Isla Verde

Break out your glitziest duds for nights in the trendy clubs and posh resorts of the famous Condado, Ocean Park and Isla Verde beaches. But also know that you're never far from a more humble spot for a cold drink overlooking the sands.

Condado is especially good for walking at night, as places are fairly close together. It becomes more scattered as you go east.

La Concha Lobby Bar BAR, CLUB
(Map p59; 1077 Av Ashford, Condado; noon-late) Take your rightful place with the beautiful people at the undisputed hot spot of San Juan. On weekend nights, the lobby bar explodes with activity while chic cocktail-bearing staff in space-age outfits and wedge heels do their best to swivel through. Things get progressively wilder as the night turns to morning, with dancing to DJs and live music.

El San Juan Hotel Lobby CLUB
(Map p66; El San Juan Resort & Casino, 6063 Av Isla Verde, Isla Verde; 8pm-2am Thu-Sat) If you want to dance but discos aren't your style, try the salsa and merengue bands here. Professional dancers move among the crowd getting everyone in motion. Dress up and mingle with the sleek clientele.

Pa'l Cielo BAR
(Map p60; 2056 Loiza, Ocean Park; 5pm-2am) Caribbean kitsch rules at this bohemian bar, which is also known for great local food (the calamari and garlic seviche stand out). Dolled up in colored lights, with artsy tropical murals, its funky mismatched tables get pushed aside after midnight for DJs or live salsa, reggae and hip-hop. It's the place to be on Sunday nights.

Mist BAR
(Map p66; 787-728-3666; www.waterbeachhotel.com; Water & Beach Club, 2 Tartak, Isla Verde; noon-3am) Stylish rooftop partying at its best. Multilevel Mist combines poolside action with sweeping beach views. White and blue mood lighting glows off the white surrounds and there are plenty of shadows in which you can escape notice. Music is cutting-edge electronic dance music and on many nights you can enjoy the reverb off surrounding condo blocks. Delicate little tapas bites are served until late.

Oceano BAR,
(Map p59; 787-724-6300; www.oceanopr.com; 2 Vendig, Condado; noon-midnight or 1am Tue-Sun) Cruise the three bars and pick your poison: from chilled-out lounge, to open-air beach bar, to dress-to-impress rooftop. Gay and straight folks alike come for elegant eats, top cocktails, DJs and dancing.

Splash Lounge GAY BAR
(Map p59; 787-721-7145; Condado 6, Condado; 5pm-3am Tue-Sun) This is a great, tiny, after-beach or pre-night-out dive for drinks and a flirt with cute patrons and bartenders. It's also got a small outdoor area. Find it across the parking lot from the Marriott Resort & Stellaris Casino.

Club Brava CLUB
(Map p66; 787-791-2781; www.bravapr.com; El San Juan Resort & Casino, 6063 Av Isla Verde, Isla Verde; cover $10-20; 10pm-late Thu-Sat) This hot club inside the El San Juan Resort gets packed with 'beautiful people' and garners rave reviews from celeb spotters and all-night dance fanatics. A mix of house, reggaetón and salsa fills the small, two-level club, and the atmosphere is electric. Dress up, bring your credit card and get ready to jive to what is touted to be the best sound system in the Caribbean.

The people-watching in the lobby beforehand is a scene in itself. Thursday and Friday are 21-plus; Saturday is 23-plus for men, 21-plus for women.

Small Bar BAR
(Map p59; 787-402-2954; 1106 Av Ashford, Condado; 3pm-5am) The name could either refer to the size of the people who will best fit into this tiny water hole or simply be self-evident. One thing that isn't small is the beer list, which is massive. A happy mix of boys, girls and couples kick back at this antidote to the nearby high-concept clubs.

Santurce & Miramar

The tiny streets around La Placita de Santurce are perfect for finding a cold beer or

FEAR & LOATHING IN SAN JUAN

Long before *Fear and Loathing in Las Vegas* and the sharp, stylized prose that gave birth to 'Gonzo' journalism, US writer Hunter S Thompson earned a meager living in 1960 as a scribe for a fledgling Puerto Rican English-language weekly called *El Sportivo*, based in San Juan. It was a wild time in the city, with Americans flooding in from revolutionary Cuba. Thompson plunged into both this wild scene and innumerable bottles of rum, and was at the center of all the mayhem, until he decamped nine months later.

The essence of the era was later to emerge rather dramatically in his seminal book, *The Rum Diary*. Published in 1998 (nearly 40 years after it was written), the novel is a thinly veiled account of Thompson's alcohol-fuelled journalistic exploits as seen through the eyes of Paul Kemp, a struggling freelance writer caught in a Caribbean boomtown that was battling against an incoming tide of rich American tourists.

Hailed today – at least by Thompson fans – as a modern classic, the book was made into a 2011 movie starring Johnny Depp, which is often as incoherently boozy as its inspiration.

cocktail, even early in the week. Calle Robert is especially atmospheric.

★La Placita de Santurce STREET PARTY
(Map p62; La Placita de Santurce; ⏲5pm-late Thu & Fri) San Juan's most exciting neighborhood for food and drink is especially unmissable on Thursday and Friday nights, when it becomes one big street party. Centered on the historic plaza, the surrounding cafes are joined by the Santurce Mercado's vendors and street kiosks, which turn the area into one huge party.

As the myriad bars fill up, ties are loosened, a salsa band lets rip from a makeshift stage, and a bright and infectious energy infiltrates the humid yet congenial surroundings. It doesn't take long for the dancing to start. A shimmy here, a holler there, and suddenly the whole square is alive with inebriated marketing reps kicking off their high heels and slick-haired business analysts salsa-ing. It's a carefree scene and in many ways, it is San Juan at its best.

Tia Maria's GAY BAR
(Map p62; 326 Av José de Diego; ⏲11am-3am) She admits to being almost 30, though the boys who pack Tia Maria's are aged across the spectrum and turn up from all over the island for the cheap drinks, good company and perhaps a game of pool. Tuesday-night karaoke.

El Patio De LiLa BAR
(Map p62; ☎787-944-7673; Robert 1360; ⏲noon-2am) This tiny blue-fronted bar sets up an array of chairs in the street come afternoon and just demands you pause for a spell. Tiny lights twinkle behind the bar; get a shot of rum and snack on one of the tasty wood-fired pizzas.

Starz GAY CLUB
(Map p62; 365 Av José de Diego; cover $5; ⏲10pm-late Sat) Make new friends across the street at popular Tia Maria's and then dance the night away at this occasionally exuberant, mostly male club. DJs spin disco, trance, techno and house.

Circo Bar GAY CLUB
(Map p62; 650 Condado; ⏲9pm-late) FREE A video bar – with a karaoke detour on Thursdays, and drag shows that get mixed reviews – this place turns sweaty and snug later at night and on weekends, when high-energy dancing gets everyone up close and personal. Amid the flashing TV screens you'll find a youngish male crowd wriggling to house beats or chilling out on the walk-through smoking patio.

☆ Entertainment

San Juan has an eclectic entertainment scene that's among the best in the Caribbean. You can walk the aesthetic streets of Old San Juan after dark and encounter a moveable feast of options. Follow your ears to a salsa performance in a backstreet bar.

Beyond the old town, the major resort hotels have live entertainment most nights. A cutting-edge nightlife scene thrives in gritty Santurce. Funky galleries and cafes offer up art films, performance art and live music.

Live Music

A number of the resort hotels have live music in their lobbies, usually on weekends. Try the El San Juan (p74) or the San Juan

Marriott Resort (p85) in Condado for salsa and merengue bands, and dancing from 8pm until late.

★Nuyorican Café LIVE MUSIC

(Map p52; ☎787-977-1276; www.nuyoricancafepr.com; 312 San Francisco, Old San Juan; ⏲8pm-late) If you came to Puerto Rico in search of sizzling salsa music, you'll find it at the Nuyorican Café. San Juan's hottest nightspot – stuffed into an alley off Fortaleza, opposite a nameless drinking hole – is a congenial hub of live Latino sounds and hip-gyrating locals. You'll get everything from poetry readings to six-piece salsa bands, and things usually get hopping around 11pm.

You'll meet people too – the Nuyorican is refreshingly devoid of pretensions or dance snobbery.

Nuestro Son LIVE MUSIC

(Map p52; 259 Tetuán, Old San Juan; ⏲6pm-late) You'll hear it before you see it, so follow your ears to this loud and proud artsy bar and live-music club concealed on a darkened backstreet. The crowd's local, the cover's always cheap, and the fervent sounds of rock, bossa nova, *bomba* and *trova* – '*anything* but reggaetón' – propel you through the door.

La Respuesta LIVE MUSIC, PERFORMING ARTS

(Map p62; www.larespuestapr.com; 1600 Av Fernández Juncos, cnr Calle del Parque, Santurce; ⏲hours vary) Check online to see what's on: usually music, alt film or poetry.

Coliseo de Puerto Rico LIVE MUSIC, PERFORMING ARTS

(www.coliseodepuertorico.com; 500 Arterial B, Hato Rey) Across the street from the Hato Rey Tren Urbano station, this 18,000-capacity arena books musical superstars from Iron Maiden to Julio Iglesias.

Classical Music, Opera & Ballet

El Centro de Bellas Artes Luis A Ferré THEATER

(Bellas Artes; Map p62; ☎787-724-4747; www.cba.gobierno.pr; Av Ponce de León, Parada 22½, Santurce) Built in 1981, this center has more than 1800 seats in the festival hall, about 700 in the drama hall and 200 in the experimental theater. The Puerto Rican Symphony Orchestra holds its weekly winter performances at the complex' newer 1300-seat Pablo Casals Symphony Hall. International stars perform here, and it's the major host of the annual Festival Casals (p69).

Theater

Amigos del Corralón THEATER

(Map p52; ☎787-226-1626; San José 109; ⏲hours vary) This great new venue is housed in a slightly grand building dating to the 18th century. Theater, dance and music can be enjoyed on a rotating schedule, and there are frequent exhibits in the gallery spaces. It's worth a look just for the ancient tiles and to see the courtyard performance space.

Teatro Tapia THEATER

(Map p52; ☎787-721-0180, 787-480-5000; Plaza de Colón, Old San Juan; tickets $10-30) A city landmark, the Teatro Tapia on the south side of Plaza Colón is an intimate neoclassical theater designed in the Italian style with three-tiered boxes and an elegantly decorated lobby. Dating from 1832, the building has long been a nexus of the island's rich cultural life and hosts big names in opera, stage and ballet from around the world.

The theater was named after the Father of Puerto Rican literature, Alejandro Tapia y Rivera, and experts today rate it as the oldest free-standing drama stage still in use in the US and its territories. The theater was restored extensively in 1949 and then again in 1976, 1997 and 2007.

The Tapia's contemporary performances are usually in Spanish and frequently feature new works from Spain or Latin America.

Cinemas

Movie theaters can be found in most of San Juan's major shopping centers. Check www.caribbeancinemas.com for most theaters and showtimes island-wide.

Movie buffs should check out the city's annual cinema festival (p69).

Fine Arts Café CINEMA

(☎787-765-2339; Popular Center, Torre Norte, Hato Rey) One of the island's few art-house cinemas, this place shows a good selection of independent films from around the world. It's across from the Hato Rey Tren Urbano station.

Fine Arts Miramar CINEMA

(Map p62; ☎787-721-4288; 654 Av Ponce de León, Miramar) This art-house cinema was once a sanctuary for adult-only movies. These days it shows independent films from around the world, as well as Hollywood blockbusters.

DON'T MISS

WINTER BASEBALL

From November through January, winter baseball is one of Puerto Rico's favorite pastimes. Top teams play during the winter, when major league action in the US is dormant, and many famous players got their starts playing here. However, the tight economics of the local baseball league mean that wages are small and post-game victory banquets may be rice and beans. Players are there for the love of the game or in the hopes of being spotted by a scout.

Going to a game is a great way to meet locals – and it's priced for the masses. The best seats in the house can usually be had for $7 and large stadiums mean you don't normally need to buy tickets in advance. Vendors wander the stands selling cold beer and mixed drinks (think watery piña coladas) for $3.

Teams have fervent support from loyal fans and games can be raucous. In San Juan, two teams worth watching are the **Cangrejeros de Santurce** (Santurce Crabbers) and **Gigantes de Carolina** (Carolina Giants). Learn more about the teams and the schedules of winter league baseball at www.mlb.com/mlb/events/winterleagues/.

Metro Cinema CINEMA
(Map p62; ☎787-722-0465; 1255 Av Ponce de León, Parada 18, Santurce) This classic restored cinema is in Santurce, edging towards Miramar. It shows a mix of popular and arty films.

Plaza Las Américas Cinema CINEMA
(☎787-767-4775; Plaza Las Américas Mall, 525 Av Franklin Delano Roosevelt, Hato Rey) In the huge mall, this 13-screen multiplex shows first-run Hollywood fare.

Casinos

San Juan has certainly developed a reputation for being Las Vegas-on-the-sea, a mantle it stole from Havana when Castro threw the mob and their gambling syndicates out of Cuba in 1959. As a result, a lot of travelers and islanders come down here purely for the action. All of San Juan's large resort hotels have casinos; the most popular include the El San Juan Resort & Casino (p74), the **San Juan Marriott Resort & Stellaris Casino** (Map p59; ☎787-722-7000; www.marriott.com; 1309 Av Ashford; r $265-325; P ❄ @ ☎ ≋) and La Concha (p72).

Most casinos offer Caribbean Stud Poker, Let It Ride, Pai Gow Poker and the Big Six Wheel, as well as the standard blackjack, roulette, craps, baccarat and minibaccarat. Casinos are typically open between noon and 4pm, and 8pm and 4am. Some are 24-hour, such as the Marriott and La Concha, plus the Condado Plaza Hotel & Casino (p73) and the Ritz-Carlton (p74).

Sports

Baseball is hugely popular in Puerto Rico; watching a game in San Juan is great fun.

Hiram Bithorn Stadium SPORTS
(☎787-725-2110; Plaza Las Américas, Av Roosevelt, Hato Rey) Hiram Bithorn Stadium seats 18,000 and is home to the Cangrejeros de Santurce. It's named after the first Puerto Rican to play in the majors. Concerts are held here, too.

Roberto Clemente Coliseum SPORTS
(☎787-754-7422; Roosevelt Ave) Roberto Clemente Coliseum is home to the Gigantes de Carolina baseball and soccer teams. It seats 12,500.

Shopping

Popular Puerto Rican souvenirs include *santos* crafts, domino sets, cigars, rum and coffee. The best arts and crafts shopping is in Old San Juan, though most of the schlocky T-shirt shops are there too. San Francisco and Fortaleza are the two main arteries in and out of the old city, and both are packed cheek-by-jowl with shops. Running perpendicular at the west end of the town, Calle del Cristo is home to many of the old city's more chic establishments.

Make time for the bustling Mercado de Rio Piedras (p62), either as a haggler for everything from plantains to pantyhose, or as a voyeur.

★Olé CLOTHING
(Map p52; ☎787-724-2445; 105 Fortaleza, Old San Juan; ⊙9am-6pm Mon-Sat) Although it's beloved by tourists, this old-school hat shop is no tourist trap. As he has for generations, Guillermo Cristian Jeffs will custom-fit you for a truly authentic Panama hat (from $60) – not some faux hipster facsimile.

Galeria Exodo ART
(Map p52; ☎787-725-4252; 200 Calle del Cristo, Old San Juan; ⊙11am-7pm) Some of Puerto Rico's best contemporary artists, including Emanuel Torres, are displayed in this gallery. The works are eclectic and not limited to local talent, but rather the theme is global images and cultures.

Bóveda JEWELRY
(Map p52; ☎787-725-0263; www.boveda.info; 209 Calle del Cristo, Old San Juan; ⊙10am-6pm) Bóveda carries locally designed jewelry, often incorporating semiprecious stones with gold, silver or cord.

Cigarros Antillas CIGARS
(Map p52; ☎787-725-5481; Juan A Corretjer, Old San Juan; ⊙9am-5pm) Cigar fans should stop by the open storefront of Cigarros Antillas to see workers roll by hand. Find it near Old San Juan's bus terminal.

Butterfly People ARTS & CRAFTS
(Map p52; ☎787-723-2432; www.butterflypeople.com; 257 Cruz, Old San Juan; ⊙11am-6pm Mon-Thu, noon-5pm Sat & Sun) This place is not for everyone, as the craftspeople use real butterflies in their art, but the artworks do make a striking impression.

Artisans Fair MARKET
(Map p52; ☎787-721-2400; Plaza de la Dársena, Old San Juan) Head here for arts-and-crafts offerings, peppered with tourist schlock. It's generally open whenever there's a cruise ship in port.

Abitto CLOTHING
(Map p59; ☎787-724-0303; 1124 Av Ashford, Condado; ⊙10:30am-6pm Mon-Sat) Drop your winnings from the casinos at Abitto, in the heart of Condado's fashion district, on world-renowned couture, such as John Galliano and Versace.

Plaza Las Américas MALL
(www.plazalasamericas.com; 525 Av Franklin Delano Roosevelt, Hato Rey; ⊙9am-9pm Mon-Sat, 11am-7pm Sun) The Caribbean's largest shopping mall has 300 stores.

ℹ Information

DANGERS & ANNOYANCES

Safety-wise, San Juan is comparable with any big city in mainland US. Though you'll hear stories of robberies, drugs and carjackings, the worst most visitors will face is tripping up over an uneven paving stone. Take all the usual precautions and you'll minimize any risk of trouble.

Never leave your belongings unguarded on the beach, don't leave your car unlocked and don't wander around after dark in deserted inner-city areas or on unpoliced beaches. Areas to avoid at night include La Perla, Puerta de Tierra, parts of Santurce (especially around Calle Loíza) and the Plaza del Mercado in Río Piedras.

Old San Juan is relatively safe and well policed. However, the enclave of La Perla just outside the north wall can be unsafe at all times.

EMERGENCY

In *any* kind of emergency, call ☎911.

Hurricane Warnings (www.nhc.noaa.gov)

INTERNET ACCESS

Almost all lodgings have wi-fi. A number of plazas in Old San Juan have free hot spots.

MEDICAL SERVICES

Drugstore chains such as Walgreen's are ubiquitous.

Ashford Presbyterian Community Hospital (☎787-721-2160; 1451 Av Ashford, Condado) The best-equipped and most convenient hospital for travelers to visit.

MONEY

ATMs are found everywhere.

POST

Old San Juan Post Office (Map p52; ☎787-724-2098; 100 Paseo de Colón, Old San Juan; ⊙8am-4pm Mon-Fri, 8am-noon Sat) Most convenient branch for travelers.

TOURIST INFORMATION

The Puerto Rico Tourism Company distributes information in English and Spanish at two venues in San Juan: the Luis Muñoz Marín International Airport (Terminal C) and near the cruise ship terminal in Old San Juan.

Puerto Rico Tourism Company (PRTC; ☎800-223-6530, 787-721-2400; www.seepuertorico.com) LMM airport (PRTC; ☎787-791-1014; www.seepuertorico.com; near Terminal C; ⊙9am-8pm); Old San Juan (Map p52; ☎787-722-1709; Edificio Ochoa, 500 Tanca; ⊙9am-6pm, extended hours in peak season)

ℹ Getting There & Away

AIR

Luis Muñoz Marín International Airport (SJU; www.aeropuertosju.com) San Juan's busy international airport is only eight miles from Old San Juan and barely 10 minutes by cab from Isla Verde. It is not a place to linger as it lacks amenities such as free wi-fi, and the places to eat, drink and shop are dire.

Aeropuerto de Isla Grande (Fernando Luis Ribas Dominicci Airport; airport code SIG) Private aircraft, charter services and some flights serving the islands of Culebra and Vieques use San Juan's close-in Aeropuerto de Isla Grande, on the Bahía de San Juan in the city's Miramar district.

CRUISE SHIP

More than a dozen cruise lines call on San Juan, with many cruisers starting and ending their voyages here. It's the second-largest port for cruise ships in the western hemisphere, serving more than a million cruise-ship passengers a year. All ships dock at the piers along Calle La Marina near the Customs House, just a short walk from the cobblestoned streets of Old San Juan.

PÚBLICO

There is almost no islandwide bus system; *públicos* (shared taxis) form the backbone of public transportation in Puerto Rico and can provide an inexpensive link between San Juan and other major cities and towns on the island.

In San Juan the major *público* centers include LMM airport, two large *público* stations in Río Piedras (Centro de Públicos Oeste and Centro de Públicos Este) and – to a lesser extent – Plaza de Colón in Old San Juan. These are the first places you should visit if you want to attempt to understand the intricacies of the useful – but difficult to fathom – *público* system.

Getting Around

TO/FROM THE AIRPORT

Fixed-price taxis serve LMM airport. The flat fees per carload (up to five passengers) include $10 to Isla Verde, $15 to Condado and Ocean Park, and $19 to Old San Juan. Add $1 for each piece of luggage, and $1 after 10pm. The taxi touts do a lot of screaming while hustling passengers into cabs, but if you find others going your way you can share the costs.

The bus is the cheapest option. Look for the 'Parada' sign outside the arrivals concourse at LMM airport. The B40 bus serves Isla Verde or Río Piedras. From Isla Verde you can connect to bus T5 to Old San Juan and Condado.

BICYCLE

With its miserable road conditions and unpredictable drivers, San Juan can be a tough place to cycle. However, cyclists can navigate a pleasant and safe cross-city route by following the shoreline from Old San Juan through Condado and Isla Verde as far as Piñones (the last part is on a designated bike lane). See p64 for bicycle hire.

BUS

AMA Metrobus (Autoridad Metropolitana de Autobuses, Metropolitan Bus Authority; ☎787-767-7979; www.dtop.gov.pr; fare $0.75; ⏲most routes 6am-10pm, reduced service Sun) operates San Juan's public buses. The buses are clean and air-conditioned, however the system itself is not easy for visitors. Route maps and information are hard to find and few bus stops have any indication of what buses stop there. Your best bet is to ask around, especially at bus stops, where veteran riders will offer advice.

The routes taken most often by travelers (bus numbers are followed by associated route descriptions) include:

- **A5** Old San Juan, Stop 18, Isla Verde (via Loiza)
- **A9** Old San Juan, Sagrado Corazón (Tren Urbano station), Río Piedras
- **C10** Sagrado Corazón (Tren Urbano station), Ocean Park (via Loiza), Condado, Stop 18, Isla Grande airport/Convention Center
- **B21** Old San Juan, Isla Grande airport/Convention Center, Condado, Sagrado Corazón (Tren Urbano station)
- **B40** Isla Verde, LMM airport, Río Piedras
- **C53** Old San Juan, Condado, Ocean Park (via McLeary), Isla Verde

Old San Juan Trolley (⏲green line 9am-6pm daily, blue & red lines 7am-7pm Mon-Fri, 9am-7pm Sat & Sun) A very useful free service links more than two dozen sights in Old San Juan. The three routes are served by buses styled like open-air trolleys and you can hop on and hop off at the 26 stops. The routes all pass by Pier 4 of the cruise ship terminal along Calle La Marina.

CAR

Try to avoid driving in the city. Roads are in poor condition and are poorly marked, while haphazard local driving habits may jangle your nerves or crinkle your fender.

In Old San Juan, there are large parking garages along Recinto Sur; rates are modest. For El Morro or the nightlife of San Sebastián, there is an underground lot beneath Plaza del Quinto Centenario off Calle Norzagaray.

All major car rental firms have offices at LMM Airport and most also have offices in resort and tourist areas.

FERRY

Ferries of **Autoridad de Transporte Marítimo** (Map p52; ☎787-758-8012; per trip $0.50; ⏲6am-9pm) connect the east and west sides of Bahía de San Juan, Old San Juan and Cataño. In Old San Juan, the ferry dock is at Pier 2, near the tourism office. Boats run every 30 minutes.

METRO

Tren Urbano (Urban Train; 866-900-1284; www.dtop.gov.pr; fare $0.75; 5:30am-11:30pm) connects Bayamón with downtown San Juan as far as Sagrado Corazón on the south side of Santurce. Modern trains run every 10 to 15 minutes, serving 16 stations. The line, which mixes elevated and underground tracks, is not especially useful for visitors with the exception of the Río Piedras stop.

TAXI

Taxi fares are set in the main tourism zones. From Old San Juan, trips to Condado or Ocean Park cost $12, and $19 to Isla Verde. Journeys within Old San Juan cost $7.

Outside of the major tourist areas, cab drivers are supposed to use meters, but that rarely happens. Insist on it, or establish a price from the start. Meter rates are $1.75 initially and $1.90 per mile or part thereof. You'll also pay 50¢ for up to three pieces of luggage. There's a $1 reservation charge; add a $1 surcharge after 10pm.

Taxis line up at the east end of Fortaleza in Old San Juan; in other places you will likely need to call one. Try **Metro Taxi** (787-945-5555) or **Rochdale Radio Taxi** (787-721-1900).

AROUND SAN JUAN

Cataño & Bayamón

Together, Bayamón and Cataño have a denser concentration of strip malls than any other area in Puerto Rico, plus there's heavy industrialization, traffic that could make you pull your hair out and air that's often fouled with noxious chemicals. Nonetheless, there are a few things worth seeing, though nothing warrants staying overnight.

About a mile north of Cataño, where Hwy 165 meets Hwy 870, you can follow the latter to a secluded picnic site amid the dramatic setting of Isla de Cabras.

Sights

Bacardí Rum Factory LANDMARK
(787-788-8400; www.casabacardi.org; Hwy 888 Km 2.6; tours 9am-4:15pm Mon-Sat, 10am-3:45pm Sun) FREE Called the 'Cathedral of Rum' because of its six-story distillation tower, the Bacardí Rum Factory covers 127

THE BACARDÍ STORY

Although today the Bacardí brand maintains its headquarters in the Bahamas and runs the largest rum factory in the world in Puerto Rico, its roots were sown several hundred miles to the west, in Cuba, a country with which the company's powerful bosses have allegedly been at loggerheads for the last 50 years.

Founded in 1862 in the city of Santiago de Cuba, the world's largest rum dynasty was the brainchild of Don Facundo Bacardí, an immigrant from Catalonia, Spain, who had arrived on the island in 1830 at the age of 16. Recognizing the unusual quality of the sugarcane in Cuba's eastern valleys, Facundo began experimenting with rum distillation using molasses until he was able to produce a refined, clear spirit that was filtered through charcoal and aged in oak barrels.

The new drink quickly caught on and, in time, Facundo passed his burgeoning rum business down to his sons Emilio and José. Emilio went on to become a well-known Cuban patriot during the Second Independence War against the Spanish and, in the 1890s, was exiled briefly for his revolutionary activities. He returned to Cuba a hero in 1898 and was promptly named as Santiago's first mayor. It was during this tempestuous period that Bacardí concocted its two famous rum cocktails, the daiquiri (named after a Cuban beach) and the Cuba *libre*, both mixed with its signature clear rum.

After the repeal of the US prohibition laws in 1932, Bacardí began expanding its operation outside Cuba, opening up a bottling plant in Mexico and establishing the Cataño distillery in Puerto Rico, a move that enabled it to combine cheap labor costs with direct entry into the American market. When the new Cuban leader Fidel Castro began nationalizing businesses island-wide in 1960, the company was promptly relocated overseas, lock, stock and rum-filled barrel, abandoning a 100-year tradition.

In the years since, a colorful web of intrigue has grown around the company (which also makes Bombay Sapphire gin and Grey Goose vodka), and political plots and conspiracy theories abound. Yet, despite controversy, Bacardí has remained the world's most popular rum, selling more than 237 million bottles annually throughout 170 countries. In Puerto Rico, the Cataño factory reigns as the so-called 'Cathedral of Rum', churning out over 70% of the company's annual global production.

beautifully situated acres near the entrance to the Bahía de San Juan, across from Old San Juan. The world's largest, most famous rum-producing family started their business in Cuba more than a century ago, and began moving their operation here in 1936. Today the distiller produces some 100,000 gallons of rum per day and ships 21 million cases per year worldwide.

The free tour (every 30 minutes, lasting about one hour) includes two free drinks and a tram tour explaining the history of the distillery.

To get to the factory from the ferry terminal in Cataño, take a *público* (about $3 per person) or walk 15 minutes along the waterfront on Calle Palo Seco (Hwy 888). At Km 2.6 north of town, look for the factory buildings to your left.

Isla de Cabras & Fuerte del Cañuelo ISLAND PARK, FORT

(Goat Island; ☎787-788-0440; www.parquesnacionalespr.com; parking $3) Isla de Cabras is perhaps the greatest seaside refuge in metro San Juan for travelers craving privacy and nature. There isn't much here except some shade trees, some gazebos for picnicking, a rocky seashore, waves and litter. You can fish, but offshore currents are too dangerous for swimming.

On the island's south end, the ruins of Fuerte del Cañuelo date from 1610. The fort once worked in tandem with El Morro across the channel to protect Bahía de San Juan.

The ruins at the north end of the island were a late-19th-century leper colony.

Reach the island at the end of Hwy 870, north of the Bacardí Rum Factory and the settlement of Palo Seco.

Museo de Oller MUSEUM

(☎787-785-6010; Plaza de Bayamón; ⏲8:30am-4pm Tue-Sat) FREE Located in the former city hall on the plaza in Bayamón's historic district, this art and history museum pays tribute to native son Francisco Oller (1833–1917), the main Latin American Impressionist. Many of Oller's great works are displayed elsewhere, but the restored neoclassical building is worth a peek, and the collection includes good Oller portraits, as well as paintings and sculptures by other Puerto Rican artists, and Taíno artifacts.

Caparra RUINS, MUSEUM

(☎787-781-4795; Hwy 2 Km 6.4, Guaynabo; ⏲9am-4pm Mon-Fri) FREE Only the foundations of a few buildings remain at Caparra, the site of Juan Ponce de León's first Puerto Rican settlement, established in 1508. Located on a highly commercial section of Hwy 2 (formerly a swamp) east of Bayamón in Guaynabo, this is a sight for only the most die-hard history buffs. The small **museum** of Taíno artifacts opens irregularly.

Getting There & Away

To get here, take the ferry from Old San Juan and enjoy a quick harbor tour along the way. The Tren Urbano links Santurce, Hato Rey and Río Piedras to Bayamón; from Old San Juan or Condado, catch bus B21 to Sagrado Corazón station and the start of the train route.

Piñones

Head east from modern San Juan and you'll find pleasantly raw and ramshackle Piñones, a series of natural beaches, forest walks in **Bosque Estatal de Piñones**, and fun seaside hangouts. Do as weekending *sanjuaneros* do and saunter Piñones' sandy curves backed by pine groves, swim in the reef-protected waters, and nosh on seafood snacks and *coco frío* (ice-cold coconut milk) at music-filled roadside stands.

Follow Rte 187 out of San Juan as it parallels the ocean and you'll know you're heading in the right direction at Punta Cangrejos, a small bridge marked by a sign saying '*Bienvenidos a Boca de Cangrejos*' (Welcome to Crabmouth Point).

After the sign, you can veer off to the left to the top of the cliff overlooking the ocean, a popular drinking spot, with fabulous views, especially at sunset. This also kicks off the run of restaurants and *friquitines* (also known as *buréns* in Piñones) – the food kiosks of all sizes that line the coastal road.

There are few accommodations, so Piñones is best visited as a day trip.

History

In the 16th century most of this fertile low-lying coastal region east of San Juan was farmed by local people. When the Spanish took over in 1719, they converted the land into huge sugarcane plantations. Captured natives were forced to provide labor, although they resisted mightily. Unable to prevent farmhands from disappearing into nearby mountains, plantation owners began shipping in African slaves, and sometimes stealing them from other Caribbean islands. Most of the 30,000 residents living in the area today are descendants of these Yoruba slaves and remain proud of their Afro-Caribbean heritage.

Beaches

Piñones' wild beaches contrast sharply with the well-raked expanses of Isla Verde not two miles to the west. Beaches run almost continuously along Rte 187, though the most picturesque, deserted ones start at around Km 9.

For swimming, avoid the coral reefs at the western end of the strand of beaches, near where the bus from San Juan stops. This is also where many of the food stands are. Instead, walk further east along the pleasant hiking/biking path.

Activities

Paseo de Piñones, a 5-mile long, first-rate nature trail and bike path runs along the beach and through the forest reserve (Bosque Estatal de Piñones).

To see a patch of the rarely viewed coastal wilderness, rent a kayak and explore the Laguna la Torrecilla (p71), with its fish, birds and occasional manatees.

If it's a good **surfing** day at Piñones, you'll spot rows of cars with board racks parked by the good breaks. Or check ahead with one of the San Juan surf shops before you go.

Eating & Drinking

The ocean vistas and open-air seating make the food kiosks terrific places to kick back with a *coco frío* or beer. At dusk, your mouth will water from the smoky smells of roadside barbecue stands.

Piñones has countless bars, restaurants and beach shacks, and places come and go. See where your senses carry you.

La Comay PUERTO RICAN $

(Rte 187 Km 8; mains $8-15; 11am-8pm Sat & Sun) Luz cooks up all manner of fried goodies (such as crab *alcapurrias)* and Puerto Rican street food on weekends at this kiosk on the inland side of Rte 187, almost to the town of Loíza Aldea.

Waterfront Restaurant SEAFOOD $$

(787-791-5989; Rte 187; mains $10-26; 10am-10pm;) Right off the bike path at Km 5, and alongside the beach boardwalk, this seaside joint has a welcoming ambience and a dynamite shrimp, octopus and lobster *asopao*. Its *mofongo* can be ordered with either seafood or soy meat.

Soleil Beach Club SEAFOOD $$

(787-253-1033; www.soleilbeachclub.com; Rte 187 Km 4.6; mains $12-29; 11am-11pm Sun-Thu, 11am-1am Fri & Sat) With a breezy oceanfront location, this upscale place has two floors from which to drink in the views and a menu of seafood-based Caribbean cuisine that's kept the buzz going for almost 18 years. Try the *mofongo* with crab, shrimp, conch or octopus, and the excellent *tres leches* cake.

Puerta del Mar PUERTO RICAN $$

(787-791-7138; mains $8-20; noon-11pm, until late Fri & Sat) Some say the folks at this low-key hang make the best *mofongo* on the island. Try it as a side to the red snapper (*chillo*) or codfish fritters.

Getting There & Away

The C45 bus picks up on Avenida Los Gobernadores near the traffic circle at Avenida Isla Verde in the Isla Verde neighborhood (connect with A5 or C53 for the rest of San Juan), and goes to the west end of the Piñones beaches. You can also cycle between San Juan and Piñones.

Loíza Aldea

After Piñones, Rte 187 breaks out of the forest, and crosses a bridge spanning the island's largest river, the Río Grande de Loíza, bringing you to the center of Loíza Aldea, commonly called Loíza. The town, a largely rural municipality in the coastal lowlands east of LMM airport, technically includes Piñones as well as three other districts.

Loíza dates from 1719 and has a rich Taíno heritage. It is named after Luisa, a powerful *cacique* (Taíno chief). Today there's little infrastructure to support tourism, the area is relatively urban, and the only two reasons for a traveler to visit are a church and a fiesta.

Sights

La Iglesia del Espíritu Santo y San Patricio CHURCH

At the northern end of Plaza de Recreo, La Iglesia del Espíritu Santo y San Patricio (Church of the Holy Ghost and St Patrick) stands proudly above the surrounding humble, modern buildings. It dates from 1646 and took its name from the patron saint of Ireland to honor Puerto Rico's famous Irish mercenaries, who designed many of Old San Juan's fortifications.

Festivals & Events

Fiesta de Santiago CULTURAL

Puerto Rico's African soul is unveiled for nine days every July and August in the Fiesta de Santiago, a cultural extravaganza of drums, masks and hybrid religious iconography relating to the Catholic Saint James the Moor Slayer.

Shopping

Handmade *vejigantes* (Puerto Rican masks) carved by local artisans are widely available in Loíza (and are generally of higher quality and are less expensive than those sold in San Juan). Wander the town center and you'll see plenty of colorful creations quite literally staring out at you.

Estudio de Arte Samuel Lind ART

(787-876-1494; www.samuellind.com; Rte 187 Km 6.6; Wed-Sun, or by appointment) It's best to call ahead to make sure this well-liked artist's studio is open. It's 2 miles south of town on Rte 187 and sells Lind's paintings, sculptures and serigraph prints. About 20 mask makers work in the area.

Getting There & Away

Públicos go from Río Piedras in San Juan to Loíza's plaza for a few dollars (recommended during the Fiesta de Santiago, when traffic on Hwy 187 and Hwy 188 is terrible). *Públicos* leave Loíza from a terminal three blocks south of the plaza, usually only during daylight hours.

El Yunque & East Coast

Includes ➡

Best Places to Eat

- Luquillo Beach Kiosks (p102)
- Pasta y Pueblo (p102)
- Las Vistas (p107)
- La Estación (p107)
- Cafe De La Plaza (p110)

Best Beaches

- Playa Luquillo (p100)
- Playa Azul (p100)
- Playa Seven Seas (p103)
- Playa Naguabo (p108)

Why Go?

The east coast is Puerto Rico shrink-wrapped, a tantalizing taste of almost everything the island has to offer squeezed into an area you can drive across in a couple of hours. Sodden rainforest teems with noisy wildlife and jungle waterfalls at El Yunque National Forest, the commonwealth's tropical gem. Down at sea level, beach-lovers bask on the icing-sugar sand of Playa Luquillo.

Golfers and those craving a one-stop holiday will find delight in the highest concentration of large, upscale resorts outside San Juan.

Unvarnished Fajardo is the island's uncrowned watersports capital, where adventurers kayak, dive, snorkel and fish, and yachters park their sailboats.

Cutting through the region like a thin, green ribbon is the Northeast Ecological Corridor, a slender tract of undeveloped and endangered pristine land featuring one of Puerto Rico's stunning bioluminescent bays at Las Cabezas de San Juan nature reserve.

When to Go

Noteworthy annual events in Luquillo include the Fiesta de los Platos Típicos (Traditional Food Festival) in November. Elsewhere along the coast your best timing depends on your priorities: peak winter season, the summer and weekends see the most places open (especially locally beloved food kiosks). But other times you'll enjoy a solitude that grows with your distance from San Juan.

Note that hurricane season – early June through late November – can bring sodden conditions to El Yunque, with the possibility of trails being closed due to mudslides and flooding.

History

Much of this region was once covered with lighter variations of the dense foliage now found only in El Yunque, but native Taíno successfully farmed the fertile land around the low-lying coasts. All that changed when the Spanish arrived en masse around 1700. The tremendous wealth of natural resources in El Yunque – lots of fresh water and timber, for example – attracted settlers, and existing farmlands were quickly turned into massive sugar plantations by colonizers.

A small gold rush added to the need for a strong labor force, and after most of the indigenous population was either wiped out by disease or forced deep into the mountains, the Spanish brought in West African slaves in considerable numbers. Descendants of those Yoruba people make up the bulk of the 30,000 residents who live in the municipalities around El Yunque today.

The next wave of colonization came when the US took control of the island in 1898, during the Spanish–American War, eventually setting up the commonwealth status that continues to this day. A region around a US military base near Fajardo that closed in 2003 has been the focus of developments like windpower farms.

Getting There & Around

Most of the east coast is traversable via Hwy 3 or Hwy 53. Once you leave San Juan, be it on Rte 187 (the scenic route via Piñones and behind Loíza Aldea) or on the main drag of Hwy 3, be prepared for bursts of concentrated development (fast-food restaurants and strip malls) and distant views of El Yunque. Públicos (shared taxis) serve most towns.

There are public vans running between Fajardo and San Juan, but to penetrate further into the countryside, a car or bike is necessary. It is easy to organize a tour into the El Yunque rainforest. The driving trip from San Juan to Fajardo takes about two hours. From San Juan to Yabucoa it's about three hours, although traffic can muck up the timings.

With its high concentration of cars, the northeast is not the most pleasant part of Puerto Rico in which to cycle. But stay off the main arteries of Hwys 3 and 66 and two-wheeled transport is possible.

Finally there are some beautiful drives through the lush mountains and hidden villages, including one along Hwy 181 (see boxed text, p111).

El Yunque

Covering some 28,000 acres of land in the Sierra de Luquillo, this verdant tropical rainforest is a shadow of what it was before ax-wielding Spanish conquerors arrived in the 16th and 17th centuries. But the ecological degradation has been largely reversed over the past 50 years, and today, under the auspices of the US Forest Service, El Yunque National Forest is once again sprouting a healthy abundance of dense tree cover.

Compared with other Puerto Rican forest reserves, El Yunque is well staffed and crisscrossed by an excellent network of signposted trails. Most of El Yunque's hikes are short, paved and relatively mild, a boon for casual visitors. Adventurers should note, however, that there's no true wilderness experience to be had here. Crowds flock to El Yunque's popular spots in peak summer season and on weekends, but if you stray off the standard routes, there are still plenty of places to slip under the radar.

Sights

Once you've entered **El Yunque National Forest** (787-888-1880; www.fs.usda.gov/elyunque; most sights 7:30am-6pm), all of the forest's visitors centers, major attractions and trailheads appear as Hwy 191 twists, turns and climbs steeply on its way south toward the summit. (It's also possible to follow Hwy 186 along the west side of El Yunque, but to experience the forest's heart, Hwy 191 is the road to take.)

In addition to short and long hiking trails in El Yunque, there are highlights directly accessible by road within the forest.

★La Coca Falls WATERFALL

(Hwy 191 Km 8.1) The first spectacular natural feature you see as Hwy 191 climbs south toward the forest peaks is an 85ft cascade as the stream tumbles from a precipice to the right of the highway onto boulder formations.

Yokahú Tower VIEWPOINT

(Hwy 191 Km 8.8) This 65ft, Moorish-looking stone tower was built as a lookout in 1962. It's the first good place for vistas of the islands to the east, but there are better vantage points higher up on the mountain. The tower often gets crowded with tour groups.

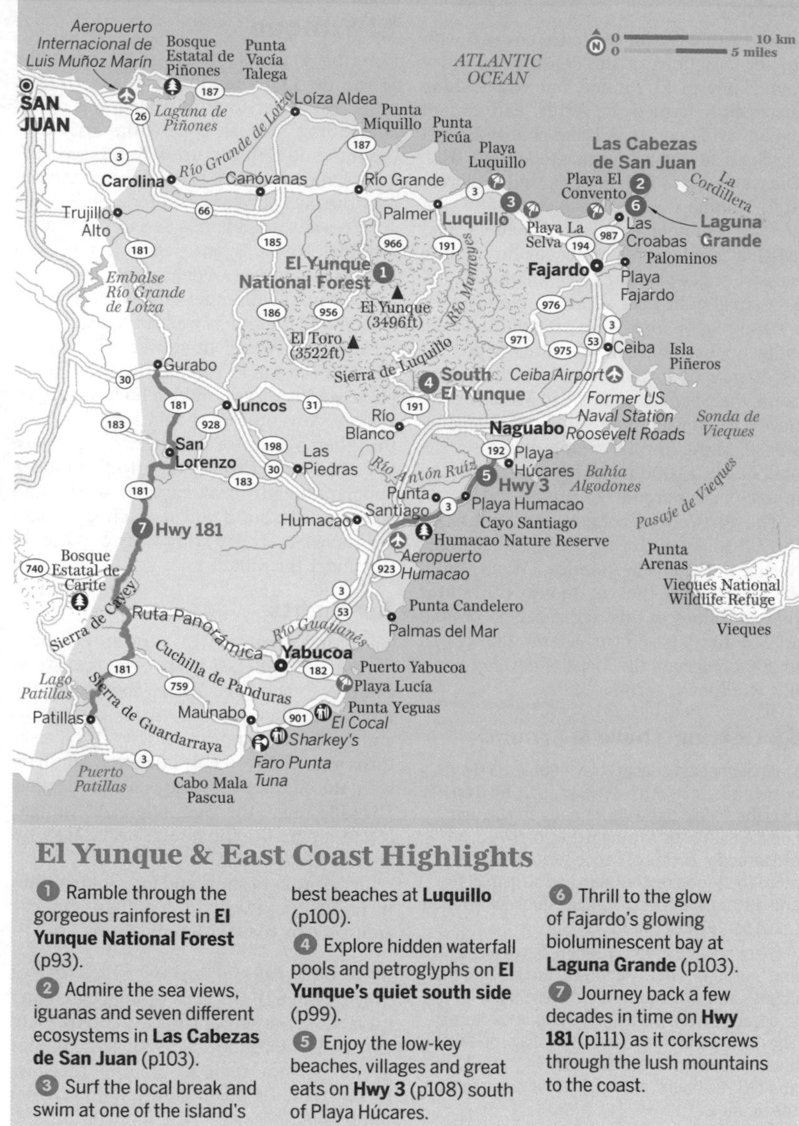

El Yunque & East Coast Highlights

1. Ramble through the gorgeous rainforest in **El Yunque National Forest** (p93).
2. Admire the sea views, iguanas and seven different ecosystems in **Las Cabezas de San Juan** (p103).
3. Surf the local break and swim at one of the island's best beaches at **Luquillo** (p100).
4. Explore hidden waterfall pools and petroglyphs on **El Yunque's quiet south side** (p99).
5. Enjoy the low-key beaches, villages and great eats on **Hwy 3** (p108) south of Playa Húcares.
6. Thrill to the glow of Fajardo's glowing bioluminescent bay at **Laguna Grande** (p103).
7. Journey back a few decades in time on **Hwy 181** (p111) as it corkscrews through the lush mountains to the coast.

Pass it by unless you have a lot of time and the view to yourself.

Baño Grande & Baño de Oro VIEWPOINT
(Hwy 191 Km 11.8) Baño Grande, a former swimming hole built during the Depression, lies across Hwy 191 from the Palo Colorado Visitors Center. A little further along the road, Baño de Oro is another former swimming hole that is now a popular spot for photo opportunities.

This second water hole takes its name from the Río Baño de Oro, which feeds the pool. The name means 'bath of gold' in English, and Spaniards gave the river this name because they mined for gold here in the 16th century.

La Mina Falls WATERFALL

To marvel at these falls or if you really want to splash in some water, take the 30- to 45-minute hike from the Palo Colorado Visitors Center down the mountain to the base of the falls. Here you'll find the 35ft water cascade, quite stunning in its natural beauty.

Come early if you want tranquillity, because it's popular with cavorting families and groups.

Activities

With more than 23 miles of well-maintained trails, and plenty of rugged terrain, El Yunque has a plethora of easy day hikes. Come prepared (think rain poncho and good shoes) and remember there are no water, trash or rest-room facilities.

It's a good idea to check in at the visitors center for the latest weather update before heading out for a trek. El Yunque's weather reflects its wet ecosystem: sudden surges of light rain can occur anytime during the year in this dense rainforest, so throw on some protective gear and get on with your day. During hurricane season El Yunque can get drenched. Some trails might be closed due to mudslides, and streams swell enormously. Winter nights in the Luquillo mountains can be damp and a little chilly.

★La Mina Trail HIKING

(Hwy 191 Km 11.7) An extension of the Big Tree Trail, this short hike starts at the Palo Colorado Visitors Center. The trail heads downhill through palo colorado forest to La Mina Falls and an old mine tunnel. Mostly paved, it's an often slippery 0.7-mile walk down, and a steep hike back up. The payoff is the falls, which drop 35ft into a perfect natural swimming pool.

Big Tree Trail HIKING

(Hwy 191 Km 10.2) Half an hour each way, this trail through tabonuco forest to La Mina Falls contains bilingual interpretive signs that highlight sights such as a 300-year-old ausubo tree. This short 0.86-mile trail is moderately difficult; its name comes from the size of the vegetation along the way. It's probably the most popular trail in the park; combine it with the La Mina Trail.

La Coca Trail HIKING

(Hwy 191 Km 8.5) To get off the beaten path, try this short but challenging trail. Wilder and less maintained than some of the more popular forest rambles, this 1.8-mile (one way) hike descends through thick tabonuco forest and enormous ferns and crosses several rocky streams. Most visitors take three to four hours for this out-and-back trek because of the slippery terrain and tempting swimming.

You'll get muddy and have to do some scrambling (long pants are recommended and good shoes are a must), but the rewards of private waterfalls and dipping pools more than make up for it.

EL YUNQUE'S FLORA & FAUNA

More than 240 species of tree and 1000 species of plant thrive in this misty, rain-soaked enclave, including 50 kinds of orchid. El Yunque is also the island's major water supply, with six substantial rivers tracing their sources here. The fauna is characterized by the presence of the critically endangered Puerto Rican parrot *(el higuaca)* and more than 60 other species of bird, nine species of rare freshwater shrimp, the coquí frog, anole tree lizards and the 7ft-long Puerto Rican boa. Night visitors can search for any of seven types of bioluminescent fungi, otherwise known as glow-in-the-dark mushrooms!

Four forest zones define El Yunque:

Tabonuco Forest Below 2000ft and receives less than 100in of rain. Features tall, straight trees and palms, orchids, flowers and aromatic shrubs.

Palo Colorado Forest Above 2000ft in the valleys and on gentle slopes, annual rainfall averages as much as 180in. This area is lush with trees more than 1000 years old, laden with vines and orchids.

Palma Sierra Forest Above 2500ft along streams and on steep valley slopes. The mountain palm tree dominates with ferns and mosses growing beneath.

Cloud Forest Grows above the Palma Sierra Forest and gets up to 200in of rain per year. Trees are twisted from strong trade winds and are less than 12ft tall. Mosses and lichens hang from trees and cover the forest floor, accented by red-flowering bromeliads.

El Yunque

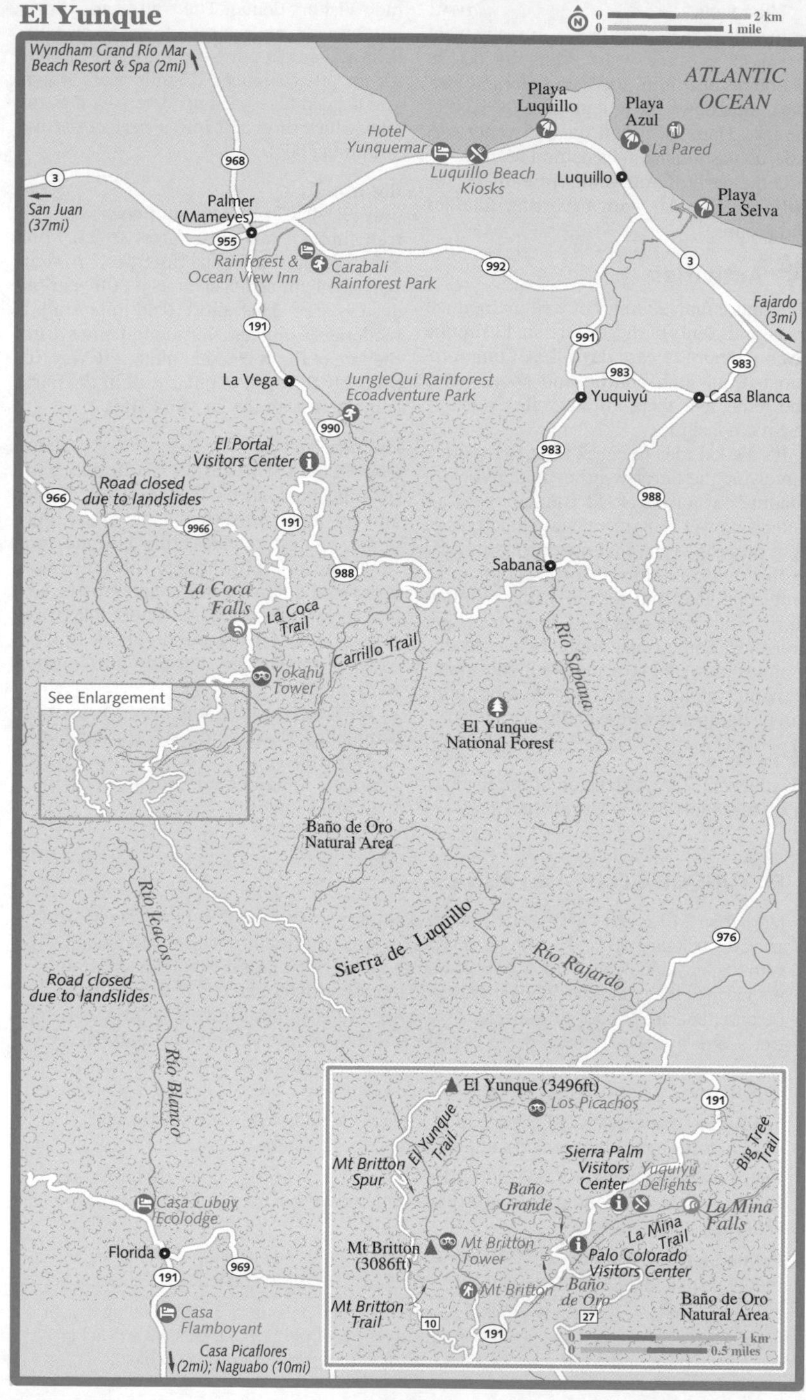

0 2 km
0 1 mile
Wyndham Grand Río Mar Beach Resort & Spa (2mi)
ATLANTIC OCEAN
Playa Luquillo
Playa Azul
La Pared
Hotel Yunquemar
Luquillo Beach Kiosks
Luquillo
Playa La Selva
San Juan (37mi)
Palmer (Mameyes)
Rainforest & Ocean View Inn
Carabali Rainforest Park
Fajardo (3mi)
La Vega
JungleQui Rainforest Ecoadventure Park
Yuquiyú
Casa Blanca
El Portal Visitors Center
Road closed due to landslides
Sabana
La Coca Falls
La Coca Trail
Carrillo Trail
Río Sabana
Yokahu Tower
See Enlargement
El Yunque National Forest
Baño de Oro Natural Area
Sierra de Luquillo
Río Rajardo
Río Icacos
Road closed due to landslides
Río Blanco
Casa Cubuy Ecolodge
Florida
Casa Flamboyant
Casa Picaflores (2mi); Naguabo (10mi)
El Yunque (3496ft)
Los Picachos
El Yunque Trail
Big Tree Trail
Mt Britton Spur
Sierra Palm Visitors Center
Yuquiyú Delights
Baño Grande
La Mina Falls
La Mina Trail
Mt Britton (3086ft)
Mt Britton Tower
Palo Colorado Visitors Center
Mt Britton Trail
Mt Britton
Baño de Oro
Baño de Oro Natural Area
0 1 km
0 0.5 miles

The trailhead is just up the road past the falls of the same name – just before the Yokahú Tower – and there is a small parking lot here.

La Coca made its mark on El Yunque history when a US college professor disappeared here for 12 days in 1997, claiming after his rescue that he got off the trail and was lost. The Forest Service, which had enlisted a search party of 60 volunteers and aircraft, was hardly amused.

Mt Britton Trail HIKING

(Hwy 930) If you are short on time and want to feel as if you have really 'summited,' take the 0.8-mile, 45-minute climb up through the palma sierra forest into the cloud forest that surrounds this peak, which is named after a famous botanist who worked here.

The trail is a continuous climb on paved surfaces to the evocative stone Mt Britton Tower, built in the 1930s. When not shrouded by clouds, the panoramic views extend over the forest to the Atlantic Ocean and the Caribbean.

The trailhead is on a dirt track, which veers off Hwy 191 for a quarter-mile at the latter's endpoint at Km 13. The more adventurous can connect to El Yunque Trail via the 0.86-mile Mt Britton Spur.

El Yunque Trail HIKING

(Hwy 191 Km 11.7) On a clear day, never-ending views extending to Vieques and Culebra reward hikers tackling the almost 1500ft of elevation gain on this trail. This is the main event for most hikers, taking you to the top of El Yunque (3496ft) in 1½ hours or longer. It starts opposite the Palo Colorado Visitors Center.

The 2.4-mile trail is mostly paved or maintained gravel as you ascend through cloud forest (with its stunted or 'dwarf' trees) to the observation deck, which is surrounded by microwave communication towers that transmit to the islands of Culebra and Vieques. If you want a rock scramble from here, take Los Picachos Trail (0.17 miles) to another old observation tower and feel as if you have crested a tropical Everest. You can return via a different route by descending down the Mt Britton Spur/Mt Britton Trail and then down a dirt track to Rte 191 and back to your start point.

El Toro Trail/Trade Winds National Recreation Trail HIKING

(Hwy 191 Km 13) Although often closed, this trail is El Yunque's best backcountry adventure. The 7.8-mile round-trip to **El Toro** (3522ft) and back is challenging due to wet conditions, thick mud and poorly maintained paths. It's an all-day excursion for most hikers (some parties even camp out overnight).

El Toro is El Yunque's highest point and the trail traverses dense jungle broken by intermittent views of both coasts. During the ascent you'll pass through all four forest zones, ending in the cloud forest at 3000ft. This haunting dwarf forest features ghostly epiphytes and ubiquitous mist.

The trailhead for the Tradewinds Trail is situated at Km 13 on Hwy 191, behind the gate where the road ends. The unpaved path climbs 3.9 miles to the summit of El Toro, from where you can either retrace your steps or continue west on the similarly vague El Toro Trail to Km 10.8 on Hwy 186 (2.1 miles from El Toro and 6 miles from Hwy 191). From here you'll need to return the way you came, or arrange for a car to pick you up.

Be sure to contact the forest visitors center for current road conditions and trail status.

Tours

There are many San Juan–based tour operators offering day trips. All transport you to and from the park, highlight the main sights and provide you with a mine of interesting information.

★ AdvenTours ADVENTURE TOUR

(☎787-530-8311; www.adventourspr.com; tours from $55) A huge range of adventures including birdwatching tours and night hikes (for nocturnal animals and bioluminescent fungi) in El Yunque National Forest. You can custom-design trips and arrange for pickup in San Juan.

Eco-Action Tours ADVENTURE TOUR

(☎787-640-7385, 787-791-7509; www.ecoactiontours.com; half-/full-day tours $58/68) This outfit is a good ecologically aware operator. It offers half- and full-day tours that can include hikes to Mt Britton and La Mina Falls. Guides are knowledgeable about the rainforest ecosystem. Tours include pickup from your San Juan hotel.

Louie's VIP Tours ADVENTURE TOUR

(☎787-379-4100; www.louieviptours.com; tours from $55) The namesake guide of these tours wins high marks for his informative and entertaining commentary. Expect to see the highlights of the forest, do a little hiking, get drenched under a waterfall and, with an optional add-on, visit a beach.

Forest Service Hikes WALKING TOUR
(787-888-1880; Hwy 191 Km 11.8; adult/child $5/3; tours 11am-1:30pm Wed-Sun) The ranger-led guided one-hour hikes from the Palo Colorado Visitors Center are worth while if you can match their limited schedule.

Sleeping

Several beautiful inns, B&Bs and guesthouses have opened up along the edges of El Yunque – not actually within the national forest, but along its fringe, which still feels very wild. The proximity to the rainforest means lots of loud animal activity: the sound of chirruping coquí will send you to sleep, and you'll wake to wild birds whistling. Some places are accessible along the north section of Hwy 191, coming from Río Grande (Luquillo beaches are only a few minutes away). Other accommodations are on the south side, also on Hwy 191. Due to mudslides, south side accommodations must be accessed from the Naguabo entrance to El Yunque. These are good choices if you want to be in close proximity to day trips in and around Fajardo. Most properties have minimum stays.

North Side

Rainforest Inn INN $$
(787-378-6190; www.rainforestinn.com; off Hwy 186; r incl breakfast $160-165; P) Bordering the national forest, this former coffee estate plantation has two two-bedroom units with beautiful (and lovely smelling) reclaimed cedar beams and luxurious details such as a claw-foot bathtub and antique mahogany and satinwood furniture. Outside, the property has views of El Yunque Peak and a private path leads to a stunning waterfall pool. No children under 12.

Carole's Rainforest Villas VILLAS $$
(787-809-4172; www.rainforestvillas.com; Rte 966; 1-/2-bedroom villa $145/270; P) Simple, remote living is the order of the day here at Carole's Rainforest Villas. Swing in your own hammock, pick bananas and mangoes from nearby trees and revel in your private small house. Shared outdoor kitchen with sweeping views, and nearby walks to waterfalls top it off. No children under eight.

South Side

★ **Casa Cubuy Ecolodge** GUESTHOUSE $$
(787-874-6221; www.casacubuy.com; Hwy 191 Km 22; r incl breakfast $120-135; P) If listening to a frog symphony, conversing around the dinner table, and relaxing on a shady balcony within hammock-swinging distance of a tropical rainforest has you dashing for jungle apparel, then this could be your place. Cocooned atop winding Hwy 191 on El Yunque's wild, isolated southern slopes, Casa Cubuy Ecolodge offers 10 cozy rooms and even has a private trail to a nearby waterfall and natural swimming pool.

For something slightly more upscale, try its three Sierra Palms rooms (doubles with breakfast $145) down the road.

Casa Picaflores INN $$
(787-874-3802; www.casapicaflores.com; off Hwy 191; studio incl breakfast $160, 3-bedroom villa incl breakfast $420; P) Spend the night in a luxurious three-bedroom house or nestled into a cozy *casita* (small house), surrounded by abundant fruit trees and majestic mahogany boughs. The lodgings feature organic linens, cleaning products are biodegradable and the grounds contain a compost-fertilized vegetable garden.

Casa Flamboyant INN $$$
(787-559-9800; www.elyunque.com/flamboy.html; Hwy 191 Km 22.2; r incl breakfast $220-275; P) Tucked way up in the mountains with panoramic views of El Yunque and three waterfalls, Casa Flamboyant makes the most of its amazing location. Three gorgeous rooms with private bathrooms and a pool are as elegant as Puerto Rico's rainforest gets. Before it became a hotel, Federico Fellini and Robert Mapplethorpe stayed here. Adults only.

CAMPING IN EL YUNQUE

There are no developed campgrounds or designated camping areas in El Yunque. Wilderness camping is allowed along most roads and trails except areas that are closed. Tents must be located at least 30ft away from any trail or body of water and at least 50ft from roads and developed picnic sites.

Most importantly, campers need a free permit that must be obtained at least 14 days before your visit. Check the website or at the visitor centers for details.

OFF THE BEATEN TRACK

GO FURTHER INTO THE COUNTRYSIDE

For pure off-the-beaten-path joy, skip El Yunque's popular highlights along the northern section of Hwy 191 and head to the region's alternative entrance off the southern portion of Hwy 191 just west of the town of Naguabo. Since mudslides closed the central section of the road in the 1970s, the southern expanse of the rainforest has remained relatively isolated and unexplored.

Spend the night at one of the wonderful south-side lodgings up the precipitous and winding Hwy 191. From there, you can procure directions to a number of nearby hiking and swimming spots, or hire local expert **Robin Phillips** (☎787-874-2138; www.rainforestfruitfarm.com; group rainforest day tour $125, group 2hr petroglyph tour $53) to guide you to some of the area's natural highlights.

Eating

Palmer, the colorful strip where Hwy 191 heads south from Hwy 3, has some attractive eating options; nearby Luquillo has myriad choices. Inside the park are a couple of good cafes and several cheerful roadside stands.

Lluvia CAFE $
(☎787-657-5186; 52 Principal, Palmer; mains $5-12; ⊙9am-6pm Wed-Sun) Among the cute galleries and artisan shops of Palmer, this creative cafe dishes up a range of tasty meals, from excellent breakfasts to thick sandwiches, salads, pizza and more at lunch. The orange juice is freshly squeezed and the coffees well-brewed.

Yuquiyú Delights PUERTO RICAN $
(☎787-396-0970; www.yuquiyudelightspr.com; Hwy 191 Km 4 & Km 11.3; mains $6-9; ⊙9am-4pm; 🅥) These small food concessions inside the park are situated next to the Sierra Palm picnic area and inside the El Portal Visitors Center. Choose from *comida criolla* (traditional Puerto Rican cuisine), burgers, baked goods, snacks and smoothies.

Information

El Portal Visitors Center (☎787-888-1880; www.fs.usda.gov/elyunque; Hwy 191 Km 4; adult/child $4/free; ⊙9am-5pm) Make this beautifully landscaped visitors center your first stop. There are interactive exhibits, a short film, a walkway through the forest canopy and a gift shop. Vending machines serve up drinks and snacks, plus there is a good small cafe. Pick up free basic maps and information, then admire some stunning tree ferns.

Sierra Palm Visitors Center (Hwy 191 Km 11.3; ⊙9:30am-5pm) This picnic area is not always staffed, but it has interesting displays, rest rooms and a tasty food concession.

Palo Colorado Visitors Center (☎787-888-1880; Hwy 191 Km 11.8; ⊙9:30am-4pm) It's worth enduring the switchbacks and steep road to get to this vistors center, which is a hub for short and spectacular hiking trails. The picnic area – which includes a series of sheltered concrete platforms hidden in the jungle, overlooking a ravine of rushing water – is hard to match anywhere on the island. A small shop offers maps.

Getting There & Away

There's no public transportation to El Yunque, which can be seen from San Juan, some 25 miles distant. Your choices are private vehicle, taxi (from $80) or a guided tour. Driving from San Juan, there will be signs directing you from Hwy 3 to Hwy 191. Turn south at Palmer and follow the signs to El Yunque National Forest.

Take note that some highway maps still show that you can traverse the forest on Hwy 191 (or access El Yunque from the south via this route). However, this section of Hwy 191 has been closed by landslides south of Km 13 for years. Some road maps also suggest that El Yunque can be approached via a network of roads along the forest's western border. Don't try it: these roads are untraveled, unmaintained tracks that dead-end in serious jungle. Be sure to check the latest conditions of El Yunque's roads on the forest service website.

El Yunque is not immune to thievery, so lock up and don't leave anything of value in plain sight in the car.

Luquillo & Around

POP 20,000

In many ways Luquillo is a typical Puerto Rican town: a physically beautiful coastal strip of magnificent beaches backed by a dull, uninspiring mishmash of condo towers, strip malls and unsightly urban sprawl. But here, in the island's congested northeastern corner, beauty easily outweighs the beast. Playa Luquillo, the mile-long crescent of surf and sand to the west of the town, is regularly touted as being the commonwealth's finest *balneario* (public beach) and the proverbial home of Puerto Rican soul food.

Surfers flock to the beach at the La Pared break, giving the area a sporty laid-back vibe. But most travelers head a mile west to Puerto Rico's so-called Riviera, the hugely popular Luquillo Beach that is as famous for its strip of permanent food kiosks as it is for its icing-sugar sand and sheltered bay.

Luquillo traces its history to an early Spanish settlement in 1797 and its name to a valorous *cacique* (Taíno chief), Loquillo, who made a brave standoff against early colonizers here in 1513. These days the 20,000-strong town is bypassed by the arterial Hwy 3 that carries traffic to Fajardo.

Because of Luquillo's popularity with *sanjuaneros* (people from San Juan), your best time to visit is on a weekday. Most of the shops and stores of interest to visitors are alongside Playa Azul, or on Fernandez Garcia, although the central town is not overblessed with charm.

Beaches

★Playa Luquillo BEACH

(Balneario La Monserrate; parking $5) Luquillo is synonymous with the fabulous Playa Luquillo. Set on a calm bay facing northwest and protected from the easterly trade winds, the public part of this beach makes a mile-long arc to a point of sand shaded by evocative coconut palms. The beach itself is an expanse of broad, gently sloping sand that continues its gradual slope below the water.

With crowds converging here at weekends and during holidays, Luquillo has always been more about atmosphere than solitude. Many come just for the famous long strip of food kiosks at its western end.

You do not have to park in the *balneario* lot if you want to visit the beach. Playa Luquillo extends at least another mile to the west. If you pull off Hwy 3 by the food kiosks, you can drive around to the ocean side of the stalls and park under the palms, just a few steps from the beach and with more cold beer and fried treats than you could consume in a year. There are decent bathrooms and public facilities.

Playa Azul BEACH

To escape the crowds of famous Playa Luquillo, head for Playa Azul, east around the headland and in the town itself, directly in front of the condominium development of the same name. While the beach is more exposed to the trade winds, seas and dangerous riptides, Playa Azul is just as broad, powdery and gently sloping as Luquillo.

Snorkellers enjoy these waters, but swim with great caution.

Scrambling over a stone jetty at the east end of Playa Azul will take you to a strand of beach and bays that stretch over 5 miles to **Playa Seven Seas** in Las Croabas.

Activities

Benefiting from a fabulous beachside location and proximity to the rainforest, Luquillo is well-positioned for both aquatic and land-based adventures. Ask locals for directions to **Las Paylas**, a pair of natural waterslides located in the hills off Hwy 983.

JungleQui Rainforest Ecoadventure Park ADVENTURE SPORTS

(787-500-7555; www.junglequi.com; Hwy 990 Km 1.2, Rio Grande; admission from $50; 9am-4pm) Organized thrills in the rainforest are the lure at this new adventure park near El Yunque. You can fly through the canopy on one of seven zip-lines or go plunging into some natural river-fed swimming holes. There are hikes and nature walks across the park, which is an old YMCA camp. Talented guides add to the fun.

Caraballí Rainforest Park ADVENTURE SPORTS

(787-889-5820; www.haciendacarabalipuertorico.com; Hwy 992 Km 5.1, Luquillo; 1st person/additional person from $50/25, horseback rides adult/child from $38/27; 9am-4:30pm) This 600-acre eco-adventure park does trail rides along the Río Mameyes and into the foothills of the rainforest; the two-hour rides include stops for swimming and a picnic. Beach rides and simple jaunts around the ranch are also offered, as well as mountain-bike tours along rainforest trails and zip-lines through the forest.

Río Mar Golf Courses GOLF

(787-888-7060; www.wyndhamriomar.com/golf; 6000 Río Mar Blvd, Rio Grande; fees from $125; 7am-dusk) The Wyndham Grand Río Mar Beach Resort & Spa is noted for two courses: the Greg Norman–branded River Course and the Tom and George Fazio–designed Ocean Course. The latter lives up to its name, hugging the Atlantic. Duffers have iguanas as their gallery.

Surfing

While not exactly hard-core, Luquillo's waves are less crowded and less daunting than the west coast's. A friendly contingent of surfers hangs out at the east end of Playa Azul – known as 'La Pared' (the Wall) – waiting for an offshore breeze to glass off a 3ft break. Pick up an 'I (heart) La Pared' bumper sticker to pose as a local. You can find breaks here year-round and there is a nice sandy bottom.

Luquillo Surfshop SURFING
(939-270-8715; La Pared; lessons per hour from $60, surfboard rentals per day from $40; hours vary) Right across from the surf beach and next to the famous surf bar Boardriders, this surf shop offers lessons and rentals of everything from stand-up to bodyboards. Look for local surfing legend Tom Ferguson checking out the action on the front terrace.

Bob's Surfing Adventures SURFING
(787-435-1760; www.rainforestrental.com; lessons from $60) Bob Roberts offers surfing lessons as well as rentals.

Kayaking

Kayaks are an ideal way to explore the beautiful bays, inlets and waterways in the east. You can usually choose from day and night tours, and operators will pick you up from your accommodations and often also rent gear for independent adventures.

★ **Enchanted Island Eco Tours** KAYAKING
(787-888-2887; www.eielecotourspr.com; tours from $68) Explore the rich life in and out of the water on kayak trips along the coast, rivers and bayous. Numerous options are available.

Las Tortugas Adventures KAYAKING
(787-809-0253; www.kayak-pr.com; tours from $55) Tour the coast by kayak and stop for snorkeling or explore the rivers flowing out of El Yunque. Reserve at least a week in advance.

Sleeping

Luquillo is a good option if you want to literally get away from the urban charms of San Juan. You're close to several top-notch beaches and close to both El Yunque and the bioluminescent bay.

During holidays and on high-season weekends, you'll have plenty of company camping at Playas La Selva and El Convento. Think twice, though, if it looks like you'll be out there alone. Groups of young men have been known to roam the area looking for vulnerable targets. Muggings do occur.

Balneario La Monserrate CAMPGROUND $
(787-889-5871; www.parquesnacionalespr.com; Hwy 3, Playa Luquillo; tent/powered sites $10/17, parking $4.50; P) The 30 campsites and the bathhouse at this Playa Luquillo spot right on the sand are very popular in summer, but best avoided in the quiet winter months (when it's often closed).

Luquillo Sunrise Beach Inn HOTEL $$
(787-889-1713; www.luquillosunrise.com; A2 Costa Azul; d incl breakfast $150-190; P) Securely midrange, the Luquillo Sunrise Beach Inn is caressed by cooling Atlantic sea breezes in each of its 17 spiffy ocean-facing rooms. There's a communal patio and all upper-floor rooms have large balconies overlooking the beach. Luquillo plaza is two blocks away and the famous *balneario* and food kiosks are a 30-minute stroll along the beach.

Hotel Yunquemar HOTEL $$
(787-889-5555; www.yunquemar.com; No 6 Calle 1, Fortuna Playa, Luquillo; r incl breakfast $110-160; P) The name Yunquemar sums it up. Lying in the shadow of El Yunque and within pebble-pitching distance of the *mar* (sea), you've got the best of both worlds here. A simple, friendly family-run hotel with its own swimming pool and beach, and a pool table and wide-screen TV tucked down in the enormous basement, it's a few minutes' drive from central Luquillo.

Rainforest & Ocean View Inn INN $$
(787-889-7430; www.rainforestoceanviewinn.com; Hwy 992 Km 4; d from $160; P) The 12 rooms at this hacienda and inn set on a hill with lovely views have dark-wood furniture, fridges, microwaves and coffeemakers, plus lofts that work well for families (up to two kids under 12 without extra charge). Drawbacks: the satellite location – you need to call the office if you need anything – and service can be spotty. There is horseback riding and mountain biking.

St Regis Bahia Beach Resort RESORT $$$
(787-809-8000; www.stregisbahiabeach.com; Rte 187 Km 4.2, Rio Grande; r from $600; P @) Luxury is the name of the game at this edition of the St Regis brand. Off the beaten path, west of Luquillo and on a broad white sand bay your biggest dilemma will be whether to lounge poolside, beachside or hit

the full-service spa. Or simply kick back in one of the 139 slightly formal, sumptuous rooms and suites.

Wyndham Grand Río Mar Beach Resort & Spa RESORT **$$$**
(787-888-6000; www.wyndhamriomar.com; 6000 Río Mar Blvd; r/ste from $200/340;) The popular Río Mar resort spreads over a mammoth 500 oceanfront acres west of Luquillo. It encompasses two golf courses, a 600-unit high-rise hotel, numerous (pricey) restaurants and a casino. Public areas and landscaping are better than some of the island's other resorts, but at the time of writing, some of the hotel was under renovation.

Eating & Drinking

The beach kiosks at Playa Luquillo deserve their fame and are a must-stop. Elsewhere, there are a few good cafes and restaurants in the center of town, especially close to the surf at La Pared.

You can also while away an afternoon or an evening with beers and cocktails at the Playa Luquillo kiosks. There are myriad people-watching possibilities, especially at weekends. For swankier options, try the Río Mar resort area.

★**Luquillo Beach Kiosks** PUERTO RICAN **$**
(Hwy 3, Playa Luquillo; dishes $3-20; hours vary, generally 11am-10pm) Luquillo's famous line of 60 or so beachfront *friquitines* (also known as *quioscos*, *kioskos* or just plain food stalls) along the western edge of Hwy 3 serve often-excellent food at very popular prices. It's a fine way to sample local food and snack culture, including scrumptious *surullitos* (fried cornmeal and cheese sticks).

The best way to start is to simply wander past the dozens of choices and see what strikes your fancy. You'll find everything from outstanding *comida criolla* to top-notch burgers to freshly blended piña coladas. The stalls themselves range from very basic to slightly stylish affairs. Most have kitchens on the parking side where you browse and tables on the beach side.

Two recommended choices are **Vejigante** (kiosk 31) for creative local fare served with flair, and upscale **La Parilla** (kiosk 2), where waiters serve excellent seafood.

★**Pasta y Pueblo** ITALIAN **$**
(Calle 14 de Julio; dishes $10-15; 5-10pm Tue-Sun;) On a gravel lot 50m south from the Luquillo Sunrise Beach Inn and a half block from Playa Azul, this unassuming little shack with fold-down windows slings some plate-licking fabulous food. There's often a crowd waiting for one of the five tables to dine on pasta laced with seafood or more traditional sauces. The guava cheesecake gets rave reviews.

Aromas Coffee & Crepes CAFE **$**
(787-355-6767; Calle 14 de Julio 60; dishes from $4; 7am-5pm) Right on the somnolent central square of what passes for central Luquillo, this sprightly cafe is the best thing for blocks around. A range of coffee drinks add zest to the day (go local with the coconut-flavored latte). There are fresh baked goods and breakfasts that include an excellent eggs Benedict; lunchtime sandwiches hit the spot.

Boardriders Surf Bar & Grill CAFE **$**
(787-355-5175; La Pared; dishes $7-20; 11am-11pm) A groovy beachside hangout festooned with Christmas lights. You can stash your board in Luquillo Surfshop next door and refuel on fish tacos, beer-battered chicken fingers and burgers before your next set. Check out the action at La Pared right in front; there's live music some nights.

La Familia Bakery 2 BAKERY **$**
(787-888-2320; Calle 1 A9, Rio Grande; meals from $4; 6am-9pm) Follow the anticipatory crowds to this sweet-smelling bakery. The breakfast pastries are luscious while the lunchtime sandwiches are splendid. Try to choose from the multitude of items in the sleek display cases, then grab a table. It's just north of Hwy 3 behind a Walgreens, 4km east of Rio Grande.

Guava's FUSION **$$**
(787-889-2222; Playa La Pared; mains from $15; 5pm-2am) A bohemia trio plays at this bar-restaurant on Sunday, and on Friday and Saturday nights the tables are cleared and you can try salsa, merengue or borchata with a splendid beach view. The food tends toward beachy versions of Latin American fare: think lots of seafood and coconut.

Getting There & Away

Hwy 3 will take you to Rte 193 (aka Calle Fernandez Garcia), which is the main artery of Luquillo.

Públicos run regularly during the week from the Río Piedras terminal in San Juan to and from the Luquillo plaza ($5 to $8). If you're going to the beach, make sure you disembark next to the food kiosks, a mile or so before Luquillo Pueblo. Taxis one-way cost $72 from San Juan.

Fajardo & Around

POP 36,500

Fajardo sprawls like an untidy suburb between the El Yunque foothills and the sea. It has many personalities: downbeat ferry port for the highly recommended islands of Vieques and Culebra; upscale yacht harbor; nature preserve; beautiful beach escape; and more. Fajardo also reigns as one of Puerto Rico's biggest water-activity centers. For water sports, join the boaters a few miles south at Puerto del Rey, one of the largest marinas in the Caribbean.

Founded in 1760, downtown Fajardo itself, which lies between Rte 194 and Hwy 3, has little to show for 250 years of history.

Around Fajardo you can do everything from diving in the waters of the coral-rich La Cordillera islands to kayaking one of Puerto Rico's three bioluminescent bays – the very popular Laguna Grande, which is part of the very worthwhile Las Cabezas de San Juan nature reserve.

The extended neighborhood of Las Croabas to the north of town is a good place to start a visit. Besides the nature reserve, it features the beguiling beach, Playa Seven Seas.

Sights

The area's best sights can be enjoyed on the beach, in or under the water, or at the nature reserve (which also has the area's one key historical site: Puerto Rico's oldest lighthouse).

★**Las Cabezas de San Juan** NATURE RESERVE
(787-722-5882; www.paralanaturaleza.org/cabezas-de-san-juan; Hwy 987 at Las Croabas; adult/child $10/7; 9am-4pm Wed-Sun, English tours 2pm) A 316-acre nodule of land on Puerto Rico's extreme northeast tip, the Las Cabezas de San Juan Reserva Natural 'El Faro' protects the **Laguna Grande bioluminescent bay** (see boxed text, p106), rare flora and fauna, lush rainforest, various trails and boardwalks, and an important scientific research center. It's popular, but you can only visit as part of a tour you book in advance by phone or via the website.

Despite its diminutive size, the reserve shelters seven – yes seven – different ecological systems, including beaches, lagoons, dry forest, coral reefs and mangroves. Animal species that forage here include big iguanas, fiddler crabs, myriad insects and all kinds of birds. Such condensed biodiversity is typical of Puerto Rico's compact island status and Las Cabezas is highlighted as an integral part of the commonwealth's vital threatened Northeast Ecological Corridor.

A historical highlight amid the natural beauty, the splendidly restored 1882 **El Faro de las Cabezas de San Juan** is Puerto Rico's oldest lighthouse. Adorned with rich neoclassical detail and topped by a distinctive Spanish colonial tower, it overlooks the peninsula's steep, craggy cliffs where the stormy Atlantic meets the Sonda de Vieques (Vieques Sound). Situated on a craggy headland, it today houses an information center and an observation deck with splendid views. It's a highlight for many tours of the reserve.

There are about 2 miles of trails and boardwalks that lead through the park, but you can't follow them on your own: you must take a guided **walking tour**. This lasts more than two hours, including a short tram ride through the dry forest section. Tours depart through the day, however most are in Spanish; the English tour is usually at 2pm.

Other tours include a **bike tour** ($20) and a **birding tour** ($12). **Night tours** (adult/child $22/12) explore the grounds, lighthouse and bioluminescent bay. Reservations are required for all tours.

You can get a glimpse of some of the reserve by simply walking east down the narrow beach from Playa Seven Seas. Better yet, take a kayak tour with a tour operator at sunset, and explore Laguna Grande after dark for the green-glowing, underwater 'fireworks' of bioluminescent micro-organisms.

★**Playa Seven Seas** BEACH
(www.parquesnacionalespr.com; parking $5.35) On the southwestern shore of the peninsula of Las Cabezas, Playa Seven Seas is a sheltered, coconut-palm-shaded horseshoe-shaped public beach. While it's not quite as pretty as Playa Luquillo, fear not – it is attractive and gets packed on weekends and during summer.

For good snorkeling or to get away from it all, follow the beach about a half mile to the northeast along the Las Cabezas property to an area known as **Playa Escondida** (aka Hidden Beach). The reefs are just offshore. Taking the trail to the west of Seven Seas eventually brings you to the nearly empty **Playa El Convento**, which has a beach house for official retreats.

Fajardo & Around

Top Sights

1 Las Cabezas de San Juan.................... B1
2 Playa Seven Seas.................... B2

Sights

3 Bahía Las Croabas.................... B2
4 El Faro de las Cabezas de San Juan.................... B1
5 Puerto del Rey.................... A5

Activities, Courses & Tours

Casa del Mar Dive Center.............(see 7)
East Island Excursions.............(see 5)
Sea Ventures Dive Center.............(see 5)
6 Traveler.................... A3

Sleeping

7 El Conquistador Resort & Golden Door Spa.................... B2
8 Fajardo Inn.................... B3
9 Moonlight Bay Hostel.................... B3
10 Playa Seven Seas Camping.................... A2
11 Sueños del Mar.................... B2

Eating

12 Calizo Seafood.................... B2
13 La Estación.................... A2
14 Las Vistas.................... B2
15 Ole-Lelolai.................... A3
16 Pasión por el Fogón.................... A3

Bahía Las Croabas VIEWPOINT

You will find this spot where Hwy 987 ends at a little seaside park rimmed by seafood restaurants and bars looking east across the water to the peaks of Culebra. There is not much of a beach here, but there's a view of the offshore islands and the air blows fresh with the trade winds.

The anchorage accommodates the fishermen's co-op and the last few *nativos*, the 'out-island' sloops that everyone around here once used for fishing and gathering conch or lobster. The fishermen here are friendly, and you can probably strike a deal with one of them for a boat ride.

Puerto del Rey MARINA

(787-860-1000; www.puertodelrey.com; Hwy 3 Km 51.4) Standing behind a breakwater in a cove 2 miles south of Fajardo and about 4.7 miles south of the ferry dock, this is one of the largest marinas (1100 slips) in the region. Many yachts stop here to take advantage of the marina's facilities. It's a hub for sailing, diving and fishing charters aimed at visitors.

The marina includes a complete village with restaurants, stores, laundry facilities, banking, car rental and all manner of boat-hauling and maintenance capabilities. This is the place to ask around if you'd like to crew on a boat headed out to the Caribbean, back to the US mainland or even across the Atlantic.

Activities

The Fajardo region is decidedly amphibian – life is as exciting in the water as it is on land. This coastal area is blessed with many tiny islands (not to mention Culebra and Vieques) that provide fabulous opportunities for swimming, diving, fishing or just relaxing on a quiet beach. Good snorkeling sites abound.

Boat Trips

Almost all sailing trips advertised for travelers on the island sail out of one of the marinas in Fajardo. Many of the trips visit **La Reserva Natural de la Cordillera**, a chain of small islands, keys and coral reefs just northeast of Fajardo. One, the 163-acre Cayo Icacos, is a popular stop and will have you doing your best talk-like-a-pirate routine.

Many tour operators will pick you up in San Juan for an extra fee.

East Island Excursions SAILING
(☎787-860-3434; www.eastwindcats.com; Puerto del Rey Marina; adult/child $69/49, transport from San Juan $15) These glass-bottomed catamarans are in high demand, so book early. All kinds of day trips to the La Cordillera islands are offered, and it even does quick runs over to St Thomas on high-speed cats. One boat has a cool water slide that launches you right into the ocean. A buffet lunch and free piña coladas seal the deal.

Traveler SAILING
(☎787-863-2821; www.travelerpr.com; Villa Marina; snorkeling tour from $65) Snorkeling tours with a guide are the highlights of this catamaran trip that also includes a lunch buffet, piña coladas and rum punch. Trips also include stops at beaches.

Kayaking

This is the most entrancing way to see the glowing bioluminescent waters at Laguna Grande. Nighttime tours typically last about two hours.

Kayaking Puerto Rico KAYAKING
(☎787-245-4545; www.kayakingpuertorico.com; Las Croabas; tours from $45) Runs numerous tours, including the bioluminescent lagoon, daytime snorkeling tours and full day trips including kayaking, snorkeling and an excursion to Culebra ($69).

Eco Action Tours KAYAKING
(☎787-791-7509; www.ecoactiontours.com; tours from $45) Offers a range of activities, though the nighttime kayak trips on Laguna Grande are the most popular. Pickups from San Juan hotels start at 5pm with a return time of about 11pm.

Island Kayaking Adventures KAYAKING
(☎787-444-0059; www.ikapr.com; Las Croabas; tours from $45) Operates nighttime Laguna Grande tours as well as adventure excursions by day. Trips include a short lesson in kayaking and light refreshments. Ask about transport from San Juan.

Pure Adventure KAYAKING
(☎787-202-6551; www.pureadventurepr.com; Las Croabas; tours from $45) All tours include a marine biologist. In addition to bioluminescence paddles, there are daytime adventures that include snorkeling in the rich waters off Playa Seven Seas. Ask about transport.

Fishing

From October to December dorado, wahoo and sailfish are found, while from January to May it's mahi-mahi, blue marlin, white marlin and some sailfish.

Captain Osvaldo Alcaide FISHING
(☎787-547-4851; www.deepseafishingpr.com) Offers half- and full-day deep-sea fishing charters out of Fajardo, and snorkeling to Icacos and Palominos islands. Beer and soft drinks are included.

Diving

Casa del Mar Dive Center DIVING
(☎787-860-3483; www.scubapuertorico.net; 1000 Ave Conquistador, El Conquistador Resort & Country Club; 1-/2-tank dives from $70/100) This PADI-certified outfit is great for all levels. Diving and snorkeling trips visit local reefs. A two-tank dive in Culebra is $125, while St Thomas is $160. Drinks and snacks included.

Sea Ventures Dive Center DIVING, SNORKELING
(☎800-739-3483, 787-863-3483; www.divepuertorico.com; Puerto del Rey Marina; dive trips from $75) Sea Ventures offers one-week PADI certification courses. There are usually trips to Palominos and Icacos daily with many more options. Snorkeling excursions are available for $45 to $60.

Sleeping

Playa El Convento is popular for informal camping. It is reached by the path heading west from Playa Seven Seas. You'll usually find at least one or two tents up at all times; avoid pitching here if there are no other campers though – muggings do occur.

Moonlight Bay Hostel HOSTEL $
(☎787-801-1578; www.moonlightbayhostel.com; 478 Calle Cometa; dm/r from $23/60; ❄︎📶) Close to the ferry dock for boats to Culebra and Vieques, this hostel is a real find. It has a fine rooftop terrace plus a modern kitchen where

DON'T MISS

LAGUNA GRANDE BIOLUMINESCENT BAY

One of the most popular sights in the east is Laguna Grande, the bioluminescent bay (or lagoon as some call it) that magically glows on dark nights. One of three in Puerto Rico (the others are Bahía Mosquito on Vieques and La Parguera Bay in the south), Laguna Grande is especially popular because of its close proximity to San Juan.

This nighttime experience is magical: by kayak you start off in a virtual cave of mangroves until you slowly break out into open sky where you are dazzled by millions of stars overhead. Then you look down into the water and voilà! The surreal glow of trillions of microscopic dinoflagellates give the water an unreal and eerie glow.

Guided kayak trips (p105) are the most popular way to experience the bay. You cause the least disruption to the water and get closest to the glow. However you also may be teamed up with kayaking amateurs whose mishaps can slow down the entire group. Other options for seeing the glowing waters include:

Electric Boat Glide across the waters with eco-friendly **Bio Island** (☎787-422-7857; www.bioislandpr.com; tours from $52), which runs tours that last a little over an hour on an eight-person boat. Guides explain why the lagoon glows.

Walking See the bay by foot on the nightime walking tours offered at Las Cabezas de San Juan (p103). You tour the grounds by foot and tram and then spend time down at the lagoon walking along boardwalks. Tours end at the lighthouse where you contrast the bay's dim glow to the encroaching luminosity of civilization.

It's important to book any tour of Laguna Grande as far in advance as possible as the tours are very popular. Note that when there's a full moon the water's glow is hard to discern. The rainy season from December to February can cause murky run-off that also diminishes the experience. Check conditions fully. Note that swimming is not allowed in the lagoon and be sure to avoid rogue operators that use non-electric boats, which can kill the dinoflagellates.

you can make free DIY pancake breakfasts. Details are well thought out with top-quality mattresses, linens and more. There's often a party vibe here, so light sleepers beware.

Playa Seven Seas Camping CAMPGROUND $

(☎787-863-8180; Hwy 987; campsites $10) One of Puerto Rico's loveliest beaches, Playa Seven Seas near Las Croabas fills up fast. Make sure you reserve in advance if you plan to come during summer or holidays. Showers and bathrooms are available and there's a cafe on the beach.

Sueños del Mar APARTMENTS $$

(☎787-435-0221; www.suenosdelmar.info; Hwy 987 Km 6.8; 4-person apt $140; ❄) Straightforward, tidy apartments are convenient for quick stops while waiting for the ferry, and have full kitchens and TVs. There are fans in the living rooms and air-con in the bedrooms. Upper-story units have good views of the bay. While there's usually a two-night minimum, you can occasionally get one night.

Ceiba Country Inn INN $$

(☎787-885-0471; www.ceibacountryinn.com; Hwy 997 Km 2.1, Barrio Seco, Ceiba; d incl breakfast from $105; P❄✆) A classic mountain retreat with friendly owners – and even friendlier pets – these nine units overlook the Caribbean and offshore islands. Picture a landscaped hillside villa with decks, barbecue grill and lounge, and the sounds of the forest coming alive at dusk. From Rte 53, take exit 5 (Ceiba North), turn right onto Rd 975, go 1 mile, turn right onto Hwy 977 and follow the signs.

Fajardo Inn RESORT $$

(☎787-860-6000; www.fajardoinn.com; 52 Parcelas Beltrán, Hwy 195; d $140-190; P❄@✆≋♿) Perched on a hill overlooking the scruffy Fajardo corridor (and distant sea views), the Spanish-hacienda-style Fajardo Inn has two beautiful swimming pools, crazy golf, a kids playground, a tennis court and a huge gym. This peach-hued parador exudes comfort and an unhurried ambience. Rooms are large and uncluttered, with cable TV, massive beds and a daily dose of complimentary Puerto Rican coffee.

El Conquistador Resort & Golden Door Spa RESORT $$$

(☎787-863-1000; www.elconresort.com; 1000 Ave El Conquistador; d from $305; P❄@✆≋♿)

A 900-unit mega resort that glitters along a steep coastal escarpment a few miles northeast of Fajardo, this minitown boasts its own cove, cable car, mock Andalusian village and a private fantasy island. Ideal for vacationers in search of golf, tennis, spa pampering, water sports, fine dining and gambling – with lots of company – this is the quintessential full-service holiday.

Note that tales that the resort was used in scenes for the James Bond classic *Goldfinger* are apocryphal (Miami Beach's Fontainbleu was the beachy star).

Eating & Drinking

Bahía Las Croabas has a string of cheap and cheerful seafood restaurants and bars looking east across the water. You can kill time until your ferry at a couple of simple outdoor cafes by the docks.

★Las Vistas CAFE **$**
(787-655-7053; www.lasvistascafepr.com; 83 Calle #2; mains $6-12; 8am-2pm Thu-Mon) Absolutely beautiful eggs Benedict vie for your attention with the panorama at this vast rooftop terrace. The menu stresses brunch with eggs in all forms plus pancakes and some pasta items for those wishing to veer lunchwards. This is a perfect stop before or after some calorie-burning activity.

★La Estación CARIBBEAN **$$**
(787-863-4481; www.laestacionpr.com; Hwy 987 Km 4; mains $9-25; 5pm-midnight Fri-Wed;) Done up like an artist's funky loft, this playfully converted gas station has a jeep dashboard bar on the patio and a candlelit dining room hung with vintage bicycles. Dining is open-air; it's near the entrance to the El Conquistador. On many nights there's live entertainment, making this a top spot for an evening cocktail.

Creative fare includes a killer skirt steak, seafood and a few good veggie items. Watch for seasonal specials. Mains come served on heavy wooden pedestals, with delicious sauces and an eye-fluttering passion-fruit vinaigrette salad dressing.

Calizo Seafood SEAFOOD **$$**
(787-863-3664; Hwy 987 Km 5.9; mains $15-35; 5-10pm Wed-Fri, 3-11pm Sat & Sun) Dine in the outdoor courtyard with umbrellas and a spreading palm tree or in the air-conditioned dining room with pretty blue- and yellow-tiled tables and work by local artists. Seafood is the highlight and wins raves.

It's on a bend in the road near Playa Seven Seas and also has non-fishy dishes including Caribbean-infused steaks (tamarind grilled mignon).

Ole-Lelolai SPANISH **$$**
(787-655-1222; www.olelelolai.com; Hwy 987 Km 2.7, Las Croabas; dishes from $7; 6-10pm) Small plates of tasty tapas lure diners to this spot along the main road in Las Croabas. Seafood from the nearby waters is a specialty, as are suitably delightful pitchers of sangria. It's all very casual and is popular with visitors after they've kayaked the nearby glowing waters of Laguna Grande.

Pasión por el Fogón PUERTO RICAN **$$**
(787-863-3502; www.pasionporelfogon.net; Hwy 987 Km 2.3; mains $15-40; 4-10pm Mon-Fri, noon-10pm Sat & Sun) Lobster medallions, filet mignon and chicken stuffed with sweet banana and bacon are among the specialties here. The snapper in garlic sauce and *mofungo* also win praise. Listed as one of Puerto Rico's leading Mesónes Gastronómicos, Pasión por el Fogón is situated across a busy road from the Villa Marina.

Entertainment

The El Conquistador Resort has a flashy casino ready to take your money in glitzy surrounds.

Information

HIMA Hospital San Pablo-Fajardo (787 653-6060; www.himasanpablo.com; Rte 194 off Av Conquistador; 24hr) The largest hospital along the east coast and your best option.

Wash-n-Post (787-863-1995; Santa Isidra shopping center; 8am-7pm Mon-Sat, 11am-5pm Sun) Across the street from the Villa Marina shopping center, this one-stop FedEx and Western Union service also does laundry.

Getting There & Away

AIR

The region's **José Aponte de la Torre-Ceiba Airport** (RVR; off Hwy 3; 24hr parking $10) is in the old Roosevelt Roads Naval Station. It replaces the old Fajardo airport, which is still mentioned in some dated literature. Services are limited to an ATM; there is no car-rental counter. It primarily has flights to Culebra and Vieques.

Via Hwy 53, take the Hwy 978 exit and follow the signs. A *público* from the airport to the Fajardo ferry terminal is fixed at $12 for up to four passengers. A taxi from San Juan is $80 for up to five people.

Air Flamenco (787-801-8256; www.air-flamenco.net) Scheduled flights to Vieques, Culebra and both San Juan airports.

Vieques Air Link (787-741-8331; www.viequesairlink.com) Offers the most daily flights to Vieques and Culebra from Ceiba.

BOAT

Ferries to Vieques and Culebra leave from the clean and modern **Maritime Transportation Authority** (787-863-0705; tickets sold before ferry sailings) terminal. It is about 1.5 miles east of town in the scruffy Playa Fajardo/Puerto Real neighborhood. A taxi from San Juan is $80 for up to five people.

CAR

Sights in the region are dispersed and you'll really need a vehicle to see things. For the ferry docks, take Hwy 195 from Hwy 3; follow signs that say 'Embarcadero' or 'ferry'. Turn north off Hwy 195 onto Hwy 987 for Villa Marina and eventually Las Croabas and the Las Cabezas de San Juan nature reserve and Laguna Grande.

There is secure outdoor parking near the ferry docks; the cost is $5 per day. Most rental car contracts prohibit taking cars on the ferry to Culebra or Vieques.

Thrifty (787-860-2030; www.thrifty.com; Puerto del Rey Marina; 8am-5pm) Located in the huge marina, call to arrange a pickup by courtesy van from either the airport or the ferry docks. One-way rentals to/from San Juan incur a $60 fee.

World Car Rental (787-863-9696; 466 Calle Union; 7:30am-8pm Mon-Fri, to 5:30pm Sat & Sun) About 200m from the ferry docks, this small office has decent cars to rent.

PÚBLICO

Públicos from the Rio Piedras area of San Juan serve the ferry terminal and parts of Las Croabas. The fare is $4 (confirm in advance) and the travel time is three to four hours depending on traffic. A trip to San Juan's international airport costs $8.

Naguabo & Around

POP 26,400

There are two parts to modern Naguabo: the so-called downtown – which you'll curse for its nutty traffic and impossible-to-understand one-way system – and the laid-back and appealing seashore.

On the water, Playa Húcares offers views and lunch in its low-key seafood restaurants. Heading south, there is a string of even more low-key seaside villages and beaches to Humacao and on to the vast upscale Palmas del Mar resort area.

Sights

There's nothing worth a detour into downtown Naguabo, but the seaside drive along Hwy 3 is very rewarding for beaches, simple foods and the nature center.

Playa Húcares VILLAGE

(Hwy 3) Playa Húcares doesn't actually have a beach – the waterfront is a long concrete and rock seawall overlooking a bay. It does, however, have a dramatic view of Vieques, 10 miles out to sea, and Cayo Santiago, closer to shore. It's worth visiting to get a look at the brightly painted sloops and for a simple seafood lunch at one of the waterfront restaurants along the pleasant promenade. It was one of the set locations for *The Rum Diary* movie.

Two Victorian mansions stand like sentinels over the waterfront walkway, officially named Malecón Arturo Corsino. One of the mansions, the Castillo Villa del Mar, is on the National Registry of Historic Places. These days it's a run-down old eyesore, but the mansion next to it has been somewhat restored, giving rise to hopes that both structures will eventually be returned to their former state of grace.

Playa Naguabo BEACH

(Hwy 3) Running along Hwy 3 beginning about a half mile south of Playa Húcares, there are about 2 miles of thin, palm-lined, vacant beaches. You can park anywhere and enjoy both quiet and lovely views out to sea and the islands. Sporadic stands sell ultra-fresh seafood at cheap prices during the day and the area is much more natural feeling than the concrete-lined shore at Playa Húcares.

Playa Humacao VILLAGE

(Hwy 3) The tiny village of Playa Humacao has a number of excellent bakeries and a noted restaurant. It's a good place to get picnic supplies and refreshments for the pristine *balneario* west of the village.

Punta Santiago VILLAGE

(Hwy 3) Punta Santiago is a local weekend and holiday hot spot. Its bright *friquitines* and kiosks offer lots of succulent treats such as *arroz con jueyes* (rice with crab chunks) and pork in all forms. During the busy season it's fun and upbeat and nowhere near as crowded as Playa Luquillo.

Humacao Nature Reserve NATURE RESERVE

(787-852-6088, gear rental 787-852-6058; Hwy 3 Km 74.3; bike/kayak rental per hour $7/12; concessions 9am-5pm Wed-Sun) Almost 3200 acres once used for a sugar cane plantation have been given back to nature at this gem of a nature reserve near the coast. Mangroves and palms shade lagoons that are havens for myriad birds and fish. Turtles and iguanas are easily spotted. You can kayak the placid waters as well as bike or walk the many nature paths. It's just west of Punta Santiago.

Activities

Most outfits are based within the gated confines of the Palmas del Mar resort area. Cayo Santiago is a popular snorkeling destination.

★**Barefoot Adventures** HANG GLIDING, KAYAKING
(☎787-850-0508; www.barefoottravelersrooms.com; Punta Santiago) The Barefoot Travelers Rooms guesthouse offers hang-gliding instruction (from $150 per tandem flight) and rentals in El Yunque. Its kayaking/snorkeling excursions (from $45 per person) to Cayo Santiago (aka Monkey Island) are very popular, particularly for the profusion of primate-spotting opportunities.

Captain Frank López FISHING, SNORKELING
(☎787-316-0441; Playa Naguabo) The captain offers fishing or snorkeling trips and sea excursions to Cayo Santiago aboard *La Paseadora*. Prices are negotiable; start your bidding at about $40.

Sea Ventures Dive Center DIVING, SNORKELING
(☎787-863-3483; www.divepalmasdelmar.com; The Marina, Palmas del Mar; 2-tank dives incl gear rental from $120) Organizes diving and snorkeling trips to Cayo Santiago and the deeper sites offshore (there are 35 within a 5-mile radius).

Rancho Buena Vista HORSEBACK RIDING
(☎787-479-7479; www.ranchobuenavistapr.com; Palmas del Mar; rides from $50) These large stables specialize in a breed local to Puerto Rico, the Paso Fino. Rides come in various durations and you can explore the lush hills or follow the beach. Pony rides for kids are $20.

Palmas del Mar Golf Courses GOLF
(☎787-656-3015; www.palmasdelmar.com; Palmas del Mar; fees from $150) The two golf links are the 6800yd Rees Jones–designed Flamboyán Course and 'the Palms', a course with waterfront holes branded by Gary Player.

Sleeping

There are several pretty guesthouses tucked into the south side of El Yunque that can be reached from Naguabo. You'll also find accommodations along the coast.

CAYO SANTIAGO

There's a monkey playground just off the coast thanks to a team of scientists who in 1938 decided to turn Cayo Santiago into a research area. Five hundred rhesus monkeys were let loose on the peaked, hazy island just offshore from Punta Santiago, and today 900 descendants of these primates run rampant on the 39 tropical acres.

Only researchers from the Caribbean Primate Research Center are permitted on the island, but visitors can eyeball monkeys from their boat (don't forget that monkeys can swim). There's fabulous snorkeling around a sunken ship not far from the shore.

Condo rentals abound at the many complexes withing the 2700 acres of the Palmas del Mar resort area. Sites like www.vrbo.com have listings.

Centro Vacacional Punta Santiago CAMPGROUND, VILLAS $
(☎787-852-1660; www.parquesnacionalespr.com; Hwy 3 Km 72.4, Playa Humacao; campsites $25-40, cabins/villas $70/115; P ❄ ≋) This spot has a *balneario*, 36 cold-water cabañas and 63 air-conditioned villas in a coconut grove on a pristine beach. Each unit can accommodate up to six people; bring your own linen.

★**Barefoot Travelers Rooms** GUESTHOUSE $$
(☎787-850-0508; www.barefoottravelersrooms.com; Punta Santiago; r $80-90; ❄ 📶 ≋ 👪) At this homey three-room guesthouse located in a gated community a block from the beach, your detail-oriented hosts really do walk around shoeless – when they're not giving hang-gliding lessons or leading snorkeling tours. Amenities include an inspirational guest kitchen, a library and a large living room with television and DVD player.

Casa Libre Puerto Rico GUESTHOUSE $$
(☎787-874-6414; www.casalibrepr.com; 188 Calle 8, Playa Húcares; r incl breakfast $100-120; P ❄ 📶 ≋) All three of the attractive rooms at this well-run guesthouse have comfortable beds and soothing decor. The Puerto Rican and Californian hosts make a tasty full breakfast and lend movies from their huge DVD library. Reserve the purple room upstairs for breathtaking El Yunque and water views.

Wyndham Garden at Palmas del Mar RESORT $$
(☎787-850-6000; www.wyndham.com; 170 Candelero Dr, Palmas del Mar; r from $155; P ❄ @ ☎ ≋) The only hotel in the Palmas del Mar resort area, this midrange property offers 107 amply furnished rooms and access to any of the resort's many amenities. There's no oceanfront lodging, but the water is just a short walk away.

Eating

From Playa Húcares south through Punta Santiago, you'll find all manner of street food priced for the masses. Look for stalls – and crowds – along Hwy 3 as you drive. Comb the kiosks and holes-in-the-wall for great *empanadillas* (dough stuffed with meat or fish), *mojito criollo* (rum, mint and lemon) sauce on fresh fish and tasty *surullitos*.

Clouds of smoke and savory smells will lead you to barbecue vendors, while cartoon-like signs will signify places with suckling pig roasted on a spit. Tops among seafood are freshly caught *chillo* (snapper) and *sierra* (kingfish).

★ **Cafe De La Plaza** FUSION $$
(☎787-852-2612; Palmas del Mar; mains $9-25; ⌚6-9:30pm Tue-Sat, 11am-2pm Sun) Buried deep beyond layers of condos within Palmas del Mar, this small, family-run bistro is worth finding. There's a large terrace outside where you can choose from its good list of bottled beers. Inside, you can dine in relaxed style on well-prepared mains like the scrumptious marinated *churrasco* (steak) or the grouper in coconut sauce.

Daniel's Seafood SEAFOOD $$
(☎787-852-1784; Calle Marina #7, Playa Humacao; mains $6-25; ⌚11am-9pm Wed-Sun) Located off Hwy 3 toward the waterfront, this long-established favorite is several cuts above the exceedingly casual (aka roofless) standard for the area. Dine in air-con comfort or on the open-air terrace. Fresh seafood in sophisticated preparations is the norm here; many come just for the lobster-stuffed fish with garlic sauce.

El Makito SEAFOOD $$
(Hwy 3, Playa Húcares; mains $12-25) From its second-story perch over the water from the *malecón* (pier), the 'little shark' has excellent views from its shaded patio seats. The menu is long, with seafood pastas, the requisite laundry list of *mofongos*, and shrimp, conch and octopus done up in myriad configurations. Locally sourced lobsters are a worthy splurge.

Restaurant Vinny PUERTO RICAN $$
(☎787-874-7664; Playa Húcares; mains $6-25; ⌚8am-7pm) Vinny does a bang-up lunch for $6 and the best *empanadillas* on the island. As is typical for Playa Húcares, seafood here is the main event and you can enjoy it with the smell of the sea for atmosphere in this completely open-air dining room.

Getting There & Away

This is car country, however *público* vans prowl Hwy 3 from Playa Naguabo (where they park near the promenade) south. For a few dollars, they go to Naguabo or Humacao, from where you can move on to Fajardo, Ponce or San Juan.

The Palmas del Mar resort can arrange for a minivan to haul you to and from San Juan's international airport – about a 45-minute trip in normal traffic. During peak season, it charges $90 to $100. For reservations call ☎787-285-4323.

Yabucoa & Around

POP 37,300

Surrounded by hills on three sides and fringed by ocean on the other, Yabucoa sits on a tract of well-watered fertile land once used to grow sugarcane. The town itself holds little for visitors, but on the periphery, Yabucoa is the starting point for two dramatic drives: the famed Ruta Panorámica (Hwy 182) west into the hills and the less heralded, but no less spectacular, Hwy 901 that tracks the coast between Playa Lucía and the Punta Tuna lighthouse.

If you are traveling south to Yabucoa from the Humacao area, take the Hwy 53 toll road to avoid the traffic on Hwy 3.

Sights & Activities

The *balneario* at **Playa Lucía**, near the junction of Hwy 901 and Hwy 9911 in Yabucoa, has great shade under its coconut trees and several beach bar-restaurants just off its premises. **El Cocal** is one of the few good surfing spots in the area (ask for directions at the *balneario*). Further southwest toward Maunabo is **Sharkey's**, another decent break where you're likely to have the waves to yourself.

Off Hwy 901 along the coast, you can ponder the ruins of **Hacienda de Santa Lucía**, an old sugar plantation a mile north of Playa Lucía. Although there are no must-see sights along this stretch, the sporadic lonely beaches glimpsed from the road are serene places for a stop.

The coastal view from the base of the **Faro Punta Tuna** (⌚9am-3:30pm Wed-Sun),

WORTH A TRIP

HIGHWAY 181 & THE RUTA PANORÁMICA

For a fine circle tour of the east, you can head south and to the coast from San Juan via Hwy 181, connecting to Hwy 182, which boasts the moniker *Ruta Panorámica* (Panoramic Route).

It's a beautiful and remote route that takes you to Yabucoa, and along this mostly narrow, bumpy and sharply curved road, you'll climb high into the tropical rainforest west of El Yunque. Expect to see canyons of bamboo arching over the road amid a plethora of verdant green, and flame trees providing vivid orange contrast against the huge, elegant tree ferns.

Travel is slow – allow at least three hours – which is all the better when you round a blind bend and find a passel of chihuahuas in the road or a bunch of schoolkids riding ponies. Amid the dense foliage you'll be dazzled by deep canyon glimpses and, eventually, views out to sea. Don't expect to find many reasons to stop for refreshments in the scattered, simple hamlets you'll encounter.

Once in Yabucoa, you can head back up the coast north and west to San Juan.

the lighthouse just southeast of Maunabo, is worth the drive. It's also a wetland reserve and nesting ground for leatherback and hawksbill turtles. From Hwy 901, take Hwy 760 toward the ocean. A path leads down to the extremely secluded **Playa Larga**.

Sleeping

There are just a few scattered places to stay along the coast south of Yabucoa.

Caribe Playa Beach Resort INN **$$**
(787-839-6339; www.caribeplaya.com; Hwy 3 Km 112, Patillas; r $98-135;) Tucked right on the shore between Maunabo and Patillas, under a slanting plantation of coconuts, this inn has 26 units, many with beachfront balconies. Most rooms have a fridge. There's a decent restaurant and a natural pool carved into the rocky coast.

Parador Costa del Mar INN **$$**
(787-266-6276; www.tropicalinnspr.com; Hwy 901 Km 5.6; d $127;) Like the other Tropical Inns paradors, Costa del Mar fits the midrange bracket. It's distinguished by its position on a grassy bluff overlooking the ocean, and its vividly colored flowers, luminous pool and brilliant-yellow paintwork. The beach is a 100m trek.

Playa de Emajaguas Guest House GUESTHOUSE **$$**
(787-861-6023; Hwy 901 Km 2.5; r from $80;) The no-frills Emajaguas Guest House nestles in verdant mountain foothills above a choice deserted beach near the El Cocal and Sharkey's surf breaks. It's light on luxuries and close to nature; you come here for the rustic surroundings and the sense of isolation. The once grand house shelters seven scruffy apartments with kitchenettes, and cats and roosters roam the property.

Eating

In this less touristy part of Puerto Rico, you'll find few places to eat that are worth a detour. Often, your best bets are simple stalls in the towns.

El Nuevo Horizonte PUERTO RICAN **$$**
(787-893-5492; Hwy 901 Km 9.8, Yabucoa; dishes $17-29; 11am-9pm Wed-Sun) Just west of the Parador Costa del Mar inn, the view rarely gets better than it does from this place. This restaurant is perched high on the mountainside overlooking the Caribbean. You can smell the *asopao de langosta* (lobster stew) cooking 200yd before you get here. A cauldron will set you back about $25 and serves at least two people.

El Mar de la Tranquilidad PUERTO RICAN **$$**
(787-839-4870; Hwy 3 Km 118.9, Patillas; dishes $10-20; noon-8pm Fri-Sun, to 5pm Tue-Thu) Heading west from Yabucoa, look for this establishment on the seaward side of Hwy 3 when it hits sea level. A beer on the outdoor terrace makes for a good driving break; you can also get *salmorejo de jueyes* (land crab in tomato sauce), lobster and some decent cocktails while enjoying fine ocean views.

Getting There & Away

Públicos link Yabucoa to Humacao ($3) and taxis can take you to Maunabo ($15). Both have onward connections to Fajardo and San Juan. Avoid the short tunnel on Hwy 53 between Yabucoa and Maunabo and stick to the scenic, oceanside Hwy 901.

Culebra & Vieques

POP 11,200

Includes ➡

Best Places to Eat

- El Eden (p122)
- Dinghy Dock (p122)
- Carambola (p138)
- El Quenepo (p137)
- Café Mamasonga (p135)

Best Beaches

- Playa Flamenco (p115)
- Playa Zoni (p116)
- Playa Caracas (p129)
- Playa La Plata (p129)
- Sun Bay (p130)

Why Go?

Separated from mainland Puerto Rico by a 7-mile stretch of choppy blue water, the two bejeweled Caribbean havens of Culebra and Vieques have an irresistible charm thanks to mellow locals, laid-back expats and itinerant sailors.

Disembark for a few days and you'll uncover a wealth of surprises – wild horses in Vieques, endangered turtles in Culebra – and people who reclaimed their prized islands from the US Navy in 1975 (Culebra) and 2003 (Vieques) after more than 50 years of military occupation.

But it's the beaches that will have you purring with delight. Between them, the two members of the Spanish Virgin Islands may have the greatest variety of truly superb beaches in the Caribbean. Many are deserted, giving you the chance for boundless frolic. Best of all, these two islands have yet to attract mass tourism, so there's nary a golf course, casino or huge resort.

When to Go

September and October can be pretty slow on the islands, with many restaurants taking a break or cutting back their hours. It's a good time to find lodging discounts and have less company on the island ferries.

The best viewing of the bioluminescent bay in Vieques is during the new moon; some operators don't go out when it's full. From April through June, wildlife fans can volunteer for a turtle-egg protection project on Culebra.

The famous Caribbean trade winds gently buffet these two islands, but it's still hot and balmy just about every day of the year.

History

Some 500 years ago the islands east of Puerto Rico, including Culebra and Vieques, were disputed territory between the Taíno and the Caribs. Groups from both tribes came and went from the islands according to the season – probably to hunt the turtles nesting here. Vieques had more fertile, flatter land for farming and therefore was the more popular island. The first real settlement came to Culebra during the early 16th century, when Taíno and Carib refugees from Borinquen gathered here and on Vieques to make peace with each other, pool their resources and mount a fierce (but ultimately unsuccessful) campaign to drive the Spaniards from the big island.

When Spain conceded Puerto Rico and her territories to the US following the Spanish–American War in 1898, both Culebra and Vieques became municipalities of the Republic of Puerto Rico. Residents are therefore recognized as US citizens (half of them are expat Americans, in any case).

Getting There & Around

There's frequent air service from San Juan to both Vieques and Culebra. Much cheaper are the regular public ferries between Fajardo and the islands. In January, ferry passengers can sometimes spot humpback whales.

There are direct flights but no ferries between Vieques and Culebra; you can go by water on a costly boat charter. Trying to connect the two islands by ferry via Fajardo will likely erase every mellow vibe you've gained.

Distances on the islands are fairly small, but some form of wheels will be needed to explore those alluring remote beaches.

Culebra

POP 1800

An elusive lizard (not seen since 1974) hides in a unique mountain 'boulder' forest, an abandoned US tank lies rusting on a paradisial beach, a sign on a shop door in the 'capital' Dewey reads 'Open some days, closed others.' Welcome to Culebra, the island that time forgot; mainland Puerto Rico's weird, wonderful and distinctly wacky smaller cousin that lies just off the east coast.

Long feted for its diamond-dust beaches and world-class diving reefs, sleepy Culebra is probably more famous for what it *hasn't* got than for what it actually possesses. There are no big hotels here, no golf courses, no casinos, no fast-food chains, no rush-hour traffic, no postmodern stress and *no problemas, amigo*. Situated 17 miles off mainland Puerto Rico, but inhabiting an entirely different planet culturally speaking, the island's peculiar brand of offbeat charm can sometimes take a bit of getting used to. It's home to rat-race dropouts, earnest idealists, solitude seekers, myriad eccentrics and anyone else who's forsaken the hassles and manic intricacies of modern life.

It's also home to a range of gorgeous natural areas, bays, snorkeling sites and all manner of fine beaches. Come, join the local vibe and explore.

OFF THE BEATEN TRACK

ISLA CULEBRITA

If you need a reason to hire a water taxi, Isla Culebrita is it. This small island, just a mile east of Playa Zoni, is part of the Culebra National Wildlife Refuge. With its abandoned and decaying 1880s lighthouse, six beaches, tide pools, reefs and nesting areas for seabirds, Isla Culebrita has changed little in the past 500 years. The north beaches, such as the long crescent of Playa Tortuga, are popular nesting grounds for sea turtles, and you may see these animals swimming near the reefs just offshore. Bring a lot of water, sunscreen, a shirt and a hat if you head for Isla Culebrita, as there is little shade here.

History

First hunting grounds for Taíno and Carib tribes, then a pirate stronghold during the days of the Spanish Empire, much of Culebra's 7000 acres has remained essentially the same ever since two-legged creatures took to walking its shores. The US Navy grabbed control of most of the island early in the 20th century and didn't cede its lands back to the locals until 1975.

Although development was threatened on the pristine lands after the military left, resident expats and native-born *culebrenses* (people from Culebra) combined forces to resist rampant growth. They've continued to work together to preserve the island's low-key vibe.

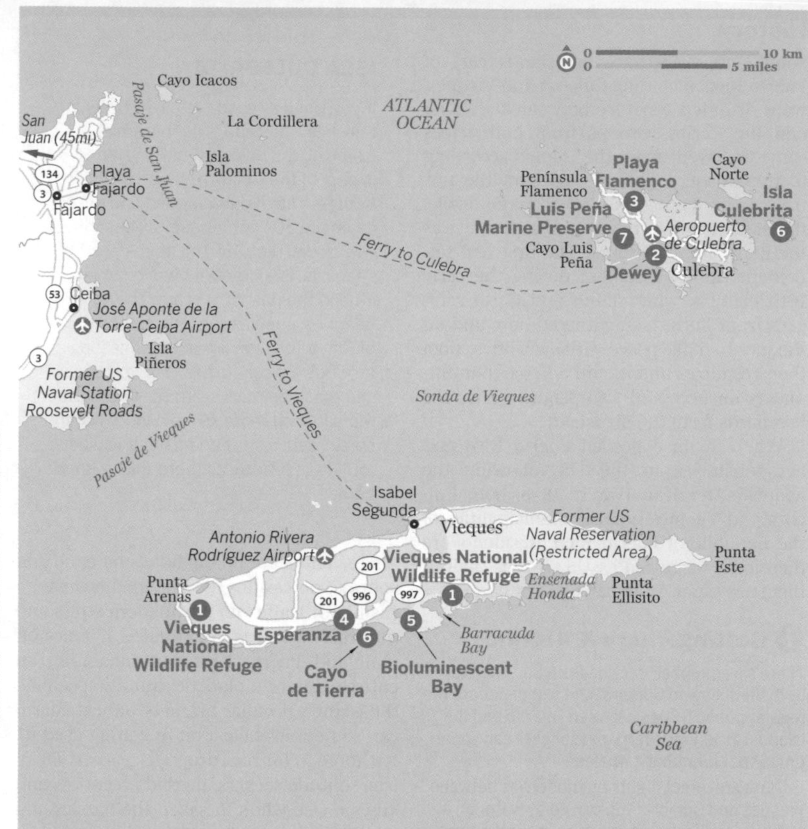

Culebra & Vieques Highlights

1. Revel in some of the best beaches in the Caribbean at the **Vieques National Wildlife Refuge** (p125), where you can find a patch of sand ideal for you.
2. Bar-hop with sailors between the trio of popular nightspots in Culebra's compact **Dewey** (p121).
3. Wander the amazing crescent of sand on paradisial **Playa Flamenco** (p115), where memories of a military past dissolve in the beautiful waters.
4. Eat, drink, play or just plain chill on the colorful oceanfront 'strip' in laid-back **Esperanza** (p127).
5. See aquatic stars on a serene but distinctly surreal evening boat tour of **Bioluminescent Bay** (p128).
6. Hike the gentle hills on the offshore islands **Isla Culebrita** (p113) and **Cayo de Tierra** (p128).
7. Plunge in and dive the reefs and sunken treasures of Culebra's clear waters best exemplified by **Luis Peña Marine Preserve** (p118).

Sights

Heading left away from the ferry dock will bring you to Calle Pedro Márquez, usually referred to as the 'main road,' which leads into Dewey, the island's principal settlement. Sights in town are modest at best.

The main road eventually leads out to the tiny airport on Rte 251; if you continue past the airport you get to Playa Flamenco. If you take Rte 250 east you'll come to turnoffs for Playas Resaca and Brava, eventually winding up at Playa Zoni. Another road, Calle Fulladoza, heads south to Punta Soldado.

Isla Culebrita and Cayo Norte are two of the more popular cays off Culebra and are easily visited; there are 18 others surrounding the island.

#200 01-12-2014 1:55PM
Item(s) checked out to p10056580.

TITLE: Puerto Rico
DUE DATE: 29-12-14

TITLE: Instant immersion Spanish crash c
DUE DATE: 29-12-14

Thanks for using North Kamloops Library.
TEL: 250 554-1124 WEB: www.tnrdlib.ca

Dewey

Nestled on a thin knob of land between two glistening bays, Dewey is Culebra's diminutive main town and the launching pad for the island's rustic attractions. A languid settlement that awakes from its slumber for the arrival and departure of the ferry, it's more of a rural backwater than delectable Caribbean idyll. Named after the US admiral who won the Battle of Manila Bay in 1898, it's a place where no one's in a hurry, and residents stop to chat about what hot commodities have turned up at the grocery store.

Belying expectations for a town so small, but reflecting Culebra's strong expat draw, Dewey has some good places to eat and even a bit of nightlife. Unfortunately a thicket of fences around the ferry terminal rob the town of what could be a lovely waterfront at sunset.

Culebra National Wildlife Refuge

More than 1500 acres of Culebra's 7000 acres are part of a national wildlife refuge, which US President Theodore Roosevelt signed into law almost 100 years ago. Most of this land lies along the **Península Flamenco** (Map p117), and from Monte Resaca east to the sea, and includes all of the coastline as well as more than 20 offshore cays, with the exception of Cayo Norte. **Monte Resaca** (Map p117), **Isla Culebrita** (Map p117) and **Cayo Luis Peña** (Map p117) are open to the public from sunrise to sunset daily, and have hidden beaches, challenging hikes and plenty of wildlife.

The **US Fish & Wildlife Service** (Map p117; ☎787-742-0115; www.fws.gov/caribbean/refuges/culebra; off Hwy 250 Km 4.2; ⏲7am-4pm Mon-Fri) administers these lands. Stop by the office on the east side of Ensenada Honda for maps, literature and permission to visit other sections of the refuge.

Ensenada Honda

Sailboat masts sway like metronomes on Culebra's sheltered central bay. You'll find fine views of the waters from all sides, including from a few good shoreside restaurants and along Hwy 250. Watch for all manner of fish – including small sharks – swimming through the crystal waters.

Museo Histórico de Culebra MUSEUM
(Culebra History Museum; Map p117; ☎787-742-3832; Rte 250; admission $1; ⏲10am-3pm Fri-Sun) Built in 1905 by the navy for use as a munitions warehouse, the little Museo Histórico de Culebra has compact but interesting displays covering nature, culture and the colorful local political history. Don't miss the historical photographs of the island and many Taíno artifacts.

Cayo Luis Peña

Less visited than Isla Culebrita, Luis Peña is the island of peaks, rocks, forests and coves you'll pass just a few minutes before the ferry lands you at Culebra's dock. This island is another part of the Culebra National Wildlife Refuge, and it has a collection of small sheltered beaches. Luis Peña is a short kayak or water taxi trip from town; it has good beaches and snorkeling all around the island.

Beaches

Culebra's beaches offer wild natural beauty. Tourist facilities vary, with plenty at Playa Flamenco and blissfully few at Playa Zoni; when venturing out to most beaches, be sure to bring lots of water and snacks.

★**Playa Flamenco** BEACH
(Map p117; Hwy 251) Stretching for a mile around a sheltered, horseshoe-shaped bay, Playa Flamenco is not just Culebra's best beach, it is also generally regarded as the finest in Puerto Rico and the Caribbean.

Backed by low scrub and trees rather than craning palms, rustic Flamenco gets very crowded on weekends, especially with daytrippers from San Juan. Alone among Culebra's beaches, it has a range of amenities. Weekdays are good for a visit, when crowds are few.

In the winter months you'll feel like Robinson Crusoe contemplating the clarity of the water here; the name comes from the nearby lagoon, which attracts flamingos in winter. Services include a collection of kiosks (selling snack food, lunches, rum punches and beer, and renting beach gear and more), toilets, outdoor showers, lifeguards, picnic tables and an often jammed parking lot. Camping is allowed.

The iconic **rusting tank** is at the beach's west end, a legacy of when troops practiced invasions here. Its swirling green and yellow stripes are the work of local artist Jorge Acevedo, who says they represent a 'dancing fish.'

You can walk here from Dewey in under 30 minutes.

★Playa Zoni BEACH

(Map p117; Hwy 250) Head to the extreme eastern end of the island and you'll eventually run out of road at Playa Zoni. From the airport junction, it's a straightforward 3-mile drive through rolling hills dotted with a growing number of large holiday homes. There's a small parking spot next to the sign alerting you to the fact that endangered turtles cross the beach. Zoni is long and straight, with beautiful islands popping up in the distance. A short walk will guarantee you solitude amid the sands.

Some locals think this is a better beach than Flamenco; it doesn't have quite the same soft sand and gentle curves, but it certainly is stunning in its own right and has idyllic views of Cayo Norte, Isla Culebrita and even Charlotte Amelie on the horizon. Check out the currents and watch out for hidden boulders in the water. Do like the savvy locals and bring a cooler for a picnic; services are nil.

★Playa Carlos Rosario BEACH

(Map p117) Remote Playa Carlos Rosario is an antidote to the crowds at Playa Flamenco and one of the best snorkeling areas in Puerto Rico.

Leave the masses behind and follow a path west from the parking lot at Playa Flamenco. A 15-minute hike over the hill will bring you to a tiny beach with no name. Continue north from here, cross the narrow peninsula, and head down to the sandy basin and shade trees.

A barrier reef almost encloses the beach; you can snorkel on either side of it by swimming through the boat channel – look for the floating white marker – at the right side of the beach. But be very careful: water taxis and local powerboats cruise this channel and the reef, and swimmers have been hit.

For really spectacular snorkeling, work your way along the cliffs on the point south of the beach, or head about a quarter mile north to a place called the **Wall**, which has 40ft drop-offs and rich colors.

Punta Melones BEACH

(Map p117; Camino Vecinal) The nearest beach to Dewey and best place to catch a sunset. Take the Camino Vecinal west from **Our Lady of Carmen Catholic Church** (Map p120; Calle Pedro Márquez) in town up and down a steep hill for about six-tenths of a mile until you see rocky Melones point with its navigation light; to the right of the point is a stony beach. Here you'll find great snorkeling at both ends.

The point's name comes from the prevalence of a species of melon cactus in this part of the island. It's a good idea to bring shoes you can wear in the water; cacti line the seafloor. There's a smattering of shady picnic tables.

Playa Brava BEACH

(Map p117) The beauty of Brava lies in the fact that there is no road here; you *have* to hike about 30 minutes along a little-used trail

FLAMENCO'S MILITARY PAST

Up until the early 1970s, Playa Flamenco was part of a live firing range used by the US Navy for target practice. First requisitioned by the military in 1902 to counter a rising German threat in the Caribbean, Culebra's beaches were used to stage mock amphibious landings and myriad ground maneuvers. In 1936, with WWII in the offing, the Flamenco peninsula yielded to its first live arms fire and the beach was regularly shelled.

Burgeoning decade by decade, the military operations reached their peak during the late 1960s at the height of the Vietnam War, with the navy simulating gun attacks and submarine warfare. When the US government hinted at expanding the Culebra base in the early 1970s, public sentiment quickly turned bellicose. In what would become a dress rehearsal for the Navy–Vieques protests 30 years later, a small committed group of Puerto Rican protesters – including Independence party leader Rubén Berríos – initiated a campaign of civil disobedience that culminated in squatters accessing the beach and having to be forcibly removed by police. Despite arrests and imprisonments, the tactics worked. In 1975 the US Navy pulled out of Culebra and the beach was returned to its natural state.

Over 40 years later you can still find evidence of the war games that once pounded Flamenco's sands. At the beach's western end, contrasting rather sharply with the diamond-dust sand and translucent water, an incongruously brightly painted yet rusting tank is a ghostly reminder of past military maneuvers.

Culebra

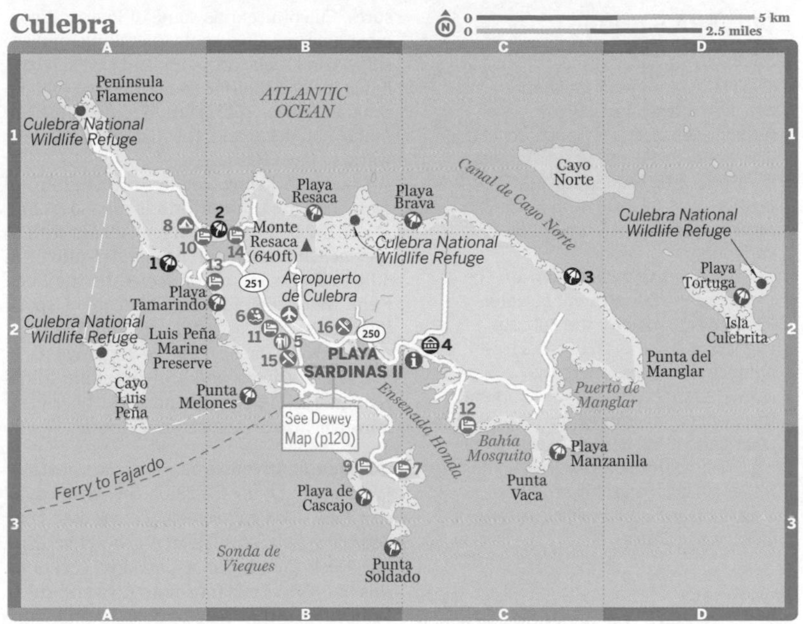

that is often overgrown with sea grape and low scrub. The rewards are immense when you finally clear the last mangrove and are confronted with an isolated but stunning swath of sand that glimmers with a fierce but utterly enchanting beauty.

To get to the trailhead, take a small road to the end off Hwy 250 past the 4km marker. Look for a turn north a little way past a cemetery. Follow this road until the pavement ends and you come up against a chain gate near a few small houses. This is the entrance to a cattle farm, but it is also a public right-of-way, so park your car or bike and head due north on the trail beyond the gate. The second half of the trail leads through a grove of trees that often attracts butterflies.

Playa Tamarindo BEACH
(Map p117) On an isolated bit of coast west of Punta Melones, this is a very good snorkeling beach; it overlooks the fish-filled waters of the **Luis Peña Marine Preserve**. It's accessible by foot by either turning off the Dewey–Flamenco Beach road at the bottom of the hill just before the lagoon, or from an unmarked trail west off the Flamenco parking lot.

This often-overlooked beach is not as flashy and fabulous-looking as others, but offers a good combination of sun and shade, gentle currents and lots of underwater life. The marine preserve protects the rich and shallow waters between Culebra and Cayo Luis Peña.

Culebra

Top Sights
1 Playa Carlos Rosario ... A2
2 Playa Flamenco ... B1
3 Playa Zoni ... C2

Sights
4 Museo Histórico de Culebra ... C2

Activities, Courses & Tours
5 Carlos Jeep Rental ... B2
6 Kayaking Puerto Rico ... B2

Sleeping
7 Bahía Marina ... C3
8 Camping Culebra ... A1
9 Club Seabourne ... B3
10 Culebra Beach Villas ... A2
11 Palmetto Guesthouse ... B2
12 Sea Breeze Hotel ... C2
13 Tamarindo Estates ... B2
14 Villa Flamenco Beach ... B2

Eating
15 Barbara Rosa ... B2
Guava ... (see 9)
16 Susie's ... B2

CULEBRA'S HUGE SEA TURTLES

Two of Culebra's most isolated beaches – Resaca and Brava – are nesting sites for the endangered leatherback sea turtle, the world's largest living sea turtle (adults can reach 7ft in length and weigh in at 1500lb). The nesting season runs from April through early June.

Each year a few volunteers are accepted by the Department of Natural Resources to monitor the delicate egg-laying process. Volunteers travel out to the beaches, where they count eggs, measure turtles, and document the event for environmental records. Locals also close nesting beaches during this time from dawn to dusk. The rather smaller hawksbill sea turtle (up to 3ft long and 250lb) also lays eggs on Culebra's beaches.

Playa Resaca BEACH

(Map p117) A *resaca* is an undertow and a metaphor for a hangover, an allusion to the state of the water perhaps, or the way you will feel after climbing up and down 640ft Monte Resaca to reach it. Not well maintained nor easy to find, the trail is a 40-minute hike that involves scrambling. The US Fish & Wildlife Service (p115) gives directions to the trailhead. Note: the beach lives up to its name and is unsafe for swimming.

Monte Resaca, the island's highest point, is characterized by an ecologically unique boulder-strewn forest on its upper slopes that harbors rare types of flora and fauna (mainly lizards). It's a tough (and sometimes prickly) climb. Bring lots of water and sturdy shoes.

Punta Soldado BEACH

(Map p117) This site on the extreme southwestern tip of the island has a rocky beach and good snorkeling. To get here, follow the road south across the drawbridge for about 2 miles, passing Club Seabourne and finally scaling a steep hill. Here the pavement stops, and it's a bumpy dirt road down to the beach. You will see the reef about 50yd offshore to the southeast. Locals bring their children to snorkel in the shallow waters here.

Activities

Diving & Snorkeling

Despite reef damage from the US Navy testing era and endemic climate-change pressures, Culebra retains some of Puerto Rico's most amazing dive spots, including sunken ships, coral reefs, drop-offs and caves. Highlights include the *Wit Power* tugboat (which sank in 1984), the Geniqui Caves, the El Mono boulders, and the fish-filled, waterworld of Cayo Ratón.

Good snorkeling can be accessed from many beaches. **Tamarindo** is a good example of the bounty on offer: it teems with a spectacular variety of fish and features a 50ft wall of coral, all protected by the **Luis Peña Marine Preserve**. Other good spots include Playas Carlos Rosario and Melones. Ask locals for the best places to plunge in.

Culebra Divers and Culebra Bike Shop rent snorkeling equipment; most boat captains will also arrange snorkel tours.

★**Aquatic Adventures** DIVING, SNORKELING

(Map p120; ☎515-290-2310; www.diveculebra.com; Calle Fulladoza; snorkeling/2-tank dives from $60/95; ⏲9am-5pm) Located just above Dinghy Dock (handy for a post-dive cocktail), this fine shop leads four-hour dive and snorkeling tours that leave about 10am. Trips include lunch.

Culebra Divers DIVING

(Map p120; ☎787-742-0803; www.culebradivers.com; Calle Pedro Márquez; 2-tank dives from $90; ⏲9am-1pm & 2-5pm) Across from the ferry dock, this is one of the island's main dive operators. It also rents out snorkeling gear (from $10 per day).

Kayaking

The usually placid waters of Ensenada Honda are ideal for a paddle; the beaches and small coves can also be fun. As well as the outfit mentioned below, you can also rent two-person kayaks (per day $50) from the gear-laden Culebra Bike Shop across from the ferry dock.

Kayaking Puerto Rico KAYAKING

(Map p117; ☎787-435-1665; www.kayakingpuertorico.com; Hwy 251; 3½-hour tours from $55) Cheerfully calling them 'aquafaris', this company's tours combine kayaks and snorkeling on the rich waters of the Luis Peña Marine Preserve. You can also start at Fajardo at the ferry port at 8am ($75, includes transfers). An office with info and gear rental is across from the airport on the way to Playa Flamenco.

Boat Trips

Return boat transfers to Isla Culebrita cost about $50 per person. Trips to Cayo Norte are generally combined with snorkeling and lunch, and start at $60 per person. You'll find captains along the waterfronts in Dewey.

Cycling

With its hills, dirt trails and back-to-nature ruggedness, Culebra is an excellent place to bike – not just for exercise but also as a handy means of transportation.

Dick & Cathie Rentals BICYCLE RENTAL
(☎787-742-0062; per day from $20) Rents good-quality mountain bikes and offers free road service. Call and they'll swiftly deliver a bike to you in their battered VW van, plus they share their love and knowledge of the island.

Culebra Bike Shop BICYCLE RENTAL
(Map p120; ☎787-742-0589; www.culebrabikeshop.com; Hotel Kokomo, Calle Pedro Márquez; rental per day from $15; ⏲9am-5pm) Located right across from the ferry dock, you can sail in and be on the road to a beach in no time.

Surfing

The island is not known for great waves, but you can sometimes catch some action at Carlos Rosario, Zoni and Punta Soldado.

Carlos Jeep Rental SURFING
(Map p117; ☎787-742-3514; www.carlosjeeprental.com; Hwy 250; per day from $40; ⏲9am-5pm) Just as kayakers enjoy Culebra's usually calm waters, so do stand-up paddlers. This car-rental outfit near the airport rents gear.

Hiking

Rejoice! The island is your oyster. The 2.5-mile hike from Dewey to Playa Flamenco is along a paved road with some inclines, but the destination is idyllic. You can veer off to Playa Tamarindo from a junction just before the lagoon. Playa Carlos Rosario is reached via a trail that starts at the west end of Playa Flamenco. The hike to Playa Brava begins at the end of a back road that cuts north from Rte 250 just past the graveyard. The trail rises to a ridge and then drops to the beach through thick scrub. The toughest hike on the island is the rough trail to Playa Resaca that traverses the eponymous mountain. The trailhead is about 2 miles from Dewey.

Sleeping

Several places to stay in budget-friendly Culebra are a short walk from the ferry dock in Dewey, otherwise you'll find options islandwide. Many have docks for boats.

Culebra has an excellent selection of rental properties of all shapes and sizes dotted around the island. **Culebra Vacation Planners** (Map p120; ☎787-742-3112; www.culebravacationplanners.com; Calle Pedro Márquez) is a local agent with a range of properties from simple rooms for $50 to beachfront stunners with views to neighboring islands ($700 a night and up).

Dewey

Hotel Kokomo HOTEL $
(Map p120; ☎787-742-3112; www.culebra-kokomo.com; Calle Pedro Márquez; r $70-150; ❄📶) This slightly scruffy banana-yellow building is right across from the ferry dock. Rooms, while basic, are clean enough, but check your room before committing – some are much better than others, and one is windowless. Two penthouse apartments are much more luxurious, sleeping four or six people.

★Palmetto Guesthouse GUESTHOUSE $$
(Map p117; ☎787-742-0257; www.palmettoculebra.com; off Hwy 250; r $95-125; ❄@📶) Run by two ex-Peace Corps volunteers from New England, this business is a super-friendly and accommodating escape. Five guest rooms have the run of two kitchens and a deck. Situated not far from the airport, it's a 10-minute stroll to Dewey. There's free pickup and drop-off from the ferry terminal or the airport.

Free snorkel gear, beach chairs, boogie boards, a handy book exchange, a sporty magazine pile, bug spray and much more are yours for the taking.

★Villa Fulladoza APARTMENTS $$
(Map p120; ☎787-742-3576; www.villafulladoza.wix.com/culebra; Calle Fulladoza; apt $75-120; 📶) Super-cute and vividly turquoise and salmon, unfussy Villa Fulladoza offers seven bright fan-cooled studio apartments with ocean breezes and plenty of room. The shared patio is shaded by a swaying mango tree, while many of the units have large terraces (get one upstairs for great views). If you are lucky enough to enjoy your own private water transportation, there's a boat dock.

Casa Ensenada GUESTHOUSE $$
(Map p120; ☎787-742-3559; www.casaensenada.com; Calle de Escudero; r $85-175; ❄📶) This pleasant guesthouse just north of town on the waterfront at Ensenada Honda is handily placed. The inn has three units (accommodating

Dewey

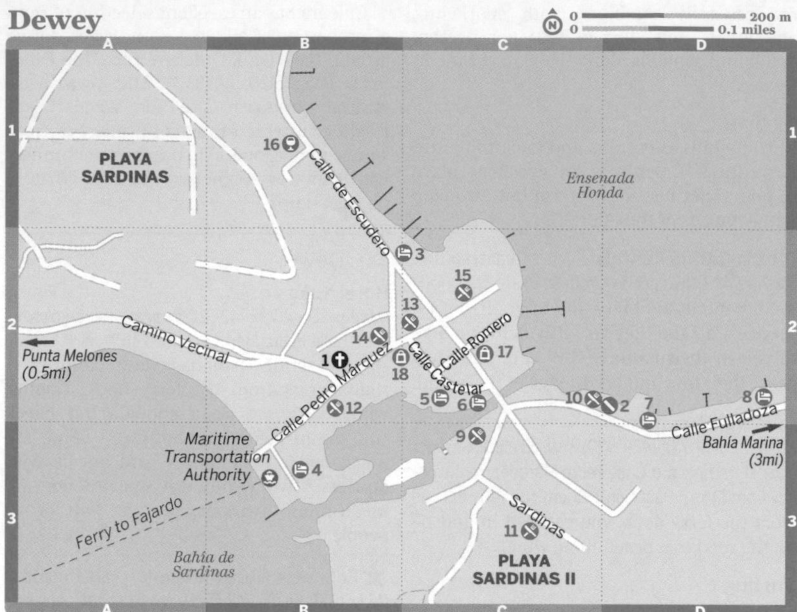

two, four or up to six people) with kitchen or kitchenette, separate entrance and air-conditioning. Unexpected extras include free use of a kayak, free boat dock, beach towels, grill, hammocks and a spacious breezy patio.

Villa Boheme HOTEL $$
(Map p120; ☎787-742-3508; www.villaboheme.com; Calle Fulladoza; r $115-175; ❄📶) This well-situated small bay-side hotel offers a communal patio, lovely water views, kayak rentals and proximity to town. A few of the colorful rooms are equipped with a kitchenette. Hang out on one of the hammocks.

Posada La Hamaca HOTEL $$
(Map p120; ☎787-742-3516; www.posada.com; Calle Castelar; r $85-155; ❄📶) Next to the infamous Mamacita's, La Hamaca has a tough act to follow for budget lodging. However, it does try to strike back with a vivid orange paint scheme. The 12 rooms are basic but comfortable, overlook the canal and have either fridges and microwaves or kitchenettes. The location is very central.

Mamacita's GUESTHOUSE $$
(Map p120; ☎787-742-0090; www.mamacitasguesthouse.com; 64 Calle Castelar; r $90-150; ❄📶) Screaming lurid pink, pastel purple, green, blue and perhaps a little yellow, Mamacita's is the raffish no-frills Caribbean crash pit you've been dreaming about. The 10 rooms are simple but attractive, the vibe in the adjacent bar fun and casual, and the on-site restaurant a humming legend. It's very central.

Outside Dewey

Camping Culebra CAMPGROUND $
(Map p117; ☎787-742-0700; www.campingculebra.com; Playa Flamenco; campsites from $20; P) The only place you can legally camp in Culebra is just feet from the famous Playa Flamenco. Campsites are in five zones: A is closest to the kiosks while E is the most distant and serene. Six people maximum per tent. There are outdoor showers with limited hours; bathrooms are open 24/7. The campground's pretty safe and reservations aren't usually necessary.

★ **Villa Flamenco Beach** APARTMENTS $$
(Map p117; ☎787-383-0985, 787-742-0023; www.villaflamencobeach.com; off Hwy 251; r $135-180; P❄) Gentle waves lulling you to sleep, a night sky replete with twinkling stars, and one of the best beaches on the planet just outside your window: this six-unit place is a winner. Enjoy the getaway with self-catering kitchen facilities, inviting hammocks and little more than palms and sand for atmosphere.

Dewey

Sights

1	Our Lady of Carmen Catholic Church	B2

Activities, Courses & Tours

2	Aquatic Adventures	D2
	Culebra Bike Shop	(see 4)
	Culebra Divers	(see 4)

Sleeping

3	Casa Ensenada	C2
	Culebra Vacation Planners	(see 4)
4	Hotel Kokomo	B3
5	Mamacita's	C2
6	Posada La Hamaca	C2
7	Villa Boheme	D2
8	Villa Fulladoza	D2

Eating

9	Colmado Milka	C3
10	Dinghy Dock	C2
11	El Eden	C3
12	Heather's	B2
	Mamacita's	(see 5)
13	Pandeli	C2
14	Vibra Verde	B2
15	Zaco's Tacos	C2

Drinking & Nightlife

16	El Batey	B1
	Spot	(see 12)

Shopping

	Artefango	(see 10)
17	Butiki	C2
18	Galería de Regalos	B2

Culebra Beach Villas APARTMENTS $$
(Map p117; 787-742-0517, 787-767-7575; www.culebrabeachrental.com; off Hwy 251; apt $150-350;) The only visible building on Playa Flamenco is a three-story Caribbean villa at this condo complex. There are 33 self-catering apartments (each individually owned – and decorated) with kitchens for two and eight people. The setting is stunning, though you'll want to stock up on provisions in Dewey. Minimum stays are two or more nights.

Tamarindo Estates APARTMENTS $$
(Map p117; 787-742-3343; www.tamarindoestates.com; r $140-280;) The Tamarindo is Culebran to the core: rustic, isolated and set facing one of the Caribbean's most serendipitous views, overlooking Cayo Luis Peña. The accommodations – which comprise 12 self-contained cottages spread over 60 acres – are no-frills. Near the water's edge there's a pool and restaurant, and remote Playa Tamarindo is a five-minute stroll away.

Club Seabourne HOTEL $$$
(Map p117; 787-742-3169; www.clubseabourne.com; Calle Fulladoza; r/villa from $170/250;) This tidy small hotel offers relaxed luxury in a garden setting. Features include an outdoor bar, a secluded swimming pool, kayak and bike rentals, and a restaurant decked out with tablecloths. The individual villas have somewhat distant sea views. Most will drive rather than walk here.

Sea Breeze Hotel APARTMENTS $$$
(Map p117; 787-504-4499; www.seabreezeculebra.com; off Hwy 250; r $180-250;) These large condos in 40 buildings on the far shore of Ensenada Honda are easily seen from every other waterside point and are a big-scale addition to the island. The fairly posh units come in two sizes, both of which are good for families. There's an upscale restaurant and a plethora of watersports, including sailing.

Bahía Marina APARTMENTS $$$
(Map p117; 787-278-5100; www.bahiamarina.net; Punta Soldado Rd Km 2.4; r $180-300;) This small condo resort has 18 two-bedroom units. Abutting a 100-acre nature preserve, balconies and terraces look out to the water some distance off from its hillside perch. It's a lengthy walk to town; the restaurant/bar has basic food. New management in 2014 should bring a needed spiff-up.

Eating & Drinking

Yes there's a lot of seafood sold in Culebra – much sourced from fishing boats tied up on the bay. Several small groceries offer up limited selections. Look for cheap, cheerful and tasty food trucks by the airport. Come sunset there's a well-trod nightlife path between Dinghy Dock, Mamacita's and the Spot.

Dewey

On Fridays, a fruit-and-vegetable vendor sets up under some shady trees near the airport, across the street from Carlos Jeep Rental.

★**Barbara Rosa** CAFE $
(Map p117; 787-742-3271; Hwy 250; dishes $8-16; 5-9pm Thu-Mon) *You* are the waiter at this diminutive cafe. You're also in Barbara's house – her front verandah to be more exact. When you've decided what you want from a fine menu featuring great burgers, seafood, fish and chips, and fab onion rings, holler

through the kitchen hatch to the busy Barbara. Bring your own booze. Cash only.

Vibra Verde CAFE $
(Map p120; Calle Pedro Márquez; mains $5-10; 8am-2pm Thu-Tue) This great little spot is hidden in a small arcade, look for the tables on the sidewalk. The menu (on a surfboard) is a delight of healthy and tasty fare. Granola breakfasts are joined by baked goods, eggs and fine coffee. Lunch includes a bevy of great sandwiches.

Zaco's Tacos MEXICAN $
(Map p120; Calle Pedro Márquez; mains $6-8; noon-8pm Mon-Fri) This cool and groovy newcomer dishes up ultra-fresh Mexican fare plus a smattering of tasty salads. Enjoy your meal in the cheery dining room or out on the back patio.

Pandeli CAFE $
(Map p120; 787-742-0296; Calle Pedro Márquez; mains $4-7; 6am-4pm;) This popular early-morning deli/cafe sells pastries, pancakes, salads, sandwiches and coffee. Come 8am it's inundated with schoolkids and stray travelers who enliven the no-frills setting.

Heather's PIZZA $
(Map p120; 787-742-3175; Calle Pedro Márquez; mains $6-20; 11am-9pm;) In the center of town, Heather's is a colorful and popular hangout at night and a great pizza parlor (with pasta and subs). It gets busy in high season, so expect a wait.

★El Eden CARIBBEAN $$
(Map p120; 787-742-0509; 836 Sardinas; dinner mains $17-25; dinner 5-9pm Wed-Sat, store 9am-9pm daily;) A liquor store with an excellent and eclectic wine selection, its restaurant is the special-occasion dinner choice for locals. Set with patio tables frocked in mismatched tablecloths, it's not an elegant place, but feels that way as owners Richard and Luz greet everyone like long-lost friends. Dishes feature creative takes on seafood and pasta, and the huge desserts are legendary.

★Dinghy Dock SEAFOOD $$
(Map p120; 787-742-0581; Calle Fulladoza; mains $10-30; 11am-11pm;) It's easy to get mesmerized by the giant tarpon that swim right up to the deck, just a couple of feet from diners. Fish is the obvious specialty here – fresh catches such as swordfish and snapper are joined by steaks and specials. The flavors are refreshingly bold.

The busy bar is a frenzy of expats nursing Medalla beers and acts as the unofficial island grapevine. Especially fun is listening into seamen discussing each other's maritime skills.

Mamacita's CARIBBEAN $$
(Map p120; 64 Calle Castelar; mains $18-22; 9am-late;) Always buzzing with activity, Mamacita's offers casual eats in a lively setting right on the water. Fish and meat plates are tasty, seasoned and creative, and the menu changes daily, as displayed on a handwritten blackboard. Fun is in the air at weekends when the *bomba* drums get warmed up.

Mamacita's has a lively happy hour and after-dinner bar scene. On weekends, locals, expats and yacht crews favor this place, with its open-air deck and Friday-night DJ. *Bomba y plena* drummers rock the patio every Saturday night; everybody dances!

Colmado Milka SUPERMARKET
(Map p120; 787-742-2253; off Calle Fulladoza; 7am-7pm Mon-Sat, to 1pm Sun) Just south of the bridge on the tiny road to the library, Colmado Milka is the island's second-largest supermarket, which means it's slightly smaller than the small 'large market' (which is out by the airport). Fresh items are hit or miss but scour the aisles for hidden gems of foodie joy.

Spot BAR
(Map p120; Calle Pedro Márquez; 6:30am-midnight Sun-Thu, to 2am Fri & Sat) This tiny bar has style – with an array of red Chinese lanterns, a checkerboard floor and a cobalt blue counter. Island restaurant workers trickle in after work on Friday nights to kick back and play darts. Food appears some nights.

El Batey BAR
(Map p120; 787-742-3828; Hwy 250; 11am-late) Not a large place, but seemingly big enough to accommodate the majority of Culebra's population at weekends, when locals swing by to shake a leg to *reggaetón* with a bit of salsa and merengue mixed in. During the week enjoy cheap burgers, cold beers and the pool table amid the stark decor. You can catch a glimpse of water across the road.

Outside Dewey

Susie's CARIBBEAN $$
(Map p117; 787-742-0574; Hwy 250; mains $20-24; 6-10pm Tue-Sun;) Beautifully presented Puerto Rican food with Asian accents, this

Culebra favorite curates a rotating collection of crowd-pleasing dishes, always including fresh fish such as grouper and snapper. Relocated to the road past the airport, the new Susie's has a vaguely hacienda feel, albeit with outdoor dining and tiki torches.

★Guava CARIBBEAN **$$$**
(Map p117; ☎787-742-3169; Club Seabourne, Calle Fulladoza; mains $16-35; ⏲6-10pm Thu-Sun) As well as being an upscale inn, Club Seabourne has an outstanding eatery in Guava. Tables are arranged around a mosquito-free screened-in porch, you can enjoy wine from the cellar and partake in the ever-changing menu of noted chef Maira Isabel. Local lobster is bliss. Watch the moon glint off Ensenada Honda framed by palms.

Shopping

★Artefango GALLERY
(Map p120; www.artefango.com; Calle Fulladoza; ⏲11am-9pm, hours vary) Perched above the Dinghy Dock, this compact gallery is the creative expression of Jorge Acevedo, a local activist and artist who's something of a celebrity. His works span many mediums and feature Culebra scenes often mixed with powerful messages for social justice. The affable artist is usually there; the T-shirts are affordable fashion statements.

Galería de Regalos SOUVENIRS
(Map p120; ☎787-742-2294; cnr Calles Pedro Márquez & Castelar; ⏲10am-5pm) A colorful gift and clothes shop that sells República de Culebra stickers and plenty of other knickknacks sure to briefly delight those left at home.

Butiki ART
(Map p120; ☎787-935-2542; cnr Calles de Escudero & Romero; ⏲9am-6pm Mon-Sat) This local art shop sells paintings, jewelry, masks, T-shirts and plenty more. Almost everything is island-made.

Information

Few establishments have meaningful street addresses on Culebra; directions tend to be descriptive. Basic island maps are handed out by hotels and car-rental agencies. Almost all services are in Dewey, including several ATMs.

DANGERS & ANNOYANCES

Culebra breeds swarms of mosquitoes, especially during the rainy season (May to November). Some of the daytime species have been known to carry dengue.

INTERNET ACCESS

Most accommodations have wi-fi, and Gretchen's Da Bar across from the ferry terminal is a handy free hot spot.

Culebra Community Library (Sardinas; ⏲10am-2pm Mon, Tue & Thu-Sat;) Across from El Eden restaurant, this welcoming volunteer-run library has computers ($5 per hour donation requested) and wi-fi. Visitors can borrow from its excellent selection of books and magazines, in English and Spanish. Excellent children's room.

MEDICAL SERVICES

Despite its small population, Culebra has good health services.

Culebra Health Center (☎787-742-3511; Camino Vecinal; ⏲24hr) In Dewey; has drugs and resident doctors. There's no pharmacy on the island, but the adjoining clinic can order prescriptions, which get flown over from the mainland.

TOURIST INFORMATION

Try www.islaculebra.com or www.culebra-island.com for good general information.

Getting There & Away

AIR

Culebra gets frequent air service from San Juan ($65 to $100 one way), Ceiba ($30 to $45) and, handily for island-hoppers, Vieques ($65 to $90).

The approach to Culebra's tiny **airport** (CPX; Map p117) over Playa Flamenco and then between two peaks is one of the world's most spectacular.

Air Flamenco (☎787-724-1818; www.airflamenco.net) Serves San Juan's Isla Grande, Culebra, Ceiba and Vieques.

Cape Air (☎800-227-3247; www.capeair.com) Fast-growing regional airline serving Culebra and Vieques from San Juan's international airport (LMM).

Vieques Air Link (☎888-901-9247; www.viequesairlink.com) Links San Juan's two airports, Culebra, Vieques and Ceiba.

BOAT

A number of companies offer charter services, which can be economical for groups.

Interisland Water Taxi (☎787-234-5897; www.interislandwatertaxi.com) Based in Fajardo, this operator offers Culebra–Vieques charters on speedboats (from $600 for six people), and service to St Thomas.

FERRY

The most popular and by far the cheapest way to Culebra from the mainland, the public ferries from Fajardo (p108) suffer from a bad rep given to them by tourists who consider cruise ships the standard of comfort.

In reality it's simple: get to the ferry terminal at least an hour early and buy your ticket (there are no reservations). Facilities are spartan but serviceable. Schedules vary by day, but there are usually at least three round trips. Check times locally or at tourist info websites.

On busy weekends, daytrippers may get bumped by island residents.

Maritime Transportation Authority (ATM; Map p120; ☎787-742-3161; Calle Pedro Márquez, Dewey; one-way $2.25; ⊙office open before sailings) Voyages take 45 minutes to two hours depending if you are on a fast ferry or cargo boat.

ℹ Getting Around

Arriving by ferry, you can easily walk to any point in Dewey proper, while another 30 minutes will take you to Playa Flamenco. Elsewhere you'll want your own transport. Bikes are fine, while scooters and golf carts are literally a breeze. Jeeps are heavily marketed, but there's no reason for such machines on Culebra's limited roads (and riding around this beautiful island in air conditioning behind glass is just wrong).

TO/FROM THE AIRPORT

Most places to stay will pick you up from the airport or ferry dock for free or charge a small fee; otherwise, $5 to $15 will get you just about anywhere on the island in a taxi.

CAR & SCOOTER

Mainland rental companies forbid you to bring a car to Culebra on the ferry. Locally, there are the unnecessary jeeps and a number of other better options such as golf carts that add to your fun.

Carlos Jeep Rental (☎787-742-3514; www.carlosjeeprental.com; Hwy 250) Rents small cars (from $60), jeeps (from $75), golf carts (from $40) and scooters (from $35). A short walk from the airport; free transport to/from the ferry dock.

Dick & Cathie Rentals (☎787-742-0062; rental per day from $50) Namesake Dick will pick you up at the airport or ferry in one of his battered but lovingly maintained open-air VW Things. He gives a good island tour to start your rental; easily the most fun way to get around.

Jerry's Jeep Rental (☎787-742-0587; www.jerrysjeeprental.com; Hwy 250) Across from the airport, rents jeeps (from $75) and golf carts (from $40).

TAXI

There is taxi service on the island, but they're basically *público* vans designed to get large parties of people back and forth between the ferry dock and Playa Flamenco for a couple of dollars per person.

Drivers include **Willy** (☎787-742-3537), who generally meets every ferry and also arrives at your door when booked.

Vieques

POP 9400

Measuring 21 miles long by 5 miles wide, Vieques is substantially bigger than Culebra and distinctly different in ambience. Though still a million metaphorical miles from the bright lights of the Puerto Rican mainland, the larger population here has meant more choice of accommodations, hipper restaurants and generally more buzz. It's renowned for its gorgeous beaches, semi-wild horses and unforgettable bioluminescent bay.

Vieques was where Puerto Rico's most prickly political saga was played out in the public eye. For over five decades the US Navy used more than two-thirds of the island for military target practice.

Since the official military withdrawal in 2003, Vieques has regularly been touted as the Caribbean's next 'big thing,' with pristine beaches and a coastline ripe for the developer's bulldozer. Fortunately, environmental authorities swept in quickly after the handover and promptly declared all of the former military land (70% of the island's total area) a US Fish & Wildlife Refuge. The measure has meant that the bulk of the island remains virgin territory to be explored and enjoyed by all.

Development elsewhere has been slow and low-key. Small hotels are the beds of choice. The island has no golf, gambling or Las Vegas–style glitz, and only one large resort. This seems unlikely to change any time soon. Vieques' residents – many of whom are US expats – are fiercely protective of their Caribbean nirvana.

History

When Columbus 'discovered' Puerto Rico on his second voyage in 1493, Taíno people were living peacefully (save for the occasional skirmish with Carib neighbors) on Vieques. With the expansion of Puerto Rico under Ponce de León, more Taíno fled to the island; Caribs joined them and the two groups mounted a fierce resistance to Spanish occupation. It failed. Spanish soldiers eventually overran the island, killing or enslaving the natives who remained.

Even so, Spanish control over the island remained tentative at best. In succeeding years, both the British and French tried to claim the island as their own. In reality, Vieques remained something of a free port, thriving as a smuggling center.

Sugarcane plantations covered much of Vieques when the island fell to the Americans in 1898 as spoils from the Spanish-American War, but during the first half of the 20th century the cane plantations failed. Vieques lost more than half its population and settled into near dormancy; the remaining locals survived as they always had, by subsistence farming, fishing and smuggling.

First requisitioned by the US military in 1941, Vieques was originally intended to act as a safe haven for the British Navy during WWII, should the UK fall to the Nazis. But after 1945 the US decided to keep hold of the territory to use as a base for weapons testing during the ever chillier Cold War. Taking control of more than 70% of the island's 33,000 acres in the east and west, the military left the local population to live in a small strip down the middle while they shelled beaches and dropped live bombs on offshore atolls. On average the military bombed Vieques 180 days a year and in 1998 alone dropped a total of 23,000 explosive devices on the island.

The US military held onto it until May 2003 when, after four years of international protests, the land was ceded to the US Fish & Wildlife Refuge. In the years since, Puerto Rican, US and international developers have been salivating at the prospect of building mega hotels and more. But for the time being, tourism, construction, cattle raising, fishing, ordnance clearing and some light manufacturing bring money and jobs to the island.

You can track the status of the navy's clean-up of the island at www.navfac.navy.mil/vieques.

Sights

Vieques is considerably more populated than its sleepy sister island, Culebra. Consequently, it has two towns to Culebra's one. The main settlement, Isabel Segunda (Isabella II), is on the north side where the ferry docks. It has lots of colonial architecture and makes for good urban strolling. (The views back to the mainland aren't bad either.)

Unfortunately, most people run through Isabel Segunda en route to Esperanza, on the Caribbean side. Esperanza is right on a lovely stretch of coast, with a public beach, and a *malecón* (waterfront promenade) lined with numerous alluring restaurants and guesthouses.

Originating in Isabel Segunda, Hwy 200 heads west past the airport as far as Punta Arenas on the island's western tip. To get to Esperanza, take either of two routes south over the mountains: Hwys 201/996 or Hwy 997. If you take the latter route, you can stop off at the wildlife refuge and its many beaches.

No matter where you go, you'll likely encounter the island's wild horses, who often canter down the road oblivious to the honks and demands of drivers.

IT'S ALL IN THE NAME

The name 'Vieques' is a 17th-century Spanish colonial corruption of the Taíno name *bieque* (small island). The Spaniards also called Vieques and Culebra *'las islas inútiles'* (the useless islands) because they lacked gold and silver. But over the centuries, residents and visitors who share affection for this place have come to call Vieques 'Isla Nena,' a term of endearment meaning 'Little Girl Island.'

Vieques National Wildlife Refuge

Lying within these protected confines are the best reasons to visit Vieques. This 18,000-acre **refuge** (787-741-2138; www.fws.gov/caribbean/refuges/vieques) occupies the land formerly used by the US military. The 3100-acre segment at the west end was used mainly as a storage area during the military occupation and is very quiet. The 14,700-acre eastern segment, which includes a former live firing range (still off-limits), has the island's best beaches along its southern shore.

The refuge protects vast tracts of largely pristine land containing four different ecological habitats: beaches, coastal lagoons, mangrove wetlands and forested uplands. It also includes an important marine environment of sea grasses and coral reefs. Many colorful species survive in these areas, including the endangered brown pelican and the Antillean manatee. Vieques' dwarfish

Vieques

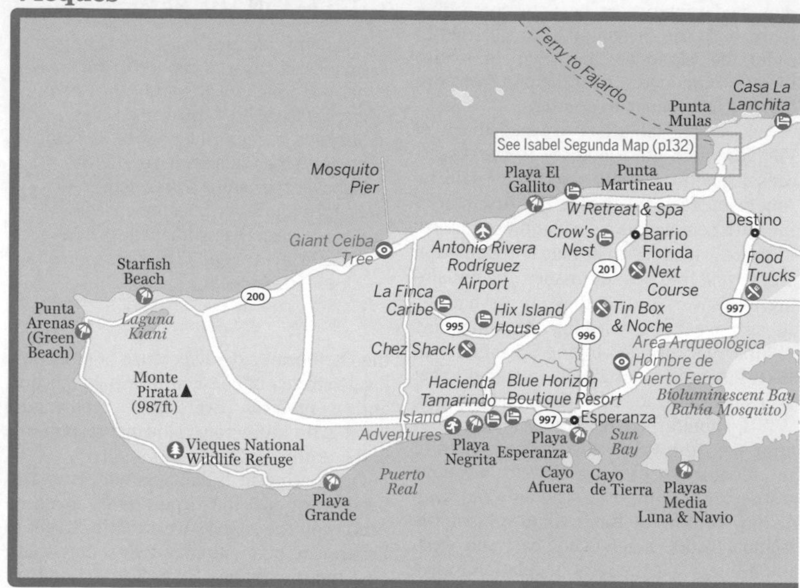

thicket-strewn forest, which includes some indigenous cacti, provides one of the best examples of dry subtropical forest in the Caribbean.

Much of the refuge's land is still officially off-limits to visitors. A potentially dangerous no-go zone is Punta Este in the far east of the island, where live ordnance is still being removed. Other restricted areas in the east include most of the north coast east of Isabel Segunda, along with the south coast east of Playa La Plata (Orchid Beach). The most easily accessible area is the ribbon of land that abuts the road leading from Hwy 997 to La Plata.

Most of the hilly western part of the refuge is open for business, and includes a lonely swath of colorful wildflowers and scores of (mostly sealed) cavernous military-style bunkers that were used to store ammunition.

Perhaps the finest **Giant Ceiba Tree** in Puerto Rico is situated on the right-hand side of the road as you head toward Punta Arenas, adjacent to the Mosquito Pier. Rumored to be 400 years old, the tree resembles a gnarly African baobab, which is probably the reason why it was venerated so much by uprooted Afro-Caribbean slaves. The ceiba is Puerto Rico's national tree.

Isabel Segunda

An intriguing coastal town dotted over low hills on Vieques' north coast, non-touristy Isabel Segunda (Isabel II) is the island's administrative center and capital. Sometimes busy, sometimes quiet – depending on ferry activity – the town is more urban than anything on Culebra (though that's not saying much). Lines of cars disgorge daily at the dock, teenagers gab in the underutilized central square, and a handful of cafes and restaurants give reasons to linger.

Though less beguiling than its southern rival Esperanza, Isabel II is no ugly duckling. Named for the enigmatic Spanish queen who reigned between 1833 and 1868, the town is the island's oldest settlement, founded in 1843. It showcases a handful of historical sights, including an 1896 lighthouse and the last Spanish fort to be built in the Americas.

Isabel Segunda hosts the bulk of the island's services, but with only 5000 residents and more wild horses than sommeliers, it's a long way from sparkling modernity.

El Faro de Punta Mulas VIEWPOINT
(off Calle F Anduce) One of Puerto Rico's 16 historic lighthouses, this pastel-shaded monu-

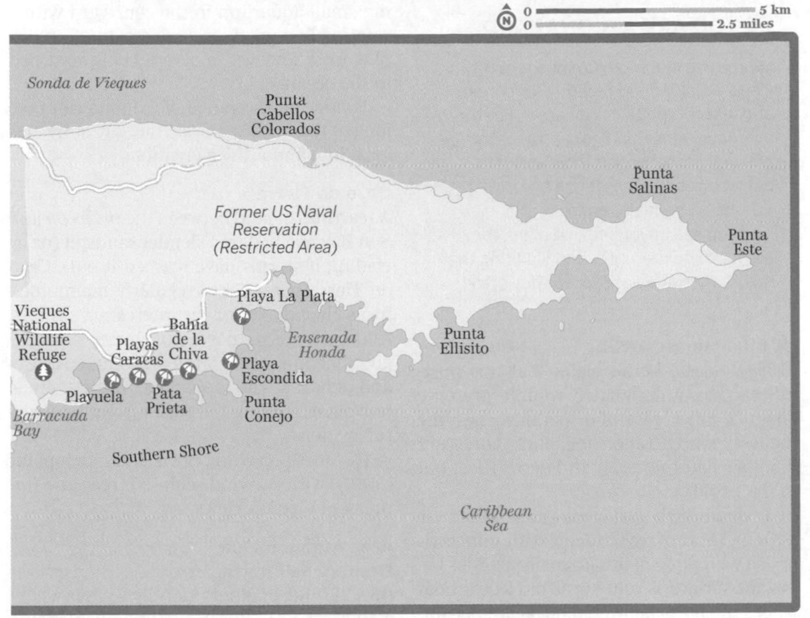

ment stands on the hilly point just north of the Isabel Segunda ferry dock. Built in 1896, it was restored in 1992 and contains a small museum that's open irregularly. Come for the vista and sunset, not the paltry exhibition.

Fortín Conde de Mirasol FORT
(787-741-1717; 471 Calle Fuerte; donations accepted; 8:30am-4:20pm Wed-Sun) This small fort, on the hill above Isabel Segunda, is the last Spanish fort constructed in the Americas (1840s). Although never completed, the fort has ramparts and a fully restored central building that houses a history and art museum. It also includes a museum that showcases the island's 4000-year-old Indian and colonial history.

Esperanza

Esperanza is the quintessential Caribbean beach town; a shabby-chic cluster of wooden shacks and colorful open-fronted restaurants that has lifted many a dampened mainland spirit. If you've been fighting your way through the traffic and suburbia of San Juan, this could be your salvation: an exotic but laid-back mélange of infectious Latin music and friendly streetside salesfolk peddling rum, reggae and bioluminescent kayaking trips.

Set on Vieques' calm southern shores, Esperanza's waters are deep, clear and well sheltered to the north, east and south by two tall, lush islands. The white concrete railings of the modern *malecón* rise quaintly above the town's narrow beach and, if you arrive at sunset, you'll be lured by the twinkling lights and ebullient music pouring from the cafes and restaurants that line the Calle Flamboyán 'Strip' facing the Caribbean.

Some 25 years ago, Esperanza was a desolate former sugar port with a population of about 1500. Its residents survived by fishing, cattle raising and subsistence farming. But then a couple of expatriate Americans in search of the *Key Largo*, Bogart-and-Bacall life discovered the town and started a bar and guesthouse called 'Bananas.' Gradually, word spread among independent travelers, and a cult following took root. Protected (rather ironically) by the presence of the US military on Vieques, Esperanza, despite a recent growth in popularity, has managed to retain much of its rustic pioneering spirit and is an evocative and fun place to visit.

YOU ARE A BIOHAZARD

Swimming in the Bioluminescent Bay is illegal and for good reason. Sunscreen and insect repellant are harmful to the dinoflagellates that light up the waters, and any immersion in the water has been banned, just as it has been in Fajardo's Laguna Grande.

If you see anyone taking a dip, they are harming the water and violating the law no matter what excuse they offer.

★Bioluminescent Bay NATURE RESERVE

(Bahía Mosquito) Locals claim that this magnificent bay, a designated wildlife preserve about 2 miles east of Esperanza, has the highest concentration of phosphorescent dinoflagellates not only in Puerto Rico, but in the world.

A trip through the lagoon – take a tour – is nothing short of psychedelic, with hundreds of fish whipping up bright-green sparkles below the surface as your kayak or electric boat passes by (no gas-powered boats are permitted – the engine pollution kills the organisms that create the phosphorescence).

You can (just!) drive east on the rough Sun Bay road (barely car-capable) and stop for a view (parking well back from the water and mangroves). However, an organized trip will give you far more opportunity to really take in the spread of phosphorescence. Guides offer a wealth of information on the phenomenon and the flora and fauna.

Reservations are essential for boat and kayak tours and rentals in high season. Trips are often cancelled if there's a full moon and clear skies.

Look for birds including pelicans, frigate and cuckoos. In the waters below, small sharks and rays are among the fish stirring up the light show.

There's another inlet to the east, Barracuda Bay, that's also filled with dinoflagellates, but tour operators don't venture out that far.

★Vieques Conservation & Historical Trust MUSEUM

(☎787-741-1850; www.vcht.org; 138 Calle Flamboyán; donations accepted; ⏲9am-5pm) Founded in 1984 to save the island's bioluminescent waters, the trust operates the tiny Museo de Esperanza, which contains intriguing exhibits on the ecological efforts of the trust, the island's natural history and its early Indian inhabitants. There's a fascinating small aquarium in the courtyard with a rotating line-up of local sea creatures on display for a few weeks before being returned to the ocean.

Pondering the range of exhibits can take longer than you'd think; the gift store has local info and artisan creations.

Cayo de Tierra ISLET

A teardrop of land between the *malecón* and Sun Bay reached by a slender sandspit (or by wading if storms have washed it out), Cayo de Tierra has a few irregularly maintained trails that make for an interesting ramble. At the northern tip is a large hyper-saline lagoon teeming with birds, including ospreys and pelicans. The most direct route there is to walk east along the beach from the Esperanza pier.

It's worth reaching the island's high point (80ft!), with its wind sculpted trees and impressive Vieques views.

Area Arqueológica Hombre de Puerto Ferro LANDMARK

(Hwy 997) Big boulders identify a grave where a 4000-year-old skeleton of an Indian known as the 'Hombre de Puerto Ferro' (usually on exhibit at the Fortín in Isabel Segunda) was exhumed.

The site is marked by a small sign on Hwy 997, east of Esperanza. About a half mile east of the entrance to Sun Bay, take the dirt road on your left (it heads inland). Drive for about two minutes on a rutted dirt road until you find the burial site.

Little is known about the skeleton, but archaeologists speculate that it is most likely the body of one of Los Arcaicos (the Archaics), Puerto Rico's earliest known inhabitants; this racial group made a sustained migration as well as seasonal pilgrimages to the Caribbean from bases in Florida.

Until the discovery of the Hombre de Puerto Ferro, many archaeologists imagined that the Arcaicos had reached Puerto Rico sometime shortly after the birth of Christ; the presence of the remains on Vieques could push that date back nearly two millennia if controversy surrounding the skeleton is resolved. Visitors can stop by the excavation site where having a healthy imagination will add interest to the boulders.

Beaches

Vieques' beaches are as legendary as Culebra's – and there are a lot more of them. The beaches in the national wildlife refuge are as good as you'll find anywhere. Elsewhere you'll find numerous strips of sand where days can easily pass into weeks.

Unfortunately many of Vieques' beaches are prone to petty theft. No matter how remote your beach, don't leave your valuables unguarded while you swim or snorkel, especially on the beach in downtown Esperanza – they'll be gone in a heartbeat.

Vieques National Wildlife Refuge

In one sense, the military occupation was a blessing in disguise, in that it has left many of the island's more remote beaches in an undeveloped and pristine state. Now protected in the national wildlife refuge, the beaches are clean, untrammeled and paradisial.

Others, encased in the former weapons-testing zones, remain closed off and are, effectively, virgin territory. Closed roads leading to contaminated areas are clearly marked as such, but if you have questions about whether an area is safe, check with the US Fish & Wildlife Service (p253).

When visiting the beaches along the **southern shore**, be aware that the main road off Hwy 997 is well-paved through the turn for Playa Caracas but then gets steadily worse as you go east. Signs make finding even secluded beaches fairly easy. Best of all, you can hop from one to another, looking for your own ideal beach, which on weekdays you may have to yourself.

Beaches on the **west end** have interesting views back to the mainland. Roads here can get muddy but are usually all car-capable.

★ Playa Caracas BEACH

(Southern Shore) Calm and clear Playa Caracas is reached on a paved road and has gazebos with picnic tables to shade bathers from the sun. Just west, **Playuela** is lesser known and has less shade, meaning that you'll find few people here and you can enjoy the view back to lovely Playa Caracas.

★ Playa La Plata BEACH

(Orchid Beach; Southern Shore) Playa La Plata (Orchid Beach) is as far east as you can go at present. This gorgeously secluded beach is on a mushroom-shaped bay, has sand like icing sugar and a calm sea that seems to shimmer in a thousand different shades of turquoise, cobalt and blue. The road here is very rough. Only a 4WD will get you close without walking.

Bahía de la Chiva BEACH

(Blue Beach; Southern Shore) Bahía de la Chiva, at the east end of the main road, is long and open, and occasionally has rough surf. There's good snorkeling here at a small island just off the coast. It's easy to find your own large patch of sand and you can get shade in the shrubs. The rough access roads here are just barely car-friendly.

If you happen upon this beach during Semana Santa (the Holy Week preceding Easter), you'll see hordes of faithful Catholics camping on the sand, where they pray and party in honor of the death and resurrection of Jesus Christ.

Playa Escondida BEACH

(Southern Shore) The deliciously deserted stretch of sand at Playa Escondida (Secret Beach) has absolutely no facilities – just jaw-dropping beauty. It's long and faces a small bay that's good for kayaking. The road here is very rough and is 4WD-only after storms.

Pata Prieta BEACH

(Southern Shore) This very tiny bay has a small patch of sand and protected waters that are excellent for snorkeling. The access road here is rough but manageable (just) by car.

Punta Arenas BEACH

(Green Beach; West End) Punta Arenas is excellent for a quiet picnic, some family-friendly snorkeling and up-close views of the big island (note the wind farm) and El Yunque across the water. To get here, pass through the rapidly vanishing former Naval

DON'T MISS

THE BEAUTIFUL INTERIOR

Yes, the coasts have beaches and nature preserves, but Vieques also has an often beautiful tropical interior of lush forests, rolling green hills, marauding horses and idiosyncratic little places worthy of a pause.

The main road through Isabel Segunda, Hwy 997, is not uncharming, but it's also rather busy by local standards. On your journeys around the island, try some of the roads less traveled such as Hwys 201, 995 and 996. Around every – often sharp – bend you'll make a new discovery and Vieques is not so big that you need to spend more than an hour or two on these forays.

Ammunitions Facility and head west for about 20 minutes through pastoral landscapes and past herds of wild horses. At the western tip of the island, the road turns to dirt and you can park in the clearings.

The strand here is not very broad and is punctuated with coral outcroppings, but there are plenty of shade trees. Snorkeling reefs extend for miles, and you can expect to have this place pretty much to yourself, except on summer weekends, when a lot of yachts out of Fajardo come here on day trips. Note, it gets very buggy here.

Starfish Beach BEACH

(West End) On the north side of Laguna Kiani is the best beach on Vieques for children, with gentle surf, crystal-clear waters and immense starfish to catch the eye lying all along the shore. It's a really good place for families to relax, and perfect for teaching youngsters the look-don't-touch approach to fragile ecosystems.

Elsewhere on Vieques

A variety of beaches ring the coast, including a great public one in the south.

★Sun Bay BEACH

(Sombé Balneario; off Hwy 997; admission $2) This long half-moon-shaped bay, less than a half mile east of Esperanza, is the island's *balneario* (public beach), with all the facilities you could hope for, including a cafe (open Wednesday through Sunday). Measuring a mile in length, Sun Bay is rarely busy. Indeed, such is its size that even with 100 people congregated in its midst it will still appear almost deserted. The beach is not always staffed, so you can often drive in for free.

Head to the east end along the car-friendly sandy tracks for shady parking places amid the palms, and few other sunbathers. The surf is gentle.

Cayo Afuera ISLET

A popular option is to journey from Playa Esperanza across to the nearby islet of Cayo Afuera, an uninhabited pinprick of land that is part of the Mosquito Bay Reserve. It's situated a few hundred yards across the bay; many intrepid locals elect to swim (not advisable unless you are a strong swimmer and are aware of the local weather conditions), while others kayak or take a boat.

There is great snorkeling here, both under the ruined pier and on the ocean side of the islet where a sunken sailboat languishes beneath the surface. Antler coral, nurse sharks and manatees have also been spotted in the vicinity.

Playas Media Luna & Navio BEACHES

If it really is isolation you're after, head east on the sandy road that runs along Sun Bay from Esperanza, and you'll enter a forest. Go left at the fork in the road. In a couple of hundred yards, you'll stumble upon Playa Media Luna, a very protected, shady beach that is excellent for kids. Beyond this on the same road is Playa Navio, where bigger waves are the domain of bodysurfers.

VIEQUES BY BIKE

Free from the mainland's legendary traffic jams and unforgiving drivers, Vieques has become a little-heralded biking center. While the main local roads are at times challenging, you can find quiet bike rides in the wildlife refuge, although bad roads mean it can be rugged and/or thrilling.

As well as renting out bikes, helmets, locks and child seats, the island's main bike outlets organize guided rides around the island. If you're up for going it alone, they can furnish you with maps, routes and insider tips. Two route suggestions:

➡ The main road from Isabel Segunda to Esperanza is Hwy 997, but head west on Hwy 200 and then south on Hwy 201 and you'll find a quieter, more pleasant alternative route. Halfway along, you can detour up Hwy 995, another lovely country road.

➡ The ultimate Vieques loop involves heading west out of Isabel Segunda on Hwy 200 all the way to Punta Arenas (the last section is unpaved). After some shore snorkeling and an idyllic picnic lunch, swing south through the old military bunkers to Playa Grande before linking up with Hwy 996 to Esperanza.

Blackbeard Sports (p131) and Vieques Adventure Company (p132) are good sources for rentals and tours.

Both of these beaches served as sets in the 1961 film version of the famous William Golding novel *The Lord of the Flies*. If you climb the rocks at the west end of Playa Navio, you'll find a path along the shore that you can follow to find petrified clams and corals dating from 50 million years ago.

Playa Grande BEACH
(Hwy 201) Playa Grande has a long, narrow strip of golden sand and wave-tossed water that drops off very quickly (not good for children or weak swimmers). If you head west on Rte 996 from Esperanza to Rte 201, you'll eventually come to a dead end where you can park and hit the sand.

Playa Negrita BEACH
(Black Sand Beach; off Hwy 201) Tired of all that powdery, blinding white sand? This beach lives up to its name with dark, sparkly sand derived from offshore volcanic rocks. It's rarely visited and has a nice line of palms along the shore. Ask locals where to turn off Hwy 201 to reach it.

Playa El Gallito BEACH
(Gringo Beach; off Hwy 200) The site of the W resort, El Gallito on the north coast has a great reef for snorkeling just 10yd offshore, but seas can be very rough here from December to March, when trade winds can blow from the northeast.

Playa Esperanza BEACH
(Calle Flamboyan, Esperanza) The advantage of slender Playa Esperanza is that it is within shouting distance of the *malecón* and Esperanza's appealing bars, restaurants and guesthouses. The downside is that it is often dirty with litter and seaweed.

Activities

All manner of activities on land and sea are on offer on Vieques. Besides Bioluminescent Bay, there are other small bays good for kayaking, especially along the southern shore of the wildlife refuge.

Snorkel sites abound and, as noted in the beach listings, many of the best are accessible from shore.

Fishing is sublime in Vieques. Imagine Florida Keys with about one-tenth of the fisherfolk and enough bonefish, tarpon and permit to stock a mini ocean. Fishing boats can also allow you access to waters off still-closed stretches of coastline in the former military zone.

Vieques is also popular for cycling.

★ Abe's Snorkeling & Bio-Bay Tours KAYAKING, SNORKELING
(☎787-741-2134; www.abessnorkeling.com; Esperanza; tours adult/child from $45/22.50) Abe's offers guided kayaking and snorkeling trips to Cayo Afuera, a few hundred yards offshore Esperanza, as well as other locations around the island. This is a great trip for beginners and families. Its Bio Bay tour is equally child-friendly, with kayaks that can accommodate families of three or four.

Blackbeard Sports DIVING, BICYCLE RENTAL
(☎787-741-1892; www.blackbeardsports.com; 101 Calle Muñoz Rivera, Isabel Segunda; 2-tank dives from $100) Blackbeard offers PADI scuba training and dive trips. You can also rent a variety of gear for reasonable rates, including snorkeling equipment, bikes, beach gear, kayaks and camping equipment. You can also arrange for adventure tours on land and sea. There's a second location within the W resort.

Fun Brothers KAYAKING
(☎787-435-9372; www.funbrothers-vieques.com; Malecon, Esperanza; kayak rental per day $35) Rents kayaks, scooters, snorkel gear, paddleboards and more. The cheery bros run a popular Bioluminescent Bay kayak tour (from $40).

Vieques Sailing SAILING
(☎787-508-7245) Captain Bill and his boat *Willo* offer a variety of sailing trips. Pick from a half-day sailing and snorkeling trip to offshore coral reefs (from $60), or an all-day sailing excursion to the south tip of the Bermuda Triangle that includes snorkeling, beach time and lunch (from $120).

Marauder Sailing Charters SAILING
(☎787-435-4858; www.viequessailing.com; Esperanza; sailing trips per person $100-250) Runs sailing excursions on a classic 34ft sloop, with two snorkel stops, a gourmet lunch prepared onboard and beverages included.

Taxi Horses HORSEBACK RIDING
(☎787-206-0122; www.taxihorses.com; Hwy 200 Km 3.8, Playa El Gallito; adult/child from $90/75) Trying to ride one of the local semi-wild horses might end your trip early, instead go for a two-hour beach jaunt on these fine steeds.

Caribbean Fly Fishing Company FISHING
(☎787-741-1337; www.caribbeanflyfishingco.com; half-day fishing trips from $375) Fish from a

Isabel Segunda

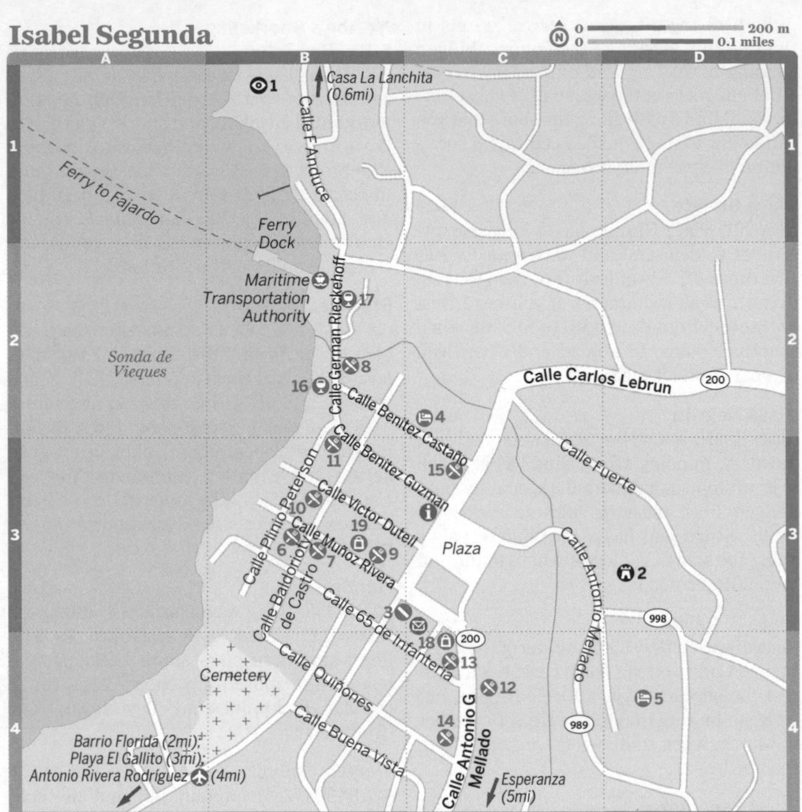

custom-designed boat or even from a stand-up paddleboard.

Tours

Bioluminescent Bay tours are the hot ticket. Many meet in Esperanza followed by a van ride over the rugged road to the glowing water. In addition to the companies listed below, Abe's Snorkeling & Bio-Bay Tours and Fun Brothers lead good Bio Bay tours.

The **Vieques Conservation & Historical Trust** (787-741-8850; www.vcht.org; Calle Flamboyán 138, Esperanza) offers occasional in-depth naturalist and cultural history tours to places including the Playa Grande sugar mill and Cayo de Tierra.

★Vieques Adventure Company ADVENTURE TOUR

(787-692-9162; www.viequesadventures.com; tours from $50) You can't miss the glowing bioluminescent waters from a clear canoe. Groups are small. It also does fly-fishing tours via kayak as well as mountain bike tours.

Island Adventures BOAT TOUR

(787-741-0720; www.biobay.com; Rte 996 Km 4.5; tours from $40) See the bioluminescent bay without paddling. Island Adventures offers 90-minute group tours in an electric boat most nights, except when there's a full moon. Schedules can change at the last minute.

Sleeping

Vieques is a rural island, expect to hear chickens, dogs, cats, cattle and horses making barnyard noises day and night. Travelers will find a range of places to stay in both of Vieques' main towns, as well as throughout the lush hills. However, there are few true beachfront properties as the wildlife refuge is off-limits to development.

Isabel Segunda

Sights

1 El Faro de Punta Mulas B1
2 Fortín Conde de Mirasol D3

Activities, Courses & Tours

3 Blackbeard Sports B3

Sleeping

4 Casa de Amistad C2
5 SeaGate Hotel D4

Eating

6 Awesome! Yogurt B3
7 Buen Provecho B3
8 Café Mamasonga B2
9 Conuco B3
10 Morales Supermercado B3
11 Panadería & Repostería Lydia B3
12 Panadería La Viequense C4
13 Roy's Coffee Lounge C4
14 Shawnaa's C4
15 Taverna C3

Drinking & Nightlife

16 Al's Mar Azul B2
17 Smoothie Stand B2

Shopping

18 Funky Beehive C4
19 Siddhia Hutchinson Gallery B3

Many places have a minimum stay during high season. Just like on Culebra, Vieques is gay-friendly. Many guesthouses and restaurants on the island are owned by lesbian or gay expats.

You can camp at **Sun Bay** (Sombé balneario; 787-741-8198; off Hwy 997; campsites $10; Wed-Sun), just east of Esperanza, which has security. If you don't require facilities or security, you can camp at Playa Media Luna or Playa Navio with a free permit from the Sun Bay office of the **Departamento de Recursos Naturales y Ambientales** (DRNA | Department of Natural Resources & Environment; 787-741-8683; off Hwy 997, Sun Bay, daily but sporadic).

If you're looking for a rental agent, try **Rainbow Realty** (787-741-4312; www.enchanted-isle.com/rainbow; 278 Calle Flamboyan) in Esperanza, which has a range of rentals, or **Vieques Fine Properties** (787-741-3298; www.viequesfineproperties.com), which has beautiful high-end homes.

Isabel Segunda

There are a few accommodations in the heart of town, easily reached on foot from the ferry. Other offerings exist just above the lighthouse on North Shore Rd, in an area called Bravos de Boston. They're an uphill trek on foot, but most places will pick you up at the dock.

★ **Casa de Amistad** GUESTHOUSE $$
(787-741-3758; www.casadeamistad.com; 27 Calle Benitez Castaño; r $75-120;) Everything a great holiday guesthouse should be. Right in the middle of town, super-friendly Casa de Amistad has nine stylish rooms for rent with air-con and private bathrooms (two economy rooms have their own bathrooms down the hall). Some have balconies to enjoy the balmy air. The ferry is a five-minute walk and there are great restaurants close by.

Everything you want has been thought of: communal areas include an honor bar, sitting room/library, kitchen, landscaped yard and swimming pool, and rooftop deck. You can also get beach gear for your outings.

Casa La Lanchita APARTMENTS $$
(787-741-8449; www.casalalanchita.com; 374 North Shore Rd, Bravos de Boston; r $125-200; P) La Lanchita turns out 12 spiffy suites with private bathroom and full kitchen on the ocean's edge. The building is a whitewashed three-story colonial beauty that resembles an old plantation house rising up over the Atlantic. Bonus features include beach gear, balconies with views, a library and a placid pool with kids' section. On clear days you can see St Thomas.

SeaGate Hotel GUESTHOUSE $$
(787-741-4661; www.seagatehotel.com; off Calle Antonio Mellado; r incl breakfast $95-200; P) Situated on a hill high above the town, the SeaGate is a hike from the ferry dock. Horses roam freely in the surrounding grounds, lush vegetation fills the garden, and views of the surrounding countryside and ocean are panoramic. Basic rooms have fridges and microwaves, for a little more you get sea views and a private balcony.

Esperanza

A row of funky small guesthouses line Calle Flamboyán, interspersed with cheery cafes. The views across to the beach and water are what holidays are for.

Lazy Hostel HOSTEL $
(787-741-5555; www.lazyhostel.com; Calle Flamboyán; dm/r from $25/65;) This somewhat dark place adjoins the boisterous

bar of the same name. It's bare-bones, but it offers a valuable budget option not far from some of the island's best beaches. Bathrooms are shared and the dorms (one female-only) have an age limit of 'about' 50.

Trade Winds Guest House GUESTHOUSE **$$**
(787-741-8666; www.tradewindsvieques.com; 107 Calle Flamboyan; r $80-120;) You'll want to blow into Trade Winds, which has a fine guesthouse to go with it's fine dining. Three of the 10 rooms in the modest guesthouse have fine bay views while the local fun is just steps away. It's not fancy, but it is good value and the deck is a winner. It's located at the far west end of the *malecón*.

Acacia Guesthouse APARTMENTS **$$**
(787-741-1059; www.acaciaguesthouse.com; 236 Calle Acacia; apt $120-160) Four airy apartments are housed in a three-story whitewashed building situated on a rise above Esperanza's beachside strip. From the 2nd- and 3rd-floor decks and rooftop patio you have spectacular views over hills and the Caribbean. Units have full kitchens and comfortable furnishings, and the friendly owners live just across the street. Cooling breezes provide comfort.

Esperanza Inn GUESTHOUSE **$$**
(787-741-2225; www.esperanzainn.com; Calle Hucar; r $100-200;) Comfortable rooms at this longtime guesthouse right near the Calle Flamboyán strip are spacious and have cable TV; you can chat with fellow travelers in the guest kitchen, at the honor bar or over coffee. Apartments with balconies and full kitchens sleep six to eight people, and a grassy backyard contains a small pool.

Villa Coral Guesthouse GUESTHOUSE **$$**
(787-741-1967; www.villacoralguesthouse.com; 485 Calle Gladiola; r $85, 2-bedroom apt $160-185;) At this six-unit Spanish-style charmer, the tranquil roof deck and pleasant bougainvillea-fringed front veranda dispel any lingering stress. Located in a quiet residential area a few minutes' walk from the action, rooms sport colorful contemporary textiles and bathroom sinks tiled like dreamy waves.

Bananas GUESTHOUSE **$$**
(787-741-8700; www.bananasguesthouse.com; 142 Calle Flamboyán; r $70-110;) This is Esperanza's original budget guesthouse-restaurant, and its seven rooms – some with air-con and/or private balconies – have an ultra-casual, cheap-and-cheerful chic atmosphere. Light sleepers should note that the house bar closes at around 1am on weekends. Rooms have no phones so there are no wake-up calls.

★ **Malecón House** INN **$$$**
(787-741-0663; www.maleconhouse.com; 105 Calle Flamboyán; r incl breakfast $160-250;) With its travertine floors, beautiful fabrics and light wood furniture, this spacious 13-room upmarket inn is a gracious choice. Looking out over the water from a quiet section of the main street, two rooms have private seaside balconies, one has a four-poster mahogany bed and all have a clean and uncluttered feel.

There's a good book library and helpful owners, plus a free poolside show in the lush garden: watching iguanas graze in the trees overhead. Enjoy baked goods in the morning on the rooftop deck. Wi-fi is limited to common areas.

El Blok BOUTIQUE HOTEL
(www.elblok.com; Calle Flamboyán) The hot news in Vieques is the 2014 opening of the landmark El Blok hotel in Esperanza. Its stunning design is sinuous and organic, with a lacy sheath over three free-flowing floors. The 22 luxurious rooms are designed to catch the breezes. Confirming the hotel's cachet: the bar/restaurant will be run by San Juan's hottest chef, Jose Enrique.

Elsewhere on Vieques

You'll find some of Puerto Rico's most interesting small and luxurious hotels dotted around the green hills and sandy coastlines of Vieques.

★ **Hacienda Tamarindo** GUESTHOUSE **$$**
(787-741-8525; www.haciendatamarindo.com; off Hwy 997; r $150-300;) Perched on a hill looking out to a fine Caribbean vista, this 17-room guesthouse has lashes of style leavened by a relaxed island vibe. Rooms are tricked out in 'Caribbean deluxe' motif, which means lots of elegant doors opening to wrought-iron balconies filled with bougainvillea. It's three-quarters of a mile west of Esperanza.

Large and delicious breakfasts are served under the namesake tamarind tree.

La Finca Caribe GUESTHOUSE **$$**
(787-741-0495; www.lafinca.com; Hwy 995, Km 2.2; r $100-140, houses from $145;) Finca Caribe is Vieques personified. Sitting high up on a mountain ridge seemingly a

million miles from anywhere (but only 3 miles from either coast), it's the kind of rustic haven stressed-out city slickers probably dream about. Its back-to-nature hippy-chic facilities – outdoor communal showers, shared kitchen and hempish decor – attract a devoted following.

Amenities include swaying hammocks, croquet, a salt-water pool, yoga, self-pick tropical fruits and more. It's located towards the west end of the island.

Crow's Nest HOTEL $$

(787-741-0033; www.crowsnestvieques.com; off Hwy 201; r from $155;) Nestled in the hills of Barrio Florida southwest of Isabel Segunda, the good-value Crow's Nest enjoys a rural airy setting with pink bougainvillea contrasting with its turquoise swimming pool. More functional than luxurious, the rooms here have lounging area and kitchenette.

★ Blue Horizon Boutique Resort BOUTIQUE HOTEL $$$

(787-741-3318; www.bluehorizonboutiqueresort.com; off Hwy 997; r $200-400;) Even though it's one of the island's few beachside resorts, the Blue Horizon still shines over the competition. With only 10 rooms harbored in separate bungalows wedged onto a stunning oceanside bluff west of Esperanza, the sense of elegance here – both natural and created – is breathtaking.

The luxury continues inside the excellent all-day restaurant and cozy communal lounge, which overlook an Italianate infinity pool fit for a Roman emperor.

Hix Island House APARTMENTS $$$

(787-741-2302; www.hixislandhouse.com; Hwy 995; apt $150-350;) Ecohip, new-age-minimalist, environmental-austere: designed by cutting-edge Canadian architect John Hix, this unique guesthouse consists of four industrial concrete blocks that arise out of the surrounding trees like huge granite boulders (or the island's abandoned navy bunkers). The 13 luxurious rooms open up to give you the feeling that you are actually living in the forest.

Amenities include fully stocked kitchens so you can rustle up your (healthy) breakfast as well as sweeping views and wi-fi in the lobby. The hotel is in the hills north of Esperanza.

W Retreat & Spa RESORT $$$

(787-741-4100; www.wvieques.com; Hwy 200 Km 3.2; r from $400;) Trendy and uberchic, Vieques' only large chain resort makes a bold statement with bursts of color and texture from striped rugs and furry pillows. All 156 rooms (not all oceanside) have open bathrooms with both showers and washing-board-styled tubs. It's located near the airport on the north shore.

Other hotel features include a full spa, a top-end organic restaurant, a beachside fire pit and two beaches (where the surf can be quite rough). In keeping with its corporate luxe pretensions, there's a hefty resort fee ($60 per day), which includes tennis, kayaks and snorkeling.

Eating & Drinking

Good food in great variety and price ranges can be found across the island. For the better places, be sure to reserve in high season.

Isabel Segunda

The island's main city also has the best selection of Puerto Rican cuisine at local-friendly prices.

★ Café Mamasonga CAFE $

(787-741-0103; 566 Calle German Rieckehoff; mains $6-15; 8am-8pm) At this bi-level tropical eatery a few steps from the ferry terminal, you can sit outside to gaze at the water and watch cars bump over the grate out front or venture to the roof for aerie views and a full bar.

Start your day with an American-style breakfast or come by later to fill up on seafood stew, fettuccini alfredo or crab cakes with mango *habañera* sauce. If dining in the tree-shaded upstairs, you may become an object of interest to some very large iguanas on the prowl.

Roy's Coffee Lounge CAFE $

(355 Calle Antonio G Mellado; mains $7-10; 8am-2pm;) At this artsy little haven on the main drag, you'll usually find a clutch of folks checking their email while sipping espresso drinks on the back garden patio. In addition to simple breakfasts, there's a full bar and grill food such as burgers and quesadillas; the big brownies and sticky cinnamon rolls are always a treat.

Panadería & Repostería Lydia BAKERY $

(787-741-8679; cnr Calles Benitez Guzman & Plinio Peterson; snacks $1-5; 4am-noon) With a 4am opening call, this veritable hole-in-the-wall bakery-cum-coffee bar is ideal for insomniacs, late-night party animals and ferry

DON'T MISS

CHEZ SHACK

What do '60s psychedelic band the Mamas and Papas and Vieques' most bohemian restaurant have in common? They both owe at least a part of their success to expat impresario and restaurateur Hugh Duffy. In the 1960s Duffy owned a restaurant called 'Love Shack' on the nearby island of St Thomas, where he hosted folk-music nights with a quartet of spaced-out hippies called the New Journeymen. It was an important first break.

But while the Journeymen changed their name to the Mamas and Papas and headed off to LA for some California Dreamin', Duffy transplanted himself just 13 miles to the west, where he opened up a string of wildly popular and wildly funky joints, including the original Bananas.

Today Duffy concentrates on **Chez Shack** (787-741-2175; Hwy 995 Km 1.8; mains $18-30; 6-10pm Mon-Fri), a quirky Caribbean hangout that rivals the luminous Bio Bay as *the* place to go on Vieques. Two decades on, both Duffy (now in his 10th decade) and the shack rustle up fine dinners that have become almost as celebrated as his erstwhile protégées. Monday is the big night, with live reggae and an outdoor grill featuring chicken, fish or steak. Reserve in advance.

Meanwhile, Duffy's son Mikie maintains family tradition with his local restaurants that include Duffy's, Tin Box and Noche.

workers on the crack-of-dawn shift. Stop by for caffeine, pastries, sandwiches and sweet bread, and vie with the locals for one of the two plastic tables that furnish the sidewalk.

Awesome! Yogurt SWEETS $

(787-517-1061; 107 Calle Muñoz Rivera; yogurt from $2; noon-9pm Tue-Fri, 4-10pm Sat & Sun) This casual cart is the place to get a cooling sweet treat to slip down your throat. The frozen yogurt is superb and the flavors pure tropical joy.

Panadería La Viequense BAKERY $

(787-741-8213; 352 Calle Antonio G Mellado; mains $3-10; 6am-4pm) If it's breakfast you're after, this is the place for early eggs or hangover-obscuring coffee. If you miss the 11am cutoff, you can feast instead on decent baked goods, tortillas and sandwiches. Service is no-nonsense and fast, the decor clean and modern, and the clientele local with a smattering of in-the-know tourists. Don't miss its photo gallery of early-20th-century Vieques.

Shawnaa's PUERTO RICAN $

(741-1434; 327 Calle Antonio G Mellado; mains $6-8; 10:30am-2pm Mon-Fri) Bring a big appetite to Shawnaa's buffet. It's full of superb *comida criolla* (traditional Puerto Rican cuisine) dishes that you can take out onto the patio or consume in the shaded interior. Don't miss the *mofungo*.

★ **Taverna** ITALIAN $$

(787-438-1100; cnr Calles Carlos Lebrun & Benitez Castaño; mains $8-20; 6-10pm) As understated as a delicate wine, this simple joint has a brick-lined dining room and makes superb thin-crust pizza. Try the pesto version or opt for seafood or any of many other variations. The wedge salad is a winner, while the pasta options include fettuccine Alfredo. Come for the great food, not the decor.

Conuco PUERTO RICAN $$

(787-741-2500; 110 Calle Muñoz Rivera; mains $12-20; 11am-2pm Wed-Fri, 6-10pm Wed-Sat) Enjoy a modern take on Puerto Rican cuisine at this cottage-styled place named for Taíno garden plots. Standouts include the *bacalaítos* (cod fritters), mahimahi with passion fruit and coconut sauce and the *pionono* (sweet yellow plantains stuffed with ground-beef stew). Romantic and refined, this is the north side's best spot for a dinner date. Try the guava cocktails.

Buen Provecho DELI

(123 Calle Muñoz Rivera; 8am-6pm Tue-Sat) Has a gourmet selection of island-scarce produce, artisan breads, Angus beef steaks and many varieties of cheese.

Morales Supermercado SUPERMARKET

(15 Calle Baldorioty de Castro; 8am-8pm) This basic grocery store has the widest (albeit) narrow selection of goods on the island. A second location is 1 mile west of town on Hwy 200 towards the airport.

Smoothie Stand JUICE BAR

(Calle German Rieckehoff; drinks from $3; 10am-4pm but hours vary) All the tropics in a glass – that's what you'll enjoy with the fabulous smoothies from this small cart right in front of the ferry terminal. Choose from an array of fruits and then enjoy the thick and eminently satisfying results.

★Al's Mar Azul BAR
(☎787-741-3400; Calle Plinio Peterson; ⏰11am-late) Al's shelters the ghosts of Charles Bukowski and Ernest Hemingway and is the nexus of local gossip. Locals come to play pool, and expats come to drink…and drink. Visitors teeter somewhere in between. Karaoke crooners fill the place on Saturday nights. Those in the know head to the narrow deck out back for sunset and stars. Food is greasy and filling.

Esperanza

Right on the Caribbean, Calle Flamboyán (aka the *malecón*) is lined with tourist-friendly cafes and bars that will provide liquid balm to anyone looking for langor. Fortunately, it's very low-key – you're about 1000 light years from Cancún here. However, a little glitter is in the offing as celebrity chef Jose Enrique of San Juan will be operating the bar and restaurant at the hip new El Blok hotel at the strip's east end.

Most places have unapologetically cliched views over the tourquoise water to Cayo de Tierra, various dawdling sailboats and beyond.

On Saturday, stop by the small **farmers market** (148 Calle Flamboyán; ⏰11am-4pm Sat) at the Vieques Conservation & Historical Trust for excellent local produce, baked goods, honey and hot sauce.

Belly Button's CARIBBEAN $
(Calle Flamboyán; mains $5-15; ⏰8am-3pm daily, 5-10pm Wed & Fri-Sun; 📶) Consisting of a small collection of alfresco tables located outside a kitchen on the *malecón,* this expat-run breakfast phenomenon conjures up enough food to keep you going until 6pm. Dinners are fresh and locally sourced; the Sunday BBQ is a tasty hoot.

Mornings, order a mug of gourmet coffee, season your eggs with locally made and sweat-inducing Komodo Dragon hot sauce, and make plans for a day of breathtaking action – or indolence.

Duffy's CAFE $
(☎787-741-7000; Calle Flamboyán; mains $10-13; ⏰11am-10pm; 📶) At this convivial bar and cafe opening out onto Esperanza's main strip, the laid-back street atmosphere infiltrates the shady interior where expats and locals mingle over a variety of bottled microbrews paired with wraps, fish tacos and burgers. Enjoy a *parcharita* – a concoction of passion fruit and tequila with a sweet and salty rim.

Bananas CARIBBEAN $
(Calle Flamboyán; mains $9-15; ⏰noon-late) Always popular for a drink, ultra-casual Bananas weighs in with excellent salads, sandwiches and seafood, as well as inexpensive daily specials. Its upstairs bar has sweeping water views, which you can just imagine as the lights grow dim and the hour grows late.

Trade Winds CARIBBEAN $$
(☎787-741-8666; Calle Flamboyán; mains $6-30; ⏰7:30am-2pm Thu-Sun, 5:30-9:30pm daily) Unpretentious dining at its finest. Sit back in a wide chair on the breezy verandah and enjoy scrumptious scrambled eggs or other breakfast delights. Lunch has a range of fresh salads, sandwiches and seafood. Island-spiced mains are the thing at night. Start with a sunset drink on the gorgeous veranda.

Orquideas TAPAS $$
(www.orquideasvqs.com; 61 Orquideas; dishes $6-15; ⏰6-10pm Nov-Apr; 🍃) Just off the *malecón*, this open-air restaurant takes the concept to new heights as there's just a hint of curtains in the large open windows and the outdoor tables barely have a swath of canvas overhead. Food is sourced locally and there is a creative and changing menu of small plates, with many veggie options.

★El Quenepo SEAFOOD $$$
(☎787-741-1215; 148 Calle Flamboyán; mains $20-32; ⏰5:30-10pm Mon-Sat) Upscale El Quenepo has a lovely interior and an equally delectable menu. The food is catch-of-the-day fresh – a family of seven brothers supplies the seafood – and the decor is stylish. Specialties include whole Caribbean lobsters, *mofongo* (mashed plantains) made with breadfruit grown in the backyard and a lovely *churrasco* (charcoal-broiled Argentinean steak). Be sure to reserve.

La Tienda Verde SUPERMARKET
(Green Store; Calle Robles; ⏰8am-8pm) This market has only a modest selection of groceries, but it does have parking and is often used as a meeting place for tours of the Bioluminescent Bay.

Colmado Lydia SUPERMARKET
(Calle Almendro; ⏰8am-6pm) Near the baseball field in the center of town, this small grocery store may have what you can't find at the town's other grocery.

DON'T MISS

THE ISLAND'S BEST FOOD TRUCKS

The second-best reason to turn off Hwy 997, the buzzing road linking Isabel Segunda and Esperanza, are two food trucks that are the finest on the island (the best reason is the amazing beaches along the southern shore of the Vieques National Wildlife Refuge). In fact, these two trucks straddle the entrance (which sometimes goes by its old name 'Garcia Gate') to the refuge and can provide you with the picnic of your dreams.

Foremost is **Sol Food** (Hwy 997; mains $5-7; 11am-3pm Sat & Sun), which sells succulent *carnitas* soft tacos that will have you making cooing noises between bites (don't miss the corn with lime butter). Nearby, **Kiosko La Taina** (Hwy 997; mains $6-8; 11am-3pm Mon-Fri) has a killer fresh-fish sandwich and empanadas that will have you saying 'more!'

Lazy Jack's Pub & Pizza BAR

(Calle Flamboyán; noon-1am Sun-Thu, to 2:30am Fri & Sat) The hardest-core of the *malecón* bars, music jams here most nights of the week. Depending on the day, you can play at an open jam, embarrass yourself over karaoke, kick back with a thin-crust pizza while grooving to a reggae band, or shake it at the Saturday-night dance party.

Bawdy expats add character, and if you drink your travel budget, the adjoining hostel is cheap.

Drinking Shacks BARS

(Calle Flamboyán; hours vary) A line of humble joints featuring a lot of bamboo architecture line the ocean side of the *malecón*. The beers are cheap and the chatter cheerful.

Elsewhere on Vieques

Tin Box FUSION $$

(787-741-7700; off Hwy 996; mains $8-20; 9am-2pm Sun, 5-9pm daily) The local Duffy family knows how to have fun and, more importantly, it knows how its patrons want to have fun. There's an eclectic collection of comfort foods here such as ribs, burgers, tacos and more. Sunday brunch is the best bet. It's sibling, Noche, is across the grassy parking lot where wild horses graze.

★ **Carambola** CARIBBEAN $$$

(787-741-3318; off Hwy 997, Blue Horizon Boutique Resort; dinner mains $24-30; 7am-10pm) Located at the lovely Blue Horizon Boutique Resort, this restaurant offers up superb cooking throughout the day. Why not start with a great breakfast with the sounds of the waves nearby? Or have dinner in a gazebo (reserve ahead), choosing from creative regional fare – watch for the island's best *mofungo* (no mean feat). It's a mile west of Esperanza.

Next Course FUSION $$$

(787-741-1028; Hwy 201; mains $22-40; 5:30-10pm Fri-Wed;) Cocooned away on Hwy 201 in the hills north of Esperanza and serenaded by a throaty chorus of frogs, this upscale place offers 'cuisine inspired by travel.' Influences come from Thai, Mexican and Persian kitchens, with an emphasis on fresh local food (some of its fruit is grown on-site). After dark, orient yourself by its tiki torches and strings of patio lights.

Noche FUSION $$$

(787-741-770; Hwy 996; mains $12-30; 5-10pm) The upscale cousin of casual dining fave Tin Box across the grassy parking lot, this is a more refined and, dare we say, romantic spot. In fact, the color theme is pink. Sophisticated fare sourced locally (often from the kitchen garden) is paired with good wines. It's a short drive north into the hills from Esperanza.

Shopping

Siddhia Hutchinson Gallery ART

(www.siddhiahutchinsongallery.com; Calles Muñoz Rivera, Isabel Segunda; 10am-4pm Mon-Sat, 11am-3pm Sun) The gallery of artist and designer Siddhia Hutchinson exhibits her first-class paintings of colorful tropical scenes and the pottery, jewelry and sculpture of other local artists.

Funky Beehive ARTS & CRAFTS

(787-741-3192; Calle Antonio G Mellado, Isabel Segunda; 10am-5pm Mon-Sat) A creative little shop that mixes souvenirs with attitude and artisan goods. A fun stop.

Gallery Galleon ART

(787-741-3078; Hwy 201; 11am-5pm Tue-Sat) Displays the works of some of the region's best artists in a lovely setting near the beaches west of Esperanza.

Information

While some actual street addresses exist on Vieques, citizens and businesses rarely use them.

DANGERS & ANNOYANCES

Vieques has a petty crime problem. Car theft happens often, especially at isolated beaches in the wildlife refuges. Belongings left on the beach vanish quickly. Leave nothing in your car and bring as little as possible to the beach so you can worry about sun exposure rather than thievery.

INTERNET ACCESS

Vieques Conservation & Historical Trust (Calle Flamboyán, Esperanza; per 30min $5; ⏲11am-4pm) Half a dozen computer terminals with a printer.

MEDIA

A good website with info for Vieques is www.enchanted-isle.com.

Vieques Events (www.viequesevents.net) A downloadable monthly bilingual magazine with comprehensive listings and good features.

MEDICAL SERVICES

Hospital Susan Centeno (☎787-741-0392; Rte 997 Km 0.4; ⏲clinic 7am-4pm Mon-Fri, emergency 24hr) Just south of Isabel Segunda on Hwy 997.

Farmacia San Antonio (☎787-741-8397; Calle Benítez Guzman, Isabel Segunda; ⏲8am-6pm Mon-Fri, 9am-noon & 1:30-6pm Sat) For basic supplies and over-the-counter remedies.

MONEY

Isabel Segunda has numerous ATMs as do Esperanza's two grocery stores.

POST

Post Office (☎787-741-3891; Calle Muñoz Rivera 97, Isabel Segunda; ⏲8:30am-4:30pm Mon-Fri, 8am-noon Sat) Across from the Banco Popular, this is the island's only post office.

Getting There & Away

AIR

Vieques gets frequent air service from San Juan ($65 to $100 one way), Ceiba ($30 to $45) and, handily for island-hoppers, Culebra ($65 to $90). Airline options include Air Flamenco (p123), **Air Sunshine** (☎787-741-7900, 800-327-8900; www.airsunshine.com), Cape Air (p123) and Vieques Air Link (p123).

Antonio Rivera Rodríguez Airport (VQS; Hwy 200, Km 2.6) has pretensions of grandeur with it's impractical two-level design, but it does have a great cafe outside, with cheap, fresh sandwiches and good rum punch.

Públicos greet most flights and will take you anywhere you want to go on the island.

FERRY

By far the cheapest way to Vieques from the mainland, the public ferries from Fajardo (p108) suffer from a bad reputation given by lofty tourists who consider a casino bus public transportation.

In reality it's simple: get to the ferry terminal at least an hour early and buy your ticket (there are no reservations). Facilities are simple but serviceable. Schedules vary by day but there are usually at least three round trips. Check times locally or at tourist info websites.

Maritime Transportation Authority (ATM; ☎787-863-0705, 800-981-2005; Ferry Dock, Calle German Rieckehoff, Isabel Segunda; one-way fare $2; ⏲office open before sailings) Fast ferries take 75 minutes between Isabel Segunda and Fajardo; the frequent cargo boats take a leisurely two to three hours.

Getting Around

BICYCLE

Vieques can be good for cycling (p130); Hwy 997 across the island from Isabel Segunda to Esperanza is less than 6 miles in length and has a few hills. However, traffic on the island's narrow roads can be a problem for casual riders. The best places are the quiet roads in the wildlife refuge, although these can be rugged in places.

CAR & SCOOTER

Cars are highly useful for exploring Vieques, as the island is large and most of the best beaches are off the main routes. Expect to pay about $50 to $70 a day for a small car or jeep. The latter is useful if you want to get to the outer beaches on the southern shore. There's no need for large and expensive air-conditioned SUVs.

Fun Brothers (☎787-435-9372; www.funbrothers-vieques.com; Hwy 200, Esperanza; scooters per day $55) Scooters are a fun way to explore the island; rentals include helmets.

Island Car Rentals (☎787-741-1666; www.islandcarrentalpr.com) Rents jeeps and minivans.

Maritza's Car Rental (☎787-741-0078; www.maritzascarrental.com) Everything from small cars to overly large SUVs.

PUBLIC TRANSPORT

Públicos usually greet both ferries and airplanes, and will take you where you need to go, just don't be in a hurry to get there. The trip between Isabel Segunda and Esperanza costs $5, with *públicos* running regularly.

TAXI

A fare of $10 to $20 should get you anywhere on the island.

741 Taxi (☎787-741-8294; www.741taxi.com)

Alba Melendez (☎787-206-0456)

Carlos & Denisse (☎787-447-8697)

Edna Robles (☎787-630-4673)

Ponce & South Coast

POP 512,000

Includes ➡

Best Places to Eat

➡ Moon's Bar & Tapas (p165)

➡ La Casa de Los Pastelillos (p155)

➡ Restaurante La Guardarraya (p159)

➡ Alexandra (p161)

➡ Café Café (p149)

Best Places to Stay

➡ Mary Lee's by the Sea (p160)

➡ Copamarina Beach Resort (p160)

➡ Hotel Meliá (p148)

Why Go?

The Caribbean-facing south coast offers the opportunity to unplug, escape the cruise-ship crowds and take a DIY journey into Puerto Rico's tempestuous, piratical past.

The proud southern capital of Ponce – the so-called Perla de Sur (Pearl of the South) – stands in elegant disrepair, where haute eateries neighbor slouching colonial facades. Along coastal Hwys 2 and 3, crumbling sugar-mill chimneys stand beside their graying industrial replacements: chemical and pharmaceutical factories. But for all these dichotomies, unpolished charm abounds in the towns, and the tatty beaches get increasingly magical as you progress west through mazes of mangroves, dry tropical forest and, finally, the surreal glow of the Bahía de Fosforescente.

When to Go

With some of the most consistent weather in the world, the dry, sunny climate is enticing, though June through August can be blisteringly hot.

With school children on holidays over summer, Puerto Rican families fill the sun-washed plazas, wander through colonial buildings and enjoy alfresco dining at the ubiquitous seafood shacks.

Although the arid, breezy atmosphere doesn't change much in winter, the typically languid pace slows to a crawl between September and May, picking up only for local festivals during the extended Christmas holiday.

History

The rolling foothills and broad coastal plains of the south coast were home to a number of indigenous tribes when colonized by Spaniards, who raised cattle and horses here for the colonial expeditions across Latin America during the 16th century. In 1630 they built the hamlet that would eventually become Ponce on a port between the mountains and the coast.

For more than a century, goods and materials flowed through the harbors. Ostensibly the port of Ponce was open only to Spanish vessels trading directly with Spain, but the watchful eyes of the island governor were far away in San Juan, and free trade flourished, bringing with it goods, currencies, and people from across the New World and Africa.

When slave revolts erupted in the neighboring French-held island of Saint-Domingue in the 1790s and in South America between 1810 and 1822, many wealthy refugees fled to the south coast of Puerto Rico, buying land to grow coffee and sugarcane. Soon they imported former slaves from Caribbean colonies to meet the ever-increasing American appetite for sugar, coffee and rum. Production and profits from agriculture skyrocketed throughout the 19th century, when sugar barons built cities with elegant town squares, neoclassical architecture and imported French fountains.

The Spanish American War ended the freebooting days, bringing with it military occupation, uniformly enforced trade laws and economic freefall. Hurricanes devastated the coffee industry, sugar prices fell, and the US government decided to develop San Juan, not Ponce, as a strategic port. When the Depression hit in the 1930s, the region went into an economic hibernation. These days the south limps along littered with contradictions between the past and the future.

Territorial Parks & Reserves

The jewel in the stash of territorial parks and reserves in this region is the Bosque Estatal de Guánica (p161), a 10,000-acre subtropical dry forest and a Unesco Biosphere Reserve. Wildlife enthusiasts can notch up some one-of-a-kind sightings.

In the east the Reserva Nacional de Investigación Estuarina de Bahía de Jobos (p155) is a mangrove-fringed coastal wilderness. Still less visited is the upland forest of Bosque Estatal de Susúa (p159), inland from Yauco.

ℹ Getting There & Around

Ponce has an airport serving a few US cities direct. The main transport artery in and out of the region is Hwy 52 from San Juan. Things get slower as you head west.

PONCE

POP 160,000

Ponce es ponce (Ponce is Ponce), runs a simple yet telling Puerto Rican saying: the explanation given as to why the nation's haughty second city does things, well, uniquely – and, as is the wont of second cities worldwide, in defiance of the capital. Native son and author Abelardo Díaz Alfaro went a step further, famously calling Ponce a *baluarte irreductible de puertorriqueñidad* – 'a bastion of the irreducible essence of Puerto Rico'. Strolling around the sparkling fountains in the central square and narrow streets of the city's historic center evokes the stately spirit of Puerto Rico's past. Unfortunately, the neighborhoods that surround the square bear witness to some woeful characteristics of Puerto Rico's present: irreducible snarls of congested traffic, economic stagnation and cookie-cutter urban sprawl.

But stick central amidst the outstanding colonial architecture and the city's dozen or so museums, or 3 miles south at the seashore-hugging, restaurant-lined boardwalk of La Guancha Paseo Tablado, and it's only Ponce's elegant, time-lost side that you need experience. Decent restaurants await, too, if you've tired of the otherwise prevalent pork and paper-plate dining culture.

History

History is better preserved in and around Ponce than almost anywhere else in Puerto Rico – both the colonial past (found downtown) and the indigenous past (just outside at the island's largest and most educational archaeological site, the Centro Ceremonial Indígena de Tibes).

The earliest European settlement saw numerous scuffles between Spanish Conquistador Ponce de León (from whom the town gets both its name and one of its nicknames, 'City of Lions') and the Taíno tribes, but the region was claimed for the Spanish Crown in 1511. The city was established around 1630, when the Spaniards built the first incarnation of the current cathedral and named it for the patron saint of Mexico, the Virgen de Guadalupe.

Ponce grew fat off the rewards of smugglers in the late 1600s. By the mid-1700s Ponce's bourgeois society wanted at least a patina of respectability and poured resources into legitimate enterprises such as tobacco, coffee and rum. Sugar, too, became an important business, and entire plains (the same denuded ones you see today) were shorn of greenery and replaced with silky, lucrative sugarcane. The added wealth and polyglot mixture of Spanish, Taíno, French and West Indian peoples helped establish Ponce as the island's earliest artistic, musical and literary center. Working-class areas pulsated to the rhythm of boisterous strains of *bomba y plena,* two distinct yet often associated types of folk music; the parlors of the bourgeoisie resonated to *danza* (a more elegant ballroom dance).

That golden age ended in 1898 when Spain rejected America's demand to peacefully observe Cuban independence. This instigated the Spanish-American War, which included an American invasion of Puerto Rico, that landed in Guánica. Under subsequent American rule, Puerto Rico's economy was drastically transformed and Ponce's sugar fields were lucrative for industrialized investors. In 1899, however, a pair of hurricanes devastated the sugar fields and Ponce's industry never fully recovered.

Decline began, and Ponce became a hotbed of civic unrest. It boiled over during the Ponce Massacre of 1937, which politically alienated Ponce from the rest of the island. Ponce was already on its knees by the time the Americans' Operation Bootstrap, an ambitious island-wide industrialization project, dealt the region a near-fatal blow by favoring the development of ports on the north coast.

Having limped along through the latter half of the 20th century through textile and cement production, tourism has recently helped turn much of the area's fortunes around, along with rum and pharmaceutical production.

Sights

Should you ever get lost in Ponce, just look to the skies for a sign from God: the town's two infallible landmarks are the towering steeples of the Catedral Nuestra Señora de Guadalupe, which sits regally at the center of the lovely Plaza Las Delicias, and an enormous concrete-and-glass cross, El Vigía, which overlooks the town to the north.

As you navigate your way through the outskirts of Ponce, its first impression, characterized by traffic jams and mini malls, is uninspiring. But the soul of Ponce is its idyllic Spanish colonial plaza and the surrounding grid of streets replete with picturesque historic buildings.

★Museo de Arte de Ponce ART GALLERY
(MAP; ☎787-848-0505; www.museoarteponce.org; 2325 Av Las Américas; adult/senior & student $6/3; ⏲10am-6pm Wed-Mon) *Brush Strokes In Flight,* a bold primary-colored totem by American pop artist Roy Lichtenstein, announces the smartly remodeled MAP, where an expertly presented collection ranks among the best in the Caribbean. It is itself worth the trip from San Juan. A $30-million renovation celebrated the museum's 50th anniversary and the smart curation – some 850 paintings, 800 sculptures and 500 prints presented in provocative historical and thematic juxtapositions – represents five centuries of Western art.

The greatest-hits collection of Puerto Rican painters is stirring (look for the wall-sized *Ponce* by Rafael Ríos Rey at the rear of the museum). The building's blanched edifice, winged central stair and hexagonal galleries were designed by architect Edward Durell Stone, who created Washington, DC's Kennedy Center. The exceptional pre-Raphaelite and Italian baroque collections are offset by impressive installations and special exhibits (which occasionally cost a small extra fee).

A complete tour of the museum takes about three hours, but if you only have time for a quick peek, spend some time sitting in awe of Edward Burne-Jones's ghostly, half-finished *The Sleep of Arthur in Avalon* (look for the unfinished, blank eyes of the attending queens) and Lord Leighton's erotic *Flaming June*, the museum's sensual showpiece. Set across from the Universidad Católica, the MAP is about 10 blocks to the south of Plaza Las Delicias.

Plaza Las Delicias SQUARE
Within this elegant square you'll discover the heart of Ponce and two of the city's landmark buildings, Parque de Bombas and Catedral Nuestra Señora de Guadalupe. The smell of *panaderías* (bakeries) follows churchgoers across the square each morning, children squeal around the majestic fountain under the midday heat, and lovers stroll under its lights at night. The **Fuente de los Leones** (Fountain of Lions), a photogenic fountain rescued from the 1939 World's Fair in New York, is the square's most captivating attraction.

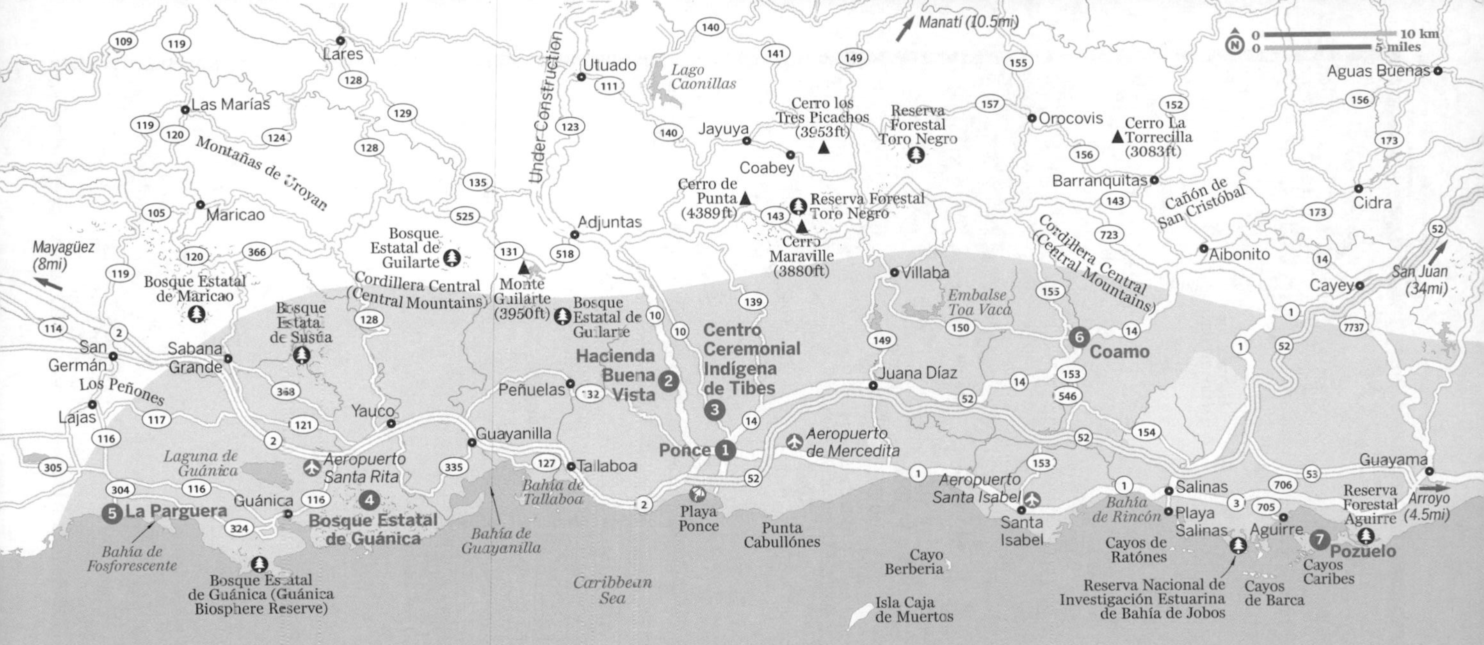

Ponce & South Coast Highlights

1. Fall in love with *Flaming June* at the **Museo de Arte de Ponce** (p142).
2. Stroll through an immaculately restored coffee plantation at **Hacienda Buena Vista** (p153).
3. Connect with the mysterious Taíno past at the **Centro Ceremonial Indígena de Tibes** (p152), the island's largest archaeological site.
4. Hike or mountain bike the dusty birding trails at **Bosque Estatal de Guánica** (p161).
5. Stagger down the crooked streets of **La Parguera** (p162) after snorkeling its cays.
6. Soak at the **Baños de Coamo** (p157), once thought to be the fountain of youth.
7. Sway on a hammock while lunching on golden, octopus-stuffed pastries at **La Casa de Los Pastelillos** (p155) in Pozuelo.

Ponce

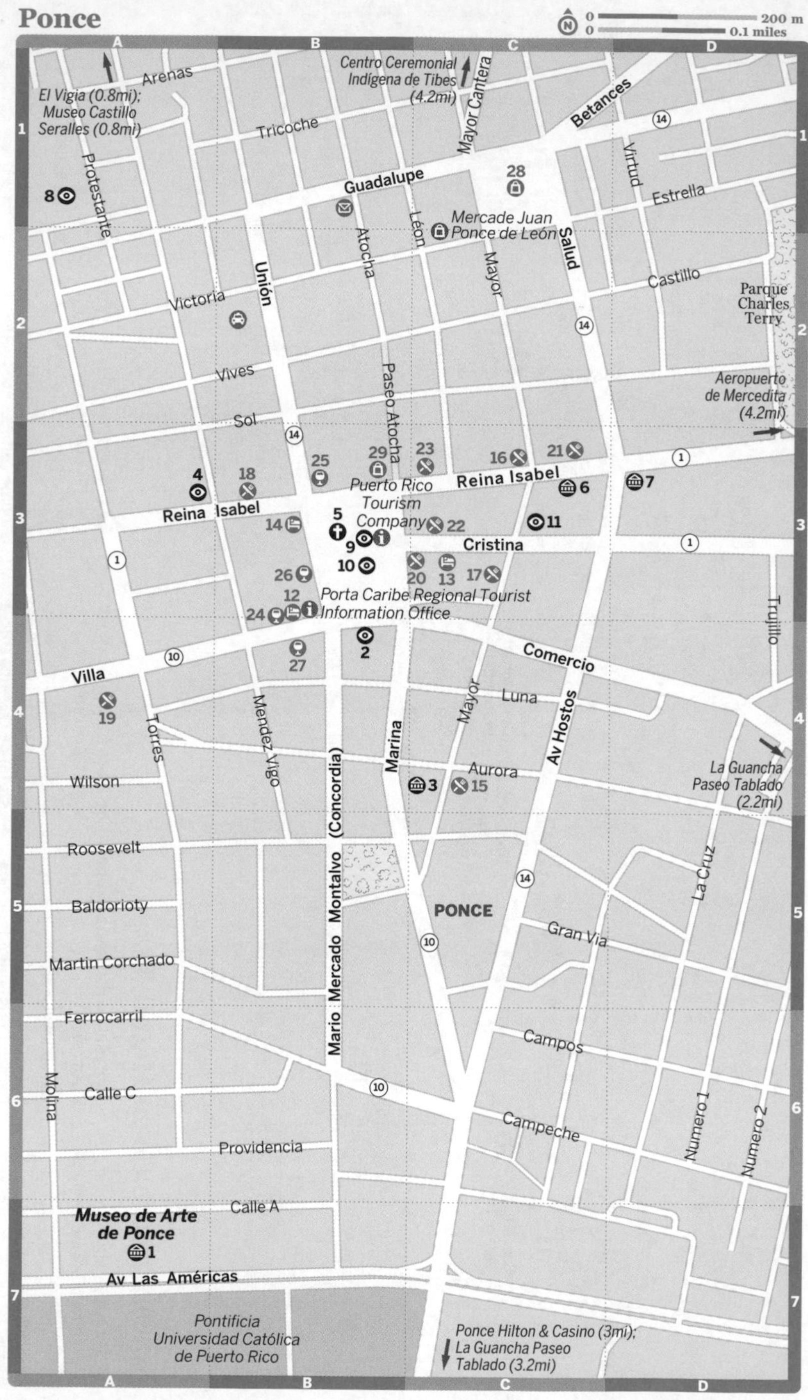

0 200 m
0 0.1 miles
Centro Ceremonial Indígena de Tibes (4.2mi)
El Vigia (0.8mi); Museo Castillo Seralles (0.8mi)
Arenas
Tricoche
Mayor Cantera
Betances
Protestante
Guadalupe
Virtud
Estrella
Mercade Juan Ponce de León
Atocha
León
Salud
Mayor
Unión
Castillo
Parque Charles Terry
Victoria
Vives
Paseo Atocha
Aeropuerto de Mercedita (4.2mi)
Sol
Puerto Rico Tourism Company
Reina Isabel
Cristina
Porta Caribe Regional Tourist Information Office
Trujillo
Villa
Comercio
Luna
Mendez Vigo
Torres
Marina
Av Hostos
Aurora
Wilson
La Guancha Paseo Tablado (2.2mi)
Mario Mercado Montalvo (Concordia)
La Cruz
Roosevelt
Baldorioty
PONCE
Gran Via
Martin Corchado
Ferrocarril
Campos
Molina
Calle C
Campeche
Numero 1
Numero 2
Providencia
Calle A
Museo de Arte de Ponce
Av Las Américas
Pontificia Universidad Católica de Puerto Rico
Ponce Hilton & Casino (3mi); La Guancha Paseo Tablado (3.2mi)

Ponce

Even as the commercial banks and the fast-food joints encroach around the edges, reminders of the city's prideful history dominate the plaza's attractions. Watch out for marble statues of local *danza* icon Juan Morel Campos and poet/politician Luis Muñoz Marín, Puerto Rico's first governor, in amidst more artsy ones of lions (the city's symbol, which doesn't take too long to realize).

Catedral Nuestra Señora de Guadalupe CATHEDRAL
(Our Lady of Guadalupe Cathedral; 6am-1pm Mon-Fri, 6am-noon & 3-8pm Sat & Sun) The twin bell towers of this cathedral cast an impression of piety over the plaza, even as young punks gather to show off skate tricks on its steps. It was built in 1931, in the place where colonists erected their first chapel in the 1660s, which (along with subsequent structures) succumbed to earthquakes and fires. Its stained-glass windows and interior are picturesque. There are several services daily.

Parque de Bombas NOTABLE BUILDING
(787-840-1045; 9am-5pm) FREE *Ponceños* (people from Ponce) claim that the eye-popping Parque de Bombas is Puerto Rico's most frequently photographed building, which is not too hard to believe as you stroll around the black-and-red-striped, Arabian-style edifice and make countless unwitting cameos in family photo albums. Since 1990 the landmark has been a tourist information center, where pleasant, bilingual staff will sell you tickets for a trolley and direct you to local attractions.

Originally constructed in 1882 as an agricultural exhibition hall, the space later housed the city's volunteer firefighters, who are commemorated in a small, tidy exhibit on the open 2nd floor.

Casa Alcaldía NOTABLE BUILDING
(Town Hall; 787-284-4141; 8am-5pm Mon-Fri) FREE Facing the south side of Plaza Las Delicias, Ponce's city hall was built in the 1840s. The last public hanging on the island happened in its courtyard, where current galleries were formerly cells. Its balcony has hosted speeches by four US presidents – Teddy Roosevelt, Herbert Hoover, Franklin Roosevelt and George HW Bush. The waggish head of Carnaval (p147), El Rey Momo, also makes pronouncements from here.

Museo de la Música Puertorriqueña MUSEUM
(787-848-7016; www.icp.gobierno.pr; cnr Reina Isabel & Salud; admission $1; 8.30am-4:30pm Tue-Sun) After the MAP, this spacious pink villa designed by Juan Bertoli Calderoni, father of Puerto Rico's neoclassical style, offers Ponce's best museum experience. A guided tour showcases the development of Puerto Rico's sound, allowing hands-on demonstrations of indigenous instruments. The collection of Taíno, African and Spanish instruments – especially the handcrafted four-string

PLAN YOUR TRIP

- Book a tour in advance at the Hacienda Buena Vista (p153).
- Call ahead to nature reserve offices to check trail conditions, as well as seasonal variations in offerings.
- Look at the www.seepuertorico.com website for information on visiting one of the south's famous festivals.

guitar-like *cuatros* and three-string *trios* – and careful explanation of Puerto Rican musical traditions are highlights. The museum also hosts a three-week seminar on drum building in July, and holds concerts in its courtyard.

Casa Wiechers-Villaronga HISTORICAL HOME
(cnr Reina Isabel & Mendez Vigo; 8:30am-4:30pm Wed-Sun) FREE Perhaps the most grand of Ponce's historic homes, this mansion was designed by Paris-educated *ponceño* architect Alfredo Wiechers. The carefully preserved Victorian details – such as the multidirectional pipeworks of the ancient shower and the hand-carved bedroom furniture – speak to the grand lifestyle of its former residents. Tours begin by request (better in Spanish, though possible in English). A twisting iron staircase ascends to the neoclassical rooftop gazebo for a bird's-eye perspective of the neighborhood.

Teatro La Perla NOTABLE BUILDING
(Pearl Theater; 787-843-4322; cnr Mayor & Cristina; lobby 8am-4:30pm Mon-Fri) FREE The restored 1000-seat Teatro La Perla was designed by Juan Bertoli Calderoni, the father of Puerto Rico's neoclassical style, and completed in the 1860s. It took 20 years to rebuild following an earthquake in 1918, but has since played a crucial role in the city's performing arts world, underscored by the nearby Instituto de Musica Juan Morel Campos, a music conservatory. It's an important performance center during festivals.

La Guancha Paseo Tablado BOARDWALK
Commonly known as 'La Guancha,' this rebuilt public boardwalk is 3.5 miles south of the city center near the relatively lonely Ponce Hilton. Refurbished in the mid-1990s, it's a haven for picnicking families and strolling couples. Its chief points of interest include a concert pavilion, a well-kept public beach and a humble observation tower. It's also the launch point for ferries to Isla Caja de Muertos (p148).

There's a handful of open-air bars and food kiosks, and a couple of fine-dining restaurants too. The place picks up with a breezy, festive atmosphere on the weekends.

Museo de la Historia de Ponce MUSEUM
(787-848-0505; 51-53 Reina Isabel; 8:30am-5pm Wed-Mon) FREE This history museum is extensive for a city of fewer than 200,000 people – evidence of Ponce's reverence for history. Located in the 1911 Casa Salazar, on the same block as the Teatro La Perla, the museum has 10 galleries displaying centuries of the city's history in ecology, economy, education, architecture, medicine, politics and daily life. A refreshingly Ponce-centric perspective on the development of Puerto Rican culture, the building itself is an architectural treasure that blends typical *ponceño criollo* detailing with Moorish and neoclassical elements.

El Vigía SCENIC OUTLOOK
(787-259-3816; 17 El Vigía; admission adult/child & senior $5.50/2.75; 9am-5:30pm Tue-Sun) It doesn't really compare with the hilltop cross in Rio de Janeiro, but the 100ft reinforced-concrete Cruceta El Vigía looking over Ponce is one of the city's more reliable points of orientation. During the 19th century the site was used by lookouts for the Spanish Crown, watching for signs of smuggling along the coast. Today, it shares grounds with the Museo Castillo Serrallés and a scrubby Japanese garden, but still offers an expansive view.

The $4 elevator ride to the top is optional; the view is probably better in the open air at the base, without the hazy obstruction of worn Plexiglas windows. Combined tickets with Museo Castillo Serrallés cost $12.50 ($5.50 for children).

Museo Castillo Serrallés MUSEUM
(Serrallés Castle Museum; 787-259-1770; www.castilloserralles.org; 17 El Vigía; adult/child & senior $8.50/4.25; 9am-5pm Tue-Sun) On the same property as the mammoth El Vigía, Museo Castillo Serrallés was the home of Ponce's rum dynasty, the Serrallés family. Docents lead bilingual walking tours through the lovely Moorish-style castle. When the somewhat exhausting hour-plus tour ends, you can order snacks and drinks at the cafe. Relax on the terrace under the red-tiled roof and enjoy a view of the city below and the quiet burble of the garden's fountains. Combo ticket options with El Vigía cost $12.50 ($5.50 for children).

Panteón Nacional Román Baldorio de Castro CEMETERY
(Frontispicio 15; ⏱8am-4:30pm Tue-Sun) FREE A fraction north of city center, in the shadow of Cruceta El Vigía, the city cemetery is a grand, mid-19th-century conglomeration of (unusually) both Catholic and Protestant tombs. The most famous incumbents are Juan Morel Campos, considered the finest exponent of the Puerto Rican *danza*, and the famous tenor Antonio Paoli.

Activities

La Guancha provides the waterside activity in Ponce, which consists of lounging in a bar, or leaving from there to check out Isla Caja de Muertos (p148) or, er, the modest beach just to the east where you can take a dip. You're doing Puerto Rico clockwise from San Juan, right? Those coming from the west's paradisical beaches will be disappointed.

In not-so-distant memory, a government boat carried swarms of people to the now-quiet beaches on Isla Caja de Muertos, but since the ferry was recommissioned to do the Fajardo–Vieques–Culebra run, the wilds have reclaimed the place. Today Island Ventures Water Excursions (p148) sends boats by reservation and offers group rides around the bay. Packages start at $25 for the return trip, and snorkeling gear can be provided for a little more. In high season look for the company's kiosk on La Guancha. Ask about dives to the Wall off the island's shore: they're magnificent with the right conditions.

Festivals & Events

Carnaval CARNIVAL
Ponce's Carnaval is a time of serious partying. Events kick off on the Wednesday before Ash Wednesday with a masked ball, followed by parades, a formal *danza* competition and the coronation of the Carnaval queen and child queen. The party ends with the ceremonial burial of a sardine (the traditional significance of which has been washed away by booze) and the onset of Lent. Each parade and all of the critical activities take place in Plaza Las Delicias in front of Casa Alcaldía. If you're planning to visit Ponce during Carnaval, make your hotel and transportation reservations at least three months in advance.

Semana de la Danza DANCE, MUSIC
Held in mid-May, this 'Week of Dance' has parades and dance events. The (humorously stuffy) Ponce Municipal Band performs in Plaza Las Delicias as well-groomed couples offer postured examples of the form of dance that accompanies 'Puerto Rico's classical music.' It's in the right place; Ponce was home to the high society and composers who made *danza* a distinctive art form at the turn of the 19th century.

Fiesta de Bomba y Plena MUSIC, DANCE
Drummers and *pleneros* (*plena* singers) arrive from all over the island to participate in this festival of *bomba y plena,* the singing, dancing and drumming style that evolved in Ponce among citizens of African descent who came en masse to work the cane fields. Held in August, with major events at the Rafael 'Caro' Maldonado baseball park.

THE PONCE MASSACRE

In the turbulent 1930s, Puerto Rico's troubled economy ignited revolutionary fervor across the island, but it was in Ponce, with its large student population and reputation for culture and sophistication, that a march for independence went terribly wrong.

The marchers had a parade permit for the demonstration, which was scheduled for the Plaza Las Delicias on Palm Sunday, March 21, 1937, but at the last minute the governor of Puerto Rico withdrew permission.

Angered, the nationalists defied the prohibition and marched anyway. Slightly fewer than 100 young men and women faced off with 150 armed police near Plaza Las Delicias. When the nationalists started singing '*La Borinqueña*' – the national anthem – a shot was fired and the entire plaza erupted in gunfire. Seventeen marchers and two police officers died. Not one civilian carried a gun, and most of the 17 marchers died from shots in the back. While the US government chose not to investigate, the American Civil Liberties Union did, and confirmed that the catastrophe warranted its popular name, 'Masacre de Ponce' (Ponce Massacre). Now a small museum, appropriately called the **Casa de la Masacre de Ponce** (cnr Marina & Aurora; admission $1; ⏱9am-4pm Wed-Sun), is housed in the building that held the offices of the Nationalist Party in 1937, keeping the memory alive.

WORTH A TRIP

ISLA CAJA DE MUERTOS

The name Isla Caja de Muertos – which translates to Coffin Island – could have been taken straight from the script of a swashbuckling adventure flick, but the big lizards here run a lazy show, trotting across dusty, cacti-lined trails and over the mangrove marsh. The morbid moniker is thought to have come from an 18th-century French author's observation that the island's silhouette looked like a casket.

There's not much to see here, but the opportunity to take a day trip from Ponce's congestion can be pleasant. It hosts some of the best snorkeling around and plenty of tranquil, if somewhat rocky, stretches of beach. Hikers wander past endangered plants and reptiles that thrive in the climate, as well as a regal 19th-century lighthouse that is occasionally used as a station for biologists. If you need more action, try a low-impact trip to scuba dive at the 40ft Wall, just offshore. The only way to make the 3-mile trip is through **Island Ventures Water Excursions** (787-834-8546; www.islandventurepr.com; round-trip $25; reservations necessary). Leave a message if there's no answer.

Los Reyes Magos de Juana Díaz RELIGIOUS FESTIVAL
Puerto Ricans arrive from all over to celebrate epiphany (January 6) in the small town of Juana Díaz, east of Ponce. There's a large procession, and people come dressed as one of the shepherds, or the three wise men who arrived late to see baby Jesus. There's a museum in town dedicated to the celebrations should you miss the actual event.

Sleeping

It's best to make your bed at one of the hotels surrounding Plaza Las Delicias, rather than one of the lackluster resorts outside the city center. The sterility of the Hilton and Holiday Inn might comfort the most cautious gringo, but local flavor is nil and prices soar for accommodations that are only questionably more comfortable. Beware: accommodation is costly here as there are, incredibly, no good options besides hotels.

Hotel Bélgica HOTEL **$**
(787-844-3255; www.hotelbelgica.com; 122 Villa; r $80-90;) Just off the southwest corner of Plaza Las Delicias, this traveler-favorite has a creaking colonial ambience, with 15ft ceilings and wrought-iron balconies. The hallways are a bit of a maze and dimly lit, but the place is charming, with delightful old furniture in many of the 20 rooms.

Rooms near the front allow you to stare out over the plaza from private balconies, but be prepared for noise on weekend nights. The wi-fi is spotty.

★**Hotel Meliá** HOTEL **$$**
(800-44-UTELL, 787-842-0260; www.hotelmeliapr.com; 75 Cristina, cnr Plaza Las Delicias; r incl continental breakfast $100-140;) Just east of the plaza, this independent, historic hotel might remind you of favorite three-star hotels in Spain and Portugal. The grand lobby is more plush than the rooms, but everything is clean and functional, and the building is monumental. What gives the Meliá the edge over its only other contender (the Ramada) is the recent refurbishment.

Continental breakfast is served on a sunny rooftop deck and the beautifully renovated pool, as well as the adjacent Mocha Coffee Shop & Bistro, are an attractive bonus. The 80 rooms are spread over four floors. Beds are big and bathrooms fully modernized. Check out the pictures on the wall for a look at Ponce in its prime - and the manager/co-owner will happily tell you the hotel's history.

Ramada Ponce HOTEL **$$**
(787-813-5050; www.ramadaponce.com; cnr Reina Isabel & Unión; s/d $109/129;) Standing grandly over a corner of the plaza, this building's colonial facade emerged from the scaffolding after years of preservationist dispute under the Ramada banner. Though it doesn't escape the bland feel of a chain, the historic building, location and clutch of amenities keeps it among the top options in town.

Of the two connected buildings, the best rooms face the square, with black-and-white-tiled floors and balconies; those in the back are clean but have little by way of atmosphere. The courtyard pool is tiny, but with the Lola restaurant (patronized by the city elite), hip design elements and an open-air bar, it's well worth a stop… for a drink, if you don't dig staying.

Howard Johnson HOTEL **$$**
(787-841-1000; www.hjdpr.com; Hwy 1 Km 123.5; s/d from $107/125;) Not much per-

sonality, but abundant in chain hotel comforts including wi-fi, an exercise room, game room and a terrific pool. A pristinely clean option very close to the airport.

Quality Inn El Tuque HOTEL $$
(☎ 787-290-2000; www.eltuque.com; Rte 2 Km 220, 3330 Ponce By Pass; r $89-119; P ❄ @ ≋) This tucked-away option with tons of space and a big pool for families adjoins a speedway and (summer) water park. In winter, your only company may be the pet turtles.

Ponce Hilton & Casino RESORT $$$
(☎ 787-259-7676; www.hilton.com; 1150 Av Caribe; r $100-280; P ❄ @ ≋) This 153-room Hilton stands within a gated area 6km south of town, near La Guancha boardwalk on the Caribbean. It's the most deluxe option in Ponce, with well-manicured grounds, on-site golf, a nightclub, enticing pools, restaurants and a casino. It suffers from a lack of local flavor; sun-pink golfers are wont to gripe about their last round and the quality of the buffet. Even so, it's the only hotel in Ponce with ocean views (for which you pay higher-end prices; cheapest rooms have pool views only).

Eating

A crop of creative chefs working in Ponce's city center are masterminding an unheralded, but varied, eating scene. For something cheap on-the-go, there are carts around Plaza Las Delicias where a hot dog with the works ($1.50) comes saddled with mustard, ketchup, onions, peppers, processed cheese, meaty chili and crispy shoestring potato chips. If you're up for a drive to the port area, *ponceños* will point you to a couple of upscale seafood places such as Pito's Seafood (p150), where white tablecloths, water goblets and waiters in vests are the order of the day. La Guancha is a good bet for open-air cafes and restaurants, which take on a festive atmosphere at sunset. Also, if you're in town on the third Friday of the month check out Ponce Fest, a culinary festival right on Plaza Las Delicias.

Sabor y Rumba CARIBBEAN $
(Reina Isabel 66; mains $9; ⏰10am-8pm) An otherwise run-down courtyard has been spruced up to provide one of Ponce's best-value restaurants. There are outside tables and generous portions of *mofongo* or *cerdo relleno* (stuffed pork). Read the electric scoreboard to find out what's cooking. There's also music classes, an espresso machine and graffiti.

King's Cream ICE-CREAM PARLOR $
(9223 Marina; cones $1-3; ⏰8am-12am) On warm evenings lines stretch down the sidewalk of this institution, located across from Parque de Bombas. Smooth-blended tropical licks overflowing with fruit are just over $1. There's another location a few blocks north of the plaza on Vives, between Unión and Marina.

Mocha Coffee Bar & Bistro CAFE $
(75 Cristina, cnr Plaza Las Delicias; snacks & lunches $3.50-10; ⏰7:30am-3:30pm) In Hotel Meliá, the newly opened art deco-decorated Mocha is the place to lounge poolside with a good frappe or brunch. Forget about the city clamor and indulge in its glamor. Chefs are showy with their presentation.

Cesar's Comida Criolla CARIBBEAN $
(near cnr Mayor & Cristina; dishes $2-14; ⏰lunch) The ultimate hole-in-the-wall joint for *comida criolla* (traditional Puerto Rican cuisine), this spot doles out oodles of pork, chicken and seafood (most served with rice and beans).

Chef's Creations FUSION $
(☎ 787-848-8384; 100 Reina Isabel; mains $6-12; ⏰lunch) The menu changes daily and leans toward international fusions of local fare, such as the delicious *paella con tostones*.

Edan Deli & Juice Bar VEGETARIAN, DELI $
(☎ 787-259-7074; cnr Villa & Torres; mains $2-7; ⏰lunch; 🌱) Within an organic grocery store, this deli offers veggie and vegan salads and sandwiches, as well as fresh juices. Healthy(ish) and cheap.

Café Tompy CARIBBEAN $
(cnr Reina Isabel & Mayor; mains $4-15; ⏰lunch & dinner) This no-frills spot has piled-high plates of assorted *comida criolla* for around $7.

★ Café Café CAFE $$
(www.cafecafeponce.com; cnr Mayor & Aurora; mains $10-18; ⏰11am-3pm Mon-Sat) 🍃 For the best coffee in Ponce and an excellent breakfast, start at this art-filled, bilingual cafe, where the clientele ranges from businessmen to skiving students. The coffee beans couldn't be fresher – they're roasted next door – and the egg scrambles are excellent. For lunch, try the *mofongo* (mashed plantains) '*a caballo,*' stuffed with corned beef and topped with a fried egg.

La Casa de Las Tias CARIBBEAN, FUSION $$
(☎787-840-4149; 46 Reina Isabel; mains $15-30; ⏰6-10pm Wed-Sat, noon-10pm Sun) In a cozy historical home, 'the aunts' kitchen is overseen by Wilda Rodriquez, one of Ponce's most creative and least-pretentious chefs. The unhurried service and atmosphere may lack a little polish, but whimsical specials (such as the fantastic midweek 'Deli & Burger Queens Night') balance traditional and fusion Puerto Rican dishes, such as the seafood stew and rib eye glazed with a guava reduction.

Okui Sushi SUSHI $$
(Cristina; sushi from $5, mains $10-20; ⏰4-10pm Tue-Wed, 4-11:30pm Thu-Fri, 2-11:30pm Sat) Coolly minimalist decor and black leather upholstery welcome you to Okui, which, despite seeming more like a small bar-club, delivers creative sushi options with a Puerto Rican spin (using plantain, for example).

Pito's Seafood SEAFOOD $$
(☎787-841-4977; Hwy 2 s/n, Sector Las Cucharas; mains $15-35) The fish dishes can't be bettered (they practically swim up to your plate) and Pito's also has one of the city's best wine cellars, making a trip out here worth the inconvenience. To get here, head west on Hwy 2 from the center for about 4 miles and you'll see it on the left after Laguna de las Salinas.

Drinking & Entertainment

Ponce nightlife is at the mercy of college crowds who pack little restaurant-cum-bars around the plaza to slam drinks and grind to reggaetón. Hot spots change often and last as long as some celebrity marriages. The scene at La Guancha is spirited; arrive too early, however, and it will be more family-focused. The best casino is at the Hilton, where there's a semblance of out-of-town nightlife that's about as Puerto Rican as Minnesota.

Kenepa's at Café Plaza BAR
(3 Unión; ⏰5pm-late) A slightly classy crowd gravitate to the sidewalk tables here, especially when the place hosts live music or DJs. When it gets late, the crowd migrates into the narrow quarters to dance.

Equilibrium BAR
(cnr Unión & Reina Isabel; ⏰9pm-late Thu-Sat) This town-center bar is a go-to option come weekends and is actually quite stylish; live DJs and various activities such as body painting, for example (around when the stylishness disintegrates). Dress smart or you might not make it inside.

Bembele Art Lounge LIVE MUSIC
(124 Villa; ⏰8pm-late Wed-Sat) For a more ambient evening, this gallery/hip bar offers experimental live performances from jazz to comedy.

La Taberna BAR
(119 Villa; ⏰4pm-late Thu-Sat) This delightfully seedy little place is right off the main square. A young crowd knocks back innumerable $1.75 Medallas, watches sports on a vintage TV and blasts music at ear-splitting levels.

Shopping

Paseo Atocha, just north of the plaza, is closed to traffic, serving as a busy pedestrian marketplace with food stands, cheap goods and street stands of suspiciously affordable designer wear.

Utopia SOUVENIRS
(☎787-845-8742; 78 Reina Isabel; ⏰7:30am-6pm Mon-Sat, from 11am Sun) Selling colorful *vejigantes* (Puerto Rican masks), *santos* (small carved figurines representing saints) and trinkets, Utopia is the nicest souvenir shop on the square. The bonus? The little bar up front serves decent coffee and will sell six-packs of beer to go: hooray!

Nueva Plaza del Mercado MARKET
(cnr Mayor & Estrella; ⏰6am-6pm Mon-Sat) Winding through crowds of shoppers on Paseo Atocha will lead you to the city's most exciting indoor market, four blocks north of the plaza. The selection of produce – freshly hacked off the vine – is marvelous. Just up the block, the slightly more crowded Mercade Juan Ponce de León has stalls hocking pan-religious voodoo charms and salsa tunes on vintage vinyl.

Information

INTERNET ACCESS

Many hotels have internet service for guests and the Plaza Las Delicias has wireless connectivity, a terrific convenience for travelers with a laptop.

Mariana Suarez de Longo Biblioteca (☎787-812-3004; cnr Marginal & Av Santiago de los Caballeros; ⏰9am-9pm Mon-Thu, 8am-6:30pm Fri, plus 10:30am-6pm Sat Jun) Three-quarters of a mile east of the plaza, this bright facility is part of Archivo Municipal de Ponce and contains an impressive $114-million digital-computing and education center. Puerto Rico Telephone footed the bill and did it right, with 50 new computers, laptop stations and wireless access.

MEDICAL SERVICES

Emergency (☎911)

Hospital Manuel Comunitario Dr Pila (☎787-848-5600; Av Las Américas, east of Av Hostos) 24-hour emergency room. Recommended.

Walgreens (☎787-812-5978; Rte 2 Km 225; ⏲24hr) The only pharmacy that can accommodate a late-night need for aloe.

MONEY

Banks line the perimeter of Plaza Las Delicias so finding a cash machine is no problem. Most of the banks are open from 9am to 4pm weekdays, plus Saturday mornings.

POST

Post Office (93 Atocha; ⏲8am-4pm Mon-Fri, 7am-noon Sat) Four blocks north of Plaza Las Delicias, this is the most central of the city's four post offices.

TOURIST INFORMATION

Puerto Rico Tourism Company (PRTC; ☎787-284-4141; www.visitponce.com; Parque de Bombas, Plaza Las Delicias; ⏲9am-5:30pm) You can't miss the big red-and-black structure in the middle of the park, where friendly, English-speaking members of the tourist office are ready with brochures, answers and suggestions.

Porta Caribe Regional Tourist Information Office (☎787-290-2911; Villa 122; ⏲8am-4:30pm Mon-Fri) This insightful office has information on the entire south coast region.

Getting There & Away

AIR

Four miles east of the town center off Hwy 1 on Hwy 5506, the Aeropuerto de Mercedita (Mercedita Airport) looks dressed for a party, but is still waiting for the guests to arrive. **JetBlue** (☎787-651-0787, 800-538-2853; www.jetblue.com) services Ponce from New York and Orlando, but there are currently no domestic flights.

CAR

Cruising to Ponce from San Juan is easy on the smoothly paved A-52 (Hwy 52), a partially toll-controlled highway called the Autopista Luis A Ferré. You'll know you've arrived when you pass through the mountains and drive through the towering letters by the roadside reading 'P-O-N-C-E.' The city center is about 3 miles from the south shore and 2 miles from the foothills of the Central Mountains to the north.

You don't have to drive through the center of town to get through Ponce – two bypass roads circle the city to the south. The inner road is Av Emelio Fagot/Av Las Américas (Hwy 163). The faster route is the outer road, Hwy 2, called the 'Ponce By Pass' which hosts the town's biggest mall and loads of American chain stores. To reach the port, take the freshly paved route just east of the square, Rte 12. It becomes a divided highway south of the Ponce By Pass. Follow the signs to La Guancha.

PÚBLICO

There's a nice, new *público* (shared taxi) terminal three blocks north of the plaza, with connections to all major towns. There are plenty of long-haul vans headed to Río Piedras in San Juan (about $20) and Mayagüez (about $10).

Getting Around

It may be possible to fly to Ponce directly, but navigating the area in depth requires a car as *público* transport can be time-consuming and maddeningly erratic.

TO/FROM THE AIRPORT

Taxis tend to gravitate to the Plaza Las Delicias. Expect to pay $15 for the 4-mile taxi trip to or from the airport.

CAR

Driving in central Ponce is a nightmare, and parking is little less of a headache. Central blocks charge for parking. Rental-car agencies are mostly located at the airport, including the following:

Avis (☎787-842-6154)

Hertz (☎787-843-1685)

TAXI

Hailing a cab at the Plaza Las Delicias is much quicker than calling for one. It's $1 to drop the flag and about $1.50 per mile, but meters are used infrequently, so ask about the price before you get an unpleasant surprise. **Coop Taxi del Sur** (☎787-848-8248) and **Ponce Taxi** (☎787-842-3370) are reliable.

TROLLEY

The city tourist office operates a trolley and a 'chu chu' train for visitors ($2), which are informative and entertaining. They supposedly both follow the same route, but the two-hour trolley ride makes stops, allowing passengers to get out and snap photos, while the train makes no stops, completing its circuit in about an hour. Of the two options, the trolley is recommended. There are supposed to be regular trips between 9am and 4:30pm, but drivers seem to change the schedule and routes on a whim. They all leave and return to the stop in front of the Casa Armstrong-Poventud, on the west side of Plaza Las Delicias. Theoretically leaving at 10am, a long-distance trolley also takes in the more distant sights of El Vigía and Centro Ceremonial Indígena de Tibes. Inquire at the tourist desk in Parque de Bombas before planning your day around a ride.

AROUND PONCE

The city around Ponce's historic center sprawls with the unsightly blandness of an American suburb, but navigate the roads into the rural areas a bit further out, and you'll find a number of sights worthy of spending an afternoon.

Sights

Centro Ceremonial Indígena de Tibes
ARCHAEOLOGICAL SITE

(Tibes Indian Ceremonial Center; ☎787-840-2255; http://ponce.inter.edu/tibes/tibes.html; Hwy 503 Km 2.2; adult/senior & child $3/2; ⏰8am-4:30pm Tue-Sun, closed major holidays) The ancient ceremonial center of Tibes is one of the Caribbean's most important archaeological sites, due largely to evidence found here of pre-Taíno civilisations, such as the Igneris. Though Tibes lacks the dramatic scale of sites such as Mexico's Uxmal, it is a quiet spot, ideal for imagining the people that once dwelt here (brought alive by enthusiastic staff and an excellent interpretation center) and is a highly recommended way to spend an afternoon. All visits include a one-hour tour, including a movie and a visit to the museum.

Puerto Rico owes the discovery of its most significant archaeological site to tropical storm Eloíse, which hit Ponce in 1975 and caused the Río Portugués to flood. When floodwater retreated from local farmland, it exposed the ruins of Tibes. The government expropriated more than 30 surrounding acres: only five of which have been fully excavated.

Current excavations have uncovered seven *bateyes* (Taíno ball courts), two ceremonial plazas, burial grounds, 200 skeletons, pottery, tools and charms. As you tour the manicured setting – with its *bateyes* and plaza rimmed by bordering stones (some with petroglyphs) – guides explain that the first settlers on this spot were Igneris, who probably arrived at Tibes from Venezuela about 300 BC.

As part of their cassava-based diet, the Igneris became fine potters, making vessels for serving and storing food. Many of these bell-shaped vessels have been found buried with food, charms and seashells in more than

THE PRE-TAÍNO PEOPLE

Much like the Inca in Peru, the Taíno in Puerto Rico rather dominate discussions about the region's pre-Columbian peoples. But the Taíno actually appeared late in the day (around AD 1200), and there is evidence of civilizations existing here for over four millennia before this date.

The island's first inhabitants are known as the pre-Ceramic people, a possibly nomadic population of hunter-gatherers whose presence in Puerto Rico can be traced to 3000 BC. Traces of their culture have been unearthed at sites such as Barceloneta, on the north coast.

By about 300 BC the Igneris were establishing themselves, heralding originally from the Orinoco region of Venezuela, and they were significantly more advanced than their predecessors on the island. One important characteristic of the Igneris was their pottery, elaborate for this era, sometimes combining carvings and multiple colours. Other hallmarks of Taíno culture, such as *cemíes* (deities and the structures built to house them) and the devices used to inhale hallucinogens facilitating communication with the supernatural world, have also been discovered at Igneris sites. The Igneris were also horticulturalists, successfully farming vegetables such as the manioc, which became a staple for subsequent pre-Columbian peoples here.

Whilst the Igneris culture appears to have been a basis of sorts for later cultures in Puerto Rico, many ways in which the Igneris were developing has led historians to refer to these people as the pre-Taíno after approximately AD 600. There were two main groups: the Elenoid, who occupied the east, and the Ostionoid, who lived in the west. Intriguingly, the Centro Ceremonial Indígena de Tibes occupies a site directly in between where these two groups lived. Excavated religious items dating from the pre-Taíno period are larger and more complex than those of the Igneris period, indicative of a more advanced society. The discovery of large *bateyes* (ball courts) for ceremonial purposes within pre-Taíno communities suggests this culture popularized the ball games the Taíno became famous for.

By the time the Taíno came along in AD 1200, many cornerstones of their culture, ranging from ceramics to living spaces to food, were already in place.

100 Igneri graves. Individuals were buried in the fetal position in the belief that they were bound back to the 'Earthmother' for rebirth. Many of the Igneri graves have been discovered near or under the *bateyes* and walkways constructed by the pre-Taíno, who probably came to the site around the first millennium.

In a tidy museum you can see some of the weapons, *cemíes* (deities) and tools that they used. You will also see reconstructed pre-Taíno *bohíos* (huts), set amid a natural botanical garden with fruit trees, including the popular *guanábana* (soursop).

Make reservations prior to visiting, particularly if you want an English-speaking tour.

Tibes lies about 2 miles north of Ponce at Km 2.2 on Hwy 503.

Hacienda Buena Vista COFFEE FARM

(787-284-7020; Rte 123 Km 16.8; adult/child $8/5; Wed-Sun by reservation) The overgrown coffee fields and lovely, rusting historic buildings of Hacienda Buena Vista make up one of the best-preserved 19th-century coffee plantations in Puerto Rico. Wandering its grounds while listening to the song of the coquí frogs makes a tranquil, historical day trip. Now, as in its heyday, the ingenuity of the irrigation and growing techniques are impressive, captured in the network of diverted waterway from the nearby Río Canas that still slowly turns the enormous water wheel and the industrial-era kitchen.

You absolutely must call in advance to book a reservation. There are several tours daily, including one in English, and a small gift shop where you can purchase locally grown beans.

Hacienda Buena Vista is 8 miles north of the city center off Rte 123. This is despite being marked by brown signs very near Ponce city center and by almost no signs further out. The winding route through the countryside takes the better part of an hour to drive. You will likely need to stop and ask for directions. Alternatively, top hotels from Ponce and San Juan can arrange taxi service to the site, as well as tours.

EAST OF PONCE

Arroyo

POP 19,000

On the southeast corner of the island, Arroyo seems to have dozed off shortly after the reign of 'King Sugar' and never awakened. It's the first town on the south coast you'll hit when heading clockwise along the island from San Juan and is typical of seaside burgs in the area, with economies that hobble along through a trickle of tourism and small commercial fishing ventures. The dusty main drag, Calle Morse, passes 19th-century structures and salt-weathered wooden homes with drooping tin roofs and shuttered windows, eventually ending at the still, blue Caribbean.

Arroyo was a rough-and-tumble smugglers' port during colonial days, when New England sea captains built many of the slouching wooden houses. Arroyo's five minutes of fame came when Samuel Morse, inventor of the telegraph, installed lines here in 1848. Citizens named the main street after Morse and praise him in the town's anthem.

Entering the village from Hwy 3 to Calle Morse, you'll notice that the upside of Arroyo's isolation is a lack of commercial development – there's not a Burger King in sight. But, despite its relative charms, the sleepy town is only worth the detour for those with time to spare.

Hwy 3, the old southern coastal road, skirts the edge of town but Hwy 753 becomes the main street, which has a smattering of watering holes/eateries near the beach end.

Sights & Activities

The narrow strand adjoining the Centro Vacacional Punta Guilarte has a **balneario** (public beach), which is the only decent beach around, even though the waters suffer from pollution. It's about 3 miles east of Arroyo. Parking costs $2.

Antigua Casa de Aduana NOTABLE BUILDING, MUSEUM

(Old Customs House; 787-839-8096; 67 Morse; 9am-4pm Wed-Sun) The elaborately carved former customs house is filled with Morse memorabilia. Call ahead, as hours vary and the building is often closed for 'renovations.'

Sleeping

Centro Vacacional Punta Guilarte CAMPGROUND, CABINS $

(787-839-3565; Hwy 3 Km 126; campsites/cabins/villas $10/65/109; P) About 2 miles east of Arroyo, this well-maintained government facility has rustic cabins and slightly more refined (read: hot water and air-con) villas, 40 basic campsites and a pool. The cabins sleep six. The place bustles during the summer months, when you should reserve a room well in advance through the San Juan office of the **Compañía de Parques Nacionales** (CPN; National Park Company; ☎787-622-5200).

Information

Arroyo Tourist Office (☎787-839-5441; 87 Morse) During peak season in summer you might get lucky and find someone in this cheerful peach building, but don't count on it: hours are erratic.

Getting There & Away

Most *públicos* bound for Guayama will take you the few extra miles into Arroyo for a nominal charge, leaving you at the terminal near the town hall on Calle Morse. It might take a while to get a *público* back to Guayama ($4), but from there you can find a connecting ride to Río Piedras in San Juan or back to Ponce.

Guayama & Pozuelo

POP 44,000

A few miles up the hill from the Caribbean coast is Guayama, Arroyo's bigger, less-attractive older sister. The two cities have been linked since colonial days when the shadowy brokering of Arroyo's ports fattened the wallets of Guayama's society families. In the century since, these sisters have grown apart, with the sprawling asphalt parking lots of big box stores and commercial development offering evidence of how Guayama has left ragged little Arroyo behind.

Today, Guayama's 44,000 residents pay the rent with jobs at pharmaceutical factories that lie west of town. The place once called the 'City of Witches' (a result of Santería worship brought here by African laborers) suffers from the contemporary spells of hasty development and heavy traffic.

During the first weekend of March the upscale **Feria Dulce Sueño** (Fair of Sweet Dreams) draws equestrian zealots for a Paso Fino horse race. Otherwise, there are a couple of impressive cultural diversions in town and some great eateries in the dreamier nearby fishing village of Pozuelo, from where you can embark on boat trips to cays and glimpse the endangered manatee (sea cow).

Sights & Activities

Centro de Bellas Artes ART GALLERY
(Rte 3 Km 138; 9am-4:30pm Tue-Sun) FREE This fine-arts center stands just west of town in the former home of the Puerto Rican High Court. The collection focuses on emerging and established Puerto Rican artists (including a somewhat humorous set of reproductions). The works are engaging in themselves but the enthusiastic tour (available in English) is worth taking for the snippets of insight into the culture that the art is themed around.

The adjoining galleries are hung with student works from the school across the street and some dusty dioramas on Taíno culture.

Museo Casa Cautiño HISTORICAL HOME
(☎787-864-9083; cnr Palmer & Vicente Pales) On the north side of the plaza, this museum was built as a *criollo*-style town house in 1887 to house the wealthy Cautiño family, who profited from cane, cattle and tobacco. Almost 100 years later, the government claimed the property for back taxes (a common event on the island, which has saved many heirlooms). Now the house has been restored to its dignified Victorian state, with Oriental carpets and period furnishings. It was closed for refurbishment at the time of writing.

★**Tropical Pirates Eco Tours** SNORKELING
(☎787-600-3594; Hwy 7710, Pozuelo) This new outfit shows visitors what they've almost certainly never seen before: boat trips exploring the nearby coast, part of the secluded Bahía de Jobos. Snorkeling requires a six-person minimum ($55 per person) and trips are six hours including a barbecue lunch. The bonus of getting water-borne with Tropical Pirates is that this is one of the best opportunities to see the Bahía de Jobos manatees. There is also kayak and mountain-bike rental.

Sleeping & Eating

Guayama's sleeping choices aren't good. If it's late and you're tired, consider pulling in here, but better sleeping options abound to the east. For eats, there's inexpensive fare in the cafeterias by the central plaza, but the best food is a few miles down the road in Pozuelo.

Hotel Brandemar HOTEL $
(☎787-864-5124; www.brandemar.com; end of Rte 748; r $75-95; P❄≋) Following a twisting road through a residential neighborhood just outside of town, you'll come to the Brandemar, a serviceable family-run hotel with no-frills rooms situated around a pool, with a restaurant across the way serving fresh seafood. There's a small beach just paces away, but it's no good for swimming.

El Suarito CARIBBEAN $
(cnr Derkes & Hostos; mains $2-5; ⏲breakfast-10pm Mon-Sat) Popular with local wags, this cafeteria dishes up eggs and toast, cheap pork chops and beer. The paintings on the walls are by regular Carlos Jun Vega, and are based on El Suarito's clientele.

Rex Cream ICE-CREAM PARLOR $
(24 Derkes; cones $1-3; ⏲9:30am-10:30pm) Exquisite ice cream made with seasonal fruit.

★**La Casa de Los Pastelillos** SEAFOOD $$
(☎787-864-5171; Rte 7710 Km 4; mains $3-30; ⏲10:30am-6pm Mon-Wed, 10:30am-10pm Thu, 10:30-11pm Fri) After seeing the sorry excuse for what passes for *pastelillos* (fried dumplings) elsewhere, you might not recognize the namesake of this seaside patio restaurant. The ambitious variations of the fried staple (shark? octopus? pizza?) are made to order, arriving as greasy, seafood-stuffed slices of heaven. More ample, healthful options are also lovingly made, based around fresh catches.

Add the view of crashing waves and dreamy hammocks tied between palms, and this is the south coast's best lunch spot.

Getting There & Away

Públicos gather at the parking structure two blocks southeast of the plaza. Local services to neighboring towns including Patillas and Salinas cost $3 and longer hauls to San Juan or Ponce are about $8. Coming by car, you can't miss town – it's at the junction of Hwy 3 and the Hwy 53 toll road.

Bahía de Jobos

Hwy 3, the slow route along the south coast, has a worthy highlight in the sprawling Reserva Nacional de Investigación Estuarina de Bahía de Jobos, which has hiking trails, and a labyrinth of mangrove canals. The marshy reserve borders a nearly abandoned sugar town, Aguirre, another compelling detour.

Sights & Activities

Reserva Nacional de Investigación Estuarina de Bahía de Jobos NATURE RESERVE
Bursting with wildlife, the National Estuarine Research Reserve at Bahía de Jobos is an enormous protected mangrove bay, one of the largest, least-visited patches of coastal wilderness in Puerto Rico. The Bahía de Jobos covers almost 3000 acres of brackish water, including associated coastal wetlands and 15 offshore mangrove cays known as Los Cayos Caribes. Though the low-lying mangrove marsh won't impress like the immediately overwhelming natural beauty of El Yunque, it's an excellent place for birdwatching and those seeking wilderness isolation.

Start at the reserve's **Lab & Visitors Center** (☎787-864-0105; Hwy 705 Km 2.3; ⏲7:30am-noon & 1-4pm Mon-Fri, 9am-noon & 1-3pm Sat & Sun), a great educational nature center where you can learn about the star billing of birdlife here: brown pelicans, great blue herons, snowy egrets, ospreys, peregrine falcons and American oyster catchers. Over 100 manatees feed here too, but far from shore so you'll rarely see them from land. To see manatees, try a trip with Guayama's Tropical Pirates Eco Tours.

You can go on a superb short hike along the **Jagueyes Forest Interpretive Trail**, which twists around mangroves, wetlands and salt flats for about 30 minutes. The path, mostly on boardwalks, can be reached from the visitors center by driving west on Hwy 3, then turning left at Km 154.6. Another short hike heads through mangroves direct from

SOUTH COAST ROAD TRIP

Since the south coast offers visitors a chance to soak up the charms of Puerto Rico's Caribbean coast at a leisurely pace, it's crucial to get off the highways and travel on the older system of back roads, Hwy 1 and Hwy 3. Weaving your way through scrappy coastal towns, you can break at the roadside kiosks for a smoky plate of pork, and join the weathered codgers for a few cold Medallas and a few bets on the mechanical horse races, known as *picas*. Don't expect much by way of beaches – the only place for any kind of quality hidden swim in the area is off Hwy 333, near Guánica – but for a deep dive into the essence of the region, you have to get off the highway.

You'll see plenty of the crumbling brick smokestacks of former sugar refineries east of Ponce. Tiny dots on the map such as Arroyo and Aguirre (a ghost town) are largely abandoned, standing in picturesque disrepair. It may not match the postcard vision of the Caribbean, but there's no chance of suffering the tourist mobs of the north.

the visitor center, skirting the ruins of old Aguirre. Signage is scant after vandalism, but both paths are good. The mangroves also make an excellent kayaking route. The only problem currently? No kayak rental.

Aguirre GHOST TOWN

Crumbling monuments to the sugar industry are evident everywhere in the southeast, but there's no more heartbreaking reminder of departed 'King Sugar' than sleepy Aguirre, which borders the Bahía de Jobos and is so far off the beaten path that it doesn't appear on many tourist maps. The moldering sugar town was booming in the early 20th century, complete with a mill, company stores, hospital, theater, hotel, bowling alley, social club, golf course, marina, executive homes and narrow-gauge railroad.

This was the planned private community of the Central Aguirre sugar company, and at its zenith in around 1960, it processed 12,500 tons of sugarcane per day. Declining prices for sugar, foreign competition and escalating production costs drove the company under in 1990 and Aguirre became a virtual ghost town. The rusting train tracks remain, as does a weedy **golf course** (787-853-4052; Rte 705 Km 1.6; tee fee weekdays $20-25, weekends $30-35; 7am-6pm Tue-Sun), which, golfers, is the island's oldest.

Getting There & Away

The only way to visit the Reserva Nacional de Investigación Estuarina de Bahía de Jobos and Aguirre is by car. Take Hwy 705 south from Hwy 3. Watch for the barely visible sign pointing to 'Historic Aguirre' opposite a closed fuel station.

Playa Salinas

Salinas proper, the town at the center of the south coast's agricultural economy, lies about a mile north of the coast and a mile south of the highway. Though it's the birthplace of baseball legends Roberto and Sandy Alomar as well as a pair of Miss Universe queens, the town itself isn't so easy on the eyes.

The coastal barrio of Playa Salinas fares better. The name is a misnomer since there's no actual sand, but the geographical features of its harbor make it an important Caribbean port. The presence of a marina, attracting lots of retired American and European yachties, together with some offshore mangrove-fringed cays, means water-themed activities are readily available.

Following Rte 701 along the coast (which becomes Cam de Playa, then Calle A), you'll pass a **tourist office** (787-824-4077; cnr Cam de Playa & Calle B; 8am-6:30pm) by the *Monumento al Pescador* (a statue of blissfully toiling fishermen), and a cluster of surf-and-turf joints before arriving at the Marina de Salinas, a complex including the Posada El Náutico hotel. Travelers looking for a berth aboard a cruising sailboat headed to the Dominican Republic, the Bahamas, the US, Cuba or Jamaica might get lucky checking the bar within the Marina de Salinas, especially in March/April. If you can't get a ride, it's still a convivial spot to watch the boats roll in and out of the harbor.

Activities

Marina de Salinas WATERSPORTS

(787-824-3185; www.marinadesalinas.com; 8-G Playa Ward) Even if you are not staying at the Posada El Náutico, most activities in the water are available through the front desk of the Marina de Salinas, where you can rent kayaks ($20 half day) and water bikes. They'll also help arrange day trips, deep-sea fishing expeditions and jaunts to the local cays.

La Paseadora BOAT TRIP

(787-824-2649; dock near El Balcón del Capitan; trips to local cays $7) With a blasting stereo and boisterous families, trips on the La Paseadora leave weekend mornings in good weather. They offer snorkeling tours and round-trips to a nearby island with a beach. It's an enjoyable trip, but temper those lofty expectations: water for snorkeling is not great, and the beaches are mostly stony or silty.

Sleeping & Eating

The mess of streets leading to Playa Salinas is confusing to navigate, but Rte 701 leads to the small commercial district of Playa Ward. From here, you can continue around the bay via largely unmarked roads. The two hotels here are peaceful and the eating scene serendipitously gourmet.

Marina de Salinas & Posada El Náutico HOTEL, MARINA $$

(787-824-3185; www.marinadesalinas.com; Playa Ward; r $95-135; P) This is the best coastal hotel east of Ponce, part of the all-in-one Marina de Salinas complex. It has clean rooms decorated with some tropical flair, a pool, playground, cafe and a slightly more upscale restaurant overlooking the harbor. It's at the end of Rte 701 after the seafood restaurants.

The snack bar near the pool is where the cruising fraternity comes for cheap breakfasts in the morning and cheap beers through the afternoon.

Manatee Eco Resort & Loco Pelicano Restaurant HOTEL, RESTAURANT $$
(☎787-824-6688; Calle A Sector Playita No 286; r $79-99; P ❄ ≋) It's not clear what efforts this self-defined 'eco' hotel makes for the environment, but it is a more economical option than the Marina de Salinas and is located across the harbor. The rooms are a bit dark, but have tiled floors, mini-refrigerators and microwaves. The restaurant turns out excellent mussels and dramatic sunset views.

You can rent kayaks ($40 a day) to navigate the bay where, according to the amiable hosts, there are scores of manatees.

★**Ladi's Place** SEAFOOD $$
(Calle A 86; ⏲11am-9pm Sun-Thu, 11am-11pm Fri & Sat) From the road, this looks like the strip's least appealing option; from inside, it's the most. Ladi's strives to offer the ideal eating/drinking environment: there's succulently cooked seafood here (fresh crab, mmmm), but it's an atmospheric bar too. And – thank goodness – the owners have realized that an open-sided bar/restaurant on the coast is a better idea than sequestering their clients away at the mercy of Arctic air-con.

It's the oldest eating joint in Playa Salinas, and claims to have invented Salinas' famous *mojo isleño* (a thin tomato-based sauce). The song list seems calibrated to please gringo sailors, and things get lively come nightfall.

El Balcon de Capitan SEAFOOD $$
(Calle 54, Hwy 701; mains $10-30; ⏲lunch & dinner) Although the slow economy has shuttered many Playa Salinas restaurants, the Capitan soldiers on, earning its Mesón Gastronómico status through fresh plates of red snapper, a good seafood-stuffed *mofongo* and tangy *mojo isleño*. Eat in a dining room often frigid with air-conditioning or on the open-air patio.

Information

Departamento de Recursos Naturales
(Department of Natural Resources; ☎787-864-0105; Playa Ward) East of town on Hwy 3 is the office of the Departamento de Recursos Naturales, which can provide information about many surrounding natural areas, as well as collect fees for visiting them.

Getting There & Away

You cannot miss where the *públicos* gather in the lot near the town plaza. You can get to Guayama for about $3 or Ponce for $6. To get to Playa Salinas and the marina, you have to walk about 1.5 miles or negotiate with your *público* driver.

From the east, Hwy 3 becomes Hwy 1 as it passes through Salinas. From Ponce, drivers should take Hwy 1 east or the Hwy 52 toll road to Hwy 1 south.

Coamo

POP 11,000

Ponce de León's obsessive search for the fountain of youth – which, according to some historians, was sought in hopes of curing sexual impotence – led not only to the discovery of North America, but perhaps also to the founding of this city, still famous for its thermal springs. León's lagging libido might be responsible for making Coamo one of the oldest colonial settlements on the island, a place that also staged a decisive battle of the Spanish-American War. The main draw for travelers continues to be the *baños* (baths) south of town.

If you're interested in poking around town after a dip, check out San Blás Catholic Church on the plaza, which has paintings by island masters Campeche and Oller, including a painting of one of Oller's girlfriends being tortured in purgatory.

Activities

Baños de Coamo THERMAL BATHS
(Coamo's Baths; admission $3; ⏲8am-6pm) After a recent facelift, the Baños de Coamo have taken on the air of a modern spa. The baths have been a destination for centuries; today, the facility has handsome changing rooms, piped-in jazz and a small cafe. It's doubtful you'll have a tranquil soak due to the close quarters, but for fans of thermal waters it is certainly worth a detour. Note that swimsuits are required – bathing au naturel isn't tolerated.

The upper pool has thermal water at about 110°F; the lower one is cooler. It's a very agreeable spot to soak away the stress of driving Puerto Rico's roads.

Sleeping & Eating

You'll pass loads of kiosks on the roads around Coamo, many of them roasting pork and seafood, and dishing out lunches for about $5.

Parador Baños de Coamo HOTEL **$$**
(☎787-825-2186; end of Hwy 546; r $85-95; P ❄ ≋) The most recent incarnation of the hotels that have stood on this site for 150 years, Parador Baños de Coamo has been here since the 1970s. Lizards scurry around the grounds and guests enjoy an open-air bar and thermal pools. Rooms are modern, if a little worn. Things are quiet in low season.

Nonguests can use the hotel's swimming and thermal pools between 10am and 5:30pm for $7/5 per adult/child. The same people are in charge of the golf course just up the hill, where there's a restaurant open Friday through Sunday.

La Ceiba MEXICAN, PUERTO RICAN **$$**
(Rte 153 Km 13; mains $7-20; 📶) After a morning at the Baños de Coamo, this breezy, brightly painted, open-air Mexican spot is a great roadside stop. It has daily specials of Puerto Rican pork, rice and beans, and passable Mexican standards, such as grilled chicken or steak burritos. This is the exception to the rule that you should never trust a restaurant with pictures of the food on the menu.

Getting There & Around

To get to the *baños* from Ponce, head north for about 3 miles and look for the sign that points off to the left (west) to the Parador Baños Coamo, which is Rte 546. Go straight on from this point to get to Coamo town or down Rte 546 to get to the *baños*. You'll pass a number of condo developments and a golf course, before coming to Parador Baños Coamo and then the *baños* lower down the hill.

There's very little public transportation to the *baños*. A *público* from Ponce will drop you at the intersection of Hwys 546 and 153, about 1 mile away ($5). For more money it may go on to the baths, but you'll need to arrange it in advance.

WEST OF PONCE

Yauco & Around

POP 40,500

Yauco is Puerto Rico's coffee capital, where well-scrubbed public squares and a hillside of brightly painted houses stand in contrast to the ragged little burgs that dot the southwest highway. Hidden up in the hills, the city was founded in 1758 by merchants tired of pillaging pirates. Now, the so-called 'City of Coffee', gleaming with a trove of colonial and Creole architecture, is a perfect supply stop before heading into one of the lonely, lovely reserves that characterize the hilly terrain hereabouts – Bosque Estatal de Susúa to the north or Guánica forest to the southwest. The region can be explored in a day trip from Ponce.

To get here, exit Hwy 2 at Km 359 and go right on Calle 25 de Julio, which runs alongside Parque Arturo Lluberas. On this plaza's east side, in the basement of the brightly painted Alejandro Franceschi Art Museum is the **tourist office** (☎787-267-0350; cnr 25 de Julio & Batences; ⏲7:30am-3pm Tue-Sun), with information about precolonial ruins and trolley tours.

Sights

A few blocks uphill from Parque Arturo Lluberas is the **Plaza de Recreo**, upon which the massive **Iglesia Católica Nuestra Señora del Rosario** casts a long shadow over domino players and strolling lovers. The plaza sits just off a bustling stretch of shops on Calle Comercio, where a number of jewelers will make gold pendants with your name on them. The two central museums are the wonderful little **Centro de Arte Alejandro Franceschi** (☎787-267-0350; cnr 25 de Julio & Batence; ⏲8am-3pm Mon-Fri, 9am-2pm Sat & Sun) FREE, and the mildly diverting **Casa Museo de la Música** (15 Calle Santiago Vivaldi Pacheco, around cnr from Casa Franceschi; ⏲8am-4pm Mon-Fri) FREE, in the former home of renowned local composer Amaury Verey Torregrosa. Outside town, motor enthusiasts will positively salivate over the prospect of **Volkylandia** (☎787-267-7774; www.thevolkyland.com; Hwy 121 Km 13.2; admission $10; ⏲9am-2pm Thu-Sun), which has one of the world's largest private collections of VWs.

Sleeping & Eating

Calle Comercio has good cheap cafeterias and cafes. Locals seem to favor **Q Lantro** (☎787-267-3854; cnr Fernando Pecheco & 25 de Julio; ⏲11am-4pm Mon & Tue, 11am-10:30pm Wed-Sat), two blocks west of Parque Arturo Lluberas, for upscale eating in the center.

Hotel El Cafetal MOTEL **$**
(☎787-856-0946; Rte 368 Km 10; r $65-105; ≋) The bizarre-looking, sole accommodation option is this motel, approached by a steeply twisting drive on a hill outside town overlooking the mountains. Try the half-decent restaurant, if you can navigate the labyrin-

WORTH A TRIP

BOSQUE ESTATAL DE SUSÚA

Juxtaposed between the dry coastal flats and the humid mountain foothills of the Cordillera Central, this foggy forest's diminutive 3300 acres are no Yellowstone, but what it lacks in acres it makes up for in solitude. Well off the main tourist trails and notoriously difficult to find, Susúa is invariably deserted year-round – save for the occassional binocular-wielding ornithologist (the forest boasts 44 bird species) and tapped-in mountain biker.

To get here, drive west out of Yauco on Rte 368, past Hotel El Cafetal to Km 2.1. Turn right and keep going until you arrive at the shack for the **Departamento de Recursos Naturales y Ambientales** (DRNA | Department of Natural Resources & Environment; 787-721-5495; 7am-3:30pm Mon-Fri, 9am-5pm Sat & Sun). There's not much in the way of amenities at the entrance – just a few picnic tables, a toilet, a scattering of fire pits and some campsites. You'd be wise to check on availability/hours before arrival; camping per tent costs $6, whilst basic cabins sleeping up to eight are $40 per night. For a DIY adventure, head up the eastern flank of the Bosque Estatal de Susúa on Rte 128 to mountain-rimmed reservoir **Lago Luchetti**, with camping and great birdwatching.

The hiking trails leaving from the entrance are typical of most on the island: poorly marked and somewhat hard to find. Rangers might help with a hand-drawn, worryingly simplistic map. For mountain bikers, there's a very challenging 6.3-mile trail that incorporates river crossings and a technical ravine reverently called La Pared (Wall). The nearest bike rental is the Wheel Shop (p181) in the town of Cabo Rojo.

thine stairs and corridors to discover it. It's no longer one of Puerto Rico's 'hourly rate' motels, but most rooms are still the boggiest of bog standard – many lack windows.

Pay $5 more to get a room with a view. There's a nice pool and – incredibly – room service.

★ Restaurante La Guardarraya PUERTO RICAN $
(787-856-4222; www.laguardarraya.com; Rte 127 Km 6; mains $7-13) You'll see the signs announcing *chuletas can-can* all over the island, but this charming 1957 institution is the place that invented the dish. What is it? A slab of pork, with the ribs and fat left on, prepared with delicate cuts so that the fat blossoms when deep-fried to resemble the underskirt of a cancan dancer. Intense? You better believe it. Sided with rice, beans and plantains it makes for an amazing (if decadent) meal.

Set on stilts in a tropical forest clearing outside of Yauco, the restaurant's historical ambience and its well-groomed waiters ensure this is among Puerto Rico's best dining experiences.

El Café de Marta CAFE $
(cnr Fernando Pacheco & Av Antonio Vivaldi; breakfast $5; breakfast & lunch) Where is all that coffee in the 'city of coffee'? At this little place, apparently. It's in the unlikely environs of the *público* terminal (you'll be waiting a while for that ride anyway) and has retained enough of Yauco's celebrated export to act as local ambassador of feisty caffeinated brews. Delicious, but the place still can't shake the island's Styrofoam cup syndrome.

Guánica & Around

POP 18,750

Not much happens in underwhelming Guánica itself, but international travelers are enticed by a plush resort east of town (Copamarina Beach Resort), beautiful nearby bays and cays, and the stunning Bosque Estatal de Guánica (p161), perched in hills above the sea. Guánica is a few miles south of Hwy 2 on Rte 116.

Activities

Rte 333 from Guánica twists past decent options for swimming before ending at the best one, **Bahía de la Ballena**, sporting a long crescent of mixed rocky and sandy shore. The road stops at the east end of the bay, and you can park along the road to picnic and sunbathe. You can also pick up the Vereda Meseta trail here, a wild 4 mile, round-trip coast-hugging trail used by hikers and bikers.

Playa Caña Gorda BEACH
(Stout Cane Beach; Hwy 333 Km 6.2; parking $3) Playa Caña Gorda is the *balneario* adjacent to the southern edge of the dry forest on Rte

Guánica & Around

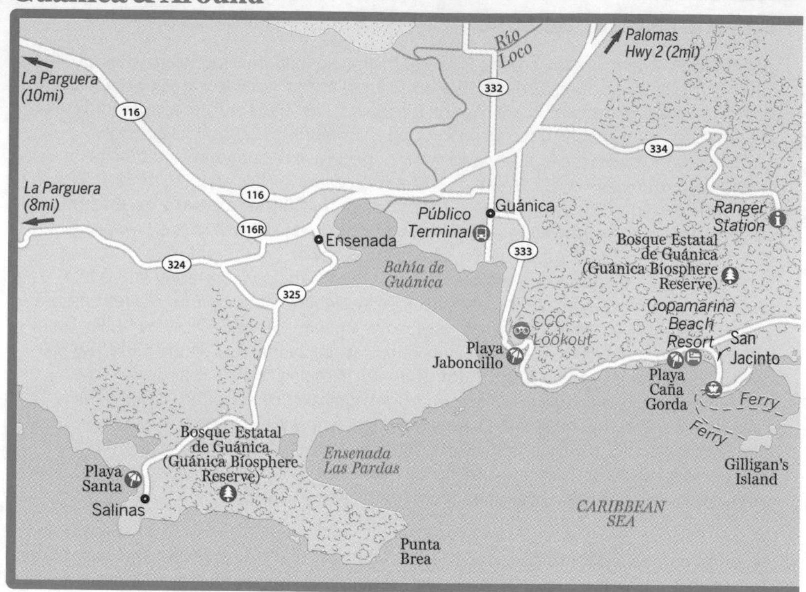

333 and is where locals come to grill fresh fish, play volleyball and lie around in the shade. The modern facilities are the most developed in the area, including a small shop with cold soda and sunblock.

Gilligan's Island BOAT TRIP
(ferry adult/child $6/3; ferry 9am-5pm Tue-Sun) Gilligan's Island and **Isla Ballena** (Whale Island) are small mangrove islands off the tip of the Caña Gorda peninsula and are technically part of the dry forest reserve. Neither is too sandy, but both offer good sunbathing and passable snorkeling. The ambitious can reach these via kayak (rentals are available at Playa Caña Gorda, the Copamarina Beach Resort and Mary Lee's by the Sea) or you can catch a **ferry** in front of Restaurante San Jacinto every hour, barring bad weather.

If Gilligan's is packed, pony up a couple more dollars to the captain and try the less-visited Ballena.

Sleeping & Eating

A community of vacation houses and guesthouses called San Jacinto dominates the highlands of the small Caña Gorda peninsula. If you're looking for a cheap option, drive up there and poke around, as some houses rent rooms.

★ **Mary Lee's by the Sea** APARTMENTS $$
(787-821-3600; www.maryleesbythesea.com; 25 San Jacinto; studios from $120, apt $250; P ❄) This immensely charming guesthouse run by Mary Lee Alverez is one of the most isolated and charming stays on the island. Set on a steep hillside overlooking the mangrove cays and the Caribbean, guests have little choice but to unplug (no cell service, no televisions) and relax. Each apartment is appointed with ultrahip, brightly colored marine-themed furnishing and many have decks, hammocks, barbecue and sea views.

One room even has a bathroom that opens out to a private garden shower. Mary Lee herself is a character, a doting host who came here to dive 50 years ago and never left. There are stairs that descend to a dock where you can relax by the water, or rent boats and kayaks for a reasonable fee.

Copamarina Beach Resort RESORT $$$
(1-800-468-4553, 787-821-0505; www.copamarina.com; Hwy 333 Km 6.5; r $130-400, villas from $800; P ❄ @) This full-service resort is the most upscale vacation retreat on the southwest coast of Puerto Rico, just east of the *balneario* on a shallow bay. It's relatively pricey but worth it: the immaculate grounds include a pair of beautiful pools,

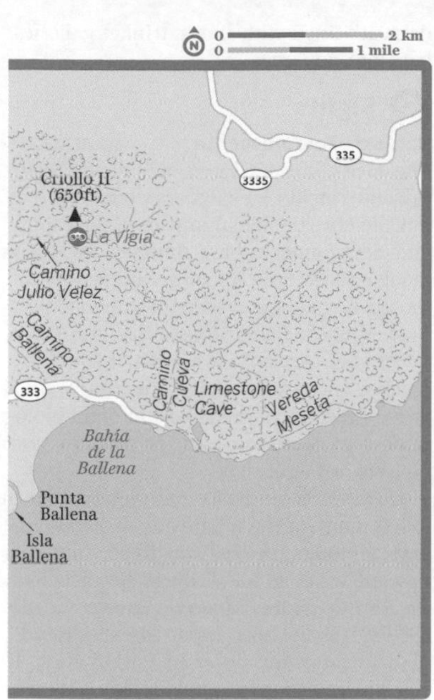

tennis courts, and two upscale restaurants. There's even an on-site dive shop and a 24-hour service desk.

Most of the plush, elegantly outfitted rooms open to ocean breezes and swaying palms, making it idyllic for honeymooners, who drag beach chairs into the shallow waters under the shade of the palm trees. The only drawback is the resort's isolation but, for those who enjoy peace and quiet, it can also be its greatest asset.

Alexandra FUSION **$$**

(☎1-800-468-4553, 787-821-0505; www.copamarina.com; Hwy 333 Km 6.5; dishes $15-35; ⊙lunch & dinner) If one dish could represent the menu at this upscale restaurant at Copamarina Beach Resort, it'd be lobster tail in mango and mustard sauce. Savory, inventive and decidedly upscale, the fusion Caribbean and New American dishes here are as elegant as the linen-draped dining room. Couples toast special occasions, and the waiters dote. Reservations are recommended.

WORTH A TRIP

BOSQUE ESTATAL DE GUÁNICA

The immense 10,000-acre expanse of the Guánica Biosphere Reserve is one of the island's great natural treasures, located in two sections just east and west of Guánica. This remote desert forest is among the best examples of subtropical dry forest vegetation in the world – a fact evident in the variety of extraordinary flora and fauna present at every turn. Scientists estimate that only 1% of the earth's dry forest of this kind remains, and the vast acreage makes this a rare sanctuary, crossed by 30-odd miles of trails that lead from the arid, rocky highlands, which are covered with scrubby brush, to more than 10 miles of remote, wholly untouched coast. Only a two-hour drive from the humid rainforests of El Yunque, this crumbling landscape and parched vegetation makes an unexpected, thrilling contrast.

Over 700 varieties of plants, many near extinction, thrive in the Reserve. Some of the unusual species here include the squat melon cactus with its brilliant pink flowers that attract hummingbirds. Another plant, with the unseemly name of the Spanish dildo cactus, grows into huge treelike shapes near the coast and attracts bullfinches and bats. Of the fauna, nine of Puerto Rico's 14 endemic bird species can be found here: including the Puerto Rican woodpecker, the Puerto Rican emerald hummingbird and – the ultimate prize for birdwatchers – the exceedingly rare 'prehistoric' Puerto Rican nightjar, of which there are estimated to be as few as 1500.

Several short trails leave from the reserve's **ranger station** (☎787-821-5706; ⊙9am-4pm), including the 1-mile **Camino Ballena** (which visits mahogany and deciduous forest and then plummets to a beach), and the 2-mile **Camino Julio Velez** (the best for birdwatchers).

To get to the eastern section of the reserve and the ranger station, which has some photocopied trail maps and brochures, follow Hwy 116 northeast from Guánica towards Hwy 2 and turn right onto Hwy 334. The southern extent of the eastern section of the forest – including Bahía de la Ballena (Whale Bay) and the ferry to Gilligan's Island – is also accessible by Hwy 333, to the south of Guánica.

Getting There & Away

Públicos stop on the plaza in Guánica, a few blocks west of the shore. Getting to either Ponce or Mayagüez costs about $7. For the last 7km to the beach you're on your own.

If you're driving to Guánica, follow Hwy 116 south from the expressway.

La Parguera

POP 1000

La Parguera is a lazy, lovable seaside town, a somewhat disorderly magnet for vacationing Puerto Ricans and US expats who spend most of the morning in bed, most of the day on the water, and most of the weekend popping open cans of Medalla. During the day, the streets empty as fishermen and divers navigate the maze of mangrove canals to the open water to catch snapper and shark, or dive the 40ft Wall.

La Parguera parties hard despite its diminutive population and for such a small community, the bars are lively. In the long summer months between Easter and September the place fills with students and travelers.

At the busy waterfront, boats shuttle tourists to the glowing waters of the town's big draw – Bahía de Fosforescente – simultaneously diminishing its glow with the pollution from their motors.

The ramshackle mix of new and old buildings has a chaotic charm, from the houses on stilts over the water to vacation condo developments that have arisen on upland fields.

Even though many of the streets don't have signs, it doesn't take long to get oriented; Rte 304 brings you into town and takes a sharp bend at the water to become the main drag. It's lined with shops, trinket galleries, bars and cafeterias.

Sights

Bahía de Fosforescente NATURE RESERVE

The once-glittering waters of Bahía de Fosforescente remain La Parguera's biggest draw, but the environmental impact of boat tours and developments have dimmed the spectacular show. Still, it can be interesting for those who have never seen the phenomenon. Boats visit the Bahía Monsio José and Bahía La Parguera, east of town, both of which are reached via narrow canals through the mangrove forest. If you come here at night bioluminescent micro-organisms in the water put on a surreal light show.

However, motorboats and pollution have killed many of the organisms in Parguera's bays, so today the best way to see bioluminescent water is on Vieques. Nevertheless, the $8 ride on the **Fondo de Cristal** (☎787-899-5891) is the least expensive way to witness this glowing water in Puerto Rico. If you are ecologically minded, skip this bay for a place where nonpolluting kayaks or electric boats are used – and tell motorized-boat operators why you're saying no.

Isla Mata la Gata & Isla Caracoles BEACH

These two mangrove cays lie less than a half mile offshore and are worth a visit after the other dusty sights nearby. The sandy strands on the seaside are really the only places in La Parguera to spend a traditional day at the beach, but both are overused and the sand is not spectacular. You can come here in your own rental boat/kayak, but the boat operators at the town docks will also take you for an $8 round-trip.

TOP FIVE CARIBBEAN VIEWS

Fuerte Caprón A hike through the brushy hills of Puerto Rico's bizarre dry forest brings you to a fort overlooking the turquoise horizon.

El Vigía (p146) This huge concrete cross on a Ponce hilltop takes in the Pearl of the South and the sea.

Rte 333 After a white-knuckled drive around Guánica, pull over to chill out on tiny beaches hidden by mangroves.

La Guancha Paseo Tablado (p146) Watch the ships roll in and out of the port at this boardwalk observation deck in Ponce.

La Casa de Los Pastelillos (p155) Swing on a hammock between palm trees and enjoy endless views at this hidden-away lunch favorite in Guayama.

La Parguera

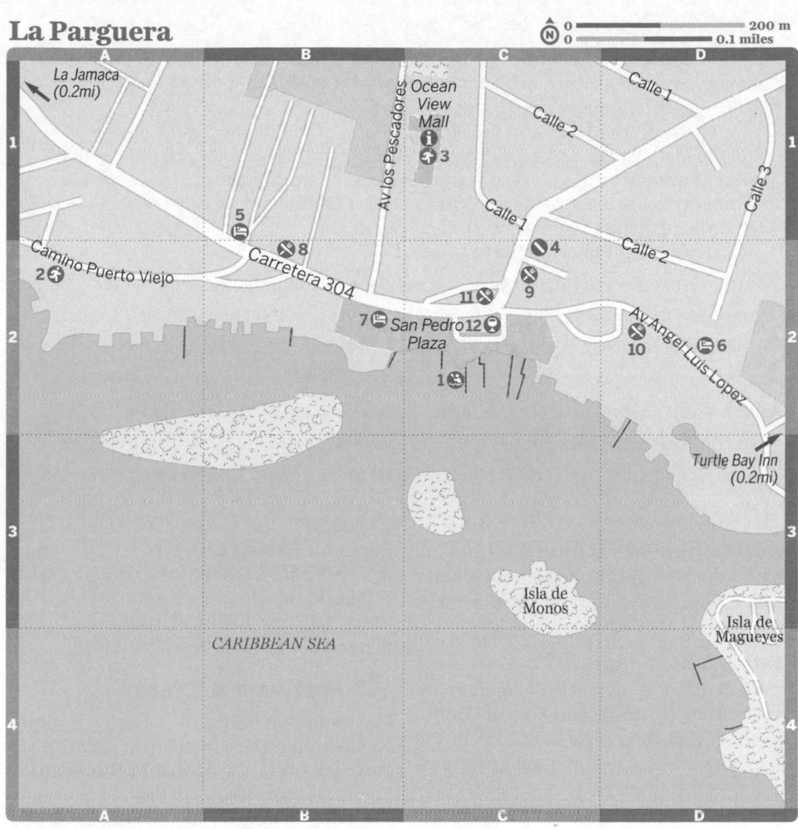

Isla de Magueyes & Isla de Monos ISLANDS
Magueyes Island lies about 20 yards south of the boat docks and is used as a marine science station for the Universidad de Puerto Rico. The island was formerly a zoo, though now it's overrun by some frighteningly large iguanas, many of which were originally brought over from Cuba. They increasingly make their way to the mainland. Monkeys held for research on Isla de Monos (Monkey Island), about a mile to the west, have also escaped and are breeding ashore – pests to local farmers, but amusement for children and tourists.

Activities

Diving & Snorkeling

West Divers DIVING, SNORKELING
(787-899-3223; www.westdiverspr.com; Rte 304 Km 3.1; 9am-6pm) West Divers is the best diving operation in the area and our favorite on the south coast. It offers three-hour

La Parguera

Activities, Courses & Tours
1 Aleli Kayak Rental ... C2
Cancel Boats ... (see 1)
2 Parguera Fishing Charters ... A2
3 Vento Lera ... C1
4 West Divers ... C2

Sleeping
5 La Parguera Guest House ... B1
6 Nautilus Hotel ... D2
7 Villa Parguera ... B2

Eating
8 La Empanadilla ... B2
9 Moon's Bar & Tapas ... C2
10 Restaurante Puerto Parguera ... D2
11 Yolanda's ... C2

Drinking & Nightlife
12 Mar y Tierra ... C2

DIVING THE WALL

Although landlubbers can have plenty of fun in La Parguera, divers know the real draw – the underwater treasure hidden 6 miles offshore.

The Wall (advanced dive, 50ft to 125ft) features a 'swim-through' at the base of an immense reef that has a sheer 60ft drop. Plenty of good diving takes place above that mark, but the real treat is wiggling in and out of the 'swim-through' hole and checking out the impressive reef structure at 80ft and below. Divers have reported seeing manatees, dolphins, manta rays and much, much more.

Other diving highlights near La Parguera:

Motor (novice, 55ft to 75ft) An unclaimed airplane motor adds mystery to a reef.

Barracuda City (novice, 60ft to 70ft) You'll get the hairy eyeball from big silver predators.

Super Bowl (intermediate, 55ft to 75ft) Swim-throughs and overhangs.

Chimney (intermediate, 55ft to 75ft) A north-facing ledge honeycombed with holes.

Black Wall (intermediate, 60ft to 130ft) A smaller version of the big coral wall.

Two for You (advanced, 55ft to 120ft) This reef looks like an underwater flower shop.

Fallen Rock (advanced, 65ft to 120ft) A magnet for abundant coral and bright-blue fish.

snorkeling trips ($50) and half-day, two-tank trips to the Wall ($115). If you're in a party smaller than three, call ahead to inquire about joining another group.

Boating & Boat Trips

Travelers have a number of vendors to choose from in this town. **Cancel Boats** (787-899-5891; boats per hr about $35), at the town docks, has a lot of loyal customers renting its 15ft whaler-type boats with 10HP engines. Competitor Torres Boat Service, nearby, has similar prices, all of which get better with larger groups.

Aleli Kayak Rental KAYAKING
(787-899-6086; 1-/2-person kayaks per hr $10/15, half day $30/40, full day $50/60) Down at the town docks, Aleli Kayak Rental is the most ecologically responsible way to see the magical waters. For any rentals, call ahead, as opening hours vary.

Kitesurfing & Windsurfing

The sheltered waters of the bay and reliable breeze makes this an excellent destination for windsurfing and kiteboarding. For all related inquiries, ask Eddie Rodríguez, who runs **Vento Lera** (787-808-0396; Ocean View Mall, Ave los Pescadores; windsurfing rentals from $45), an excellent water-sports shop.

Fishing

You can fish the reefs for grouper, snapper and mackerel, or head into deeper water for blue marlin, tuna and dorado.

Parguera Fishing Charters FISHING
(787-382-4698; Camino Puerto Viejo) Parguera Fishing Charters runs half- and full-day trips (from $175) on its 31ft Bertram from a well-marked dock at the west end of town.

Festivals & Events

Fiesta de San Pedro PARTY
Named after the abundant pargo fish, La Parguera hosts the Fiesta de San Pedro to honor the patron saint of fishermen in June. The party takes over the main street, where there's live music, food kiosks, children's activities and vendors who pour untold gallons of Medalla.

Sleeping

There are plenty of sleeping options within walking distance of La Parguera, so unless it's the peak of summer or during a festival, it won't be hard to find a comfortable place to sleep for under $100. Guesthouses and a pair of larger, slightly more polished hotels are within walking distance of the dock.

Nautilus Hotel HOTEL $
(787-899-4004; www.nautiluspr.com; 238 Av Angel Luis Lopez; r Mon-Fri $65, Sat & Sun $70-90; P) Just east of the center of town, the Nautilus is a well-appointed modern place with 18 rooms: the best deal in town.

★**La Jamaca** INN $$
(787-899-6162; Reparto Lo Borde, off Rte 304; r $95-120; P) Ah, imagine it. *Jamacas* (hammocks) swinging in a breezy location

on a verdant hill above town, amidst a courtyard replete with plants and a pool on hand. La Jamaca has been dishing out little pieces of paradise to its guests for a quarter of a century. It's nothing fancy, mind, but it is blissful.

To get here, continue on Rte 304 uphill past La Parguera Guest House and the boatyard for three quarters of a mile, and follow signs up a minor road to your right.

La Parguera Guest House MOTEL **$$**
(787-899-3993; www.pargueraguesthouse.com; Carretera 304 Km 4; r $85; P ❄ @) This cheerfully painted guesthouse is right on the strip with 18 clean, small rooms all with a small refrigerator and cable TV. There are also two apartments; one sleeps six and goes for $120, another sleeps eight and can be had for around $150. Prices go up during peak season.

Turtle Bay Inn INN **$$**
(787-899-6633; www.turtlebayinn.com; 153 Calle 6; s $79-99, d $109-125; P ❄) This obtrusively yellow building, the newest accommodation in town, has an inconvenient location a few blocks away from the waterside action, but the 12 rooms here are very comfortable, and rates include a continental breakfast. There's a pool, and the whole place is powered solely by solar paneling.

Villa Parguera HOTEL **$$**
(787-899-7777; www.villaparguera.net; Carretera 304 Km 3.6; r $107-187; ❄ @) On the main street across from the church, this two-story hotel with 63 units is a longtime favorite of travelers, and the closest to luxury you will find in the town. It's a modern and reliably clean choice, and many rooms have been recently renovated.

There is a gourmet restaurant (flat on ambiance but with varied dishes) and nightclub on-site, which does a campy show on the weekends.

Eating & Drinking

It's easy to follow your nose here; there are plenty of bars and food kiosks at the waterfront. Nightlife in La Parguera is an outdoor affair: people drink, eat and stroll from one end of the waterfront road to the other.

★**Moon's Bar & Tapas** TAPAS **$**
(Carretera 304 Km 3.2; tapas $3-8; 3am-midnight Thu-Sun, 3am-2am Fri & Sat) This intimate, open-air spot serves decent tapas, bruschetta, scrumptuous thick soups and homemade hamburgers. Or you can perch at the bar and enjoy a cocktail or maybe (not so common hereabouts) a glass of good wine.

La Empanadilla CAFETERIA **$**
(Carretera 304, near La Parguera Guest House; empanadas $1-2; lunch until late) The best place for cheap empanadas in town – nothing costs over two bucks. The empanadas with *pulpo* (octopus) are the best.

Yolanda's CARIBBEAN **$**
(Carretera 304 Km 3.2; mains $6-13; lunch until late) The high-pitched roof and wood trim give Yolanda's a South Seas atmosphere. It serves savory lunch specials and stiff drinks. In the evening the patio makes a great place to party.

Restaurante Puerto Parguera SEAFOOD **$$**
(Av Angel Luis Lopez; mains $10-20; 11am-8pm Mon-Thu, 11am-11pm Fri & Sat) Turning sharp left by the raucous Mar y Tierra pool hall, you'll spot this refreshingly unpretentious place on the right before Hotel Nautilus. It does a mean $15.95 red snapper or, for 20 bucks, great *mofongo* with a classic combo stuffing of octopus and shrimp.

Mar y Tierra BAR, POOL HALL
(Carretera 304; 4pm-midnight, later on weekends) Mar y Tierra stands out among the cluster of places packed between the main street and the docks – primarily through the eardrum-busting Latin rock and salsa it pumps out.

Information

Ocean View Mall (Ave los Pescadores) One block off Rte 304, Ocean View Mall has a book exchange; a well-stocked, brightly lit grocery store; and a contract post office.

Getting There & Away

Públicos come and go irregularly from a stop near the small waterfront park and boat piers in the center of the village. Service is basically local and travels to nearby towns such as Lajas ($1), where you can move on to bigger and better van stands in bigger and better municipalities.

The fastest way here is on Hwy 116, off Hwy 2, from Guánica or San Germán. Follow the signs for the last couple of miles on Hwy 304.

West Coast

POP 353,000

Includes ➡

Best Places to Eat

- Horned Dorset Primavera (p175)
- La Copa Llena (p175)
- La Rosa Inglesa/English Rose Inn (p175)
- El Bohió (p182)
- Annie's Place (p185)
- Costa (p179)

Best Places to Stay

- Tres Sirenas (p174)
- Blue Boy Inn (p173)
- Villa Vista Puerto (p184)
- Casa Islena (p173)
- Horned Dorset Primavera (p174)
- Centro Vacacional Boquerón (p184)

Why Go?

West is best – at least as far as those quintessential snapshots of Puerto Rico go. Here the languid, azure ocean takes on a visceral palpability because this is the place to get in it: paddling like mad to catch a ride on one perfect wave after another, or swimming off sandy shorelines that regularly grace 'world's best beach' lists. The region's pièce de résistance is Rincón, a surfin' safari outpost (named in a Beach Boys song, for goodness' sake!) where grizzled beach bums and stoned locals catch waves in the salty dawn, and mingle around beach bonfires at twilight.

As well as taking the drop on flawless surf, Porta del Sol (Gateway to the Sun) is a land of stormy shorelines, low-key resorts and down-to-earth fishing villages. Grab a few cold ones, bite down on a conch fritter or three, and get ready to brave the waves, bask in the stunning sunsets and absorb the mellow spirit of slacker independence.

When to Go

Welcome to the endless summer: the west coast is pleasantly hot all year round. It gets heavy rain in late summer and early fall, but otherwise, expect it to be sunny, breezy and around 80°F nearly every day.

If you're here to surf, winter is an ideal time to visit, although surfing competitions kick off from mid-October. Around this time cold fronts bring big waves to the western beaches, when average crests of 5ft or 6ft can grow as large as 25ft. In December and February, you may also spot migrating whales offshore.

Those who aren't here to ride the waves will find the calmer waters more inviting for swimming and deep-sea fishing in summer.

History

The consensus is that Columbus first arrived in Puerto Rico in November 1493 and docked somewhere off the west coast (though there is some dispute as to actually *where*). Fifteen years later he was followed by Juan Ponce de León, who landed near Cabo Rojo before heading off east to found the settlement of Caparra. San Germán, the island's second-oldest city, was founded near Mayagüez in 1511, and moved to its present site in 1573.

More recently, the west has spawned many great liberal thinkers including Dr Ramón Emeterio Betances, the inspiration behind the revolutionary Grito de Lares in 1868. The details of this abortive rebellion were fine-tuned in a series of safe houses near Mayagüez.

Territorial Parks & Reserves

The Refugio Nacional Cabo Rojo (p186), part of the 4775-acre Bosque Estatal de Boquerón, is a favorite with casual outdoor enthusiasts; it's great for birdwatchers, and the flat, guided trails are easy to manage for young children. There're visitor centers and guided hikes, plus sublime Caribbean views. The Refugio de Boquerón (p183) has mangrove wetlands and excellent birdwatching opportunities. Nature lovers should nevertheless remember that the ultimate treat is a short jaunt southeast in Bosque Estatal de Guánica (p161).

Getting There & Around

Mayagüez is the regional hub and has its own airport (flights from San Juan and the US Virgin Islands only). You can fly direct from the US into Aguadilla airport 30 minutes' northeast of Rincón. The Cabo Rojo area southwest of Hwy 2 has Puerto Rico's best cycling: undulating, blissfully traffic-free roads and a top-notch bike shop (p181).

Rincón

POP 15,000

You'll know you've arrived in Rincón – 'the corner' – when you pass the group of sun-grizzled gringos cruising west in their rusty 1972 Volkswagen Beetle with surfboards piled on the roof. Shoehorned far out in the island's most remote corner, Rincón is Puerto Rico at its most unguarded, a place where the sunsets shimmer scarlet and you're more likely to be called 'dude' than 'sir.' This is the surfing capital of the island, and one of the premiere places to catch a wave in the northern hemisphere.

For numerous Californian dreamers this is where the short-lived summer of love ended up. Arriving for the World Surfing Championships in 1968, many never went home. Hence Rincón became a haven for draft-dodgers, alternative lifestylers, back-to-the-landers, and people more interested in riding the perfect wave than bagging $100,000 a year, living in a Chicago suburb.

Breaking anywhere from 2ft to 25ft, Rincón's waves are often close to perfect. The names are evocative: Domes, Indicators, Spanish Wall and Dogman's. The crème de la crème is Tres Palmas, a white-tipped monster frequently dubbed the 'temple' of big-wave surfing in the Caribbean.

Though Rincón is crawling with American expats, the tourist/local divide is more seamless and less exclusive than in the resorts out east. However, with a new, more affluent surfing generation demanding a higher quality of living than their hippie parents, Rincón has developed a clutch of boutique hotels and gourmet restaurants aimed at surfing Gen X yuppies.

History

Rincón traces its history to the 16th century and a few low-key sugarcane plantations. The municipality is actually named after one of the area's original planters, Don Gonzalo Rincón. For most of its history, the town survived on cane farming and cattle-raising.

Things changed when the World Surfing Championships arrived in 1968. Glossy images of Rincón were plastered over international media – the word was out. Every year since then has seen successive generations of wave riders make the pilgrimage. And while they pursued an endless summer, they began to invest in the community, building their own restaurants, guesthouses and bars. Eventually, Rincón's perfect surf and permanent beach bums lent the place the vibe it retains today, something similar to a Hawaiian surfing outpost.

Sights

Rincón is more of a region than a town, encompassing a municipal center surrounded by clusters of commercial areas. The municipal center is only about four square blocks, encircling the Catholic church and the Presbyterian church that face each other across the traffic-crowded Plaza de Recreo. This

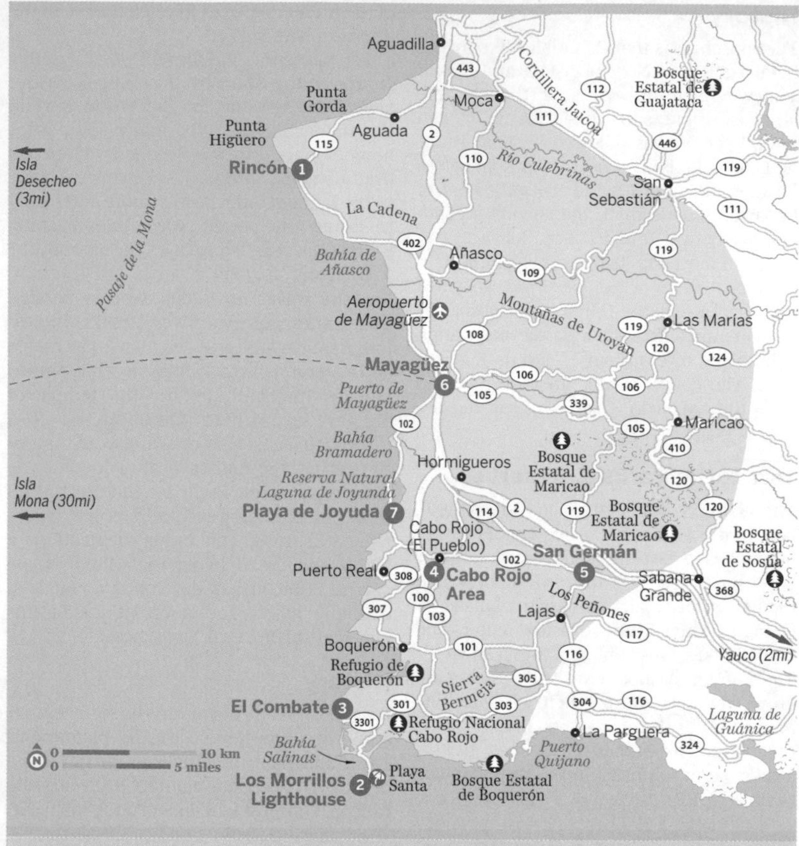

West Coast Highlights

1. Surf beside beach bums and vacationing businesspeople on the legendary breaks of **Rincón** (p169).
2. Peer at the endless sea from the top of the **Los Morrillos Lighthouse** (p186), overlooking idyllic Playa Santa, then cool off with a swim.
3. Chow down on conch fritters at **Annie's Place** (p185), one of Puerto Rico's most idyllic beach bars in hidden-away El Combate.
4. Hire a bike at the west's best **bike shop** (p181) in Cabo Rojo (El Pueblo), then pedal the beach-hugging byways of the Cabo Rojo Area.
5. Explore historic streets and some of the west's best food in **San Germán** (p187).
6. Get giddy on **Sangria de Fido** (p179), the local punch of Mayagüez.
7. Lunch on fresh seafood in **Playa de Joyuda** (p182), Puerto Rico's 'Gourmet Golden Mile'.

core has essential services but most inns, restaurants and beach attractions lie north or south.

The best swimming beaches are south of the village, as are many of the larger hotels. A number of different snorkeling and surfing sites lie north and west of town, along Hwy 413. Moving further north, Hwy 413 climbs into steep hills similarly scattered with eating and sleeping options, that may turn eyes away from the swell: for a while at least.

Punta Higüero Lighthouse LIGHTHOUSE
(10am-2pm) FREE Nicknamed El Faro, the Punta Higüero lighthouse dates from 1892 and rises almost 100ft. It was restored in

1922 after being severely damaged by a tsunami set off by the devastating 1918 earthquake. The 26,000-candlepower light has been automated since 1933 and still helps ships navigate the Pasaje de la Mona. The principal reason to come here, however, is the view. Five great surf breaks are nearby, and sometimes humpback whales come within 100yd of the coast.

The historic lighthouse crowns **Parque Pasivo El Faro**, a pleasant city park that makes a breezy place for a sunset picnic, or to spy migrating whales during winter.

Bonus Nuclear Power Plant LANDMARK
A curious landmark, this green dome poking out from behind the palm trees behind the Punta Higüero Lighthouse once housed the Caribbean's first nuclear-powered electricity-generating facility. Back when the Beach Boys led the surfin' safari, the Boiling Nuclear Superheater Plant (known half-sarcastically by the acronym of Bonus) was a prototype of the superheater reactor. In its short life from 1960 to 1968, it suffered a reactor failure and drew scorn from environmentalists.

The US government tried converting the building into a museum, only to discover – shocker – that a failed nuclear power facility wasn't popular with tourists.

Subsequently Bonus became a rusting relic of the nuclear age and a favorite canvas for graffiti artists, who scrawl slogans to vilify nukes or praise marijuana. Locals named a surf break after it: Domes, one of Rincón's most consistent breaks. It currently opens only by appointment through the **Puerto Rican Electric Power Authority** (787-521-3434; www.aeepr.com).

Activities

Surfing

Surfing is the prime attraction, so if you're arriving in high season, make arrangements for rentals or lessons as early as possible. If you're just looking for a casual arrangement,

SURF BEACHES

As far as surfing folklore goes, Rincón wins the ultimate accolade: it's mentioned in a song by the Beach Boys. Released in 1962, 'Surfin' Safari' names Rincón as the place where 'they're walking the nose,' surfer slang for moving forward on the board toward the front. For walking the nose or simply taking in the action from shore, here's a guide to Rincón's hottest surf beaches (running south to north):

Little Malibu Just north of the marina. OK in winter, with easy 4ft breaks. Good for beginners.

Tres Palmas The big kahuna, with breaks of up to 25ft. Requires *bon courage* and a long paddle out. Handle with care.

Steps Also known by its Spanish name, *Escalera*, this is the 'inside' break to Tres Palmas' 'outside' break. Good snorkeling spot when it's calm.

Dogman's A local favorite that is anything but predictable. Expect waves that are high and hollow.

Maria's A good right, but needs a decent swell. Three times a year the waves break big, but otherwise it's average.

The Point In front of the lighthouse, this one is not for amateurs. Waves can break big here while Maria's is lying flat.

Indicators Good powerful rights. Watch out for rocks and a pipe and coral bottom.

Domes Named for the nearby former nuclear facility. Good rights with the occasional left. A strong undercurrent, but probably the most consistent spot in Rincón.

Spanish Wall A beautiful secluded spot only reachable by a rough path, this place gets up in winter and can be particularly fabulous after a cold front.

Pools Offers a few shallow reef-break peaks that can occasionally barrel.

Sandy Beach Good beginner's beach with decent waves when the swell is right.

Antonio's Used heavily during the 1968 World Surfing Championships, this has a right wall with a shorter left. Two take-off points spread the crowd.

Rincón & Around

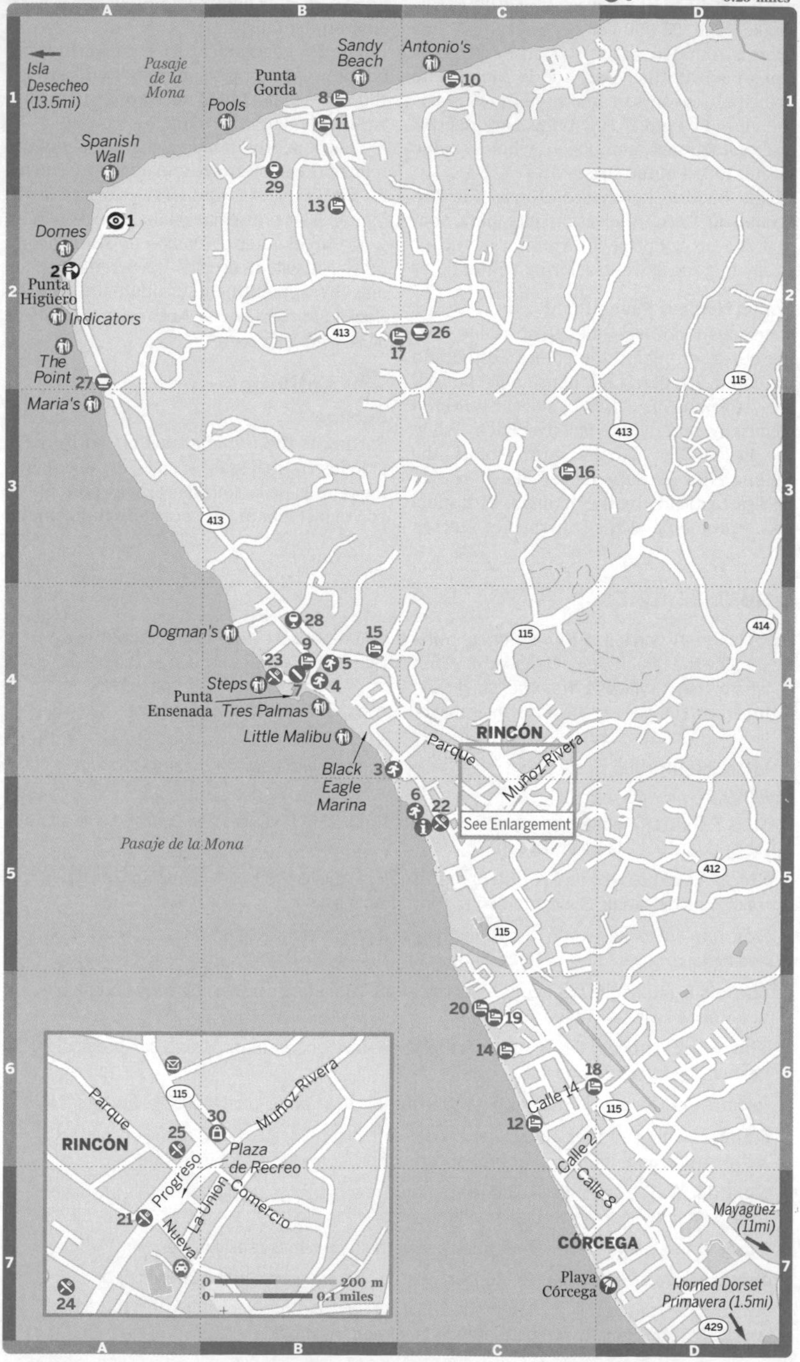

0 500 m
0 0.25 miles

A B C D
1 2 3 4 5 6 7

Isla Desecheo (13.5mi)
Pasaje de la Mona
Sandy Beach
Antonio's
Punta Gorda
Pools
8
10
11
Spanish Wall
29
13
1
Domes
2
Punta Higüero
Indicators
413
17
26
The Point
27
Maria's
115
413
16
413
28
Dogman's
15
115
414
9
23
5
Steps
4
Punta Ensenada
7
Tres Palmas
Little Malibu
RINCÓN
Parque
Muñoz Rivera
Black Eagle Marina
3
6
22
See Enlargement
Pasaje de la Mona
412
115
20
19
14
18
Calle 14
115
12
Calle 2
Calle 8
Mayagüez (11mi)
CÓRCEGA
Playa Córcega
Horned Dorset Primavera (1.5mi)
429

115
Parque
Muñoz Rivera
30
RINCÓN
25
Plaza de Recreo
Progreso
La Union
Comercio
21
Nueva
24
0 200 m
0 0.1 miles

Rincón & Around

there are shacks with boards to rent by the major surfing areas. There are numerous surf schools: some great, many poor. Only the following two come especially recommended. If neither can assist, they'll point you in the direction of those who can.

Rincon Surf School SURFING, YOGA
(☎787-823-0610; www.rinc[illegible]surfschool.com) Rincon Surf School often does lessons at Sandy Beach and is a good option for beginning adults. Also on offer are surf-and-yoga combo packages, and lessons specifically for women.

Surf 787 SURFING
(☎787-448-0032; www.surf787.com) The coolest kid on the block, Surf 787 has a suite of packages, all-inclusive surf vacations, adult getaways and a kids' surf camp. The instructors here, who are all CPR and water-safety certified, also offer lessons for couples and small groups.

Diving & Snorkeling

Because of the rough water this is not a great place for snorkeling, but snorkelers will fare much better in summer, when the water is calmer. Head for either **Playa Shacks** or **Playa Steps** near Black Eagle Marina for the best of what the beaches have to offer.

Rincón has many dive shops thanks to the popularity of diving the pristine reefs around Rincón and Isla Desecheo.

Taíno Divers DIVING, SNORKELING
(☎787-823-6429; www.tainodivers.com; Black Eagle Marina; 2-tank dive $149, snorkeling $95) Located inside the little marina north of town, this is probably the best outfit on the west coast; the guides here are responsible, professional and environmentally aware. It does almost daily runs to Desecheo (8am to 2pm) and shorter trips to nearby reefs (8am to noon). Snorkel trips, one-tank dives, whale-watching and sunset cruises are also available, as well as chartered deep-sea fishing trips.

Swimming

The surf is often too rough for swimming at many sites along the coast. Fortunately, there's the safe and newly renovated **Rincón Balneario** (public beach) about half a mile from the Plaza de Recreo. Here you'll find restrooms, showers, temporary food shacks and a new mall, which contains the tourist office, harbor restaurant and lookout tower.

Many of the hotels and guesthouses on the water south of the town center have decent swimming from the thin, thin stretch of sand out front.

Kayaking

You can rent kayaks from **Capital Water Sports** (☎787-823-2789; Sunset Village, Rincón Balneario), and if you're short on anything from paddleboards to fishing tackle, these guys should be able to help. Use the kayaks anywhere around the *balneario*. Taíno Divers (p171) also rents kayaks. Fees at both are approximately $25 per hour per kayak.

Fishing & Whale-Watching

Taíno Divers (p171) runs responsible **whale-watching tours** (about $50 per person for a two-hour tour). Boats are required to keep a minimum distance from the gentle giants, but less scrupulous operators don't always adhere to that rule. Taíno Divers can also take you on half-day deep-sea fishing excursions for about $600 per chartered boat (eight people maximum). Whale-watching is also possible from the Punta Higüero lighthouse park (p168) in December.

Makaira Charters FISHING
(☎787-299-7374; www.fishrinconpr.com; half/full day $575/850) Captain Pepi Alfonso is a licensed US Coast Guard who runs deep-sea fishing charters for up to six people and can sometimes split charters if your party is smaller. Drinks are included, but bring your own food – no bananas though (an old fishing superstition)!

Horse Riding

Pintos R Us HORSEBACK RIDING
(☎787-516-7090; www.pintosrus.com; Hwy 413 opp Black Eagle Marina; two-hour ride $60) Horseriding along the beach is a romantic way to enjoy the coast here, and this outfit runs relaxed tours doing just that for groups of up to 12 people.

Cruises

Katarina Sail Charters SAILING
(☎787-823-7245; www.sailrinconpuertorico.com; Black Eagle Marina; 3hr snorkel/sail adult/child $75/37.50) How about enjoying the wide skies and drop-dead gorgeous sunsets from the water a little less frenetically? The Katarina offers several such possibilities. Even on the three-hour cruise you'll get the chance to snorkel, sunbathe, spot manatees (and whales in season) and cast a line for a fresh fish lunch. There are sunset cruises (adult/child $55/27.50) and full moon booze cruises ($55, adults only).

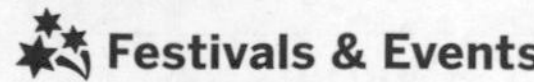

Festivals & Events

Rincón Triathlon SPORTS
(www.trialoderincon.com; Jun) This triathlon has been going since 1982, which is pretty much ancient history in the triathlon world. Held every June, it's a classic ironman contest that's starting to draw some quality international athletes – it makes for a serious fiesta for spectators.

Sleeping

Rincón has some of the best-value accommodations on the island, especially in its small, boutique properties. Reservations are recommended, particularly in high season (November to February), when the town is overrun by surfers.

Rincón is also awash with vacation-rental properties of all shapes and sizes. You can enlist the services of **Island West Properties** (☎787-823-2323; www.rinconrealestateforsale.com), which maintains an office on Hwy 413 about a mile out of town toward the lighthouse. Villa rentals with one to eight bedrooms go for between $120 and $700 per night. The nearest campground is at **Tres Hermanos** (☎787-826-1610; Hwy 115 Km 5; campsites $17) on the Bahía de Añasco, a 15-minute drive south.

Accommodations are either south of town (marginally better-connected to the center) or north of town via Hwy 413 (where steep hills and twisting lanes give an extra degree of isolation and add several premature grey hairs to drivers' heads). Several lanes branch off Hwy 413 to the properties on the north-facing beach.

Many of the accommodations (as well as restaurants and pubs) do not have street addresses per se.

North of Town

Most of the following accommodations, and some other scrappy options not listed, are along Hwy 413, north of town.

Beside the Pointe HOTEL $
(☎787-823-8550; www.besidethepointe.com; r $75-125; P ❄ 📶) The social centerpiece of Sandy Beach, this guesthouse has a happening bar and restaurant – Tamboo Tavern (p176), rooms that are outfitted like small apartments, and lots of unpretentious character. Despite the seafront location few rooms have good views, but one has cooking facilities, and all have nice tiled floors and flat-screen

televisions. And, of course, you're right near that surf.

★Casa Islena HOTEL **$$**

(☎787-823-1525; www.casa-islena.com; Hwy 413, Beach Rd; r incl breakfast $125-205; P ❄ @ 📶 🏊) A high-class option in the heart of Rincón's best surfing, Casa Islena is an elegant, Mediterranean-style guesthouse on a magnificent, moody stretch of ocean. It's a magnet for discerning jet-setting surfers; guests work out their sore muscles at morning yoga under palms and navigate the walled-in gardens to nine large, lovely sea-view rooms.

Breakfast is served at the bar, next to the sparkling pool. Afternoon snacks and dinner are available at the on-site Island House restaurant, where the spectacular dinnertime show is made up of roaring surf and setting sun. As with all of Rincón's best places, you'll certainly want to book early.

★Blue Boy Inn HOTEL **$$**

(☎787-823-2593; www.blueboyinn.com; 556 Black Eagle St; r $185-215; P ❄ 📶 🏊) This elegant little inn near the old marina is an excellent mid-priced option with very private rooms. This isn't a good place for families (it suggests no children under 12), nor is it ideal for avid surfers (the best breaks are further north of town), but the tiled terraces are hidden among leafy gardens and exude a romantic, secluded atmosphere.

In the evening guests can cook in the outdoor kitchen near the pool or sit around the crackling fire pit before retiring to their rooms, where high-thread-count sheets cover sleigh beds. It has boogie boards and bikes for its guests to use, free of charge.

Dos Angeles del Mar Guesthouse GUESTHOUSE **$$**

(☎787-823-1378; http://dosangelesdelmar.com; off Hwy 413; r $99-149; P ❄ 📶 🏊) This guesthouse has five immaculate rooms in a lofty house surrounded by a candidate for Puerto Rico's loveliest garden. The sea's a short way off, but the four top-floor rooms have spectacular views from the balconies and are impeccably kept. There's daily maid service and a wonderful little pool. The website has driving directions (which you'll need; it's a nightmare to find otherwise).

Lazy Parrot Inn HOTEL **$$**

(☎787-823-5654; www.lazyparrot.com; Hwy 413 Km 4.1; r $125-165; P ❄ @ 🏊) Claiming the middle ground between high quality and high quirky, the Lazy Parrot is a venerable inn crammed full with all kinds of parrots – including real ones, carved ones, inflated ones and stuffed ones. It occupies the high country above Rincón. Rooms are comfortable, but not flashy and there's an inviting pool.

There are two great restaurants on-site: **LPR** (☎787-823-5654; mains $16-21; ⏲noon-9:30pm) on the upper level and the wonderful Mi Familias Pizzeria (p175) poolside.

La Rosa Inglesa/English Rose Inn B&B **$$**

(☎787-823-4032; www.larosainglesa.com; follow signs from Hwy 413 interior; r incl breakfast $125-210; P ❄) High in the hills, this B&B meets a high standard of cleanliness and comes with the best breakfast in town.

Casa Verde Hotel HOTEL **$$**

(☎787-823-5600; www.casaverdehotel.com; Beach Rd off Hwy 413, Sandy Beach; r/ste $150/320; P ❄ 🏊) This recently refurbished hotel has made the leap – slightly underwhelmingly in our opinion – from guesthouse to small-scale hotel. Its desirable location near Sandy and Pools beaches makes it a good bet for surfers.

South of Town

Rincón Inn Hostel HOSTEL **$**

(☎787-823-7070; www.rinconinn.com; Hwy 115 Km 11.6; dorm $25) Here it is – the cheapest accommodations in the west shy of camping or dossing on the beach. This is a slightly dim, but perfectly clean, little place with a self-catering kitchen. It's a block back from the water and a mile south of the center.

Coconut Palms Guesthouse GUESTHOUSE **$$**

(☎787-823-0147; www.coconutpalmsinn.com; 2374 Calle 8, Comunidad Estela; r $75-150; ❄ 📶) Sandwiched between Rincón's more upscale southern resorts lies this unpretentious guesthouse in a residential neighborhood just off Hwy 115. The Coconut's best feature is its fern-draped and bird-filled courtyard along with its lovely setting right on a calm, nonsurfing stretch of beach. It has a number of adjoining rooms, many with pull-out futons and little lounge areas. Paper-thin walls mean noise from other guests can travel.

Hotel Villa Cofresí HOTEL **$$**

(☎787-823-2450; www.villacofresi.com; Hwy 115 Km 12.3; r $119-199; P ❄ 🏊) There's nothing too fancy at this expansive complex, but it's the most reasonable of Rincón's actual hotels. Despite fabulous customer service and

LOCAL KNOWLEDGE

JOAQUIM CRUZ: RINCÓN SURFER

Rincoń was the first place in Puerto Rico to sponsor surfing in a big way after the 1968 World Championships. It also embraces surfing culture in its entirety, with friendly people, plenty of places to stay, a decent local mayor, rural tranquillity and an excellent array of other sports. Ten years ago I was surfing with my friend, Rasta, up at Crash Boat Beach near Aguadilla. The swell was so awesome that the local dudes with boogie boards were actually fighting with each other for space in the water. I took a gorgeous wave and dropped down, turning as I went, hand on the wall. I think I took the tube three times before I ran out of water and hit the shore. There was this guy behind me watching and whooping. I'm not sure whether he was wishing he was up there with me or he was just sharing in the moment.

Favorite Surf Spot

Dogman's, because the waves there are really hollow. Often the waves elsewhere are just as high, but Dogman's invariably has the best tubes.

Best Time of Year

From the second week in October through April.

After-Surf Party

Go to bars like the Calypso (p175), where you can hear good bands playing Latin, rock, salsa and reggae.

As told to Brendan Sainsbury

squeaky-clean rooms (in which you can fit at least four, making this a deal), the overall feel is that of a Days Inn just landed in the tropics. There's a large pool and water-sports concession on the property, and a pretty good restaurant-bar.

★Tres Sirenas GUESTHOUSE **$$$**
(☎787-823-0558; www.tressirenas.com; 26 Sea Beach Dr; r incl breakfast $150-280; ❄📶🏊) All things weighed up, this is Rincón's best guesthouse. A stone's throw from two of the bigger, more luxurious municipality hotels, true indulgence awaits you at this serene end-of-street detached house, from the freshly-brewed coffee in your room to the lovingly-prepared breakfasts served to all guests as they gaze over the pool out to the glimmering ocean.

The rooms, with heavy wood furniture, are spacious; the penthouse has a 40ft private balcony and a Jacuzzi. For those on a budget, the studio apartment (no breakfast included), a few houses back from the sea, can sleep six to eight. The wonderful hosts can put you in touch with all manner of activities, including horse riding on Paso Fino horses.

★Horned Dorset Primavera RESORT **$$$**
(☎787-823-4030; www.horneddorset.com; Hwy 429 Km 0.3; ste from $1270; P❄@📶🏊) Undoubtedly the best small resort in Puerto Rico, and perhaps the Caribbean, this place rightly claims to offer the 'epitome of privacy, elegance and service'. There are 30 suites in private villas furnished with hand-carved antiques, and with their own private plunge pools (in case you get bored of the communal infinity pool, which overlooks the setting sun).

This serene spot with its understated Moroccan design elements is favoured by an affluent international set of travelers who are quite comfortable with life's finer things. Dripping with exclusivity, the Horned Dorset doesn't accept children under 12 years of age, shuns TVs in the rooms and encourages people to dress up – especially for dinner. It's a long way from Rincón's surf scene, but it's blissful.

Rincón of the Seas RESORT **$$$**
(☎787-823-6189; www.rinconoftheseas.com; Hwy 115 Km 12.2; r $165-295; P❄@🏊) This modern resort with all the usual upscale touches is set in a swath of beautifully landscaped grounds. Regular rooms go for under $200 in summer, but travelers with a penchant for art deco can fork out for the special ocean-view suite. There are tons of on-site amenities and staff are more than willing

to hook you up with snorkeling and diving adventures.

Eating

A lot of Rincón's guesthouses and hotels also serve food. Outside of San Juan, Rincón's varied eating options are almost without equal on the island.

Self-caterers can shop at **Rincón Cash & Carry** (10am-6pm Mon-Sat, 10am-4pm Sun), in the town center, across from the Plaza de Recreo.

★Mi Familias Pizzeria PIZZA $
(787-823-0103; Hwy 413 Km 4.1; pizzas & pastas $7-18; 11:30am-10pm) Sometimes the best things in life are the simple ones and this new Italian restaurant, located poolside at the Lazy Parrot Inn (p173) but masterminded by different people, is our favorite pizza stop on the island. Pizzas are straight out of a wood-fired brick oven and prepared with bundles of TLC.

★La Rosa Inglesa/ English Rose Inn BREAKFAST $
(787-823-4032; www.larosainglesa.com; follow signs from Hwy 413 interior; breakfast $4.50-11; breakfast) The trick to this exceptional breakfast place are the crusty homemade breads and savory home-stuffed sausages, which turn the egg dishes into a real event. Upscale surfers shovel down breakfast burritos and poached eggs after surfing the morning away. It's kind of a pain to get here, situated as it is up in the hills above town, but the town's best breakfast and great views are ample reward.

To find it, look for signs off Hwy 413...or follow the crowd.

La Cambija PUERTO RICAN $
(Cambija 17; mains $4.50-12; 11:30am-9pm) In a town where so many successful restaurants are expat-owned, it's nice to see Puerto Rican–helmed La Cambija doing so well. Locals and tourists mix around the bar, or at the informal, open-air tables, feasting on *pinchos* (marinated pork and plantain kebabs, mmm) or a fillet of mahimahi.

Libanesa Bakery BAKERY $
(52 Muñoz Rivera; snacks $3-7) Rincón's best bakery, in the heart of downtown.

★La Copa Llena INTERNATIONAL $$
(787-823-0896; http://attheblackeagle.com; Black Eagle Marina; mains $18-40; 3-9:30pm Wed-Sat, 11am-9:30pm Sun) Is your glass half empty or half full? It's hard not to look on the bright side of life at La Copa Llena (the full cup). Down by the marina, this is one of the best restaurants in town, both for the elegantly understated interior and seafronting patio but mostly for the innovative food. How about shredded papaya, peanut and shrimp salad followed by a cashew nut and catch-of-the-day fish curry?

Das Alpen GERMAN, ITALIAN $$
(www.dasalpencafe.com; Plaza de Recreo, south side; mains $14-22; 5-10pm Thu-Mon) Like a condensation of European culinary goodness, Das Alpen has arrived to ratchet the restaurant quality in central Rincón up by several notches. The varied menu, from bratwurst-topped bruschetta to goulash to strudel, reads like a best-of culinary tour of Central Europe, and the German beer range should stave off cravings for Oktoberfest.

★Horned Dorset Primavera FRENCH FUSION $$$
(787-823-4030; www.horneddorset.com; Hwy 429 Km 0.3; mains $30-50; dinner) Elegant and exclusive, this is among Puerto Rico's best fine-dining options – where you climb the sweeping staircase to the black-and-white-tiled dining room of lined drapes and an atmosphere right out of a colonial Caribbean culinary dream. The stunning French-influenced daily menu focuses on seasonal dishes that marry seasoned duck and tropical fruit reductions, grilled mahimahi, chateaubriand and delicately prepared seafood dishes.

The clinking wine glasses toast marriage proposals and business deals, and patrons outfit themselves accordingly. Smart casual attire is required.

Drinking & Nightlife

★Banana Dang CAFE
(www.bananadang.com; Hwy 413 Km 4.1; 7am-4pm Wed-Mon;) Banana Dang comes pretty close to delivering the best shots of caffeine on the island. Next door to the Lazy Parrot Inn in the hills above Rincón, it's well worth stopping off here to – in the words of the owners – think, drink and link (yes, there are computer terminals and wi-fi access). Bananas – converted into delectable smoothies – are the owners' other obsession.

Calypso Tropical Café CAFE, BAR
(787-823-4151; cnr Hwy 413 & lighthouse road; noon-midnight) Wall-to-wall suntans, svelte girls in bikini tops, bare-chested blokes

nursing cold beers, and syncopated reggae music pumping out beneath the sun-dappled palm trees: the Calypso is everything you'd expect a beachside surfers' bar to be and *the* place to find out about surf gossip. All that's missing is a prepsychedelic-era Brian Wilson propping up the jukebox (then again, Brian never *could* surf).

Lucky 13 BBQ BAR
(Hwy 115, cnr Calle 14; 9am-late) Starting early and staggering home late, you could spend your entire day in Lucky 13. In fact, many people seem to. By the time breakfast is done it's time for the midday cocktails, after several of which a slather of barbecued meat seems the most natural choice in the world. It's colorful, it's popular and its unappealing location, right on the main road, puts no one off whatsoever.

Tamboo Tavern BAR
(www.besidethepointe.com; Sandy Beach; noon-midnight) The patio bar of the Beside the Pointe guesthouse (p172) overlooks some of the best sand in Rincón. With a congenial après-surf scene and a young and vivacious local crowd who drink a little too much and dance a little too close, it was shortlisted by *Esquire* among the best bars in America, and it's easy to see why.

A rooftop terrace now makes it still more appealing.

La Carta Buena JUICE BAR
(Hwy 413 Km 1.2; 8am-3pm) Good coffee and better smoothies are served from a bright orange booth cunningly designed to trap you as you head out toward the lighthouse.

Pool Bar & Sushi BAR
(787-823-2583; http://poolbarsushi.com; off Hwy 413; 5pm-late Wed-Mon) This bar does exactly what it says on the tin: has a pool and serves sushi. It often shows surf films on a big screen. It's just back from Pools Beach. Take the first left-hand turn off Hwy 413, then immediately bear left again and follow the road downhill, asking directions where you can.

Shopping

Uncharted Studio ART, CLOTHING
(www.theunchartedstudio.com; Plaza de Recreo; 10am-5pm) This hip gallery, right on the central square, sells the work of local artists, as well as cool custom T-shirts, screen prints and paintings.

Parrotphernalia SOUVENIRS
(787-823-5654; www.lazyparrot.com; Lazy Parrot Inn, Hwy 413 Km 4.1; 9am-6pm) In the Lazy Parrot Inn (p173), this shop is a must-stop for parrot lovers. You will see handmade sea-glass jewelry here, which makes for one of Puerto Rico's more unique souvenirs.

Information

EMERGENCY

Police Station (787-823-2020) In the south corner of the village, off Nueva.

INTERNET ACCESS

Almost every place to stay and many restaurants have free wi-fi.

Banana Dang (www.bananadang.com; Hwy 413 Km 4.1; per 30min $3; 7am-7pm Mon & Wed-Sat, 9am-7pm Sun) Wi-fi and terminals available.

MEDICAL SERVICES

Rincón Centro de Salud (787-823-3120, 787-823-2795, 787-823-5171; 28 Muñoz Rivera) In town next to Paco's Grocery, this health center is a block south of Plaza de Recreo.

MONEY

There are ATMs in the lobby of almost every hotel and in many bars, so finding cash won't be a problem.

Banco Popular (9am-2:30pm Mon-Fri, 9am-noon Sat) Downtown near Plaza de Recreo. Has an ATM.

POST

Post Office (787-823-2625; 7:30am-4:30pm Mon-Fri, 8:30am-noon Sat) A quarter mile north of the Plaza de Recreo on Hwy 115.

TOURIST INFORMATION

The Tourism Association of Rincón puts out a great, amusing map, complete with site descriptions and essential phone numbers (it's completely not to scale). You can get one from your innkeeper: sometimes free, sometimes for $1.

Tourist Information Center (787-823-5024; Sunset Bldg, Cambija St; 8am-4:30pm Mon-Fri) In the Sunset Building adjacent to Rincón public beach.

Rincon Tourism Information (www.rincon.org)

Getting There & Away

Rincón doesn't have its own airport, but there are two in the area. If you are coming from San Juan, fly into Mayagüez. Aguadilla's Aeropuerto Rafael Hernández generally has a couple of flights a day from the New York area or Miami.

The *público* stand is just off Plaza de Recreo on Nueva. Expect to pay around $5 if you are headed north to Aguadilla or $3 to go south to Mayagüez (you can access San Juan from either of these cities). Both trips take about 40 minutes.

The easiest way to approach the town is via the valley roads of Hwy 402 and Hwy 115, both of which intersect Hwy 2 south of the Rincón peninsula.

Getting Around

Rincón – despite its mantle as an 'alternative' beach haven – has little provision for nonmotorized transport. A spread-out community with minimal public transport, Rincón has few sidewalks and almost no facilities for bicycles (the nearest bike rental is in Aguadilla). The only reliable way to get around the area is by rented car, taxi, irregular *públicos* or – if you're energetic and careful – walking. You will pay around $40 for a taxi from either the Aguadilla or Mayagüez airports. Car rentals can also be found at both of these destinations.

Mayagüez

POP 86,500

Like many of Puerto Rico's midsized cities, it takes some digging to discover the charm of Mayagüez. The 'Sultan of the West' is largely a transportation point for visitors to the west or those making the weekend junket to the Dominican Republic. The commonwealth's third biggest city, behind San Juan and Ponce, it has few comparable attractions. Still, there's plenty of vibrancy here, mostly thanks to a hard-partying student population and some ambitious restoration projects.

Founded in 1760 by émigrés from the Canary Islands, Mayagüez started inauspiciously, getting by on fruit production and agriculture. Even today the city remains noted for the sweetness of its mangoes. In the mid-19th century Mayagüez developed a contrarian nature and sheltered numerous revolutionary thinkers including Ramón Emeterio Betances, architect of the abortive Grito de Lares. Disaster struck in 1918 when an earthquake measuring 7.6 on the Richter scale all but destroyed the central business district, but the city rose from the rubble.

Mayagüez today boasts a large university over 13,000 students strong (specializing in sciences), various historic buildings (including the delightful Yagüez Theater), Puerto Rico's only zoo and planetarium, and a lovely central plaza. But its gastronomy and drinking scene alone would be enough to warrant a visit. Local treats include the delicacy known as *brazo gitano* (gypsy's arm; a jam sponge cake presented in the style of a Swiss roll) and an insanely sweet rum-and-wine cocktail known as Sangria de Fido. And when night falls, students descend Thursday through Saturday on a lively bar scene.

Sights

Catedral de Nuestra Señora de la Candelaria CHURCH

(Plaza Colón) Consecrated in 1760, Mayagüez' original Catholic church was replaced by the current model in 1836. The cathedral suffered many blows over the subsequent 80 years, culminating in the 1918 earthquake. Despite ambitious schemes, full refurbishment wasn't actually completed until 2004. The cathedral now sparkles afresh and survives as one of Puerto Rico's most evocative ecclesial monuments, with gilded scenes from the life of Christ behind the altar.

Zoológico de Puerto Rico ZOO

(787-834-8110; Bario Miradero, Hwy 108 interior; adult/child $10/5, parking $3; 8:30am-4pm Wed-Sun) The only real zoo on the island, with a recent multimillion-dollar top-to-bottom renovation, boasts over 600 species of reptiles, birds, amphibians and mammals. The highlight is the brightly polished arthropod and butterfly house, where kids squeal at glass enclosures of giant tropical cockroaches and brightly painted butterflies that flutter about. The latest thing is zoo nights, giving visitors the chance to observe the nocturnal behavioral patterns of animals. Off Hwy 108, the zoo is just northeast of the university in the same neighborhood as the agricultural research station.

★**Estación Experimental Agrícola Federal** AGRICULTURAL CENTER

(787-831-3435; http://eea.uprm.edu; Av Paris; 7am-4pm Mon-Fri) Wandering through the Estación Experimental Agrícola Federal, the tropical agricultural research station of the US Department of Agriculture, is a bit like wandering through a geeky botanical garden, what with the neatly-labeled plantations of yams, plantains, bananas and imported tropical 'cash crops' such as cinnamon trees from Sri Lanka. Today, the station also throws many of its federal grants behind biofuels and tropical medicine.

Mayagüez

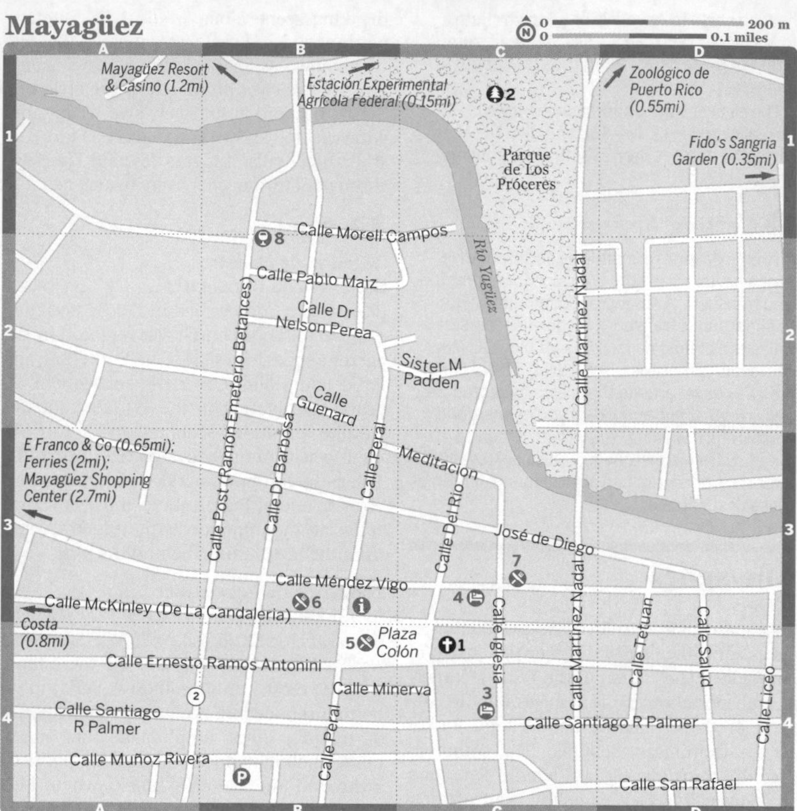

Mayagüez

Sights
1 Catedral de Nuestra Señora de la Candelaria C4
2 Parque de los Próceres C1

Sleeping
3 Hotel Colonial C4
4 Howard Johnson Downtown Mayagüez C3

Eating
5 Friends Cafe B4
6 Rex Cream B3
7 Ricomini Bakery C3
Stoa's .... (see 4)

Drinking & Nightlife
8 El Garabato B2

The adjacent city park known as **Parque de los Próceres** (dawn-dusk), on the south side of Hwy 65, also has verdant walkways and together these make an interesting stroll. These grounds lie just southeast of the university campus.

Sleeping

Hotel Colonial HOTEL **$**
(787-833-2150; www.hotelcolonial.com; 14 Calle Iglesia; r incl breakfast $49-99; P) With negotiation, these 29 rooms can be an affordable option in the center of town. Rooms are a bit bleak, but retain some haughty 'colonial' dignity and it's under half the price of any other overnight option. There's local charm in the long staircases and Moorish tiling of these historic digs, especially considering the building was once a home for nuns. A renovation is on the cards.

Howard Johnson Downtown Mayagüez HOTEL $$

(787-832-9191; www.hojo.com; 70 Calle Méndez Vigo; d $116-177;) This place was once a monastery but any spirituality here has long been superseded by rampant capitalism: it is firmly geared toward the business traveler. Rooms get corresponding facilities such as desks, mini-refrigerators and flat-screen televisions. Perks include a small courtyard pool and the absolutely enormous collection of wine at the on-site bar-restaurant, Stoa's. For discounts, book online.

Mayagüez Resort & Casino HOTEL $$$

(787-832-3030; www.mayaguezresort.com; Rte 104 Km 0.3; r $195-365;) This hotel-and-casino combo is the plushest option in town and locals pack into the casino to drink and play slots. Located off Hwy 2 north of town, the 140-unit property, with tennis courts and pool, stands on 20 lovely acres of tropical gardens – actually an adjunct to the nearby agricultural research station.

Eating & Drinking

Another culinary hit for Mayagüez: the first-ever store of national ice-cream chain **Rex Cream** (60 Calle McKinley; cones $1-3) is here – grab a cooling-down cone and retire to the plaza to indulge. The Mayagüez Resort & Casino is a sure-fire bet for upscale entertainment, and many other highly regarded restaurants and beach bars can be found southwest of the center on the **Boulevard Guanajibo**. The nightlife scene is notoriously hard to pin down, with students regularly switching allegiances between here-today-gone-tomorrow bars and clubs. The only way you are going to gauge the latest scene is by asking locals.

E Franco & Co BAKERY, CAFE $

(787-832-0070; www.brazogitano.net; 3 Manuel Pirallo; dishes $7-16) This salt-of-the-earth grocery-store-cum-cafe, stocked with fresh-baked goods and opulent hampers, has been here more than 150 years and is still drawing in punters from as far away as San Juan for a monthly stock up. Cocooned in the waterfront warehouse district, Franco's is an upmarket place with tables scattered around a deli counter reminiscent of an old English tearoom.

Order your lunch from a set menu and you'll receive a complimentary *brazo gitano* that washes down well with a cup of fine Puerto Rican coffee. Stocked with assorted condiments.

Stoa's SPANISH, BAR $

(70 Calle Méndez Vigo; dishes $2-8; breakfast, lunch & dinner) Don't be fooled by the simple first impression of this lunch counter, located in the lobby of Howard Johnson: Stoa's has one of the best wine selections in western Puerto Rico. There's a diverse offering by the glass, and by the bottle the sky's the limit, with imports from Italy, Spain, France and California.

The food is nothing exceptional – a menu of grilled sandwiches and hot/cold tapas – but it's all elegantly prepared.

Ricomini Bakery BAKERY, CAFE $

(101 Calle Méndez Vigo; dishes $2-8; 5am-1am) The Ricomini bakery and deli has been on this corner for well over a century. With a lunch counter, some tables and basic groceries, this is a de facto social hub of downtown Mayagüez: deals are made, relationships forged (and broken), and gossip boisterously exchanged.

Roll up for steaming coffee, scrambled eggs, a slice of the famous *brazo gitano* or a delicious toasted Cubano sandwich, stacked with ham, roasted pork, cheese and pickles.

Friends Cafe CAFE $

(Plaza Colón; snacks $1-4; 8am-11pm;) An unmissable little place, right on the plaza, Friends serves knock-out coffee, great smoothies and wonderful ricotta-and-spinach *empanadillas* (dough stuffed with meat or fish).

★**Costa** INTERNATIONAL $$

(787-519-6647; Plaza de las Banderas; mains $19-36; 11am-11pm) Right by the sea, Costa is a jewel in an otherwise underwhelming Mayagüez waterfront. Affluent residents chill in a minimalist space buffeted by icy air-con that wouldn't look amiss in a New York contemporary art museum. There's a large patio with an open-air bar and select cool-sounding (and pretty good-tasting) dishes like *filete mignon* of Angus. It's perfect for weekend brunch, too.

Fido's Sangria Garden BAR, CAFE

(75 & 78 Calle Dulievre, off Hwy 106; 11am-late Wed-Sat, to 6pm Sun) Wilfrido 'Fido' Aponte became a local legend for his potent sangria – a blend of Bacardi 151 and extraordinarily sweet tropical fruit juice. The drink garnered such a cultish following that,

according to locals, Bacardi offered a king's ransom for the recipe, which Fido refused. His heirs still produce several varieties of the 'wine cocktail' and sell them out of a garage in a residential neighborhood of Mayagüez.

Across the street from here is Fido's Sangria Garden where food can help soak up the booze. The sangria is delicious stuff, but the high sugar content ensures a memorable hangover. To find this place, head northeast out of town on Hwy 106 and turn right into a residential neighborhood on Arturo Gigante. Make a left on Dulievre.

El Garabato BAR

(102 Calle Post; ⏲1pm-2am) El Garabato is more of a typical pub than a club. Here students swing by for a quick one between classes or stop to play dominoes with the regulars; wild nights are saved for **Red Baron Pub**, the city's classic dance club, which is upstairs in the same building.

The way to do it is to get tanked up in El Garaboto before staggering upstairs to jump to the reggaetón, rap, hip-hop and Spanish rock. El Garaboto's happy-hour prices get you $1 beer but you'll be charged around $6 to get into the Red Baron if there are live bands.

Information

Hospital Dr Ramón Emeterio Betances (Mayagüez Medical Center; ☎787-652-9200; Rte 2 cnr Carolina)

Tourist Information Office (☎787-833-1650; cnr Calles McKinley & Peral; ⏲8am-4pm Mon-Sat) On the main square; well stocked with local maps.

Getting There & Away

AIR

The Aeropuerto de Mayagüez is about 3 miles north of town, just off Hwy 2. **Cape Air** (☎800-352-0714; www.flycapeair.com) currently has three to four flights daily to and from San Juan ($49 to $89 one-way). **Continental Airlines** (www.continental.com) flies directly to Mayagüez from several US cities.

CAR & MOTORCYCLE

Hwy 2, part of the island's nominal ring road, brings you to town from the north or south. While this is a four-lane road, it is plagued by traffic lights. Hwy 105 is the west end of the Ruta Panorámica, which leads from Mayagüez into the mountains and to Maricao.

FERRY

America Cruise Ferries (☎787-832-4800; http://acferries.com) currently does the 12-hour run between Mayagüez and Santo Domingo just once each week, departing Mayagüez Wednesdays at 8pm, and Santo Domingo Tuesdays at 8pm. The other two weekly journeys between Santo Domingo and Puerto Rico go direct to San Juan.

At the time of research, one-way tickets from Mayagüez started at $104.50 for a sleeping chair. Cabins are an additional 50 bucks while vehicles cost from $250 on top of that.

PÚBLICO

The *público* terminal is in Barrio Paris, about four blocks north of Plaza Colón. *Públicos* make the trip to west-coast beach towns such as Aguadilla and Rincón (each about an hour away), and the long trek to San Juan ($20 to $28, plan on four hours at least).

Getting Around

A few taxis usually show up at the airport when the flights arrive from San Juan; if none are there, or if you need to get to the airport, call **White Taxi** (☎787-832-1154). The one-way fare to town is about $8.

To rent a car you will find vendors at the airport as well as in Mayagüez Shopping Center, 2.7 miles south of town on Hwy 2. The shopping center has an **Enterprise** (☎787-805-3722).

Cabo Rojo Area

Cabo Rojo (Red Cape) is the name of both a small administrative town (10 miles south of Mayagüez and 8 miles west of San Germán) and the wider municipality that surrounds it. To add to the confusion, it is also the name used to describe the rugged coastline that constitutes Puerto Rico's extreme and rarely traveled southwestern tip. Got it?

This is a remote region of coastal mangroves, wildfowl-packed lagoons, dry forest and, further south, extensive salt pans. Included in the Cabo Rojo municipality are the Playa de Joyuda area (noted island-wide for its gastronomy), the grungy coastal village of Boquerón, and the more idyllic fishing village of El Combate, but these serve as mere trailers to the big-screen event: the lonely Refugio Nacional Cabo Rojo and its surrounds. This reserve covers the southern tip of mainland Puerto Rico, characterized by the Los Morrillos Lighthouse, rising out of a rugged headland on the southernmost point near what locals claim to be the island's best stretch of beach.

Busy Hwy 2 cuts inland between Mayagüez and Yauco, leaving this rather isolated corner of the island refreshingly untrodden. There's an extensive patchwork of wildlife refuges here, along with trails to hike, some unusual birds and mammals to spot and a quiet network of country roads that make for excellent cycling.

The best selection of accommodations lie in Boquerón and the best restaurants are divided between Boquerón and Playa de Joyuda.

Cabo Rojo (El Pueblo)

The *pueblo* (town) of Cabo Rojo will more likely depress than inspire you, what with its manicured but bland center and surrounding sea of strip malls on Hwy 100. It is, however, notable for three things that will come in useful as you commence exploration of the area: a fine museum, an excellent bike shop, and the regional tourist information office.

Its one attraction, within a park on the south side, is the **Museo de los Próceres** (787-255-1560; Hwy 312; 9am-4pm Mon-Fri) FREE. A grand, colonnaded facade announces this engaging, well-kept museum, dedicated to local heroes such as Ramón Emeterio Betances, the father of Puerto Rico's independence movement, and Roberto Confresí, a once notorious local pirate. The town also hosts one of the best cycle shops, the **Wheel Shop** (787-255-0095; www.wheelshoppr.com; Hwy 100 Km 5.9), and the regional office of the **Puerto Rico Tourism Company** (PRTC; 787-721-2400; www.seepuertorico.com; Hwy 100 Km 6.6, Galeria 100 mall next to El Mesón restaurant; 8am-4pm).

El Pueblo is Cabo Rojo's transport 'hub'. As well as having the only connections to the more remote places in the area (although it's asking a lot of the terrible *público* connections just to get to Boquerón), from here you can catch a van to Mayagüez ($5, 40 minutes), Ponce ($9, two hours) or San Germán ($5, 20 minutes).

Playa de Joyuda

South of Mayagüez and just north of Boquerón, little Joyuda is a dining destination, famous for its string of seafood restaurants and known islandwide as the Milla de Oro del Buen Comer (Gourmet Golden Mile). It might be a bit generous to call these places 'gourmet,' but the seafood can be very fresh, and more than a dozen family-owned establishments line a 3-mile oceanfront stretch of Hwy 102, specializing in oysters, crab and shrimp. Often, you can get a seat right over the water and look down at startlingly large carp who loll up to lazily beg for table scraps.

While Joyuda isn't a beach haven, there are plenty of accommodation options in this ramshackle west coast outpost, and with a couple of decent sailing and dive operators and a nearby nature reserve, there's enough outdoor adventures to work up an appetite for an evening of shellfish. Just offshore, the tiny **Isla de Ratones** has a white sandy beach and is great for snorkeling.

Sights & Activities

Reserva Natural Laguna de Joyuda NATURE RESERVE

The heart of the 300-acre Reserva Natural Laguna de Joyuda is a sizeable saltwater lagoon with a depth that rarely exceeds 4ft. The sanctuary is of great importance to waterfowl and other migratory birds that come here to prey on more than 40 species of fish. Humans come here for the same reason.

The reserve is also home to one of Puerto Rico's famous bioluminescent bodies of water, like those in La Parguera and Vieques, but is free of commercial tourism. After dark, microorganisms give the dark water a green glow. Travelers with access to a kayak can launch a nighttime exploration of the lagoon; watch for the access road off Hwy 102 near Parador Perichi's.

Tourmarine Adventures (787-375-2625; www.tourmarinepr.com; Rte 102 Km 14.1) is the outfit to ask about renting kayaks to go out on the *laguna*. It also runs trips around the area on a 33ft lobster boat. If you've got a big enough group, the owner might arrange trips to Isla Mona...if you can get a permit. Then there are snorkeling trips around the nearby cliffs ($40 without equipment), deep-sea fishing in the Pasaje de la Mona ($500 per half-day charter) and diving off Isla Desecheo ($75 per person).

Sleeping

Hotel Costa de Oro Inn HOTEL $

(787-851-5010; Rte 102 Km 14.7; r $55-85; P) A tiny pool and spotless rooms make this little guesthouse the best value within miles. There are no big luxuries on the property, but you'll be very comfortable. There's also a small cafeteria on site where mains come for a $4 bargain.

Parador Joyuda Beach HOTEL $$
(☎787-851-5650; Hwy 102 Km 11.7; r $70-125; P❄≋) Up the road from the Joyuda Plaza, this hotel is actually *on* a narrow strand of beach. Snorkeling right offshore is OK, as long as the wind stays southerly. The hotel has a restaurant, a swimming pool and 41 unsurprising rooms with those ubiquitous flowery bedspreads and terracotta tiled floors.

Parador Perichi's HOTEL $$
(☎787-851-3131; www.hotelperichi.com; Rte 102 Km 14.3; r from $96; P❄≋) Close to Joyuda Plaza, Perichi's is Joyuda's fanciest place, which isn't saying much. Although it has definitely seen better days, the 41 rooms have air-con, and there's a large pool and a restaurant you won't need given the nearby 'gourmet' offerings.

Eating

Joyuda is a great place for a bit of culinary exploration, and it would take weeks of tasting to settle on a favorite. Park your car or bike, stroll up and down the strip a few times and see where your nose leads you. For informal dining, locals swear by El Bohió, Raito and Vista Bahía. Others champion El Gato Negro. You might end up in all or none of these, sampling lobster, *mofongo* (mashed plantains), oysters or crab. Joyuda's restaurants aren't always fancy in terms of decor, but the food is legendary.

★**El Bohió** SEAFOOD $
(www.restauranteelbohiojoyuda.com; Hwy 102 Km 13.9; dishes $9-21; ⊙lunch & dinner Thu-Tue) The best seafood in town is the subject of fierce debate among locals, but this place is a certain contender, with a long list of shellfish and fresh fillets done in a variety of styles and waitstaff offering recommended fresh catches. What really puts El Bohió over the edge is the atmosphere – it's perched on stilts right above the crystal water.

El Gato Negro SEAFOOD $
(☎787-851-2966; Hwy 102 Km 13.6; dishes $9-22; ⊙lunch & dinner) El Gato Negro vies with El Bohió for the most locally-popular joint. It's not as fancy as Island View nor does it have so idyllic a waterfront terrace as El Bohió, but it somehow feels a more authentic Puerto Rican experience than either, patronized by everyone from gossiping old *abuelas* (grandmothers) to weekending families from San Juan. Stewed conch is a solid choice.

Island View SEAFOOD $
(☎787-851-9264; Hwy 102 Km 13.8; dishes $7-21; ⊙lunch & dinner Thu-Tue) Great views of the few small cays that dot the water off the coast and big steaming dishes of seafood specialties, such as rice and crab, have made Island View (the sophisticated diner's choice) very popular.

Getting There & Away

Joyuda isn't on a regular *público* route, but you can drive here easily enough from either Mayagüez or Cabo Rojo on Rte 102. Alternatively, take a taxi or hire a bike from the Wheel Shop (p181) in Cabo Rojo (El Pueblo).

Boquerón

POP 2000

Boquerón is something of the wild child of west coast fishing towns, a place that pulses with the beats of the Caribbean, and colorful characters who wander among wooden-shack restaurants and open-air food stalls. It boasts a well-regarded and sheltered *balneario* and a marina, but the best diversions lie out of town: either diving or paying a visit to the surrounding Boquerón verdant patchwork of refuges, nature reserves and state forests – plus several palm-shaded beaches within a short drive.

Historically, Boquerón's legacy is possibly even older than Caparra's. Certain scholars have claimed that this is where Columbus first set anchor when he 'discovered' the island of Puerto Rico in 1493. Back in the day (well, maybe the early '90s), Boquerón was the place to hang hereabouts, but those days are gone. It lacks El Combate's comparatively untouched charms, La Parguera's intimate vibe or Rincón's world-class water sports, and the overall feel is of a worn once-hip village surfing on the back of its past reputation.

But it does attract travelers of all types, from wealthy yachters to brightly dressed Rastafarians, has the best array of accommodations in the area, and the closest semblance to nightlife in the southwest. At night the two main roads are shut to traffic and people can indulge in that favorite Caribbean pastime of *limin'* – hanging out, chilling, and moving between bars with a drink in hand.

A NIGHT AT THE BEACH

Camping on Puerto Rico's beaches is illegal, but some of the large, developed facilities at public beaches around the island, including Balneario Boquerón, have government-operated cabanas to rent. These facilities vary in quality – some are little more than cinder-block apartments with a kitchenette and a grill, others are a bit more plush, with balconies and barbecue grills. Still, they make an affordable way to stay on the beach. Here's the catch: since they are mostly for Puerto Rican families, they are poorly marketed to tourists, and guests have to bring their own linen. Contact the Centro Vacacional Boquerón (p184).

Sights

Refugio de Boquerón NATURE RESERVE

The western part of the Bosque Estatal de Boquerón is protected as the Refugio de Boquerón, a 400-acre patch of mangrove wetlands, about 2 miles south of town between the coast and Hwy 301. This is an excellent area for birdwatching; more than 60 species are commonly sighted, including migratory ducks, ospreys and mangrove canaries. An excellent way to see this sanctuary is to rent a kayak and paddle south across Bahía de Boquerón (Boquerón Bay).

The **main office** (787-851-7260; Rte 101 Km 1.1, Boquerón; 7:30am-3:30pm) can provide information on the *refugio* and has a 700ft walkway leading into the mangroves. Or stop at Km 1.1 just off Rte 101 and start walking along the trail you see there. Insect repellent is a must-carry in dry season, as is water, and always watch where you put your feet: tiny crabs scuttle about.

Beaches

Balneario Boquerón BEACH

(parking $5) Just south of town, the Balneario Boquerón ranks among the best public beach facilities in Puerto Rico. The mile-long arc of sand gets insanely busy on high-season weekends, but it's still big enough to carve out a relatively quiet space, and the beach area is backed by coconut palms and ample grassy lawns and showers, changing rooms, toilets and picnic tables. It's designated as one of only five Blue Flag beaches in Puerto Rico.

To get there, turn left (heading toward town) off Hwy 101 at the Boquerón Beach Hotel and proceed along a small spur road for a quarter-mile. You can also reach the beach on foot from downtown Boquerón; a small footbridge connects at the end of Calle José de Diego.

Playa Buyé BEACH

Playa Buyé is a small palm-fringed beach that's about 2.5 miles north of town off Hwy 307.

Activities

Diving & Snorkeling

Nearby La Parguera has good diving and snorkeling opportunities.

Mona Aquatics DIVING, SNORKELING

(787-851-2185; www.monaaquatics.com; Calle José de Diego) Next to the *club náutico* (marina), west of the center of town, Mona Aquatics has a 40ft dive boat – *Orca Too* – that takes you on local dives (two-tank dives from $75, one-tank night dives $50) or longer excursions to Isla Desecheo (from $115). Prices include snack, weights, instruction and two dives, and get cheaper if you have a group. It also rents out snorkeling gear.

Kayaking

Along Calle José de Diego, there are a number of vendors renting kayaks and other gear to get in the water. This is a great option if you want to explore the mangroves east of town.

Boquerón Kayak Rental KAYAKING

(787-255-1849; Calle José de Diego) Has pedal boats and surf bikes, as well as kayaks (all from $15 per hour). Cash only.

Sleeping

There are a number of private homes with rooms or apartments to rent, look for signs nailed to telephone poles along Calle José de Diego.

Buyé Beach Resort CABINS $

(787-255-0358; Hwy 30 Km 4.8; cabins $75;) Located on a popular beach north of town, this clean and simple operation has 16 cinder-block-and-tile cabins on the beach. Each one accommodates three to four people and includes a private bathroom and kitchen. There is a coin laundry here, too. Parking is $3 (refunded if you stay).

★Villa Vista Puerto ECOLODGE $$
(☎787-255-4144; off Hwy 307; r from $100; P) This hand-built ecolodge is a unique choice for travelers looking to get off the beaten path and book an environmentally sensitive stay. It's set high on a hillside overlooking Puerto Royal and the surrounding jungle, about halfway between Boquerón and Cabo Rojo (El Pueblo) on Hwy 307.

There's a guesthouse for two and a rustic-chic, canvas-topped cabana, both of which have hand-built driftwood furniture, a spacious indoor area, a great outdoor cooking area and use of a jungle shower. The place is perfect for couples who want to really get away, and though it's isolated from dining and entertainment options, it's in the heart of some stunning nature.

★Centro Vacacional Boquerón CABINS $$
(☎787-851-1900, reservations 787-622-5200; apt $75-115) This excellent, enormous government-operated complex is the best of its kind in Puerto Rico – a sprawling village of basic apartments that hold six people and have a bathroom, kitchen, bunk beds and ceiling fans. They come in two classes – cabanas, a basic option with no air-con, and villas, which are more modern and have air-con. The rooms are a bit like summer camp – you even have to provide your own linen – but the beach outside your door ranks among the island's best.

The place gets booked a year in advance for summer and holidays, but stands half-empty in low season.

Adamari's Apartments APARTMENTS $$
(☎787-851-6860; Calle José de Diego; r from $133; P ❄) Adamari's is the tall building right next to Parador Boquemar, with a launderette out the front. The nine clean apartments (each with a kitchenette and many with ocean views) are serviceable and good value for the price. They all have cable TV, which is nice, and mattresses covered in some kind of protective plastic, which is not.

Parador Boquemar HOTEL $$
(☎787-851-2158; Calle José de Diego; r $107-133; P ❄) A bit of a rabbit-hutch feel pervades in the 60 generic rooms here, piled on top of each other over three crowded stories in a building that has seen better days. That said, because you're essentially 'downtown,' the Boquemar is rather popular. Rooms are clean, but about what you might expect from a slightly worn American motel. There's a pool, an above-average on-site restaurant and friendly, down-to-earth service.

Wildflowers INN $$
(☎787-851-1793; www.wildflowersguesthouse.com; 13 Calle Muñoz Rivera; r $100-125; P ❄) A Victorian-era house right in central Boquerón, Wildflowers feels like a misplaced New England B&B. Doubling as a gallery, the cozy rooms and sleek communal areas display the work of local artists. There's no maid service or breakfast, but rooms can sleep up to four and there's shared use of a microwave and coffee machine along with private refrigerators. Dark-wood floors and furnishings add a dash of 19th-century romance.

Cofresí Beach Hotel HOTEL $$
(☎787-254-3000; www.cofresibeach.com; 57 Calle Muñoz Rivera; apt $129-219;) For families this is a nearly uniform recommendation – each unit is fully equipped with a microwave and TV, and its location in a residential neighborhood is a bit removed from the downtown craziness. There's a limited maid service available by prearrangement, and a view of the bay from the pool.

Eating & Drinking

The cheapest eats are from the kiosks along Calle José de Diego, where vendors stand proudly beside piles of oysters and clams, which are shucked open, juiced with fresh lemon or hot sauce and slurped down on the spot. *Pinchos* (kebabs with grilled chicken, pork or seafood) are another option. None of it is above $4.

★Los Remos Restaurant & Beach Club INTERNATIONAL, BAR $
(Calle José de Diego; breakfasts $6-8, mains $11-20; ⌚8am-11pm) It's actually rare in Puerto Rico for a place to offer everything from breakfast through to late-night drinks and do it well. Long may Los Remos continue in this vein. Plopped right in the center of the strip, it opens up onto the water out back. Creative breakfasts feature the likes of coconut French toast, while lunch and dinner can be anything from fajitas to mahimahi fillet.

The cocktails can't be bettered in Boquerón.

Terramar ITALIAN $
(Cnr Calles José de Diego & Hermgenes Pou; mains $5-16; ⌚2-11pm) A great new option on the small back road that loops off the main drag from next to Wildflowers guesthouse around to Los Remos Restaurant & Beach Club. Terramar has the vibe of a cozy Madrid tapas bar and Italianesque fare almost unequalled in western Puerto Rico.

La Marea SEAFOOD, CARIBBEAN $
(5 Calle José de Diego; mains $8-15; ⌚lunch-10pm) La Marea is a lofty notch above most alfresco dining on the strip and the dishes – shrimp-stuffed plantains and cuts of fresh fish – are a good match for the unpretentious elegance. The bar serves labor-intensive mojitos and spot-on piña coladas.

Galloway's Bar & Restaurant SEAFOOD, BAR $$
(Calle José de Diego; dinner mains $12-24) 'Snowbirds Welcome' reads the sign out the front, but those four-seasoned spring-breakers from Minneapolis you've just spied on the waterfront deck aren't the only birds pecking at the food. Small black-feathered creatures will make a beeline for any spare tasty morsel, so hold on to your freshly prepared octopus. Something of a local legend, Galloway's combines great seafood with a picturesque waterfront setting on Boquerón's rustic downtown strip.

All pretense of being a restaurant is dropped by 9pm on weekends, when a fun-loving yuppie crowd shows up for live 1980s and '90s rock. There's also occasional Spanish guitar music.

Pika-Pika MEXICAN $$
(☎787-851-2440; 224 Calle Estación; mains $12-24; ✍) Although discerning fans of Mexican cuisine might be a bit underwhelmed by the cheese-covered Puerto Rican/Tex Mex fusions, this high-class cantina located on the road in and out of Boquerón is a place to escape the thumping. Here for donkey's years, it's dimly lit and cool, and patronized by families and groups of friends. Deep-dish burritos and tacos can be prepared vegetarian-style. The margaritas are lethal!

Getting There & Away

The easiest way to get to Boquerón by *público* is via the town of Cabo Rojo (El Pueblo). From April to August, it's easy to find one for about $3.

If you're driving from El Pueblo or Mayagüez, follow Hwy 100 south to Hwy 101 and turn right (west). Driving from San Germán, it's a straight shot west on Hwy 101, south of Lajas.

El Combate

Remember that saying about first appearances being deceptive? Thus it is with El Combate. Named after a 1759 colonial turf war to control the lucrative salt flats to the south, El Combate (The Battle) is the last village heading south before the Los Morrillos Lighthouse, and as you skirt it the community appears nothing more than a sprawl of backyard trailer camping sites and dreary condos. Alight in its tiny center, however, and a different feeling shines through. Here, the dreamy beach village vibe that Boquerón long since lost lingers yet. Appropriately, you'll find one of western Puerto Rico's best beach bars, Annie's Place, a couple of tawdry guesthouses, and the gorgeous 3-mile-long strip of sand that affronts the Pasaje de la Mona. This beach is perfect for swimming and is perennially popular with vacationing Puerto Rican families.

Sleeping & Eating

You won't find luxury, but then again, visitors here spend little time indoors.

Combate Beach Hotel & Restaurant HOTEL $
(☎787-254-2358; www.combatebachresort.com; Hwy 3301 Km 2.7; r $140-201; P ❄ ≋) A favorite oasis in El Combate, this hotel is right on the beach about a quarter of a mile from all the development in town. The motel-style rooms are simple but clean, with private bathrooms. They're also the best rooms you're going to get in town.

There's a casual restaurant serving seafood and *comida criolla* and the whole place runs smoothly under the watchful eyes of the proprietors.

★**Annie's Place** RESTAURANT, BAR $
(Hwy 3301 Km 2.9; mains $5-15) Breezes from the ocean drift into the mellow, open-walled Annie's, a bar and restaurant with sensational *empanadillas*, lobster soup, fish salad and homemade burgers. Overlooking the long public beach, this has the best atmosphere of El Combate bars, and it gets popular in the evening, when couples come by to watch the sun set and check out the gringo-centric live music that's often on.

Getting There & Away

Públicos run frequently to and from the town of Cabo Rojo (El Pueblo) from April to the end of

August ($3), where you can connect to Mayagüez ($4, 30 minutes) or Ponce ($8, two hours).

If you're arriving by car, El Combate is at the end of Hwy 3301. Go west at the turnoff from Hwy 301.

Refugio Nacional Cabo Rojo & Around

Rolling hills tumble into mangroves and crystalline salt pans. Rust-red limestone cliffs fall precipitously away into the ocean or drop to beaches reckoned by many to be the epitome of Caribbean paradise. Quiet lanes and well-marked trails twist and turn tempting cyclists and hikers into blissfully car-free exploration, and interpretation centers leave travelers insightfully informed about what they're seeing. This is the Refugio Nacional Cabo Rojo, the southernmost extent of Puerto Rico, crowned by its iconic Los Morillos Lighthouse.

Whilst the main approach to the peninsula on which the lighthouse sits is via Hwy 301 from Hwy 100, there is a more adventurous option. For a lonely drive through undeveloped coastal plains or a cycling adventure, approach from La Parguera via Hwy 304, Hwy 305 and Hwy 303. Then follow Hwy 301 south until it turns to dirt and stops.

Sights & Activities

Centro de Visitantes de Pesca y Vida Silverstre de Cabo Rojo NATURE RESERVE
(Refugio Nacional Cabo Rojo; ☎787-851-7258; Hwy 301 Km 5.1; 9am-4pm Mon-Sat) This refuge is about a mile north of the Hwy 301 turnoff to El Combate. Its visitors center contains displays on local wildlife and wildlife management techniques. Outdoors you will find birdwatching trails among the ruins of an old farmstead in the Valle de Lajas (Lajas Valley). The area around the plains and shores of Cabo Rojo is a major winter ground for migratory ducks, herons and songbirds, and more than 130 bird species have been sighted here.

You can arrange guided hikes through the refuge at the Centro Interpretativos Las Salinas de Cabo Rojo.

Corozo Salt Flats NATURE RESERVE
Vast salt flats surround the rocky, dramatic narrow peninsula that heralds your approach to the southwestern tip of the island. You'll pass pools of evaporating brine and mounds of salt waiting to be shipped to market alongside the dirt road as you head south toward the Los Morillos Lighthouse. This can be a bizarre, picturesque and adventurous place to explore, a place where scrub forest gives way to an elevated headland surrounded by steep limestone cliffs and amazing views of the ocean.

The best place to get a handle on this salty domain is the **Centro Interpretativos Las Salinas de Cabo Rojo** (☎787-851-2999; Hwy 301 Km 11; 8:30am-4:30pm Wed-Sat, 9:30am-5:30pm Sun). This visitor center is staffed by knowledgeable, ecosensitive guides who give thorough explanations of local flora and fauna. Across the road is a three-story wooden lookout tower that offers a bird's-eye view of the salt pans, a major bird migratory corridor. There is also a small network of hiking and mountain-biking trails here (though no place to rent a bike), which lead to a stretch of very long beach on the island's west side. This is not perfect sand – much of it is dotted with mangrove forest – but it is excellent for private swimming.

Los Morrillos Lighthouse LIGHTHOUSE
(10am-6pm Wed-Sun, with seasonal variations) FREE From this smartly remodeled lighthouse at the bone-rattling end of PR 301 just past the salt pans, there's not much fur-

SALT WARS

The salt pans that you'll see as you head out toward the Los Morrillos Lighthouse are part of a legacy many centuries old. Humans have been gathering salt on Cabo Rojo since AD 700. When the Spanish arrived they were quick to see the potential of the evaporation pools used by the Taíno people to make salt, and they expanded the business. Salt production became such a lucrative force in the area that locals fought over it. The very name of El Combate (aka The Battle) references a war between El Combate folks and factions from the nearby town of Lajas over control of the salt flats. Many of those heralding from El Combate may still refer to themselves as *los mata con hacha* (those that kill with axes) whilst Lajas citizens, who purportedly responded to the axes with stones, are often known as the *tira piedras* (stone throwers).

ther you can go: you're as south as it gets in Puerto Rico. The lighthouse stands sentinel on the headland of Punta Jagüey, with some dramatic cliff formations right beyond the outer walls. An observation deck overlooks the surreal turquoise of Playa Santa's water and across the expanse of Caribbean.

If a volunteer is on hand at the lighthouse, they might offer a casual history of the area (largely revolving around salt). The final stretch of unmetalled road is not passable for cars but a 10-minute walk from the parking lot will have you at the door.

Playa Santa BEACH

From the same parking space as that of Los Morrillos Lighthouse (or from another a little further on down the track to the left), you can follow the trails out to an immaculate crescent beach known as Playa Santa, where a protected bay makes excellent swimming for both humans and manatees. The beach here is touted as one of western Puerto Rico's best (and given greater accolades by some): one thing it most certainly has is a welcome feeling of isolation.

Trails from here circle back up to the lighthouse, or you can continue exploring around the windswept headlands.

Sleeping & Eating

Parador Bahía Salinas Beach Resort & Spa RESORT $$

(787-254-1213; www.bahiasalinas.com; Hwy 301 Km 11.5; r incl breakfast $90-200; P ❄ @ ≋) As if the location wasn't enough – rust-red cliffs, salt flats and an adjacent wildlife refuge – the rooms in this gorgeous, palm-shaded boutique parador have balconies, sleigh beds and tropical flowers. The serene grounds are immaculate too – drape-covered sun loungers and canopy beds look over an undisturbed stretch of ocean and the infinity pool that frames some of the island's most spectacular sunsets.

As to the service, it's been resting on its laurels recently but it remains an outstanding (indeed, the only) choice hereabouts. The award-winning Aqua al Cuello Restaurant is on-site. During high season there can be a three-day minimum stay; to get lower rates, book via the website.

Aqua al Cuello Restaurant CARIBBEAN, FUSION $$

(787-254-1212; www.bahiasalinas.com; Parador Bahía Salinas Beach Resort & Spa, Hwy 301 Km 11.5; meals $8-28; lunch & dinner) On a beautiful deck over the water, this breezy dining destination cooks up equally beautiful food that has bagged Puerto Rico's best Mesón Gastronómico award in recent years. The mahi-mahi in Creole sauce is plated with style and backed up by some surprising specials. Ever tried kangaroo?

Information

For information on the entire Cabo Rojo area, the Porta del Sol branch of the Puerto Rico Tourism Company (p181) is located in Cabo Rojo (El Pueblo).

Getting There & Around

This is one of the best opportunities for exploration without a car in Puerto Rico. You can hire a bike in Cabo Rojo (El Pueblo) at the Wheel Shop (p181). The town is connected to Ponce and Mayagűez by *público*. Public transport does not reach the Refugio Nacional Cabo Rojo area. The closest you can get is El Combate, which is served in season (April to September) by *públicos* and seldom if at all outside of these months.

San Germán

POP 34,500

Puerto Rico's second-oldest city (after San Juan), San Germán is also one of its best preserved. Founded in 1511 near present-day Mayagüez on the orders of Juan Ponce de León, the original coastal settlement was moved twice in its early life to escape the unwelcome attention of plundering French corsairs. The current town, which lies about 10 miles inland from the Cabo Rojo coast, was established in 1573 and once administered a municipality that encompassed the whole western half of the island. Downsizing itself over the ensuing four centuries, contemporary San Germán (named for Germaine de Foix, the second wife of Spain's King Ferdinand) is far more unassuming than the colonial capital of yore, although the historical buildings – some of which date from the 17th century – retain a quiet dignity. For those interested in colonial Creole architecture, this little town can only be bested by Ponce and Old San Juan.

Despite its rich architectural heritage and lofty listing on the National Register of Historic Places, San Germán is largely ignored (wrongly) by its modern inhabitants and by tourists. As a result, the classic four-square-block colonial center – laid out in an

San Germán

San Germán

Top Sights
1 Iglesia de Porta Coeli D1

Sights
2 Casa Acosta y Flores D2
3 Casa de Lola Rodríguez de Tió A1
4 Casa Morales C1
5 Casa Perichi C2
6 Catedral de San Germán de Auxerre B1
Iglesia de Porta Coeli Museum ..... (see 1)
7 Viejo Alcaldía C1

Sleeping
8 Parador Oasis B2

Eating
9 Chateaux De Auxerre B1
10 De Lirious C2
11 Tapas Café C2

unusual irregular pattern – is a veritable ghost town after dark. The city's one downtown hotel sports cobwebs and few of the numerous historic buildings are open for public viewing.

But there is a clutch of excellent restaurants and, fortuitously, San Germán's semi-abandonment lends it an air of authenticity. It is far more absorbing to stroll around than any other town or city west of Ponce, being one of the few settlements in Puerto Rico where the central city core hasn't been demeaned by thoughtless development.

Sights

★Iglesia de Porta Coeli — CHURCH

(Heaven's Gate; Plaza Santo Domingo) This small, squat building might not look like much, but it is actually one of the oldest surviving ecclesial buildings in the Americas. Originally constructed between 1606 and 1607 on the orders of Queen Isabella of Spain, it served as the chapel for a Dominican monastery that stood on this site until the 1860s. Atop a long, steep flight of steps overlooking Plaza Santo Domingo, the current structure dates from 1692.

The Porta Coeli has an interior with ausubo pillars and roof beams, and a ceiling made from palm wood, which is typical of construction in Puerto Rico during the 17th and 18th centuries. Inside, a small **museum** (Plaza Santo Domingo; admission $1; ⌚8:30am-4:30pm Wed-Sun) displays statues of the black Virgin of Montserrat, folksy carvings of Christ imported from the early days of San Juan, choral books dating back 300 years and other curios.

Catedral de San Germán de Auxerre — CHURCH

(⌚8-11:30am & 1-3pm Mon-Fri, 8-11am Sat, Mass 7am & 7:30pm Mon-Sat, 7am, 8:30am, 10am & 7:30pm Sun) San Germán's cathedral is named for the town's patron saint and is noticeably grander than the diminutive Porta Coeli. Facing Plaza Francisco Mariano Quiñones, it dates back to 1739, but major restorations and expansions over the years (especially in the 19th century) have created a mélange of architectural styles, including colonial, neoclassical and baroque elements.

This is an active parish; if you visit for a Saturday or Sunday service, take note of the crystal chandelier that helps to light the main nave and the trompe l'oeil fresco.

Viejo Alcaldía HISTORIC BUILDING
The old city hall, which acts as a dividing line between the city's two central squares, is a classic example of a 19th-century colonial municipal building, with its stately facade and cool inner courtyard. The building currently serves as a police station and the headquarters for San Germán's rather low-key tourist office.

Universidad Interamericana UNIVERSITY
(Luna) Founded in 1912, this university is now the largest private facility of its kind in the western hemisphere. The 267-acre campus just west of San Germán is probably the most attractive college setting in Puerto Rico and it draws about 6000 students from all corners of the globe. There are branch campuses in San Juan, Arecibo, Barranquitas, Bayamón, Fajardo, Guayama and Ponce.

Casa de Lola Rodríguez de Tió MUSEUM
(☎787-892-3500; 13 Dr Santiago Veve) Built in 1843 in a neoclassical Creole style and said to be an excellent example of local 19th-century domestic architecture, this house is reputedly the town's most continually occupied residence. Its most famous resident was a 19th-century poet and patriot named Lola Rodríguez de Tió, who was exiled in the 1860s for her revolutionary activities. Lola's mother was a descendant of Ponce de León. The house is supposed to act as a museum, but is often closed. Phone ahead.

Historic Homes

The following historic homes are not open to the public, but are beautifully preserved examples of valuable architectural heritage.

Casa Perichi HISTORIC BUILDING
(94 Luna) Situated on the main drag, this 1920s estate has been on the National Register of Historic Places since 1986. Its eclectic architectural style featuring wrap-around balconies and decorative wood trim has been called 'Puerto Rican ornamental artisan.'

Casa Morales HISTORIC BUILDING
(38 Ramos) This Victorian-era house was built soon after the American occupation in 1898. With its gables, porches and roof turrets, it is redolent of a Queen Anne–style structure from the plush neighborhood of a US mainland city.

Casa Acosta y Flores HISTORIC BUILDING
(70 Dr Santiago Veve) Built in a crisscross of styles, this house, dating from 1917, exhibits elements of Creole, Victorian and art-nouveau architecture and looks like a wedding cake.

Sleeping

Parador Oasis HOTEL $
(☎787-892-1175; 72 Luna; r $75; P❄@≋) If you wanted luxury, you've come to the right place – the catch is you're 20 years too late. Hidden under the cobwebs of the lackluster modern-day Oasis is a once grand dame of Puerto Rican paradores. Today, the place is down on its luck and seemingly bereft of guests, with the air of Miss Havisham's house in Charles Dickens' *Great Expectations*.

There's carpet that is coming up at the seams and artwork that is downright bizarre. Still, the Italianate pool glistens invitingly and the staff try hard to plug the gaps. Framed testimonies on the wall highlight favorable reviews from years past; the most recent dates from 1984.

Villa del Rey HOTEL $$
(☎787-642-2627, www.villadelrey.net; Rte 361 Km 0.8; r $85-110; P❄≋) Your only alternative to the antiquated Oasis is this family-run country inn just north of town. A sturdy midrange option, it has big rooms, suites with kitchenettes, and an unhurried west-coast ambience (you may have to holler to raise the receptionist). Certainly fit for the kids – though perhaps not for a *rey* (king).

Eating

Tapas Café SPANISH $
(48 Dr Santiago Veve; tapas $4-11; ⏲dinner Wed-Fri, lunch & dinner Sat & Sun) The food and atmosphere are both great at this cafe, which seems like it'd fit in among the Triana district of Seville. Flamenco drifts under the high ceilings, and bullfighting paraphernalia adorns the walls, while the kitchen turns out delicious fare such as *albondigas* (meatballs), *queso manchego* (Manchego cheese), *tortilla española* (Spanish omelette) and *jamon serrano* (cured Spanish ham).

★**De Lirious** INTERNATIONAL $$

(55 Dr Santiago Veve; mains $4.50-24; ⏰afternoons & evenings) Given its refined ambience, delicious and originally prepared food, and consistent opening, this is San Germán's best choice for a meal. They kick you off with an array of delicious soups, such as Argentine sausage and plantain, then graduate you to enticing mains, such as the veal cutlets stuffed with apricots and cheese then drenched in cilantro sauce.

When the sun shines, there's a serene outside courtyard lending itself well to a glass of white wine. Like everywhere in San Germán, it's often deserted.

Chateaux De Auxerre CARIBBEAN, FUSION $$

(16 Estrella; dishes $15-25; ⏰6-10pm Wed & Thu, 6pm-midnight Fri & Sat, 11am-4pm Sun) A feast in the courtyard of this centrally located 19th-century town house rewards a tough day of west coast exploration. Sunday brunch dishes are exceptional – strong coffee, and eggs with fresh, seasonal vegetables – and in the evening the menu assumes a French classicism. Watchful servers and linen table dressings also elevate this to one of the region's most upmarket dining experiences.

Despite specific opening hours posted on its door, hours seem to be at the whim of the owners.

Information

The government recently changed the name of Calle Luna to Av Universidad Interamericana; nobody uses it, however, so addresses still refer to Luna.

San Germán Tourism Office (☎787-892-3790; Viejo Alcaldía, Plaza Francisco Mariano Quiñones; ⏰8am-4pm Mon-Fri) This office also runs the San Germán trolley bus around the town's main sights, but schedules are erratic.

Getting There & Away

San Germán enjoys frequent *público* services to and from Ponce ($7, 90 minutes) and Mayagüez ($5, 45 minutes). It lies just south of the Hwy 2 expressway, so if you are driving here from the west coast, follow Hwy 102 from the town of Cabo Rojo (El Pueblo).

Isla Mona

Few wilderness adventures in the Caribbean can compare with a trip to Isla Mona, a wild, deserted speck in the ocean some 50 miles to the west of the main island. And although few people ever visit Mona, the 14,000-acre island looms large in the imagination. It's a place where the beauty of limestone caves and turquoise water coexists with the dangers of a rugged environment. Then there's the island's long, romantic history, told in Taíno petroglyphs and swashbuckling stories about sunken galleons, treasures of gold and skeletons of 18th-century pirates.

A nature reserve since 1919 and uninhabited for more than 50 years, Mona is very difficult to visit. Concerns about safety caused the **DRNA** (Department of Natural Resources; ☎787-999-2200; www.drna.gobierno.pr; Rte 8838, Km 6.3, Sector El Cinco, Río Piedras) to close the island to visitors for months, so if you are even considering a trip here, start your inquiries as soon as possible – it can take about four months of planning to secure permits and transportation.

While the DRNA provides toilets and saltwater showers at Playa Sardinera, Mona is a backcountry camping experience. You're required to pack everything in and out – including bringing your own water and hauling out your garbage. The rangers and police detachment (in an occasionally manned station at Playa Sardinera) can provide basic first aid and have radio contact with the main island, but beyond that, you are on your own in a beautiful – if hostile – environment.

Isla Mona is almost a perfect oval, measuring about 7 miles from east to west and 4 miles from north to south. Most of the island's coastline is made up of rough, rocky cliffs, especially along the north side. The south side, meanwhile, has a number of narrow beaches that fringe the highlands. The most approachable of these beaches is **Playa Sardinera**, where you will find toilets, showers and the concrete living quarters of the rangers and police detachment.

The island's terrain consists of a broad rim of coastal plain rising gently to a central mesa. Because the land is flat and overgrown, it is difficult to find landmarks on the horizon. More than a few people have gotten lost here – including the pirate William Kidd and a boy scout who died from dehydration and exhaustion in 2001. The basic photocopied map you get from the DRNA in San Juan is useless; the US Geological Survey (USGS), an agency of the US Department of the Interior, publishes a better map.

ISLA MONA WILDLIFE

Although the dry, semitropical climate might suggest an area with little variety in vegetation, Mona claims about 600 species of plants and 50 species of trees. Four of the plant species are endemic, unknown to the rest of the world. If you are exploring here, wear protective clothing. Mona has four types of venomous trees and bushes: indio, papayo, manzanillo and carrasco. Almost 3000 acres of the island consist of cactus thickets, while 11,000 acres are in scrub forest.

The biggest stars of the island's wildlife menagerie are the giant rock iguanas, *Cyclura stejnegeri* (similar to the iguanas at Anagada in the British Virgin Islands and Allan's Cays in the Bahamas), ferocious little buggers with sharp teeth and claws, that charge when threatened.

Between May and October, Isla Mona's beaches are important nesting grounds for a number of species of marine turtle, including the chronically endangered Carey turtle.

History

Mona was first settled about 1000 years ago as pre-Columbian peoples migrated north through the Caribbean archipelago. Petroglyphs in some caves and the subtle ruins of *bateyes* (Taíno ball courts) are the chief remnants of the Indian presence. Columbus stopped here on September 24, 1494 (at the end of his second New World voyage) and remained several days to provision for the long trip back to Spain. When the Spaniards returned in 1508, with an expedition led by Juan Ponce de León, Mona had become a sanctuary for Taíno people escaping slavery.

The Spanish eventually claimed the island to guard the ship traffic to and from the gold coast of the Americas, but abandoned it after two decades when they couldn't afford it. Uninhabited and defenseless, Mona was a haven for pirates by the late 1500s, when French corsairs used it as staging ground for their attacks on the Spanish colony at San Germán.

During the next 300 years, Mona became the refuge of a host of privateers, including Sirs Walter Raleigh and Francis Drake, John Hawkins, William Kidd and the Puerto Rican buccaneer Roberto Cofresí.

In the early 20th century it was mined for bat guano (exceptional agricultural fertilizer!) and made headlines when a German submarine fired on the island, thinking it was a post for the Allies, in the early 1940s.

Following Civilian Conservation Corps (CCC) activities on the island, the comings and goings of treasure hunters, WWII and a scam to turn Mona into an airbase, the government of Puerto Rico slowly began to take seriously its duty to protect the island as a nature preserve, and eventually prohibited development. Finally, after almost a millennium of human interference, Mona returned to her wild state.

Activities

You will find spectacular 150ft visibility (or better) for **diving** in the waters around the island. There are excellent barrier and fringe-reef dives filled with lagoons and ruts on the south side of the island. Divers particularly enjoy the sharp drop-off along one reef that creates an overhanging wall; some fascinating creatures come to drift in its cool shadow.

Aside from diving, the only other activity is geeking out on the flora and the fauna.

Tours

Acampa Nature Adventure ADVENTURE TOUR
(☎787-706-0695; www.acampapr.com) Organizes four-day trips of the island with guided hikes; billed as 'roughing it with all the comforts.'

Adventures Tourmarine BOAT CHARTER
(☎787-375-2625; www.tourmarinepr.com; Rte 102 Km 14.1, Playa de Joyuda) The esteemed Captain Hernández is based in Joyuda in Cabo Rojo and is an old Mona hand; call for prices and availability.

Getting There & Away

The only way to get to Isla Mona is by boat, and it's almost impossible unless you are part of an organized trip. It is also extremely expensive; about $800 per person for groups of 10 people. If you are prone to seasickness, beware that the Pasaje de la Mona makes for a rough crossing.

North Coast

POP 970,000

Includes ➡

Best Places to Eat

- Ola Lola's (p208)
- One Ten Thai (p207)
- Heladería de Lares (p203)
- Villa Dorada d'Alberto Seafood Restaurant (p195)
- Eclipse (p208)

Best Places to Stay

- Casa Grande Mountain Retreat (p201)
- TJ Ranch (p201)
- Ritz-Carlton Reserve Dorado Beach (p195)
- Villa Tropical (p205)

Why Go?

Veering from a manicured coast of plush golf resorts and posh surf spots, this region rears up into the less-visited vine-tangled crags of karst country, where landscapes seem positively prehistoric with yawning cave systems, *mogotes* (vegetated, steep-sided hillocks) and lonely spreads of forest. However renowned the teeing in the east and the paddle-boarding in the west might be, don't make the mistake of forgoing what lies in between.

The sights here have neither the untouched exotic natural spectacle of El Yunque nor the rustic allure of the central mountains, but the north has more than enough DIY adventures for travelers with no fixed timetable, plus its own generous share of world-class diversions. Goggle at the world's largest radio telescope, clamber inside some of its largest caverns, relax at serene eco-retreats or strike out on a trail in some of Puerto Rico's remotest forest – and still, should you wish, make your dinner reservation in San Juan.

When to Go

Outside of the island's rainy months (late summer to early fall), the north coast is generally sunny.

Big Atlantic storms can barrel in out of nowhere to whip the waves into white-capped frenzy. The arrival of low pressure systems come late fall starts the big waves a-rolling and October's international surf tournament in Isabella starts drawing the surfers as surely as wasps to nectar.

Inland, the humidity increases, but on the shore the 80°F temperatures aren't at all oppressive. As there's only a difference of a few degrees between the coldest month, January, and the warmest, August, the region offers consistently sunny, breezy days year-round.

History

The north coast contains one of the island's largest and oldest Native American ceremonial sites near Utuado, an archaeological find offering dramatic proof that a well-organized Taíno culture thrived on the island before the arrival of the Spanish. Though Arecibo is the third-oldest city on the island, there is little of historical note remaining on the north coast outside of a couple of picturesque Spanish-colonial lighthouses. The 20th century saw a burgeoning of San Juan's suburbs westward into satellite towns such as Vega Alta and Manatí. At the same time a concerted effort has been made to protect karst country through tree-planting projects and the formation of half a dozen forest reserves in the 1940s.

Territorial Parks & Reserves

The north coast is dotted with small karst-country parks and reserves, although they're not nearly as well-equipped (or as well trodden) as El Yunque. They vary in size from the diminutive 1000-acre Bosque Estatal de Cambalache to larger reserves such as the 5000-acre Bosque Estatal de Río Abajo. This particular park has better-maintained trails and a wider range of facilities, but still pales in comparison to the Parque de las Cavernas de Río Camuy, one of Puerto Rico's most oft-visited tourist attractions. Nestled in the northwest, the Bosque Estatal de Guajataca has caves, *mogotes* and plenty of signposted trails.

Getting There & Around

Aguadilla has an international airport widely used by vacationers heading for the west coast beaches and scientists keen to study the stars at the Observatorio de Arecibo. Erratic *públicos* run between the smaller coastal towns and from San Juan out to the main population centers along Hwy 2. Renting a car is easily the best option for getting around, although reliably scheduled public buses connect Dorado to San Juan's Tren Urbano metro system. The Isabela region is good for cycling.

Dorado

POP 37,000

For those who love golf, Dorado is pure gold, legendary for its exceptional courses. It boasts five championship-standard golf courses that are an international draw. If your interest in the fairways wanes, several stunning local beaches offer a welcome break from the clubhouse banter. If you're only interested in beaches, bypass Dorado for locales further west.

Founded in 1842, Dorado first became a resort town in the early 1900s when the Rockefeller family started building a Caribbean Shangri-la. The venture went public in 1958 when Laurance Rockefeller, the well-known philanthropist and conservationist, opened up the region's first hotel, the Dorado Beach, a pioneering ecoresort where no building was taller than the surrounding palm trees. Today, although there have been some formidable resorts here over the years, many golfers opt for time-shares and condo rentals, robbing the hotel scene of its once-ritzy image.

Away from the resorts, Dorado has a timeless public beach in town and an even prettier free option a few miles to the west at Cerro Gordo. Back in town, the original 19th-century settlement, with its teardrop-shaped lights rimming the main plaza, is a pleasant spot to while away a lazy afternoon.

El Dorado's urban core is spread out, and the route between PR 22 and the coast is almost entirely developed. Rte 165 turns into Calle Méndez Vigo, the town's central road.

Sights

Dorado has a trio of small museums, none of which is too remarkable, but a decent breather between golf rounds. The **Museo y Centro Cultural Casa del Rey** (787-796-5740; Calle Méndez Vigo; 8am-4.30pm Mon-Fri) is an old Spanish garrison that displays antique furniture; the **Museo del Plata** (787-796-9031; Industria; 8am-4pm Mon-Sat) showcases local art, sculpture and paintings; and the **Museo de Arte e Historia de Dorado** (787-796-5740; cnr Calles Méndez Vigo & Juan Francisco; 8am-3:30pm Mon-Sat) gives you the rundown on local history and archaeology. Admissions are free.

Beaches

Balneario Manuel Morales BEACH

(parking $3) Although nobody is advertising it, there is, in fact, a public beach in Dorado where you can swim. Balneario Manuel Morales is at the end of Rte 697. But it's a rather boring bit of sand surrounded by rocky

North Coast Highlights

1 Surf the storied waves at **Playa Jobos** (p205).

2 Put a mountain-sized ear to the heavens at **Observatorio de Arecibo** (p198).

3 Trot along in the sand and snorkel with **Tropical Trail Rides** (p204) at Playa Shacks.

4 Get into the swing of things with a round on one of the north coast's world-class golf courses, like the newly opened **Royal Isabela** (p204).

5 Picnic near the most spectacularly rough north coast beach, **Playa Mar Chiquita** (p197).

6 Embark on a DIY cave hike at the lonely **Bosque Estatal de Guajataca** (p201).

7 Sample far-eastern flavors or sip artisan ales in one of Hwy 110's varied eateries such as **One Ten Thai** (p207).

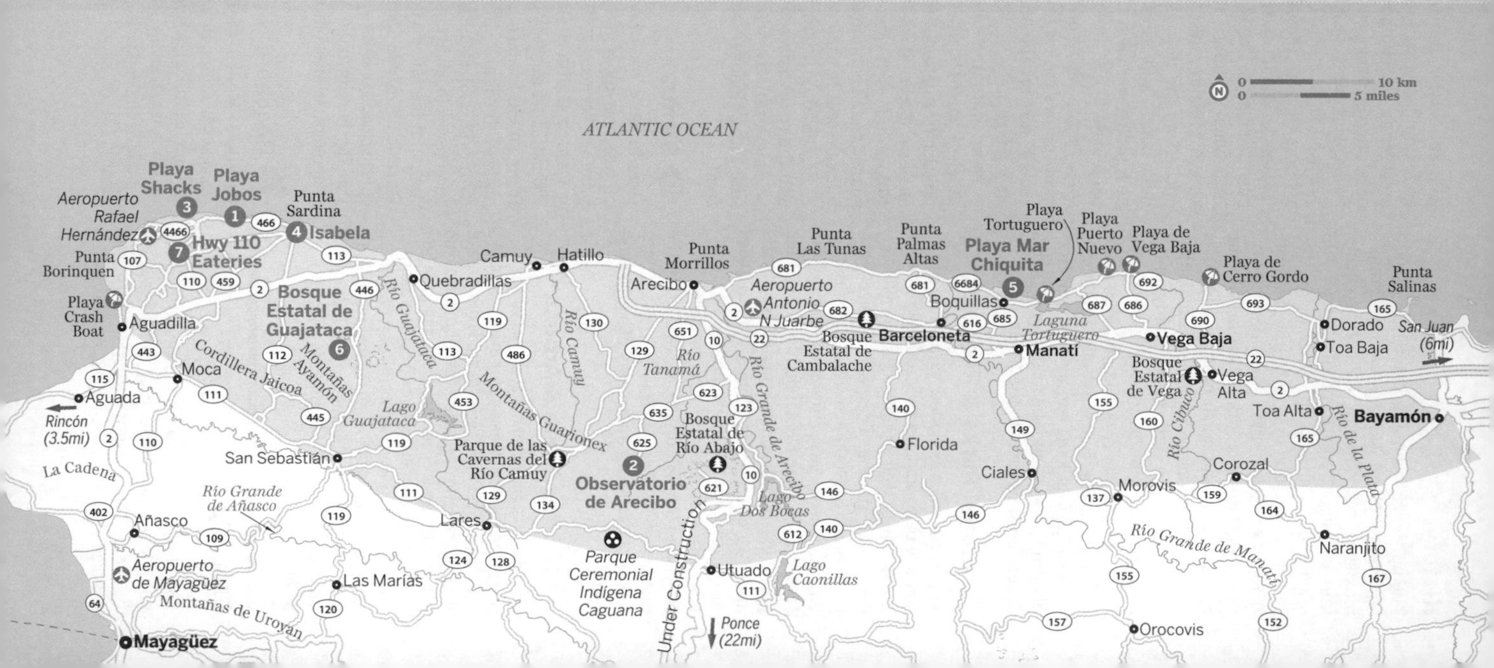

outcrops and marred by litter. For a far better experience try Playa de Cerro Gordo, several miles to the west.

Punta Salinas BEACH

Toa Alta's beach, Punta Salinas, lies about 20 minutes east of Dorado on Rte 165. It's got food kiosks, lifeguards, restrooms and basketball courts.

Playa de Cerro Gordo BEACH

(parking $3) Lying at the end of Hwy 690, this palm-dotted expanse of sand was once the north coast's best-kept secret, but word is definitely out; the government just pumped several million dollars into creating restrooms, showers, fire pits and the like to put Cerro Gordo on the tourist map. Camping is possible here.

Activities

With expertly groomed holes, impeccably maintained greens and gentle Atlantic breezes, Dorado has the best golf courses in the Caribbean, period. There are five 18-hole courses here and all remain open despite the changes to the hotel that used to administrate them.

Dorado Beach Club GOLF

(787-626-1001; www.doradobeachclubs.com; 7:30am-5pm) Four of the most famous courses are now under the umbrella of the Dorado Beach Club, an upscale vacation facility housed partially in a former Hyatt. The famed **East Course** is the green jewel – Jack Nicklaus ranked its 540yd 4th hole, a double dogleg with a pair of ponds and amazing views, among the world's best. It's also listed among the planet's finest golf courses by *Golf Digest*.

Next door lies the equally famous 6975yd **West Course**, while across the road you'll find the **Pineapple** and **Sugarcane** courses (usually the most reasonably priced to play) at the Plantation Club. Booking tee time at any of these can be done through the **Plantation Club Pro Shop** (787-626-1010; www.doradobeachclubs.com; 8am-5pm) or through its website.

Dorado del Mar GOLF

(787-796-3070; http://embassysuites3.hilton.com; 7:30am-5pm) Dorado's fifth and newest course is the Chi Chi Rodríguez–designed Dorado del Mar at the Embassy Suites. Greens fees at these courses range from $100 to $200 depending on tee times.

Sleeping & Eating

Dorado's guests mostly stay in time-shares and eat at the American fast-food restaurants lining the main roads, or inside the golf resorts. If you're here to golf and have a taste for something more adventurous, try the area by the public beach, where open-air snack bars sell lots of deep-fried delights and cold beer.

Embassy Suites Dorado del Mar Beach & Golf RESORT $$

(787-796-6125; www.embassysuitesdorado.com; 201 Dorado del Mar Blvd; r $120-300; P ❄ @) Close to town amid a phalanx of gated communities, the Embassy Suites has a Chi Chi Rodríguez–designed golf course, a business center, a gym, tennis courts and specialty restaurants.

The open-plan lobby is a fountain-filled state-of-the-art extravaganza where smooth-talking salespeople in Hawaiian shirts leap from behind pillars and try to sell you time-shares. If you can survive this relatively innocuous form of initiation, you could be in for a ball.

★ Ritz-Carlton Reserve Dorado Beach RESORT $$$

(787-626-1100; www.ritzcarlton.com; 100 Dorado Beach Dr; r $750-4000; P ❄) There's some wealthy types coming to town, clearly, because the dreamy 1000-sq-ft-average Ocean Reserve rooms, with walk-in wardrobes and private balconies, are the lead-in choice at the lavish Ritz-Carlton. The hotel opened its doors in December 2012 as one of only a handful of Ritz-Carlton Reserve properties worldwide.

There are many more spacious apartments ('residences') offering anything from one to five rooms, graduating up to the pièce de résistance – an old plantation hacienda, that's been converted into a sumptuous $20,000-a-night private villa with its own infinity pool.

Among several restaurants here, the stand-out is **Mi Casa** by José Andrés, a casual yet sophisticated beachside locale that creatively combines Puerto Rican and Spanish flavors. Mi Casa can get very crowded.

★ Villa Dorada d'Alberto Seafood Restaurant SEAFOOD $$

(787-278-1715; 99 Calle E; dishes $12-30; 11am-9pm Tue-Thu & Sun, to 11pm Fri & Sat) With gentlemanly waiters in black tie and linen napkins, this classy joint serves seafood platters to a soundtrack of schmaltzy elevator music. On the weekends it's a scene as tables of locals buzz with date night, and it remains one of the only places around that draws vacationers from their all-inclusive slumber.

Afterwards you can wander out to the public beach, where guitarists play romantic Puerto Rican and Cuban classics.

El Ladrillo SEAFOOD $$

(☎787-796-2120; 334 Calle Méndez Vigo; dishes $15-35; ⊙noon-10pm) El Ladrillo has been a culinary anchor of downtown Dorado for decades. It exudes old-world charm, with dark wood, exposed brick and thick steaks. Naturally, it serves seafood as well – everything from octopus salad to lobster *asopao* (an island specialty, a delicious thick stew). It also functions as a mini art gallery; the walls are crowded with colorful local paintings.

Getting There & Away

It is easy to get a *público* or bus to and from either Río Piedras in San Juan (40 minutes) or Bayamón (for the Tren Urbano to San Juan; 20 minutes). There are also *públicos* to the ferry terminal in Cataño (about $4, 20 minutes).

DON'T FORGET THE QUARTERS

If you're making the day trip across the north coast, don't forget to bring enough change for the tolls...in cash! The total one-way trip along PR 22 (San Juan to Hatillo) is currently $6.25, with a toll increase likely some time in 2014. If you get caught without cash, you'll have to pull over, complete a pile of paperwork and find another toll booth to pay later – a doubly unpleasant detour. Those with exact change get the fast lane, marked 'Autos Cambio Exacto Con Monedas.'

The best option if you're hiring a car to travel around Puerto Rico for more than a few days is to pay your rental company the $50-odd one-off charge to activate the AutoExpresso tag, which means you can cruise straight through the automatic lane in tolls island-wide without stopping and frantically rummaging for small change.

Manatí & Around

POP 42,000

Modern Manatí, which was named for the endangered manatee (sea cow) that once prospered in these waters, is an industrial hub for workers in local pharmaceutical factories and a nearby pineapple-canning plant. But skirt the industrial eyesores and you'll uncover some little-heralded beaches, along with two inland forest reserves among the sinkholes and limestone *mogotes* of karst country.

The beaches and Laguna Tortuguero lie on a thin coastal strip to the north of Expressway 22, which skirts Manatí. The Bosque Estatal de Cambalache is situated 5 miles west of Manatí. Another rarely explored reserve is the Bosque Estatal de Vega, approximately 6 miles to the east.

Sights & Activities

Laguna Tortuguero LAKE

(☎787-844-2587; ⊙8am-4pm Wed-Fri, 6am-6pm Sat & Sun) This lagoon is one of only two natural lakes in Puerto Rico, making its protection extra precious. It is also one of the most ecologically diverse areas on the island, listing 717 species of plant and 23 different types of fish. Hiking around this pretty spot yields ocean views, and you can also fish and kayak in the lake – though you'll have to bring your own equipment.

One of the lake's problems is a caiman infestation, with unfortunate results for the ecosystem; rangers have an extermination program to get the population under control. In theory, caimans only hunt at night, but be alert for them.

To get to Tortuguero from Hwy 22, take Exit 41, take a right on Hwy 2, then left on Rte 687 until you see a big sign for the lagoon on your left.

Bosque Estatal de Cambalache NATURE RESERVE

Cambalache covers an area of just 1000 acres, making it smaller than a lot of Puerto Rican resort hotels. West of Barceloneta, the forest is ecologically varied and characterized by distinctive karstic formations; countless *mogotes* pop straight up from the landscape to heights of 160ft. Its many caves provide homes for fruit bats, which often swarm like bees into the evening sky. The forest has a picnic area, 8 miles of hiking trails, two (poorly maintained) mountain bike trails and camping.

Note that a permit is required for cycling, but on our last visit there was no one checking for them and no way to obtain them in advance, except for calling the Departamento de Recursos Naturales y Ambientales in San Juan. Basic on-the-ground information can be obtained at the **ranger station** (787-878-7279; Hwy 682 Km 6.6; 7:30am-4pm) to the right of the entrance gate.

Beaches

In addition to the following, **Playa de Vega Baja** is another lonely beach off Hwy 692 (where the Río Cibuco meets the sea), often good for surfing.

★Playa Mar Chiquita — BEACH

An anomaly among Puerto Rican beaches, Playa Mar Chiquita isn't alongside a main thoroughfare, has no long strand and isn't good for swimming and surfing. Still, the pure drama of this place makes it a favorite. Two huge coral formations protect a small, shallow cove and tidal pools from the raging crash of the Atlantic, which sprays foam in unpredictable bursts. In the aftermath, the coral rushes with a network of tiny waterfalls into the protected tidal pools.

This is the kind of beach for just standing in awe of nature, chilling in the small sandy area with a book or picnicking alongside Puerto Rican families. There are also caves along this stretch of coast, though it can be almost impossible to see them from the land.

There's a barely visible sign to the beach off Hwy 685, about 2 miles north of Manatí and just beyond the entrance to the town of Boquillas. If you miss the sign, go north on Hwy 648 (about a mile east of Boquillas). This road takes you over a steep hill to the beach.

Playa Tortuguero — BEACH

Heading east on the seaside road (Hwy 686) from Playa Mar Chiquita, you'll pass through a coastal forest. When the road creeps back to the edge of the coast, a long strand – Playa Tortuguero – will be on the left.

Just a little further along lies a *balneario* (public beach) known as **Playa Puerto Nuevo**. This narrow crescent of sand is sheltered by a broad headland to the east and surrounded by clusters of beach homes.

DON'T MISS

PLAYA MAR CHIQUITA

With foaming, furious waves, bizarre rock formations and a protected wading pool, Playa Mar Chiquita is the most spectacular beach on this coast.

Sleeping

Camping in this area, like much of the rest of the island, is not an easy option, due to unmanned ranger stations, conflicting information and erratic office hours. With persistence, the best option is **Playa de Cerro Gordo** (787-883-2515; campsites $13; beach 8am-6pm) campground, with around 100 berths right on one of the north coast's best beaches. There are lifeguards on the beach, and food kiosks. Parking is $3.

Getting There & Away

While you can get to and from Manatí by *público* (about 45 minutes from San Juan), you'll need wheels to avoid being stuck in the undesirable town with no way of getting around the sights. By car, Manatí can be reached from the east or west via Hwy 2, or by taking Hwy 149 south from Hwy 22.

Arecibo & Around

POP 94,000

As you approach Arecibo in the crawl of traffic, it's hard to imagine that this sprawling modern municipality of nearly 100,000 people is Puerto Rico's third-oldest city, after San Juan and San Germán. Founded in 1556, the original town was named after an esteemed *cacique* (Taíno chief). Little of historical note remains in the present-day city, save a restored cathedral and Spanish-colonial lighthouse in a campy amusement park. Veer further inland and the view gets a lot more interesting.

Arecibo's greatest claim to fame is the world's largest and most sensitive radio telescope, the Observatorio de Arecibo, several miles up into the hills to the south, in the heart of karst country. Harboring a fascinating museum and a view worthy of a futuristic James Bond film set, the observatory is open for public viewing and reigns as one of the island's most rewarding must-sees.

Just west at Hatillo, the popular **Hatillo Mask Festival**, held on December 28, is one of Puerto Rico's most symbolic ceremonies whose innovative masks and costumes adorn the front of numerous books, postcards and tourist literature.

Sights & Activities

★ Observatorio de Arecibo NOTABLE BUILDING
(787-878-2612; www.naic.edu; adult/child $10/6; 9am-4pm daily mid-Dec–mid-Jan, Jun & Jul, Wed-Sun rest of year) The Puerto Ricans reverently refer to it as 'El Radar.' To everyone else it is simply the largest radio telescope in the world. Resembling an extraterrestrial spaceship grounded in the middle of karst country, the Arecibo Observatory looks like something out of a James Bond movie - probably because it is (007 aficionados will recognize the saucer-shaped dish and craning antennae from the 1995 film *GoldenEye*).

The 20-acre dish, operated in conjunction with Cornell University, is set in a sinkhole among clusters of haystack-shaped *mogotes*, like earth's ear into outer space. Supported by 50-story cables weighing more than 600 tons, the telescope is involved in the SETI (Search for Extraterrestrial Intelligence) program and used by on-site scientists to prove the existence of pulsars and quasars, the so-called 'music of the stars.' Past work has included the observation of the planet Mercury, the first asteroid image and the discovery of the first extra-solar planets.

NORTH COAST GRAND SLAM

Despite the precipitous terrain, the north coast showcases some of Puerto Rico's biggest outdoor attractions, many of which can be tackled in an ambitious day trip from San Juan. A 'grand tour' for weekend warriors includes the Río Camuy caves, the Observatorio de Arecibo (the largest radio telescope in the world) and the Parque Ceremonial Indígena Caguana – all must-sees on any itinerary and all consequently crawling with day-trippers. For an alternative escape, forge south into the mountain foothills around Río Abajo, where placid lakes and out-of-the-way retreats make a tranquil respite from the island's congestion and provide the best overnight option hereabouts: Casa Grande Mountain Retreat.

Top scientists from around the world perform ongoing research at Arecibo, but an informative visitor center with interpretative displays and an explanatory film provide the public with a fascinating glimpse of how the facility works. There's also a well-positioned viewing platform offering you the archetypal 007 vista.

To get to the observatory follow Hwys 635 and 625 off Hwy 129. It's only 9 miles south of the town of Arecibo as the crow flies, but the roller-coaster ride through karst country will make it seem more like 90.

Parque de las Cavernas del Río Camuy CAVE
(787-898-3100; Hwy 129 Km 18.9; adult/child $12/6, parking $2; 8am-5pm Wed-Sun & holidays) The beguiling networks of stalagmite-ornamented caves at Río Camuy are the third-largest of their kind in the world, formed by the soft karstic limestone that shapes the hills on this remarkable part of the island. This park is *big* – it's spread over 10 miles with multiple entrances. A visit here can be an unearthly, slightly creepy diversion from the typically sunny shore – if you have the time and patience to put up with the terrible crowds.

Over the years, the caves have been shelters for indigenous people, home to millions of bats that help keep the island's insect population under control, and a source of fertilizer. But no modern explorers went to the trouble of making a thorough investigation of the caves until 1958. In 1986 the attraction opened as a tourist facility.

Call the park for local conditions (too much rain causes closures), and arrive before 10:30am to avoid crowds or waits of upward of an hour standing in line. Don't expect much contact with the spectacular underground formations either. Your visit begins with a film at the visitor center and a trolleybus through the jungle into a 200ft-deep sinkhole to **Cueva Clara de Empalme** (Clear Cave Junction), where you take a 45-minute guided walk. Here you walk past enormous stalagmites and stalactites. At one point the ceiling of the cavern reaches a height of 170ft; at another you can see the Río Camuy rushing through a tunnel.

After leaving the cave from a side passage, you take another tram to the **Tres Pueblos sinkhole**, which measures 650ft across and drops 400ft. Forty-two petroglyphs that you can now inspect have been found in **Cueva Catedral** (Cathedral Cave).

The last tour leaves at 2pm if you want to see all three areas. All told, the fun of the visit here depends on the size of the crowds, your patience and the tour guide (some of them seem bored stiff).

You can get off the beaten path underground by joining **Expediciones Palenque** (☎787-407-2858; www.expedicionespalenque.com; full-day tour $90), which offers daylong caving trips, and a host of other cool trips hiking, rappelling and body rafting the Río Camuy.

Parque Ceremonial Indígena Caguana PARK

(☎787-894-7325; adult/child $2/1; ⏰8:30am-4:20pm) Like the archaeological site at Tibes near Ponce, this Taíno ceremonial site, off Hwy 111, has no monumental ruins; the power of the place comes from the natural botanical garden of ceiba, ausubo and tabonuco trees that shade the midslopes of the central mountains. There are 10 ceremonial *bateyes* (Taíno ball courts), dating back about 800 years.

Stone monoliths line many of the courts, and quite a few have petroglyphs, such as the famous Mujer de Caguana, who squats in the pose of the traditional 'earth mother' fertility symbol. Caguana is a place to walk and reflect, not to be thrilled by exhibits or enormous ancient monuments. Nevertheless, there is a small **museum** with artifacts and skeletons on the property, and a gift shop that sells inexpensive but attractive reproductions of Taíno charms, including the statues called *cemíes*.

Lagos Dos Bocas & Caonillas LAKE

These two lakes – each more than 2 miles long – fill a deeply cleft valley at a point where karst country gives way to the jagged spine of the central mountains, east of Hwy 10 and north of Utuado. The lakes are the principal reservoirs for the north-central part of the island, and they can provide a tranquil escape if the beaches are too congested.

In calm weather, you can ride Dos Bocas' free launch, which serves as a taxi service to the residents in the area. The boat landing is on Hwy 123, on the west side of the lake. Boats leave almost every hour. You can disembark at restaurants around the lake or just sit back and enjoy the two-hour ride. You can similarly pick up the boat launch on the other side of the lake at the end of Hwy 612, about 3 miles beyond the Casa Grande Mountain Retreat. Along the shore there are several *comida criolla* (traditional Puerto Rican cuisine) restaurants, some of which hire kayaks.

Bosque Estatal de Río Abajo NATURE RESERVE

(☎787-880-6557; ⏰visitors center 8am-4pm) This 5000-acre forest has a visitors center just off Hwy 621, halfway between Utuado and Arecibo, and some of the island's most rugged terrain. In the heart of karst country, the forest's altitude jumps between 700ft and 1400ft above sea level. The steep sides of the *mogotes* are overrun with vines, and the forest features fine tropical hardwoods, including Honduran mahogany and Asian teaks, beside huge clumps of bamboo.

The remains of the lumber roads cut by the loggers and the Civilian Conservation Corps (CCC) workers have now become trails. The two best are the **Visitors Center Trail** (a 500m-long stroll with three gazebos set up along the way) and **Las Perdices** (about 2km long). Others are often poorly maintained. Inquire at the visitors center and you should be able to piece together a more substantial hike through karst country.

To reach Bosque Estatal de Río Abajo from San Juan, take Hwy 22 west toward Arecibo. Turn south on Rte 10 toward Utuado. Turn west on Hwy 621 and continue to Km 4.4 and the park entrance.

The ranger station is near the entrance, where Hwy 621 snakes into the forest. At the end of this road, there is a picnic and recreation area and an aviary, where the DRNA is working to reintroduce the Puerto Rican parrot and other endangered species.

Faro y Parque Histórico de Arecibo AMUSEMENT PARK

(☎787-880-7540; Rte 655; adult/child $12/10; ⏰9am-6pm Mon-Fri, 10am-7pm Sat & Sun) This gimmicky, overpriced theme park off Hwy 2 nevertheless offers a glimpse of the historic Arecibo lighthouse, and is a good place to break up the long drives across the north coast if you're traveling with kids, who will likely get into the pirate-themed stuff.

Perched on a headland on the hill at Punta Morrillos, east of Arecibo, the whitewashed **Faro de los Morrillos**, dating from 1897, is an excellent example of Spanish neoclassical

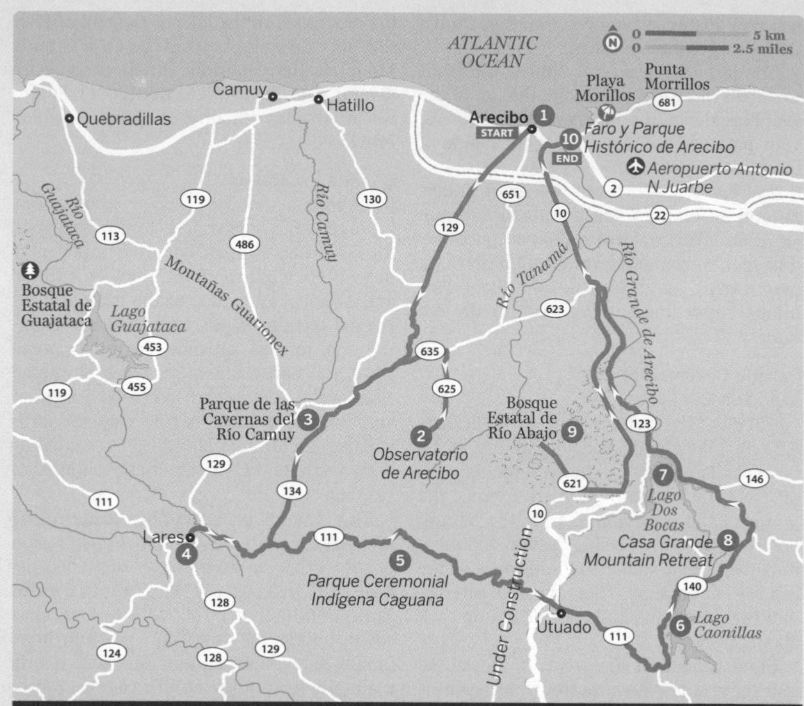

Driving/Cycling Tour
Karst Country

START ARECIBO
END FARO Y PARQUE HISTÓRICO DE ARECIBO
LENGTH 60 MILES; FOUR HOURS WITHOUT STOPS

Start in ❶ **Arecibo** (p197), a town perfectly situated to fuel up for the trip, and head south toward Lares, birthplace of the *independenista* movement. Take a scenic detour along the way to the ❷ **Observatorio de Arecibo** (p198), the world's largest radio telescope and a surreal sci-fi vision in the jungle. Afterwards, stop at the ❸ **Parque de las Cavernas del Río Camuy** (p198), where you'll find a network of dripping caves that can be a great place to cool off. Honing in on Lares, you'll want to stop in the main plaza for ice cream from the renowned ❹ **Heladería de Lares** (p203). Next, head east on Hwy 111 (up and down lots of ridges) to the ❺ **Parque Ceremonial Indígena Caguana** (p199), a quiet park that was once used for worship and ball games by indigenous Taíno people. After a quiet walk, follow signs toward Utuado, after which you can turn off for a short detour to either of the visually stunning mountain lakes in the area: ❻ **Lago Caonillas** (p199) or ❼ **Lago Dos Bocas** (p199). Regular boats ply the lakes and ramshackle restaurants sell all the regular Puerto Rican favorites. You'll find serene accommodations and early morning yoga nearby at the ❽ **Casa Grande Mountain Retreat** (p201).

On the way back toward Arecibo, you can divert down to Rte 621 and ❾ **Bosque Estatal de Río Abajo** (p199), where former lumber roads have been converted to trails. Leaving the park, head back north on Hwy 10 and, as it approaches the edge of Arecibo city, hook up with Hwy 681. This will bring you down to the ❿ **Faro y Parque Histórico de Arecibo** (p199), where a picturesque lighthouse stands guard over the Caribbean.

architecture. Inside, a museum displays artifacts salvaged from shipwrecks. There are fantastic views of the Atlantic Ocean and karst country from the roof.

Beaches

The best beach around Faro de los Morrillos is the **Balneario Morrillos** (parking $3), a quarter of a mile past the lighthouse turning. It has dunes and surf, but better beaches lie along the coast to the east.

Sleeping & Eating

★Casa Grande Mountain Retreat GUESTHOUSE **$$**
(787-894-3900/39; www.hotelcasagrande.com; Hwy 612 Km 0.3; r $95-125;) Materializing in the heart of Puerto Rico's gorgeous karst country, the Casa Grande is the perfect place to escape the daily grind. Nestled in its own steep valley, the ecologically congruous hotel stops you in your tracks and forces you to slow down. While there are no TVs or phones in any of the 20 rooms, there are daily yoga classes and a scrumptious on-site **restaurant** (mains $12 to $14).

Each room has a porch where you can swing along on the hammock and watch the mist roll across the hills. This is a place to completely unplug. Note that its website also has an option for work-exchange stays.

★TJ Ranch CABINS **$$**
(787-880-1217; http://tjranch.com; Rte 146; s/d $100/135;) A charming stop on any karst country driving or cycling tour, TJ Ranch is a little-known Eden that harbors three beautiful cabins surrounded by lush foliage next to Lago Dos Bocas. It's actually a working coffee plantation and the congenial hosts are known to be formidable cooks who will concoct all sorts of mini-feasts from the ultimate Puerto Rican cookbook.

Punta Maracayo Hotel HOTEL **$$**
(787-544-2000; www.hotelpuntamaracayopr.com; Hwy 2 Km 84.6; r from $99;) With excellent service, modern rooms and lots of colorful common spaces, there's no contest that Punta Maracayo is the best option along the dreary north coast highways. Although the facility itself is a bit similar to a quality highway hotel in the US, it does well to dress things up with fresh tropical flowers in the lobby, wicker furniture and bold modern art.

The pool area in back is a great option for people traveling with children, as it is spacious.

Lighthouse Bay Restaurant PUERTO RICAN **$$**
(787-815-0910; Hwy 655; dishes $6-19; noon-10pm;) Right near the Faro y Parque Histórico de Arecibo lighthouse, this is a good stop for lunch or dinner when you are in the area. It's $18 for a large platter of *mariscos* (four types of shellfish).

Getting There & Away

Arecibo's city center is trapped between Hwy 2 and the Atlantic Ocean – it's a thin strip of restaurants and strip malls. The main attractions lie about 15 to 20 minutes outside of town in karst country, just off Hwy 129. It is accessible from San Juan or Aguadilla by the Hwy 22 expressway, or from Ponce by Hwy 10. Catch a *público* just east of the plaza to San Juan ($10, two hours) or Aguadilla ($8, 1½ hours).

Lago Guajataca

Serene Lago Guajataca has some of Puerto Rico's best fishing – on the north side of the lake are two clubs for anglers hoping to catch the tucunaré fish stocked in this lake. Right in the middle of karst country, the easiest approach to the lake is along Hwy 2 to Rte 119, and then into the forest to the **DRNA** (787-896-7640; Rte 119 Km 22.1; 6am-6pm Tue-Sun). You'll need to get a permit here if you want to fish and you can pick up a loaner bamboo fishing pole (no bait) from the office. You are also free to use the bathrooms (with showers) and picnic tables. Kayaking is allowed on the lake (it's best to bring your own kayak), but swimming is prohibited.

Bosque Estatal de Guajataca

Despite its diminutive size (2300 acres) and proximity to the northwestern coastal towns, the Bosque Estatal de Guajataca contains more trails (27 miles) than any other forest in Puerto Rico – including El Yunque – and it's the best place for a wild hike in the region. Set in dramatic karst country, the distinctive local terrain rises and falls between 500ft and 1000ft above sea level and is characterized by bulbous *mogotes* and rounded *sumideros* (funneled depressions). Covered by a moist subtropical forest and watered annually by 75in of rainfall, there are 45 species of bird to be found here along with 186 different types

QUICK GREEN ESCAPES

- Bosque Estatal de Guajataca (p201)
- Laguna Tortuguero (p196)
- Bosque Estatal de Río Abajo (p199)
- Lagos Dos Bocas & Caonillas (p199)

of tree. One of the highlights of the forest is the limestone **Cueva del Viento** (Cave of the Wind), which is rich with stalactites and stalagmites. There is also a pair of observation towers, which have some picnic tables where locals gather around grills, and plantations of blue mahoe trees. The area is a favorite habitat of the endangered Puerto Rican boa.

Compared to other Puerto Rican forests and parks, the trails in Guajataca are relatively well marked, though it's wise to procure a map beforehand to see how the various paths link up. True to form, the **ranger station** (787-872-1045; Rte 446; 8am-5pm) near the trailheads, 5 miles into the forest, is not always open, and when rangers do emerge they don't always have much in the way of printed information. The moral: come prepared. The best bet is to call the DRNA in San Juan before you arrive at the forest, find things closed and feel a little lost. Be warned that 'official' maps of the area are usually hand-drawn, photocopied and not to scale.

The nearest eating facilities are a bakery and a supermarket at the intersection of Hwys 446 and 457.

Sights & Activities

Most of the main hikes depart from, or near, the ranger station on Rte 446. The most popular is the 1.5-mile **Interpretative Trail** that passes the **observation tower** and several other points of interest (be sure to hike to the observation tower to get the best views of the surrounding countryside). It's a moderate walk that takes about two hours. **Trail Number One** breaks off from the Interpretative Trail and heads toward **Cueva del Viento**. There, wooden stairs will take you down into the depths of the dark cave (bring a flashlight). Let rangers know if you are going into the caves.

Sleeping

Nino's Camping & Guesthouse CABINS, CAMPGROUND $
(787-896-9016; www.ninoscamping.com; Rte 119 Km 22.1; campsites $25, cabins up to 8 people $199;) Near Lago Guajataca, this is a nice lakeside option, operated by a friendly family. The little cabins for four to 12 people have everything except sheets and utensils. Discounts are given for longer stays and there's a swimming pool and an activities room onsite. It also rents kayaks and operates fishing ventures for groups.

Getting There & Away

There are no buses to Guajataca. If you're driving, take the narrow Rte 446 south of Hwy 2 and follow it for 5 miles. Bike hire is available at Aquatica Dive & Surf near the Ramey Base.

Isabela & Aguadilla Area

POP 103,000

Nicknamed 'Garden of the Northeast' for its local cheeses and elegant Paso Fino horses, Isabela and its surroundings boast an invitingly rugged coastline blessed with a handful of classic surfing beaches such as Jobos and Shacks that rival anything in Rincón, especially in winter. With accommodations and eating joints (mostly scattered along Rtes 466 and 4466) that have come on a pace to match Rincón, too, the 'scene' here begs to be checked out.

After the ghastly urban sprawl on Hwy 2, the miles of sand dunes, inlets and untrammeled beaches that lie sandwiched between the lashing Atlantic and a 200ft coastal escarpment are a sight for sore eyes. You can scan the water from high cliffs for whales or charter whale-watching tours, which are also available down the coast during winter.

If you avoid the main roads, Isabela is great cycling country (the beach area even has a spanking new cycling path). Alternatively, you can explore the web of back roads skirting the edge of karst country around the Bosque Estatal de Guajataca and Lago Guajataca. The former has some well-signposted hikes (unusual in Puerto Rico), while the latter offers kayaking and fishing.

Hanging on to the coattails of Isabella in an unruly sprawl of highways and strip malls and with a center sapped of life, larger Aguadilla is most notable for its international airport. Entrenched in a former Cold War command center known as the Ramey Base, this will (unfortunately) be many visitors' first impression of Puerto Rico. But, besides one of the island's best bike rental shops, there is one overwhelming reason to stop by: Hwy 110 near the airport has become one of Puerto Rico's most eclectic dining destinations, and the quality of restaurants here is high and delightfully varied.

Sights

To get some crashing waves and lonely sands to yourself, head 5km east of Isabela on Avenida Noel Estrada. When you hit Hwy 2 at the carving of the *cacique* (Taíno chief), turn left then left again to reach the beach again near the old Guajataca Tunnel. Swimming here can, however, be dangerous: get local advice first.

Palacete Los Moreau HISTORIC SITE
(☎787-830-4475; Hwy 464 Km 2.6, Moca; ⏰grounds 9am-5pm, tours Thu-Mon) FREE Here's an intriguing diversion from the beach scene: a 19th-century tenderly restored French hacienda, exquisitely furnished within and with lush grounds to stroll about, usually open to the public and with enthusiastic tours of the property provided for free.

The serene two-towered mansion was frequented by one of Puerto Rico's most prolific writers, Enrique Laguerre, who is buried within the grounds. Phone ahead to secure a tour.

Activities

Surfing

While Isabela might lack the surfer-chic of Rincón, the waves here are just as legendary. Some say Playa Jobos has the best breaks on the island, while other favorite spots include **Surfer's Beach** (preferred location for local contests, with diverse breaks from multiple directions and strong northwestern swells), **Table Top** (named for a flat, exposed reef that looks like a table with a round barrel coming up against cliffs) and **Gas Chambers** (known as Puerto Rico's best 'right tube,' these waves head right for a sharp and unforgiving cliff). Also check out **Secret Spot**, **Sal Si Puedes**, **Shore Island** and **Las Dunas**.

To get the scoop on what's breaking and where, stop by **Wave Riding Vehicles** (☎787-669-3840; www.waveridingvehicles.com; Rte 110 Km 7.3; ⏰10am-6pm) at Jobos Beach. You can hire boards for $20, snorkeling gear for $10 or get a two-hour lesson for about $65.

Serious surfers will also find a number of custom board builders in the area. Of these, **MHL** (☎787-609-6198; www.mhlcustom.com;

WORTH A TRIP

INDEPENDENCE & ICE CREAM

For unbiased visitors, sleepy **Lares** is famous for two reasons. First, it was the site of the short-lived Grito de Lares independence call in 1868, and second, it sells some of the best ice cream on the island, if not in the Caribbean.

To the chagrin of modern-day *independistas*, the bulk of the people who visit the town these days come to consume large quantities of ice cream rather than plot surreptitious rebellion – and what better place to do it? Their fixation is the understated **Heladería de Lares** (☎787-897-3290; Plaza de Recreo, Lecaroz; per scoop $2; ⏰10am-5pm Mon-Fri, 9am-6pm Sat & Sun), an ice-cream store that occupies the ground floor of a three-story building in the town's pleasant main plaza. Though it may not have sparked any history-shaping insurrections since its inception four decades ago, the store's crafty concoction of over 1000 exotic ice-cream flavors, including avocado, *arroz con pollo* (chicken with rice) and – urghhhh – garlic, could certainly be seen as revolutionary.

Wacky, wonderful or just plain weird, Heladería de Lares today is celebrated across the island and is well worth a mile or two's diversion from a karst-country driving tour for a sample. If you prefer your garlic in a curry rather than a cone, don't worry: there are plenty of delicious traditional flavors to choose from such as chocolate, almond and vanilla.

Rte 4466 Km 1.2, beyond Villa Montaña) has an impeccable reputation for hand-crafted boards.

Diving & Snorkeling

Puerto Rico Technical Diving Center DIVING

(☎787-997-3483; www.technicaldivingpr.com; Hwy 107 Km 4, Aguadilla; guided dive $49, snorkeling from $50) Whilst its location on a dreary Aguadilla highway makes it more inconvenient than some of the operators nearer the water in Isabella, there's really no point going anywhere but the best, and this outfit most certainly has that reputation. It's the best-equipped dive facility and welcomes clients of all ages and skills.

Cycling

Hit the ocean road on or around Rtes 466 and 4466 for some of the best bike rides on the north coast, part of which is connected by – yep, really – an actual cycle lane. There are plenty of decent circuits in the Aguadilla/Isabela area that steer clear of the main roads and incorporate some magnificent rural scenery. There are also a couple of moderately difficult single-track trails in the area.

Aquatica Dive & Surf CYCLING

(☎787-890-6071; www.aquaticapr.com; Rte 110 Km 10, Aguadilla; 2 dives incl gear $95; ⏲9am-5pm Mon-Sat, 9am-3pm Sun) Outside Gate 5 of Ramey Base near the airport is one of Puerto Rico's best bike-rental establishments. The staff here can also help you with route planning. Aquatica also, as its name suggests, rents surfing gear.

Horseback Riding

A horseback ride along a nearly deserted beach is one of the joys of Isabela and an excellent experience.

Tropical Trail Rides HORSEBACK RIDING

(☎787-872-9256; www.tropicaltrailrides.com; Rte 4466 Km 1.8; 2hr ride $50; ⏲twice daily) You can take a ride along the fields, dunes and beaches with Tropical Trail Rides, which works out of stables at Playa Shacks.

Golf

The arrival of the Royal Isabela has put Isabela up there on the golfing circuit with Dorado.

Royal Isabela GOLF

(☎787-609-5888; www.royalisabela.com; 396 Av Noel Estrada; per day $250, caddie fee $90) Little touches, like a replicated Scottish burn (stream), a tee over an ocean inlet toward a cliff (supposedly shaped like a Taíno chief's face) and a finish playing around sugar plantation ruins, show indications of the creativity that went into the course design here. The course also conserves some important wildlife, including many rare butterfly species, and there is a self-guided tour of the fauna you might spot.

ISLA DESECHEO

The island appearing alluringly on the horizon in spectacular west-coast sunsets is Isla Desecheo, a 1-sq-mile knob of prickly cacti and bushy scrub situated 13 miles off Puerto Rico's northwest coast. One of four outlying islands making up the Puerto Rican archipelago (the others are Culebra, Vieques and Mona), Desecheo was 'discovered' by Columbus in 1493, but remained unnamed until Spanish explorer Nuñez Alvarez de Aragón passed through in 1517. Buccaneers and pirates frequented it during the 16th and 17th centuries to hoard booty and hunt the feral goats introduced by the Spanish, and over the years it's been home to lizards, seabirds and a few monkeys, introduced for an adaptation experiment. From WWII to the early 1950s, Desecheo was – surprise, surprise – used as a bombing range by the US military who left behind a cache of unexploded ordnance, a fact that makes the island remain officially off-limits to visitors (trespassers will be arrested – or perhaps blown up).

But all is not lost. Thanks to its favorable position to the west of the geologically important Puerto Rican Trench, the waters around Desecheo are free from murky river run-off from the main island. As a result the sea here is unusually clear (visibility is generally 30m to 45m), making it one of the best spots for diving in the Caribbean. Desecheo was declared a US Fish and Wildlife Refuge in 1976 and a National Wildlife Refuge in 1983. Taíno Divers (p171) in Rincón offers diving trips to Isla Desecheo.

Non-members *must* contact the club in advance to see if there are available tee times. Sip a few cocktails in the elegant 19th hole, positioned to give the perfect course overview, or eat in the Moroccan-decorated La Casa restaurant afterwards.

Beaches

Playa Jobos BEACH

The wonderfully dramatic crescent of Playa Jobos is protected by a large headland of dead coral to the east, and the surf breaks pretty consistently off this point. The site of the 1989 World Surfing Championships, Jobos is a good place to surf or watch professional athletes doing their wave thing. There is also fine swimming off the eastern beach, where the point protects you from the surf.

The bar-restaurants on the south side of the cove offer a laid-back après-surf scene, especially on weekends.

Playa Shacks BEACH

Playa Shacks lies less than a mile west of Playa Jobos, near Ramey Base on Rte 4466. There are good submarine caves here for snorkeling.

Playa Crash Boat BEACH

This is the next must-go beach, north up the coast from Aguadilla. An undulating road winds down to a car park, snack stands, a lively bar, a pier (off which you can swim) and a swath of ocher sand. It got its name because the air force used to keep rescue boats here to pick up crews from the Strategic Air Command's bombers that didn't make the runway. It's on the looping Rte 458, which branches off Hwy 107.

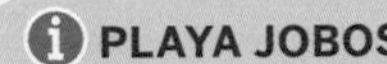

PLAYA JOBOS

What locals refer to as Playa Jobos is actually one long coastline made up of different beaches – Jobos is the biggest one, at the intersection of Rtes 466 and 4466. That's also where you will find most hotels and restaurants.

Sleeping

★Villa Tropical APARTMENTS $$

(☎787-872-7172; www.villatropical.com; 326 Bo Bajuras, Playa Shacks; $100-170; P ❄ ⓦ) Sea views hit you vividly from all sides at the impeccably designed Villa Tropical, where accommodations in huge, light, airy apartments will make you pinch yourself to check you're not teleported to an affluent Californian coastal enclave, and big balconies act as stages to watch the wicked surf action on a rarely traipsed stretch of sand just shy of Playa Shacks.

Villa Tropical's apartments also have remarkably well-equipped kitchens, making them ideal for families. For the best experience, grab a room in the end building, a block down from the reception. There's a launderette on-site, and snorkel-gear rental available.

Hacienda El Jibarito HOTEL $$

(☎787-280-4040; www.haciendaeljibarito.com; Rte 445 Km 6.4; r from $110; P ❄ ≋) Opened in 2006, this innovative ecolodge bills itself as an 'agro-tourist complex,' that is, a hotel doubling up as a *hacienda* (agricultural estate). Although facilities retain suitably rustic touches such as hammocks, rocking chairs and antique farming implements, it's a bit softer than the back-to-nature experience you get in the hills.

Comfortable rooms sport TVs, phones and bathtubs, and a laid-back poolside bar shakes up refreshing piña coladas, but the hacienda's real forte lies in its beautifully landscaped grounds and positive environmental practices. The adjacent *granja* (farm) – which guests may visit – makes use of its own chickens, cows, shrimp farm and greenhouse to send produce directly to the on-site restaurant. The hacienda is 8 miles south of Isabela heading along Hwy 112.

Parador Villas del Mar Hau CABINS $$

(☎787-872-2045; www.paradorvillasdelmarhau.com; Rte 466 Km 8.3; cabins $150-230; P ❄ ≋) A clutch of brightly painted beach huts lie scattered like bucolic homesteads along a breathtaking beach where offshore coral islets create bathing lagoons: welcome to this rustic retreat run by the Hau family for nearly 50 years. Here you can ride a horse, go cycling, kayak, snorkel, hike the beach or sleep undisturbed under a palm tree. The kiteboarding outside the front door is the best on Puerto Rico.

The villas are 4 miles west of Isabela. Rates in low season can drop by almost $50.

Hotel Restaurante Ocean Front HOTEL **$$**
(☎787-872-0444; www.oceanfrontpr.com; Rte 4466 Km 0.1; r $85-150; P ❄) Imagine a classic Caribbean-style beach hotel situated on a tempestuous stretch of sand popularly regarded by aficionados as being surfers' heaven. That's the Ocean Front: small, compact, suitably modern, but not too flashy. Rooms have balconies and good views of the incoming surf and there's a popular on-site restaurant-bar that hosts occasional live music.

Room rates are lowest Monday to Friday. The hotel is situated 5 miles west of Isabela on Playa Jobos.

Hotel El Guajataca HOTEL **$$**
(☎787-895-3070; www.hotelelguajataca.com; Hwy 2 Km 103.8; r $118-162; P ❄ ≋ 👪) About 5 miles east of Isabela in Quebradillas, El Guajataca is a run-of-the-mill parador – ie slightly dog-eared rooms, keen-to-please staff and good family facilities – notable for its stupendous north-coast setting. Perched on a grassy cliff overlooking the Atlantic, this is Puerto Rico at its wildest and most romantic, although the fairly bland hotel hardly emulates the location.

There are two nice pools, a tennis court and easy access to a great surfing (but not swimming) beach.

Courtyard by Marriot Aguadilla HOTEL **$$**
(☎787-658-8000; www.courtyardaguadilla.com; cnr W Parade & W Belt, Aguadilla; d from $139; P ❄ 📶 ≋ 👪) It's only worth staying here if flight arrivals/departures make other options inconvenient, but hey ho: you could easily do worse in Aguadilla. It's an above-average chain option, but two things besides its location a mere couple of blocks from the Aguadilla airport terminal give it the edge: a nice casino with a schedule of live performers and events, and a splash park in the courtyard.

What the rooms lack in personality is made up for by an exceptional, modern facility.

Royal Isabela RESORT **$$$**
(☎787-609-5888; www.royalisabela.com; 396 Av Noel Estrada; r $650-1150; P ❄ 📶 ≋) 🍃 Luxury melds with a strong environmental ethos at the Royal Isabela, the new golf resort that many are whispering is the superior of anything Dorado can offer for teeing, dining and – should your wallet stretch – staying. The vision of Stanley and Charlie Pasarell has risen out of a former sugarcane plantation into an enticing tract of vegetated cliffs, rocky coves and undulating, copse-fringed greenery.

The 20 *casitas* (small houses) are cocooned away within the folds of this estate, so hidden that you can barely see one from the next. Needless to say, they're a soliloquy in style, with dark-wood flooring, carved beds, walk-in four-jet showers and Gilchrist & Soames toiletries. Each has its own private plunge pool and paths wind down to private alfresco dining areas – ideal for honeymooners.

As for the 19th hole, the vista across the grounds, sweeping to the sea, is magnificent. Next to the open-air bar is the terracotta-roofed restaurant **La Casa**, where dishes ($20 to $38) are concocted with produce from the Royal Isabela's own private farm.

Villa Montaña RESORT **$$$**
(☎787-872-9554; www.villamontana.com; Rte 4466 Km 1.2; villas $250-325; P ❄ @ ≋) This resort is something of an anomaly in Puerto Rico – a high-end stay that works gracefully within its stunning environment. Here, 48 brightly painted plantation-style villas, coming with one, two or three bedrooms, look across the lawn to the tempestuous crash of Playa Shacks. Tucked away amid the tropical foliage, you'll find a tennis court, a gym, a spa and the Moroccan-themed Eclipse restaurant.

It also has bikes for guests to borrow. Our last visit found standards had dropped marginally: complacent staffing and a hint of tumbleweed a-blowing. But it was off-season and accommodations in high season get booked up fast.

Eating

In addition to the following, don't forgo the culinary pampering of Hwy 110's eateries close by. For top dining in Isabela itself, head to La Casa at the Royal Isabela.

★ **Ola Lola's** BREAKFAST **$**
(☎787-872-1230; Hwy 4446, Playa Shacks, just before Villa Tropical; breakfasts $5-10; ⏲breakfast 7am-2pm Fri-Tue, bar 4-9pm Fri-Mon) It claims to have the world's best piña colada, and the bar here is a great place for an ice-cold afternoon drink, but Ola Lola's is probably best known now as one of the north coast's most serendipitous breakfast joints, where fresh-brewed coffee, omelettes or the 'wafflewich' sandwich-waffle combo make darned good fueling for surfers starting early.

HIGHWAY 110'S BIZARRE BUT BOUNTIFUL EATERIES

Somehow, inexplicably, where elsewhere main highways in Puerto Rico are the sorry domain of ubiquitous fast-food franchises, Hwy 110, which runs between Aguadilla's Aeropuerto Rafael Hernández and Hwy 2, has become a haven of varied world cuisines, hippy healthy-eating joints and bold new culinary ventures that will leave your palate feeling better about itself. Choose from Thai, Middle Eastern or creative takes on Caribbean classics and round it off with artisanal beer.

★ **One Ten Thai** (787-890-0113; www.onetenthai.com; Hwy 110 Km 7; mains $8-15; 5-10pm Wed-Sun;) After all the stick-to-your-ribs Puerto Rican cuisine, it's hard not to fall head over heels for the refreshing flavors of One Ten Thai, a restaurant that began when the owners started doing word-of-mouth Thai meals for friends from their home kitchen. Ingredients are locally sourced from a community garden and local fishermen.

The adjoining microbrew bar has one of the most ambitious beer lists on the entire island and the dishes are simple, elegant and delicious. The small dining area is clearly a DIY affair, but buzzes with great energy. People come from as far afield as San Juan to eat here.

Paprika (787-658-6442; Hwy 110 Km 9.8; mains $8-15; 11am-2pm & 5-8pm Tue-Fri, noon-9pm Sat;) The owner here traces his heritage back to Egypt and Israel and thus-themed this wonderful menu unfolds: dishes are bright with healthy ingredients, delicate seasoning and eye-catching presentation (Israeli fish balls, baba ghanoush, stuffed vine leaves) and there's craft beers to boot.

Beer Box (787-384-8522; Hwy 110 Km 9.8; noon-7pm Mon-Wed, noon-midnight Thu-Sat, noon-5pm Sun) Tacked on to the edge of a supermarket parking lot, the Beer Box has Puerto Rico's best selection of craft beers, period. There's a surprising variety of Puerto Rican labels available, besides American and European ones, and despite it being primarily a beer shop, often a cask is left open to have a glass or three siphoned off. Just as a taster, of course.

Sau Seige (787-560-9906; Hwy 110 Km 9.2; deli items from $5; 3-7pm Mon-Fri) At this unassuming deli with just a couple of eat-in tables some truly wondrous gastronomic surprises await, such as spring rolls made with *ropa vieja* (shredded beef marinated in tomato sauce) or colorful quinoa salad. Every day yields different treats.

Cocina Creativa (787-890-1861; Hwy 110 Km 9.2; snacks $5-7, mains $7-16; 9am-4pm Mon, 9am-4pm & 5-10pm Tue-Sat;) Tucked rather incongruously behind a gas station on one of the northwest's ubiquitous big box strips, Cocina Creativa boasts a fresh, cozy, homegrown vibe. You can realign your chakras here with a kind of organic-meets-European-meets-Jamaican menu, and even buy a new pair of flip-flops. Try the yucca and fishcakes, the jerk chicken with mango chutney or the amazing bruschettas.

Panadería Los Cocos BAKERY, CAFE $
(787-895-6932; PR 484 Km 0.2, just north of Hwy 2, Quebradillas; sandwiches $3; 6am-10pm) The rosy-cheeked ladies behind the counter at this bakery will claim that they're baking in Puerto Rico's oldest bakery. They might be right. The bakery has been cooking continually for 140 years and still uses wood-fired ovens to turn out fresh bread with a thick, floury crust. Their champion dishes include a slightly sweet bread stuffed with roasted pork, cakes sweetened with fresh fruit and killer sandwiches.

Finding the place is difficult. It is just east of Quebradillas. Look for a sign painted on a surfboard advertising lessons.

Pedro's Pescado SUSHI $
(787-872-4716; Hwy 4446 Km 1; sushi plates $10-15; 5-9pm Fri & Sat) If you're lucky enough to find these guys open, this place is well worth a visit: sublime sushi does not come with a beach setting this good anywhere else in Puerto Rico. Smoked salmon rafter rolls, with avocado and cream cheese, or coconut and shrimp rolls with piña colada sauce are stand-outs.

LOCAL KNOWLEDGE

REVOLUTION BREWING: CRAFT BEER IN PUERTO RICO

Jorge Castro, owner of the Beer Box (p207) on Hwy 110, talks brews and breweries in Puerto Rico.

How did you come to champion craft beer?

I got into craft beer thanks to friends from New York who suggested I try Westmalle Tripel. I was instantly blown away by the beer's complexity (having been used to drinking super-light yellow fizzy beer) and I tried as often as I could to find that beer again. Then I learned the story of the Trappist monasteries and Belgian beer tradition in general. A little after that I discovered American craft beer styles and started catching up with all of them and with the community surrounding them. That, together with my travels through Europe and America, inspired me to set up Puerto Rico's first craft beer store, the Beer Box.

How popular is craft beer in Puerto Rico?

It's grown incredibly over the past five years! The only brand available before the 'explosion' was Sam Adams, but it's grown so much that even the local big brewery – Cervecera de Puerto Rico (CPR), which brews the popular Medalla – has started a craft beer program. Restaurants and supermarkets that would never sell the stuff are now pretty much forced to carry at least a few bottles, because of the huge demand.

What are your favorite Puerto Rican beers and why?

Definitely the Boqueron Brewing Co (BBCo) beers: a one-man operation out of the sleepy town of Cabo Rojo, in southwestern Puerto Rico. BBCo beers are simple American styles (mostly) and they have kept distribution largely on the west coast of the island, triggering outrage from the San Juan crowd, who think it's ridiculous BBCo is not distributing its beers in the capital. I think it's a genius move! It drives demand through the roof and helps the economy of the west coast. Also, the long-thriving Old Harbor Brewery out of Old San Juan is mandatory for beer aficionados: it has survived almost 10 years in this hostile environment for microbrews.

My favourite BBCo beer is the Boqueron Caja de Muerto Summer Ale: it's a crisp, surprisingly medium-bodied wheat beer brewed for the summer months.

What is the future for craft beer in Puerto Rico?

For me, the future of craft beer in Puerto Rico is the imminent growth of local breweries. The law allows for breweries to distribute themselves, which is a big help. There's already a lot of quality products on the market, but it's all in its infancy. There will be a bunch of new breweries coming out here in the next five years and the market will grow with the locals. Local breweries like Boqueron and Old Harbor are our best-selling beers at the moment. It is also worth noting that CPR will enter the craft beer market when it releases its new beers in 2014.

★Eclipse CARIBBEAN, FUSION **$$**
(☎787-872-9554; www.villamontana.com; Rte 4466 Km 1.2; dishes $10-40; ⊙noon-10pm Sun-Thu, to 11pm Fri & Sat) The alfresco atmosphere – furious waves and gentle breezes, bright tropical flowers and elegantly rustic furniture – is nearly outpaced by the creative flavors of seafood and fresh, locally sourced vegetables at this on-site restaurant of Villa Montaña. Start with the fried brie and seaweed salad or the octopus salad with golden plantains before moving on to mains of pan-Latin steak and seafood.

The menu changes daily. Nice, but overpriced.

Hotel Restaurante Ocean Front SEAFOOD **$$**
(☎787-872-0444; www.oceanfrontpr.com; Rte 4466 Km 0.1; dishes $6-22; ⊙noon-10pm) Tiny glowing lights and wavy green plants give this restaurant a relaxed, romantic atmosphere that complements the seafood dishes. The indoor setting is surprisingly formal, but the deck hosts casual surfers in for a drink. The owner is famous for his secret salmon recipe. Live music nightly. Rooms available.

Information

Puerto Rico Tourism Company (PRTC; 787-890-3315; Aeropuerto Rafael Hernández Terminal Bldg, Aguadilla; 8am-4:30pm Mon-Fri) For more information about this region, check out this helpful office at the Aguadilla airport on the old Ramey Base.

Getting There & Away

The easiest way to access the region from San Juan is via the four-lane Hwy 22, which becomes Hwy 2 after Hatillo. Keeping anticlockwise, Hwy 2 continues to link Aguadilla with the branch road to Rincón (Hwy 115), Mayagüez and eventually Ponce.

Scheduled airline services to Aguadilla's Aeropuerto Rafael Hernández change seasonally. Flights come in from New York and Newark (US) and the Dominican Republic about three times a week.

The *público* terminal in Aguadilla, right off the central plaza, is your best chance of an onward ride. Expect to pay $20 to San Juan (about three hours).

However, to really enjoy this area (and its lack of traffic), you need to get off the main highway and explore the back roads, where there are no *públicos* (this includes the best beach areas such as Playa Jobos).

Central Mountains

POP 340,000

Includes ➡

Best Places to Eat

- ➡ El Rancho Original (p218)
- ➡ Vaca Brava (p218)
- ➡ Casa Bavaria (p221)
- ➡ Restaurante Toro Verde (p218)
- ➡ El Burén (p222)

Best Places to Stay

- ➡ Las Casas de la Selva & Tropic Ventures (p214)
- ➡ Jájome Terrace (p214)
- ➡ Hacienda Gripiñas (p222)
- ➡ Parador Villas de Sotomayor (p223)

Why Go?

Those who explore these winding roads gain a dramatically different perspective on the island and a chance to commune with Puerto Rico's old soul. Rough around the edges and best approached with a flexible agenda, this is a place of Taíno legends and sugarcane moonshine, muddy hillside towns and misty afternoons.

The whole thing is strung together by the Ruta Panorámica, a vine-covered ribbon of potholed blacktop that rolls like a roller coaster along the island's rugged spine. Following rusty road signs, it winds through ragged agricultural towns, humid patches of jungle and past cliff-edge vistas where birds of prey glide in lazy circles. Between fog-covered valleys and the sharp scent of fresh-roasted beans, visitors get a whiff of the endangered cultural essence of Puerto Rico – moving decidedly more in time with their less-developed Caribbean neighbors than the paved-over hustle of the States.

When to Go

Unlike the reliably sunny shores, the mountains catch all kinds of weather, and are considerably cooler.

Cerro Maravilla in the Toro Negro forest records average temperatures 10°F to 15°F lower than San Juan. In winter, towns in the hills can be downright chilly, sometimes dropping to 45°F. There's no rainy season, per se, but the dampness gets into the bones, making layered clothing a must.

Mornings are clearer, making simultaneous views of the north and south coast possible, but the Ruta Panorámica will still often be blanketed in mist.

History

Legend has it that native Taíno survived here until the mid-19th century and, even today, Indian traditions run strong in the festivals and artisan workshops scattered along the Ruta Panorámica. In more recent times, notoriety has struck these mountains twice. In 1950 an unsuccessful uprising in Jayuya marked the death knell of the Puerto Rican independence movement as an effective political force. Further scandal erupted in 1978 when two young independence supporters were shot by police posing as revolutionaries on Cerro Maravilla in an incident that uncovered corruption, ballot-box fraud and an alleged FBI cover-up.

Territorial Parks & Reserves

The Central Mountains is one long chain of protected reserves, give or take the odd road. By far the best for hiking are Bosque Estatel de Carite in the east, Reserva Forestal Toro Negro in the middle of the Ruta Panorámica and, biggest of the lot, the Bosque Estatel de Maricao in the west.

Getting There & Around

The Ruta Panorámica, a chain of 40 mountain roads, travels 165 miles across the roof of Puerto Rico, from Yabucoa in the east to Mayagüez in the west. It is generally well-marked with distinctive brown road signs, and highlighted on almost all commercial maps of the island. If driving, be careful and never drive after dark.

Major towns in the central region – Aibonito, Barranquitas, Jayuya and Adjuntas – are accessible by *público* from either coast. Some of the more remote places, however, are a little more difficult to reach and, if you're without a car, you may require lifts, taxis or plenty of forward planning. Bikes can be precarious on the Ruta Panorámica, where drivers are famously erratic. Riders should stick to the wider link roads such as Rte 15 between Cayey and Guayama and listen to local advice.

Caguas

POP 80,000

Large, smart, modern Caguas, just 20 miles south of San Juan, is a misleading introduction to Puerto Rico's central massif (which although large is neither smart nor modern). The thickly forested hills seem far away here, despite it being the best place to pick up supplies for mountainous sojourns such as Bosque Estatel de Carite. La Ciudad Criolla (the Creole City) is, however, a worthy half-day stop for its proud cultural scene, evidenced in a clutch of museums near leafy Plaza Palmer. This central square is where you will find the attractive cream-colored cathedral, dating from the 1930s and, amid the foliage, an intriguing floral clock and a statue of José Gautier Benítez, one of Puerto Rico's best-known poets.

Sights

★Museo Artes Populares de Caguas — MUSEUM

(787-258-3505; cnr Betances & Luis Padial; 9am-noon & 1-5pm Tue-Sat) FREE A leading contemporary Puerto Rican artist, Edwin Báez Carrasquillo, specializes in creating *retablos,* three-dimensional scenes of Puerto Rican life full of fascinating minute detail, and his work forms the bulk of this riveting little museum. Subjects covered here range from the museum's founder in his study piled high with curios to the devastation of the 1918 hurricane.

Centro de Bellas Artes de Caguas — ARTS CENTER

(787-653-8833; cnr Luis Padial & Segundo Ruiz Belvo; 9am-5pm) FREE On the west side of Calle Luis Padial, spreading along a grand walkway replete with fountains and sculptures, the former premises of the General Cigar Company has been converted into an impressive three-tier cultural center, with artwork by Caguas artists and two dedicated performance spaces. With its bold art installations, including striking vestibule stained glass remembering Caguas author Abelardo Díaz Alfaro, it is one of the island's most impressive arts venues. The ground-floor cafe offers the city's best caffeine fix.

Museo del Tobacco — MUSEUM

(787-744-8833; cnr Betances 87 & Luis Padial; 9am-noon & 1-5pm Tue-Sat) FREE Puerto Rico's tobacco industry might be outshone by Cuba's, but the island produced plenty of its own tobacco back in the day, which was then often shipped to Cuba for manufacture into cigars. Tobacco growing, cutting, drying and processing was once an economic mainstay of Caguas and this museum offers a history of all of it. There is a reconstruction of a tobacco ranch and tobacco rolling demonstrations. Oh, and you can buy handmade smokes here, too.

Central Mountains Highlights

1 Load up on fresh coffee and navigate the roller-coaster curves of the **Ruta Panorámica** (p216).

2 Hurtle through the treetops on some of Latin America's best zip lines at **Toro Verde Nature Adventure Park** (p217).

3 Inhale the aroma of homegrown Puerto Rican coffee in **Hacienda San Pedro** (p221).

4 Join the spontaneous street party hosted by *lechoneras* in **Guavate** (p218).

5 Bushwhack your way up an overgrown trail in the **Reserva Forestal Toro Negro** (p219).

6 Descend into the sheer gorges and crashing waterfalls of **Cañón de San Cristóbal** (p215).

7 Study the stunning *retablos* of Edwin Báez Carrasquillo in the art museums of **Caguas** (p211).

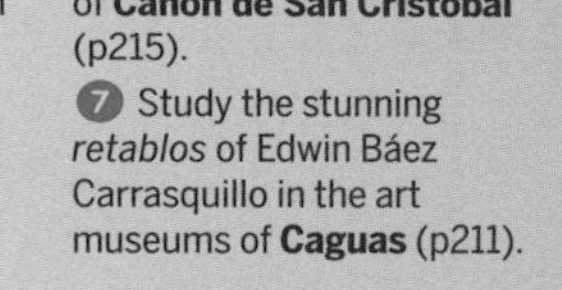

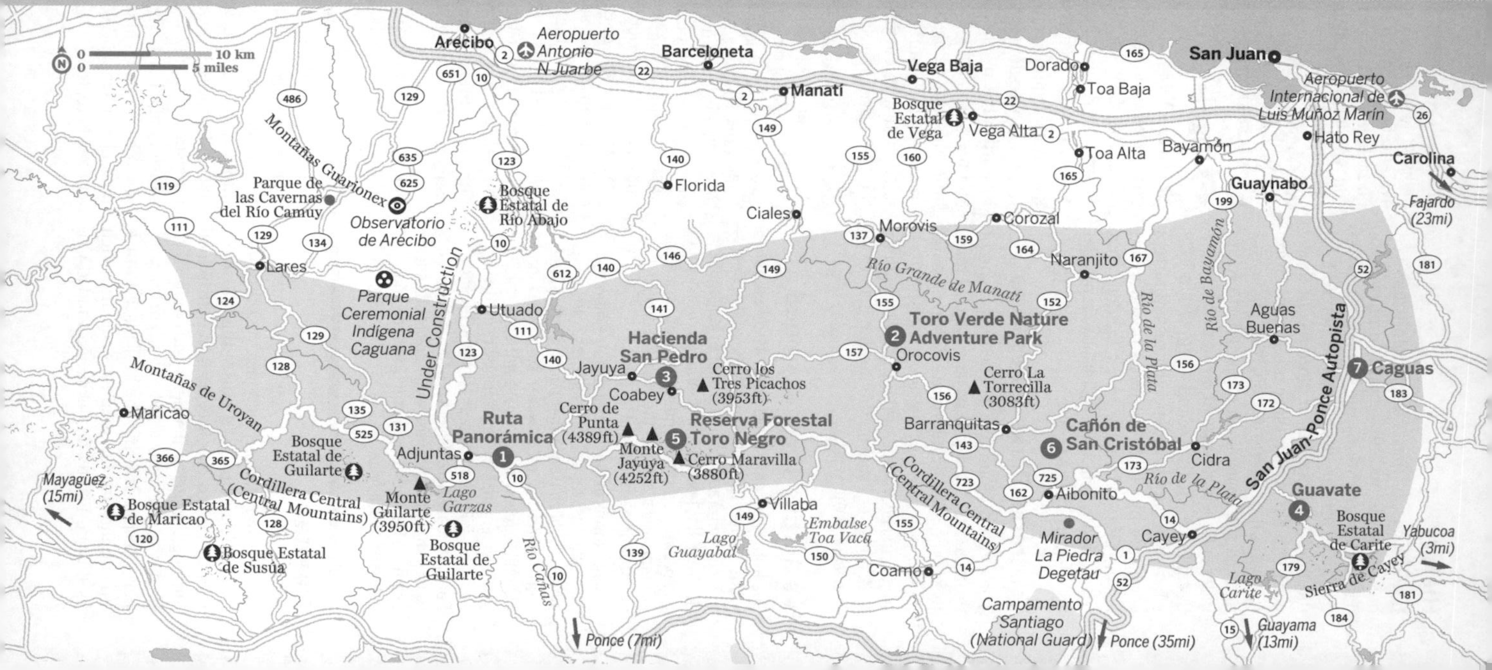

Museo de Arte MUSEUM
(☎787-744-8833; Luis Padial, opp Centro de Bellas Artes; ⊙9am-noon & 1-5pm Tue-Sat) FREE This museum, pleasant for a serendipitous stop, focuses on contemporary art. Most notable is the work by Carlos Osorio, an artist behind the establishment of Museo del Barrio in New York.

Jardín Botánico y Cultural de Caguas PARK
(cnr Rte 156 & Ave Zafiro; ⊙10am-4pm Thu-Sun) FREE Whilst beelining for a botanical garden with the flora-rich mountains beckoning might seem counterintuitive, this verdant area on a meander of the Río Caguitas, 4km west of the center on Rte 156, is the rival of any San Juan park. The highlight is an arboretum of plants known to and utilized by the Taíno.

Getting There & Away

Públicos to San Juan and other destinations use a terminal two blocks northeast of Plaza Palmer on Calle Acosta. It's a 30-minute ride to Río Piedras in San Juan. The much-talked-about light rail link to San Juan, connecting to Cupey station on the San Juan–Bayamon railway, is projected for completion by 2016.

Bosque Estatal de Carite

Less than an hour south of San Juan, the **Bosque Estatal de Carite** (Carite Forest Reserve; ☎787-747-4545; Rte 184 Km 27.5; ⊙7am-3.30pm Mon-Fri) was created in 1935 to protect the watersheds of various local rivers from erosion and urbanization. Measuring 6000 acres in area, the mountain reserve is easily accessed from the San Juan metro area. It can get crowded on weekends and during the summer when *sanjuaneros* come here to enjoy the 72°F temperatures, leafy shade and mutiple *lechoneras* (restaurants specializing in smoky, spit-roasted suckling pig) that line Hwy 184 as it approaches the northern forest entrance. The forest is one of the first points of interest you will hit if you are traversing the Ruta Panorámica from east to west.

As with most Puerto Rican forest reserves, facilities are spartan and ranger stations are often unmanned. If you are intending to stay here, make arrangements in advance and bring water, insect repellent and food; no supplies are sold inside. The only way to enter the forest is by car. From the north, take Hwy 52 to the Cayey Este exit to Hwy 184. From the south, take the Ruta Panorámica from Yabucoa. You can also reach the forest from Patillas on the south coast via Hwy 184.

Sights & Activities

Carite can be a great place for hiking, camping, fishing and cooling off in pools and streams, as long as you're up for some DIY adventure. There are 49 species of bird here – including the endangered native *falcón de sierra* (mountain hawk) – and a variety of trees.

Hurricanes have wreaked havoc on Carite's trails in the past and most paths have been destroyed. The only trail maintained by rangers is Charco Azul, though with a bit of bushwhacking you can probably get through on the El Radar and a couple of others that lead upstream from Charco Azul. It's best to phone ahead to check current conditions if you're a serious hiker, though you may well reach a park employee who knows nothing about the trails.

At Las Casas de la Selva, managers can provide information and guides for long hikes through Carite, including the six-hour trek through **Hero Valley**, which descends to a river of slick boulders and is suggested for experienced hikers only. There are three main *areas recreativas* (recreational areas) good for a picnic: **Charco Azul** (near the southern entrance on Hwy 184), **Real Patillas** (also in the south on Hwy 184) and **Guavate** (above the *lechoneras* in the north).

Charco Azul Trail HIKING
After several storms destroyed trails here, rangers decided to clear and maintain only this one, the reserve's most popular trail. It leads to a hazy blue swimming hole and camping/picnic area of the same name. It is an easy half-mile walk from Hwy 184, near the southeast corner of the forest. The swimming hole is about 15ft deep with a rocky bottom. It can be a madhouse on summer weekends, but relatively lonely in the winter. Beyond the swimming area there is another, sketchier trail leading to the top of Cerro La Santa (2730ft), Carite's highest point.

El Radar Trail HIKING
El Radar trailhead departs to the south, off Hwy 184 near the northwest corner of the forest, and makes a steep, 1-mile climb to the peak of Cerro Balíos. If you look beyond the ugly Doppler radar weather station, you'll be rewarded with vistas of the north and south coasts, and hills that roll off toward El Yunque.

TAKING A HIKE

Fine, we'll just say it: Puerto Rico can bedevil the ambitious hiker. Despite the lush natural areas and acres of natural reserves there's something about traipsing trails that just simply doesn't jibe with Puerto Rican culture – one park ranger suggested it was because people don't like getting their shoes dirty! Trails are often unmarked and poorly maintained and there are few reliable maps available locally. If you want to do a lot of hiking it's a good idea to order detailed topographical maps before you leave home, have no expectations for word-of-mouth route suggestions and arrive with an ample supply of patience.

Sleeping

The options for staying over in the forest are divided between upscale ecolodges and two **camping areas** (campsites per person $4, children under 10 free). At the northwest corner of the reserve is the Guavate Camping Area, with room for six tents and 30 people. Charco Azul, the more attractive choice, is the pondside camping area at the southeast end of the reserve. It can accommodate 10 tents and 50 people. Both areas have toilet and bathing facilities. Reserve 15 days in advance with the Departamento de Recursos Naturales y Ambientales (DRNA).

★Las Casas de la Selva & Tropic Ventures CAMPGROUND, CABINS $

(787-839-7318; www.eyeontherainforest.org; Hwy 184 Km 16.1; campsites $15, cabins $50-80) This reserve is on the south slope of the Sierra de Cayey in the Río Grande de Patillas watershed. Once a coffee plantation, it became a sustainable-growth tree farm 20 years ago, and continues to be a leading institution for rainforest study.

The 1000-acre reserve is mostly for ecological and environmental research and volunteers but, if there is space, visitors can come for a rustic vacation and sleep in the heart of the forest (tent hire – $25 for two people – is also available).

Advance arrangements are necessary, preferably through its website, since its phone lines are not reliable. Note: the gate will be locked unless you make a reservation. To find Las Casas de la Selva, follow Hwy 184 southeast toward Patillas through the Bosque Estatal de Carite to Km 16.1, where you will see a sign for the reserve.

Jájome Terrace HOTEL $$

(787-469-3939, 787-738-4016; www.jajometerrace.com; Rte 15 Km 18.6; r incl breakfast $110-124;) With no TVs, phones or cell phone reception and a miles-from-anywhere feel, the lush Jájome sits 2800ft up in the mountains of the Cordillera Central with satellite map views over towards Ponce. In business since the 1930s, the place has hosted national icon Luis Muñoz Marín and Miss Universe contestants.

Almost wiped out by Hurricane George in 1998, the wooden Jájome was revamped in sturdy brick in 2002 and reopened with its 10 fully renovated rooms and popular open-terrace restaurant fresh with nouveau rustic charm.

Getting There & Around

Públicos out here are not much more common than blue moons. Getting to the insanely popular restaurant strip of Guavate is your best bet – the forest's northern gate (plus trails and camping access) is half a mile from here. The most popular way of seeing the mountains in their entirety is still a rental car.

Aibonito & Around

POP 25,000

Once the de facto capital of Puerto Rico, after Spanish Governor Romualdo Palacios González established residence here in 1887, Aibonito has long been a retreat for the island's political leaders and most wealthy citizens. The town has a number of other claims to fame that include being the island's highest town (at about 2000ft) and home to an impressive flower festival. For these reasons, and because it's on the Ruta Panorámica, Aibonito is Puerto Rico's most visited mountain town.

The town has a euphonious name that suggests a Spanish exclamation meaning 'Wow, how beautiful,' but the name is probably derived from a Taíno word. Today, travelers should associate Aibonito with a very limited definition of beauty. Terrible traffic jams on the narrow streets are a daily occurrence and, whilst thriving flower-growing, poultry-raising and poultry-processing industries have brought prosperity, it has come with precious little thought to urban planning.

Yet the extraordinary spectacle of Puerto Rico's deepest canyon, the Cañón de San Cristóbal, lying north of town in a deep volcanic rift, alone warrants a visit here. More serene views, this time from above, await at the Mirador La Piedra Degetau.

Aibonito-lovers claim that the weather in their town is perpetually spring-like. They are not exaggerating: the average temperature is 72°F. Gentle showers are common.

Most drivers approach Aibonito via the Ruta Panorámica. A less-traveled and more dramatic route (if you like hairpin turns) is to take Hwy 173 and Hwy 14 south from Cidra.

Sights

★Cañón de San Cristóbal — CANYON

This canyon is so unexpected – both in location and appearance – that it may take your breath away. The deep green chasm seems to drop out of nowhere, its rocky crags hiding a veil of falling water. Only 5 miles north of Aibonito and cutting more than 500ft down through the central mountains, you'll probably only see the canyon right as you approach its edge; the rift is so deep and narrow that the fields and hills of the surrounding high-mountain plateau disguise it.

The highest waterfall on the island is here, where the Río Usabón plummets down a sheer cliff into a gorge that is deeper, in many places, than it is wide. For fit outdoor enthusiasts, the descent into the canyon is a first-class thrill, whether you take steep trails or make the technical descent – recommended only for those with mountaineering experience.

You can catch a glimpse of the canyon from a distance by looking east from the intersection of Hwy 725 and Hwy 162. Getting into the canyon is a bit trickier. One way is to take side roads off Hwy 725 or Hwy 7725 and then cross private land to approach the rim of the canyon. It's essential to get permission to cross private property. Cañón de San Cristóbal has sheer cliffs that are prone to landslides, and the trails into the canyon are a slippery death wish when they get wet (and it rains a lot around here).

The best way to visit the canyon is to plan ahead, make reservations and join an organized trek with **Go Hiking Puerto Rico** (☎787-857-2094; www.barranquitaspr.net/tours), run by local historian and geographer Samuel Oliveras Ortiz. Trips run on weekends and holidays and vary from a three- to four-hour basic tour ($100) to a five- to six-hour adrenalin-junkie fest with rock climbing and rappelling ($135 to $160 depending on number of people). Another outfit that comes recommended is **Montaña Explora** (☎787-516-6194; montanaexplora@yahoo.com), with similar prices. Wear secure shoes and layer appropriate clothing that you can take off at the canyon floor, where temperatures can be more than 10°F warmer than up on the brink. Of course, you will need water and snacks for the return trip up the canyon wall (where you get to climb up through a waterfall).

Mirador La Piedra Degetau — VIEWPOINT

This nest of boulders crests a hilltop alongside the Ruta Panorámica (Hwy 7718 here) at Km 0.7, just south of Aibonito. Once the 'thinking place' of Ponce-born writer Federico Degetau y González, this must have been a truly sublime place in its day, with its views of the mountains, the Atlantic and the Caribbean.

On a clear evening you can actually see cruise ships leaving San Juan more than 20 miles to the north and the lights of Ponce glowing to the south.

Sadly, a lookout tower (that dwarfs the actual rocks), myriad picnic shelters, a playground and a paved parking lot hinder the lyrical ruminations of potential poets today. It's still an awe-inspiring view, but one can't help feeling that Degetau must be turning in his grave.

Festivals & Events

Festival de Flores — FLOWERS

The Festival de Flores (Flower Festival) at Aibonito has grown into a major rite of summer during the last 30 years. Today it draws hundreds of commercial growers and amateur horticulturists and tens of thousands of flower-lovers to see the town and surrounding countryside ablaze with roses, carnations, lilies and begonias. Of course, along with the flowers there are food and craft stalls and the requisite beauty pageant.

This event takes place at the end of June and often runs into the July 4 holiday (US Independence Day), so you had better plan to get here before the crowds or expect to spend your holiday in a traffic jam. Remember to check the regulations of the Department of Agriculture if you're planning to bring back plants to the United States.

Eating

Restaurante Asador Isla Bonita PUERTO RICAN $$
(☎787-735-8151; Hwy 162 Km 0.6; mains $10-20; ⊙lunch Fri-Sun) Location, location… Come here for the 2700ft-high sublime views over the hilly greenery known as Tetas de Cayey (Cayey Tits) that mean it doesn't matter if the food, such as *mofongo* or *paella jíbara*, is only average. It's located near the junction with Hwy 1.

Restaurante El Cantinflas PUERTO RICAN $$
(☎787-735-8870; cnr Rte 162 & 7718; mains $8-18; ⊙8am-10pm) With decent honest Puerto Rican offerings, this option lies at the junction of Rtes 162, 772 and 7718.

Getting There & Away

Públicos will take you to Aibonito from Cayey or Caguas for about $5. These cities have connections to the Río Piedras district of San Juan (another $5 or so).

Barranquitas & Around

POP 29,000

One of Puerto Rico's most quintessential mountain towns, Barranquitas is a diminutive, picturesque settlement clinging to the muddy slopes of the rain-lashed Cordillera Central. Lying on the north side of the Cañón de San Cristóbal, about a 20-minute drive out of Aibonito on Hwy 162 (or an even shorter detour off of the Ruta Panorámica via Hwy 143), the town is known locally as the Cuna de Próceres (Cradle of Great People) for its historical propensity to produce poets, politicians and governors of national (and international) distinction. Most notable in this list is the legendary Muñoz clan, Puerto Rico's substitute 'royal' family whose evocative mausoleum has made Barranquitas a pilgrimage site for local patriots and curious visitors.

This is not, however, a fairy-tale village of architectural heirlooms. Hurricanes and fires have ravaged Barranquitas several times (the name translates to 'Place of Little Mud Slides'), and the oldest structures, such as the church, date only from the early 20th century.

Barranquitas' charm rather lies in its narrow streets, tightly packed with shops and houses, which fall away into deep valleys on three sides of the plaza. Indeed, the view as you descend the mountain road into town with the afternoon sun setting the church tower ablaze above the dense architectural jumble of the central neighborhood, is truly memorable. The best range of restaurants in the Central Mountains also lies here.

Sights & Activities

Plaza de Recreo de Barranquitas PLAZA
Barranquita's central plaza is laced with wrought-iron railings, and guarded by the **Parroquia de San Antonio de Padua**, a small church first constructed in 1804. The original church was destroyed by two catastrophic hurricanes (the first of which wiped out the whole town), but was rebuilt in 1933 in a quaint post-colonial style.

The church was recently renovated and now gleams amid the surrounding mountain greenery. The centerpiece of the plaza

RUTA PANORÁMICA

Traveling the Ruta Panorámica can be a fun detour or a maddening frustration. Here, distances suddenly become mysteriously elongated as the island appears to double in size and you crawl along the curving lines of the map at a snail's pace. Drives that would take 20 minutes on the coast turn into two- to three-hour odysseys. Only a few brief glimpses of the faraway ocean remind you that you haven't disappeared into the Amazonian jungle. First-timers beware: this is no Sunday-afternoon dawdle. Maneuvering through dense rainforest and sleepy mountain villages, the Ruta's roadsides are populated by posses of stray dogs, horse-riding *jíbaros* (country people) and – most chillingly – the burnt-out wrecks of hundreds of abandoned cars. The latter should be enough to remind wannabe speed-freaks to steer carefully (never at more than 25mph). Unfortunately, the locals aren't always so fastidious, often taking the precarious hills and tricky chicanes at 35mph or more.

Drive defensively and be on your guard, and remember to sound your horn around blind corners. And don't get ruffled if you can't find signs for the 'official' Ruta Panorámica – signs are often obscured or moved by local business owners hoping to lure traffic.

is a decorative wrought-iron gazebo adorned with distinctive art nouveau flourishes, surrounded by four classical fountains.

Casa Museo Luis Muñoz Rivera MUSEUM
(☎787-857-0230; cnr Calles Muñoz Rivera & Padre Berrios; admission $1; ⏱8:30am-4:20pm Wed-Sun) This tin-roofed house honors the so-called grandfather of Puerto Rico's autonomy movement and the 20th-century architect of the Puerto Rican commonwealth. This is where Luis Muñoz Rivera was born in 1859, and it contains a collection of furniture, letters, photographs and other memorabilia, including his death mask. The coolest thing on display is Muñoz' 1912 Pierce-Arrow motorcycle, which carried him to his mausoleum.

Mausoleo Familia Muñoz Rivera MUSEUM
(7 Calle Padre Berrios; ⏱8:30am-4:20pm Tue-Sun) FREE Just south of the plaza is a family tomb holding the remains of Muñoz Rivera, his famous son Luis Muñoz Marín and their wives. Photographic displays at the tomb evoke the funeral of Luis Muñoz Marín, and the brightly colored frescos on the walls are an aptly powerful testament to the man himself. See the box on p220 for more information.

★Toro Verde Nature Adventure Park ADVENTURE SPORTS
(☎787-867-7020; www.toroverdepr.com; Carretera 155, Barrio Gato, sector Los Santiago, Orocovis; ⏱8am-5pm Fri-Mon) This park was completed in 2010, and offers a suite of adventures among a stunning patch of forest near the little town of Orocovis, north of Barranquita. The affordable, adrenaline-soaked zip-line tours and single-track mountain-bike circuit make it the best facility of its kind on the island – and possibly in the Americas.

There are several zip-line tours to choose from, but even the standard canopy zip-line tour ($85, three hours) is a rush – sending you sailing over a valley connected to eight lines.

The longest line on the standard tour is over 2500ft long and 600ft in the air. The other packages offered are a good option for those who want something a bit different, including the two-minute ride on 'La Bestia' ($65), which harnesses you superman-style into one of the longest zip lines in the world, and a hanging-bridges tour ($100, two hours), in which you rush across wildly swinging bridges (while strapped to a safety cable). Note that for the zip lines and bridge tour there are weight and age requirements (the youngest available for kids over 12).

The 8-mile-long mountain-bike circuit ($25) is far and away the best-maintained trail ride on the mountain, designed by pro mountain-biker Marla Streb. Its single-track trails are challenging, with lots of tight lines and good drops.

LECHÓN LINGUISTICS

- *Cuerito* – Smoky, crispy pig skin
- *Cuchifrito* – Deep-fried pork delicacies, including ears and tails
- *Morcillas* – Dark pork and rice-stuffed blood sausage

Sleeping & Eating

★Delia Aponte B&B $
(☎787-857-1782; Padre Berrios 7; s/d incl breakfast $30/60) Delia Aponte's tastefully decorated double room is reminiscent of Cuba's *casas particulares:* beautiful old furnishings, a sprightly host and a delicious breakfast are included in the price. Given Puerto Ricans seem disinterested in this type of accommodation, it is one of the best bargains in Puerto Rico for those who are game. It's right in the heart of Barranquitas. Phoning ahead to make a reservation is preferred.

El Cañon GUESTHOUSE $$
(☎787-375-4309; Rte 719 Km 1; s/d/tr $79/89/99; P ❄) And the prize for Puerto Rico's strangest combination of business ventures goes to...this slickly finished, ultra modern cluster of rooms and apartments in little Barranquitas, above a furniture store and opposite a steakhouse run by the same people.

El Navideño BOUTIQUE HOTEL $$$
(☎787-867-6900; www.elnavideno.com; Pedro Arroyo 3, Orocovis; r from $200; ❄ 📶) It's *navidad* (Christmas) all year round at Puerto Rico's oddest boutique hotel, but once you've got over the festive songs and the *coquitos* (traditional rum-and-coconut drinks) being dished out at the bar, you'll find this place very comfortable, if OTT in almost every aspect (including the price).

The gaudy suites upstairs come with super-plump beds, wi-fi, flatscreen TVs and DVD/Blueray players. Energy flow has been corrected by the same people who did Madonna's feng shui. Breakfast is served in

WORTH A TRIP

GUAVATE

Puerto Ricans invariably speak of Guavate in reverential tones. During the week, it's just an unkempt strip of scruffy, shack-like restaurants abutting the Carite Forest. But come on the weekend for a heady transformation – a free-wheeling atmosphere united around good food, spontaneous dancing and boisterous revelry that earns it the designation of the 'Ruta del Lechón.'

A cherished place for traditional Puerto Rican cooking, Guavate is the spiritual home of the island's ultimate culinary 'delicacy,' *lechón asado,* or whole roast pig, locally reared and turning on a spit. And, although the myriad *lechoneras* that pepper the roadside might look a little rough around the edges (Styrofoam plates, Formica tables), appearances can be deceiving and the crowds tell another story. Everyone from millionaire businessmen to cigar-puffing *jíbaros* (country people) congregate for the best in authentic Puerto Rican cuisine and culture. If it's the island's uninhibited soul you're after, look no further.

The best action is on weekend afternoons between 2pm and 9pm, when old-fashioned troubadours entertain crowds, and live salsa, *meringue* and *reggaetón* music summons diners to the makeshift dance floors for libidinous grooving. With over a dozen restaurants and stalls all offering similar canteen-style food and service, your best bet is to come hungry and follow the crowds. Standards include *arroz con grandules* (rice and pigeon peas), *pasteles* (mashed plantain and pork) and – brave, this one – *morcillas* (rice and pigs blood).

If you can't choose which *lechonera,* try **El Rancho Original** (☎787-747-7296; Rte 184 Km 27.5; plates $6-7; ⏲10am-8pm Sat & Sun), where they serve consistently perfect pork that's heavenly, smoky and covered in crispy skin. But, truth be told, standards on the 'Pork Highway' are very high and most places along the route have dedicated fans who swear their place is best.

To get to Guavate from San Juan, follow expressway 52 to exit 31, halfway between Caguas and Cayey. Turn east onto Hwy 184.

an inviting central patio. El Navideño is in Orocovis, near Toro Verde Nature Adventure Park.

Andante Fusion Culinaria PUERTO RICAN **$**
(☎787-477-4229; off Calle Nuevo Barranquitas, above Rte 152; mains $5-15; ⏲lunch & dinner) The Andante has been a gastronomic success since its opening in 2013, boasting imaginative food (chicken stuffed with spinach and guava sauce, for example) and drop-dead gorgeous views. It's up in what's become the most distinctive landmark hereabouts: the garish windmill above town, also accessible via a flight of some 320 steps from central Barranquitas.

★**Restaurante Toro Verde** INTERNATIONAL **$$**
(☎787-867-7020; Rte 155 Km 33, Barrio Gato, Sector Los Santiago, Orocovis; mains $5-22; ⏲11am-6pm Mon-Thu, 11am-9pm Fri-Sun) It's not so common to find fine dining *and* a fine view in the Central Mountains, but this newly opened restaurant at the adventure park will wow you on both counts. The marinated steak in a cilantro, orange and chimichurri sauce or the famous Orocovis sausage with a side of red beans and plantains are both as heavenly as the location.

Most of the veg comes from Toro Verde's own farm. A tip: probably best to eat after you have done 'the beast.'

Vaca Brava STEAKHOUSE, BBQ **$$**
(☎787-857-2628; Rte 771 Km 9.3; mains $9-28; ⏲11am-11pm Thu-Sun) There's a certain brazen spectacle to the pure carnage at Vaca Brava, an open-air restaurant that serves *enormous* platters of steak, fish and chicken, many constructed in whimsical, carnivorous sculptures. This is a restaurant where gluttony is nearly mandatory. If you want to test your limits, try the half-stack of beef ribs, some 3ft tall, which seems rather like something out of *The Flintstones.*

Masochists should opt for the Vaca Acosta Challenge, an 8lb platter of sirloin cocooned by French fries and soaked in mushroom sauce. Finish it and you'll get it free, but note that previous winners can be counted on one hand (the travel channel's *Man v. Food* host Adam Richman was a televised loser). The unapologetic gluttony is a bit shocking, but brings a long line of locals. Just don't end up in the hospital.

Getting There & Away

Públicos to/from surrounding towns stop on Calle Padre Berrios, three blocks south of the plaza past the Mausoleo Familia Muñoz Rivera (in the center, downhill, incidentally, is east!). You'll pay $1 to go to Aibonito, or $10 for the long (plan on four hours) roller-coaster ride to/from San Juan (Río Piedras terminal, often changing in Caguas).

Reserva Forestal Toro Negro

Covering 7000 acres and protecting some of Puerto Rico's highest peaks, the Toro Negro Reserve provides a quieter, less-developed alternative to El Yunque. Bisected by some of the steepest, windiest parts of the Ruta Panorámica (Hwy 143 in this section), the area is often shrouded in mist and blanketed by dense jungle foliage. This is where you come to truly escape the tourist throngs of the coast. But don't expect El Yunque's polish. Toro Negro's ragged facilities – which comprise a campground, a few trails and a recreation area – are spartan and poorly staffed and the signs are rough. It's best to plan ahead and ask about current conditions at the DRNA in San Juan, as mudslides are common. Properly prepared and with a decent topographical map, you should be able to carve out some memorable DIY adventures in the mountains. There are also organized tours.

Cerro de Punta, at 4389ft, is the tallest point in the reserve and Puerto Rico's highest peak. You can almost drive to the top on the Ruta Panorámica or, alternatively, attempt to bushwhack your way up from Jayuya on an infuriatingly unkempt (and vague) trail. Other notable peaks include Monte Jayuya and Cerro Maravilla, where two pro-independence activists were notoriously shot by Puerto Rican police in 1978.

Sights & Activities

Cerro de Punta MOUNTAIN

Rising to 4389ft, the summit of Cerro de Punta lies in Toro Negro Forest Reserve just off Hwy 143 (the Ruta Panorámica). Most people drive to the top. Although there's a narrow, unmarked, fairly treacherous cement road to the peak, it's better to stop in a parking lot on the northern side of Hwy 143 and take the last 1.5 miles by foot, soaking up the sights and sounds of the surrounding jungle.

The summit is crowned by communication towers, though the view north is stupendous – clouds permitting. Cerro de Punta lies in the west of the reserve, almost 10 miles of tortured driving from Area Recreativa Doña Juana.

The challenge for hikers has nothing to do with the difficulty of the terrain: the absence of marked trails underscores Puerto Rico's disinterest in the activity. Before committing to a hike, understand that you'll waste a lot of time looking for trailheads. Theoretically, a trail leaves from behind Hacienda Gripiñas, close to the town of Jayuya. If you find it, good luck following it: it is badly signposted and poorly maintained. Locals are of little help here – since hiking is so uncommon, most don't know anything about the trail, which is a steep and sweaty two- to three-hour grunt.

Area Recreativa Doña Juana RECREATION AREA

This is the area of about 3 sq miles at the eastern end of the park surrounding the ranger station, with picnic sites, toilets, showers, a camping area and a half-dozen short trails branching off Hwy 143. One trail leads to the swimming pool, open in summer only. Three others lead to the observation tower, less than a half-mile south of the highway.

Hiking

There are approximately 11 miles of trails around Doña Juana, but mostly they are short walks to the swimming pool. Always consult with the ranger station for longer hikes.

Camino El Bolo HIKNG

Across from the visitor's center at Area Recreativa Doña Juana, you'll spot a narrow trail heading uphill. That's El Bolo, a 2.5-mile jaunt taking you up to a mountain ridge and great southern views, and then crossing Vereda La Torre to elevate you even higher. It's best to come back down on the same path rather than the narrow Hwy 143, the other alternative.

Vereda La Torre HIKING
A very popular and easy path that starts in the Area Recreativa Doña Juana, La Torre goes up to an observation tower with great views. The 2-mile trail starts at the picnic tables and slowly gets more hilly and rough as you ascend. You'll see a tiny road feed into Vereda after about 20 minutes of walking – that's Camino El Bolo. Take a slight left to continue to the observation tower.

Tours

Acampa Nature Adventure Tours HIKING
(787-706-0695; www.acampapr.com; 1221 Av Jesús T Piñero, San Juan) Offers one day hiking/adventure tours to the Toro Negro rainforest. The excursion involves hiking/scrambling along the Quebrada Rosa River, rappelling off a 60ft cliff and zip-lining 200ft across the treetops. Prices start at $159 per person (six-person minimum) and include transportation from San Juan, equipment and lunch.

Sleeping

Los Viveros CAMPGROUND $
(Hwy 143 Km 32.5; campsites per adult/child $4/2) In the forest, just north of the ranger station in the Area Recreativa Doña Juana, this is a designated camping area with enough space for 14 tents. You will need a permit from the DRNA in San Juan. Apply 15 days

THE MUÑOZ CLAN

While America spawned the legendary Roosevelt dynasty, Puerto Rico produced its very own influential establishment family, the iconic Muñoz clan: two generations of charismatic politicians who changed the course of the island's postcolonial history and set the commonwealth on the road to modernity.

Born in the mountain town of Barranquitas in 1859, Luis Muñoz Rivera was the son of a former town mayor and the grandson of an enterprising Spanish sea captain. With politics planted firmly in his DNA, he formed the Autonomist Party in 1887, an organization that called for Puerto Rican autonomy within the confines of the Spanish colonial system. Three years later he upped the ante further by founding a newspaper, *La Democracia*, to act as a journalistic mouthpiece for his cause.

With the Spanish driven out by a US military government in 1898, Muñoz Rivera switched his focus to the United States. Initially an advocate of outright independence, he dropped his claims in the early 1900s to ensure a more equitable relationship with the US. Although Muñoz Rivera died a year before its implementation, he was considered instrumental in drafting the new laws (granting US citizenship to Puerto Rican nationals) and is still revered as one of Puerto Rico's most influential homegrown personalities. His mausoleum in Barranquitas remains an important and oft-visited historical monument.

A chip off his father's block, Rivera's son, Luis Muñoz Marín, was a prodigious poet and journalist who studied law in the United States. Returning to Puerto Rico in 1916, the younger Muñoz became a leading advocate for Puerto Rican independence. But like his father before him, Luis reneged on his initial promises during a spell as president of the Puerto Rican senate in the mid-1940s in order to enlist US economic backing for an ambitious industrialization campaign codenamed 'Operation Bootstrap.'

In 1949 Muñoz Marín became Puerto Rico's first democratically elected governor, a position he held for an unprecedented four terms (until 1965). During his time in office he orchestrated Puerto Rico's economic 'miracle,' transforming the island from a poverty-stricken agrarian society into a thriving economic powerhouse based on tourism, manufacturing and pharmaceuticals. Often touted as the 'father of modern Puerto Rico,' Muñoz commanded huge popularity at home for his efforts in tackling poverty while, at the same time, extracting greater freedoms from the United States. Other more nationalistic voices depict him as a turncoat who was coerced out of his independence ideals by a belligerent US military establishment.

Today, the Muñoz legacy is still evident across Puerto Rico, from the mausoleum and museums of Barranquitas to the island's Aeropuerto Internacional de Luis Muñoz Murín (LMM international airport), named in honor of its most celebrated native son.

WORTH A TRIP

CASA BAVARIA

You might not believe your eyes when you stumble upon **Casa Bavaria** (☎787-862-7818; www.casabavaria.com; Carr 155 Km 38.3, Barrio Perchas, Morovis; ⏰noon-8pm Thu, Fri & Sun, to 10pm Sat), a German-Creole surprise of a restaurant perched 2105ft high in the mountains near Morovis in the center of the island. The menu mixes typical cuisine from the Bavarian region of Germany with meaty specialties of Puerto Rico. The outdoor seating and misty views draw bikers and road-trippers galore, and fans include President Bill Clinton, who stopped by in 2008 to order the schnitzel.

in advance. If you bring charcoal and lighter fluid you can cook your food over one of the open-air picnic grills at the Area Recreativa Doña Juana.

Information

The Ruta Panorámica (Hwy 143) is your artery to and from the forest, and it is none too wide. Honk your horn when approaching blind curves and drive with caution.

All of the forest's public facilities lie at the east end of the reserve in the Area Recreativa Doña Juana at Km 32.4 on Hwy 143.

The **ranger station** (☎787-867-3040; Hwy 143 Km 32.5; ⏰8am-noon summer, reduced hours winter) has blurry photocopies of park literature, and some of this material is extremely misleading. The trail map lacks useful detail and the compass rose has been rotated so north is not at the top of the page.

You're not likely to get anything better in San Juan from the DRNA, nor is it easy to get USGS maps on the island. You can get a USGS map from map suppliers in the US or mail-order one on the island.

Barranquitas is an hour away. Come prepared: bring ample food and water and some insect repellent. Public transport is, of course, nonexistent.

Jayuya

POP 16,000

Puerto Rico's unheralded mountain 'capital' lies a few kilometers north of the Ruta Panorámica in an isolated steep-sided valley overlooked by three of the island's highest peaks – Cerro de Punta, Cerro los Tres Picachos and Cerro Maravilla. Verdantly beautiful, the precipitous geography here has protected many of the island's traditions. If you're bent on finding Puerto Rico's last authentic *jíbaro* (country person), this is a good starting point.

Steeped in Taíno legend, the original settlement of Jayuya had little contact with the rest of the island until 1911, when it was declared a municipality. In 1950 local nationalist leader Blanca Canales led a revolt against US occupation known as the 'Jayuya Uprising.' Rebels sacked the police station and declared a Puerto Rican republic from the town square. The rebellion lasted just three days before US planes bombed the town, causing widespread destruction. Still, even today, Jayuya is one of the island's most un-Americanized towns.

Efforts to keep Taíno culture alive include a festival of music, food and games, and a Miss Taíno pageant.

Sights

Jayuya is the heart of coffee country, making a visit to one of the outlying plantations requisite. Besides the distillery, the sights below require short drives outside town.

Pitorico Rum Distillery DISTILLERY
(☎787-828-1300; Rte 141 Km 0.7; ⏰9am-4pm Mon-Fri) FREE It's certainly not Bacardí, nor even Don Q, that does it for Jayuya folks – not compared to their very own artisan rum, which comes in delicious flavors like passionfruit and coconut. The amenable staff here will give you a complimentary tour of their distillery plus a few tastings (it's kind of protocol to then buy something in the shop afterwards, but then you'll most likely want to anyway). To add to the illicitness, this rum is technically moonshine (because of the size of the still used).

★**Hacienda San Pedro** FARM
(☎787-828-2083; www.cafehsp.com; Rte 144 Km 8.4; ⏰8am-6pm Mon-Fri, 10am-5pm Sat & Sun) San Pedro is a small, working coffee farm with an attached museum and tasting room where you can get a fascinating insight into

the whole coffee-making process from green bean to dark-roast espresso. Tours are also available upon request. The gourmet blends served here are some of the best brews you'll taste anywhere. Rustically packaged beans are sold on-site. True gourmands can also buy green coffee beans to try their hand at roasting.

Casa Museo Canales MUSEUM
(☎787-828-4094; Rte 144 Km 9.3; adult/child $1.50/1; ⊙noon-4pm Sat & Sun) In a small park in the barrio of Coabey, this reconstructed 19th-century coffee *finca* (rural smallholding) nestles in the shadow of the surrounding mountains. With quintessential *criollo* features and interesting antiques, it belonged to Jayuya's first major, Rosario Canales.

Rosario spawned two famous offspring. His son, Nemesio, is recognized as a great Puerto Rican poet, playwright and political activist who pushed for legal rights for women. Meanwhile his daughter, Blanca Canales Torresola, became a notorious figure in the Puerto Rican nationalist movement when she led an independence revolt against American-backed authorities in Jayuya in 1950.

Museo del Cemí MUSEUM
(☎787-828-1241; Rte 144 Km 9.2; adult/child $1.50/1; ⊙9:30am-4pm Mon-Fri, to 3pm Sat & Sun) In the same park as Casa Museo Canales, in Coabey, this is perhaps the oddest building on the island. Designed by Río Piedras architect, Efrén Badía Cabrera, the weird fish-like structure supposedly represents a gigantic *cemí* or native talisman. The exhibits inside are made up mostly of Taíno artifacts – including an *espâtula vomita,* a tool Taíno used to make themselves vomit before they took hallucinogenic drugs.

La Piedra Escrita ARCHAEOLOGICAL SITE
(Rte 144 Km 7.3) Supposedly one of the island's best-preserved native petroglyphs is carved on a large rock in the middle of the Río Saliente. Forming a natural bathing pool, it has become a popular stopping-off point for curious (and hot) travelers. There's a small parking lot and restaurant.

Sleeping & Eating

There are a few very basic restaurants in town, though several *panaderías* (bakeries) serve sandwiches. For a cafe better than most San Juan can muster, head to Hacienda San Pedro.

★Hacienda Gripiñas HOTEL $$
(☎787-828-1717; www.haciendagripinas.com; Hwy 527 Km 2.5; s/d $77/90, incl breakfast & dinner $104/148; P ❄ ☎ ≋) Ensconced in this beautifully restored coffee hacienda dating from 1858 and nestled in the shadow of Cerro de Punta, guests wander over creaking floors, rock in wicker chairs on the breezy balconies and take mouth-watering lunches in the black-and-white-tiled dining room.

Furnished with antiques and historic coffee posters, the hotel has a few modern touches – like wi-fi and a pair of swimming pools – but the historical building is dignified and timeless. Yet don't expect coastal-style luxury; the rooms are very simple, and some are much nicer than others. The three-day packages include meals, but mid-week rates are by far the best bargain. Even if you're not staying, the dining room has excellent views and good, if pricey, food. Prices increase at weekends.

Posada Jayuya HOTEL $$
(☎787-828-7250; 49 Guillermo Esteves; s/d incl breakfast $79/89; P ❄ ☎ ≋) This place in the town center is a good comfortable sleepover with 27 rooms that include TVs and refrigerators. The air-con might sound like the inside of a 1956 Buick, but at least it'll work, and the passable downstairs restaurant sometimes hosts live music.

El Burén PUERTO RICAN $
(☎787-828-2589; Hwy 528 Km 5.4; mains $11-16; ⊙2-10pm Thu, noon-10pm Fri & Sun, noon-11pm Sat) A host of Puerto Rican classics await you in an atmosphere reminiscent of a *jíbaro* ranch, but with the quiet confidence of an establishment that knows people know how well it cooks. Try *longaniza* (a chorizo with a vivid red hue from annatto seeds) and rice or seafood *mofongo,* and don't forgo the *sorullitos* (Puerto Rican corn fritters) to start with.

Adjuntas & Around

POP 19,000

Although calling Adjuntas the 'Switzerland of Puerto Rico' is a bit of an overstatement, the surrounding silhouetted mountains earn this attractive agricultural hub a more accurate moniker, the 'town of the sleeping giant.' After the discovery of copper near here in the 1960s, local community groups fought successfully to prevent their cool subtropical jungle haven from being turned into a huge open-cast mining pit. Instead, today Adjuntas has become something of an environmental steward whose livelihood remains rooted in bananas, coffee and citrus fruits.

Marking the spot where one of the island's major north–south arteries (Hwys 123 and 10) crests the Central Mountains, Adjuntas is a traffic bottleneck in the summer. The central plaza is a good place to wander while you cool the engine and there are several places on its border for a quick bite.

The main attraction hereabouts is the Bosque Estatal de Guilarte, with a good peak and remote cabins.

Sights

Casa Pueblo VISITOR CENTER
(787-829-4842; www.casapueblo.org; 30 Rodolfo Gonzáles; donation $2; 8am-4pm) Casa Pueblo is Adjuntas' tenacious environmental organization, the primary obstructer of a plan to blight the area with an open-pit mining operation. These days, it also concentrates on sustainability issues and rainforest protection. It has an artisan's shop and a grassy butterfly garden. This is an excellent place to inquire about local volunteer opportunities.

Sleeping

Parador Villas de Sotomayor CABINS $$
(787-829-1717; www.paradorvillassotomayor.com; Hwy 123/10 Km 36.3; r $113-250;) This campus of small cabins along a rock river is the best spot for families in the area, with an on-site horseback-riding stable, bright swimming pool, basketball and tennis courts and plenty of space to run around. There are 26 slightly worn but decent villas and a well-regarded restaurant with a varied menu (mains $9 to $21) and a delicious rabbit fricassee.

Bosque Estatal de Guilarte

This forest, west of Adjuntas, actually consists of a number of parcels of land totaling about 4500 acres. Most is rainforest dominated by sierra palms. Coming from the east, you first see Lago Garzas, a fishing site. West of the lake, the road rises toward the park's ranger station, near the intersection of Hwys 518 and 131, where there's a picnic area with shelters, cooking grills and toilets. There's also a trail to the top of Monte Guilarte (3950ft) and five cabins.

The **DRNA** (787-829-5767, 787-724-3647; cabins $20) maintains the basic cabins (sleeping up to six), toilets and shower facilities. Cooking facilities are outdoors and there's no electricity. You must bring all your own gear, including bedding. Make your reservations 15 days in advance with the DRNA in San Juan. Camping is not permitted in Guilarte.

Maricao

POP 6000

Fog-swathed Maricao is the smallest municipality on the main island of Puerto Rico, and a gem of a mountain retreat near the western end of the Ruta Panorámica. This is a town of little commerce, with rushing streams, gorges, bridges, terraced houses, switchback roads, and weather so cool and damp that some houses have stone fireplaces to take the nip out of the air. Outside town lies beautiful mountain terrain and the largest state forest in Puerto Rico, the Bosque Estatal de Maricao.

Maricao is just the kind of place in which legends take root. Some claim that it was the strong coffee grown here that woke up the devil on the island. Another story tells of 2000 Taíno that survived here into the 19th century, centuries after the last native Puerto Ricans were thought to have disappeared.

Stopping here is probably as close as travelers can come to experiencing the charms of the legendary *jíbaro*'s existence. Maricao hosts a popular coffee-harvest festival in mid-February, with crafts and traditional coffee-making demonstrations.

Sights

Bosque Estatal de Maricao NATURE RESERVE
This forest of more than 10,000 acres lies along the Ruta Panorámica south of Maricao. The drive is spectacular, with sharp curves snaking over ridges as the mountainsides fall away into steep valleys. En route there are pull-offs at trailheads leading into the woods or down steep inclines.

Curiously, few trails are maintained or mapped and guides are difficult to come by. If you are coming here to hike, bring a topo map from a supplier in the US, or order one from the USGS.

While the landscape is categorized as high-mountain rainforest, scientists note that the 845 species of plant here are less 'exuberant' than tropical rainforests such as El Yunque. Birds are the most studied fauna, with 44 identified species. Tanagers, cuckoos and warblers are some of the remarkable types spotted in the forest.

Sleeping

Parque Ecológico Monte de Estado en Maricao CABINS **$**
(787-873-5632, reservations 787-622-5200; Hwy 120 Km 13.1; cabins from $65;) East of Maricao, this campground has 24 remodeled cabins sleeping between three and six, mostly with refrigerators, fireplaces and hot water. The area also has a swimming pool, basketball courts, restrooms, showers and an observation tower. Make reservations as far in advance as possible by calling the Compañía de Parques Nacionales in San Juan. Parking here is $3.

Getting There & Away

Públicos leave the town's plaza on the Maricao–Mayagüez run and charge $5. As usual, the vans leave when they are full or on the driver's whim. You can approach Maricao from the east or west on the Ruta Panorámica. You can also connect to points north and south via Hwys 119 and 120, which involve a spectacular climb into the mountains on twisting roads.

Understand Puerto Rico

Puerto Rico Today

Drive any distance on Puerto Rico's deplorable roads and your teeth will rattle to the perfect metaphor for the commonwealth: it's on a very bumpy path. Its finances have gone from bad to worse and it is at risk of following Detroit into bankruptcy. Meanwhile, its best-educated workers see greater opportunity in the United States. And the very relationship with the giant to the north shows no sign of being resolved any time soon.

Best in Print

When I Was Puerto Rican (Esmeralda Santiago) This memoir tackles immigration and cultural assimilation.

Parrots Over Puerto Rico (Susan L Roth & Cindy Trumbore) A beautiful and lyrical look at the island's people, nature and parrots.

Simone (Eduardo Lalo) A moody meditation set amid the neighborhoods of San Juan.

Spiks (Pedro Juan Soto) These short stories concern the struggle of Puerto Rican emigrants to the US in the '50s.

Best on Film

Maldeamores (2007) Luis Guzmán stars in this film about love's little ironies.

Lo que le pasó a Santiago (1989) Nominated for an Oscar, this is a mysterious, lyrical tale of unexpected love.

Rum Diary (2011) Johnny Depp as Hunter S Thompson in his booze-filled days in San Juan as depicted in his book of the same name.

La guagua aérea (1993) A rueful comedy about Puerto Ricans who moved to the US in the '60s.

Economic Woes

Like so many other places in the world, Puerto Rico's economy was sent in a downwards spiral with the global financial crisis that hit hard beginning in 2007. The effect on the commonwealth was immediate and stark: employment soared to 16%, a level unthinkable just a few years earlier when the island was touted as an economic miracle. Meanwhile, recession in the US depressed tourism and many long-time visitor haunts closed, from Old San Juan to the furthest reaches of the south and west coasts. (You can still see these commercial corpses, even today as tourism recovers.)

Meanwhile government spending rose as efforts were made to prop up the economy. The budget deficit in 2012 was a whopping $2.2 billion. Efforts by the governor, Alejandro García Padilla, to raise taxes and limit spending have met with mixed results. As the red ink has flowed, Puerto Rico has taken a far more blasé approach than other places facing economic ruin such as Ireland and Greece. Why? Well you only need to look north to the US to see the salvation that most locals complacently assume will come.

Bailing out Puerto Rico, however, carries no political gain for President Obama or either party in Congress, plus with US spending down, there's little money for a bailout anyway. Instead, Puerto Rico's finances may survive because it is too big to fail. For years the commonwealth's municipal bonds have been beloved by mutual funds and other investors, lured by their high interest yields and supposed security. Were Puerto Rico to collapse, it would have disastrous consequences for some of the world's largest financial institutions. By 2014, it was clear to many investors that Puerto Rico's debt load might not be fatal and it was able to again sell bonds to avoid insolvency. Though this is merely a lifeline and hardly a cure.

Energy & the Environment

Energy issues have long sparked debate among Puerto Ricans, whose energy costs are twice that of their US neighbors (three times for electricity). A 2010 law promised 12% in renewable energy sources by 2015, but this lofty goal was quickly abandoned amid the economic turmoil. Getting 6% of the commonwealth's energy from renewable sources by 2014 became the new goal, and there was little time to meet this target. Also, like other places, securing new sources of energy is not easy. Wind turbines near Ceiba in the east offer nighttime shows of spinning hazard lights, but turbines in the southwest were only narrowly approved after conservationists protested the impact on the critically endangered Puerto Rican nightjar bird.

While the pause in tourism has slowed coastal development, environmentalists look at the many pristine stretches of shore with deep concern. Rumors of new developments abound, especially on the fairly untouched paradisiacal beaches of Vieques. It's hard to argue against a new resort when so many jobs are needed.

The 51st State?

A commonwealth of the United States of America, Puerto Rico is a semi-autonomous territory whose constitutional status has long been a political oxymoron. Puerto Ricans enjoy many protections and benefits that US citizens have, but they are not allowed to participate in federal elections and have only a nonvoting 'Resident Commissioner' in the US House of Representatives. Puerto Rico's status is a major point of contention for local political leaders and the people in general.

A non-binding resolution in 2012 showed that the majority of the island's voters favor statehood with the US. President Obama has committed to funding an 'official' referendum that would decide Puerto Rico's political fate. The cost, a mere $2.5 million, is subject to congressional debate. A bill that would link a majority vote for statehood with a mandated admission process to the US as the 51st state spent 2013 wandering through Congress. Its fate depends on tepid Republican party support, since the consensus is that Puerto Rico would elect Democrats and that would have a major impact on the politically divided and deadlocked US Congress.

POPULATION: **3.7 MILLION**

POPULATION GROWTH RATE: **0.47%**

GDP PER CAPITA: **$16,300**

LIFE EXPECTANCY: **78.3 YEARS**

LITERACY RATE: **94.1%**

UNEMPLOYMENT: **13.5%**

belief systems

(% of population)

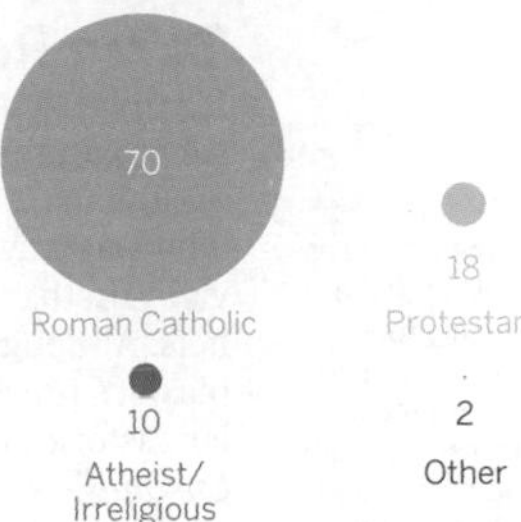

if Puerto Rico were 100 people

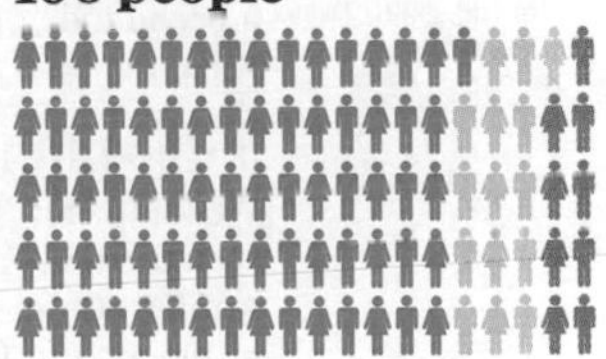

76 would be White
12 would be Black
3 would be Mixed
9 would be Other

population per sq mile

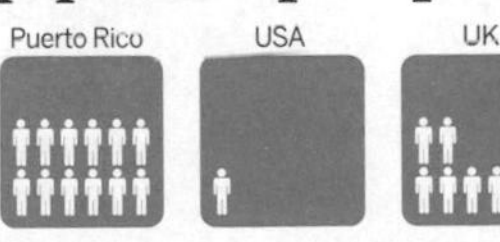

History

Puerto Rico occupies a crucial juncture in the geographical and political history of the Americas. The most defining event in its annals was the nearly 400-year rule of the Spanish, whose checkered history of colonization, genocide, military triumph and defeat is seen everywhere, especially at El Morro fort in Old San Juan. Then there's the dramatic arc of the commonwealth's struggle to define itself after the US occupation in the late 1800s. Protests, terrorism, and passion have fueled the debate.

Taíno Roots

It's unfortunate that, similar to so many other indigenous peoples of the Americas, the best record of Taíno culture is written by those who would annihilate it. Through the journals of Ramón Pané, a Catalonian friar who was traveling with the second Columbus expedition, we are given a vivid firsthand account of the Taíno lifestyle, customs and religious beliefs. Although told with an unintentionally comic cultural and religious bias, it's precious information and often more accurate than other similar histories in the Americas. In his 1505 *Account of the Antiquities – or Customs – of the Indians,* Pané gives a breathless report of Puerto Rico's native residents, describing cities with wide, straight roads, elaborate religious rituals and small communities of 'artfully made' homes behind walls of woven cane. Their diet was derived from tropical fruit grown in orchards that grew oranges and citron that reminded Pané of the ones in Valencia or Barcelona. The beauty of the Taíno culture only exists as an echo today, but it had an indelible influence on contemporary Puerto Rico.

Some historians claim that a small group of Taíno escaped the 16th-century Spanish genocide and hid in Puerto Rico's central mountains where they survived until the early 19th century, but there's no proof of this claim.

Taíno Life on Puerto Rico

We know now that the Taíno were an Arawakan Indian group who had societies that were well established on Puerto Rico and the other Greater Antilles (Cuba, Hispaniola and Jamaica) when Columbus first turned up in the area in 1493. Arawaks first settled the island around AD 700, following a migration north from the Orinoco River delta in present-day

TIMELINE

2000 BC

Puerto Ferro Man, a native from the Ortoiroid culture that had migrated north from the Orinoco basin in present-day Venezuela, lives on the island of Vieques.

430–250 BC

The Ortoiroids are displaced by the Saladoids, a horticultural people skilled at pottery. Saladoids laid the early building blocks for a singular Caribbean culture.

AD 1000

The Taíno – who also come from the Orinoco basin – emerge as a dominant culture; they name the island Boriken, meaning 'the Great Land of the Valiant and Noble Lord.'

Venezuela. By AD 1000 a distinctive Taíno culture had emerged based on agriculture, fishing, hunting and the production of cassava bread.

Pané speaks in depth about the complex religious cosmology of the Taíno, a system that had creation stories that often surprised Pané with their Christian parallels. They believed in a single, eternal god who was omnipresent and invisible, and often also worshiped the mother of this god, who was known by a number of names. Each home held a stone or wood idol, usually about 3ft tall, called a *cemí,* which would receive their prayers. The practice of making these statues translated seamlessly into Christianity. Today *santos* (carved figurines representing saints), of the same height, are available across the island.

The native Taíno belief in the afterlife was quite different from the Christian dogma though, and in it there are some basic elements that would survive in other hybrid religions in the islands. Take for instance the Taíno belief in the walking dead, which bears a certain resemblance to famous tenants of Haitian Vodou. According to Taíno, the dead can return from the afterlife, a place called Coaybay, and walk among the living. In Taíno belief the dead walked through the villages and forests at night so they could eat tropical *guanábana* fruit. They also believed that women from Coaybay could have sexual communions with living men. The only way to tell the living from the dead was to touch someone on the belly, as they believed that the dead had no navel.

One recent genetic study of 800 Puerto Ricans found 61% had mitochondrial DNA from a female Amerindian ancestor, 27% inherited mitochondrial DNA from a female African ancestor and 12% had mitochondrial DNA from a female European ancestor.

The small, round wooden huts of the Taíno people were called *bohios,* where they smoked *cohibas* (cigars) and slept in *hamacas* (hammocks). They called their newly adopted island Borinquen (Land of the Noble Lord) and made pottery, wove baskets and carved wood. The native society was relatively democratic and organized around a system of *caciques* (Taíno chiefs) who oversaw a rank of medicine men, subchiefs and, below them, workers.

For leisure, the Taíno built ceremonial ball parks where they played a soccer-like game with a rubber ball between teams of 10 to 30 people. At Tibes near Ponce in the south, and at Caguana near Utuadu in the north, archaeologists discovered impressive courts, marked by rows of massive stone blocks. Drums, maracas and güiros provided the game's percussive accompaniment – instruments that resound in Puerto Rican traditional and popular music today.

The first black person to arrive in Puerto Rico was Juan Garrido, a conquistador allied to Juan Ponce de León. He first set foot on the island in 1509.

Colonization of the Taíno

Columbus first saw Puerto Rico on November 19, 1493 – a date simultaneously celebrated and mourned today. Columbus' 17 ships landed on the island's west coast for water, somewhere in the area near Rincón. But the visit was extremely brief, as Columbus' main base in the region was on Hispaniola (known today as Haiti and the Dominican Republic). There

1493

On November 19, during his second voyage to the New World, Christopher Columbus lands on Puerto Rico's west coast. He christens the island *San Juan Bautista.*

1508

Juan Ponce de León leads Spanish colonists to Puerto Rico in search of gold. He establishes the island's first colony – Caparra – in the north on swampy land close to San Juan harbor.

1509

Ponce de León becomes first governor of San Juan Bautista (Puerto Rico) after Spain refuses to grant Columbus' son, Diego, rights to the lands discovered by his (recently deceased) father.

1511

Subjected to brutal exploitation, the Taíno stage their first unsuccessful revolt against their Spanish overlords. Ponce de León is subsequently replaced as governor in favor of Diego Columbus.

was a period of relative quiet between his 'discovery' of Puerto Rico and the arrival of Ponce de León, who landed on the island in the August of 1508. León was here for good; he was sent by the Spanish crown to set up a colonial base for the Caribbean in Puerto Rico and look for gold. At first, León's expedition was amicably received by the chief of all chiefs, a *cacique* called Agüeybana.

But the good relationship didn't last long. Approximately 100 years before the Spanish arrived, Taíno culture was challenged by the Caribs, a warlike tribe from South America who raided Taíno villages for slaves and fodder for cannibalistic rites. The simmering tensions between the Taíno and Caribs were still evident when Ponce de León took possession of the island and sometimes misinterpreted by the Spanish as Taíno aggression. In reality the Taíno were a friendly, sedentary people who put up little resistance to the new colonizers. Although León's letters to the crown describes this as a period of relative peace, he had difficulty making the Taíno understand that he was now in charge, and indigenous people were understandably resistant to their newfound roles as subservient laborers.

When León was unable to get the Taíno to fall in line with the arduous tasks of mining and farming for the Spanish, Queen Isabella issued an edict in simple terms: 'You will force the said Indians to associate with the Christians of the island.' Though the Spanish crown issued paltry monetary payments for the labor, it was tantamount to slavery.

By 1511 the forced labor and religious conversion of the Taíno had destroyed any shred of initial goodwill that may have existed between tribal leaders and the Spanish. When Agüeybana died, his nephew, called Agüeybana II, took over and tensions came to a head. Though accounts differ about the lead-up to the first Taíno uprising, the most colorful version goes like this: in an effort to test the Spaniards' suggestion of

AGÜEYBANA

Agüeybana (meaning 'Big Sun') was the most powerful *cacique* (Taíno chief) in Puerto Rico when Europeans first discovered the island. A trusting character who was curious about the European travelers, Agüeybana's close relationship with Juan Ponce de León was instrumental in Spanish colonization of the Caribbean. Told in a prophecy about the coming of a 'clothed people,' Agüeybana warmly received the Spanish explorer in 1508; some historical accounts, notably written by the Spanish, claim that he believed the Europeans were deities. He hosted a ceremony of friendship and led León and a delegation of his men on a scouting expedition of the island, from which Puerto Rico's first maps were drawn. But León struggled to convince Agüeybana to assist him with his two main priorities: mining Puerto Rico for gold and converting indigenous people to Christianity.

1513

Following the decimation of the local Indian population through disease and outright slaughter, the first West African slaves arrive on the island to work in the new economy.

1521

The city of San Juan is founded on its present site and the island changes its name from San Juan Bautista to Puerto Rico.

1595

With permission from the Queen of England, British privateer Sir Francis Drake attempts to attack and loot San Juan with 26 ships but is repelled by the city's formidable defenses.

1598

On a revenge mission, George Clifford, earl of Cumberland, lands in Santurce to attack San Juan by land. He occupies the city for several months before an outbreak of dysentery forces retreat.

religious protection and life beyond death, Agüeybana II lured a Spanish soldier to a lake where he was promised a number of women would be bathing. Instead, a Taíno warrior drowned him while tribal leaders watched. Soon greater aggression was planned.

A few small raids on new Spanish settlements in the south went in favor of the Taíno, but as soon as León learned of the incidents, he unleashed his technologically advanced soldiers on the Taíno warriors. The battle that quelled the uprising was shocking in its brutality. An estimated 11,000 Taíno were killed in military campaigns by a Spanish force numbering only 100.

Testimonies vary as to how many Taíno inhabited Borinquen at the time of the Spanish invasion, though most anthropologists place the number between 20,000 and 60,000. In 1515 – after nearly a decade of maltreatment, a failed rebellion, disease and virtual slavery – only 4000 remained. Thirty years later a Spanish bishop put the number at 60.

While Taíno blood may have all but disappeared in modern Puerto Rico, native traditions live on. Puerto Rican Spanish is dotted with native words like yucca (a root vegetable), iguana, *manatí* (manatee – a sea mammal), maracas and ceiba (Puerto Rico's national tree); and some terms have even found their way into modern English: think *huracan* for hurricane and *hamaca* for hammock.

The Invaders

It's easy to imagine Puerto Rico's disparate invaders scheming in the shadowy ports of the Caribbean and the gilded halls of Europe. To evade the guns of El Morro and sack the San Juan harbor would write history – for pirates and princes alike. Not long after the fort was commissioned by Spanish King Charles V in 1539, it came under siege from those seeking strategic power in the Caribbean. Everyone from daring British dandy Francis Drake to storied cutthroats like Blackbeard tried their luck against San Juan's formidable defenses.

One of the colony's earliest invaders, Francis Drake first arrived in Puerto Rico in 1595 pursuing a stricken Spanish galleon – holding two million gold ducats – that took shelter in San Juan harbor. While the plucky Brit may have singed the king of Spain's beard in Cádiz a decade earlier, the Spaniards quickly got revenge in Puerto Rico when they fired a cannonball into Drake's cabin, killing two of his men, and – allegedly – shooting the stool from underneath him. Drake left the island empty-handed and died the following year of dysentery in Panama.

San Juan was attacked by the British navy again three years later under the command of the third earl of Cumberland. Learning from Drake's mistakes, Cumberland's 1700-strong army landed in what is now Condado and advanced on the city via land from the east. After a short battle,

1598

Spain's Phillip III forbids growing ginger, which is more lucrative for farmers, commonly smuggled and traded for slaves. The king demands they grow sugar to benefit the crown.

1625

The Dutch navy besieges San Juan and burns it to the ground, but they are prevented from taking total control by Spanish forces manning the fortifications in El Morro.

1797

A third and final attempt by the British to take San Juan is led by General Abercromby during the Seven Years' War, but the Spanish once again stand firm.

1825

Spanish authorities hire American schooner *Grampus* to capture 'El Pirata Cofresí', Puerto Rico's nautical Robin Hood, who robbed rich foreign ships to feed Cabo Rojo's poor; he's executed at El Morro.

the city surrendered and the British occupied it for the next 10 weeks, before a dysentery epidemic hit and forced an ignominious withdrawal.

In response to frequent British incursions, San Juan's defensive walls were repeatedly strengthened, a measure that helped repel an ambitious attack by the Netherlands in 1625. The Dutch fired over 4000 cannonballs into the city walls before landing 2000 men at La Puntilla. Although the invaders managed to occupy the city temporarily and take the Fortaleza palace, the Spanish held El Morro fort and, after less than a month, the Dutch retreated, razing the city as they went.

San Juan's second great fort, San Cristóbal, was inaugurated in the 1630s and the city saw no more major attacks for almost two centuries. It wasn't until 1797 that the British, at war again with Spain, tried one last time. Still, even though the armada had over 60 ships and 10,000 men they eventually withdrew in bloodied and breathless exasperation.

Smuggling, Sugar & Spain

Just look at a map and Puerto Rico's strategic position – between the shores of North, Central and South America – is immediately evident. During Spain's early settlement in the 16th century, the empire knew that Puerto Rican harbors were key to transporting the limitless wealth of the Americas. But the crown's insistence on a centralized government was an arrogant political position that would cost Spain dearly, and shape the development of Puerto Rico.

In the mid-1500s Spain insisted that all imports and exports from its growing empire be trafficked through ports in Spain. But Seville was some 2½ months away by sail and the policy was immediately inadequate for controlling the island's many ports. A number of forces – including new Spanish colonies in gold-rich Peru and Mexico – led to the rise of an enormous, well-organized black market in Puerto Rico.

This unchecked flow of goods and money hastened the development of Puerto Rico's *other* ports – Ponce and Arroyo among them – where sugarcane and goods from the Americas were moved out of sight of Spanish authorities.

The power vacuum was quickly filled by merchants operating with their own agenda. Through the 16th and 17th centuries, cities of the south grew rich from trade with Caribbean neighbors – certainly illegal, but completely unknown to the distant king.

Even after Spain gave more power to local authorities in San Juan in the 18th century, the brisk black-market exchange of sugar, ginger and slaves between Puerto Rico and its neighbors (including the young United States) continued in the south, funding many of the majestic homes and fountains tourists visit today.

1850–67

The Puerto Rican liberation movement gathers strength under the inspirational leadership of Ramón Emeterio Betances, a poet, politician, diplomat and eminent surgeon.

1868

Revolutionaries inspired by Betances take the town of Lares and declare a Puerto Rican republic, but the uprising is repelled within hours by Spanish forces sent from nearby San Sebastián.

1873

In the wake of the Grito de Lares, the Spanish authorities institute various political and social reforms in Puerto Rico, including the abolition of slavery, freeing 30,000 slaves.

1898

US forces blockade San Juan and land a 16,000-strong force unopposed at Guánica on the south coast, ending the Spanish–American War; Spain cedes Puerto Rico to the USA.

JUAN PONCE DE LEÓN

Soldier, sailor, governor, dreamer and politician, the life story of Juan Ponce de León reads like a *Who's Who* of late-15th- and early-16th-century maritime exploration. Aside from founding the Spanish colony of Puerto Rico in 1508, this daring, yet often short-sighted, Spanish adventurer partook in Columbus' second trans-Atlantic voyage, charted large tracts of the Bahamas, discovered the existence of the Gulf Stream, and was the first recorded European to set foot in what is now known as Florida.

Born in Valladolid, Spain, in 1460, de León served his military apprenticeship fighting against the Moors during the Christian reconquest of Granada in 1492. The following year he arrived in the New World on Columbus' second expedition and settled on the island of Hispaniola, where he was proclaimed deputy governor of the province of Higüey. Following Columbus' death in 1506, the Spanish crown asked de León to lead the colonization of Borinquen, an island first explored by Columbus in 1493.

Despite initially currying favor with the native Taíno Indians, the Spaniard's relationship with his new neighbors quickly deteriorated. In 1512 he was replaced and given a new task: explore the region. After circumnavigating the Bahamas, de León elected to divert northwest and, in the process, inadvertently 'discovered' Florida.

After several forays along Florida's coast (which de León thought was an island), the explorer returned to Puerto Rico via Cuba and Guadalupe in 1515 and stayed there for the next six years. In 1521, de León organized another trip to Florida. This time they landed on the west coast of Florida but were quickly beaten back by Calusa Indians. Wounded in the thigh by a poisoned arrow, de León was shipped back to Havana where he died in July 1521. His remains were returned to Puerto Rico where they are interred in the Catedral de San Juan.

African Roots

As throughout the Caribbean, slavery was the engine of the Puerto Rican economy through the late 18th and early 19th centuries, and has left an indelible mark on Puerto Rican culture. The two types of slaves that were brought to the island – *ladinos*, born and acculturated in Spain, and *bozales* and Yoruba people, brought from Africa – first mined meager gold and silver deposits. Once these deposits were depleted, slaves propped up the sugarcane industry and agriculture on the coastal areas of the island. While the rest of the island's population experienced normal growth, the slave population skyrocketed throughout the late 18th century. A census figure in 1765 shows 5400 slaves in Puerto Rico; by 1830 it had increased to more than 31,000, mainly due to the introduction of new slaves directly from Africa and other parts of the Caribbean.

1900

US Congress passes the Foraker Act, granting a US–run government in Puerto Rico; American Charles Allen is installed as governor, aided by an 11-man executive council that includes five Puerto Ricans.

1917

The Jones Act makes Puerto Rico a territory of the US and unilaterally grants islanders US citizenship and a bill of rights; English becomes the official language.

1933

Cockfighting becomes legal in Puerto Rico. Though states in the US and neighboring islands subsequently ban the pastime, its popularity in Puerto Rico booms.

1937

Student *independentistas* (independence advocates) clash with police on Palm Sunday; 19 people die and over 100 are injured in what becomes known as the 'Masacre de Ponce.'

However, despite these increases, by 1795 the majority (more than 60%) of black and mulatto people living in Puerto Rico were free. This trend, unusual for the Caribbean, is often attributed to an asylum policy that granted freedom to fugitive slaves from throughout the region.

By the late 1830s, after years of racial violence in the Caribbean and abolitionist movements, it became clear that slavery was increasingly less justifiable. Sugar barons combined their slave holdings with low-wage workers called *jornaleros* and continued to accrue immense wealth.

Many slave uprisings occurred and began to intertwine with a political movement for emancipation led by Julio Vizcarrondo, a Puerto Rican abolitionist living in Spain, as well as island-based political leaders such as Segundo Ruiz Belvis, Román Baldorioty de Castro and Ramón Emeterio Betances. After years of struggle the Spanish National Assembly abolished slavery on March 22, 1873.

Described by the late cultural and social writer Jose Luis González as *el primer piso,* or 'the first floor' of Puerto Rican culture, influences from the commonwealth's history of slavery continue to shape the country today. In Puerto Rico's music, art and religious icons, African traditions are powerfully felt.

From Spanish Colony to American Commonwealth

As two Greater Antilles islands ruled by Spain for nearly four centuries, Cuba and Puerto Rico share a remarkably similar history. Both were colonized in the early 1500s, both retain vestiges of their indigenous Taíno culture, both were heavily influenced by the African slave trade and both remained Spanish colonies a good 80 years after the rest of Latin America had declared independence. The irony, of course, lies in their different paths after 1898 and the fact that today Puerto Rico is intertwined with the US. Cuba's relationship with the US has stayed chilly since it was considered a former Soviet satellite and 'public enemy number one.'

The total number of American soldiers killed in Puerto Rico during the Spanish–American War of 1898 was four.

Two Wings of the Same Dove

While the bulk of Spain's South American colonies rose up under the leadership of revolutionary emancipator Simón Bolívar in the 1820s, Puerto Rico and Cuba's conservative Creole landowners elected to stay on the sidelines. But, as economic conditions worsened and slavery came to be regarded as an ailing colonial anachronism, the mood started to change.

During the 1860s links were formed between nationalists and revolutionaries on both islands, united by language and inspired by a common foe. The cultural interchange worked both ways. Great thinkers like Cu-

1942

A German submarine fires on Isla de la Mona, a largely uninhabited island off Puerto Rico's west coast. It was one of the few incidents of WWII in the Caribbean.

1948

With US Congressional approval, Puerto Ricans craft their own constitution and elect their first governor, Luis Muñoz Marín, former president of the Senate, who holds the post for 16 years.

1950

A nationalist revolt in the mountain town of Jayuya is suppressed by the US Air Force; in response, two nationalists in Washington, DC try unsuccessfully to assassinate President Harry Truman.

1952

The constitution of Puerto Rico is approved by referendum, making the island an Estado Libre Associado (a US commonwealth); the Puerto Rican flag is flown – legally – for the first time.

ban national hero José Martí drew early inspiration from Puerto Rican surgeon and nationalist Ramón Emeterio Betances, while Mayagüez-born General Juan Rius Rivera later went on to command the Cuban Liberation Army in the 1895–98 war against the Spanish.

It was Puerto Rican nationalists who fired the first shot, proclaiming the abortive Grito de Lares in 1868. Following Puerto Rico's lead two weeks later, Cuba's machete-wielding *mambises* (19th-century Cuban independence fighters) unleashed their own independence cry. Both ultimately failed.

Cuba and Puerto Rico's political divergence began in 1900 when the US Congress passed the Foraker Act, making Puerto Rico the first unincorporated territory of the US. Cuba, meanwhile, thanks to the so-called Teller Amendment (passed through Congress before the Spanish-American War had started), gained nominal independence with some strings attached in 1902.

Resistance to the new arrangement in Puerto Rico was spearheaded by the Partido Unión de Puerto Rico (Union Party), which for years had been demanding greater democratic rights. The Union Party was led by Luis Muñoz Rivera, one of the most important political figures in the history of Puerto Rico and a diplomat who was willing to compromise with the US on key issues. Under pressure from President Woodrow Wilson

Former leader of the Puerto Rican Nationalist party, Pedro Albizu Campos was of African, Taíno and Basque descent. He graduated from Harvard University with a law degree in 1921 and was fluent in eight languages.

GRITO DE LARES

As well as boasting the world's largest radio telescope and its youngest-ever boxing champion, Puerto Rico also holds the dubious distinction of having created history's shortest-lived republic. The independent republic of Puerto Rico, proclaimed during the abortive Grito de Lares (Cry of Lares) in 1868, lasted slightly less than 24 hours.

Worn down by slavery, high taxes and the asphyxiating grip of Spain's militaristic rulers, independence advocates in the Caribbean colonies of Puerto Rico and Cuba were in the ascendancy throughout the 1850s and '60s.

The main Puerto Rican attempt at armed insurrection came on September 23, 1868. Over 600 men and women marched defiantly on the small town of Lares near Mayagüez, where they were met with minimal Spanish resistance. Declaring a Puerto Rican republic from the main square, the rebels named Francisco Ramírez Medina head of a new provisional government. But the glory didn't last. Marching next on the nearby town of San Sebastián, the poorly armed liberation army walked into a Spanish military trap and were quickly defeated by superior firepower.

This failed revolution did lead to some long-term political concessions. In the years that followed, the colonial authorities passed liberal electoral reforms, granted Puerto Rico provincial status and offered Spanish citizenship to all *criollos* (island-born people of European descent).

1953

Immigration from Puerto Rico to the US peaks as an estimated 75,000 Puerto Ricans move to New York City. Almost one in 10 New Yorker residents are from Puerto Rico.

1967

Puerto Rico holds first plebiscite on the issue of Puerto Rican statehood, but votes overwhelmingly to remain a commonwealth; the independence parties gain only 1% of the votes.

1970

Marisol Maralet becomes the first Puerto Rican to win the title of Miss Universe. Over the next 40 years, four more Puerto Ricans win the title, the most of any country in the contest's history.

1978

Two independence supporters are shot by police posing as revolutionary sympathizers in the Central Mountains; the incident exposes deep political fissures and government corruption.

he ultimately ceded on his demand for outright independence in favor of greater autonomy via an amendment to the Foraker Act.

In 1917, just months after Muñoz Rivera's death, President Woodrow Wilson signed the Jones Act. It granted US citizenship to all Puerto Ricans and established a bicameral legislature whose decisions could be vetoed by the US president. No Puerto Ricans were involved in the debate over citizenship.

A special cask of high-grade rum was set aside by a brewer in 1942 with orders that it be opened only when Puerto Rico becomes an independent nation. When (or if) that happens, free drinks for everyone!

A Question of Status

Questioned by many before the ink had even dried, the Jones Act failed to provide any long-term solutions. On the contrary, the debate over Puerto Rico's relationship with the US continued to intensify, defining the political careers of two major figures who would emerge on the island in the late 1920s and early '30s: Pedro Albizu Campos, leader of the pro-independence Partido Nacionalista (Nationalist Party), and Luis Muñoz Marín, who established the Partido Popular Democrático (PPD; Popular Democratic Party) in 1938.

As son of the widely respected Muñoz Rivera, Luis Muñoz Marín took a conciliatory approach to challenging the colonial situation. While the US Congress sidestepped the status question, Muñoz Marín's PPD pressed for a plebiscite to allow Puerto Ricans to choose between statehood and independence. In the late 1930s and early 1940s, the majority of the PPD favored independence. However, neither President Franklin D Roosevelt nor the Congress seriously considered it as an option, and laws were enacted to criminalize independence activities.

Rather than take to the mountains to fight – as Fidel Castro in Cuba later did – Muñoz Marín adopted a strategy that incorporated the status question with other issues affecting the Puerto Rican people, such as the dire economic and social effects of the Great Depression. His deciding moment came in 1946 when he rejected independence and threw his political weight behind an effort to grant the island a new status. In 1948, with Marín's support, Congress granted Puerto Rico the status it has today as an Estado Libre Associado, or ELA, the Free Associated State. This was intended to give the island more political autonomy, despite close ties with the US.

Blanca Canales, leader of the abortive Jayuya Uprising in 1950, is popularly considered to have been the first woman to have led an armed revolt against the US government.

In 1952, this status description was approved by a referendum held on the island. Voters also approved Puerto Rico's first constitution that was written by islanders. Muñoz Marín became the first governor of Puerto Rico to be elected by Puerto Ricans. The new status and newly granted US citizenship for Puerto Ricans led to what is commonly known as the 'Great Migration.' Attracted to better economic opportunities in the US, Puerto Ricans left the island by the tens of thousands. In 1953 alone an estimated 75,000 Puerto Ricans arrived in New York City. Miami and Chi-

1985

A mudslide following Tropical Storm Isabel kills 129 people in the hills near Ponce, making it the island's worst natural disaster in a century.

1999

Major protests break out on the island of Vieques against the US Navy, following the killing of islander David Sanes Rodríguez during military target practice.

2000

Puerto Ricans elect ex San Juan mayor Sila Maria Calderón of the Popular Democratic Party as the first woman governor of the commonwealth.

2003

After four years of protests and 60 years of occupation, the US Navy pulls out of Vieques; the former military land is promptly designated a US Fish & Wildlife Refuge.

cago also hosted large Puerto Rican populations and the period would forever transform the face of urban communities of the United States.

Nevertheless, despite claims by the new governor and his supporters that the status question was finally resolved with ELA, for all intents and purposes, nothing changed: the US Congress still had plenary powers over Puerto Rico. Although islanders became exempt from paying federal income taxes, they still had no representation in Congress (apart from a nonvoting delegate), could not vote in US national elections, and were still being drafted into the US Armed Forces to fight alongside young Americans in foreign wars.

A popular vote in 1990 making Spanish the official language in Puerto Rico was revoked just two years later to reinstate both Spanish and English as joint commonwealth languages.

Over the years a number of referenda and plebiscites have been held, ostensibly to allow the Puerto Rican people to decide the future of the island's status. Two official plebiscites, in 1967 and 1993, resulted in victories for 'commonwealth' status, that is, the ELA. Other votes have been held, with the status options, as well as the approach to self-determination, defined in different ways. All of these popular votes have been shaped by the ruling party at the time of the vote, either the pro-ELA PPD, or the pro-statehood Partido Nuevo Progresista (PNP; New Progressive Party). None have been binding for the US Congress.

In 1998, as the island was getting ready to mark the 100th anniversary of US control, Congress acknowledged that the current status was no longer viable. A bill called for a plebiscite on the island where Puerto Ricans would vote on only two status options: either statehood or independence. It did not provide ELA or any other form of 'enhanced commonwealth' as an option, angering members of the PPD. Ultimately, the legislation went nowhere.

In 2012, a non-binding vote on the island's political status was held on Puerto Rico and drew an impressive turnout of 78% of eligible voters. A majority favored statehood, which sends the issue squarely back to the US government for resolution.

2005

Guerrilla pro-Independence leader Filiberto Ojeda Rios is killed in a shootout with US federal agents. The incident causes widespread anger and demonstrations on the island.

2006

An acute budgetary crisis forces the shutdown of schools and government offices across the island for two weeks as legislative officials try to address a $740-million deficit in public funds.

2009

Sonia Sotomayor becomes the 111th Justice of the US Supreme Court. Of Puerto Rican descent, Sotomayor is the first Hispanic justice in the history of the court.

2012

In a non-binding referendum, 54% of voters favored rejecting Puerto Rico's status as a territory of the US. In a separate question about preferred status, 61% favored statehood.

Life in Puerto Rico

Puerto Rican culture is a kaleidoscope with four constantly overlapping influences – Taíno, Spanish, African and American – and, as such, the dynamic culture is incredibly hard to classify. One side of the street looks like the Bronx, while the other side is all Latin America, with bananas sold out of the back of a truck. The commonwealth exports over half of its population to the east coast of the United States, but still the expatriates exhibit a fierce loyalty to the island they call home.

Lifestyle

Most Puerto Ricans live a lifestyle that weaves together two primary elements: the commercial and material values of the United States and the social and traditional values of their 'enchanted' island. Because of the strong connection to the mainland United States, Puerto Ricans have espoused many of the same social values as their cousins in New York. Even so, the Puerto Rican flags that fly from the fire escapes of NYC leave no doubt that many Puerto Ricans will never fully lose themselves to mainstream American culture.

Annually, 4.3 million international visitors to Puerto Rico supply the economy with approximately $2.3 billion. More than one third of these tourists are made up of cruise-ship passengers.

Modern practicalities of the island's political and cultural position have meant that, for three or four generations now, many Puerto Ricans have grown up bouncing between mainland US cities and their native soil. Even those who stay put assimilate by proxy: young people in a wealthy San Juan suburb may wander the mall past American chain stores and chat about Hollywood blockbusters; obversely, their counterparts living in the uniformly Puerto Rican neighborhoods of New York or Chicago may have a day-to-day existence that more closely resembles Latin America. This makes the full scope of their bilingual and multicultural existence difficult to comprehend for outsiders. Many Puerto Ricans are just as comfortable striding down New York's Fifth Ave for a little shopping during the week as they are visiting the *friquitines* (roadside kiosks) with their families at Playa Luquillo on the weekend.

Where Puerto Rico and the US most diverge in a practical sense may be in economics. A glance beyond the shiny buildings of San Juan shows the toll taken by worldwide recession coupled with the island's own woes. A large number of manufacturing jobs left the island over the last decade, taking skilled managers with them and leaving factories to rust. With an unemployment rate about double the US (currently 13.5%) and average salaries around $17,000 (about half the US), the local aphorism is that if you need a job, fly to Orlando – a journey made easy by their US citizenship.

From Rincón to Vieques, visitors will find Puerto Ricans to be incredibly friendly and open; they like nothing better than to show off their beloved Borikén (the island's Taíno name). You'll also note that, despite their obsession with big American cars and big shopping complexes, Puerto Ricans are much more into genuine experiences than material things. A favorite island pastime is to wade into warm ocean waters just before sunset – beer in hand and a few more in the cooler – to shoot the breeze with whoever else is out enjoying the glorious spectacle of changing skies. The next day, there's a good chance the afternoon will be spent standing around the grill (again, usually with a beer in hand) and savoring the scent of a favorite family recipe. Bank executive, schoolteacher, fisherman or even visiting gringo – it doesn't matter who you are, as long as you share an appreciation for how good life can be in Puerto Rico.

Multiculturalism

Like most Caribbean cultures, Puerto Ricans are genetically an ethnic mix of Native American, European and African. About 76% of the island classifies itself as white (meaning of Spanish origin, primarily), 12% as black, 3% as mixed, and 9% as other, which includes Taíno. Along the coast of Loíza Aldea, where African heritage is most prominent, distinct features from the Yoruba people abound, while in the mountains, a handful of people still claim distant Taíno bloodlines. Many of them are right; advanced ethnographic study of Puerto Ricans in recent years uncovered a strong connection to the island's first settlers.

Puerto Ricans might tell you that ethnic discrimination doesn't exist on their island, but politically correct Spanish speakers may be aghast at some of the names Puerto Ricans use to refer to each other – words like *trigueño* (wheat-colored) and *jabao* (not quite white). It may sound derogatory (and sometimes it is), but it can also simply be a less-than-thoughtful way of identifying someone by a visible physical characteristic, a habit found in much of Latin America. You'll also hear terms like *la blanquita,* for a lighter-skinned woman, or *el gordo* to describe a robust man. Identifying which terms are racial slurs, rather than descriptive facts, will be a hard distinction for non-islanders to make, and it's wisest to steer clear of all such vernacular. Compared with much of the Caribbean, Puerto Rico is remarkably integrated and even-keeled about ethnicity.

READING UP ON PUERTO RICAN CULTURE

From sexual revolution to struggles for the commonwealth's independence to island-saving eco-activism, start your cultural journey to Puerto Rico in the pages of a book.

Down These Mean Streets (Piri Thomas) Peppered with the street slang of Spanish Harlem, this gritty classic takes a cold and sober look at the challenges of violence, drugs and racism during the first wave of Puerto Rican immigration to New York City.

Boricuas: Influential Puerto Rican Writings – An Anthology (edited by Roberto Santiago) This collection of essays and stories presents an incredibly diverse and wide-ranging insight into Puerto Rican authors, many of whom are scarcely translated into English. If you read one book to sample Puerto Rican writing, this is it.

The Disenchanted Island – Puerto Rico & the United States in the Twentieth Century (Ronaldo Fernández) Required reading for Latin American studies students, this chronicle of the island's struggle for independence is passionately told, putting the relationship between Puerto Rico and the United States under a microscope.

Imposing Decency: The Politics of Sexuality & Race in Puerto Rico, 1870–1920 (Eileen J Suárez Findlay) This brassy, bold historical reading of Puerto Rico feminism is rooted in Puerto Rico's working-class sexual revolution during the turbulent years of the American colony.

Islands Under Fire: The Improbable Quest to Save the Corals of Puerto Rico (Kevin McCarey) The US Navy was bombing much of Culebra in the 1970s and damage to the coral reefs was becoming too extreme. McCarey joined up with an oddball band of activists to bring the destruction to a halt. It's a romp of a book you'll be unable to put down.

The island's most important challenge is to correct the historical fact that the poorest islanders – those descended from the slaves and laborers who were kept from owning land until the early 20th century – have been short-changed when it comes to higher education. As in the United States, the issue of racial and economic inequality in Puerto Rico – while still visible – has improved immeasurably in the last 50 years. While urban deprivation and a lack of provision of housing are ongoing issues, the relative economic conditions in modern Puerto Rico are significantly better than in most other countries in the Caribbean.

According to a recent World Values Survey, Puerto Ricans were among the happiest people on the planet, with a 'happiness rating' of 4.67 out of five. The United States came 15th with a rating of 3.47.

Religion

Like many former Spanish colonies, Roman Catholicism is practiced widely, with an estimated 70% of Puerto Ricans identifying as Catholic. But both Catholics and Protestants – the second-largest religious group – have been widely influenced by centuries of indigenous and African folkloric traditions. Slaves brought from West Africa between the 16th and 19th centuries carried with them a system of animistic beliefs that they passed on through generations of their descendants.

The *santos* (small carved figurines representing saints) that have been staple products of Puerto Rican artists for centuries descend to some degree from Santería beliefs in the powers of the saints (although many Puerto Ricans may not be aware of the sources of this worship). Many Puerto Ricans keep a collection of their favorite *santos* enshrined in a place of honor in their homes, similar to shrines that West Africa's Yoruba people keep for their *orishas* (spirits), like Yemanjá, the goddess of the sea.

Belief in the magical properties of small carved gods also recalls the island's early inhabitants, the Taíno, who worshipped little stone *cemíes* (figurines) and believed in *jupías,* spirits of the dead who roam the island at night to cause mischief.

Tens of thousands of islanders consult with *curanderos* (healers) when it comes to problems of love, health, employment, finance and revenge. Islanders also spend significant amounts of money in *botánicas:* shops that sell herbs, plants, charms, holy water and books on performing spirit rituals.

Practice your Spanish by reading *El Nuevo Día,* Puerto Rico's biggest-selling daily newspaper, online at www.elnuevodia.com.

Women in Puerto Rico

Puerto Rican culture, like much of Latin American, is too often stigmatized as a 'macho' world where women play traditional roles, bearing children, cooking meals and caring for the home. Stereotypes paint Puerto Rican men in a similarly simplistic light – possessive, jealous and prone to wild acts of desperation when in love. Although many women generally perform all those duties (and more) in the most traditional Puerto Rican family structures, recent history has seen the island break significantly with the punitive gender discrimination that can be common in other Latin American countries and throughout the Caribbean.

PUERTO RICO'S BEAUTIES

On most progressive issues of gender equality, Puerto Rico can shame other Latin American countries...at least until it's time to dust off the rhinestone tiara and satin sash and crown a beauty queen. Puerto Rico simply adores that time-honored ritual of female objectification, the beauty pageant. The island's near obsession with pageants has paid off, too. In the big enchilada, the annual Miss Universe, Puerto Ricans are something of a cinch. The island has brought home a stunning five wins in the pageant's history, the most recent in 2006.

In some sense, both sexes seem to enjoy the drama that comes along with these intertwined roles – pay close attention to couples twirling on the dance floor to a salsa song or, better yet, a steamy bolero, and you'll see clearly what game they are both happily playing. But a more substantive look at Puerto Rican culture reveals a much greater complexity to the role of women in contemporary Puerto Rico.

Puerto Rican women have excelled at business, trade and, most importantly, politics – often with more measurable achievement than their counterparts in the United States. San Juan elected a female mayor decades before a woman won a comparable office in the US, and, in 2000, Sila María Calderón was elected governor of Puerto Rico. She ran on a campaign that promised to end government corruption, and clean house she did. In the US, Supreme Court Justice Sonia Sotomayor is of Puerto Rican descent and has strong ties to the island.

El Boricua is an online monthly bilingual cultural magazine for Puerto Ricans worldwide. It can be found at www.elboricua.com.

Other women's issues that tend to be loaded with political and social baggage in the United States have a relatively progressive position in Puerto Rican culture. For instance, abortion is legal in Puerto Rico (although the rest of the Caribbean, outside of Cuba, is uniformly opposed to it). In Puerto Rico, even socially conservative politicians remain acutely aware of the effects of a high birthrate on family living and quality of life. The facts of life are taught early in the home, but it's worth noting that high-school-aged Puerto Rican girls wait longer to have sex than their US counterparts.

The effect that the relatively progressive place women have in Puerto Rican society has on travelers is very noticeable for women traveling alone. Although typical safety precautions should be followed, solo women travelers attract much less attention than in other corners of Latin America.

Sports

Though the silent, stone-lined Taíno ball courts of Tibes and Caguana pay homage to Puerto Rico's long dedication to sports, they speak nothing of the ferocious energy that fires the competitive spirit of islanders today. For such a geographically small place, Puerto Rico plays a disproportionately large role in modern sport, especially in boxing and baseball.

Boxing

Puerto Rico has spawned enough fighters to fill its own boxing Hall of Fame, including the youngest world champion in boxing history and one of the sport's greatest-ever knockout specialists.

Legal since the 1930s, *peleas de gallos* (cockfighting) is a passionate pastime for Puerto Ricans. Abhorred by animal rights groups, the 'sport' entails placing specially bred and trained *gallos de pelea* (fighting cocks) in a pit to battle each other to the death, in fights lasting about 20 minutes.

The standard was set in the 1930s when wily bantamweight Sixto Escobar became the first Puerto Rican to win a world championship belt, knocking out Mexican Baby Casanova in Montreal in 1936. In his homeland, Escobar – from Barceloneta on the north coast – became an overnight hero.

The 1970s introduced the two Wilfredos – Benitez and Gómez. Wilfredo Benitez, nicknamed 'The Radar,' was a Puerto Rican childhood boxing sensation. Raised in New York City, he became the youngest-ever world champion when he defeated Colombian Antonio Cervantes in a World Junior Welterweight championship bout in San Juan in 1976. Benitez, just 17 at the time, defended his title three times before losing to Sugar Ray Leonard in 1979. Gómez, known affectionately as Bazooka, was a punching phenomenon from San Juan who retains one of the highest knockout ratios, with 42 knockouts in 46 fights. Rated number 13 in *Ring* magazine's list of all-time best punchers, Gómez was the subject of the 2003 documentary *Bazooka: The Battles of Wilfredo Gómez*.

As much a showman as a fighter, Hector 'Macho' Camacho was Puerto Rico's most flamboyant star. Born in Bayamón but raised in New York, Camacho aped the style of Muhammad Ali by leaping into the ring dressed as Captain America before a fight. During a 20-year career he fought everyone from Roberto Duran to Julio César Chávez and tested loyalties in his homeland in an all–Puerto Rican world-title fight against Felix Trinidad.

Trinidad, from Cupey Alto, is another modern boxing legend who won world titles at three different weights, including a 1999 victory over Oscar de la Hoya, after which he received a hero's welcome at San Juan's airport.

Puerto Ricans continue to score well in boxing. One of the greatest recent stars is Danny García, son of legendary trainer Angelo García. He's been on a roll since he won the world welterweight title in 2010. José Pedraza has also achieved fame after winning the super featherweight title in 2011.

Baseball

Puerto Rico's official pastime is *béisbol* (baseball), a modern game that bears a vague resemblance to the ceremonial *batú* of Taíno ancestors and draws telling parallels with the island's contemporary economic and cultural relationship with the US. As much as Puerto Rico's beleaguered economy is reliant on support from the US federal government, the *Liga de Béisbol Profesional Roberto Clemente* (Professional Baseball League Roberto Clemente; www.ligapr.com) – named after the legendary player of the early 1970s – is bankrolled by America's own Major League Baseball (MLB).

Players with island roots often make their most significant contributions to the Puerto Rican diaspora while working in New York and Chicago. The pros that rise from the island's stadiums are often celebrated as icons when they make it to the big time in the US.

While the official pastime gets plenty of lip service and Puerto Ricans follow the US Major Leagues avidly, the great passion for baseball is found in school and amateur leagues, although the Puerto Rican pros play a full season, November to January. These winter league games, as they are called, attract diehard fans, and – importantly – scouts from the major league teams in the US. Currently there are six teams in the league. Catching a winter league game (p85) can be a terrific cultural experience and it's dirt cheap by American standards. Tickets are usually under $10 and a cold beer will only set you back $3. San Juan is a great place to watch a game.

US Major League teams also hold spring training camps in Puerto Rico and regularly use the island's league as a farm team. Early-season exhibition games are held in spring, including the televised San Juan Series, at San Juan's Hiram Bithorn Stadium.

The Sounds of Puerto Rico

The music of Puerto Rico is a sonic reflection of the destination itself, a sound shaped by a dynamic history of revolution, colonialism, and the cultural crosscurrents that blow between the island, New York City, Spain and Africa. The sound synonymous with Puerto Rico is certainly salsa, but that which pounds from the open doorways of most of the island's nightspots these days is usually reggaetón, a blazing blend of hip-hop and thudding Caribbean syncopations.

Popular Music & its Roots

To cram for your history lesson on Puerto Rican music in under four minutes, cue up 'Tradicional A Lo Bravo,' a hugely popular single from Puerto Rican reggaetón hitmaker Tego Calderon. Calderon's rapid-fire lyrical delivery and the pounding syncopated bass line is emblematic of the reggaetón movement, but the song also borrows a little something from the important musical traditions of the island. The brassy horns pay homage to salsa bands from the 1960s. The nylon string guitar nods to colonial traditions and *jíbaro* (rural troubador) music. The loping syncopation of the hand drums reference African-rooted Puerto Rican *bomba*. Somewhere, hidden among Calderon's potent swagger, you'll even hear the grinding scrape of a güiro, a percussion instrument made from a notched, hollowed gourd, which was a part of the musical battery of indigenous Taíno tribes.

From the lilt of precolonial folk music to the macho assault of reggaetón, Puerto Rican music has been an evolving part of, not a departure from, past traditions. Puerto Rico has also always been a musical melting pot and remains so today. The island's musical genres can shift as quickly as they are defined, shaped by strong influences from the US, Europe and across Latin America. These dynamic hybrids, whether present in reggaetón or contemporary rock, are a fundamental quality of the music. Then and now, these traditions often place as much importance on dancefloor expressions as on the sound itself.

The Puerto Rican Cuatro Project (www.cuatro-pr.org) is a nonprofit organization that has adopted the island's national instrument as a means of keeping its cultural memories alive. Its website is a must for those seeking to learn about Puerto Rican musical traditions.

Bomba y Plena

The bewildering conflux of traditions that collide in Puerto Rican music can be seen in the earliest popular music on the island, *bomba y plena,* two distinct yet often associated types of folk music. With origins in European, African and native Caribbean cultures, this is the basis for many of the sounds still associated with Puerto Rico and, like salsa, a musical form inexorably tied with dance.

The most directly African in origin is the *bomba,* a music developed by West and Central African slaves who worked on sugar plantations. A typical *bomba* ensemble included drums made from rum barrels and goatskin, *palitos* or *cuás* (wooden sticks that are hit together or on other wooden surfaces), maracas and sometimes a güiro. In the oldest forms (documented as early as the 1680s), dancers led the band, furiously competing with each other and the percussionists in an increasingly frenzied physical and rhythmic display. The tunes ended when either dancer or drummer became too exhausted to continue. Loíza Aldea, on the northeast coast, claims *bomba* as its invention, and the streets rumble with it throughout summer, particularly during the Fiesta de Santiago, which begins during the last week of July.

Plena, which originated in the more urban region around Ponce, is also drum-based but with lighter textures and a less forceful beat. Introduced by *cocolocos,* slaves who migrated north from islands south of Puerto Rico, *plena* uses an assortment of handheld percussion instruments. Locals once referred to the form as *el periodico cantado* (the sung newspaper), because the songs typically recounted, and often satirized, current events. The *plena* beat has strongly syncopated African roots and is a close cousin to calypso, *soca* and dancehall music from Trinidad and Jamaica.

Bomba y plena developed side by side on the coastal lowlands, and inventive musicians eventually realized the call-and-response of *bomba* would work well with *plena*'s satirical lyrical nature, which is why the forms are often played back-to-back by ensembles. If you catch *bomba y plena* today, a historically accurate performance will be rare; in the 1950s a modernization of the sound paved the way for salsa by often adding

PUERTO RICO PLAYLIST

It's nearly a crime to distil three generations of Puerto Rico's vibrant club music into an iPod playlist, but the following romp includes singles spanning half a century, from classic salsa to contemporary reggaetón. If nothing else, use this as a starter to discover the diverse and unexpected charms of Puerto Rican music.

Tito Puente 'Ran Kan Kan,' *Babarabatiri* (1951)

Cortijo Y Su Combo 'El Bombon De Elena,' *...Invites You to Dance* (1957)

Celia Cruz 'Chango Ta Vani,' *La Incomparable* (1958)

Willie Colón 'Te Conozco,' *Cosa Nuestra* (1969)

El Gran Combo De Puerto Rico 'No Hay Cama Pa' Tanta Gente,' *Nuestra Musica* (1971)

Ismael Marinda 'Se Casa La Rumba,' *Abran Paso!* (1972)

Eddie Palmieri 'Nunca Contigo,' *The Sun of Latin Music* (1973)

Fania All-Stars 'Ella Fue (She Was the One),' *Rhythm Machine* (1977)

Frankie Ruiz 'Me Dejo,' *Mas Grande Que Nunca* (1989)

Marvin Santiago 'Fuego A La Jicotea,' *Fuego A La Jicotea* (1991)

Vico C 'Calla,' *Aquel Que Había Muetro* (1998)

Yuri Buenaventura 'Salsa,' *Yo Soy* (2000)

Tego Calderon 'Guasa, Guasa' from *Abayarde* (2003)

Daddy Yankee 'Gasolina,' *Barrio Fino* (2004)

Tito El Ambino 'El Tra,' *It's My Time* (2007)

Don Chezina 'Songorocosongo,' *Tributo Urbano A Hector Lavoe* (2008)

Calle 13 'No Hay Nadie Como Tú,' *Los de Atrás Vienen Conmigo* (2009)

Kany Garcia 'Feliz,' *Boleto De Entrada* (2009)

Cultura Profética 'Baja La Tension,' *La Dulzura* (2010)

Marlow Rosado y La Riqueña 'Fuego A La Jicotea,' *Retro* (2012)

horns and other European instruments, pan-Caribbean rhythmic elements and the clatter of Cuban percussion.

Salsa

For most gringos, salsa's definition as a catch-all term for the interconnected jumble of Latin and Afro-Caribbean dances and sounds isn't easy to get a handle on, but for those who live in its areas of origin – Puerto Rico, Cuba and New York City – it's as much a lifestyle as a genre, with cultural complexities that go well beyond the 'spicy' jargon that's often bandied about.

Salsa tunes might sound vastly different from one another. They can be slow or brisk, flippant or heartrending. Salsa was born in the nightclubs of New York City in the 1960s and remains an iconic sound today.

The Source of the Sauce

In addition to the mishmash of African traditions that spread through the islands via the slave trade, Cuba's *son* – a traditional style that was widely reintroduced to global audiences in the '90s through *Buena Vista Social Club* – is a crucial ingredient in salsa. Originating in eastern Cuba, *son* first became popular in the 1850s, mixing guitar-based Spanish *canciōns* and Afro-Cuban percussion, a fundamental formula that still makes the foundation of many salsa songs. Variations include the rumba, mambo and cha-cha.

Another element of salsa is merengue, which took root in Puerto Rico's neighboring island, the Dominican Republic, where it is the national dance. With its even-paced steps and a signature roll of the hips, it's probably the easiest Latin dance for beginners. Compared with salsa, the rhythmic underpinning has a more rigid structure, and though the music can gallop along at a wild pace, dancers keep their upper body in a graceful, poised stance.

Of all the variations that helped bring salsa into being, none is more important than the mambo – a flamboyant style of music and dance that marries elements of swinging American jazz with *son*. Again, the musical dialogue of the Caribbean islands is evident right down to the style's name; mambo is a Haitian word for a vodou priestess. It started in Cuba in the 1930s and soon spread to Puerto Rico and the US, where mambo became a cross-over fad.

The Birth & Near-Death of Salsa

It's wonderfully appropriate that salsa is called just that, given the number of sound styles that melded in Puerto Rico to produce the sound that was then exported to the world.

In 1964, Johnny Pacheco, a visionary producer, created Fania Records, a label that helped make salsa a wildly popular commercial success. Scores of Puerto Rican, Cuban and Nuyorican singers became household names in the '60s, and when Carlos Santana's now-ubiquitous rock song 'Oye Como Va' hit the music stores in 1969, it may have marked the crest of the Latin wave.

Though the craze left a mark on American pop and jazz traditions, the crowds dwindled in subsequent decades as musical tastes shifted radically in the late 1970s. While Puerto Rican youth turned to rock-and-roll imports from the US through the '80s, traditionalists celebrated the sappy *salsa romantica* typified by crooners such as José Alberto.

Salsa Today

Though salsa's faithful took plenty of solace in Fania records from the '80s, it wasn't until the 1990s that a modern Nuyorican – salsa crooner

Menudo was one of the original boy bands conceived by producer Edgardo Díaz in 1977. It went on to record phenomenal worldwide success with a brand of light teen pop music and celebrated former members such as Ricky Martin.

Best Salsa Recordings

Willie Colón and Ruben Blades: Siembra (1978) – An essential in any salsa collection.

Celia Cruz and Johnny Pacheco: Celia & Johnny (1974) – Deliriously sassy and brassy.

Ismael Miranda: Asi Se Compone Un Son (1973) – A romp through salsa standards.

Marc Anthony, aka ex-Mr JLo – brought salsa back from the brink of obscurity and into a blinding popular spotlight, braiding its traditional elements with those of sleek and shiny modern Latino pop.

Although Anthony and Lopez remain salsa's premier couple, American audiences have also had fleeting infatuations with Ricky Martin (Mr 'La Vida Loca') and hunky Spaniard Enrique Iglesias. More recent Puerto Rican pop stars, like the smart, jazz-fused group Cultura Profética, pick and choose the elements of the island's traditional sound to weave into contemporary records.

But the neo-traditionalist salsa from Bronx-born Puerto Rican singer India and heartthrob crooner Manny Manuel carry the torch from the graying generation who invented it. There are a number of new ensembles who keep turning out the salsa hits in rotation on Puerto Rican radio, though most of them hail from New York City. Watch for the superb El Gran Combo de Puerto Rico, a large group of masters who've packed festivals in the US and on the island for over 50 years. Also huge – and very cutting edge – is Marlow Rosado y La Riqueña, fronted by the namesake composer/producer who mixes salsa, reggaetón, rock and more. And Marc Anthony continues to release chart-topping albums, most recently *3.0,* a salsa album featuring 'Vivir Mi Vida.'

Puerto Rico's national anthem, 'La Borinqueña,' is actually a *danza* that was later subtly altered in order to make it sound more grandiose and anthem-like.

Reggaetón

The raucous bastard-child of reggae, salsa and hip-hop is reggaetón, a rough-and-tumble urban sound that took over the unpaved streets of Loíza Aldea, the Caribbean's answer to the ethos of American thug life. On a trip to a Puerto Rican nightclub, reggaetón dominates the turntables, and you'll likely wake up the next morning with your ears ringing.

As the name suggests, it draws heavily on reggae, though the simplest reduction of its sound is a Spanish-language hip-hop driven by the crushing bass of Jamaican raga, a bossy, electro-infused spin on reggae. An aggressive strain of reggaetón developed in urban areas of Puerto Rico in the 1980s, circulated underground on self-released mix tapes. In the 1990s it incorporated thunderous elements of Jamaican raga and came unto its own. Toss in the thud of a drum machine and some X-rated lyrics and you have yourself a bona fide musical revolution.

Unlike most traditionally postured Puerto Rican music/dance combos, reggaetón dancefloors feature a deliriously oversexed free-for-all, with its

SALSA STAR TITO PUENTE

Puerto Ricans and Cubans jovially argue over who invented salsa, but the truth is neither island can claim to be the commercial center of salsa success. That honor belongs to the offshore colony known as El Barrio: the Latin Quarter, Spanish Harlem, New York City. In the euphoria following the end of WWII, New York's nightclub scene boomed as dancers came in droves to bump and grind to the sound of mambo bands. At the time, the music carried a basic Latin syncopated beat, punctuated by horn sections that were typical of the great swing bands of Stan Kenton and Count Basie.

Then young Puerto Rican drummer Tito Puente came into the picture. After serving three years in the US Navy during the war and attending New York's Juilliard School of Music, Puente began playing and composing for Cuban bands in New York City. He gained notoriety for spicing up the music with a host of rhythms with roots in Puerto Rican *bomba*.

Puente became a star and the face of the salsa boom, bridging cultural divides with his music decades before multiculturalism was even considered a real word. Shortly after the legendary five-time Grammy winner's death in 2000, at the age of 77, a stretch of road in Harlem – East 112th St at Lexington Ave – was renamed Tito Puente Way.

PUERTO RICAN MUSIC: ALIVE & KICKING

Through slush and snow, you've been daydreaming all winter about that idyllic Puerto Rican night on the town, when rum flows like water, the band is hot as a tin roof and the likelihood of dislocating something on the dancefloor is high. Catching live traditional music isn't as easy as you might hope, but the following San Juan nightspots are known for salsa.

Nuyorican Café (p84) San Juan's coziest dancefloor hosts live combos playing traditional favorites.

Club Brava (p82) In a resort but known for its mix of house, reggaetón and salsa.

La Placita de Santurce (p83) The infamous Friday-night street party that attracts salsa bands.

El San Juan Hotel Lobby (p82) Live salsa and meringue bands belie the seemingly staid surrounds.

most popular move known as *perreo,* or dog dance – which leaves little to the imagination. Reggaetón stars such as Tego Calderon, Daddy Yankee, Don Omar and Ivy Queen have hit the mainstream.

Puerto Rican Folk

The earliest folk music on the island started with the percussion and wind instruments of the Taíno, and grew to incorporate elements as disparate as the island's ethnic composition: Spanish guitars, European parlor music and drums, and rhythms from West Africa. Indigenous instruments include at least half a dozen guitar-like string instruments that are native to the island, such as the aptly named four-string guitar-like *cuatro*.

José Feliciano, a six-time Grammy award winner, taught himself to play guitar despite being born blind. He remains one of Puerto Rico's most successful crossover pop stars.

In the mountains, sentimental and twangy folk music was played on *cuatros* by rural troubadours, called *jíbaros,* whose costume often includes a ragged straw hat. A number of traditional *jíbaro* songs – mostly rooted in some kind of Western European parlor music – are still popular at island weddings and family gatherings. An *aguinaldo* is sung by groups of wandering carolers at Christmastime, with lyrics that often explain the traditions of the holiday (perhaps unsurprisingly, many of the most famous ones include singing about pork).

Perhaps the most structurally complex of the island's folk music, *danza* is considered Puerto Rico's classical music. *Danza's* exact lineage is unknown, but it's generally considered to be modeled after *contradanza,* a social music and dance from Europe. *Danza* popularity blossomed in 1840 when it incorporated new music and dance steps called *habaneras* (another export of Cuba).

Arts in Puerto Rico

Although no match for the island's iconic music, the rest of Puerto Rico's arts still have profiles that vividly reflect the vibrant local culture. Fittingly, Puerto Rico's writers use both Spanish and English to describe local life and issues around poverty, freedom, colonialism and the country's netherworld status within the US. Movies tend to reflect the screen-friendly local colors, as do the always energetic visual arts. With dance, Puerto Ricans express physically the rhythms of their music.

Literature

Puerto Rico was without a printing press until 1807, and Spain's restrictive rule kept literacy rates low for almost 400 years. But indigenous literature developed nonetheless; the 19th and 20th centuries gave rise to writers who penned the island's identity: Alejandro Tapia y Rivera, Manuel Alonso, Dr Enrique Laguerre and Julia de Burgos.

As more islanders migrated to the US in the 1950s, Puerto Rican 'exiles,' known as Nuyoricans, produced powerful fiction. One of the most successful writers was Pedro Juan Soto, whose 1956 collection *Spiks* (a racial slur aimed at Nuyoricans) depicts life in the New York barrios with biting realism. Miguel Algarín, Miguel Piñero and Pedro Pietri started a Latino beatnik movement on Manhattan's Lower East Side at the first Nuyorican Poets Café.

Esmeralda Santiago's 1986 memoir, *Cuando era puertorriqueña* (When I Was Puerto Rican), became a standard in US schools for its eloquent portrayal of her childhood on the island and how the lessons learned there have shaped her success.

ICONS OF PUERTO RICAN LITERATURE

Alejandro Tapia y Rivera (1826–82) The 'Father of Puerto Rican literature' wrote poems, stories, essays, novels and plays. Long, allegorical poems include *Sataniada*, 'A Grandiose Epic Dedicated to the Prince of Darkness.'

Manuel Alonso (1822–89) Alonso wrote *El gíbaro* (1849), a collection of vignettes about cockfights, dancing, weddings, politics, race and the *espiritismo* (spiritualism) that characterize the island *jíbaro* (an archetypal witty peasant).

Dr Enrique Laguerre (1906–2005) Puerto Rico's first important international novelist. Published in 1935, *La llamarada* (Blaze of Fire) is set on a sugarcane plantation, where a young intellectual struggles with US corporate exploitation.

Julia de Burgos (1914–53) A major female poet, she responded in outrage when the island became US territory. Her work embodies two fundamental elements of Boricua identity: intense, lyrical connection to nature and fiery politics.

Giannina Braschi (b 1953) One of the biggest names among the many Puerto Rican writers living in New York, Braschi writes about the state of freedom in her homeland – or lack thereof. Her three novels, *Empire of Dreams* (1994), *Yo-Yo Boing!* (1998) and *United States of Banana* (2011), have won international acclaim.

PUERTO RICO ON FILM

For movies set in Puerto Rico or the barrios of New York, seek out:

Carlito's Way Starring Al Pacino and Sean Penn, this popular 1993 drama follows the exploits of Carlito Brigante, a Puerto Rican drug dealer in New York who struggles to go straight after his release from prison.

Rum Punch Shot entirely on location in 2011, Johnny Depp plays Hunter S Thompson in his early yet still-dissolute days when he worked as a journalist in San Juan during the early 1960s.

Angel Written and directed by Jacobo Morales (who also stars), this drama follows the story of a corrupt police captain and the man he wrongly imprisoned. It narrowly missed out on a 2008 Academy Award nomination.

Eduardo Lalo is best known for his Romulo Gallegos Prize–winning novel *Simone* (2012), which, through an unusual narrative style, sets an almost hypnotic tone for its ramble through the city of San Juan. His first book, *En el Burger King de la calle San Francisco* (In the San Francisco Street Burger King), is a lyrical exploration of Old San Juan.

Zoé Jiménez Corretjer, another San Juan writer, has won many awards for her contemporary poetry. Two other poets, Luz María Umpierre-Herrera and Sandra María Esteves, are particularly known for their poetic dialogue in which they each wrote two works to the other debating the roles of women in Puerto Rican society.

Rita Moreno (born in Humacao, 1931) managed the rare feat of winning an Academy Award *(West Side Story)*, a Grammy *(The Electric Company Album)*, a Tony *(The Ritz)* and two Emmys *(The Muppet Show* and *The Rockford Files)*. Only 11 others have won all four.

Cinema

Puerto Rico's balmy weather, historic architecture and modern infrastructure attract Hollywood productions, but a homegrown industry only started to flourish in the late 1980s, thanks largely to one director: Jacobo Morales. He wrote, directed and starred in *Dios la cría* (God Created Them). The movie, offering a critical look at Puerto Rican society, was lauded by critics and fans. His next offering, *Lo que le pasó a Santiago* (What Happened to Santiago), won an Academy Award nomination in 1990 for best foreign film (the irony!). *Linda Sara* (Pretty Sara), his 1994 follow-up, earned him another.

Director Marcos Zurinaga also made a name for himself in the 1980s, first with *La gran fiesta* (The Big Party) in 1986, which focuses on the last days of San Juan's biggest casino, and the acclaimed *Disappearance of Garcia Lorca* (1997).

The most widely distributed and successful Puerto Rican film is probably Luis Molina Casanova's 1993 tragicomedy, *La guagua aérea* (Flight of Hope), which explores the reasons behind Puerto Ricans' emigration in the 1960s. On the artistic front, *Mi santa mirada,* a 2012 short drama by Alvaro Aponte, follows a Puerto Rican drug dealer who decides to change his life. It was recognized at the Cannes Film Festival.

Puerto Rico's screen celebrities include Raúl Juliá (1940–94), and the smoldering Benicio del Toro (b 1967), who won an Oscar for *Traffic*. Though divorced in 2012, Jennifer Lopez (b 1969) and Marc Anthony (b 1968) are both Nuyoricans with strong island ties.

Better known by the nickname Diplo, Ramón Rivero was the king of Puerto Rican comedy and kept islanders laughing through times of intense economic hardship in the 1940s and '50s. He also starred in one of Puerto Rico's finest films, *Los peloteros* (The Baseball Players).

Visual Arts

San Juan's Museo de San Juan is a symbol of Puerto Rico's dedication to the visual arts, which can be traced back to the early days of Spanish colonization. The first great local artist to emerge was self-taught painter José Campeche (1751–1809). Masterpieces such as *Dama a caballo* (Lady on Horseback) and *Gobernador Ustariz* (Governor Ustariz) demonstrate

TRIO OF PUERTO RICAN FOLK ART

Search out examples of these folk-art treasures in some of the better shops on the quieter streets of Old San Juan.

Santos Drawing on the artistic traditions of carved Taíno idols called *cemíes,* these small statues represent religious figures and are enshrined in homes to bring spiritual blessings to their keepers.

Mundillo Made only in Spain and Puerto Rico, this fine lace was imported with early nuns, who made and sold it in order to finance schools and orphanages. Renewed interest in island folk arts, generated by the Instituto de Cultura Puertorriqueña, has revived the process.

Máscaras These frightening and beautiful headpieces are worn at island fiestas, and are popular pieces of folk art. The tradition of masked processions goes back to the Spanish Inquisition, when masqueraders known as *vejigantes* brandished balloon-like objects (called *vejigas;* literally, 'bladders'), terrifying sinners into returning to the church. In Puerto Rico, it merged with masking traditions of African slaves.

Campeche's mastery of landscape and portrait painting, often inspired by the story of Jesus.

Another master, Francisco Oller (1833–1917) did not gain recognition until the second half of the 19th century. Oller was very different from Campeche; he studied in France under Gustave Courbet and was influenced by acquaintances including Cézanne. Like his mentor Courbet, Oller dedicated a large body of his work to scenes from humble, everyday island life. Bayamón, Oller's birthplace, maintains a museum to its native son, and many of his works are in San Juan's Museo de Arte de Puerto Rico. Both Oller and Campeche are honored for starting an art movement inspired by Puerto Rican nature and life, and they gave a distinct cultural and artistic identity to the island.

For eye-popping examples of Puerto Rico's vivid visual art, head to San Juan's Santurce district. Museums, galleries, outdoor art and impromptu graffiti combine for a visual riot as vibrant as the best salsa.

After a storm of poster art that covered the island in visual and verbal images during the 1950s and '60s, serious painters such as Julio Rosado del Valle (1922–2008), Francisco Rodón (b 1934) and Myrna Báez (b 1931) evolved a new aesthetic in Puerto Rican art, in which images rebel against the tyranny of political and jingoistic slogans. Báez is one of a new generation of female artists building on Puerto Rico's traditions to create exciting installation art. Her work is exhibited in many San Juan galleries.

One of the island's most famous contemporary artists was actually a Nuyorican – Rafael Tufiño (1922–2008), who was born in Brooklyn to Puerto Rican parents. Using vivid colors and big canvases, Tufiño was considered the 'Painter of the People' because of his unflinching depiction of poverty on the island. His work has joined the permanent collection of the Museum of Modern Art, the Metropolitan Museum of Art and the Library of Congress.

Dance

The rolling gait of salsa is inexorably linked with the Puerto Rican identity, and the island's attitude toward dance often has a refreshing lack of North American reserve.

Over time, many classifiable musical forms – *bomba,* salsa, *plena* and *danza* – have evolved complementary dances based on syncopated rhythms and melodies. An early example was the formal *danza,* an elegant ballroom dance imported from Cuba. *Bomba* is another colorful import, with influences brought via African slaves. Boisterously energetic, *bomba* has spawned a plethora of subgenres such as *sica, yuba* and *holandes,* and is both spontaneous and exciting to watch.

Puerto Rico's signature dance is certainly salsa. With its sensuous moves and strong African rhythmic base, it seems like the perfect expression of Puerto Rico's cultural DNA – loose-limbed locals make it look as simple as walking.

To see the best free-form Puerto Rican dance, head to San Juan's steamy nightclubs, where being seen with the best moves is a matter of searing personal pride.

Puerto Rico's Landscapes

Puerto Rico is grouped with the Caribbean's three largest islands – Cuba, Jamaica and Hispaniola – in the Greater Antilles, the most substantial of a series of islands that dot the waters of the Caribbean and North Atlantic. But at 100 miles by 35 miles, Puerto Rico is quite clearly the Greater Antilles' lesser sidekick, even with its four principal satellite islands – Mona and Desecheo to the west, Culebra and Vieques to the east – and a host of cays hugging its shores.

Geology

Like almost all of the islands that sprang from the Caribbean Basin, Puerto Rico owes its existence to a series of volcanic events. These eruptions built up layers of lava and igneous rock and created an island with four distinct geographical zones: the central mountains, karst country, the coastal plain and the coastal dry forest. At the heart of the island, running east to west, stands a spine of steep, wooded mountains called the Cordillera Central. The lower slopes of the cordillera give way to foothills, comprising a region on the island's north coast known as 'karst country.' In this part of the island, erosion has worn away the limestone, leaving a karstic terrain of dramatic sinkholes, hillocks and caves.

The San Fermin earthquake that hit western Puerto Rico in October 1918 measured 7.6 on the Richter scale and triggered a 20ft tsunami. The event caused more than $4 million worth of damage to the cities of Mayagüez and Aguadilla. It killed 116 people.

Forty-five non-navigable rivers and streams rush from the mountains and through the foothills to carve the coastal valleys, particularly on the east and west ends of Puerto Rico, where sugarcane, coconuts and a variety of fruits are cultivated. The island's longest river is the Río Grande de Loíza, which flows north to the coast.

Territorial Parks & Reserves

Puerto Rico has more than a dozen well-developed and protected wilderness areas, which offer an array of exploration and a few camping opportunities. Most of these protected areas are considered *reservas forestales* (forest reserves) or *bosques estatales* (state forests), although these identifiers are often treated interchangeably in government-issued literature and maps. Commonwealth or US federal agencies administer most of the natural reserves on the island, and admission to these areas is generally free.

Private conservation groups own and operate a few of the nature preserves, including Las Cabezas de San Juan and Humacao Nature Reserve in the east. The best time to visit nearly all of the parks is from November to March; however, Bosque Estatal de Guánica is an inviting destination year-round.

Major Parks & Reserves

El Yunque National Forest The emerald 28,000-acre highlight of the island's parks is this misty, magnificent rainforest. Dotted with idyllic waterfalls and covered in dense flora, it's home to some of Puerto Rico's most wild and

PARK & NATURE RESERVE AGENCIES

Departamento de Recursos Naturales y Ambientales (DRNA; Department of Natural Resources; ☎787-999-2200; www.drna.gobierno.pr) Puerto Rico's natural resources agency administers all of the island's *bosques estatales* and *reservas forestales,* and issues camping permits.

National Park Service (NPS; www.nps.gov) Oversees the San Juan National Historic Site, which includes the stunning El Morro and San Cristóbal forts.

US Fish & Wildlife Service (☎787-741-2138; www.fws.gov/southeast/maps/vi.html) Manages several refuges, including those at Cabo Rojo, Culebra and Vieques. The emphasis is on preserving places where wildlife breed, migrate or simply live.

US Forest Service (USFS; ☎campground & reservation info 800-280-2267; www.fs.fed.us) Manages the use of El Yunque, which as a national forest is less protected than the national parks, with commercial exploitation in some areas allowed (usually logging or privately owned recreational facilities).

endangered animals. With the island's best trails, El Yunque's lush forests and sun-splashed peaks are ideal for hiking and mountain biking.

Bosque Estatal de Guánica An immense patch of 10,000 acres on the southwest coast, this huge park is home to a tropical dry-forest ecosystem and a Unesco biosphere forest. Its arid scenery and beautiful birds make it good for hiking, swimming, biking and birdwatching.

Reserva Forestal de Toro Negro This ruggedly beautiful, central, mountainous park has landscapes that are only slightly less spectacular than El Yunque's, but with none of the infrastructure. If you want to get off the map (literally), this is the place.

Las Cabezas de San Juan This notable 316-acre coastal preserve is at the northeast corner of Puerto Rico. The El Faro (lighthouse) stands guard over the offshore cays. Its paved trails and interpretive centers make this a fine place for families, and it's a great spot to view the Laguna Grande bioluminescent bay.

Bosque Estatal de Río Abajo Densely forested and dotted with development, this state forest covers 5000 acres in karst country near the Observatorio de Arecibo. It has hiking trails and an aviary, where the Department of Natural Resources is working to reintroduce the Puerto Rican parrot and other endangered species.

Isla Mona The most isolated of Puerto Rico's nature sanctuaries lies about 50 miles west of Mayagüez, across the often-turbulent waters of Pasaje de la Mona. This tabletop island is sometimes called Puerto Rico's Galápagos or Jurassic Park because of its isolation. It's a tag made all the more eerie by the island's 200ft limestone cliffs, honeycomb caves and giant iguanas. Come here for solitude, hiking and caving.

Vieques National Wildlife Refuge Glimmering to the east are the 'Spanish Virgin Islands,' Culebra and Vieques, both of which have large tracts of land designated as National Wildlife Refuges under the control of the US Fish & Wildlife Service. At 18,000 acres, the Vieques refuge is the largest protected natural reserve in Puerto Rico and home to wild turtles and iguanas. It has some of the Caribbean's best beaches; activities include snorkeling, swimming, hiking and cycling.

Puerto Rico – mainland and islands – claims approximately 3500 sq miles of land, making the commonwealth slightly larger than the Mediterranean island of Corsica and slightly smaller than the US state of Connecticut.

Other notable parks and reserves include Bosque Estatal de Carite, which offers easy hikes through pristine forest, as well as kayaking and camping in the central mountains; the Bosque Estatal de Guajataca and Parque de las Cavernas del Río Camuy on the north coast, for hiking, caving and petroglyphs; and Culebra National Wildlife Refuge, which US President Theodore Roosevelt signed into law a century ago.

Environmental Issues

Puerto Rico has suffered from a number of serious environmental problems, including population growth and rapid urbanization, deforestation, erosion of soil, water pollution and mangrove destruction. While Puerto Ricans still have a long way to go toward undoing generations of damage and preserving their natural resources, the past few decades have seen an increase in the level of awareness, resources and action dedicated to conservation efforts.

Tourism

Unchecked development has long been Puerto Rico's biggest environmental threat. Big developers and hotel companies regularly eye the country's lush coastline and pristine beaches in search of their next site. As economically beneficial as tourism might be, its continued expansion could lead to a law of diminishing returns.

The National Astronomy & Ionosphere Center website (www.naic.edu) has information about the Observatorio de Arecibo for the general public as well as for academic types.

Population Growth & Urbanization

Population growth and rapid urbanization have also been huge threats to the island's environment for many years, although this has moderated somewhat, simply because the population is falling as people head to the US mainland looking for work. Still, Puerto Rico currently has a higher population density than any of the 50 US states, with an average of 408 people per sq km. It also supports one of the highest concentrations of roads in the world (certainly the bumpiest).

Deforestation & Soil Erosion

Clear-cut logging operations ended in the 20th century, leaving untold acres of rich mountain topsoil plugging the mouths of rivers and streams. In the 1920s and '30s, conservationists and the US colonial government set aside and reforested an extensive network of wilderness reserves, mostly in karst country and the Cordillera Central. Today these reserves are mature forests and cover nearly the entire central part of the island – about one-third of Puerto Rico's landmass. Meanwhile, the demands of development continue to threaten unprotected natural areas.

ENVIRONMENTAL GROUPS

Many organizations working to protect Puerto Rico's environment also offer excellent tours or activities that visitors can join.

Corporación Piñones Se integra (COPI; ☎787-253-9707; www.copipr.com) A very busy nonprofit that works to preserve and restore San Juan's urban waterways and lagoons through activism and awareness (including kayak tours; see p71).

Para la Naturaleza (www.paralanaturaleza.org) Operates a number of private nature reserves, including the very popular Cabezas de San Juan in the east near Fajardo. Part of the Conservation Trust of Puerto Rico, it hopes to protect fully one-third of the island in the coming decades. Check for its many excellent tours.

Sierra Club (www.puertorico.sierraclub.org) The Puerto Rico branch of the huge environmental group runs frequent bike rides, kayak trips and other tours of natural spots across the island.

Surfrider Foundation (www.surfrider.org) Has chapters in San Juan and Rincón; organizes plastics and beach cleanups, and runs public education programs.

Water Issues

Many streams, rivers and estuaries on the coastal plain have been polluted by agricultural runoff, industry, and inadequate sewer systems. Environmental groups lobbying for the cleanup of these cesspools have made little headway. Visitors should not be tempted to swim in rivers, streams or estuaries near the coast. On a positive note, efforts are being made to clean up San Juan's urban estuaries.

Mangrove Conservation

Widespread economic development after WWII devastated vast mangrove swamps, particularly along the island's north shore. In the 1990s, progress was made in reversing this damage, including the creation of a 2883-acre nature reserve at Bahía de Jobos on the south coast.

Environmentalists had more reason to celebrate in 2013 with the creation of the Corredor Ecológico del Noreste (Northeast Ecological Corridor), which will protect some 3000 acres of mangroves, beaches and sea turtle nesting sites on the north coast east of Luquillo.

Heavy-Metal Pollution

Both the land and sea life around Vieques were literally under siege from the US government during the years of naval bombardment. The US Navy left Vieques in 2003 and the island was deemed a Superfund site shortly after the pullout. Though progress has been made, much of the Vieques National Wildlife Refuge is closed to the public until heavy metals, unexploded ordnance and leftover fuels and chemicals can be taken care of.

Wildlife of Puerto Rico

Seeking out the wildlife of Puerto Rico can be very rewarding. The island's jungle-clad mountains and surreal variety of terrain – including some of the wettest and driest forests in the subtropical climate – have a bit of everything (albeit no huge beasts or flocks of colorful birds). The island's most famous creature is the humble common coquí. The nocturnal serenade of this small endemic frog is the sound of the island, an ever-present reminder of Puerto Rico's precious natural environment.

Amphibians & Reptiles

Puerto Rico's long coastline is one of its most inviting environments to both human and animal visitors. Despite heavy development, a handful of the island's beaches are still nesting sites for two of the world's most critically endangered turtles, the hawksbill and leatherback sea turtles. An excellent place to view the nesting process is on the isolated northern beaches of the island of Culebra.

The hawksbill and leatherback sea turtles are among the 61 species of reptiles and 25 species of amphibians on the island – one of the most diverse collections of such animals in the world. Certainly the most famous amphibian is the tiny but highly vocal coquí frog (its distinctive nighttime croak has been measured at 10 decibels), which has been adopted as a national symbol.

Learn all about the coquí frog and other animals that inhabit Puerto Rico in *Natural Puerto Rico* by Alfonso Silva Lee, an exhaustive but entertaining book on island wildlife.

Iguanas are often kept as semiwild pets and pose unlikely obstacles on numerous Puerto Rican golf courses. The most notable wild species is the Mona ground iguana, which still survives in large numbers on the western island of Mona – often dubbed the Galápagos of the Caribbean because of its unique biological diversity. You'll find other iguanas lazily eyeing your lunch at outdoor cafes on Vieques and Culebra, domesticated to the point where French fries from tourists seem to comprise most of their diet (although human food can be deadly).

Though not native to the island, spectacled caimans have become somewhat of a pest in the areas around Laguna Tortuguero on the north coast. Introduced as a macho pet in the 1990s, many of these minicrocs were abandoned by their owners and dumped in the vicinity of Puerto Rico's only freshwater lake, where they have played havoc with the fragile ecosystem.

Puerto Rico boasts 11 varieties of snake, none of which are poisonous. The most impressive is the Puerto Rican boa, which averages 7ft in length; it is also endangered, but hikers may spot one in the karst region of the northwestern state forests and in El Yunque.

Marine Life

Spending time in the water off Puerto Rico's shores at the right time of year can reveal excellent marine life. Pods of humpback whales breed in the island's warm waters in winter. In the late winter of 2010, southern shores off the island also saw more orca (killer whales) than ever before recorded. Local fishermen attribute this to the relatively warm waters of the Caribbean bringing more dolphins for the orca to eat. Most whale-watching tour operators leave from Rincón, with the tour season usually beginning in early December and ending in March.

Though looking for whales may be a hit with tourists, the Antillean manatee (the town of Manatí, on the north coast, is named after the mammal) is more dear to Puerto Ricans. These so-called sea cows inhabit shallow coastal areas to forage on sea grasses and plants. Manatee numbers have dropped in recent decades due to habitat loss, poaching and entanglement with fishing nets, but they are generally thought to be coming back. To see a manatee, rent a kayak and float along the mangrove-lined shores in the southeast of the island, near Salinas.

Of course, the majority of travelers are captivated by seeing the tropical fish and coral off the island's shores. The continental shelf surrounds Puerto Rico on three sides and blesses the island with warm water and excellent coral reefs, seawalls and underwater features for diving and snorkeling. Especially off the west coast, the water is clear and filled with fish, including parrot fish, eels and sea horses. An abundant supply of sea grass is home to crabs, octopus, starfish and more.

There are seven known regions worldwide that are phosphorescent – meaning they glow in the dark thanks to micro-organisms called dinoflagellates living in the water – but Puerto Rico's are considered among the brightest and the best. Head to Bioluminescent Bay (Bahía Mosquito) in Vieques, Bahía de Fosforescente at La Parguera and Laguna Grande north of Fajardo.

Mammals

Very few of the land mammals that make their home in Puerto Rico are native to the island; most mammal species – from rats to cows – have been accidentally or intentionally introduced to the island over the centuries.

Bats are the only native terrestrial mammal in Puerto Rico. They exist in large numbers in the caves of karst country, but most travelers will only catch glimpses at dusk while visiting Bosque Estatal de Cambalache or the Cavernas del Río Camuy.

Puerto Rico is also home to the distinctive Paso Fino horse, a small-boned, easy-gaited variety. The Paso Finos have been raised in Puerto Rico since the time of the Spanish conquest, when they were introduced to the New World to supply the conquistadors on their expeditions throughout Mexico and the rest of the Americas. The horses are most dramatic on the island of Vieques, where they roam in semiwild herds across the landscape.

Other mammals of interest to travelers are two small colonies of monkeys, both introduced by scientists. The first lives on the 39-acre Cayo Santiago where a group of rhesus monkeys arrived for scientific study in 1938. Today they've burgeoned into a community of more than 900 primates and can be spotted from snorkeling tour boats. The second scientific monkey colony that grew out of control is on Isla de Monos off La Parguera, which is a standard part of the tour of the mangrove canals.

For birdwatchers heading to Puerto Rico or the Caribbean, *A Guide to the Birds of Puerto Rico and the Virgin Islands* by Herbert Raffaele is a must-have. If you don't luck out and spot a wild Puerto Rican parrot, one of the 10 most endangered species in the world, there are over 300 in captivity in various zoos and sanctuaries.

Birds & Bugs

With more than 250 species spread over 3500 sq miles, Puerto Rico is an excellent place to dust off your binoculars and engage in a bit of tropical birdwatching. The commonwealth's most famous bird is also one of its rarest: the elusive Puerto Rican parrot (aka the Puerto Rican Amazon). Numbers of the bright-green bird were down in the mid teens during the 1970s, but thanks to concerted conservation efforts the wild population has recovered to a still-precarious 60 to 80. The parrots exist in the wild in the El Yunque and Río Abajo forest reserves, although seeing one is akin to winning a lottery ticket.

Another endemic bird is the Puerto Rican tody, a small green, yellow and red creature that frequents the moist mountains of the Cordillera Central and the dense thickets of the south coast where it feeds on insects.

HIKING FOR THE BIRDS

Exotic birdlife is the wildlife of choice to spot on nature hikes. The most obvious destination for budding ornithologists is El Yunque National Forest, situated close to the capital. The El Portal Visitors Center on Hwy 191 has good, basic information on the local birdlife.

The island's richest species diversity can be spied in the Cabo Rojo area, particularly around Las Salinas salt flats, where migratory birds from as far away as Canada populate a unique and highly varied ecosystem. Call in at the Centro Interpretativos Las Salinas de Cabo Rojo to speak with informed local experts.

The coastal dry forest of Guánica might be the biggest draw for serious birdwatchers looking to whittle down their life list. It features more than 130 bird species, comprising largely of songbirds. Some of these are migratory birds, such as the prairie warbler and the northern parula. Many are nonmigratory species, including the lizard cuckoo and the critically endangered Puerto Rican nightjar. One of the joys of winter beachcombing is watching the aerial acrobatics of brown pelicans as they hunt for fish.

The island also has a supply of unusual flying and crawling insects, including a large tropical relative of the firefly called the *cucubano,* and a centipede measuring more than 6in in length with a sting that can kill. Much to the chagrin of generations of foreign visitors there are also zillions of blood-hungry mosquitoes.

Flora

Puerto Rico's tropical climate and unique rain patterns create a veritable greenhouse for a huge variety of plant life, which thrives on tropical heat, tons of rain and lots of moisture in the air. As soon as you leave San Juan's urban zone and head into the mountains, you'll see green everywhere.

Mangrove swamps and coconut groves dominate the north coast, while the El Yunque rainforest, at the east end of the island, supports mahogany trees and more than 50 varieties of wild orchid. Giant ferns thrive in the rainforest as well as in the foothills of karst country, while cacti, mesquite forest and bunchgrass reign on the dry southwest tip of the island, resembling the look of the African savanna. The dry forests near Guánica grow a variety of cacti, thorny scrub brush and plants equipped for harsh, dry conditions.

The hills of the Cordillera Central are densely forested and flowering trees punctuate the landscape. Look for the butterfly tree, with its light-pink flower resembling an orchid, the bright orange exclamation of the African tulip and the deep red of the royal poinciana, which are cultivated near the Christmas season.

Exotic shade trees have long been valued in this sunny climate, and most of the island's municipal plazas sit beneath canopies of magnificent ceibas or kapoks (silk-cotton trees), the *flamboyán* (poinciana), with its flame-red blossoms, and the African tulip tree.

Islanders often adorn their homes with a profusion of flowers, such as orchids, bougainvillea and poinsettias, and tend lovingly to fruit trees that bear papaya, *uva caleta* (sea grape), *carambola* (star fruit), *panapen* (breadfruit) and *plátano* (plantain). Of course, sugarcane dominates the plantations of the coastal lowlands, while farmers raise coffee on the steep slopes of the Cordillera Central.

Survival Guide

Directory A–Z

Accommodations

You can find all types of accommodations in Puerto Rico – from huge resorts to humble guesthouses to remote mountain retreats. Compared to the rest of the Caribbean, however, you won't find as many all-inclusive resorts, where food and drinks are included in the price. Hostels are also rare, as are the chain motels that are common in the US. There is a burgeoning number of B&Bs, a previously unknown category on the island.

Lodging rates in Puerto Rico vary, sometimes by more than 30%, from season to season. In general, rates are highest from mid-December through to the end of April. They are also high from mid-June to August, when many island families take their vacations. Rates are lowest from September to mid-December.

Camping

Camping is a difficult proposition in Puerto Rico, as reservations must usually be made at least 15 days in advance, reservation offices and ranger stations have maddeningly erratic hours, and the quality of facilities varies greatly.

Beach camping You can find campsites on or near the sand on Vieques and Culebra. It's also possible at some of the beaches along the northeast coast, moving from Luquillo east.

National forests & forest reserves Contact the **Departamento de Recursos Naturales y Ambientales** (DRNA, Department of Natural Resources & Environment; ☎787-999-2200; www.drna.gobierno.pr) at least 15 days in advance for reservations and a permit. Commonwealth-run forest-reserve campgrounds are likely to have showers and RV hookups available; national forest campgrounds tend to be less developed.

Guesthouses

Places calling themselves 'guesthouses' can differ vastly from one to the next. While some guesthouses may have as few as two rooms, others may have dozens. One guesthouse may look like a roadside motel, another may be a beach house with a pool, a bar and a restaurant. Most are midrange in price.

Hotels

Puerto Rico has many top-end resort hotels and a growing number of boutique options. Most major chains have properties in San Juan and elsewhere. Despite financial difficulties, there are new resorts opening, most notably the lavishly restored and expanded Condado

SLEEPING PRICE RANGES

The following price ranges refer to a double room with bathroom in high season. Unless otherwise stated, a tax of 9% to 15% is included in the price.

$ less than $80

$$ $80–200

$$$ more than $200

CAMPING TIPS

- Bring anything you might need from home; outdoor outfitters are rare on the island.
- Use caution camping alone at a site without a guard.
- Camping reservations through state agencies require a valid credit card.
- Summer is high camping season; during other seasons public camping areas are often closed (although sometimes you can just set up camp for free and no one will bother you).

Climate

Barranquitas

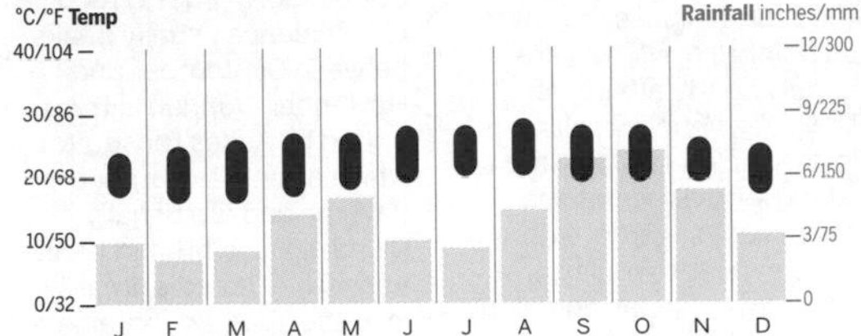

Mayagüez

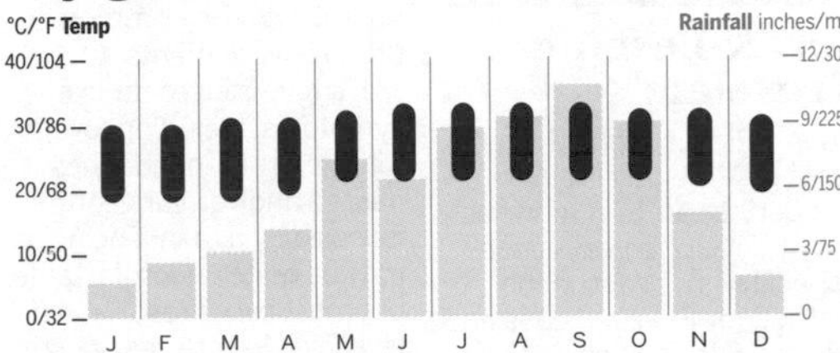

Ponce

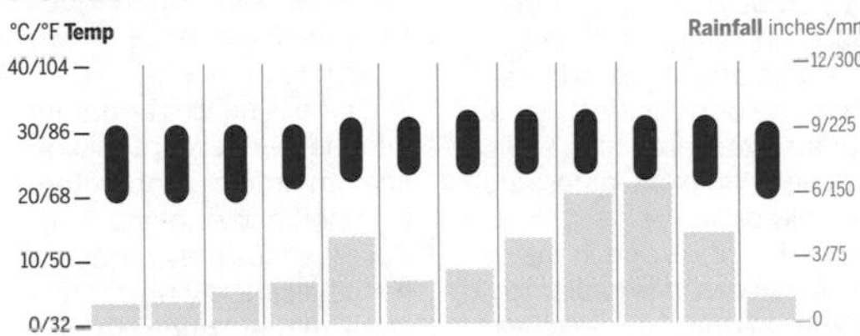

Vanderbilt Hotel in San Juan and the swanky Ritz-Carlton Reserve Dorado Beach Resort to the west.

At busy times, expect to pay $150 a night or much more for a room. Watch out for mandatory 'resort fees' that can add charges of $60 a day or more to room prices. Service charges are also common at resorts.

Paradores

The Puerto Rico Tourism Company (PRTC; www.seepuertorico.com) endorses about 20 paradores (inns) scattered across the island and they are a mixed bag. Some are modern and generic hotels, others are quaint, oozing with charm. Some are beautifully housed in old coffee plantations.

Vacation Rentals

All those condo towers lining San Juan's beautiful beaches have owners within hoping to rent out their units to visitors, often at rates much better than hotels. Consult airbnb.com and vrbo.com for scores of listings in a variety of locations and price ranges.

BOOK YOUR STAY ONLINE

For more accommodations reviews by Lonely Planet authors, check out http://lonelyplanet.com/hotels/. You'll find independent reviews, as well as recommendations on the best places to stay. Best of all, you can book online.

Customs Regulations

Goods brought into the US in greater quantity than the duty-free customs allowances are subject to taxes and tariffs and must be declared at customs.

Cigarettes Each person over 18 can bring 200 cigarettes duty free into Puerto Rico or the US.

Currency US law permits you to bring in or take out as much as $10,000 in US or foreign currency, traveler's checks or letters of credit without formality.

Gifts US citizens are allowed to import, duty free, $400 worth of gifts from abroad, while non-US citizens are allowed to bring in $100 worth.

Liquor Each person over the age of 21 can bring 1L of liquor duty free into Puerto Rico or the US.

Plants Declare any plants, fruits or vegetables at the airport. The US department of agriculture restricts many island plants.

Electricity

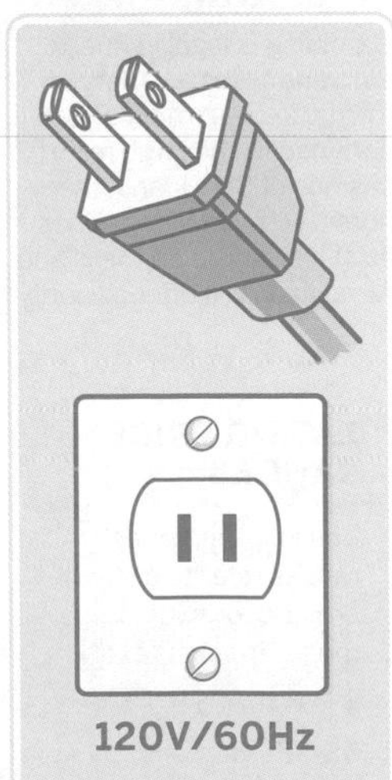

Food

Food is an intrinsic part of Puerto Rican culture and the commonwealth offers a flavorsome array of dining options, from side-of-a-dusty-road food trucks to trendy farm-to-table bistros. For more on Puerto Rico's cuisine, see p32.

Gambling

Gambling is legal in Puerto Rico and takes a variety of forms. Though most of it is confined to the large resort casinos of San Juan, other hotels with smaller casinos exist elsewhere on the island. All casinos will offer a variety of slot machines, and some table games. There is a horse track and cockfighting arena in San Juan. Elsewhere on the island, places to watch cockfights *(galleras)* are largely seedy affairs. You'll likely see vendors selling lottery tickets around the island, and a mechanical horse-racing game, with rules similar to roulette, at small town fiestas and along the side of the road.

EATING PRICE RANGES

The following price ranges refer to a standard one- or two-course meal. Tipping is extra.

$ less than $15

$$ $15–30

$$$ more than $30

Gay & Lesbian Travelers

Puerto Rico is probably the most gay-friendly island in the Caribbean. San Juan has a well-developed gay scene, especially in the Condado district, for Puerto Ricans and visitors. Other cities, such as Mayagüez and Ponce, have gay clubs and gay-friendly accommodations as well. Vieques and Culebra have become popular destinations for an international mix of gay and lesbian expatriates and travelers.

In the cities and in major resort areas, it is easier for gay men and women to live their lives with a certain amount of openness. As you travel into the middle of the island, it is more difficult to be out, as people are not used to seeing same-sex couples holding hands or displaying affection publicly.

Recently, Puerto Rico's legislature has debated extending various rights, such as adoption, to single-sex couples.

Health

For medical emergencies, dial ☎911.

Availability & Cost of Health Care

Cities and larger towns will have at least one high-standard hospital. Elsewhere there is usually at least one good clinic.

Dengue Fever

Dengue fever is a viral infection found throughout the Caribbean. In Puerto Rico the incidence usually peaks between September and November. Dengue is transmitted by Aedes mosquitoes, which often bite during the daytime and are usually found close to human habitations. They breed primarily in artificial water containers such as jars, barrels, plastic containers and discarded tires. Dengue is common in urban environments.

Dengue causes flu-like symptoms, including fever, muscle aches, headaches, nausea and vomiting, often followed by a rash. The aches may be quite uncomfortable, but most cases resolve in a few days. Severe cases usually occur in children under age 15 who are experiencing their second dengue infection.

There is no treatment for dengue fever except taking acetaminophen/paracetamol (Tylenol) and drinking fluids. Severe cases may require hospitalization. The cornerstone of prevention (there is no vaccine) is protection against insects, so use bug repellant.

Environmental Hazards

Animals Do not attempt to pet or feed any animal, except domestic animals known to be free of infectious diseases. Spiny sea urchins and coelenterates (coral and jellyfish) are a hazard in some areas.

Mosquitoes Except for infrequent outbreaks of Dengue fever, mosquito-borne illnesses are usually not a concern in Puerto Rico. A bug spray containing DEET is best to ward off insects, but use sparingly as it kills natural organisms in island bays and inlets.

Sandflies The notorious 'no-see-ums.' These invisible bugs come out mostly in the early evening. Culebra and Vieques can be

INTERNATIONAL VISITORS

Entering the Region

- International travelers will most likely transit through an East Coast hub such as New York City or Miami.
- Puerto Rico subscribes to all the laws that apply to traveling and border crossing in the United States.
- Visitors from other countries must have a valid passport.
- You only need a visa to enter Puerto Rico if you need a visa to enter the US.
- Countries participating in the Visa Waiver Program – the EU, Australia, New Zealand and much of Latin America – don't need visas to get into Puerto Rico.
- The US State Department (www.state.gov) has current information about visas, immigration etc.
- US citizens can enter the commonwealth with proper ID such as a driver's license, a passport or a birth certificate, although there are no special checks for this.

Embassies & Consulates

Most nations' principal diplomatic representation is in Washington, DC. Consulates in Puerto Rico tend to be the honorary kind that have very limited services – if any – for travelers.

Canadian Consulate (787-759-6629; Suite 1111, 268 Ponce de Leon, Hato Rey Center, San Juan) Offers limited services.

Money

- Major bank offices in San Juan and Ponce will exchange foreign currencies. There are also exchange desks at San Juan's Luis Muñoz Marín International Airport and major resorts (which offer terrible rates).
- ATMs are easily found in all but the smallest towns.
- Tipping in restaurants averages 15% to 20%.

Post

Post offices run by the US Postal Service (www.usps.com) are found in towns and cities large and small. International postal rates are very reasonable.

Practicalities

TV & Radio American TV is broadcast across the island. Radio is mostly in Spanish. Places to stay will have the full complement of US cable/satellite channels.

Weights & Measures Puerto Rico follows the American imperial system with two exceptions: all distances on road signs are in kilometers and gas is pumped in liters.

Telephone

To call home from Puerto Rico:

- First dial 011, the international dialing prefix in the US.
- Dial the country code of the country you want to call. For Australia, dial 61; the UK, 44; Ireland, 353; New Zealand, 64.
- Dial the rest of the number.

Time

Puerto Rico is on Atlantic Standard Time. Clocks in this time zone read an hour later than the Eastern Standard Time zone, which encompasses such US cities as New York and Miami. There is no Daylight Saving Time observed on the island.

particularly thick with them, so lay on the DEET.

Sun Yes, it's subtropical, so apply high-protection sunscreen liberally.

Water Tap water in Puerto Rico is safe to drink.

Insurance

Check your health and/or your homeowners' insurance to see what is and is not covered in terms of problems that may arise on the road. You may want to consider travel insurance for lost luggage, trip cancellations and delays, health coverage and more.

Worldwide travel insurance is available at www.lonelyplanet.com/travel_services. You can buy, extend and claim online anytime – even if you're already on the road.

Internet Access

Wi-fi is common in places to stay, cafes and many public places and squares. In this book, the wi-fi symbol (wi-fi) means that wi-fi is available throughout the property unless otherwise noted, while the internet symbol (@) means there are public internet terminals available.

Legal Matters

- Puerto Rico follows US laws in all criminal and most legislative matters. If you are arrested, you have the same rights as you would elsewhere in the US.
- If you are stopped by the police, remember there is no system of paying fines on the spot. Don't attempt to pay the officer.
- Although English is widely spoken, many police in rural areas do not speak English.

Drinking Laws

Alcohol is deeply ingrained in the island's social scene – more so than in parts of the US and Europe. Puerto Rico has few 'blue laws' prohibiting the times and places where alcohol can be consumed.

- Minors are not permitted in bars and pubs, even to order nonalcoholic beverages.
- Old San Juan has laws to prevent drinking in the streets, and violators are subject to heavy fines.
- Driving while under the influence of alcohol will result in stiff fines, jail time and penalties.
- Drinking on the beach is legal.

Maps

Apps from Apple and Google have Puerto Rico well covered. There are also many free maps available that will do in most cases. Otherwise you'll find more detailed maps at drug and convenience stores.

US Geological Survey (USGS; www.usgs.gov) An agency of the US Department of the Interior publishes very detailed topographic maps of Puerto Rico, at various scales up to 1:250,000. Maps at 1:62,500, or approximately 1in = 1 mile, are ideal for backcountry hiking and backpacking. Some bookstores and outdoor-equipment specialists on the island carry a selection of topographic maps.

Opening Hours

Businesses are usually open 8am to 5pm, but there are certainly no set rules. Nearly all museums in Puerto Rico close on Mondays. Some also remain closed on Tuesdays.

Banks	8am-4pm Mon-Fri, 9:30am-noon Sat
Bars	2pm-2am, often later in San Juan
Government offices	8:30am-4:30pm Mon-Fri
Post offices	8am-4pm Mon-Fri, 8am-1pm Sat
Shops	9am-6pm Mon-Sat, 11am-5pm Sun, later in malls

Public Holidays

US public holidays are celebrated along with local holidays in Puerto Rico. Banks, schools and government offices (including post offices) are closed, and transportation, museums and other services are on a Sunday schedule. Holidays falling on a weekend are usually observed the following Monday.

New Year's Day January 1

Three Kings Day (Feast of the Epiphany) January 6

Eugenio María de Hostos' Birthday January 10

Martin Luther King Jr Day Third Monday in January

Presidents' Day Third Monday in February

Emancipation Day March 22

Palm Sunday Sunday before Easter

Good Friday Friday before Easter Sunday

Easter A Sunday in late March/April

José de Diego Day April 18

Memorial Day Last Monday in May

Independence Day/Fourth of July July 4

Luis Muñoz Rivera's Birthday July 18

Constitution Day July 25

José Celso Barbosa's Birthday July 27

Labor Day First Monday in September

Columbus Day Second Monday in October

Veterans' Day November 11

Thanksgiving Fourth Thursday in November

Christmas Day December 25

Safe Travel

Hazards in the Water

The currents of Puerto Rico's beaches can be deadly, with the biggest hazards being riptides and dangerous ocean currents. Obey all posted signs on beaches. If you get caught in a riptide that carries you away from shore, never panic or swim against it, you'll only get worn out. Instead, swim parallel to the shoreline and when the current lessens make your way back to shore.

Hazards on the Road

Puerto Rican drivers are more aggressive than drivers on the mainland US, and rules of the road are taken as more of a suggestion. Remember to keep your cool and proceed with caution. If you're driving and see a police car with its blue lights on, don't worry, police in Puerto Rico are required to have their lights lit whenever driving. Police will sound a siren during emergencies. Mountain roads can be very narrow, have sudden drop offs, and rough surfaces. Beep before driving into blind curves. If you come to a point in the road too narrow for both cars to pass, the car on the uphill side should reverse and let the other driver pass.

Hiking & Camping

➡ Don't ever head into the forest without leaving someone your planned itinerary.

➡ Minor cuts and scrapes can get infected easily in this climate; carry disinfectant with you.

➡ Getting lost is easy; invest in a good topographical map for serious hikes.

Weather & Natural Disasters

Although somewhat predictable, Puerto Rico can get pounded with tropical storms and hurricanes, which can result in a number of serious disruptions for visitors, including washed-out roads and trails, and shuttered attractions. Hurricane season is usually between the beginning of June and the end of November. If you're visiting during this time there's still likely nothing to worry about.

Telephone

The good news for US cell phone users is that Puerto Rico is treated as just another state in terms of coverage and roaming fees.

Tourist Information

Puerto Rico Tourism Company (PRTC; Map p132; www.seepuertorico.com) is the commonwealth's official tourist bureau. It has a fair range of general interest materials and a decent website. Privately produced tourist magazines and brochures are abundant.

Travelers with Disabilities

Travel to and around Puerto Rico is becoming easier for people with disabilities as the country is subject to the Americans with Disabilities Act (ADA). Public buildings (including hotels, restaurants, theaters and museums) are now required by law to be wheelchair-accessible and to have appropriate restroom facilities.

Public transportation services (buses, trains and taxis) must be made accessible to all, including those in wheelchairs, and telephone companies are required to provide relay operators for the hearing impaired.

Many banks now provide ATM instructions in Braille. ADA-compliant curb ramps are common, and some of the busier roadway intersections have audible crossing signals. Playa Luquillo has a beach especially for the mobility-impaired, and ferries to Culebra and Vieques are accessible.

Volunteering

As a relatively rich country in close geographic and economic proximity to the United States, Puerto Rico offers limited opportunities for volunteering.

Rainforest management The Earthwatch Institute (www.eyeontherainforest.org) partners with Las Casas de la Selva to run one- to three-week research missions to the Bosque Estatal de Carite, where participants learn forest management skills and aid in the rejuvenation of the tropical rainforest. Volunteers stay in tents in the Casas de la Selva complex inside the park and spend their time planting seedlings, studying trees and monitoring local frog populations. Some of the trips are family friendly.

Turtle watching The US Fish and Wildlife Refuge runs a volunteer turtle watch on Culebra's Playa Brava during nesting season. You can access this project through Coralations (www.coralations.

org), a nonprofit organization that is involved in coral reef protection.

Wildlife protection The **Vieques Conservation & Historical Trust** (787-741-8850; www.vcht.org; Calle Flamboyán 138, Esperanza) accepts volunteers for a wide variety of projects, including assisting with animals and reefs, maintaining a tank of rescued marine animals, and feeding animals.

Women Travelers

Puerto Rico's status as a US commonwealth means that women have a position in society not dissimilar to the United States.

Puerto Rican women crisscross the island by themselves all the time, so you won't be the only solo woman on the ferry or public bus, but as a foreigner you will attract a bit more attention. Most of it will be simple curiosity, but a few may assume you'd much rather be with a man if you could. If you don't want the company, most men will respect a firm but polite, 'no thank you.'

Transportation

GETTING THERE & AWAY

Air

Airports & Airlines

Puerto Rico is the most accessible island in the Caribbean. It has air service from most major American hubs and all the major airlines serve San Juan. There is very limited international service to other airports in Puerto Rico, although you can fly to the US Virgin Islands from Culebra and Vieques.

San Juan is a hub for Caribbean flights. The growing regional carrier, **Seaborne Airlines** (www.seaborne airlines.com), relocated its main operations to San Juan in 2014.

Luis Muñoz Marín International Airport (SJU; www.aeropuertosju.com) San Juan's busy international airport is only 8 miles from Old San Juan and barely 10 minutes by cab from Isla Verde. It is not a place to linger as it lacks amenities such as free wi-fi, and the places to eat, drink and shop are dire.

Sea

Cruise Ship

San Juan is the second-largest port for cruise ships in the western hemisphere (after Miami). More than 25 vessels call San Juan their home port or departure port and over one million cruise-ship passengers pass through the ports in Old San Juan annually.

All the major cruise-ship lines operate cruises from San Juan.

Ferry

A new ferry service connects the Dominican Republic with Puerto Rico. **America Cruise Ferries** (☎Mayaguez 787-832-4800, San Juan 787-622-4800; www.acferries.com; one-way adult from $90, with car from $250) is running the large *Caribbean Fantasy* from the Don Diego port near Santo Domingo in the Dominican Republic. It serves San Juan (13 hours) two days a week and Mayagüez (12 hours) in the west one day a week. The ferry is large and luxurious (it has extra-cost cabins).

Yacht

- Crewing aboard a yacht destined for the West Indies from North America or Europe is a popular way of getting to Puerto Rico.
- Marinas are located at most major resorts and at principal ports around the Puerto Rican coast.

CLIMATE CHANGE & TRAVEL

Every form of transport that relies on carbon-based fuel generates CO_2, the main cause of human-induced climate change. Modern travel is dependent on airplanes, which might use less fuel per mile per person than most cars but travel much greater distances. The altitude at which aircraft emit gases (including CO_2) and particles also contributes to their climate change impact. Many websites offer 'carbon calculators' that allow people to estimate the carbon emissions generated by their journey and, for those who wish to do so, to offset the impact of the greenhouse gases emitted with contributions to portfolios of climate-friendly initiatives throughout the world. Lonely Planet offsets the carbon footprint of all staff and author travel.

➡ Upon reaching the island you *must* clear immigration and customs unless you are coming directly from a US port or the US Virgin Islands.

➡ There are numerous online clearinghouses for those seeking yacht-crew positions (both experienced and inexperienced), including **Crewfinders** (www.crewfinders.com) and **Yacht Crew Register** (www.yachtcrewregister.com).

GETTING AROUND

Air

Because Puerto Rico is such a small island, its domestic air transportation system is basic. Daily flights connect San Juan, Ponce, Aguadilla and Mayagüez. Most domestic flights link San Juan to the offshore islands of Culebra and Vieques.

Bicycle

Bicycles should be considered a recreational, rather than practical, form of transportation for all but the most ambitious of travelers. Cycling hasn't traditionally been a popular means of getting around the island and the bad road conditions make this unlikely to change soon.

The hazards of cycling in Puerto Rico include nightmare traffic, dangerous drivers and a general lack of awareness about cyclists' needs. Most natives simply aren't used to seeing touring bikes on the road. Never cycle after dark. For further advice contact the Puerto Rican Cycling Federation.

You can usually rent a bike in tourist areas.

Boat

Charter Yacht

All of the island's major resorts have marinas where you can charter yachts or powerboats, either with a crew or 'bareboat.' Crewed boats come with a skipper and crew, and you don't need any prior sailing experience. With bareboat charters, you rent the boat and be your own skipper.

Charter companies include the following:

Erin Go Bragh (☎787-860-4401; www.egbc.net) Only offers short-term charters with crew.

Sail Caribe (☎787-889-1978; www.sailcaribe.com; Marina Puerto del Rey, Fajardo; yacht rental per week from $3500) Has a large range of boats and yachts for rent.

Ferry

Public ferries link Fajardo with Culebra and Vieques.

Car

Despite the occasional hazards of operating a car in Puerto Rico, driving is currently the most convenient way to get around the countryside, see small towns, cross sprawling suburbs and explore wide, open spaces. This is particularly relevant to roads such as the Ruta Panorámica where public transport is scant and cycling deemed too dangerous.

Car Rental

Car-rental rates in San Juan are very competitive, elsewhere, not so much. A car costing $30 or less a day in San Juan will cost $60 or more in smaller cities and on the islands. Most companies prohibit taking rentals from the mainland to Culebra and Vieques.

All of the major international car-rental companies operate on the island, especially at the airport in San Juan. There are also local firms, especially in smaller cities and on the islands. Local San Juan firms include the following:

Charlie Car Rental (☎787-728-2418; www.charliecars.com) Has offices in San Juan plus Aguadilla and Caguas.

Target (☎787-728-1447, 800-934-6457; www.targetrentacar.com) Large local firm has offices across San Juan plus numerous other cities.

Driver's Licenses

Any valid driver's license can be used to rent and operate a car or scooter in Puerto Rico. If you stay longer than 90 days, residency laws require you to get a Puerto Rican license.

Fuel

Major oil companies maintain gas stations across the island, which generally stay open until about 7pm. Don't let your tank go dry, though, because the next station could be a long way up the road. In rural areas, stations may close on Sunday.

GETTING AROUND ON CULEBRA & VIEQUES

You can rent vehicles, scooters and bicycles easily on Culebra and Vieques. Also, 'taxi' vans or *públicos* shuttle people around the islands for between $3 and $5 each. *Públicos* meet travelers at the docks; prices for common destinations are usually fixed.

ROAD DISTANCES (MILES)

	Aguadilla	Aibonito	Arecibo	Cabo Rojo Point	Fajardo	Mayagüez	Ponce	Rincón
Aibonito	95							
Arecibo	33	61						
Cabo Rojo Point	70	122	70					
Fajardo	115	69	83	145				
Mayagüez	17	80	49	22	142			
Ponce	63	34	45	50	95	46		
Rincón	11	94	43	35	125	14	60	
San Juan	83	46	52	122	38	100	74	93

Parking

Finding parking can be a real problem in San Juan. Do not park at curbs painted red or yellow. Parking fees at the hotels average about $20 per day.

Road Conditions & Hazards

➡ Puerto Rico's roads are in an abysmal state. Expect bumps, potholes, broken guard rails and worse.

➡ Puerto Rico has more cars per square mile than any other place on earth – twice as many as Los Angeles County – so expect traffic jams.

➡ Puerto Ricans' driving habits are casual in the extreme; a sure sign of a tourist driver is the use of turn signals. Sudden stops, turns in front of oncoming traffic and other unsafe moves are common. Drivers often ignore stop lights and signs.

➡ Watch out for island animals – dogs, chickens, horses, pigs – that wander across the roads, particularly in the mountains and on Culebra and Vieques.

➡ Secondary roads through the mountains are in generally poor condition, with lots of rough surfaces and very narrow passes.

➡ Police always keep warning lights on. Emergency situations are signaled by a siren.

➡ Puerto Rico's best roads are its Expressway toll roads, which include numbers 22 (San Juan–Arecibo), 66 (San Juan–Canóvanas), 52 (San Juan–Ponce) and 53 (Fajardo–Yabucoa). Have correct change, usually 50¢ to $2, ready at toll booths.

Road Rules

➡ Driving rules here are basically the same as they are in the US: traffic proceeds along the right side of the road and moves counterclockwise around traffic circles.

➡ It is legal to turn right at a red light, except where signs state otherwise.

➡ It is legal to ignore red lights (if safe to do so) between midnight and 5am.

➡ Watch for school zones, where the speed limit is 15mph (strictly enforced during school hours).

➡ Most highway signs employ international symbols, but distances are measured in kilometers, while speed limits are posted in miles per hour.

➡ Seat belts and motorcycle helmets must be worn; children younger than four years must travel in child safety seats.

Hitchhiking

Hitchhiking is rare in Puerto Rico and not recommended.

Local Transportation

Public Transportation

San Juan has an efficient bus system and a metro (Tren Urbano), which will eventually expand to cover places like Caguas. Elsewhere services are more casual.

Públicos

Públicos are essentially public minibuses that run prescribed routes during daylight hours. Traveling via *público* offers a great local experience, but requires a lot of patience and time. Some *públicos* make relatively long hauls between places such as San Juan and Ponce or Mayagüez, but most make much shorter trips, providing a link within and between communities.

Comfort Van rides are not especially comfortable, as drivers will try to put as many passengers in one van as possible. Vans can be old, stinky and extremely hot and crowded. Travel can be slow as the driver stops frequently to let people on and off.

Cost *Público* is by far the most inexpensive way to travel long distances in Puerto Rico. The longest ride on the island will not cost more than $15, though something around $4 or less is much more common. Pay extra if you want the driver to take you to a destination that is off the route.

Destinations The destination will be clearly written in the front window of the van. If you go to an unusual destination, you will likely be stranded for a return trip.

Frequency *Públicos* will leave when the van is full. In the early morning and evening, when people are going to and from work, the terminals will be most busy. Some *públicos*, such as the ones that run to popular beaches, may only operate on the weekend.

Schedules For fares and schedules, inquire with locals any place *públicos* stop. There is no central source of info.

Terminals There will be major *público* terminals near the center of every midsized or large city. Elsewhere, *públicos* make their pickups and drop-offs at a van stand on or near a town's central plaza.

Taxi

Taxis are available in most of the midsized to large cities on the island. Often, flagging a taxi in a public plaza is faster than calling for one. Drivers almost never use meters, so establish the cost before beginning your journey. San Juan is the exception to this: its government-regulated 'tourist taxis' have fixed rates.

Language

Spanish spelling is phonetically consistent, meaning that there's a clear and consistent relationship between what you see in writing and how it's pronounced. Most Latin American Spanish sounds are pronounced the same as their English counterparts – if you read our blue pronunciation guides as if they were English, you'll be understood just fine. Note that the kh in our pronunciation guides is a throaty sound (like the 'ch' in the Scottish loch), v and b are similar to the English 'b' (but softer, between a 'v' and a 'b'), and r is strongly rolled. Some Spanish words are written with an acute accent (eg días) – this indicates a stressed syllable. In our pronunciation guides, the stressed syllables are in italics. Spanish nouns are marked for gender (masculine or feminine). Endings for adjectives also change to agree with the gender of the noun they modify. Where necessary, both forms are given for the phrases in this chapter, separated by a slash and with the masculine form first, eg perdido/a (m/f).

When talking to people familiar to you or younger than you, use the informal form of 'you', *tú*, rather than the polite form *Usted*. In all other cases use the polite form. The polite form is used in the phrases provided in this chapter; where both options are given, they are indicated by the abbreviations 'pol' and 'inf'.

BASICS

Hello.	*Hola.*	o·la
Goodbye.	*Adiós.*	a·dyos

WANT MORE?

For in-depth language information and handy phrases, check out Lonely Planet's *Latin American Spanish Phrasebook*. You'll find it at **shop.lonelyplanet.com**, or you can buy Lonely Planet's iPhone phrasebooks at the Apple App Store.

How are you?	*¿Qué tal?*	ke tal
Fine, thanks.	*Bien, gracias.*	byen *gra*·syas
Excuse me.	*Perdón.*	per·*don*
Sorry.	*Lo siento.*	lo *syen*·to
Yes./No.	*Sí./No.*	see/no
Please.	*Por favor.*	por fa·*vor*
Thank you.	*Gracias.*	*gra*·syas
You're welcome.	*De nada.*	de *na*·da

My name is ...
Me llamo ... me *ya*·mo ...

What's your name?
¿Cómo se llama Usted? *ko*·mo se *ya*·ma *oo*·ste (pol)
¿Cómo te llamas? *ko*·mo te *ya*·mas (inf)

Do you speak English?
¿Habla inglés? *a*·bla een·*gles* (pol)
¿Hablas inglés? *a*·blas een·*gles* (inf)

I (don't) understand.
Yo (no) entiendo. yo (no) en·*tyen*·do

ACCOMMODATIONS

I'd like to book a room.
Quisiera reservar una habitación. kee·*sye*·ra re·ser·*var oo*·na a·bee·ta·*syon*

How much is it per night/person?
¿Cuánto cuesta por noche/persona? *kwan*·to *kwes*·ta por *no*·che/per·*so*·na

Does it include breakfast?
¿Incluye el desayuno? een·*kloo*·ye el de·sa·*yoo*·no

campsite	*terreno de cámping*	te·*re*·no de *kam*·peeng
hotel	*hotel*	o·*tel*
guesthouse	*pensión*	pen·*syon*
youth hostel	*albergue juvenil*	al·*ber*·ge khoo·ve·*neel*
I'd like a ... room.	*Quisiera una habitación ...*	kee·*sye*·ra *oo*·na a·bee·ta·*syon* ...

single	*individual*	een·dee·vee·*dwal*
double	*doble*	*do*·ble

air-con	*aire acondicionado*	*ai*·re a·kon·dee·syo·*na*·do
bathroom	*baño*	*ba*·nyo
bed	*cama*	*ka*·ma
window	*ventana*	ven·*ta*·na

DIRECTIONS

Where's ...?
¿Dónde está ...? — *don*·de es·*ta* ...

What's the address?
¿Cuál es la dirección? — *kwal* es la dee·rek·*syon*

Could you please write it down?
¿Puede escribirlo, por favor? — *pwe*·de es·kree·*beer*·lo por *fa*·vor

Can you show me (on the map)?
¿Me lo puede indicar (en el mapa)? — me lo *pwe*·de een·dee·*kar* (en el *ma*·pa)

at the corner	*en la esquina*	en la es·*kee*·na
at the traffic lights	*en el semáforo*	en el se·*ma*·fo·ro
behind ...	*detrás de ...*	de·*tras* de ...
far	*lejos*	*le*·khos
in front of ...	*enfrente de ...*	en·*fren*·te de ...
left	*izquierda*	ees·*kyer*·da
near	*cerca*	*ser*·ka
next to ...	*al lado de ...*	al *la*·do de ...
opposite ...	*frente a ...*	*fren*·te a ...
right	*derecha*	de·*re*·cha
straight ahead	*todo recto*	*to*·do *rek*·to

EATING & DRINKING

What would you recommend?
¿Qué recomienda? — ke re·ko·*myen*·da

What's in that dish?
¿Que lleva ese plato? — ke *ye*·va e·se *pla*·to

I don't eat ...
No como ... — no *ko*·mo ...

That was delicious!
¡Estaba buenísimo! — es·*ta*·ba bwe·*nee*·see·mo

Please bring the bill.
Por favor nos trae la cuenta. — por fa·*vor* nos *tra*·e la *kwen*·ta

Cheers!
¡Salud! — sa·*loo*

I'd like to book a table for ...	*Quisiera reservar una mesa para ...*	kee·*sye*·ra re·ser·*var oo*·na *me*·sa *pa*·ra ...

KEY PATTERNS

To get by in Spanish, mix and match these simple patterns with words of your choice:

When's (the next flight)?
¿Cuándo sale (el próximo vuelo)? — *kwan*·do *sa*·le (el *prok*·see·mo *vwe*·lo)

Where's (the station)?
¿Dónde está (la estación)? — *don*·de es·*ta* (la es·ta·*syon*)

Where can I (buy a ticket)?
¿Dónde puedo (comprar un billete)? — *don*·de *pwe*·do (kom·*prar* oon bee·*ye*·te)

Do you have (a map)?
¿Tiene (un mapa)? — *tye*·ne (oon *ma*·pa)

Is there (a toilet)?
¿Hay (servicios)? — ai (ser·*vee*·syos)

I'd like (a coffee).
Quisiera (un café). — kee·*sye*·ra (oon ka·*fe*)

I'd like (to hire a car).
Quisiera (alquilar un coche). — kee·*sye*·ra (al·kee·*lar* oon *ko*·che)

Can I (enter)?
¿Se puede (entrar)? — se *pwe*·de (en·*trar*)

Could you please (help me)?
¿Puede (ayudarme), por favor? — *pwe*·de (a·yoo·*dar*·me) por fa·*vor*

Do I have to (get a visa)?
¿Necesito (obtener un visado)? — ne·se·*see*·to (ob·te·*ner* oon vee·*sa*·do)

(eight) o'clock	*las (ocho)*	las (*o*·cho)
(two) people	*(dos) personas*	(dos) per·*so*·nas

Key Words

appetizers	*aperitivos*	a·pe·ree·*tee*·vos
bar	*bar*	bar
bottle	*botella*	bo·*te*·ya
bowl	*bol*	bol
breakfast	*desayuno*	de·sa·*yoo*·no
cafe	*café*	ka·*fe*
children's menu	*menú infantil*	me·*noo* een·fan·*teel*
cold	*frío*	*free*·o
dinner	*cena*	*se*·na
food	*comida*	ko·*mee*·da
fork	*tenedor*	te·ne·*dor*
glass	*vaso*	*va*·so
highchair	*trona*	*tro*·na

Signs

Abierto	Open
Cerrado	Closed
Entrada	Entrance
Hombres/Varones	Men
Mujeres/Damas	Women
Prohibido	Prohibited
Salida	Exit
Servicios/Baños	Toilets

hot (warm)	*caliente*	kal·*yen*·te
knife	*cuchillo*	koo·*chee*·yo
lunch	*comida*	ko·*mee*·da
main course	*segundo plato*	se·*goon*·do *pla*·to
market	*mercado*	mer·*ka*·do
menu (in English)	*menú (en inglés)*	me·*noo* (en een·*gles*)
plate	*plato*	*pla*·to
restaurant	*restaurante*	res·tow·*ran*·te
spoon	*cuchara*	koo·*cha*·ra
supermarket	*supermercado*	soo·per·mer·*ka*·do
vegetarian food	*comida vegetariana*	ko·*mee*·da ve·khe·ta·*rya*·na
with/without	*con/sin*	kon/seen

Meat & Fish

beef	*carne de vaca*	*kar*·ne de *va*·ka
chicken	*pollo*	*po*·yo
duck	*pato*	*pa*·to
fish	*pescado*	pes·*ka*·do
lamb	*cordero*	kor·*de*·ro
pork	*cerdo*	*ser*·do
turkey	*pavo*	*pa*·vo
veal	*ternera*	ter·*ne*·ra

Fruit & Vegetables

apple	*manzana*	man·*sa*·na
apricot	*albaricoque*	al·ba·ree·*ko*·ke
artichoke	*alcachofa*	al·ka·*cho*·fa
asparagus	*espárragos*	es·*pa*·ra·gos
banana	*plátano*	*pla*·ta·no
beans	*judías*	khoo·*dee*·as
beetroot	*remolacha*	re·mo·*la*·cha
cabbage	*col*	kol
carrot	*zanahoria*	sa·na·*o*·rya
celery	*apio*	*a*·pyo
cherry	*cereza*	se·*re*·sa
corn	*maíz*	ma·*ees*
cucumber	*pepino*	pe·*pee*·no
fruit	*fruta*	*froo*·ta
grape	*uvas*	*oo*·vas
lemon	*limón*	lee·*mon*
lentils	*lentejas*	len·*te*·khas
lettuce	*lechuga*	le·*choo*·ga
mushroom	*champiñón*	cham·pee·*nyon*
nuts	*nueces*	*nwe*·ses
onion	*cebolla*	se·*bo*·ya
orange	*naranja*	na·*ran*·kha
peach	*melocotón*	me·lo·ko·*ton*
peas	*guisantes*	gee·*san*·tes
(red/green) pepper	*pimiento (rojo/verde)*	pee·*myen*·to (*ro*·kho/*ver*·de)
pineapple	*piña*	*pee*·nya
plum	*ciruela*	seer·*we*·la
potato	*patata*	pa·*ta*·ta
pumpkin	*calabaza*	ka·la·*ba*·sa
spinach	*espinacas*	es·pee·*na*·kas
strawberry	*fresa*	*fre*·sa
tomato	*tomate*	to·*ma*·te
vegetable	*verdura*	ver·*doo*·ra
watermelon	*sandía*	san·*dee*·a

Other

bread	*pan*	pan
butter	*mantequilla*	man·te·*kee*·ya
cheese	*queso*	*ke*·so
egg	*huevo*	*we*·vo
honey	*miel*	myel
jam	*mermelada*	mer·me·*la*·da
oil	*aceite*	a·*sey*·te
pasta	*pasta*	*pas*·ta
pepper	*pimienta*	pee·*myen*·ta
rice	*arroz*	a·*ros*
salt	*sal*	sal
sugar	*azúcar*	a·*soo*·kar
vinegar	*vinagre*	vee·*na*·gre

Drinks

beer	*cerveza*	ser·*ve*·sa
coffee	*café*	ka·*fe*
(orange) juice	*zumo (de naranja)*	*soo*·mo (de na·*ran*·kha)
milk	*leche*	*le*·che

tea	*té*	te
(mineral) water	*agua (mineral)*	*a*·gwa (mee·ne·*ral*)
(red/white) wine	*vino (tinto/ blanco)*	*vee*·no (*teen*·to/ *blan*·ko)

EMERGENCIES

Help!	*¡Socorro!*	so·*ko*·ro
Go away!	*¡Vete!*	*ve*·te
Call ...!	*¡Llame a ...!*	*ya*·me a ...
a doctor	*un médico*	oon *me*·dee·ko
the police	*la policía*	la po·lee·*see*·a

I'm lost.
Estoy perdido/a. — es·*toy* per·*dee*·do/a (m/f)

I had an accident.
He tenido un accidente. — e te·*nee*·do oon ak·see·*den*·te

I'm ill.
Estoy enfermo/a. — es·*toy* en·*fer*·mo/a (m/f)

It hurts here.
Me duele aquí. — me *dwe*·le a·*kee*

I'm allergic to (antibiotics).
Soy alérgico/a a (los antibióticos). — soy a·*ler*·khee·ko/a a (los an·tee·*byo*·tee·kos) (m/f)

Numbers

1	*uno*	*oo*·no
2	*dos*	dos
3	*tres*	tres
4	*cuatro*	*kwa*·tro
5	*cinco*	*seen*·ko
6	*seis*	seys
7	*siete*	*sye*·te
8	*ocho*	*o*·cho
9	*nueve*	*nwe*·ve
10	*diez*	dyes
20	*veinte*	*veyn*·te
30	*treinta*	*treyn*·ta
40	*cuarenta*	kwa·*ren*·ta
50	*cincuenta*	seen·*kwen*·ta
60	*sesenta*	se·*sen*·ta
70	*setenta*	se·*ten*·ta
80	*ochenta*	o·*chen*·ta
90	*noventa*	no·*ven*·ta
100	*cien*	syen
1000	*mil*	meel

SHOPPING & SERVICES

I'd like to buy ...
Quisiera comprar ... — kee·*sye*·ra kom·*prar* ...

I'm just looking.
Sólo estoy mirando. — *so*·lo es·*toy* mee·*ran*·do

May I look at it?
¿Puedo verlo? — *pwe*·do *ver*·lo

I don't like it.
No me gusta. — no me *goos*·ta

How much is it?
¿Cuánto cuesta? — *kwan*·to *kwes*·ta

That's too expensive.
Es muy caro. — es mooy *ka*·ro

Can you lower the price?
¿Podría bajar un poco el precio? — po·*dree*·a ba·*khar* oon *po*·ko el *pre*·syo

There's a mistake in the bill.
Hay un error en la cuenta. — ai oon e·*ror* en la *kwen*·ta

ATM	*cajero automático*	ka·*khe*·ro ow·to·*ma*·tee·ko
credit card	*tarjeta de crédito*	tar·*khe*·ta de *kre*·dee·to
internet cafe	*cibercafé*	see·ber·ka·*fe*
post office	*correos*	ko·*re*·os
tourist office	*oficina de turismo*	o·fee·*see*·na de too·*rees*·mo

TIME & DATES

What time is it?	*¿Qué hora es?*	ke *o*·ra es
It's (10) o'clock.	*Son (las diez).*	son (las dyes)
It's half past (one).	*Es (la una) y media.*	es (la *oo*·na) ee *me*·dya
morning	*mañana*	ma·*nya*·na
afternoon	*tarde*	*tar*·de
evening	*noche*	*no*·che
yesterday	*ayer*	a·*yer*
today	*hoy*	oy
tomorrow	*mañana*	ma·*nya*·na
Monday	*lunes*	*loo*·nes
Tuesday	*martes*	*mar*·tes
Wednesday	*miércoles*	*myer*·ko·les
Thursday	*jueves*	*khwe*·ves
Friday	*viernes*	*vyer*·nes
Saturday	*sábado*	*sa*·ba·do
Sunday	*domingo*	do·*meen*·go

January	*enero*	e·ne·ro
February	*febrero*	fe·*bre*·ro
March	*marzo*	*mar*·so
April	*abril*	a·*breel*
May	*mayo*	*ma*·yo
June	*junio*	*khoon*·yo
July	*julio*	*khool*·yo
August	*agosto*	a·*gos*·to
September	*septiembre*	sep·*tyem*·bre
October	*octubre*	ok·*too*·bre
November	*noviembre*	no·*vyem*·bre
December	*diciembre*	dee·*syem*·bre

PUBLIC TRANSPORTATION

boat	*barco*	*bar*·ko
bus	*autobús*	ow·to·*boos*
plane	*avión*	a·*vyon*
train	*tren*	tren
first	*primero*	pree·*me*·ro
last	*último*	*ool*·tee·mo
next	*próximo*	*prok*·see·mo

I want to go to ...
Quisiera ir a ... kee·*sye*·ra eer a ...

Does it stop at ...?
¿Para en ...? *pa*·ra en ...

What stop is this?
¿Cuál es esta parada? kwal es *es*·ta pa·*ra*·da

What time does it arrive/leave?
¿A qué hora llega/ sale? a ke o·ra *ye*·ga/ *sa*·le

Please tell me when we get to ...
¿Puede avisarme cuando lleguemos a ...? *pwe*·de a·vee·*sar*·me *kwan*·do ye·*ge*·mos a ...

I want to get off here.
Quiero bajarme aquí. *kye*·ro ba·*khar*·me a·*kee*

a ... ticket	*un billete de ...*	oon bee·*ye*·te de ...
1st-class	*primera clase*	pree·*me*·ra *kla*·se
2nd-class	*segunda clase*	se·*goon*·da *kla*·se
one-way	*ida*	*ee*·da
return	*ida y vuelta*	*ee*·da ee *vwel*·ta
airport	*aeropuerto*	a·e·ro·*pwer*·to
aisle seat	*asiento de pasillo*	a·*syen*·to de pa·*see*·yo
bus stop	*parada de autobuses*	pa·*ra*·da de ow·to·*boo*·ses
cancelled	*cancelado*	kan·se·*la*·do
delayed	*retrasado*	re·tra·*sa*·do
platform	*plataforma*	pla·ta·*for*·ma
ticket office	*taquilla*	ta·*kee*·ya
timetable	*horario*	o·*ra*·ryo
train station	*estación de trenes*	es·ta·*syon* de *tre*·nes
window seat	*asiento junto a la ventana*	a·*syen*·to *khoon*·to a la ven·*ta*·na

DRIVING AND CYCLING

I'd like to hire a ...	*Quisiera alquilar ...*	kee·*sye*·ra al·kee·*lar* ...
4WD	*un todo-terreno*	oon to·do·te·*re*·no
bicycle	*una bicicleta*	*oo*·na bee·see·*kle*·ta
car	*un coche*	oon *ko*·che
motorcycle	*una moto*	*oo*·na *mo*·to
child seat	*asiento de seguridad para niños*	a·*syen*·to de se·goo·ree·*da* *pa*·ra *nee*·nyos
diesel	*petróleo*	pet·*ro*·le·o
helmet	*casco*	*kas*·ko
hitchhike	*hacer botella*	a·*ser* bo·*te*·ya
mechanic	*mecánico*	me·*ka*·nee·ko
petrol/gas	*gasolina*	ga·so·*lee*·na
service station	*gasolinera*	ga·so·lee·*ne*·ra
truck	*camion*	ka·*myon*

Is this the road to ...?
¿Se va a ... por esta carretera? se va a ... por *es*·ta ka·re·*te*·ra

(How long) Can I park here?
¿(Por cuánto tiempo) Puedo aparcar aqui? (por *kwan*·to *tyem*·po) *pwe*·do a·par·*kar* a·*kee*

The car has broken down (at ...).
El coche se ha averiado (en ...). el *ko*·che se a a·ve·*rya*·do (en ...)

I have a flat tyre.
Tengo un pinchazo. *ten*·go oon peen·*cha*·so

I've run out of petrol.
Me he quedado sin gasolina. me e ke·*da*·do seen ga·so·*lee*·na

GLOSSARY

aldea – village, hamlet
Arcaicos – Archaics; first known inhabitants of Puerto Rico

bahía – bay
balneario – public beach
barrio – neighborhood, city district
bateyes – Taíno ball courts
boca – mouth, entrance
boleros – ballads
bomba – musical form and dance inspired by African rhythms and characterized by call-and-response dialogues between musicians and interpreted by dancers; often considered as a unit with *plena*, as in *bomba y plena*
Boricua – Puerto Rican; a person of Puerto Rican descent
Borinquen – traditional Taíno name for the island of Puerto Rico
bosque estatal – state forest
botánica – shop specializing in herbs, icons and associated charms used in the practice of Santería

cacique – Taíno chief (male or female)
callejón – narrow side street, alleyway
capilla – chapel
Caribs – original colonizers of the Caribbean, for whom the region was named
casa – house
cayos – cays; refers to islets
cemíes – small figurines carved from stone, shell, wood or gold, representing deities worshipped by the Taínos
centros vacacionales – literally 'vacation centers'; form of rental accommodation popular with island families, with facilities ranging from basic wooden cabins on the beach to two-bedroom condos
cerro – hill, mountain
Changó – Yoruba god of fire and war believed to control thunder and lightning; one of several principal deities worshipped in Santería (see also *orishas*)
comida criolla – traditional Puerto Rican cuisine
Compañía de Parques Nacionales – CPN; National Park Company
coquí – a species of tiny tree frog found only in Puerto Rico; the island's mascot
cordillera – a system of mountain ranges
criollo – island-born person of Spanish parentage; in colonial times considered inferior by peninsular Spaniards (see also *mestizo*)
culebrenses – residents of Culebra
curandero – healer

danza – form of piano music and stylized figure-dance with Spanish origins, fused with elements of island folk music
Departamento de Recursos Naturales y Ambientales – DRNA; Department of Natural Resources & Environment

espiritismo – spiritualism
Estado Libre Asociado – associated free state; the term describes Puerto Rico's relationship with the USA

fiesta patronal – the annual celebrations staged in Puerto Rican cities and towns to honor each community's patron saint
fortaleza – fortress
friquitines – roadside kiosks
fuerte – fort

galería – gallery
garitas – turreted sentry towers constructed at intervals along the top of Old San Juan's fortifications
gringo – term used on the island to describe Americans

hacienda – agricultural estate, plantation

iglesia – church
Igneris – Indian group of the Arawakan linguistic group; early settlers of Puerto Rico
independentistas – advocates for Puerto Rican independence

jíbaro – country person, often cast as archetypal Puerto Rican

laguna – lake or lagoon
lechonera – eatery specializing in suckling pig
LMM – abbreviation for San Juan's Luis Muñoz Marín International Airport

malecón – pier, waterfront promenade
máscaras – masks (see also *vejigantes*)
mercado – market
Mesónes Gastronómicos – a Puerto Rico Tourism Company–sponsored program involving a collection of restaurants around the island that feature Puerto Rican cuisine
mestizo – person of mixed ancestry; usually Indian and Spanish (see also *criollo*)
mogotes – hillocks
mundillo – traditional form of intricately woven lace, made only in Puerto Rico and Spain

norte – north
Nuyoricans – Puerto Rican 'exiles' in the US

orishas – Yoruba deities worshipped in Santería, often associated with Catholic saints (see also *Changó*)

palacio – palace
parador – country inn

parque – park

pasaje – passage

playa – beach

plazuela – small plaza

plena – form of traditional Puerto Rican dance and song that unfolds to distinctly African rhythms beat out with maracas, tambourines and other traditional percussion instruments; often associated with *bomba*

pleneros – *plena* singers

ponceños – residents of Ponce

PRTC – Puerto Rico Tourism Company

públicos – shared taxis, usually minivans equipped with bench seats, which pick up passengers along a prescribed route and provide low-cost local transport islandwide

puerta – gate, door

puerto – port

punta – tip, end

reserva forestal – forest reserve

ron – rum

sanjuaneros – residents of San Juan

Santería – Afro-Caribbean religion representing the syncretism of Catholic and African beliefs, based on the worship of Catholic saints and their associated *Yoruba* deities or *orishas*

santero – an artist who carves *santos*; one of many names for practitioners of the rites of *Santería*

santos – small carved figurines representing saints, enshrined and worshipped by practitioners of *Santería*

sonda – sound

supermercado – supermarket

sur – south

Taínos – indigenous Puerto Ricans

tienda – store

turismo – tourism

turista – tourist

universidad – university

urgente – urgent

valle – valley

vegetales – vegetables

vejigantes – traditional Puerto Rican masks (see also *máscaras*)

ventana – window

vereda – path, trail

vino – wine

Yoruba – West Africans brought to Puerto Rico as slaves

zoológico – zoo

Behind the Scenes

SEND US YOUR FEEDBACK

We love to hear from travelers – your comments keep us on our toes and help make our books better. Our well-traveled team reads every word on what you loved or loathed about this book. Although we cannot reply individually to postal submissions, we always guarantee that your feedback goes straight to the appropriate authors, in time for the next edition. Each person who sends us information is thanked in the next edition – the most useful submissions are rewarded with a selection of digital PDF chapters.

Visit **lonelyplanet.com/contact** to submit your updates and suggestions or to ask for help. Our award-winning website also features inspirational travel stories, news and discussions.

Note: We may edit, reproduce and incorporate your comments in Lonely Planet products such as guidebooks, websites and digital products, so let us know if you don't want your comments reproduced or your name acknowledged. For a copy of our privacy policy visit lonelyplanet.com/privacy.

OUR READERS

Many thanks to the travelers who used the last edition and wrote to us with helpful hints, useful advice and interesting anecdotes:

Keith Bailey, Lorilee Crisp, Diane Davis, Andrew Miller, Pamela Miller, Marcia Nielson, Kelly Tek, Paul Tibbitts, Renate van Bemmelen, Sarah Whittington.

AUTHOR THANKS

Ryan Ver Berkmoes

A *mofungo* of thanks to the following: the many locals who answered my persistent questions with good humor, thinking I was just a somewhat irritating tourist, and to the cafe owner who spotted me dinner after the power failed and the ATMs and credit card machines quit working. At Lonely Planet, huge affection and thanks to the former commissioning crew in Oakland who roped me into this. Big thanks to Brana Vladisavljevic and all the rest who came through after things went off the rails. Finally, true love for my golden sweetheart and fellow Vieques star-gazer Alexis Averbuck.

Luke Waterson

A particular *gracias* and a whole load of *abrazos* to Ali in Orocovis, Benjamin and Dalma in Jayuya, Nadine in Ponce, Maritza in Cabo Rojo, Harry, Lisa and Dario in Rincón, Jorge in Aguadilla, Trevor in Isabela and Eddy in San Juan – all of whom proved truly exceptional human beings in terms of their help and hospitality. And espresso thanks to all Puerto Rico's coffee growers – you've created a serendipitous world-class product and truly done the island proud.

ACKNOWLEDGMENTS

Climate map data adapted from Peel MC, Finlayson BL & McMahon TA (2007) 'Updated World Map of the Köppen-Geiger Climate Classification', *Hydrology and Earth System Sciences*, 11, 163344.

Cover photograph: Puerto Rican fishing boat, George Oze / Alamy.

THIS BOOK

This 6th edition of Lonely Planet's *Puerto Rico* guidebook was researched and written by Ryan Ver Berkmoes and Luke Waterson. The 5th edition was written by Nate Cavalieri and Beth Kohn; the 4th edition was written by Brendan Sainsbury and Nate Cavalieri. This guidebook was commissioned in Lonely Planet's Oakland office, and was produced by the following:

Commissioning Editors Catherine Craddock-Carrillo, Suzannah Shwer

Destination Editor Brana Vladisavljevic

Product Editor Elizabeth Jones

Senior Cartographer Mark Griffiths

Book Designer Virginia Moreno

Assisting Editors Michelle Bennett, Melanie Dankel, Lauren Hunt, Saralinda Turner

Assisting Cartographers Corey Hutchison, Valentina Kremenchutskaya, Alison Lyall

Cover Researcher Naomi Parker

Thanks to Sasha Baskett, Elin Berglund, Brendan Dempsey, Bruce Evans, Ryan Evans, Larissa Frost, James Hardy, Kate Mathews, Kathleen Munnelly, Claire Naylor, Karyn Noble, Martine Power, Ellie Simpson

Index

Map Pages **000**
Photo Pages **000**

F

G

H

I

J

K

Map Pages **000**
Photo Pages **000**

Map Pages **000**
Photo Pages **000**

OUR STORY

A beat-up old car, a few dollars in the pocket and a sense of adventure. In 1972 that's all Tony and Maureen Wheeler needed for the trip of a lifetime – across Europe and Asia overland to Australia. It took several months, and at the end – broke but inspired – they sat at their kitchen table writing and stapling together their first travel guide, *Across Asia on the Cheap*. Within a week they'd sold 1500 copies. Lonely Planet was born.

Today, Lonely Planet has offices in Franklin, London, Melbourne, Oakland, Beijing and Delhi, with more than 600 staff and writers. We share Tony's belief that 'a great guidebook should do three things: inform, educate and amuse'.

OUR WRITERS

Ryan Ver Berkmoes

Coordinating Author, San Juan, El Yunque & East Coast, Culebra & Vieques Ryan first visited Puerto Rico in 2004. On his visits since, he has criss-crossed the islands, always wondering where he'll next find the perfect beach. Recent thrills included trying to find an authentic daiquiri (no blenders ever!) and getting lost in El Morro. He succeeded in one but not the other. Off-island, Ryan splits his time between the US and Europe and writes about travel and more at ryanverberkmoes.com. Follow him on Twitter via @ryanvb.

Read more about Ryan at:
lonelyplanet.com/thorntree/profiles/ryanverberkmoes

Luke Waterson

Ponce & South Coast, West Coast, North Coast, Central Mountains Whether it's the spontaneous street parties, the sun-kissed spirit of revolution or the wicked coffee, Luke and Latin America are in love. Having authored Lonely Planet guidebooks from *Cuba* to *Peru*, he relished tracking down the Latino soul of the USA's Caribbean outpost (finding lots of street parties, revolution and coffee). Hiking in the central mountains and caffeine-refuelling at hidden haciendas were his top experiences this time round. (Well, the cold box of beer with the off-duty marines on that idyllic cay wasn't bad.) Luke lives in Slovakia; examples of his work can be found on his blog at http://englishmaninslovakia.com.

Read more about Luke at:
lonelyplanet.com/thorntree/profiles/lukewaterson

Published by Lonely Planet Publications Pty Ltd
ABN 36 005 607 983
6th edition – October 2014
ISBN 978 1 74220 445 1

10 9 8 7 6 5 4 3 2 1
Printed in China

Map Legend

Sights
- Beach
- Bird Sanctuary
- Buddhist
- Castle/Palace
- Christian
- Confucian
- Hindu
- Islamic
- Jain
- Jewish
- Monument
- Museum/Gallery/Historic Building
- Ruin
- Sento Hot Baths/Onsen
- Shinto
- Sikh
- Taoist
- Winery/Vineyard
- Zoo/Wildlife Sanctuary
- Other Sight

Activities, Courses & Tours
- Bodysurfing
- Diving
- Canoeing/Kayaking
- Course/Tour
- Skiing
- Snorkeling
- Surfing
- Swimming/Pool
- Walking
- Windsurfing
- Other Activity

Sleeping
- Sleeping
- Camping

Eating
- Eating

Drinking & Nightlife
- Drinking & Nightlife
- Cafe

Entertainment
- Entertainment

Shopping
- Shopping

Information
- Bank
- Embassy/Consulate
- Hospital/Medical
- Internet
- Police
- Post Office
- Telephone
- Toilet
- Tourist Information
- Other Information

Geographic
- Beach
- Hut/Shelter
- Lighthouse
- Lookout
- Mountain/Volcano
- Oasis
- Park
- Pass
- Picnic Area
- Waterfall

Population
- Capital (National)
- Capital (State/Province)
- City/Large Town
- Town/Village

Transport
- Airport
- Border crossing
- Bus
- Cable car/Funicular
- Cycling
- Ferry
- Metro station
- Monorail
- Parking
- Petrol station
- Subway/Subte station
- Taxi
- Train station/Railway
- Tram
- Underground station
- Other Transport

Note: Not all symbols displayed above appear on the maps in this book

Routes
- Tollway
- Freeway
- Primary
- Secondary
- Tertiary
- Lane
- Unsealed road
- Road under construction
- Plaza/Mall
- Steps
- Tunnel
- Pedestrian overpass
- Walking Tour
- Walking Tour detour
- Path/Walking Trail

Boundaries
- International
- State/Province
- Disputed
- Regional/Suburb
- Marine Park
- Cliff
- Wall

Hydrography
- River, Creek
- Intermittent River
- Canal
- Water
- Dry/Salt/Intermittent Lake
- Reef

Areas
- Airport/Runway
- Beach/Desert
- Cemetery (Christian)
- Cemetery (Other)
- Glacier
- Mudflat
- Park/Forest
- Sight (Building)
- Sportsground
- Swamp/Mangrove